Short-Term Psychotherapy and Brief Treatment Techniques

An Annotated Bibliography
1920 – 1980

Short-Term Psychotherapy and Brief Treatment Techniques

An Annotated Bibliography 1920–1980

Harvey P. Mandel

York University
Downsview, Ontario, Canada

Plenum Press · New York and London

Library Congress Cataloging in Publication Data

Mandel, Harvey P.
  Short-term psychotherapy and brief treatment techniques.

  Includes indexes.
  1. Psychotherapy, Brief—Bibliography. I. Title. [DNLM: 1. Psychotherapy, Brief—
Bibliography. ZWM 420 M271s 1920-80]
Z664.N5M36 [RC488.5]   016.61689'14   81-221
ISBN 0-306-40658-6   AACR2

© 1981 Plenum Press, New York
A Division of Plenum Publishing Corporation
233 Spring Street, New York, N.Y. 10013

Printed in the United States of America

The editor and publisher gratefully acknowledge the permission to reprint abstracts granted by the publications listed below. The numbers before and after the colon are, respectively, the volume and page numbers of the articles in the original publications. The numbers in parantheses are the serial numbers of the abstracts in this bibliogaphy.

Advances in Behavior Research, 1:231 (1530)
American Journal of Clinical Hypnosis, 1:3 (399); 5:81 (804); 13:17 (109); 12:1 (754); 16:23 (980); 17:143 (400); 19:231 (16); 19:251 (336); 20:76 (1179); 21:38 (82); 22:54 (1368)
American Journal of Mental Deficiency, 78:241 (70)
American Journal of Nursing, 70:1484 (1431)
American Journal of Psychiatry, 114:68 (162); 116:737 (1323); 117:35 (1507); 117:1088 (371); 120:533 (1017); 120:1097 (744); 121:1176 (682); 122:135 (1493); 122:267 (1544); 123:548 (505); 123:664 (253); 123:786 (239); 123:1069 (1239); 123:1394 (1552); 124:371 (117); 124:924 (947); 124:1535 (1086); 124:1668 (278); 125:136 (1518); 125:458 (164); 125:877 (1273); 125:1040 (1317); 126:789 (1107); 126:1024 (249); 126:1093 (156); 126:1461 (426); 126:1628 (1183); 127:825 (351); 127:908 (1356); 127:1221 (920); 127:1327 (231); 127:1357 (532); 127:1386 (1134); 127:1391 (779); 127:1626 (1070); 128:480 (1357); 128:718 (1245); 128:882 (1168); 129:220 (210); 129:710 (1198); 129:715 (1164); 129:721 (474); 129:725 (315); 130:961 (1521); 130:1103 (869); 130:1107 (546); 131:47 (591); 131:56 (1305); 131:271 (445); 131:1103 (555); 132:373 (1277); 132:413 (620); 132:1207 (755); 133:418 (919); 133:509 (518); 133:515 (519); 133:518 (1122); 133:896 (177); 133:1043 (1371); 134:134 (1280); 134:1104 (556); 135:592 (572); 136:149 (901); 136:427 (1210); 136:555 (1461); 136:1283 (128); 137:1 (503); 137:409 (904)
Archives of General Psychiatry, 3:593 (1402); 6:56 (870); 9:61 (467); 9:105 (402); 9:113 (1200); 13:133 (526); 13:269 (229); 14:536 (711); 15:190 (871); 16:727 (605); 17:176 (50); 17:584 (914); 18:178 (157); 18:428 (1399); 18:532 (1400); 18:552 (1195); 18:718 (674); 21:546 (602); 21:620 (1458); 22:462 (592); 23:65 (1394); 25:110 (1088); 26:51 (635); 28:111 (378); 29:719 (877); 30:249 (653); 30:363 (516); 30:830 (1369); 32:110 (884); 32:127 (1348); 32:995 (862); 33:78 (517); 33:87 (346); 33:96 (786); 33:548 (1118); 33:1291 (577); 36:177 (208); 36:1125 (1351)
Archives of Sexual Behavior, 5:313 (810)
Behavior Research and Therapy, 1:53 (57); 1:69 (791); 1:139 (1000); 2:217 (1055); 2:245 (204); 3:87 (583); 3:235 (740); 3:245 (1103); 4:1 (1104); 4:139 (464); 4:209 (793); 5:1 (1397); 6:31 (1310); 6:83 (794); 7:275 (558); 8:21 (630); 8:347 (906); 9:7 (175); 10:319 (296); 11:91 (655)
British Journal of Medical Psychology, 42:81 (14); 47:1 (1271); (in press) (911)
Child Psychiatry and Human Development, 7:254 (803)
Cognitive Therapy and Research, 3:61 (684)
Comprehensive Psychiatry, 4:333 (808); 7:39 (1331); 10:44 (1517); 10:275 (687); 11:108 (241); 13:459 (1499); 18:585 (631)
Drug Forum, 1:137 (1464); 3:239 (267)
Family Life Co-ordinator, 17:165 (868)
Group & Organizational Studies: The Journal for Group Facilitators, 3:483 (730)
Health and Social Work, 3:105 (819)
International Journal of Group Psychotherapy, 12:503 (412); 15:81 (713); 15:465 (1172); 18:220 (1328); 23:204 (1135); 29:3 (692)
International Journal of Psychiatry in Medicine, 6:349 (1111); 6:523 (199)
Journal of Applied Behavior Analysis, 4:89 (66)
Journal of Applied Behavioral Science, 13:7 (552)
Journal of Behavioral Medicine, 1:25 (1363)
Journal of Child Psychology and Psychiatry, 9:61 (1420); 19:119 (734)
Journal of Child Psychology and Psychiatry and Allied Disciplines, 19:1 (129)
Journal of Marital and Family Therapy, 87: (585)
Journal of Nervous and Mental Disease, 123:53 (1470); 124:535 (935); 126:441 (990); 127:330 (1158); 132:189 (1506); 134:316 (1508); 136:272 (790); 137:349 (1430); 147:124 (633); 149:270 (778); 149:281 (1476); 150:18 (1276); 150:27 (664); 151:75 (344); 152:303 (140); 157:420 (994); 159:164 (1402a); 159:234 (636); 159:325 (446); 160:204 (615)
Journal of Psychiatric Education, 2:62 (606)
Journal of Psychiatric Research, 2:267 (632)
Journal of Psychosomatic Research, 3:303 (1437)
Journal of the American Academy of Child Psychiatry, 8:140 (968); 8:154 (1097)
Journal of the American College Association, 23:304 (706)
Journal of the American College Health Association, 24:186 (1142)
Journal of the American Medical Association, 174:2214 (119); 192:21 (850); 195:626 (454)
Medical Care, 7:55 (28)
Mental Hygiene, 44:169 (1234); 45:57 (335); 54:301 (1345)
New England Journal of Medicine, 266:283 (235)
New York State Journal of Medicine, 72:2743 (1177)
Perceptual Motor Skills, 34:199 (4); 41:555 (1216)
Psychiatric Quarterly, 26:414 (476); 39:1 (168); 40:80 (1455); 42:271 (1241); 42:358 (1411); 42:751 (1175); 47:341 (837); 48:230 (1490)
Psychiatric Quarterly Supplement, 37:230 (874)
Psychiatry, 16:21 (365); 20:387 (1347); 22:277 (1182); 34:198 (537); 40:315 (64)
Psychiatry in Medicine, 1:349 (1398); 3:311 (1031); 4:77 (1110); 4:273 (1550)
Psychological Reports, 4:231 (549); 13:275 (435); 18:995 (77); 23:663 (138); 32:75 (383); 35:1093 (952); 41:79 (1219); 42:481 (611)
Psychosomatics, 2:1 (131); 9:81 (815); 15:160 (1178); 19:425 (200)
Seminars in Psychiatry, 3:264 (907)
Social Work, 5:91 (507); 12:28 (1343); 12:44 (1027); 13:81 (1213); 14:38 (430)

All other material cited as journal abstracts, summaries, or conclusions is reprinted by permission of the sources specified in the body of the bibliography

Time strengthens as it
weakens,
Space contracts as it
expands,
Love grows as it
dies,
And new structures emerge.

Dorothy Mandel
Toronto, 1980

And still we are blessed with more
real time than any other creature,
and cursed with enough awareness
and intelligence to measure it.

N.J. Berrill
Man's Emerging Mind

Acknowledgements

There are many who deserve special thanks for their direct and indirect contributions which have lead to this volume. Space permits listing but a few; I trust those not mentioned will understand.

To Ida, Bernard, and Rhoda, for having shared in meaningful beginnings and continuing bonds;

To my wife Dorothy, whose companionship before, during, and after a miraculous sabbatical in California's libraries and along its beaches and mountains has led me to know the pain of too much happiness;

To York University, for allowing me both the time and peace of mind to contemplate, reintegrate, and renew;

To Youthdale Treatment Centres of Toronto, where I have had the privilege of working with dedicated professional mental health workers and troubled teenagers and their families;

To the staff of the Counselling and Development Centre at York University, for their interest in and curiosity about briefer therapies; specifically, to Lucie Cantrell, Cheryl Legare Simon, Joan Green, and Charlene Denzel, for their active support during more than four years of this project;

To the staff of the Del Mar Psychiatric Clinic in California, and especially to Gerry Nelson, Len Sperry, Orville Coonce, and Richard Lewak, all of whom enjoyed the stimulation of a range of therapy approaches;

To Ed Shafransky in San Diego, who acted as my legs at the Biomedical Library of UCSD and for his proving that kindness begets kindness; to Deborah Schuller in Toronto, for her valuable contributions to this work;

To Dr. Alan Chin, for his continued friendship during periods of change;

To the many hundreds of professional authors/practitioners, who have provided the impetus for new directions by sharing a part of themselves through their journal articles and books;

To the people at Plenum Publishing, and especially to Leonard Pace and Patricia Vann, for their warm and valuable guidance throughout the course of this project;

And a very special word of thanks to Ms. Helen Musikka, my secretary, without whom this volume would not have come to be. This text as it appears is directly the result of her conscientious concern for detail. The process by which this book has been mass produced demanded that the original typed copy in fact be set up as the final copy, to be photographed rather than typeset. The magnificent layout of this book is to her credit, and I wish to thank her publicly.

And finally, to all of my patients, who have provided me with new depths of understanding into the essense of the process of change - the struggle between the fear and the magnetic pull of opportunity.

Contents

INTRODUCTION

The Scope of Brief Therapy

Within the last two decades there has been a dramatic expansion in the uses of short-term treatment (Grayson, 1979, Small, 1979). Brief therapies have been and continue to be widely used with a number of different patient populations in a broad variety of service settings. They have been reported in use with children, adolescents, adults, and the aged; in groups, families, and individual treatment; on college campuses, high schools, in community mental health centers, in child guidance clinics, in private psychiatric clinics, in hospitals as part of out-patient or in-patient therapy, in programs of preventive community mental health; with the rich, the middle class, and the poor (Barten, 1971, 1972; Caplan, 1961, 1964; Small, 1979; Wolberg, 1965).

Further, short term methods of therapy range across all of the major and well-known theoretical orientations found in the broader field of psychotherapy. There are some unique theoretical contributions which can be found within this field as well. A brief list of some of the theoretical systems represented includes: psychoanalysis and its derivatives (Adler, 1972; Alexander, 1951; Alexander and French, 1946; Malan, 1979; Sifneos, 1979), rational-emotive (Ellis, 1971, 1978), existential therapy (Frankl, 1966), hypnotherapy (Erickson, 1954), learning theory approaches utilizing a wide range of techniques, such as systematic desensitization (Lazarus, 1971; Wolpe, 1973; Wolpe and Lazarus, 1966), and implosive therapy (Frankel, 1972; Stampfl and Levis, 1967), non-directive and Rogerian approaches (Shlien, 1964), problem-solving approaches

including some of the newer sex therapies (Kaplan, 1974;
Neiger, 1972) and crisis intervention techniques (Ewing,
1978), systems and communication orientations (Halevy, 1963;
Watzlawick, 1978), transactional analysis (Brechenser, 1972)
and other related approaches, etc., etc., etc.

Brief forms of therapy have also been used in dealing
with the widest possible range of human problems. They
have been used in problems of abortion, adoptions, of
alcoholism, or anorexia nervosa, as an adjunct to the treatment of cancer, in dealing with problems of childhood such
as encopresis and enuresis and various phobias, in dealing
with adult phobias, for coronary patients, in the rehabilitation of criminals, for problems created by or related to
death or dying, for depression, for drug problems, grief
reactions, to aid those who have just experienced natural
disasters such as floods, fires, and earthquakes, etc., in
dealing with obesity, for psychosomatic difficulties, to
aid those who have been raped, in the treatment of sexual
dysfunctions, disorders, and variances, to help decrease
the frequency of smoking, to alleviate specific speech
difficulties, to help suicide attempters and those who have
suffered the loss of a loved one through suicide, for underachievement problems both in school and in industry, in
dealing with the horrors of war, in helping mothers and
fathers of premature infants, etc., etc., etc. Brief
therapy has been used to treat psychoses, neuroses and
personality disorders (Small, 1979).

In summary, brief therapy has been used and is
currently being used by a diversity of mental health
professionals in dealing with an extremely wide range of
human problems. It is no longer a question of whether
briefer methods of psychotherapy will survive to be accepted
by the wider professional community or the public ar large.
The only questions remaining, and they are by no means easy
questions to answer, include concerns about the types of
patients who are best suited to specific forms of brief
therapy, the need for more vigorously controlled outcome
and follow-up studies, and a deeper understanding of how
and why change comes about with these shorter forms of
therapy.

Historical Influences and the Emergence of Brief Therapy

From a review of the literature it is apparent that briefer forms of therapy were being practiced in the 1930's and 1940's. Yet a number of interrelated factors have converged within the last fifteen years to give a strong impetus to the emergence of short term therapies. First, the development of the community mental health movement in the late 1950's and the early 1960's resulted in new treatment populations which had been underserviced or had not been serviced at all by the more traditionally oriented psychotherapy systems (Caplan, 1961, 1974; Minuchin, 1967). This new movement raised the need for new and effective ways of dealing with such a clientele, methods which up to that time had not been widely used or fully developed. Along with this came the push to deinstitutionalize the mental health system across North America.

A second and related factor was the development of crisis intervention and crisis management programs which began to flourish as a result of the new community mental health orientation (Ewing, 1978). The major focus in these programs became the assistance to either individuals, families, or groups in crisis in order to reestablish as quickly as possible a prior level of psychological functioning. Stress was placed on the rapid resolution of presenting difficulties, usually within a six to eight week period.

Third, the seeming unlimited funding of mental health programs in the 1950's and 1960's came to an abrupt end in the 1970's. There is an accelerating external political pressure based on economic necessity to hold the line on budgets and to cut back drastically on some mental health programming. With this has come the demand for increased accountability of mental health professionals. The terms "evaluation and feedback" can be heard across the professional landscape. In the 1950's this push for greater efficiency led to the emergence of the group therapy movement; in the 1970's it has led to the emergence of brief models and methods.

Fourth, throughout the course of the last two decades there has been a veritable explosion in the use of drug therapies. From the introduction of minor tranquilizers to the new breakthroughs in the use of antipsychotic drugs, drug therapy has been subtly and consistently juxtaposed against the longer term psychotherapies. The issue of time has been raised, either explicitly or implicitly, when comparisons between drug therapy and psychotherapy results are drawn.

Fifth, there has been a burgeoning of diverse theoretical systems which place increased importance on ego psychology and the reality - and task-oriented, forms of psychotherapy. These forms tend to be more active and confrontive, and shorter in duration than the traditional forms of treatment. Although many of these newer systems do not deny the value of thought, insight, or understanding, they all stress the importance of action in the process of change.

Sixth, third-party payment agencies, such as insurance companies, have begun to limit the total benefits payable in coverage of psychotherapy. This has already resulted in a trend toward fewer sessions. With the number of studies most recently reporting at least equal efficacy in outcome of longer term and shorter term therapies, the pressure on the part of these organizations for briefer therapy will increase (Cummings, 1977; Reed, 1972).

Seventh, the medical profession has undergone dramatic changes in the last twenty years in terms of the kinds of expectations for provision of service. Many of us are well aware that house calls, as an example, have become a thing of the past except on rare occasions. Likewise, there has been a dramatic change in the use of emergency departments at many community hospitals. These departments are seeing an increasing number of psychiatric emergencies, and many have now included psychiatric emergency back-up as part of their standard staffing. These emergency departments use crisis intervention techniques and approaches as part of their ongoing practice (Miller, 1968; Straker, 1971).

Setting Brief Therapy Apart

All of the above factors have contributed to the emergence and continuing growth of a wide range of short term therapies. Even with all of this diversity, however, one can still discern a number of common characteristics or elements in these brief therapies. Regardless of the particular theoretical orientation of the individual practitioner, brief therapy can generally be characterized in the following manner: it tends to be active, focussed on circumscribed patient concerns, and demands a level of involvement, enthusiasm, intensity, and risk on the part of the therapist.

There is no one operational definition for brief or short term therapy, in terms of an agreed number of sessions. The average number of therapy sessions reported within the field usually is less than twenty. Exactly how these sessions are spread out will vary greatly across therapists, across different presenting problems and population (e.g., one session per day for four weeks; one session per month for one year; one long weekend marathon, etc.). The common bond in this diversity is the limited amount of therapy.

Remaining Questions

Over the last forty years, an impressive list of questions have been addressed regarding briefer forms of therapy. Contained in this bibliography are some of the answers to a range of challenging questions. Among these are included: (1) Is brief therapy to be used only in crisis or emergency situations? (2) Is brief therapy merely a palliative measure, helping clients/patients return to a previous level of psychological stability, or can deeper, more pervasive personality change result from a brief therapy encounter? (3) How long do the positive effects of brief therapy last? (4) What requirements does a brief therapy approach place on the client or on the therapist? What changes in outlook are necessary for a therapist or agency to change from a longer term approach to a shorter approach? (5) What types of patients and presenting problems can be effectively dealt with within a brief therapy model? (6) What types of supervision are necessary in the training of

therapists in the use of briefer forms of therapy? (7) What
changes in various theoretical systems of therapy need to be
made to accommodate a briefer approach? etc.

History of Brief Therapy

The following series of statements and dates provide
an overview of the major developments and influences in the
field of brief therapy and short term treatment techniques.
I apologize to those individuals or organizations who have
not been included and who should have been. It is hoped
that future editions of this text will correct any such
errors.

1900-1930:

a. Freud reports on brief analytic treatments.

b. Psychoanalytic treatment progressively gets
    longer due to research and personality theory
    development; some break away from trend to
    set up shorter treatment approaches with
    different populations (e.g., Adler, Ferenczi,
    Stekel, Fenichel).

c. Adler establishes child guidance centers
    in Austria.

1930-1940:

a. Early and immediate access psychiatric
    services established in Holland.

b. Psychiatric emergency service established
    at the Massachusetts General Hospital in
    1934 by Stanley Cobb.

1940-1950:

a. Impact of World War II on the study of
    brief interventions (Grinker and Kardiner
    study effect of brief treatment on war
    neuroses)-early 1940's.

b.   Birth of crisis intervention principles
     (rapid diagnosis and intervention, and
     preventive role of brief treatment –
     Lindemann – 1944 and the Coconut Grove
     Fire).

c.   Council on Brief Therapy meets in Chicago,
     1942, 1944, 1946, as part of the work of
     the Chicago Institute of Psychoanalysis.

d.   Further refinements of psychoanalytic
     principles for briefer treatment –
     (Alexander and French) – 1946.

                    1950–1960:

a.   Acute psychiatric service initiated by
     Lindemann at Massachusetts General
     Hospital.

b.   Peter Sifneos initiates large scale
     brief therapy program on an outpatient
     basis at Massachusetts General Hospita.

c.   Continued formulation of preventive
     intervention principles, community
     mental health principles, and crisis
     intervention principles (Caplan,
     Rapoport, Klein and Lindemann et al.)

d.   Efficacy studies reported on briefer
     treatment in social casework (Kogan).

e.   VA Hospitals set up contract for short
     term psychiatric treatment limiting
     coverage for number of sessions.

f.   24-hour Trouble Shooting Clinic opened
     at Elmhurst City Hospital in Queens,
     N.Y. (Bellak and Small), 1958.

g. Precipitating Stress Project at Langley-Porter Neuro-Psychiatric Institute opens in San Francisco, 1958. (Kalis, Harris, et al.).

h. Emergency Walk-in Psychotherapy Unit at Bronx Municipal Hospital opens, 1959 (Coleman and Zwerling).

i. Rapid increase in use of Behavior Therapies and efficacy studies involving their uses in the treatment of phobias, obsessions/compulsions, etc. (Wolpe, etc.).

j. Rapid increase in the use of drug therapies, shortening both treatment and hospitalization length.

k. Mental Health Act passes in England, affecting psychiatric unit functioning (i.e., admissions, management/therapy, outcome) - 1959.

1960-1970:

a. Walk-in Clinic, Metropolitan Hospital, East Harlem, opens, 1962.

b. Benjamin-Rush Center for Problems in Living, open with focus on early-access, brief treatment (Jacobson et al.) - 1962.

c. Young People's Counselling Service attached to adolescent unit of the Tavistock Clinic opens - London, England.

d. University Counseling Centers across North America called upon to expand services, emphasizing shorter-term treatment programs for larger numbers of clients.

e. Insurance companies begin to experiment
    with limiting coverage of length of
    treatment, thereby influencing treatment
    process.

f. Community Mental Health Act passes in U.S.,
    requiring emergency care for services
    receiving Federal funds, opening the door
    to further expansion of patient populations
    served - 1964.

g. Boston University Medical School and
    Medical Center opens a short term treatment
    clinic in order to decrease long waiting-
    lists (Mann, et al.).

h. Family Treatment Unit, Colorado Psychiatric
    Hospital opens, Denver, 1964 (Langsley et al.).

i. Strong emergence of ego-oriented, reality-
    based treatment approaches.

j. Mental Research Institute, Brief Therapy
    Center established in Palo Alta, California
    (Watzawick, Weakland, Fisch, et al.) - 1966.

k. Tavistock Clinic London England, reports on
    research findings from brief focal psycho-
    therapy (Balint, Malan, et al.).

l. Continuing formulations of crisis inter-
    vention principles and models (Parad,
    Levy, Rusk, Pittman, et al.) - mid-1960's.

m. Montreal General Hospital, Department of
    Psychiatry, reorganizes to reduce delays/
    waiting time for treatment based on a
    brief treatment approach (Straker et al.) -
    1968.

n. St. Vincent's Hospital, N.Y., sets up
    emergency psychiatric services with
    similarities to Montreal General
    set-up - 1968.

o. Philadelphia Child Guidance Clinic
    reports on work with socio-economically
    deprived patient populations (Minuchin,
    Haley, et al.).

p. Explosion of research/treatment of
    sexual dysfunctions by briefer forms
    of therapy (Masters and Johnson, Kaplan,
    et al.).

                    1970-1980:

a. Davanloo continues and expands work in
    brief analytic treatment at Montreal
    General Hospital.

b. Sifneos moves from Massachusetts
    General Hospital to Beth Israel
    Hospital to continue work on STAPP
    for specific patients.

c. Continued research findings on the
    specific parameters of structure for
    time-limited therapy (patient types,
    length and spacing of sessions, etc.
    (Mann, Malan, et al.).

d. Reports of impact of short-term therapy
    on later adjustment from Kaiser-Permanente
    Prepaid-Plan, indicating powerful positive
    impact of briefer therapy (Cummings et al.).

e. Re-emergence of popularity and use of
    hypotherapy (Erickson et al.), with
    emphasis on shorter treatment approaches.

f. Neurolinguistic Programing emerges
    (Randler and Grinder, et al.), with
    emphasis on shorter treatment methods.

g. Proceedings of the first and second
    international symposia on short-term
    dynamic psychotherapy published
    (Davanloo et al.).

   h. Continuing budgetary restraints produce
       pressure on individuals and mental health
       agencies to maximize resources, including
       developing short-term treatment approaches.

About this Bibliography: (Instructions)

      This annotated bibliography on brief therapy approaches
has taken over four years to complete. Over 1,500 sources
are cited, published between 1920 and the end of April,
1980. More than 125 different professional journals are
presented, as is the work of over 1,000 mental health
professionals.

      Non-English titles are not included in this volume.
Perhaps a future volume will contain references to the many
fine articles written in other languages.

      All articles and books are cross-referenced through
the subject index at the back of the book. Thus, an article
which is about brief therapy with children and their
families carried out in a child guidance clinic using an
analytically-oriented approach will be listed separately
under the following headings: "children"; "family";
"child guidance clinic"; and, "analytically-oriented".

      I sincerely request anyone finding errors within this
text to write me with the information. Obviously, in an
undertaking of this kind, some slips are inevitable even
though great care has been taken by a number of people to
avoid any serious mistakes. I apologize in advance for
any inconvenience caused by such errors.

      I wish to conclude on a personal note. About seven
months prior to the completion of the work for this book,
I broke my leg and was forced to wear a full-length cast
for about six months. Fortunately, my wife and a number
of friends helped out, and I was able to finish the task
within a few months of the original deadline. Yet, as a
result of the accident and in combination with my impending

middle age, I have suddenly become acutely aware of time -
its importance, nature, role and impact in both my personal
and professional life. It was a personal experience which
has added a dimension to the work in this book.

Toronto
September, 1980   Harvey P. Mandel

1.   Abend, S., et al., Reactions of adolescents
      to short-term hospitalization, American
      Journal of Psychiatry, 1968, 124, 949-954.

The authors report on the results of providing short-term
hospitalizatton for 928 adolescents at the Bronx Municipal
Hospital Center. Involvement of family and friends was
encouraged as part of the therapy. The average length of
stay in the hospital was 3 weeks, with an upper limit of
6 weeks. Adolescents between the ages of 12 and 18 are
eligible for admission to the program. The authors uncovered 3 distinct stages in the adolescents' adjustive
reactions to the therapy program. I. Pre-engagement: this
stage was characterized by anger, denial of the need for
treatment, anxiety, etc.; II. Engagement: this stage was
characterized by conformity to the program, the admitting
of the need for help, decrease in acting out behavior,
serious working on issues; III. Disengagement: this
stage was precipitated by impending discharge from the
program, and was characterized by one of two reactions -
aggression or depression. Three cases are presented to
highlight these stages.

2.   Abramson, H.A., LSD-25 as an adjunct to
      brief psychotherapy with special reference
      to ego enhancement, Journal of Psychology,
      1956, 41, 199-229.

The author reports on the use of LSD-25 as an adjunct to
individual and group psychotherapy in non-psychotic
ambulatory patients. Specific reference is made to issues
of ego enhancement, and verbatim transcripts are used to
illustrate some of the issues discussed.

3.   Ackerman, M., and Ackerman, S., Emergency
      psychodrama for an acute psychosomatic
      syndrome, Group Psychotherapy, 1962, 15, 84-88.

The authors report on a one session emergency psychodrama
session with a female patient who was exhibiting severe
psychosomatic symptoms (dizziness, head pounding, confused
thinking, etc.). The specific techniques used are described and a reasonable adjustment reported.

4.   Adams, H.B., et al., Individual differences
      in behavioral reactions of psychiatric
      patients to brief partial sensory
      deprivation, Perceptual and Motor Skills,
      1972, 34, 199-217.

30 hospitalized psychiatric in-patients exposed to a few
hours of partial sensory deprivation (SD) showed a wide
range of individual differences in their reactions.
Reduced symptoms and improved intellectual functioning
after SD were the predominant group trends, but some
individuals showed substantial changes in opposite
directions. Individual differences in behavioral reactions
during and after SD were significantly related to MMPT
personality characteristics. Symptom reduction after SD
was a function of characteristics quite different from
those usually associated with prognosis for conventional
verbal psychotherapy. The results suggested that many
persons unlikely to benefit from traditional therapeutic
procedures might show improved personality and intellectual
functioning after a brief exposure to SD. There were many
other complex relationships between personality variables
and reactions to SD. (Journal abstract).

5.   Adelman, C.S., Teaching police crisis
      intervention techniques, Victimology,
      1977, 2, 123-126.

Presents a summary of a workshop on the use of crisis
intervention by police. Typical kinds of issues and
experiences which arose from the experiences of about 20
police officers are discussed.

6.   Adler, K.A., Techniques that shorten
      psychotherapy: Illustrated with five
      cases, Journal of Individual Psychology,
      1972, 28, 155-168.

Presents a series of techniques and approaches which
Adlerian psychology has contributed to the field which act
to shorten the length of psychotherapy. Specifically
focussed on are: purposiveness of symptoms, unity of

personality, issues of differential diagnosis, early recollections, birth order, dreams, life style, face-to-face encounter between therapist and patient, as well as five case histories to illustrate many of these approaches.

7.   Adsett, C.A., and Bruhn, J.G., Short-term group psychotherapy for post-myocardial infarction patients and their wives, Canadian Medical Association Journal, 1968, 99, 577-584.

The authors report on a study of 10 patients who had experienced coronary disease, and who were having some difficulty in adapting to their situation. A short-term, focussed group therapy approach was instituted for 6 of the 10 patients. Ten bi-weekly sessions were held, along with simultaneous wife group therapy in a separate group. The types of feelings and perceptions expressed by the patients were summarized, as well as a summary of the types of emotions experienced by the wives of the cardiac patients. More extensive follow-up is suggested by the authors, but they reveal encouraging initial results, especially when compared with the changes occurring in those four patients who refused the brief, group therapy experience.

8.   Affleck, D.C., and Garfield, S.L., Predictive judgements of therapists and duration of stay in psychotherapy, Journal of Clinical Psychology, 1961, 17, 134-137.

Fifteen variables to psychotherapy assets were rated by therapists on the basis of the intake information of out-patient candidates for therapy. A specific prediction of duration of stay was also made. Despite evidence that experience increases the reliability of these judgements, particularly those dealing directly with the therapy situation, the ratings were not significantly related to actual duration of stay. A general bias in the direction of being over-optimistic about patient length of stay resulted in marked difficulty in the correct identification of the early terminator.

9.   Aguilera, D.C., Sociocultural factors:
      Barriers to therapeutic intervention,
      Journal of Psychiatric Nursing and Mental
      Health Services, 1970, 8, 14-18.

This paper addresses some of the general socio-cultural
factors therapists must keep in mind in their work with
any ethnic groups or individuals from these groups.
Specifically, crisis intervention is described in detail
as an appropriate time-limited approach in community mental
health work. Such an approach used at the Benjamin Rush
Center in Los Angeles involves a here-and-now focus,
directive participation by the therapist, a time limit of
approximately 6 sessions, with the aim of helping the
client solve a specific problem. The phases of intervention are described (assessment, client perceptions of
crisis, actual intervention, crisis resolution and future
planning). A case report is also presented to highlight
the points made.

10.   Aguilera, D.C., Crisis: Moment of truth,
       Journal of Psychiatric Nursing and Mental
       Health Services, 1971, 9, 23-25.

The author focusses on the crisis of death and dying as a
moment of truth for those involved, including professionals
involved in the case. Issues of importance for nurses and
others dealing with those dying are reviewed, including
analysis of previous patterns of coping with stress,
meaning of the event for the patient, and situational
supports (their extent and strengths and weaknesses).

11.   Aguilera, D., and Messick, J., Crisis inter-
       vention: Theory and methodology, C.V. Mosby,
       St. Louis, 1974.

The authors provide an historical perspective of the
evolution of crisis theory and a model for understanding
theory and intervention in crisis situations. The authors
deal with crisis intervention, long term and short term
therapy, and provide case material to highlight their
point of view.

12. Aguilera, D.C., and Messick, J.M., Crisis
     intervention, in, Clark, A.L., and Assonso,
     D., (eds.), Childbearing and the nurse,
     Philadelphia, F.A. Davis Co., 1975.

13. Aguilera, D.C., Crisis intervention, impli-
     cations for community nursing, in, Quinn, M.,
     and Reinhardt, A., (eds.), Current practice
     in community nursing Vol. 1, St. Louis, Mo.,
     The C.V. Mosby Co., 1977.

14. Ahumada, J.L., On limited-time group
     psychotherapy, British Journal of Medical
     Psychology, 1976, 42, 81-88.

In her review of Bion's ideas on groups, Rioch (1970)
remarked that the shift in perspective from the individual
to the group, though often given lip service, is difficult
in actual practice but essential in order to grasp social
phenomena. This paper attempts to conceptualize the
evolution of the total group, as well as members within it,
in limited-time closed groups. The vicissitudes of ideal-
ization, first of the therapist defining the dependence
phase, then of the other members and the group itself in
the group symbiosis phase, as well as the ulterior contacts
with internal and inter-personal reality, bringing about
individuation, are described. A clinical outlook is chosen
to attain some clarity in the description of complex but
relevant phenomena. (Journal summary).

15. Ahumada, J.L., et al., On time-limited
     group psychotherapy: I. Setting, admission,
     and therapeutic ideology, Psychiatry, 1974,
     37, 254-260.

The work of a team of mental health professionals at the
Department of Psychopathology of the Center of Medical
Education and Clinical Investigations of the University of
Buenos Aires is described. The use of initial individual
and group interviews (2 each) is detailed as an integral
part of the admission program to limited-time group psychotherapy (1 session/week) 75 minutes duration, for 18 months.

16.   Aja, J.H., Brief group treatment of obesity
       through ancillary self-hypnosis, American
       Journal of Clinical Hypnosis, 1977, 19,
       231-234.

This treatment paradigm was developed to increase subjects'
control over food intake while considering the economics
of time and expense to the client. A three session treatment was provided for 40 subjects. A standard trance
induction was followed by a series of behavior specific
suggestions related to control eating. Mean weight loss
was 12.6 pounds three months posttreatment and 9.5 six
months posttreatment. A discussion of the treatment merits
and deficits follows the verbatim therapy procedure.
(Journal abstract).

17.   Albronda, H.F., et al., Social class and
       psychotherapy, Archives of General Psychiatry,
       1964, 10, 276-284.

This paper reports on five years of teaching experience
with medical students who served as therapists for 384
patients who requested therapy. The patients varied over
a wide range socioeconomically. No selection of patients
was done according to models of treatment, differences
among socioeconomic variables, etc. The authors compared
patients according to whether they remained in treatment,
those who did not enter into on-going therapy, and those
who dropped out at some point prior to completion of
therapy. They found no significant differences across the
three groups re the variable of social class, but they did
find some differences in the degree of stability of social
adjustment across the three groups. The article also
compares results with other published reports from medical
and psychiatric teaching centers.

After 30 interviews, upper and lower class individuals
experiences were similar; i.e., they both had a better
chance of improving had they stayed in therapy longer.
Initially, upper class patients tend to gain socially in
adjustment by the 21st session, but by the 30th, they are
no different than lower class levels of adjustment. Authors
conclude that it may take lower class individuals slightly
longer to learn of the value of psychotherapy, but that
they can learn such fairly easily.

Conclusion: Regardless of social class, the longer a
person stayed in therapy, the more he/she benefitted by it.

18.   Aldrich, C.K., Brief psychotherapy: A
       reappraisal of some theoretical assumptions,
       American Journal of Psychiatry, 1968, 125,
       585-592.

The author, using a psychoanalytic framework, presents a
discussion of parental expectations and how they are manifested in their children. Specifically, the author focusses
on middle and upper class children and teenagers who exhibit
behavioral disorders of various kinds, and traces their
difficulties to the parental expectations of the children.
The term superego lacunae is used to describe and explain
the youngsters behavior.

The author summarizes some of the assumptions that psychoanalysts should question about their views of briefer forms
of therapy (e.g., that it is more dangerous and riskier;
that improvements early in therapy are "flights into health"
and indicate that client is now ready for more intensive
work).

The author extends the Johnson and Szurek concept of superego lacunae and parental expectation by discussing issues
revolving around symptom choice, society and therapist
expectations (not just parental expectations), and the
value in decreasing the length of time needed for psychotherapy.

19.   Aldrich, C., The long and short psychotherapy,
       Psychiatric Annals, 1975, 5, 507-512.

The author raises the point that in many cases short-term
or time-limited therapy is the treatment of choice. The
author cites a study of long term therapy in which deterioration in the patients was reported. This may be due to
the continuing dependency on the therapist over a long
period of time. Short term approaches, however, clearly
let the patient know that the expectations are that his/her
synptoms will probably soon disappear, and that therapy
will be ending within a specified period of time. The
author presents some discussion on the role of psychoanalytic

model in tending to prolong therapy, advocating increased
clarity around its use. There is also some discussion
about when longer term and shorter term therapies are
inappropriate, as well as suggestions for future research
in this area.

20.   Aldrich, C.K., Office psychotherapy for
       the primary care physician, in, Friedman,
       D.X., and Dyrud, J.E., (eds.), American
       handbook of psychiatry, 2nd edition, New
       York, Basic Books, 1975.

The "primary care physician" occupies a particular strategic
position in the treatment of mild and relatively uncompli-
cated mental health problems. Although the PCP may have
developed some knowledge of management of the psychological
aspects of illness, he often needs help in understanding
psychiatric principles and practice and their relationship
to his patients and his therapeutic milieu. In this chapter from the American handbook of psychiatry, Aldrich's
prime focus is on the PCP's psychotherapeutic care of
relatively acute conditions in which the psychiatric factor
is primary, and on the consulting, teaching and referral
relationships between the PCP and the psychiatrist. The
author examines both the diagnostic process and many aspects
of psychotherapeutic procedures potentially utilized by a
PCP, while focussing insightfully on some of the differences
between attitudes and styles helpful in psychotherapeutic
procedures and those frequently exhibited by the PCP in
treatment of more organic conditions. (Abstract by Deborah
Schuller).

21.   Alexander, F., Principles and techniques
       of briefer psychotherapeutic procedures,
       Research Publication of the Association of
       Nervous and Mental Disease, 1951, 31, 16-20.

22.   Alexander, F., Principles and techniques of
       briefer psychotherapeutic procedures, in,
       Wortis, S., Herman, M., and Hare, C., (eds.),
       Psychiatric treatment, Baltimore, Williams
       and Wilkins, 1953.

23.   Alexander, F., The dynamics of psychotherapy
       in the light of learning theory, American
       Journal of Psychiatry, 1963, 120, 440-449.

The author summarizes in detail the assumptions all psychoanalysts can agree on, and then proceeds to question some
of these. Alexander stresses the relationship between the
patient's past relationships and the kind of interaction
set up between therapist and patient in the present. It is
the difference between the two which permits new emotional
adjustments to develop. Thus focus on the past is always
reconnected back to the present, a position shared by Rado.
The author also questions whether longer analyses produce
better, more long lasting results. His claim is that long
analyses foster greater dependencies in the patient. He
discusses his technique of "experimental temporary interrup-
tions", in which sessions are cancelled for a period of
time, during which the patient discovers many strengths
hitherto unused. Further, the sessions which follow such
an interruption usually are very productive, for they bring
to the forefront much unconscious material previously
defended against. The role of countertransference is also
discussed, and its positive and negative aspects presented.

Further, the value of keeping the patient as much as
possible at an adult level of functioning is discussed.
While regression is seen as critical, an over-emphasis on
it without the reconnecting back to the present is seen as
harmful. The author concludes with a discussion of the
principles of learning theory, and shows how they can be
used to explain the processes of therapy.

24.   Alexander, F., and French, T.M., Psycho-
       analytic therapy, New York, Ronald Press
       Co., 1946.

One of the classic books in the field of shorter-term
therapies, and a dramatic break with the more traditional
psychoanalytic approaches of its time. The book was
originally criticized for many of its innovations at the
time it was published. The book includes case illustrations
which reflect the positive outcome of briefer forms of
therapy. Alexander and French show how the therapist becomes
active from the very first encounter with the patient. They
indicate that all the old, unresolved conflicts arise in

the transference situation, and they point to the differences between the parents reactions and the therapist's
reactions as the key to producing change for the patient.
Unlike the parent, the therapist's attitude is more objective and understanding. This results in a corrective
emotional experience, which is the secret of success in
short-term therapy. Over time in the therapy context, the
therapeutic results become part of the individual's new
ways of life. Alexander and French suggest another change
from classic analytic therapy - spacing out sessions,
rather than bunching them together. This allows for the
working through of repressed material than if daily sessions
were held.

25.   Alexander, J.F., and Parsons, B.V., Short-
       term behavioral intervention with delinquent
       families: Impact on family process and
       recidivism, Journal of Abnormal Psychology,
       1973, 81, 219-225.

Based on prior family interaction studies and a systems
conceptualization of deviant behavior, a specific, short-
term behaviorally oriented family intervention program
designed to increase family reciprocity, clarity of communication, and contingency contracting was developed for
delinquent teenagers. The results indicated that 46 families
receiving the program demonstrated significant changes in
three family interaction measures at the end of therapy,
and also significantly reduced recidivism rates at follow-
up when compared to 30 families receiving alternate forms
of family therapy and a total of 52 families receiving no
professional treatment. The study emphasized the utility
of a therapy evaluation philosophy that includes a clear
description of intervention techniques, a description of
expected process changes, stringent nonreactive outcome
measures, and control for maturation and attention placebo.
(Journal abstract).

26.   Allgeyer, J.M., The crisis group-- its
       unique usefulness to the disadvantaged,
       International Journal of Group Psychotherapy,
       1970, 20, 235-240.

In this brief article, Allgeyer states the rationale and
theoretical treatment design underlying a multidisciplinary,
community-based, walk-in clinic. She presents an example
of the dynamics of a specific crisis group seen at such a
clinic. The author concludes that the crisis group is
uniquely helpful in reaching persons underrepresented in
clinical practice, namely, those of divergent racial, cultural, and socioeconomic backgrounds. The existential
understanding by group members of the conditions affecting
each other's lives and their ability to aid one another
emphatically and practically appears therapeutically effective. Finally, the middle class therapists benefitted
directly by experience with disadvantaged group members,
and were enabled to provide more meaningful treatment to
minorities and the poor. (Abstract by Deborah Schuller).

27.   Alpern, E., Short clinical services for
       children in a child guidance clinic,
       American Journal of Orthopsychiatry, 1956,
       26, 314-325.

This article summarizes clinical work done with 200 families
in a psychiatric child guidance clinic. A detailed description of the diagnostic and process variables is presented
as they relate to outcome measures. Progress in the children
is intimately connected to parental activity, in the sense
that the more that parents can seperate out their own problems
from those of their children, the greater the possibility
that their children will improve. The author also reports
that quite frequently, the children begin to progress prior
to changes in their parents or support from them. Lack of
progress was seen in those children with extreme resistance
to change, and whose family situations included serious
marital difficulties, negative environmental conditions,
and/or serious educational or biological difficulties.

The key element here is emphasis on immediate service
(including the diagnostic work-up), and an early requirement
for clarity of purpose of treatment, both on the part of the
parents and the therapists.

28.   Alpert, J.J., et al., The types of families
       that use an emergency clinic, Medical Care,
       1969, 7, 55-61.

This study relates the results of a detailed examination of
the users of one hospital's emergency clinic. Four types
of utilizers are differentiated: (a) families with a stable
relationship with a physician; (b) families with a stable
relationship with the hospital; (c) families with an
unstable relationship with a physician; and, (d) families
with an unstable relationship with the hospital. Social
characteristics of each of these groups are distinguished.
The degree of reliance on any medical facility appears
correlated with advantaged socioeconomic status. The group
characterized by unstable relationships with the hospital
is more frequently comprised of disadvantaged families.
The use of such a typology in screening emergency clinic
patients might increase knowledge about the motivations for
seeking medical care and lead eventually to ways of improving
overall health care patterns. (abstract by Deborah Schuller).

29.   Alvord, J., Home token economy: An incentive
       program for children and their parents,
       Champaign, Illinois, Research Press, 1973.

In a 20 page booklet, Alvord outlines briefly the rationale
and history of this token economy program. He addresses
parents, by providing detailed instructions for initiating
such a system in the home. He explains procedures for
choosing desirable and undesirable behaviors, and provides
rules concerning privileges, bonds, incorporation of allow-
ances in the program and setting of token amounts. He
suggests means of modifying the system so that it best meets
a family's particular needs, and includes a short case study.
His program is sufficiently flexible to be applicable to
most families in which the parent is able to enforce the
contract. The token economy is not viewed as effective with
those children whom parents cannot control physically or
emotionally. Professional guidance is recommended to adjust
and audit the system on a weekly basis for problem children.
(abstract by Deborah Schuller).

30.   Amada, G., The paucity of mental health
        services and programs in community colleges:
        Implications of a survey, Journal of the
        American College Health Association, 1975,
        23, 345-349.

To gain an overview of the extent and nature of mental
health services throughout the community college system in
California, the author addressed thirteen-item questionnaires
to the 100 private and public junior colleges comprising the
system. Amada relates and discussed the findings in this
article. Most significantly, also two-thirds of these
junior colleges do not provide on-campus mental health
services, although 85% of this group indicated an appreciable
need for such services. The implications of the study extend
to the rest of the U.S., and Amada recommends state and
federal legislation to allocate to junior colleges the funds
necessary for organizing mental health programs wich the
colleges appear to need. In this way they could provide an
immediate, confidential, and intensive service to help
students. (abstract by Deborah Schuller).

31.   Amada, G., Crisis-oriented psychotherapy:
        Some theoretical and practical considerations,
        Journal of Contemporary Psychotherapy, 1977,
        9, 104-111.

The author's experience in organizing and implementing a
community college psychological service which offers
primarily short-term psychotherapy led him to identify the
distinguishing characteristics of crisis-oriented therapy.
Amada believes that a therapist risks little in assuming
that most psychiatric clients are indeed in a state of crisis
at the time they seek psychotherapeutic help. He adumbrates
the prime features of short-term therapy with regards to
entailed tasks, the need to maintain a positive relationship
with the client via the use of the contemporary context,
the role of apparel and speech, the relinquishment of
anonymity, flexible scheduling, and telephone accessibility.
Further, the therapist provides intellectual "anchors" which
provide the client with the ballast of a psychological
working vocabulary. The author concludes that the standard
of clinical adeptness and sophistication requisite for undertaking short-term psychotherapy is unique, and perhaps even
more difficult to achieve thn that which inhere in long-
term therapy. (abstract by Deborah Schuller).

32.   Amster, F., Therapeutic techniques with
       emphasis on client participation and with
       potentialities for economy in therapy,
       American Journal of Orthopsychiatry, 1951,
       21, 367-377.

Writing from a dynamic stance, the author illustrates with
four case studies a therapeutic technique which emphasizes
the client's active participation in his struggle for self-
maintenance and maximal functioning. The therapeutic
approach begins with an acceptance of each client as a
composite of positive and negative adaptations to his social
reality, and a definition of therapy as a process for which
the client shares active responsibility. Emphasis is placed
on demonstrating to the client the degree to which his
current life is dominated by his past. This affords
opportunities for release and diminution of anxiety, as well
as for a strengthening of independent strivings. Definition
and directive use of ego-challenging therapy which sets
disciplines on the exploitation of childhood investments
appears to have distinct advantages, including the potential
for economy in the therapeutic process. (abstract by
Deborah Schuller).

33.   Amster, F., Some therapeutic implications
       of short-term therapy, Journal of Psychiatric
       Social Work, 1952, 22, 13-19.

The author poses four questions pertinent to the development
of a realistic professional approach to meet increased
public demand for therapeutic service of a particular type
--i.e. short-term, and oriented towards "speedy recovery"
in circumscribed problem areas. These questions concern
definition of therapist responsibility with regards to
clients experiencing temporary difficulties; therapeutic
services possible with this group; and general therapeutic
implications of short-term therapy. Amster examines six
cases to assess the validity and potential of short-term
treatment. She condludes that brief work offers specific
gains to clients; that it meets requests for service made
by the majority of individuals seeking help; and that it
may be therapeutically beneficial for a large segment of
the population. However, this type of approach requires
reorientation. flexibility, and discipline on the part of
the therapist. (abstract by Deborah Schuller).

34. Anchor, K.N., Personality integration
     and successful outcome in individual
     psychotherapy, Journal of Clinical
     Psychology, 1977, 33, 245-246.

Successful and unsuccessful outcomes in twenty-four therapy
dyads were analyzed according to client-therapist personality
integration (pi). Results indicated that successful outcome
was most likely to occur when both client and therapist
were high pi. Failure was most frequent among mixed sex
dyads with discrepant pi differences. Implications for
effective client-therapist matching were discussed.
(Journal abstract).

35. Anchor, K.N., and Sandler, H.M.,
     Psychotherapy sabotage revisited: The
     better half of individual psychotherapy,
     Journal of Clinical Psychology, 1976, 32,
     146-148.

This study examined the amount of actual client self-
disclosure emitted and the pattern of its occurrence within
and across individual therapy sessions. An earlier finding
showed that many clients avoided self-disclosure until the
session's closing minutes early in therapy. These data
revealed that in the middle stages of short-term therapy
for a university population (N=26) clients continue to
engage in the highest proportion of self-disclosure during
the latter half of the therapy hour. The position that
there are ways in which psychotherapy sabotage can be
reduced was discussed. (Journal summary).

36. Andolfi, M., Paradox in psychotherapy,
     American Journal of Psychoanalysis, 1967,
     34, 221-228.

The author briefly describes the concept of paradox, its
definition, and its use in individual, marital, and family
therapy. Specific examples highlight the points raised,
and demonstrate the use of paradox to shorten the course
of therapy.

37.   Andolfi, M., A structural approach to a
       family with an encopretic child, Journal
       of Marriage and Family Counseling, 1978,
       4, 25-29.

This article describes brief therapy using a structural
approach. During the course of therapy, the encopretic
behavior of a pre-adolescent boy was observed in relation
to the interaction and structure of the family system. The
presenting problem was analyzed as a sign of family dysfunction and of the stress consequent to the parents separation.
The success of the theory did not consist of only the disappearance of the encopretic behavior, but also in the dis-
covery of different modalities of relating which produced
a liberating effect on the identified patient and on other
members of the family. (Journal abstract).

38.   Andrews, D.A., and Young, J.O., Short-
       term structured group counseling and
       prison adjustment, Canadian Journal of
       Criminology and Corrections, 1974, 16,
       5-13.

A study intended as a demonstration of the effect of short-
term structured group counseling in a correction facility
is reported. Andrews and Young review the literature on
correctional intervention--especially, criteria traditionally
used in evaluating counseling programs, and the lack of
empirical support of post-treatment effects. Subjects were
forty-seven delinquent males, with sentences ranging from
six to nine months. Twenty-four inmates were randomly
assigned to experimental groups, and participated in two,
one and one-half hour discussion sessions. Dependent
variables were attitude measures, number of reported mis-
conducts over five post-treatment weeks, and officers'
ratings. Results indicate fewer misconduct reports among
younger (aged sixteen and seventeen) residents who took
part in the counseling sessions; with no significant effect
shown among older (eighteen - twenty-one years) youths.
Attitude and officer ratings failed to uncover any differential treatment effects. The authors briefly discuss the data.
(abstract by Deborah Schuller).

39. Annon, J., The behavioral treatment of
sexual problems, Vol. I: Brief therapy,
Honolulu, HI., Enabling System, 1974,
(also reprinted by Harper Row, New
York, 1976).

This text reviews various behavioral approaches in the treatment of human problems, and then focusses on the behavioral
approaches to the treatment of sexual difficulties. The
author details a variety of issues related to the background
information and knowledge for such an approach, as well as
presenting a conceptual scheme for such treatment (the
PLISSIT Model). Issues relating to the treatment process
include such items as permission (thoughts, fantasies, dreams,
feelings, etc.), limited information by clients about sexual
facts, specific suggestions for males and females. The text
concludes with a number of self-study programs, and a list of
readings in the area of sexuality.

40. Annon, J., The OLISSIT Model: A proposed
conceptual scheme for the behavioral treatment of sexual problems, Journal of Sex
Education and Therapy, 1976, 2, 1-15.

The P-LI-SS-IT model is constituted by four levels of
approach: (a) permission; (b) limited information; (c)
specific suggestions; and, (d) intensive therapy. The first
three levels can be viewed as brief therapy, as contrasted
with the fourth. Utilization of this model has distinct
advantages. It may be used in a variety of settings and
adapted to available client time. Because each level requires
increasing professional experience, this model allows the
individual to gear his approach to his own particular level
of competence, and more easily determine when referral is
appropriate. The model provides a framework for discriminat-
ing between those problems which require intensive therapy
and those amenable to briefer therapy. While the brief
therapy portion of the model is not intended to resolve all
sexual problems, it may handle many. Intensive therapy is
seen as highly individualized, necessary because standardized
treatment was not successful. The author provides practical
suggestions for applying the four levels of treatment, stating
both advantages and limitations of each. (abstract by Deborah
Schuller).

41.   Annon, J., and Robinson, C.H., The PLISSIT
       approach to sex therapy, Tape cassette E-7,
       American Association of Sex Educators,
       Counselors, and Therapists, 5010 Wisconsin
       Ave., N.W., Washington, D.C., 200016, 1977.

42.   Annon, J., and Robinson, C.H., The use of
       vicarious learning in the treatment of
       secual concerns, in, LoPiccolo, J., and
       LoPiccolo, L., (eds.), Handbook of sex
       therapy, New York, Plenum Press, 1978.

43.   Ansbacher, H.L., Adlerian psychology: The
       tradition of brief psychotherapy, Journal
       of Individual Psychology, t972, 28, 137-151.

Presents the view that the tradition of brief psychotherapy
is in fact the tradition of Individual Psychology, and its
originator, Alfred Adler. He discusses the attributes of
brief therapy (time factor, exogenous factors, focussed
interview, importance of the first interview, relationship
with the patient, public health aspect) and shows how all
of these attributes specifically expressed themselves through
Adler's system of therapy. He concludes by summarizing the
differences in the concept of man and its implications for
psychotherapy between Freud and Adler, by touching on the
following comparisons: pragmatism versus positivism;
becoming versus being; humanism versus mechanism; community
feeling versus superego.

44.   Applebaum, S.A., Parkinson's Law in
       psychotherapy, International Journal of
       Psychoanalytic Psychotherapy, 1975, 4,
       426-436.

Describes the importance of the issue of time psychotherapy,
with a special emphasis on Parkinson's Law - activity
contracts or expands to fill the amount of time available
to complete the activity.

Focusses on issues of separation and individuation, important developmental issues and critical issues for psychotherapy. Compares open-ended psychotherapy and the issue of timelessness, with short-term set series of sessions, and suggests that the same issues and patterns emerge in groups whether they meet for only a few sessions or over a period of years.

He also cautions against the use of either short-term or long-term therapy as an automatic decision.

45. Argles, P., and Mackenzie, M., Crisis intervention with a multi-problem family: A case study, Journal of Child Psychology and Psychiatry, 1970, 11, 187-195.

The authors initially summarize some of the basis principles of crisis intervention and crisis theory, and concepts of adjustment and maladjustment. Characteristics of individuals or families in crises are: (a) great emotionality at time of crisis with increased ability or desire to accept outside aid or support; (b) greater accessibility to past problems or unconscious information.

The major characteristics of multi-problem families were: (a) deniel of feelings, especially that of depression with a concomitant inability to help members of the family; (b) mistrust of authority, and skill in using agencies or individual professionals; (c) lack of insight into feelings, and choice to act out rather than reflect, thus producing difficulty in acceptance to help from outsiders; (d) lack of willingness to commit themselves to on-going treatment. This last factor lead the team to offer a time-limited, clearly defined, goal-oriented approach, which the family was able to use constructively; (e) these families are acutely aware of their inadequacies - setting attainable goals helps in allowing for development of some sense of competency.

46.   Argyle, M., et al., Social skills training
       psychotherapy: A comparative study,
       Psychological Medicine, 1974, 4, 435-443.

In this study, two forms of treatment were compared. Brief
psychotherapy and a social skills approach were used, the
social skills program based in learning theory. The number
of Ss was seven, and six of the seven showed marked improvement in the clinical and social areas, although both
approaches produced improvement. Social skills training
effects tended to last for a longer period of time than
those of the brief psychotherapy, even though those Ss in
the psychotherapy group had about twice the number of
sessions as those in the skills group.

47.   Argyris, C., Intervention theory and method:
       A behavioral science view, Reading, Mass.,
       Addison-Wesley, 1970.

48.   Arthur, G.L., et al., Domestic disturbances:
       A major police dilemma, and how one major
       city is handling the problem, Journal of
       Police Science and Administration, 1977, 5,
       421-429.

This article describes the structure, process, and research
outcome results of the Family Crisis Intervention Program
of the Columbus, Georgia, Police Department.

49.   Atkins, M., et al., Brief treatment of
       homosexual patients, Comprehensive
       Psychiatry, 1976, 17, 115-124.

The authors describe a brief treatment service, focussed
specifically on the short-term treatment (three sessions)
of sixteen homosexual patients. Treatment in some cases
involved strengthening the homosexual relationship or in
making it less uncomfortable for the individual. Case
examples were included along with a discussion of some of
the similarities and differences between homosexual patients
and other patients. (e.g. "coming out).

50.   Atkins, R.W., Psychiatric emergency
       service, Archives of General Psychiatry,
       1967, 17, 176-182.

Different types of psychiatric emergency care aiming to
render various kinds of service have been described in the
literature. The one described here provides immediate and
rapid clinical evaluation, first aid, and disposition. It
is manned by second-year psychiatric residents, supervised
by faculty, and supported by all the other services of a
general hospital. In order to operate successfully it
depends heavily on three hospitals (Stron Memorial,
Rochester State, and Monroe County) to which patients are
admitted, outpatient clinics, and social agencies, which
make possible prompt appropriate disposition, thereby
facilitating the accommodation of a large number of patients
and their families. In two years, 7,684 patient visits were
recorded and extensive data collected on each one. The
demographic, educational, occupational, diagnostic, therapeutic, and dispositional data are recorded in this report.
(Journal summary).

51.   Auerbach, S., and Kilmann, P.R., Crisis
       intervention: A review of outcome
       research, Psychological Bulletin, 1977,
       84, 1189-1217.

Crisis intervention studies conducted in suicide prevention/
crisis intervention programs, in psychiatric settings, and
with surgical patients are critically evaluated. In the
first area the impracticality of suicide as an outcome
measure and the need for shifting evaluation emphasis from
crisis worker performance to client behavior change measures
is stressed. Also, the virtual impossibility of demonstrating overall program impact on the community and the need for
developing internal program evaluation procedures is noted.
Studies in psychiatric settings suffer from considerable
methodological shortcomings that prohibit definitive conclusions; studies operationally specifying treatment
components are greatly needed here. Studies with surgery
patients indicate the necessity for developing intervention
techniques most appropriate for individuals differing in
their typical manner of dealing with stress. In all settings,
outcome measures should be appropriate to the situation and
logically related to the goals of intervention. (Journal
abstract).

52.   Auerbach, R., and Kilmann, P.R., The
       effects of group desensitization on
       secondary erectile failure, Behavior
       Therapy, 1977, 8, 330-339.

Sixteen subjects were assign to group desensitization (SD)
or treatment control groups. The groups were balanced with
respect to age, education, severity of disorder, duration
of disorder, number of sexual partners, cooperativeness of
female partner, and marital status. The SD group received
fifteen forty-five minute sessions of relaxation plus a
common hierarchy of secual scenes, while the control group
received fifteen sessions of relaxation alone. Subjects
in the SD group reflected significant positive changes when
compared with control subject on measures of sexual performance and satisfaction with nonsexual aspects of their
relationships with their most frequent sexual partner.
These gains were maintained over a three month follow-up
period. The control subjects who received subsequent treatment made substantial gains which persisted over three
months. Implications and suggestion for future research
are discussed. (Journal abstract).

53.   Augenbraun, B., et al., Brief intervention
       as a preventive force in disorders of early
       childhood, American Journal of Orthopsychiatry,
       1967, 37, 697-702.

The authors describe a brief psychotherapeutic family
intervention model (three sessions, follow-up six to nine
months later) they have developed in the context of a
pediatric practice. The specific characteristics of the
therapists are described in the context of an active,
educational model for a variety of child focussed problem
areas (e.g., behavior problems, sleep and feeding difficulties, crying problems; G.I. tract difficulties).

They report that in many cases, the child's symtomatology
disappeared rapidly, and a shift in focus occurred related
to the disturbances in interaction between the parents of
the children. Case material from two families is presented
to highlight points made. Most families responded positively to the program. None of the children treated in
this program had conditions with an organic base.

54.   Avnet, H.H., Short-term treatment under
        auspices of a medical insurance plan,
        American Journal of Psychiatry, 1965,
        122, 147-151.

Avnet relates impressions from a two to three-year follow-
up study of a non-profit community insurance plan to provide
ambulatory psychiatric coverage. Four-fifths of patients
responding to the follow-up questionnaire who utilized the
program for a maximum of fifteen individual therapy sessions
report recovery or improvement. The author presents information about the plan, data from the follow-up, and implications. She concludes that the brief psychotherapy
offered under the plan appears worthwhile. (abstract by
Deborah Schuller).

55.   Axelrod, B.H., Mental health considerations
        in the pediatric emergency room, Journal of
        Pediatric Psychology, 1976, 1, 14-17.

The emergency room setting provides opportunities for
psychosocial intervention with children and their families,
and yet this area of patient contact has been neglected in
most training programs throughout the U.S. This paper
shares the experience of the emergency room setting from
the perspective of both house officers and staff and the
families and children who seek care under adverse conditions.
Suggestions for intervention that can be made regardless
of professional discipline are offered. (Journal abstract).

56.   Ayer, W.H., Implosive therapy: A review,
        Psychotherapy: Theory, Research, and
        Practice, 1972, 9, 242-250.

Ayer reviews theoretic rationale and general outcome research of implosive therapy--noting the disparity between
published case reports which appear to support the method
and the majority of experimental approaches, which do not.
He examines the literature to report current status of
concepts pertinent to implosive therapy--i.e. psychoanalytic concepts in IT theory and practice; the role of
visual imagery; and side effects. Relevant animal research
is discussed, although the author states that most of this

research has been only superficially related to the IT
paradigm. He concludes that the efficacy of IT as an
enduring clinical technique and the range of its applicability need yet to be determined. Ayer cites a variety
of issues which bear further empirical investigation.
(abstract by Deborah Schuller).

57.   Ayllon, T., Intensive treatment of
       psychotic behavior by stimulus satiation
       and food reinforcement, Behavior Research
       and Therapy, 1963, 1, 53-61.

This investigation demonstrates that extensive and effective
behavioral modification is feasible without costly and
lengthy therapeutic treatment. In addition, the often heard
notion that another undesirable type of behavior will replace the original problem behavior is not supported by the
findings to date. (Journal summary).

58.   Ayllon, T., and Azrin, N.H., The
       measurement and reinforcement of
       behavior of psychotics, Journal of
       Experimental Analysis of Behavior,
       1965, 8, 357-383.

An attempt was made to strengthen behaviors of psychotics
by applying operant reinforcement principles in a mental
hospital ward. The behaviors studied were necessary and/or
useful for the patient to function in the hospital environment. Reinforcement consisted of the opportunity to engage
in activities that had a high level of occurrence when freely
allowed. Token were used as conditioned reinforcers to
bridge the delay between behavior and reinforcement.
Emphasis was placed on objective definition and quantifi-
cation of the response and reinforcers and upon programming
and recording procedures. Standardizing the objective
criteria permitted the ward attendants to administer the
program. The procedures were found to be effective in
maintaining the desired adaptive behaviors for as long as
the procedures were in effect. In a series of six experiments, reinforced behaviors were considerably reduced when
the reinforcement procedure was discontinued; the adaptive
behaviors increased immediately when the reinforcement
procedure was re-introduced. (Journal abstract).

59.   Ayllon, T., and Azrin, N.H., The token
       economy: A motivational system for therapy
       and rehabilitation, New York, Appleton-
       Century-Crofts, 1968.

60.   Ayllon, T., and Haughton, E., Control
       behavior of schizophrenic patients by
       food, Journal of Experimental Analysis of
       Behavior, 1962, 5, 343-352.

Operant-conditioning principles using food as a reinforcer
were applied to control the behavior of 45 chronic schizophrenic patients. The investigation was conducted in a
psychiatric ward in which there was 24-hr. environmental
control. In order to use food as a reinforcer for controlling psychotic behavior, it was necessary first to deal
with the eating deficits in the patients. Approximately 50%
of the ward population was selected because of a history of
refusal to eat. Their refusal to eat had remained relatively
unaffected by one or more of these treatments: spoonfeeding,
tubefeeding, intravenous feeding, and electroshock. These
treatments were discontinued and the patients were left alone
at mealtimes. The results show that social reinforcement in
such forms as coaxing, persuading, and feeding the patient
tend to shape patients into eating problems so they are
conditioned to eat only with assistance. When refusal to
eat was no longer followed by social reinforcement, the
patients soon started eating unassisted. When access to the
dining room was made dependent upon a chain of responses
including a motor and social component, all patients learned
these responses. (Journal abstract).

61.   Ayllon, T., and Kelly, E., Reinstating
       verbal behavior in a functionally mute
       retardate, Professional Psychology, 1974,
       385, 393.

The article describes the use of behavioral techniques in
restoring the functional speech of an eleven year-old girl
who had not spoken in the classroom for ever eight months.
The entire procedure took less than four hours to complete.
(Journal abstract).

62.   Ayllon, T., and Rosenbaum, M., The
      behavioral treatment of disruption and
      hyperactivity in school settings, in,
      Lahey, B., and Kazdin, A. (eds.),
      Advances in child clinical psychology,
      New York, Plenum Publishing, 1977.

63.   Ayllon, T., and Skuban, W., Accountability
      in psychotherapy: A test case, Journal of
      Behavior Therapy and Experimental Psychiatry,
      1973, 4, 19-30.

An attempt was made to determine empirically the feasibility
of therapy on a contract basis between therapist and client.
The case was of a 9-yr-old autistic child whose major problems were temper tantrums and refusal to obey adults'
requests. Therapeutic goals and criteria were defined to
the satisfaction of therapist and client (the parents) as
was the duration of treatment (35 days). An important
feature of the intervention was the decision to develop
social behaviors outside and not inside the clinic, thus
obviating the problem of transfer. (Journal abstract).

64.   Ayllon, T., et al., Behavioral treatment
      of childhood neurosis, Psychiatry, 1977,
      40, 315-322.

The present study attempted to use behavioral treatment to
eliminate the neurotic symptoms of a 5-year-old child. The
child's symptoms were assessed on a pre- and post-treatment
basis, and in addition, ongoing observations of the child's
symptoms allowed daily evaluation of the treatment program.
Behavior therapy focused on altering the current symptom-
environment relationships experienced by the child. Follow-
ups on the resolution of the child's problems were conducted
two months and two years after behavior therapy and indicated
that the child was symptom-free. Therapeutic attempts to
resolve the historical conflicts of early childhood and to
resolve the contemporary conflicts of current social interaction are discussed as viable but not mutually exclusive
therapeutic strategies. (Journal abstract).

65.   Azrin, N.H., Improvements in the community-
       reinforcement approach to alcoholism,
       Behavior, Research and Therapy, 1976, 14
       339-348.

This study evaluated a modified Community-Reinforcement
program for treating alcoholics. The previously tested
Community-Reinforcement program included special job, family,
social and recreational procedures and was shown to reduce
alcoholism. To increase the effectiveness of the program
further, the present study incorporated a Buddy system, a
daily report procedure, group counseling, and a special
social motivation program to ensure the self administration
of Disulfiram (Antabuse). The alcoholics who received the
Improved Community-Reinforcement program drank less, worked
more, spent more time at home and less time institutionalized
than did their matched controls who received the standard
hospital treatment including Antabuse in the usual manner.
These results were stable over a 2 year period. The program
appeared even more effective and less time-consuming than
the previous program. The present results replicate the
effectiveness of the Community-Reinforcement program for
reducing alcoholism and indicate the usefulness of the
additions to the program. (Journal summary).

66.   Azrin, N.H., and Foxx, R.M., A Rapid
       method of toilet training the institi-
       tutionalized retarded, Journal of Applied
       Behavior Analysis, 1971, 4, 89-99.

Incontinence is a major unsolved problem in the institutionalized care of the profoundly retarded. A reinforcement and social analysis of the incontinence was used to
develop a procedure that would rapidly toilet train
retardates and motivate them to remain continent during the
day in their ward setting. Nine profoundly retarded adults
were given intensive training (median of four days per
patient), the distinctive features of which were artificially
increasing the frequency of urinations, positive reinforcement of correct toileting but a delay for "accidents", use
of new automatic apparatus for signalling elimination ,
shaping of independent toileting, cleanliness training,

and staff reinforcement procedures. Incontinence was
reduced immediately by about 90% and eventually decreased
to near zero. These results indicate the present procedure
is an effective, rapid, enduring, and administratively
feasible solution to the problem of incontinence of the
institutionalized retarded. (Journal abstract).

   67.   Azrin, N.H., and Nunn, R.G., Habit-
          reversal: A method of eliminating
          nervous habits and tics, Behavior
          Research and Therapy, 1973, 11, 619-628.

No clinical treatment for nervous habits has been generally
effective. The present rationale is that nervous habits
persist because of response chaining, limited awareness,
excessive practice and social tolerance. A new procedure
was devised for counteracting these influences: the client
practiced movements which were the reverse of the nervous
habit, he learned to be aware of each instance of the habit
and to differentiate it from its usual response chain and
he was given social approval for his efforts to inhibit the
habit. The treatment was given during a single session to
12 clients who had diverse nervous habits such as nail-
biting, thumb-sucking, eyelash-picking, head-jerking,
shoulder-jerking, tongue-pushing and lisping. The habits
were virtually eliminated on the very first day for all 12
clients and did not return during the extended follow-up
for the 11 clients who followed the instructions.
(Journal summary).

   68.   Azrin, N.H., and Nunn, R.G., A rapid
          method of eliminating stuttering by a
          regulated breathing approach, Behaviour,
          Research and Therapy, 1974, 12, 279-286.

The Habit Reversal Procedure for eliminating nervous habits
was applied to the problem of stuttering. In the new
procedure the speaker interrupted his speech at moments of
actual or anticipated stuttering and at natural pause points,
and resumed speaking immediately after breathing deeply
during the pause. In addition to this regularized pausing
and breathing, the program included other factors such as
formulation of one's thoughts prior to speaking, identifi-

cation of stutter-prone situations, identification of
mannerisms associated with stuttering, speaking for short
durations when tense or nervous, daily breathing exercises,
relaxation procedures for anxiety, immediate display of
improved speaking and enlisting family support for progress.
Fourteen stutterers were given training in the program
during a single counseling session of about two hours
duration. The next day, the average number of stuttering
episodes decreased by 94 per cent at the end of one month,
and by 99 per cent during the extended follow-up. Each of
the clients was improved by at least 93 per cent. The new
procedure appears to be more rapid and effective than
alternative procedures. (Journal summary).

69.   Azrin, N.H., and Thienes, P.M., Rapid
       elimination of enuresis by intensive
       learning without a conditioning
       apparatus, Behavior Therapy, 1978, 9,
       342-354.

Recent studies have shown that enuresis can be eliminated
very rapidly by a method based on an operant approach.
Modifications were made in the method to make it more convenient to use, especially by eliminating the use of
conditioning apparatus. The new method consisted of 1 day
of intensive training including reinforcement for inhibiting
urination, practice in appropriate urination, bladder-
awareness training, copious drinking, self-correction, and
positive practice for accidents, awakening training, and
family encouragement. All 50 children, aged 3-14 yrs.,
who used the new method ceased bedwetting. Accidents were
reduced to 25% on the very 1st night and decreased further
to 10% after 1 month and to 2% at 1 year. The average
child (median) had only 4 accidents before achieving 2 weeks
of dryness. Relapses were infrequent (20%) and always
reversed by a 2nd training session. This reduction was far
greater than was achieved by Ss in a control condition
using the standard pad and buzzer conditioning method. It
is concluded that the method provides a convenient means
of eliminating enuresis rapidly and durably for almost all
enuretic children over 3 years of age. (Journal abstract).

70.   Azrin, N.H., et al., Autism reversal:
       Eliminating stereotyped self-stimulation
       of retarded individuals, American Journal
       of Mental Deficiency, 1973, 78, 241-248.

Stereotyped self-stimulation by retarded persons is a
common problem for which no practical treatment exists.
Based on the theory that this autistic behavior is caused
by a deficit of environmental reinforcement for outward-
directed activities, a reinforcement program was devised
for use with retarded adults. This reinforcement program
reduced self-stimulation by about two-thirds. Further
reduction was attempted using an overcorrection procedure.
The overcorrection procedure, when combined with the
reinforcement program, reduced the self-stimulation by 95
per cent after two days and virtually eliminated the problem
thereafter. The combined procedure was maintained as a
feasible ongoing ward program. (Journal abstract).

71.   Azrin, N.H., et al., Reciprocity counseling:
       A rapid learning-based procedure for marital
       counseling, Behavior Research and Therapy,
       1973, 11, 365-382.

Existing martial counseling procedures have not been
experimentally evaluated or generally have not been based
on an experimentally derived theory. The present study
formulated a model of marital discord based on reinforcement
theory, developed a marital counseling procedure based on
that theory and experimentally evaluated its effectiveness.
The model viewed marital discord as the resultant of non-
reciprocated reinforcement. The counseling procedures
attempted to establish general marital reciprocity of
reinforcement by teaching reciprocity in several specific
areas of marital unhappiness. The reciprocity procedure
was conducted for about 3-4 weeks with 12 couples, after
first conducting a catharsis-type counseling as a control
procedure. The results showed that the reciprocity procedure
increased reported marital happiness, whereas the control
procedure did not. Once reciprocity was achieved in a
specific problem area, the benefits generalized somewhat
to other yet-to-be counseled areas. The increase in marital
happiness occurred for each of the specific areas of marital

interaction, for 96 percent of the clients, and was maintained and increased during the available follow-up period.
These results indicate that the procedure is an effective,
rapid and enduring method of producing marital happiness.
(Journal summary).

72.   Azrin, N.H., et al., Dry bed: A rapid
       method of eliminating bedwetting (enuresis)
       of the retarded, Behavior Research and
       Therapy, 1973, 427-434.

Bedwetting has been a major and unsolved problem for the
severely retarded. To solve this problem, an intensive
training program was designed similar to a recently
developed program for daytime toilet training of the
retarded. Some distinctive features of the new procedure
were frequent positive reinforcement for correct toileting,
a negative reinforcer for accidents, positive practice in
night time toileting, increased level of urination by forcing
drinking, immediate detection of correct and incorrect
toileting and Positive Practice for accidents. Of twelve
retarded adult bedwetters, the average bedwetter required
only one night of intensive training. Several days of
apparatus monitoring were used following the training but
proved unnecessary for two-thirds of the trainees.
Accidents were reduced by about 85% during the first week
after training, and almost entirely (95%) during the fifth
week with no relapse during a 3 month follow-up. No reduction of accidents resulted when the same bedwetters
were given a control procedure that provided no positive
or negative reactions other than the sounding of an alarm
upon bedwetting. The Dry-Bed procedure appears to be a
very rapid solution to the problem of enuresis among the
retarded and may be applicable to other difficult populations
and also to normals. (Journal summary).

73.   Azrin, N.H., et al., Dry-bed training:
       Rapid elimination of childhood enuresis,
       Behavior Research and Therapy, 1974, 12,
       147-156.

Enuresis has been treated with moderate effectiveness by the
urine-alarm method which requires many weeks of training.
The present procedure used a urine-alarm apparatus but

added such features as training in inhibiting urination,
positive reinforcement for correct urinations, training in
rapid awakening, increased fluid intake, increased social
motivation to the nonenuretic, self-correction of accidents,
and practice in toileting. After one all-night training
session, the 24 enuretic children averaged only two bed-
wettings before achieving fourteen consecutive dry nights
and had no major relapses. Little or no reduction in bedwetting occurred within the first two weeks for matched-
control enuretics who were given the standard urine-alarm
training. The results of a control-procedure showed that
the new procedure did not involve Pavlovian conditioning.
The new method appears to be a more rapid, effective and
different type of treatment for enuresis. (Journal abstract/
summary).

74.   Azrin, N.H., et al., Elimination of
       Enuresis without a conditioning apparatus:
       An extension by office instruction of the
       child and parents, Behavior Therapy, 1979,
       10, 14-19.

A new and effective method of training enuretic children
without a conditioning apparatus has relied on a special
trainer during the first day of training. The present study
determined whether a single office session would suffice to
teach the parents to conduct training themselves. Forty-
four enuretic children 3 to 15 years of age were treated.
The results were similar to those obtained when using the
special trainer. All of the children stopped bedwetting.
A median of four accidents occurred before achieving 2 weeks
of dryness. Bedwetting was reduced to 18% on the first day
and decreased progressively to 4% at the 1-year follow-up.
Relapses were infrequent (7%), and none of the children
"dropped out." The new method appears to be very effective
when taught in a single, usual office counseling situation
without the need for a special trainer. (Journal abstract).

75.   Azrin, N.H., et al., Comparison of
      regulated-breathing versus abbreviated
      desensitization on reported stuttering
      episodes, Journal of Speech and Hearing
      Disorders, 1979, 44, 331-339.

This study was an investigation of the regulated-breathing
method for controlling stuttering as compared to a placebo-
control method consisting of abbreviated desensitization
training. The regulated-breathing procedure, given to 21
stutterers, taught the speaker to breathe smoothly and
deeply, to pause at natural juncturing points, to plan
ahead for the content of the speech, and to relax chest and
neck muscles. Several general behavioral procedures were
also used including relaxation training, self-correction
for errors, social support, daily home practice, and
response awareness, which are components of the general
habit reversal procedure for diverse habits. Training was
given in one or two sessions plus regular follow-up telephone calls. Daily self-recordings were obtained of the
number of stuttering episodes during everyday speech, to
determine the generalized effect of the treatment. The
regulated-breathing method reduced the reported stuttering
episodes by 94% on the first day after training and by 97%
during the fourth week and the three-month follow-up. The
control procedure reduced reported stuttering only slightly
(about 10%). The results indicate substantial effectiveness
of the regulated-breathing method for reducing reported
stuttering episodes in everyday speech as compared with an
alternative treatment of equal duration. (Journal abstract).

76.   Babad, E.Y., and Salomon, G., Professional
      dilemmas of the psychologist in an organ-
      izational emergency, American Psychologist,
      1978, 33, 840-846.

The limitations of the common models of organizational
development (OD) when applied to organizations undergoing
an extreme emergency are discussed in light of the authors'
experiences as front-line psychologists in the 1973 Israeli-
Arab war. The working assumptions underlying common OD
cannot be met in an emergency, hence another approach,
emergency organizational development (EOD) is proposed.

It differs from OD in orientation (direct problem solving
rather than facilitation of changeability), work methods,
and the conception of the psychologist's role. In addition
to laying the first foundations toward the development of
an EOD conception, the authors describe and discuss some of
the most pressing personal problems and dilemmas facing
the psychologist who is expected to provide psychological
services to an organization in an extreme emergency.
(Journal abstract).

77.   Bach, G.R., The marathon group: Intensive
       practice of intimate interaction, Psychological
       Reports, 1966, 18, 995-1002.

Briefly are described the schedule, contents, the psychosocial processes, and the therapeutic effects of Marathon
Therapy which is a living-in, intensive interaction experience in which so-called "patients" and so-called "psychotherapists" involve each other as persons in reciprocal
influence-pressures to improve their styles of life.
(Journal summary).

78.   Bailey, M.A., et al., A study of factors
       related to length of stay in psychotherapy,
       Journal of Clinical Psychology, 1959, 15,
       442-444.

Personal data cards and treatment folders of 247 psychosomatic patients and 211 psychotherapy patients were
reviewed to study the relationship between certain normative
data and length of stay in treatment. A chi square test
revealed a highly significant relationship between improvement in psychotherapy and length of stay in treatment.
Although no statistically significant relationships were
obtained between normative data and length of stay in
treatment in the psychosomatic clinic, several trends were
found which established some relationship between length of
stay in treatment and low socio-economic status, diagnosis
of psychosis, and somatic orientations. Length of stay in
psychotherapy was found to be significantly related to
number of years of schooling, and amount of previous
experience in psychotherapy. On the basis of these findings
it appears that most criteria for assignment used in this
clinic are not valid in predicting the length of stay in
treatment. (Journal summary).

79.   Baker, E., Brief psychotherapy, Journal of
       the Medical Society of New Jersey, 1947,
       44, 260-261.

80.   Baldwin, B.A., Crisis intervention in
       professional practice: Implications for
       clinical training, American Journal of
       Orthopsychiatry, 1977, 47, 659-670.

Crisis intervention as a therapeutic model has had multiple
roots, and is presently defined in a sound body of principles
that provides an effective framework for professional practice. However, there are several areas of ambiguity that
have prevented effective use of this model by clinicians,
and have hindered its inclusion in professional training
programs. Strategies toward the development of an effective
training model for crisis therapists are suggested. (Journal
abstract).

81.   Baldwin, B.A., A paradigm for the classi-
       fication of emotional crises: Implications
       for crisis intervention, American Journal
       of Orthopsychiatry, 1978, 48, 538-551.

A model is presented, in which six classes of crises are
detailed. A short review of classification schema for crisis
intervention is presented as well, prior to the classification by Baldwin. The present system breaks crises into
the following: 1) Dispositional crises; 2) Crises related
to anticipated life transitions; 3) Traumatic stress crises;
4) Maturational/developmental crises; 5) Crises reflecting
underlying psychopathology; and, 6) Crises in which there
has been a complete psychological breakdown of normal
functioning. A short case summary is presented to highlight
each of these six classes of crisis. General comments pertaining to differential treatment focus are also presented.

82.   Baldwin, B.A., Crisis intervention and
       enhancement of adaptive coping using
       hypnosis, American Journal of Clinical
       Hypnosis, 1978, 21, 38-44.

Crisis intervention as a therapeutic modality is widely
accepted, yet little attention has been directed to
integrating this therapeutic modality and hypnosis.
Hypnosis is compatible with the goals and structure of
crisis intervention by: (a) helping clients attain a
relaxed milieu for therapy that counters many of the
negative effects of the crisis state, (b) potentiating the
effects of a range of therapeutic techniques associated
with various therapeutic orientations, and (c) providing
additional techniques unique to hypnosis that are useful in
facilitating adaptive crisis resolution.   Hypnosis enhances
adaptive coping while catalyzing client progress toward the
primary goal of crisis intervention: the restoration of
client functioning to at least a precrisis level as quickly
as possible. (Journal abstract).

83.   Baldwin, B.A., Crisis intervention: An
       overview of theory and practice, The
       Counseling Psychologist, 1979, 8, 43-52.

This paper is an overview of "established principles of
crisis intervention in theory and practice for the mental
health practitioner who has not been exposed to this
approach in the past." The author brings together, from
a variety of sources, those concepts that define the crisis
model. He first delineates and notes four distinct phases
in the life cycle of an emotional crisis. He outlines 10
basic corollaries to crisis theory. Baldwin then offers a
classification paradigm consisting of six basic types of
emotional crises falling along a continuum. As one progresses from Class1 to Class 6, crises become more serious
and the locus of stress moves from external to internal,
reflecting greater psychopathology. Each of the six classes
is defined and a general treatment strategy basic to each
presented. The author then lays out a four-stage model for
conceptualizing crisis intervention, defined by the affective
and cognitive tasks of the therapist. He concludes by
presenting six general principles of crisis therapy which
transcend setting, target population, and type of problem.
(abstract by Deborah Schuller).

84.   Baldwin, B.A., Training in crisis
       intervention for students in the mental
       health professions, Professional Psychology,
       1979, 10, 161-167.

Crisis intervention is a model for very brief psychotherapy
that has steadily gained in both acceptance and application
among mental health professionals. Based on many of the
concepts developed by Caplan, Lindemann, and others, this
model has been refined into an effective therapeutic framework that has now become the treatment of choice for many
patients seeking professional help. However, although
widely used, this approach is not often systematically
taught to mental health professionals during their graduate
training. One interdisciplinary training program in crisis
therapy designed specifically to meet this need of psychologists and other mental health professionals is described in
terms of its teaching model, its structure and its implications for facilitating professional growth. (Journal
abstract).

85.   Baldwin, K.A., Crisis-focussed casework
       in a child guidance clinic, Social Casework,
       1968, 49, 28-34.

This article describes the role of the social worker in
relation to parents who seek help with a child at a time of
family stress. Experience at the Greater Lawrence Guidance
Center (Lawrence, Mass.) has shown that timely help, given
a client to actively seek solutions to current situational
or developmental stresses, can improve problem-solving
skills and result in the client's personal and psychological
growth. Three cases are presented to illustrate the activity
of the caseworker. Methods of intervention are described,
including a rapid delineation of the sources of stress, a
focus on the stressful situation, and, where indicated, an
unlinking of the present problem from unresolved conflicts
in the individual's past. When the client is helped to
discharge tension appropriately, adaptive coping mechanisms
are strengthened, and frequently the child is freed from
being an object of displacement. Crisis intervention can
prevent further regression and disruption of personal
relationships; it can be a meaningful service when help is
given at the time it is requested and needed. (Journal
summary).

86.   Balint, M., et al., Focal psychotherapy,
       London, Tavistock Publications, 1972.

87.   Ball, J.D., and Greiger, R.M., Leader's
       guide to time-limited rational-emotive
       group psychotherapy, Catalog of Selected
       Documents in Psychology, (MS-1688),
       Washington, American Psychological
       Association, 1978.

88.   Balson, P.M., The use of behavior therapy
       techniques in crisis-intervention: A case
       report, Journal of Behavior Therapy and
       Experimental Psychiatry, 1971, 2, 297-300.

In the case of a man with an acute onset of stuttering and
massive free-floating anxiety following an automobile
accident, a variety of behavioral techniques, including
relaxation training, assertive training, graded rehearsal
and modification of behavioral operants were employed, with
the complete eradication of the symptons in five, 50 minute
sessions. The use of behavioral techniques in crisis-
intervention is discussed. (Journal summary).

89.   Bandler, B., Health oriented psychotherapy,
       Psychosomatic Medicine, 1959, 21, 177-181.

One of the major focusses in this author's approach to
psychotherapy is the active mobilization and generation of
healthy, non-pathological aspects of patients' personality
make-up. Further, a simultaneous neutralizing of the
pathological aspects in the patient is recommended. An
example of such an approach in dealing with an alcoholic
husband and his wife is presented, in which a shift in
focus in therapy from the drinking behavior and the difficulties in the marital relationship to a focus on the
children or other potential areas of satisfaction is
effected. The primary goal of therapy within this context
is to restore or aid in the establishment of new subli-
mations.

90.   Bandler, B., The concept of ego-supportive
       psychotherapy, in, Parad, H.J., and Miller,
       R.R., (eds.), Ego-oriented casework, New
       York, Family Service Association of America,
       1963.

91.   Bandura, A., et al., Vicarious extinction
       of avoidance behavior, Journal of Personality
       and Social Psychology, 1967, 5, 16-23.

This experiment was designed to investigate the extinction
of avoidance responses through observation of modeled
approach behavior directed toward a feared stimulus without
any adverse consequences accruing to the model. Children
who displayed fearful and avoidant behavior toward dogs
were assigned to 1 of the following treatment conditions:
1 group of children participated in a series of brief
modeling sessions in which they observed, within a highly
positive context, a fearless peer model exhibit progressively
stronger approach responses toward a dog; a 2nd group of Ss
observed the same graduated modeling stimuli, but in a
neutral context; a 3rd group merely observed the dog in the
positive context, with the model absent; while a 4th group
of Ss participated in the positive activities without any
exposure to either the dog or the modeled displays. The 2
groups of children who had observed the model interact non-
anxiously with the dog displayed stable and generalized
reduction in avoidance behavior and differed significantly
in this respect from children in the dog-exposure and the
positive context conditions. However, the positive context,
which was designed to induce anxiety-competing responses,
did not enhance the extinction effects produced through
modeling. (Journal abstract).

92.   Bard, M., and Berkowitz, B., Training
       Police as specialists in family crisis,
       Community Mental Health Journal, 1967,
       4, 315-317.

This article reviews an experiment in the training of police
to function effectively as family crisis experts. A total
of 18 police were involved in the project, all of whom had

a minimum of three years of police work experience. The
trainers were professional psychologists, who had provided
a three phase educational approach to crisis intervention
methods and theory.

93.   Barrera, M., An evaluation of a brief
       group therapy for depression, Journal
       of Consulting and Clinical Psychology,
       1979, 47, 413-415.

A brief group therapy for treating depressed outpatients
was evaluated. As an adjunct to group therapy, clients
used written self-instructional materials to guide them in
monitoring and increasing their frequency of pleasurable
activities. Twenty depressed clients were randomly assigned
to one of two conditions, and immediate (IT) or delayed
(DT) group. Results did not support the effectiveness of
IT. However, after receiving treatment, DT clients successfully increased activities and decreased depression relative
to IT. Effects were largely maintained through the 7-month
follow-up. Factors that could account for these results
are discussed. (Journal abstract).

94.   Barrett, C.L., Systematic desensitization
       versus implosive therapy, Journal of
       Abnormal Psychology, 1969, 74, 587-592.

Systematic desensitization (SDT) and implosive therapies
(IT) were compared for their effectiveness and efficiency
in reducing snake phobic behavior in otherwise normal
adult human beings. SDT and IT Ss differed significantly
from control Ss in posttreatment avoidance of a snake and
in change of reported discomfort. SDT and IT, however, did
not differ in effectiveness. These results held at a 6
month follow-up. IT was more efficient in that treatment
was completed in 45% of the time required for SDT. Results
were qualified by the finding that SDT had a consistent and
continuing effect across Ss and across time whereas IT was
more variable. Occurrence of unusual disturbance of Ss
during SDT and of IT Ss sessions was discussed. (Journal
abstract).

95.   Barten, H.H., The 15-minute hour: Brief
       therapy in a military setting, American
       Journal of Psychiatry, 1965, 122, 565-567.

The focus of this article is on the use of 15 minute interviews, a few times each week/patient. The active role of
the therapist in structuring is stressed, with major
emphasis on the present problem and current interpersonal
difficulties. The wide range of patients seen by the author
in this way is reviewed, including the types of patients for
whom such an approach would be most useful. Specifically,
those patients for whom exploratory psychotherapy appears
inappropriate, either by choice or necessity, would be good
candidates for very brief therapy sessions. The specific
setting in which such a practice was reported in this
article was a military hospital.

96.   Barten, H.H., The coming of age of the
       brief psychotherapies, in Bellak, L., and
       Barten, H.H., (eds.), Progress in community
       mental health, New York, Grune and Stratton,
       1969.

This chapter is a discussion of techniques of verbal
psychotherapy based on some degree of dynamic understanding
of the patient. Barten reviews a representative sample of
emerging models of brief therapies, including crisis intervention, six to ten session psychotherapy, some slightly
lengthier techniques, brief follow-up procedures and 15
minute sessions. He examines the nature of brief therapies
and reviews common selection criteria. He discusses the
role of brief therapies in community mental health,
practical approaches to psychosocial pathology, early
preventive therapy and brief screening techniques, treatment,
of the poor and emergency services. He concludes that brief
psychotherapy is a flexible, multi-faceted tool which offers
preventive, corrective and amelorative benefits disproportionate in magnitude to the brevity of the therapeutic
endeavour. (abstract by Deborah Schuller).

97.   Barten, H.H., Brief therapies, New York,
       Behavioral publications, 1971.

This edited book of readings in brief therapy covers a
wide range of approaches with a varied collection of human
problems. The book is divided into sections on concepts
and strategies of brief therapy, its use in community
mental health operations, techniques and approaches for
specific patient populations, family, group, and hospital
practice, etc.

98.   Barten, H.H., Children and their parents
       in brief therapy, Behavioral Publications,
       N.Y., 1972.

An edited book of readings in the brief therapy of children
and adolescents, covering such diverse approaches as family,
individual, group, hospitalization, etc. All articles
except for the introductory chapter had appeared in
professional journals and are reprinted in this collection.

99.   Barten, H.H., Comments on "Adlerian Psychology:
       The tradition of brief psychotherapy", Journal
       of Individual Psychology, 1972, 28, 152-153.

A review of the article by Ansbacher. Barten adds that
brief methods of therapy must emphasize the positive aspects
of an individual, with a focus on the future rather than on
the past.

100.   Barten, H.H., and Barten, S.S., New pers-
       spective in child mental health, in, Barten,
       H.H., and Barten, S.C., (eds.), Children
       and their parents in brief therapy, New
       York, Behavioral Publications, 1973.

An introductory chapter to the collected works of other
authors in the area of brief therapy approaches with
children and adolescents. The authors review some of the
more important aspects of brief therapy, such as an active,
focussed, intervention strategy on the part of the therapist.
The major emphasis in working with children in a short-term

context often becomes a focus on the parents, (i.e., "change
the system and you change the child"). The advantages of
each approach in dealing with children and their families
is reviewed (i.e. individual versus family), as well as the
educative aspects of therapy (e.g., helping parents learn
to anticipate crises so as to diminish the impact of them).
The effectiveness of these various approaches is also
reviewed.

101.   Bartoletti, M.D., Conjoint family therapy
        with clinic team in a shopping plaza,
        International Journal of Social Psychiatry,
        1969, 15, 250-257.

The author explains the nature of family therapy as practiced
in a small, tax-supported community mental health service
available to pre-school and school-age children and their
families. The therapeutic plan utilized is divided into two
segments, each spread over an eight-week period. The clinic
team, composed of a psychiatrist, psychologist, and social
worker, stresses "working periods" between sessions during
which the family is expected to practice improving their
functioning as a unit. This plan is still in its evolutionary phases, and the hope is that it will increase the
clinic's effectiveness in family therapy. (abstract by
Deborah Schuller).

102.   Bartoletti, M.D., Conjoint family therapy
        with clinic team in a shopping plaza,
        Psychotherapy: Theory, Research and
        Practice, 1969, 22, 203-211.

103.   Bartolucci, G., and Drayer, C.S., An
        overview of crisis intervention in
        the emergency rooms of general
        hospitals, American Journal of
        Psychiatry, 1973, 130, 953-960.

This article addresses itself to the use of principles of
community mental health in hospital emergency rooms. The
development of crisis principles is reviewed with a overview of military and civilian applications. A discussion
of Caplans's crisis conceptualization is presented, in which

the limitations of such a view for emergency room application
is pointed out. Specifically, Caplan's focus on universal
characteristics of all crisis, with the deemphasis on an
individual's social and interpersonal factors is questioned.
A reformulation of Caplan's perspective, in which specific
recommendations for a medico-psycho-social team in emergency
rooms are made, is presented on being more appropriate for
such locations.

   104.   Bauer, F., and Balter, L., Emergency
           psychiatric patients in a municipal
           hospital, Psychiatric Quarterly, 1971,
           45, 382-393.

The authors present summary data which describe the
characteristics of patients seen through the emergency
department for psychiatric reasons. Among the major
characteristics is the fact that over 16% expressed their
opinion that they were not ill, and almost 40% had not come
to the mental health facility on their own initiative. Some
of the difficulties in dealing with such a population are
discussed.

   105.   Baum, C., Brief group therapy for single
           mothers: Some observations by a para-
           professional, American Journal of
           Orthopsychiatry, 1974, 44, 214-215.

The author reports briefly on a service for single mothers,
a short-term (two hours/week for six weeks) group therapy
program, focussed on the specific problems of the single
mother. The groups described deal with both psychodynamic
and social issues relating to the reality of their life
situation. Although no statistical measures are reported,
clinical impressions are that these groups provide an
important maturing and mobilizing function for the participants.

106.   Baum, M., Extinction of avoidance responding
        through response prevention (flooding),
        Psychological Bulletin, 1970, 74, 276-284.

The resistance of extinction of avoidance responding is
discussed, and a treatment for hastening extinction is
described. The treatment, known as response prevention
(flooding), consists of thwarting the avoidance response
while forcing the subject to remain in the situation which
it fears. Behavior therapy analogues to response prevention
are reviewed, and the various factors which determine the
efficacy of response prevention are noted. Three theories
(two-process theory, competing response, theory, and a
relaxation analysis), which attempt to explain why and how
response prevention works, are discussed, and it is concluded
that no one theory provides an adequate account of all of the
results obtained. (Journal abstract).

107.   Baum, O.E., and Felzer, S.B., Activity
        in initial interviews with lower class
        patients, Archives of General Psychiatry,
        1964, 10, 345-353.

The focus of this project was to study variables related to
the high drop-out rates seen in lower class patients. The
results were gathered over a two year period from patients
seen by third year residents in an outpatient clinic. The
approach used was interdisciplinary and dynamic, focussing
on both psychological and psychosocial aspects of treatment.
The specific procedures used are presented, including methods
of assessing patient motivation, intelligence, and ability
for fantasy. Difficulties which arose between therapists
of middle class background and patients of lower class
background are discussed. The need for the therapist to
actively reach out so that the patient can begin to understand his/her own situation and feelings, is stressed. The
therapist must be flexible, using language that is understandable and clear. The ways a therapist can be too active
are also presented, such as lecturing at the expense of the
patient's needs, etc. Further, some of the similarities
among all patients irrespective of their social class are
also discussed such at the need to work through and resolve
symptom formation.

108.   Baum, O.E., et al., Psychotherapy, dropouts,
        and lower socioeconomic patients, American
        Journal of Orthopsychiatry, 1966, 36,
        629-635.

This research report focussed on various factors which
contribute to the dropping out of therapy of lower socioeconomic patients. Drop out was defined as leaving therapy
before six sessions had been held. Among the variables
looked at were comparisons between experienced versus less
experienced therapists, patient characteristics, and aspects
relating to the referral source. Certain aspects in the
inexperienced therapists contributed to a higher patient
drop-out rate. Inappropriate referrals, or inadequate
patient preparation by the referring agency also contributed
to higher patient drop-out rates.

109.   Baumann, F., Hypnosis and the adolescent
        drug abuser, American Journal of Clinical
        Hypnosis, 1970, 13, 17-21.

This paper reports the results obtained with an accidentally
discovered technique of hypotherapy over a five year period
with adolescent drug abusers in private practice (revivi-
fication of a previous "good trip" or happy drug experience
in short-term therapy). Results appeared to depend markedly
upon the motivation of the subjects. Those who really wanted
to make a change because of possible harm to their physical
health were more likely to succeed than others who felt that
their drug was essentially harmless. This is the probable
explanation for the fact that marijuana smokers were not
significantly helped, whereas users of LSD, amphetamines
and barbiturates made considerable improvement. The methodology and outcome are described and discussed. (Journal
abstract).

110.   Beahan, L.T., Emergency mental health
        services in a general hospital, Hospital
        and Community Psychiatry, 1970, 21, 81-84.

Although emergency mental health services are known to
shorten or avert the need for psychiatric hospitalization,
established hospitals sometimes find it difficult to alter

customary administrative and treatment procedures to offer such services. Using suicide as the prototypal psychiatric emergency Beahan describes the manner in which suicidal patients formerly were handled in the hospital's emergency room, new approaches introduced, and some of the difficulties encountered in effecting the changes. The new approaches used were based on clearly understanding the system of getting a suicidal patient into psychiatric treatment, the immediacy of treatment, the extension of treatment beyond the hospitalization period, and the importance of well-trained personnel. The article concludes with 12 suggestions for those considering organizing a psychiatric emergency service in a general hospital. (abstract by Deborah Schuller).

111.   Beahan, L.T., Evolution of a psychiatric emergency service, Frontiers of Hospital Psychiatry, 1970, 38-40.

112.   Beahan, L.T., et al., The evolution of a co-ordinated emergency service, Hospital and Community Psychiatry, 1971, 22, 214-216.

This article describes the steps by which one community hospital moved from an inpatient psychiatric service to a vertically co-ordinated organization. This change allowed the hospital to provide continuity of care between the psychiatric emergency, outpatient and inpatient departments. The establishment of a crisis clinic and the creation of this co-ordinated service drastically reduced the number of psychiatric patients admitted to the hospital, while permitting an increase in the total number of patients seen over a five-year period. Measures to prevent routine admission to the hospital of chronic patients en route to the state hospital, and of prisoners who could be assessed at a jail, were also implemented. (abstract by Deborah Schuller).

113.   Beck, A.T., and Greenberg, R.L., Brief
        cognitive therapies, Psychiatric Clinics
        of North America, 1979, 23-37.

Current cognitive therapies vary in placement of emphasis
and use diverse techniques, but hold in common these
fundamental assumptions: that behavior and affect are
mediated by cognitive processes: that maladaptive behavior
and affect correlate with maladaptive cognitions; and that
the task of the therapist is to identify these cognitions
and provide learning experiences which will modify them.
A number of these therapies are designed to be brief
therapies. (Journal abstract).

114.   Beck, B.M., and Robbins, L.L., Short-term
        therapy in an authoritative setting, N.Y.,
        Family Service Association, 1946.

115.   Beck, D.F., Research findings on the
        outcomes of marital counseling, Social
        Casework, 1975, 56, 153-181.

Among other things reviewed in this survey of research
results in the field of marital therapy, is the value of
brief interventions in the treatment of marital difficulties,
including such approaches as structured communication
training, and behavior modification.

116.   Beers, T., and Foreman, M., Intervention
        patterns in crisis interviews, Journal of
        Counseling Psychology, 1976, 23, 87-91.

This exploratory study compared the response patterns of
two groups of counselors experienced in crisis intervention.
One group (n=5) was trained according to the Rusk model and
the other (n=5) in the brief, focal therapy approach.   Judges
were trained to rate the occurrence of four therapist intervention - explicit empathy, information gathering, consensual
formulation and problem solving - across interview segments.
With the exception of explicit empathy, no between-group
differences in frequency of interventions were found.
Across time segments, each intervention followed a distinct

pattern as hypothesized by Rusk. The study concludes that
the combined patterns of interventions may provide counselors
with a cognitive map of process goals as they proceed through
a crisis interview. (Journal abstract).

117.   Behrens, M.I., Brief home visits by the
        clinic therapist in the treatment of
        lower-class patients, American Journal of
        Psychiatry, 1967, 124, 371-375.

Brief and occasional home visits by the therapist have not
only proved feasible but have had notably successful results
in the treatment of lower-class clinic patients. They
provide a better understanding of family dynamics and result
in the development of improved patient-therapist relationships. They may also aid in the prevention of hospitalization. The home visit is of greatest value when made by
the person directly responsible for patient care and not by
an intermediary. (Journal abstract).

118.   Bellak, L., The emergency psychotherapy
        of depression, in, Bychowski, G., and
        Despert, J.L., (eds.), Specialized
        techniques in psychotherapy, New York,
        Basic Books, 1952.

119.   Bellak, L., A general hospital as a focus
        of community psychiatry: A trouble-
        shooting clinic combines important
        functions as a part of a Hospital's
        emergency service, Journal of the American
        Medical Association, 1960, 174, 2214-2217.

The psychiatry department of a general hospital can serve
a preventive as well as a therapeutic function. The Trouble-
Shooting Clinic here described combines the two aspects,
serving in major emergencies as well as in minor problems
involving guidance, on a walk-in basis, around the clock.
Aiding the "lonely crowd" that exists in every community,
it should become part of every hospital emergency service.
An attempt is also made to propagate pyschiatric understanding by seminars for key people of the community. A
year-long course for general practitioners is given. Each

week chaplains discuss psychiatric aspects of their work,
and guidance teachers present cases. A seminar for lawyers
focuses on psychiatric aspects of their daily clientele.
Other programs are in preparation. (Journal abstract).

> 120.   Bellak, L., The role and nature of
>   emergency psychotherapy, American
>   Journal of Public Health, 1968, 58,
>   344-347.

The author presents an extremely brief outline of the nature
and role of brief psychotherapy, and specifically relates
these to primary, secondary, and tertiary prevention.

> 121.   Bellak, L., The therapeutic relationship
>   in brief psychotherapy, American Journal
>   of Psychotherapy, 1979, 33, 564-571.

My conception of the therapeutic process and the therapeutic
relationship in brief psychotherapy is clearly based on an
explicit conceptual framework, embedded in the psychoanalytic theory of personality, its theory of psychopathology,
and its theory of therapeutic technique. There is a heavy
emphasis on careful conceptualization and interrelations of
the patient's personality, history, and current life situation. These data are then related to a set of general and
specific propositions concerning the therapeutic process
generally and the therapeutic relationship specifically for
a given patient, combined with a readiness to introduce whatever modifications seems necessary as we go along. Above all,
I believe that in brief therapy the therapist's general
dynamic knowledge and precision are the most important components of his expertise. It also helps if the therapist is
not too scared and not too obsessive so he can be emotionally
available, and also has an appropriate touch of the Dr.
Kildare syndrome - or a rescue fantasy. (Journal summary).

122.   Bellak, L., Brief and emergency
        psychotherapy, in, Karasu, T.B., and
        Bellak, L., (eds.), Specialized
        techniques in individual psychotherapy,
        New, York, Brunner/Mazel, 1980.

The authors begin this chapter by presenting some basic
propositions related to brief and emergency psychotherapy.
They review the methods used in such approaches, such as
interpretation, catharsis, reality, testing, sensitization,
education, support, etc. Issues relating to the therapeutic
alliance, transference/countertransference, and the therapy
contract are all detailed, and related to each of the first
five sessions. The use of brief therapy as a method of
intake is also discussed. A detailed sample interview
transcript is provided at the end of the chapter to highlight many of the theoretical points raised.

123.   Bellak, L., and Barten, H.H., (eds.),
        Progress in Community Mental Health,
        New York, Grune and Stratton, 1969.

124.   Bellak, L., and Small, L., Brief
        psychotherapy and emergency psycho-
        therapy, 2nd edition, New York, Grune
        and Stratton, 1978.

125.   Bellak, L., et al., Psychiatry in the
        medical surgical emergency clinic: The
        incidence and management of psychiatric
        problems in patients in the medical-
        surgical clinic of a general hospital,
        Archives of General Psychiatry, 1964, 10,
        267-269.

The authors present the results of assigning a psychiatrist,
psychologist, or social worker to the Medical-surgery
Emergency Clinic at City Hospital Center at Elmhurst, Queens,
New York. The aim of the project was to revaluate the degree
of psychiatric problems which are presented to the Medical-
surgery Clinic, and to provide immediate, emergency psycho-

therapy where appropriate. A significant percentage of the
presenting patients suffer from emotional problems, and the
positive initial results of the mental health group involvement in the emergency clinic strongly suggests adopting such
practice at other general hospitals.

126.   Belleville, T.P., et al., Conjoint
        marriage therapy with a husband and
        wife team, American Journal of
        Orthopsychiatry, 1969, 39, 73-83.

The authors report on conjoint marriage and/or family therapy
with couples who presenting problems were either sexual
difficulties or child-parent relationship difficulties. The
maximum number of sessions was 16, with a husband/wife treatment team. The actual number of couples completing the
treatment was 27, and a large proportion of these reported
success. Of the original 44 couples, seven decided to proceed with divorce, 21 were rated as successfully treated.

Issues such as the advantages of heterosexual co-therapy are
presented, including increased observation with two people
rather than only one, less need for out-of-session collaboration between each of the individual therapists who would
normally be seeing partners separately, etc. Further, the
advantage of treating couples as a unit are also presented,
including each member of the couple to know first hand what
the nature of the difficulties with his/her partner are,
decreased feelings of being left out, etc. Some of the
important issues related to transference-countertransference
dimension are presented and suggestions given for the
handling of such issues. A brief discussion is also
included focussed on the qualities necessary in selecting
potential therapists for the kind of professional practice
outlined in the article.

127.   Benady, D.R., and Denham, J., Development
        of an early treatment unit from an
        observation ward, British Medical Journal,
        1963, 2, 1569-1527.

The authors present data covering a block of two, one year
periods (1955-56 and 1960-61), in which they discuss the
changes in admissions and treatment on an observation ward

brought on by the passage of the Mental Health Act in England
in 1959. Policy changes in the ward are presented, with a
shift toward more immediate and short-term treatment. The
results of such a shift are discussed, including a greater
number of patients returning to their communities and their
own homes. Implications for general hospitals and community
mental health programming are also detailed.

   128.   Bennett, M.J., and Wisneski, M.J.,
           Continuous psychotherapy within an HMO,
           American Journal of Psychiatry, 1979,
           136, 1283-1287.

Describes the long-term psychotherapy program developed by
the Harvard Community Health Plan, focusing on its planning,
implementation, and monitoring. The inclusion of coverage
for chronic conditions in a health maintenance organization
practice led to the development of a range of extended
treatment services, exploratory as well as supportive, and
to the enhancement of short-term methods. The control of
utilization and cost is effected through the willingness
of the provider group to adapt treatment methods to patient
needs, rather than through the benefit structure. With the
broad range of treatment methods available in this plan,
only 1-2% of patients require long-term continuous psychotherapy. (Journal abstract).

   129.   Bentovim, A., and Kinston, W., brief
           focal family therapy when the child is
           the referred patient: I. Clinical,
           Journal of Child Psychology and Psychiatry,
           and Allied Disciplines, 1978, 19, 1-2.

This paper describes a style of family work which initially
derived from the brief individual psychoanalytic therapy
developed at the Tavistock Clinic by Malan and co-workers.
The approach is highly suitable for use in busy Child
Guidance Clinics where the alternatives are no treatment at
all, or occasional supportive interviews with counselling.
Even where resources are available, the method may prove a
treatment of choice offering opportunity for the improvement

of the context of the individual's emotional life. The
approach emphasizes seeing the whole family or marital
couple, determining a few dynamic hypotheses which organize
the salient facts from the history with observations of
family interaction, and then constructing a focal plan.
This plan links with the hypotheses but is operational and
serves as a guide and reference point for the therapist in
his work with the family. The frequency of sessions varies
from one- to six-weekly, and period of contact is between
3 and 9 months. The therapeutic technique is an active
one which does not rest on any rigid theoretical ideas. A
contract and working alliance are set up in the initial
sessions which also provide further opportunity for alter-
ation of the hypotheses or plan. The role of the workshop
group in supporting the therapist and helping the therapeutic work is emphasized. Two cases with very different
psychopathology and family pathology have been described
as examples of the clininal process. (Journal conclusions).

130.   Berblinger, K.W., Brief medical
        psychotherapy and the question of the
        psychiatric referral, Maryland State
        Medical Journal, 1956, 5, 269-273.

The author defines medical psychotherapy as a form of treatment which occurs as a result of a close personal interaction
or relationship between patient and doctor. The general or
family physician is closer to the patient than medical
specialists, and is able to continue to provide therapeutic
care. Issues of self-awareness, communication techniques,
psychological responses, etc. are discussed as part of the
understanding necessary by the medical practitioner if he/
she is to be an effective preventive force for mental health.
Some of the difficulties in making a psychiatric referral
are also discussed.

131.   Berblinger, K.W., Psychotherapy for the
        non-psychiatrist, Psychosomatics, 1961,
        2. 1-4.

The integration of medical psychotherapy with the daily
practice of medicine conceives of the psychological

variable as communication therapy. Its initiation, conceptualization, objectives and limitations have been described
in terms of the recognition of psychological clues and
doctor-patient interaction. (Journal summary).

132.   Berblinger, K.W., Brief psychotherapy and
        psychiatric consultation, Psychosomatics,
        1967, 8, 6-10.

The author reviews several considerations which may lead to
brief psychotherapy as a treatment of choice, rather than
mere expediency. While premising empathic learning within
a distinct social setting as a base common to all therapies,
he distinguishes brief from long term therapies by focussing
on three factors: a) the definition of the social field;
b) the impact of the initial psychiatric intervention; and
c) the ccntinuous awareness of an agreed upon reality.
Berblinger, while not advocating the abandonment of in-depth
treatment for focal contacts, he does propose the use of the
psychiatric consultation (i.e., the briefest form of brief
therapy) as an important teaching device. Such a device may
increase perceptiveness as well as understanding of the
patient within a short time span, and lead to a correct
assessment of the patient's personality profile as well as
a formulation of realistic treatment goals. (abstract by
Deborah Schuller).

133.   Berg, D.E., Crisis intervention concepts
        for emergency telephone service, Crisis
        Intervention, (Supplemert) 1970, 2, 11-19.

134.   Berlin, I.N., Crisis intervention and
        short term therapy: An approach in a
        child psychiatric clinic, Journal of the
        American Academy of Child Psychiatry, 1970,
        9, 595-606.

The author presents a short-term approach to working with
children, adolescents, and their families. Three specific
cases are presented (an infant problem at a well-child
clinic; a child with an asthma problem; and a family

struggling with a teenager on probation). The types of
formulations used are discussed. The types of questions
asked by the staff of themselves include: what brought the
family for help? Why now? Who in the family is affected
by the crisis and how? What were the methods of coping
prior to the request for help? How can intervention be
made effectively given the presenting dynamics? What are
the covert issues? Where are the family strengths which
can be utilized to precipitate change? How can the gains
achieved by consolidated? Some of the characteristics
of the therapist needed to effectively carry out such work
are briefly presented.

135.   Berliner, B., Short psychoanalytic
        therapy, Bulletin of the Menninger
        Clinic, 1941, 6, 183-189.

136.   Berliner, B., Short psychoanalytic
        psychotherapy, Bulletin of the Menninger
        Clinic, 1945, 9, 155-161.

The author continues to elaborate on an earlier article on
short-term analytic therapy. The main focus of this approach
is on character analysis and on the analysis of interpersonal
relationships. When little or no analysis of the transference is needed with a particular patient, then brief therapy
is recommended. Such patients are those who are able to
discuss their central conflict without necessarily reliving
it or acting it out in connection with the therapist-patient
relationship. A case report of a 36 year old male with a
travel phobia is presented in some detail, in which the
phobia resulted from a homosexual panic. The author points
out that the reason patients are in fact able to distinguish
the core conflict from the relationship between therapist
and patient is due to what he terms "high morale", or a
solid sense of reality. A brief discussion of depression,
and the dynamics involved in it is presented.

137.   Bernard, H.S., and Klein, R.H., Some
        perspectives on time-limited group
        psychotherapy, Comprehensive Psychiatry,
        1977, 18, 579-584.

The authors review a range of issues pertinent to time-
limited group psychotherapy. They summarize the development
of such a treatment approach, and discuss guidelines for
time-limited groups, (e.g., patient selection, motivation,
resistance, external environment, psychodynamic conflicts
and treatment goals, patient preparation, therapeutic
techniques, and issues of termination).

138.   Bernard, J.L., Rapid treatment of gross
        obesity by operant techniques, Psychological
        Reports, 1968, 23, 663-666.

This paper reports the application of operant techniques in
the treatment of a case of gross obesity. The patient
weighed 407 lbs. at the initiation of the program, was
schizophrenic, and probably had metabolic and/or endocrine
dysfunction as contributing factors. Over a period of 6
months, of which the last 6 weeks were an extinction period,
she lost 102 lbs. at a relatively stable rate. At the end
of the extinction period, the loss rate had slowed somewhat
but showed no indications of reversal. The rapid weight
loss, compared to that in earlier studies, is attributed
to positive reinforcement for weight lost, in addition to
control of caloric intake. (Journal summary).

139.   Bernard, J.L., et al., Some effects of a
        brief course in the psychology of adjust-
        ment on a psychiatric admissions ward,
        Journal of Clinical Psychology, 1965, 21,
        322-326.

The authors report on a research study in which a series of
five, one hour lectures entitled, "The psychology of adjustment", was presented to newly admitted female psychiatric
patients. Both a control and experimental group were formed.
Approximately 40 patients completed the program in each
group. The change measures used consisted of MMPI and
structured interviews, and the results point to the value
of such lectures in influencing certain pathological
attitudes on the part of the patients.

140.   Bernstein, N.R., and Tinkham, C.B., Group
        therapy following abortion, Journal of
        Nervous and Mental Disease, 1971, 152,
        303-314.

The authors arranged short-term group therapy with single
and married women who had obtained therapeutic abortions.
They were generally women from high socioeconomic backgrounds, and educationally sophisticated, but they showed
a wide variety of differences in personality and in their
individual psychological disturbances. Older and more
socially established women were more able to view the
experience in perspective and to discuss their own values
and reactions to termination of pregnancy. Younger, single
girls seemed to have more trouble in separating the event
from their current interactions with men and their present
social insecurities and emotional liability. They also felt
intimidated by the older women. The groups discussed
attitudes toward hospitalization and surgery, the search
for someone to perform the abortion, and the attitudes of
internists, psychiatrists, and surgeons with whom they
dealt. Religion, sexuality, personal guilt, and the rights
and meaning of feminity in this and other cultures were all
examined, and the idea of killing a living thing received
heavy emphasis. The groups served to reduce guilt, to
enhance assimilation of the experience, and helped put the
experience into proportion for its members. A combination
of older and married women in such groups is important to
stabilize and sustain the groups. (Journal abstract adapted).

141.   Berzins, J.I., et al., A-B therapist
        distinction, patient diagnosis, and
        outcome of brief psychotherapy in a
        college clinic, Journal of Consulting
        and Clinical Psychology, 1972, 38, 231-237.

Prior clinical studies have suggested that therapists' A-B
status interacts with patient diagnosis in determining the
outcome of psychotherapy, but this interaction hypothesis
has been studied almost exclusively in laboratory analogues,
not in actual clinical practice. To discern whether this
hypothesis would apply to brief psychotherapy in a college
clinic, the "outcomes" obtained by three A and three B
therapists with their schizoid and neurotic patients (N=57)

were examined in a 2 x 2 factorial design. Analysis of
variance computed for three dependent measures based on
therapists' and patients' posttherapy ratings revealed
considerable support for the hypothesis, primarily with
respect to therapists; appraisals of their own effectiveness. The B therapists also obtained much lower improvement and rapport ratings from schizoid than neurotic
patients, whereas A therapists obtained equally satisfactory
results with both. The interaction hypothesis is characterized A-B performance differences better than an alternate
"prognostic" hypothesis tested via the inclusion of two
additional diagnostic categories (adjustment reaction,
passive-aggressive personality). (Journal abstract).

142.   Beutler, L.E., and Anderson, L.,
        Characteristics of the therapist in
        brief psychotherapy, Psychiatric Clinics
        of North America, 1979, 2, 125-137.

In an attempt to distill some of the qualities of therapists
which maximize their therapeutic influence, the authors
synthesize from research data the findings they consider to
be most practical an salient as well as most reliable and
valid. Characteristics are reviewed under four headings,
reflecting the role of fixed characteristics, the role of
personal qualities which are attributed to the therapist by
the patient, the impact of the therapist's patterns of
communication, and the results of efforts to match patients
with therapists. (Journal abstract).

143.   Bieliauskas, V.J. Short-term psycho-
        therapy with college students: Prevention
        and cure, Confina of Psychiatrica, 1968,
        11, 18-33.

The author describes the functioning of a psychological
student center at a university. The primary mode of treatment is short-term, with most cases being seen in no more
than eight sessions. Out of a total referral list of 562
students (constituting 11% of the total student body), a
sample of 139 was selected at random for the study.
Statistical measures are presented related to source of

referral, year of study, distribution of number of counseling sessions, presenting problem, tests administered, focus of therapy, results of each case based on therapist nctes, and outcome ratings of therapists. Therapists rated 73% of the sample as having been helped by the short-term treatment.

144.   Bierenbaum, H., et al., Effects of
         varying session length and frequency in
         brief emotive psychotherapy, Journal of
         Consulting and Clinical Psychology, 1976,
         44m 790-798.

This study examined the role of emotional catharsis in brief emotive psychotherapy and its differential effects within three time frames. Forty-one patients at a University Health Service were seen in one of three ways: (a) 1/2 hour, twice a week; (b) 1 hour, once a week; or (c) 2 hours, every other week. Duration of therapy (number of weeks) and amount of therapy (number of hours) were not varied. Outcome was assessed using (a) the sum of MMPI scales, D, Pt, and Sc; (b) a personal satisfaction interview; and (c) behavioral target complaints. The amount of emotional catharsis produced in each session was also measured. Patients in the 1-hour group produced the most catharsis and improved the most on the personal satisfaction interview and behavioral target complaints, with high-catharsis patients showing the greatest improvement. Patients in the 1/2 hour group improved the most on the MMPI scales, irrespective of the amount of catharsis produced. These findings are seen as supporting the contention that within a specific time frame emotional catharsis can lead to certain positive outcomes in brief emotive pyschotherapy. (Journal abstract).

145.   Binder, J.L., Modes of focusing in
         psychoanalytic short-term therapy,
         Psychotherapy: Theory, Research, and
         Practice, 1977, 14, 233-241.

It is now established that psychoanalytic theory and technique can be fruitfully applied to short forms of psychotherapy. Even though focusing on a delimited area of conflict is fundamental to the conduct of brief treatment,

psychoanalytic models generally have not attempted to explain
the complex and subtle internal activities of the therapist
for searching for a focus. After a brief review of the
history of focusing in psychoanalytic brief therapy, this
report attempts to study the process of therapist focusing
by constructing a typology of several forms of focusing.
The typology is conceptually organized around the relative
emphasis on the therapist's conscious, cognitive activity
or his preconscious, empathic-intuitive activity. The modes
of focusing to be examined include the search for common
clinical syndromes associated with stressful conditions, the
the articulation of more individualized conflicts precipitated by current stress, the use of historical material to
formulate transference interpretations, and the use of early
empathic reactions of the therapist to some of the patient's
inner objects. Clinical material is used to illustrate
each mode of focusing. The relationship of focusing to
selection criteria and the therapeutic influence in brief
treatment is discussed. (Journal abstract).

146.   Binder, J., Treatment of narcissistic
        problems in time-limited psychotherapy,
        Psychiatric Quarterly, Vol. 51, No. 4
        (in press).

Narcissistic conflicts are frequently perceived as
impervious to time-limited therapy. Although the author's
final suggestion is to refer such patients for long-term
psychotherapy, his experience in treating within a time-
limited frame, demonstrates that such symptoms as those
associated with fantastic expectations of perfection can be
alleviated by circumscribed reorganization of ego defenses
(from lower to higher order) and learning of ego coping
skills of abstract analysis and synthesis. Unconscious
greed, envy, and rate can be controlled to some extent,
although profound problems of intimacy remain. The author
details one case study based on a 16 session contract. He
concludes that long-term therapy is still the treatment of
choice due to the severity of the distortion of object
relations. However, brief dynamic psychotherapy can resolve
more problems than many analytic therapists had previously
believed possible. (abstract by Deborah Schuller).

147.   Binder, J., and Smokler, I., Early
        memories: A technical aid to focusing
        in brief psychotherapy, Psychotherapy:
        Theory, Research, and Practice, 1980,
        (in press).

Development of a thorough dynamic focus entails two therapist
tasks: a) determination of a conflict or cluster of conflicts responsible for most of the patient's current difficulty, and, b) translation of this dynamic formulation into
one or more interventions that help the patient articulate
in affectively meaningful terms what he can presently understand about the nature of his conflict. This paper emphasizes
the technique of focusing, and, as an aid to focusing, the
valuable role of early memories, particularly as they reflect
the range and qualities of the patient's internalized
repertoire of interpersonal relationship paradigms. Early
memories may help to crystallize initial hypotheses into a
dynamic picture of distorted object relations. Such memories
may help to improve the specificity of the focus, thus making
it a more compelling area of work for the patient. They also
provide an historical context in which to place current painful feelings. The authors present five case vignettes to
illustrate their ideas on focusing and their methods of using
early memories in time-limited uncovering therapy. Training
and clinical implications are also discussed. (abstract by
Deborah Schuller).

148.   Binder, J.L., and Weisskopf, S.,
        Facilitating ego mastery in brief
        psychotherapy with medical students,
        American Journal of Psychotherapy, 1975,
        29, 575-592.

Four related techniques for doing brief psychotherapy with
medical students are described, which capitalize on styles
of ego adaptation and defense characteristic of this population. These styles involve the use of intellectual mastery
and intellectualization. The therapeutic use of a frequently
occurring form of positive ego-ideal transference is also
discussed. (Journal abstract).

149.   Bindstock, W.A., et al., The role of brief
       psychotherapy, in Proceedings of the 4th
       World Congress of Psychiatry, Part I.,
       Excerpta Medica Foundation, 1966.

150.   Birger, D., et al., The evolution and
       demise of a crisis intervention program
       in a state hospital, Hospital and Community
       Psychiatry, 1974, 25, 675-677.

A crisis intervention team in a state hospital offered
professional services to approximately 27 patients before
it was disbanded 6 months of operation. The authors describe the evolution of the team, discuss the conflicts that
led to its demise, and evaluate the experience. (Journal
abstract).

151.   Birnbaum, F., et al., Crisis intervention
       after a natural disaster, Social Casework,
       1973, 54, 545-551.

The authors describe a natural disaster and its effects on
the inhabitants of a town, the nature of social work intervention and outreach, and the experience of professional
social workers attempting to help. Problems in a delivery
of services and projections for future cases of intervention
after natural disasters are discussed. The authors'
experiences demonstrated the value of professional casework
intervention, although they believe that the potential for
such intervention was unrealized. They suggest means by
which social workers would move more quickly into an
affected area in order to become a visible and effective
force throughout the period of rescue, relief, and restoration. The authors emphasize a professional responsibility
to apply theoretical and practical knowledge of crisis to
large scale emergencies. (abstract by Deborah Schuller).

152.   Blaine, G.B., Short-term psychotherapy
       with college students, New England
       Journal of Medicine, 1957, 256, 208-211.

The author presents a variety of techniques which can be
effectively used in the short-term treatment of college

students. The reasons why such a brief approach is often
effective with this age group are presented, including
verbal fluency, lack of rigid defenses, etc. Techniques
discussed include environmental manipulation, giving information, getting out information or emotion, and the
effective use of transference and insight, along with
reality testing. Short case vignettes are presented to
highlight the techniques discussed.

153.   Blais, A., and Goerges, J., Psychiatric
        emergencies in a general hospital out-
        patient department, Canadian Psychiatric
        Association Journal, 1969, 14, 123-133.

A pilot study of 350 patients who made 408 visits to the
emergency department of an urban general hospital over an
eight month period was conducted to determine: 1) individual
and social-cultural characteristics of patients seeking help;
2) the nature of their problems; 3) how best to meet patient
needs through treatment and preventive services; 4) how to
organize psychiatric emergency services to meet those needs.
Data from the study are presented and discussed briefly.
The authors review the literature pertaining to therapy with
lower socio-economic status, since such clients comprised
the majority of the sample. The issue of high patient drop-
out rate following the initial interview was discussed.
The authors conclude that an immediate access, brief therapy
walk-in psychiatric emergency service is a valuable approach.
(abstract by Deborah Schuller).

154.   Blane, H., and Muller, J., Acute
        psychiatric services in the general
        hospital, II. Current status of
        emergency psychiatric services,
        American Journal of Pyschiatry, 1967,
        124, 37-45.

The authors present a survey of those facilities which offer
treatment for those individuals who present themselves to
general hospital emergency units. The authors conclude that
only a few of these institutions have novel community-
oriented programs to meet the needs of these patients. The

potential and value of being able to help a large number
of individuals who turn more readily to such hospital
emergency units is discussed.

155.   Blaufarb, H., and Levine, J., Crisis
        intervention in an earthquate, Social
        Work, 1972, 17, 16-19.

Following an earthquake in 1971, a child guidance center
provided crisis therapy for approximately 300 families.
The aim was to decrease anxiety levels and to restabilize
family units. The treatment was carried out over a period
of five weeks, and although no follow-up was done, the
clinical sense from professionals involved indicated value
to such a crisis family intervention caused by the exposure
to natural disasters.

156.   Blinder, B.J., et al., Behavior therapy
        of anorexia nervosa: Effectiveness of
        activity as a reinforcer of weight gain,
        American Journal of Psychiatry, 1970, 126,
        1093-1098.

The authors present a technique for weight restoration in
a condition that is often highly refractory to therapy,
with mortalaity rates up to 15 percent. Operant reinforcement was applied to three consecutive patients by making
access to physical activity contingent upon weight gain.
Treatment of from 4 to 6 weeks resulted in rapid weight
restoration. Modification of the technique, illustrating
variations in operant reinforcement, are also reported.
A total of five cases are presented, three in detail.
Further, clinical observations indicated positive changes
in mood and interpersonal relationships following the
initiation of treatment. (Journal abstract adapted).

157.   Bloch, H.S., An open-ended crisis-
        oriented group for the poor who are sick,
        Archives of General Psychiatry, 1968, 18,
        178-185.

This paper describes a particular kind of group experience
that was set up to meet the needs of lower socioeconomic
groups, trying to adapt what is known and thought about

their use of psychiatric personnel and their own behavior
to their needs. It was found that such a group could serve
multiple functionst including crisis and short-term management, intermittent supportive care, and long-term intensive
group therapy. (Journal summary).

158.   Bloom, B.L., Definitional aspects of
        the crisis concept, Journal of Consulting
        Psychology, 1963, 27, 498-502.

8 expert judges reacted to a series of 14 miniature case
histories of stress experiences which had been constructed
so that it was possible to study the differential effects
of 5 variables upon judgements of the presence or absence
of "Crisis". The variables studies were: (a) knowledge or
lack of knowledge of a precipitating event, (b) rapidity of
onset of reactions, (c) awareness or lack of awareness on
the part of the heor of inner discomfort, (d) evidence of
behavioral disorganization, and (e) rapidity of resolution.
The results indicated that to these judges, a crisis was
defined as an episode beginning with a known precipitating
event following by either no discernible reaction or by
some reaction which required a month or somewhat longer to
resolve. Within a group of episides in which precipitating
events were known, there appeared to be no way by which
crises could be reliably judged on the basis of subsequent
reactions. In view of the apparent lack of clarity of the
crisis concept, further refinement is indicated before
attempts to assess the effectiveness of crisis intervention
are undertaken. (Journal abstract).

159.   Bloom, B., Perspectives on crisis
        intervention, Internal Journal of
        Psychiatry, 1968, 6, 380-382.

The author focusses on three major strategies of the
community mental health movement, namely, crisis intervention, consultation, and anticipatory guidance. The importance of providing crisis intervention at the time when an
individual is in crisis and therefore more susceptible to
change is stressed. The scarcity of trained mental health
professionals has led to the development of mental health
consultants, whose knowledge can be shared with para-

professionals who are working directly with clients.
Anticipatory guidance involves the knowledge that there are
normative stressful life experiences which can be predicted
(e.g., pregnancy and childbirth, marriage, adolescence,
etc.), and which have common characteristics for many
individuals who are experiencing them. Such knowledge can
be shared with individuals who are about to go through such
predictable crises in order to help lessen the trauma
experienced.

160.   Bloom, B.L., Social and community
        intervention, Annual Review of Psychology,
        1980, 31, 111-142.

In this review chapter of various social and community
interventions, the author summarizes work done in the field
of planned short-term therapy (PSTT). PSTT is presented in
an historical perspective, the rationale for PSTT is reviewed
(i.e., economy, changing conceptualizations in the field of
therapy, results of outcome studies), a short section on
single-session therapy is presented, and the implication
for PSTT are discussed.

161.   Boehm, B., Characteristics of brief
        service and long-term cases: A
        comparative study, Mimeographed report:
        Family and Children's Services, Minneapolis,
        Minn., April, 1961.

162.   Bogen-Tietz, E., and Jordan, J.H., Rapid
        treatment of the psychotic patient
        integrating electronarcosis and psycho-
        analytic psychotherapy, American Journal
        of Psychiatry, 1957, 114, 68-72.

The psychotic patient, no matter what his underlying
character structure may be, reacts against deprivation with
the defense of a break with reality. Intensive electronarcosis (electrically-induced seizure prior to a few minutes
of subconvulsive electrical stimulation) quickly produces a
state in which gratification of infantile needs become the
basis for reality contact. While reality is sustained with

maintenance electronarcosis, re-education leads to a secure
basis for restructuring psychotherapy. This, in turn, makes
the defensive break with reality unnecessary. (Journal
summary adapted).

   163.   Boileau, V.K., New techniques in brief
           psychotherapy, Psychological Reports,
           1958, 4, 627-645.

Boileau presents theoretic and clinical considerations for
an ahistorical, need-oriented approach to therapy. He
compares different psychotherapeutic systems (orthodox
Freudian, neo-Freudian, character analysis, and non-
directive) on the basis of focus of attack on the symptom
formation process, essential nature of the therapist's
intended communication, and underlying therapeutic assumption. The author shifts the treatment focus by emphasizing
the basic, blocked need which underlies the process of
symptom formation. He describes the techniques employed in
"need-integrative" therapy under the organizational headings
of need acceptance, transference, handling of defense and
resistance, acting out, and motivation. Clinical excerpts
illustrate his discussion. (abstract by Deborah Schuller).

   164..   Bolman, W.M., Preventive psychiatry for
           the family: Theory, approaches, and
           programs, American Journal of Psychiatry,
           1968, 125, 458-472.

From a theoretical framework which conceives of the family
as a flexible social system subject to stress from its biological, intrapsychic and social environments, Bolman
systematically links general programmatic concerns with
specific programs related to family-oriented preventive
psychiatry. Included are tables identifying approaches to
providing for family health, psychosocial, and economic
needs through community facilities. For each broad type
of care, he details target population, the intended goal
of the service, type of approach (e.g., whether primary,
secondary, or tertiary prevention; and community-wide,

milestone, or high-risk). Specific examples are also
provided for each. The fourth group of preventive
approaches highlighted focusses on the problems of
adolescents. (abstract by Deborah Schuller).

165.   Bonime, W., Some principles of brief
        psychotherapy, Psychiatric Quarterly,
        1953, 27, 3-18.

The author presents case material focussed on a 37 year
old male who was suffering from a war neurosis, brought on
by his experiencing the torpedoing of his ship. Within a
psychoanalytic orientation, and with a focus on dream
interpretation, a brief course of treatment was successfully
completed. The specific case is generalized to highlight
the principles of brief therapy.

Among the principles covered are such items as: active
role of therapist; collaboration between therapist and
patient; focus on pertinent and accessible personality
difficulty and the need to clarify the areas covered; the
avoidance of interpretative exhibitionism; a careful
evaluation of situational factors, by themselves and in
relation to trends; a focus on the good qualities (i.e.,
positive assets) of each patient as well as a careful
uncovering of the low-levels of self-esteem of many
patients, etc.

166.   Bonnefil, M.C., Therapist, save my child:
        A family crisis case, Clinical Social
        Work Journal, 1979, 7, 6-14.

This paper describes five sessions (the total treatment
contact) with a mother and her 15-year old daughter who
was suddenly refusing to attend school. They were a very
insecure and inhibited mother and daughter in an intensely
dependent relationship involving much ambivalence on both
sides. Not only was the immediate school problem resolved,
but the clients developed some awareness of their own underlying conflicts related to the developmental phase of the
family and of how their ways of handling these conflicts
related to the developmental phase of the family and of how
their ways of handling these conflicts affected one another.
(Journal abstract).

167.   Bonnefil, M., Crisis and diagnosis:
        Infantile autism, Clinical Social Work
        Journal, 1976, 4, 276-288.

This paper outlines a theoretical model for presenting
diagnoses to parents of autistic children. The model is
based on crisis theory. Actual professional practice, as
determined by interviews with the parents of 22 autistic
children of various ages, is compared with the theoretical
model. This study demonstrated that professional practice
did not seem to have given adequate recognition to mourning
reactions but did show a tendency toward increased involvement of parents in treatment. The failure to recognize or
encourage adaptive mourning is seen as fostering denial
which might impair the ability of the parents to cope
effectively with the problem. (Journal abstract).

168.   Bonstedt, T., Psychotherapy in a public
        psychiatric clinic: An attempt at
        "adjustment", Psychiatric Quarterly, 1965,
        39, 1-15.

The public psychiatric clinics are facing a demand for
services which is far out of proportion to their existing
manpower resources. This paper describes approaches
(modifications) tried by the author in the area of psychotherapy as a treatment tool of decisive importants:
1. Increased individualization of treatment to permit more
tolerant use of less "orthodox" approaches if they fit the
patient, for example, "limited goal clinics" and "15-minute
hours."
2. Empirical orientation, such as willingness to try new,
more effective techniques.
3. Greater attention to symptoms which are alarming to the
patient and his community - less exclusive preoccupation
with basic personality changes.
4. Simplification of the referral and "staffing" procedure,
thereby permitting early application of therapeutic skill.
5. Increased acceptance of patients who are difficult to
treat but represent a heavy burden to the community (psychotics, alcoholics, persons with borderline intelligence).
6. Careful early screening of therapeutic goals, to keep
them within more realistic limits.

7.   Increased attention to techniques of improving motivation for treatment.
8.   Greater tolerance toward direct contact with the
patients' real life situations.
9.   Removal of an automatic expectation of a lengthy treatment in a majority of cases. (Journal summary modified).

169.   Bonstedt, T., Crisis intervention or
        early access brief therapy? Diseases of
        the Nervous System, 1970, 31, 783-787.

In this paper a brief comparison is made of crisis intervention and early access brief therapy approaches, as they
are conceptualized at present. While they have an area of
overlap in terms of rapid application, focus or environment
and current events, and needed sensitivity of the clinician,
they also show important differences in terms of the underlying frameworks of reference. Crisis intervention is built
upon crisis theory, with relatively more emphasis upon the
environment, with its more optimistic view of the role of
crises in individual lives, and opportunity to utilize these
insights in anticipatory guidance through other professionals.
Early access brief therapies are built upon the modifications
of ego psychology, with some attention toward various aspects
of social psychiatry. It is important to distinguish between
the two approaches, if they are both to produce their optimum
results. (Journal summary).

170.   Bonstedt, T., and Baird, S.H., Providing
        cost-effective psychotherapy in a health
        maintenance organization, Hospital and
        Community Psychiatry, 1979, 30, 120-132.

The authors share responsibility for providing psychotherapy
for adults and children who are subscribers to the Health
Maintenance Plan, Cincinnati. The limited resources in such
a setting led them to combine the general-system-theory
proposition that the least expensive defenses against stress
should be used first with the principle of effective par-
simony, which calls for a particular sequence of action in
providing mental health care. Thus their approaches include
involving the patient in planning the frequency of therapy

sessions, including entire families in the sessions, and
setting reasonable goals and time frames for meeting the
goals. They also use non-medical mental health professionals, under the supervision of a psychiatrist, and other
primary providers in the HMO who are interested in psychotherapy and are willing to call on a psychiatrist when
necessary. (Journal abstract).

171.   Boreham, J., Brief psychotherapy:
        termination and follow-up - the
        conclusion of a case study, British
        Journal of Projective Psychology, 1975,
        20, 1-9.

The author reports on the use of a psychoanalytically-based
brief therapy approach. Twelve sessions of focal psychotherapy with a 30 year old individual with sexual indiffer-
ence were held, and outcome measures taken. Success at
termination was reported and a follow-up about 1 1/2 years
after termination supported the original positive evaluation.
(Journal abstract).

172.   Borkovec, T.D., Effects of expectancy
        on the outcome of systematic desensi-
        tization and implosive treatments for
        analogue anxiety, Behavior Therapy, 1972,
        3, 29-40.

Fifty college female subjects, selected on the basis of
their pretest avoidance of a snake, were randomly assigned
to four conditions (a) desensitization, (b) implosion,
(c) avoidance response, and (d) no-therapy. Half of the
subjects received therapeutic instructions to establish a
positive expectancy of improvement while the other half
received instructions designed to avoid establishing
expectancy of improvement. After four sessions, the posttest
was administered. It was found that desensitization and
implosion both resulted in decreased pulse rate. The
expectancy manipulation strongly affected overt, behavioral
measures of fear. Implosion was most influenced by the
expectancy effects, while positive expectancy implosion
showed the most improvement over the traditional no-therapy
group. (Journal abstract).

173.   Bos, C., Short-term psychotherapy Canadian
       Psychiatric Association Journal, 1959, 4,
       162-165.

Bos raises some issues pertinent to brief therapy and its
role in the panoply of available therapeutic techniques.
He repudiates the view of brief therapy as inferior to long-
term treatment, while reiterating the notion that therapeutic success may be a function of the therapist's
personality rather than of a specific technique. Thus, he
stresses the need to refine diagnostic techniques and to
understand better the role of intuition, empathy, and
motivation. He notes the eclecticism and practical orientation of brief therapy, and how these inform the attitudes
of a therapist vis a vis a patient. Bos examines the two-
fold function of the first session (i.e. reassurance and
diagnosis) and suggests that interviews with the patient or
family member follow along the lines of a medical case
history. (abstract by Deborah Schuller).

174.   Boudewyns, P.A., Is 'milieu therapy' in
       a short-term inpatient psychiatric setting
       worth the money?, International Mental
       Health Research Newsletter, 1974, 16, 7-8.

175.   Boulougouris, J.C., et al., Superiority
       of flooding (implosion) to desensitization
       for reducing pathological fear, Behavior
       Research and Therapy, 1971, 9, 7-16.

Flooding was compared to desensitization as a fear-reducer
in 16 phobic patients who were treated in a cross-over
design with 6 sessions of each procedure. Flooding was
significantly superior to desensitization on clinical and
physiological measures and improvement has been maintained
over 12 months followup. Flooding is a promising technique
for the reduction of fear in anxious phonic patients. The
essential therapeutic components of flooding still have to
be determined before it can be used routinely. (Journal
summary).

176.   Brady, J.P., Metronome-conditioned
relaxation: A new behavioral procedure,
British Journal of Psychiatry, 1973, 122,
729-730.

The author describes a modification of a progressive
relaxation technique in which a metronome is used as part
of the treatment process. Metronome-conditioned relaxation
(MCR) is used as part of a systematic desensitization
process in an attempt to get the patient to relax deeply
while pairing the anxiety hierarchy with is anxiety-
inhibiting state. In two case examples are given, both
successful, and both using a small number of sessions.

177.   Brady, J.P., Behavior therapy and sex
therapy, American Journal of Psychiatry,
1976, 133, 896-899.

Behavior therapy is characterized by the way in which
clinical data are collected, analyzed, and used in the
treatment program - specifically, the application of the
methods of experimental and social psychology. A case
history of the behavioral treatment of a sexual problem is
presented to illustrate this process. Many people have
assumed that the "new sex therapy" is behavior therapy
because of its focus on the here and now and similarities
in particular treatment maneuvers. However, the author
notes that sex therapy is behavior therapy only to the
extent that it deals comprehensively with environmental,
interpersonal, and organismic factors that operate to
maintain the sexual problem. (Journal abstract).

178.   Brandon, S., Crisis theory and possibilities
of therapeutic intervention, British Journal
of Psychiatry, 1970, 117, 627-633.

The author reviews the work of Caplan in some detail,
focussing on the nature and processes observed during crises.
The work of others is also interwoven in the discussion
(e.g., Erikson, Lindemann, Tyhurst). Once an individual is
in crisis, a number of intervention principles come into
play, including issues of dependency between therapist and
client, maintaining a reality focus, etc. The implications
for psychiatric practice of these issues are also presented.

179.   Brandon, S., Crisis therapy, Current
        Psychiatric Therapies, 1975, 15, 243-246.

In this short article, the author summarizes some of the
more important developments in the field of crisis therapy,
and presents some of the major postulates held in the field
(e.g., early and rapid treatment at times of crisis, etc.).

180.   Brechenser, D.M., Brief psychotherapy
        using a transactionsl analysis, Social
        Casework, 1972, 53, 173-176.

A transactional approach used in a crisis ward of a hospital
is described. The average stay is three weeks, with two
individual therapy sessions/week, and one TA group therapy/
week. The value for the patients of using the Parent, Adult,
Child model is discussed. Improvements in the patient
population are reported in general terms, and recommendations
for longer term therapy once the crisis passes are reviewed.

181.   Bridges, P.K., Psychiatric emergencies:
        Diagnosis and management, Springfield,
        Ill., C.C. Thomas, 1971.

182.   Brink, T.L., Geriatric counseling: a
        practical guide, Family Therapy, 1976,
        3, 163-169.

The author provides a brief overview of the use of short-
term geriatric counseling, with its specifically defined
objectives. Techniques focussed on include the initial
interview structure and typical remarks, methods of identifying problems, and ways of helping to find solutions to
very practical problems.

183.   Brink, T.L., Brief psychotherapy: A
        case report illustrating its potential
        effectiveness, Journal of the American
        Geriatrics Society, 1977, 25, 273-276.

The advance of industrialization in Mexico and elsewhere has
brought about psycho-social problems of aging similar to
those encountered in the United States. A case study is

presented of a 64 year old Mexican widow who had suicidal
thoughts and feelings of uselessness. External constraints
on the therapist dictated that psychotherapy be completed
within 15 days. A strategy of brief psychotherapy was
adopted. The focus was not on establishing transference,
probing the unconscious or reconstructing the patient's
personality, but on identifying problems and formulating
practical solutions promptly. Hour hour-long sessions were
sufficient to gather information and to counsel the patient
and her family. The diagnosis was depression. The initial
success of these measures made for a good prognosis. Both
patient and family were advised of the availability of
antidepressant drugs, and advised against relocating the
patient. (Journal abstract).

    184.   Brink, T.L., Guidelines for counseling the
            aged, The New Physician, 1977, 25, 31-33.

This is a guide for primary care physicians interested in
brief, problem-centered counseling of the aged.

    185.   Brink, T.L., Pastoral care for the aged:
            a practical guide, Journal of Pastoral
            Care, 1977, 31, 264-272.

This is a guide for the clergy interested in brief, problem-
oriented counseling for the aged.

    186.   Brink, T.L., Depression in the aged:
            dynamics and treatment, Journal of the
            National Medical Association, 1977, 69,
            891-893.

Depressed elders can be treated in various ways: medication,
ECT, and psychotherapy. Brief therapy by a primary care
physician is recommended.

187.   Brink, T.L., Dream therapy with the aged,
       Psychotherapy: Theory, Research, and
       Practice, 1977, 14, 354-360.

Dreams are a useful technique in helping elder clients cope
more effectively with problems they confront. Dreams can
be used in short term work as well as with OBS patients.

188.   Brink, T.L., Geriatric rigidity and its
       psychotherapeutic implications, Journal
       of the American Geriatric Society, 1978,
       26, 274-277.

Many depressed elders are rigid, and the rigidity is
frequently symptomatic of maladjustment to the stresses of
old age. However, the best approach in brief psychotherapy
is not to attack the client's rigidities, but to accept
them and work with them, directing therapy toward effective
coping with specific problems. Two case studies are
presented.

189.   Brink, T.L., Geriatric psychotherapy,
       New York, Human Sciences Press, 1979.

Psychotherapy for older persons can be performed by
psychiatrists, clinical psychologists, social workers,
clergy, or primary care physicians. Geriatric psychotherapy
must be brief, problem-centered, and team oriented, Many
of the Freudian and Rogerian theories and techniques cannot
be fruitfully applied. The book outlines the basic
strategies, approaches, and specific techniques, including
group therapy, family therapy, dream therapy, milieu
therapy, and adjunctive treatments (somatic and behavioral).

190.   Brockopp, G.W., Crisis theory and
       suicide prevention, Crisis Intervention,
       1970, 2, 38-42.

191.   Brodskey, L., Anger provocation as a
        crisis intervention technique, Hospital
        and Community Psychiatry, 1977, 28, 533-536.

The author describes the use of anger provocation, a technique that encourages patients to express their repressed
anger to a therapist who makes himself the target for their
anger. He presents 5 case examples to illustrate the positive effects of the technique in crisis and emergency
situations. Three of the patients were depressed and withdrawn, one was suffering from conversion hysteria, and one
was a paranoid schizophrenic. The author cautions that the
technique must be used with discretion only in those cases
where the repression of anger is producing major incapacitating symptomatology, but where the anger is not the major
source of disorganization. (Journal abstract).

192.   Brothwood, J., The work of a psychiatric
        emergency clinic, British Journal of
        Psychiatry, 1965, 111, 631-634.

The aim of the present study was to evaluate various patient
population characteristics of the Maudsley Hospital Emergency
Clinic in comparison to patients seen on an out-patient basis
by appointment at the hospital. The total sample was 100
patients, 53 women and 47 men. Detailed demographic data
were presented. The results indicated that both populations
were similar in characteristics, and differed from a third
sample population of observation ward patients. The functions of the Emergency Clinic as they have evolved naturally
are listed as: (a) psychiatric evaluation without delay
from referring family physicians; (b) allocation of patients
for appropriate services; (c) a continuing advisory service
for previous or current patients.

193.   Brown, V.B., Drug people: schizoid
        personalities in search of a treatment,
        Psychotherapy: Theory, Research and
        Practice, 1971, 8, 213-215.

This paper describes two group treatment methods used to meet
specific needs of the "Drug People". The first is a modification of crisis group treatment (Strickler and Allgeyer,
1967; Morley and Brown, 1969): the second is a community-
oriented, self-help approach. (Journal introduction).

194.   Brown, V.B., Community crisis intervention:
        the dangers of and opportunities for change,
        in Parad, H., et al., (eds.), Emergency and
        disaster management, Bowie, Maryland, The
        Charles Press, 1976.

The author states that to meet the mental health needs of
a community, the crisis intervenor must move along a
continuum from individual treatment through community
intervention; yet little attention has been paid to the
broader social frame of reference. Conceptualizing
community hazards as entailing losses or shifts in power
within a number of interlocking systems, the author examines
interventions in such events as loss of community leader,
loss of community program, homicide of community member,
changing of racial balance of school, urban redevelopment
and relocation, and allocation of funds to one group over
another. Brown briefly outlines high-risk interfaces
within the community, and various roles and strategies the
crisis intervenor may use to help reduce crisis potential
within low-income and minority communities. She concludes
by illustrating with two specific situations (the assassi-
nation of Martin Luther King and a community drug crisis)
the types of interventions which can be carried out by
community mental health professionals. (abstract by
Deborah Schuller).

195.   Browne, S.E., Short psychotherapy with
        passive patients: An experiment in
        general practice, British Journal of
        Psychiatry, 1964, 110, 233-239.

An account is given of an active and brief form of psychotherapy in general practice with 21 patients of the passive
personality type, which was found in 71% of all patients
interviewed. Treatment was directed towards increasing
self-assertiveness and self-acceptance which were regarded
as basic aspects of a unitary process of recovery through
greater self-realization. It involved the use of hypnotic
techniques and the playing-back of tape-recorded interviews;
reassurance, clarification and interpretation of the patient's
attitudes to himself and others and active persuasion and
suggestion were the main elements in therapy. Sixteen

patients were considered on follow-up two years later to
be much or considerably improved. It is suggested that
this method of psychotherapy is simple and effective enough
to be of value to general practitioners, as well as in
psychiatric practice. (Journal summary).

196.   Bruch, H., Brief psychotherapy in a
       pediatric clinic, Quarterly Journal of
       Child Behavior, 1949, 1, 2-8.

197.   Bruck, M., An example of the use of
       psychodrama in the relieving of an acute
       symptom in a psychiatric children's clinic,
       Group Psychotherapy, 1953, 6, 216-221.

Bruck describes his work with an eight-year old child who
had suffered from tics and a partial paralysis for six
months prior to referral to a clinic. The intake process
with the mother yielded information regarding onset of
symptoms and features of the child's familial context. To
reduce anxiety within a situationally-circumscribed number
of sessions, psychodrama was chosen as the treatment mode.
The author relates the session in which the boy's symptoms
disappeared. Bruck notes on the basis of follow-up over
18 months that the symptoms have not returned. (abstract
by Deborah Schuller).

198.   Bryt, A., Emergency psychotherapeutic
       assistance, American Journal of Ortho-
       psychiatry, 1962, 32, 399-403.

The author present an account of the theoretical framework
(drawing from Sullivan, Allport, and Ackerman) within which
an experimental program of very brief psychotherapy was
implemented in selected adolescent cases. The program is
designed to attend to disorders of adaptation which manifest themselves as acute disturbances in adjustment through
behavioral symptomatology. The goals of E.P.A. are defined
as the re-establishment of a state of prior emotional
adaptation, neurotic as it may have been. Five sessions
each for patient and parent are the approximate maximum.
(abstract by Deborah Schuller).

199.   Buchanan, D.C., Group therapy in kidney
        transplant patients, International
        Journal of Psychiatry in Medicine, 1975,
        6, 523-531.

A short-term, open membership therapy program for kidney
transplant patients and their families is described. The
content and process of this group is related to the ten
curative factors described for psychiatric patients. The
primary benefits for the patients seemed to be the opportunity to observe others cope with similar problems and
to learn of the adaptive strategies used by others. The
patients were able to offer advice to others, to overcome
their tendency toward seclusion and in general, experience
a feeling of hope for the future. The family members gained
more from a sense of group cohesiveness than did the patients.
Both family and patients utilized the meetings to ventilate
their anger and frustrations with chronic illness and to
learn more about transplantation. A more realistic expectation of the future was provided. The group did not seem
long enough to measurably improve the interpersonal relations
between patients and their families nor did the group members
comment upon maladaptive behaviors exhibited between family
members within the meetings. (Journal abstract).

200.   Buchanan, D.C., Group therapy for chronic
        physically ill patients. Psychosomatics,
        1978, 19, 425-431.

Some of the emotional stresses and coping styles most often
seen in patients with chronic physical illness are reviewed,
and a two-phase group therapy program designed to suit their
needs is described. The program consists of several initial
didactic or educational group meetings, followed by meetings
that stress insight-oriented psychotherapy (usually 10-15
meetings in total). (Journal abstract modified).

201.   Buchanan, D.C., Psychotherapeutic inter-
       vention in the kidney transplant service,
       in Levy, N., (ed.), Psychological factors in
       hemodialysis and transplantation, New York,
       Plenum Press, (in press).

This chapter focusses on the psychotherapeutic properties
inherent in interaction between transplant service personnel
and the transplant patient, and attempts to develop them
further. Buchanan describes two complementary psychotherapeutic techniques that can be easily implemented by a
transplant service: group psychotherapy and individual
brief therapy. A two-phase model of group therapy (the
first aimed at patient and family education, the second
with a predominantly psychological focus) comprising 10-15
weekly or bi-weekly sessions can serve as a major thrust
in the prevention and alleviation of emotional stress. The
group meeting may uncover reactions which can be effectively
treated through individual brief psychotherapy by the transplant staff. The most prevalent psychological problem of
transplant patients is depression. The author provides
information on recognizing and understanding depression,
and describes techniques of interaction with the depressed
patient. Buchanan concludes that depression proves amenable
to brief supportive psychotherapy, and that such a technique
can be capably applied by the transplant service. (abstract
by Deborah Schuller).

202.   Buchanan, F.S., Notes on them-centered
       time-limited group therapy, in, Ruitenbeek,
       H.M., (ed.), Group therapy today, New York,
       Atherton Press, 1969.

The author describes in detail a time-limited theme-centered
group therapy approach, based on the pioneering work of
Ruth Cohn. The group is limited to 10 sessions and uses
a theme (e.g., isolation; or, alone, lonely, and single
theme) to form the context of group interaction. The use
of media (music, poetry, etc.) is presented, along with
some actual exchanges in transcript form, and comments by
the author about the process over the course of the 10
sessions.

203.   Buda, B., Utilizatton of resistance and
       paradox communication in short-term psycho-
       therapy, Psychotherapy and Psychosomatics,
       1972, 20, 200-211.

The author presents a summary of eight theoretical foundations of short-term therapy and focusses on the need for
proper patients selection (great tension, distress and
emotional upheaval accompanied by heightened problem
awareness), and greater effectiveness of the therapeutic
operations themselves. Among the principles are personality
viewed as an open system with built-in capacities for growth,
description of what happens when these tendencies are
blocked, and a focus on the quality of the relationship
between therapist and client within the short-term context.
Resistance and its meaning in brief therapy are highlighted,
and the use of paradoxical communication to control and
utilize this resistance is discussed. Examples from other
therapists are cited which elucidate the use of paradoxical
communication in therapy.

204.   Burchard, J., and Tyler, V., The modification
       of delinquent behaviour through operant con-
       ditioning, Behaviour, Research and Therapy,
       1965, 2, 245-250.

The frequent antisocial behaviour of a 13-year-old delinquent boy was hypothesized as resulting from contingencies
between such behaviour and social reinforcements provided
by staff and peers. Systematic use of such operant techniques as time-out from reinforcement, differential reinforcement and discrimination training over a five-month
period resulted in a declining rate of antisocial behaviour
together with a decrease in seriousness of offenses. Five
months of operant conditioning was more effective in
modifying and controlling his behaviour than the more
conventional types of psychotherapy utilized during the
pervious four years of his institutionalization. (Journal
summary).

205.   Burdon, A.P., Principles of brief psycho-
        therapy, Journal of the Louisiana Medical
        Medical Society, 1963, 115, 374-378.

The author presents a psychoanalytically oriented discussion
on brief therapy. The major strength of the paper is its
application to everyday psychiatric practice. Among the
issues discussed is the view that it is not the severity
of the pathology but the stability of the premorbid
personality that facilitates the use of a brief therapy
approach. The author outlines five principles of brief
therapy. These are: a) the development of basic trust,
especially involving issues of patient expectancy re therapy;
b) the patient's wish for meaningful change, especially
involving the wish for one's own inner personality change;
c) the process of emotional exposure (catharsis) linkage
in the patient's mind of past conflicts/events so that new
solutions can be sought; d) the potential for mastery of
the present conflict situation the patient finds him/herself
in; e) the development of a new perspective, in which not
only insight plays a role, but new and real action on the
patient's part occurs. The author also briefly indicates
those patients for whom brief therapy is indicated (acutely
situationally disturbed individual with stable and purposive
premorbid equilibrium, even if this stability was based on
formidable defenses), as well as those for whom it is
contraindictated (massive psychotic regression; chronic
character disorder).

206.   Burdon, A.P., and Neely, J.H., Chronic
        school failure in boys: A short-term,
        group therapy and educational approach,
        American Journal of Psychiatry, 1966,
        122, 1211-1220.

The authors report on a five year study involving the treatment of 55 boys and their families. The students did not
exhibit any neurological deficits based on psychological
test results and physical examination. They did exhibit
repeated school failure, age range of the sample was 7-12
years. At least average in intelligence as measured by
I.Q. tests, the absence of psychotic symptomtalogy, and
the high level of motivation of the parents were criteria
for inclusion in the sample. The therapy program lasted

between 3.5-5 months. Fathers, mothers, and children were involved; fathers and mothers separately in group therapy once/week for 90 minutes/session, with children attending regular school in the morning and the clinic-school in the afternoon. The specific type of therapy used and the focus of the sessions is summarized. A follow-up was done one and two years after the conclusion of treatment, on a total of 46 children and their families. Separate information was gathered from teachers, parents, and the children themselves. Teachers indicated the increase in student co-operativeness and a decrease in the need for disciplinary action, and a steady and modest increase in school performance. 90% of the parents indicated the value of the program in changing patterns within the family. The students indicated a marked improvement in their attitudes toward school. The authors conclude by stressing the value of an intensive and comprehensive program for dealing with chronic school failure in school children.

207.   Burgess, A.W., and Holmstrom, L.L., Crisis
       and counseling requests of rape victims,
       Nursing Research, 1974, 23, 196-202.

A study of 146 adults and pediatric victims of sexual assault in the greater Boston area revealed a positive response by the victims to psychological intervention during the crisis period. Victims were interviewed at a hospital immediately following the assault, and were followed up with telephone calls from the investigators/ counselors. Immediate crisis requests of the rape victims were conceptualized as medical interventions, police intervention, psychological intervention, control and undertain. The telephone counseling follow-ups of these crisis requests revealed victims' needs changed to emotional and supportive services. The counseling requests were: confirmation of concern, ventilation, clarification, advice, and wants nothing. The victims' requests were considered important factors in negotiating the professional-client relationship. The counselors listened carefully to each request and responded appropriately. (Journal abstract).

208.   Burke, J.D., et al., Which short-term
        therapy? Archives of General Psychiatry,
        1979, 36, 177-186.

In recent years, numerous forms of short-term psychotherapy
have been developed, without clear guidelines for choosing
among them. There are three major approaches in terms of
both their techniques and their criteria for patient
selection. The "interpretive" method stresses the use of
insight produced by a therapist's interpretations, the
"existential", the maturational effect of a brief empathic
encounter with the therapist, and the "corrective", the
behavioral changes resulting from patient management by the
therapist. The question facing a short-term therapist is
how to choose a particular method for a particular patient.
A fremework is proposed based on developmental phases of
adult life to help therapists match patient and method.
(Journal abstract).

209.   Burks, H.L., and Hoekstra, M., Psychiatric
        emergencies in children, American Journal
        of Orthopsychiatry, 1964, 34, 134-137.

The present study was initiated to answer questions pertaining to psychiatric emergencies in children at a
university medical center (Michigan). The control group
consisted of randomly selected 110 children from a total
sample of 600 children who had been seen at the clinic as
non-emergencies; the experimental group consisted of 110
children referred to the clinic during the same period on
an emergency basis, the existence of an emergency being
defined by the referring agent. Compared to the control
group, the emergency group was significantly different in
terms of duration of illness, age, source of referral, and
nature of precipitating events. Implications of each of
these factors are discussed.

210.   Burnell, G.M., et al., Postabortion group
        therapy, American Journal of Psychiatry,
        1972, 129, 220-223.

Two hundred and fifty women who had had a therapeutic
abortion attended a group therapy program after discharge
from the hospital. Each group was led by a psychiatrist-

gynecologist team and consisted of three to five women.
The authors concluded that the program was beneficial,
helping patients to cope with guilt feelings and the clear
areas of misinformation about sexual function and contra-
ception. This program also provided an opportunity to
combine educational, therapeutic, and preventive aspects
of gynecological and psychiatric practice. (Journal
abstract).

211.   Burns, D., and Brady, J.P., Stuttering
        and speech disorders, Psychiatric Clinics
        of North America, 1978, 1, 335-348.

The stuttering syndrome is here defined as a self-
perpetuating system with behavioral, cognitive, and emotional
components. The sense of failure when attempting to speak
results in the stutterer's viewing himself as inadequate or
inferior. This belief engenders anxiety, emotional tension
that results in increased stuttering, and maladaptive
behavior such as interpersonal withdrawal and decreased
assertiveness. Increased dysfluency and social isolation
in turn help maintain the negative self-image. Burns and
Brady relate a four-phase model of metronome-conditioned
speech restraining and adjunctive techniques, such as
systematic desensitization, assertive training, and
regulated breathing techniques. As a result of such interventions, the stuttering cycle fades out and a fluency
cycle emerges, which leads to a diminution of anxiety and
enhanced self-esteem. (abstract by Deborah Schuller).

212.   Burnside, I.M., Crisis intervention
        with geriatric hospitalized patients,
        Journal of Psychiatric Nursing and
        Mental Health Services, 1970, 8, 17-20.

During the year of my group work with aged persons in a
convalescent hospital, group members frequently experienced
stress situations. Using some of the principles of brief
psychotherapy and crisis intervention, I have presented a
simplified guide that I used while working with these aged,
hospitalized patients. It is well to remember that the
theme of loss will be the most familiar theme heard from

the aging person, and though the losses are many and varied,
the main loss includes death of a "significant other."
Understanding the dynamics of depression in the aged
individual, and the ability to operationalize the classic
work of Lindemann in grief work, are useful to the nurse-
therapist working with the aged individual in stress
situations. (Journal summary).

213.   Butcher, J.N., and Kolotkin, R.L.
        Evaluation of outcome in brief psycho-
        therapy, Psychiatric Clinics of North
        America, 1979, 2, 157-169.

The authors review some of the research on the effectiveness of brief psychotherapy and examine some of the issues
related to conducting sound outcome research. Special
considerations for evaluation of effectiveness are reviewed,
including selection of appropriate criterion measures,
determination of appropriate points during and post-treatment
for evaluation of outcome; and the necessity of evaluating
negative effects. The need to tie measures of outcome to
specific features of brief therapy, particularly to the
concrete nature of goals and the directive nature of treatment is examined. The authors include a table comparing
some of the characteristics of brief versus long-term psychotherapy. They note that a special issue in evaluating the
effectiveness of time-limited treatment concerns the use
of direct intervention techniques with individuals under
conditions of high arousal or transitional pathology.
(abstract by Deborah Schuller).

214.   Butcher, J.N., and Koss, M.P., Research
        on brief and crisis-oriented therapies,
        in, Bergin, A., and Garfield, S., (eds.),
        Handbook of psychotherapy and behavior
        change, 2nd edition, New York, Wiley, 1978.

In this comprehensive overview, the authors provide some
historical background developments that influenced the
emergence of brief therapy methods. (Psychoanalytically-
oriented, behavioral, and crisis intervention, and various
brief verbal therapies). Elements common to all of these

approaches are summarized (time factors, limited goals,
focussed interviewing techniques and orientation on present
central issue, active involvement of therapist, early and
rapid assessment, maintaining flexibility, immediacy of
intervention, value of ventilation, issues of patient
selection, and the nature of the therapy relationship).
They review the types of process variables which are
important in briefer forms of therapy (e.g., role of
interpretation, the role of patient expectations, role of
crisis in the process of change, limitation of time and its
effect on the process, concrete behavioral focus, etc.).
They conclude this chapter with an overview of the results
of outcome research in the area of brief therapy. Approximately 250 references are included.

215.   Butcher, J.N., and Maudal, G.R., Crisis
        intervention, in, Weiner, I.B., (ed.),
        Clinical methods in psychology, New York,
        Wiley, 1976.

In one of the most comprehensive reviews of the area of
crisis intervention, the authors summarize the origins of
crisis intervention (e.g., influence of World War II;
disaster grief work and the early crisis clinics; suicide
prevention; free clinics). They then provide an overview
of the various theoretical formulations of crisis intervention, the characteristics of competent crisis intervention,
and the differences between crisis therapy and psychoanalytic psychotherapy, and crisis therapy and other short-
term therapy approaches. The goals of crisis therapy are
clearly laid out (symptom relief, re-establishing the
previous adjustment balance, developing an understanding
of the precipitating events) and how these factors combine
with the person's past and present personality dynamics.
Methods of gathering the type of information needed to do
effective crisis intervention work are presented, along
with a summary of the range of tactics available to the
crisis intervention worker (e.g., offering emotional
support, allowing catharsis, setting a tone of optimism,
being actively involved in the problem issues, selective
listening, being willing to use factual information, being
focussed, advice giving, setting limits, using confrontation
where appropriate, supporting the health and adaptive

aspects of the individual's personality, setting up concrete
goals, and being willing to use outside community resources.
The importance of follow-up work is also stressed. Approximately 150 references are included.

216.   Caffey, E.M., et al., Brief hospital
        treatment of schizophrenia:-early results
        of a multiple-hospital study, Hospital
        and Community Psychiatry, 1968, 19,
        282-287.

The authors report on a study in which 203 schizophrenic
patients were studied. Patients were provided with an
intensive, brief hospital stay, followed by an outpatient
aftercare program. The findings point to the value of
time-limited hospital treatment. Patients who had received
brief treatment did not exhibit significantly greater readmission rates compared to those who had received longer
term hospitalization. The value of the aftercare program
was also stressed.

217.   Calsyn, R.J., et al., Correlates of
        successful outcome in crisis intervention
        therapy, American Journal of Community
        Psychology, 1977, 5, 111-119.

The present study examines the correlates of successful
outcome (subsequent inpatient or outpatient treatment) of
305 outpatient cases treated by crisis intervention therapy.
Although the two measures of outcome were correlated with
each, the respective relationships with the predictor
variables were sometimes different. Demographic variables
and therapist's characteristics were not correlated with
either outcome measures. Past responses to stress (prior
state hospitalization and suicidal behavior) were predictors
of subsequent inpatient treatment, but not subsequent outpatient treatment. On the other hand, current precipitating events did not predict inpatient treatment, but did
predict subsequent outpatient treatment. Several statistically nonsignificant relationships which either replicate
or disagree with previous findings are also discussed.
(Journal abstract).

218.   Cameron, W., and Walters, V., The emergency
        mental health service, Southern Medicine,
        1965, 58, 1375-1379.

219.   Campbell, D.D., A short-term psychotherapy
        for depression: A second controlled study,
        Dissertation Abstracts International, 1974,
        1974, 35, 2B, 1039.

220.   Campbell, R.J., Psychotherapy in a
        community mental health center, American
        Journal of Psychiatry, 1965, 122, 143-147.

The author summarizes establishment and running of a
community mental health center connected to St. Vincent's
Hospital and Medical Center in New York City. The hospital
services the Greenwich Village, Chelsea, and waterfront
areas of the city. The impact of such a center on the
traditional practice orientations of psychiatry and psychiatric trainees is discussed, including the difficulty
in setting limited and specific goals at the beginning of
therapy. A wide range of approaches is used, including
drug therapy, counseling, environmental manipulation,
family conferences, etc. The value of contact with and
involvement with other community service agencies is highlighted. The sources of resistance to briefer forms of
therapy on the parts of both therapist and patient are
described.

221.   Campbell, R.J., Facilitation of short-
        term clinical therapy, Current Psychiatric
        Therapies, 1967, 7, 186-196.

The author describes the changes, including resistances on
the part of staff members to instituting a short-term outpatient clinic in New York City. The types of patients
seen are described, including a special group from the
Greenwich Village area. The steps taken to institute a
briefer approach to therapy are detailed, including changes
in intake procedures, supervision, professional seminars,
etc. The author concludes by listing those variables which

appear to be related to success of brief therapy. Among
these are accessibility (i.e., rapid intake and involvement),
flexibility on the part of the therapy staff, and the use
of community resources as part of the on-going treatment
plan.

222.   Campbell, R.J., Brief psychotherapy in
       an outpatient clinic, American Journal
       of Psychiatry, 1968, 124, 1225-1226.
       (discussion).

223.   Campbell, R.J., and Thompkins, H.J.,
       Brief psychotherapy, Proceedings IV
       World Congress of Psychiatry, Madrid,
       Spain, September, 1966, 407-415.

224.   Caplan, G., An approach to community
       mental health, N.Y., Grune and Stratton,
       1961.

The author presents a systematic approach to dealing with
mental health concerns within a community mental health
model. Primary prevention techniques are outlined. Further,
details are provided regarding the ways of helping individuals experiencing life crises. The effective use of many
community resources is stressed. The theoretical under-
pinnings of the conceptual approach lie within ego psychology
developments, and particular emphasis is placed on issues of
grief and anxiety in human crises, relating to loss and danger
respectively. Stages of human reaction to stress are outlined
as well, connected specifically to stress of pregnancy, birth,
and the developing mother-child relationship. Throughout the
text, concrete examples of techniques are used to illustrate
the approach suggested.

225.   Caplan, G., (ed.), The prevention of
       mental disorders in children, New York,
       Basic Books, 1961.

226. Caplan, G., Principles of preventive psychiatry, N.Y., Basic Books, 1964.

227. Caplan, G., et al., Four studies of crisis in parents of prematures, Community Mental Health Journal, 1965, 1, 149-161.

This study focussed on the reactions of 86 families to the premature birth of a child. The major focus was on attempts to continue to understand the nature of crisis and how individuals react to crisis. Specific coping patterns of behavior were identified by the researchers, and the results were related both to issues of mental health and illness as well as to issues of prevention.

228. Capone, M.A., et al., Crisis intervention: A functional model for hospitalized cancer patients, American Journal of Orthopsychiatry, 1979, 49, 598-607.

A model for psychosocial rehabilitation of hospitalized oncology patients, found to be effective in use with gynecologic patients, is described. It is suggested that the contribution of mental health professionals to the health delivery system of an oncology ward is essential to the maintenance of comprehensive care. (Journal abstract).

229. Carlson, D.A., et al., Problems in treating the lower-class psychotic, Archives of General Psychiatry, 1965, 13, 269-274.

This paper discusses some of the problems encountered in outpatient psychiatric treatment of severely disturbed lower-class patients. Their special needs and ways of relating were described. The major problem in providing care to these patients revolved around the difficulties the residents had in reconciling an indicated directive treatment approach with the values implicit in expressive psychotherapy. From the point of view of comprehensive training the residents should have an experience of working with all types of patients in order to develop his capacity to find the treatment modality appropriate to each patient's

needs. To make use of the opportunity to treat a wide
range of treatment problems, residents will require much
support and supervision - more than is needed in a clinic
whose function is clearly either psychotherapy on the one
hand or management on the other. (Journal summary).

230.   Carney, F.J., Evaluation of psychotherapy
        in a maximum security prison, Seminars in
        Psychiatry, 1971, 3, 363-375.

The author reports the results of a psychotherapy research
project in which the effects of treatment were studied as
they related to recidivism rates of prisoners incarcerated
in a maximum security facility. Overall, there were significant decreases in recidivism rates for those who participated in the therapy program. More specifically,
however, inmates with a shorter previous record of offenses
and older inmates benefitted more, and the longer these
inmates remained in psychotherapy, the lower the recidivism
rates. Those inmates who were younger but who had significantly greater offense rates did not benefit from the treatment program; more specifically, this latter type of
prisoner had a higher recidivism rate the longer they
remained in treatment. The value of longer term treatment
using a group therapy approach and shorter term treatment
using an individual treatment approach was stressed.

231.   Carpenter, W.T., et al., Emergency
        psychiatric treatment during a mass
        rally: The march on Washington,
        American Journal of Psychiatry, 1971,
        127, 1327-1332.

The authors present a rationale for establishing emergency
psychiatric facilities during mass demonstrations. Special
aspects or attributes such as trust, confidentiality, the
authoritarian role of the physician, legal complications,
the management of potentially violent patients, and the
evaluation of thought processes are discussed. The low
incidence of psychiatric casualties and the relative rarity
of adverse drug reactions during the November, 1969 March

on Washington are documented: The majority of the most
disturbed patients came to Washington for idiosyncratic
reasons and did not regard themselves as antiwar protestors.
(Journal abstract).

232.   Carrera, R.N., and Lott, D.R., The effect
        of group implosive therapy on snake phobias,
        Journal of Clinical Psychology, 1978, 34,
        177-181.

Snake phobic Ss groups of 10 were presented with a verbal
fantasy similar to those used in individual Implosive
Therapy (IT) in order to explore the adaptability of the
procedure to group use. A single 25-minute implosive
presentation of the same material on audio tape was effective in reudcing snake phobias in about the same percentage
of Ss as individual IT. It was concluded that IT can be
adapted to group use, but that care should be taken to
ensure an opportunity for extinction to occur through
repated presentation of the fantasy material. (Journal
abstract).

233.   Cartwright, D., et al., Length of therapy
        in relation to outcome and change in
        personal integration, Journal of Consulting
        Psychology, 1961, 25, 84-88.

The authors report on a replication of an earlier study
(Standal and van der Veen, 1957). Eighty-seven clients
were used in this study, all having been seen in therapy
at the University of Chicago Counseling Center. There were
52 males, and 35 females, with an average of 28.5 years.
The average number of therapy sessions was 29.5, covering
an average number of 31.9 weeks. The type of therapy used
was client-centered in orientation. The first finding was
that there was a moderate linear relationship between
change in personal integration and number of therapy
sessions, confirming the previous study's findings.

234.   Case, J.D., Community participation and
        short-term treatment needs citizen
        participation, Group Psychotherapy, 1967,
        1967, 20, 196-197.

The author presents a discussion of the importance of
having community agencies available to provide immediate
support and service to clients. The main focus of the
article is on a short-term, intensive approach to treatment
in a local prison.

235.   Castelnuovo-Tedesco, P., The twenty-
        minute "hour": An experiment in medical
        education, New England Journal of Medicine,
        1962, 266, 283-289.

Experience in the teaching of basic psychiatric principles
to medical residents is described. The instruction has
centered about the use of a simple, supportive psychotherapeutic technic, called the twenty-minute "hour". By this
approach the patient is seen, after an initial period
devoted to a standard medical work-up and psychiatric
history taking, for several twenty-minute psychotherapeutic
sessions spaced at weekly intervals. Usually, symptoms
are at least moderately alleviated after approximately ten
such sessions. The reasons why psychotherapeutic management of patients is infrequently attempted by internists
and general practitioners in a planned and systematic way
are also examined, and it is concluded that lack of time,
although usually given as the chief reason, is probably of
less consequence than other factors less often discussed.
These include lack of familiarity with, and lack of confidence in, short-term psychotherapeutic technics, together
with a number of attitudes about the doctor-patient
relationship that make the physician reluctant to consider
psychotherapy as a medical technic and to share with the
patient the responsibility for the outcome of his emotional
distress. (Journal summary).

236.   Castelnuovo-Tedesco, P., The twenty minute
        hour: A guide to a brief psychotherapy
        for the physician, New York, Little, Brown,
        and Co., 1965. (also printed in Italian,
        L'Ora di venti minute: Guida alla psi-
        coterapia per il medico practico, Editore
        Boringhiere, Torino, Italy, 1972).

237.   Castelnuovo-Tedesco, P., Brief psychothera-
        peutic treatment of the depressive reactions,
        The Quarterly of Camarillo, 1965, 1, 16-28.
        (also reprinted in, International Psychiatry
        Clinics, 1967, 3, 197-210).

Although cautioning that "depression" may be an omnibus
term used to represent a heterogeneous group of reactions,
the author relates criteria of selection for brief therapy
of patients suffering depressive reactions. He outlines
the dynamics of depression, noting the presence of dis-
appointment or regret, anger, guilt, dependency, and a
sense of helplessness. To illustrate, two brief case
histories are presented. He concludes by examining
characteristics and conditions of brief treatment of
depressive reactions; therapeutic focus (on the present,
and especially on the relationships which currently are
disappointing), the physician's response to the patient as
a function of certain aspects of the psychopathology of
depression, and the issue of time limits. (abstract by
Deborah Schuller).

238.   Castelnuovo-Tedesco, P., Brief psycho-
        therapy: Current status, California
        Medicine, 1967, 107, 263-269.

In the past decade, stimulated by public concern with
issues of mental health, there has been a new spurt of
interest in techniques of brief treatment with circumscribed goals. These are applicable to groups as well as
to the single patient. There are still differences of
opinion about the effectiveness of brief psychotherapy,
particularly the lastingness and depth of the results
obtained, yet it is often highly beneficial, especially
to previously well-functioning individuals who are

involved in a situational crisis. Although probably the
best results of brief psychotherapy are with disturbances
of moderate severity and recent onset, in practice, it is
often tried with a wide spectrum of patients. Brief psychotherapy aims at relief of the patient's major current
conflicts rather than at change of his personality structure, which generally requires long-term treatment. Brief
psychotherapy is of special relevance to the general
physician because the patients whom he sees in large
numbers are precisely those best suited for this form of
treatment. (Journal abstract).

239.   Castelnuovo-Tedesco, P., The twenty-
        minute hour: An approach to the post-
        graduate teaching of psychiatry, American
        Journal of Psychiatry, 1967, 123, 786-791.

Approaches to the teaching of psychologic medicine to non-
psychiatrist physicians have varied greatly. The author
describes an approach based on brief, supportive psychotherapy; it is his conviction that psychotherapy is the
chief instrument the practitioner needs to learn if he is
to discharge his responsibilities to his patients in the
area of psychologic medicine. Emphasis in this training
program for residents in internal medicine is on actual
contact with a patient. Problems that commonly arise are
reviewed. (Journal abstract).

240.   Castelnuovo-Tedesco, P., Brief psycho-
        therapy: Therapia universalis? Seminars
        in Psychiatry, 1969, 1, 405-410.

The author examines the question of why brief therapy has
become the center of so much interest. He suggests that
its current popularity is not explained fully by its
unique merits, but rather that this trend toward regarding
brief therapy as the universal therapy reflects serious
doubts over the intrinsic value of psychotherapy itself.
A common manifestation of this questioning has been a view
of brief therapy as essentially and even ideally the
removal of symptoms and return to the status quo ante.
Underlying this skepticism is a tendency to stress the

relationship with the therapist as the major or sole beneficial factor in therapy, with a simultaneous undervaluing
of the technical aspects of therapy. The author affirms
the complementarity of brief and longer forms of therapy -
both in their respective applicability to the variety of
problems encountered and with regards to the training of
therapists. (abstract by Deborah Schuller).

241.   Castelnuovo-Tedesco, P., The twenty
        minute hour revisited: A follow-up,
        Comprehensive Psychiatry, 1970, 11,
        108-122.

A questionnaire dealing with the use of psychotherapy by
non-psychiatrists was distributed to 50 internists who,
during their residency, took part in a psychotherapy course
for medical residents. Forty-one physicians, whose average
age was 35 years replied. The majority were in private
practice. Anywhere from 3-60 per cent of patients are seen
as having a primarily psychiatric disorder. The majority
of the patients with emotional difficulties are treated
by the physician himself. The consultative advice received
from psychiatrists generally is regarded as satisfactory.
Most of the emotionally upset patients treated are psychoneurotic and the most frequently employed treatment methods
are psychotropic drugs with simple reassurance, or brief
psychotherapy with drugs. Brief psychotherapy alone or
long-term, non-intensive psychotherapy are used also, but
much less often. The "20-minute hour" is regarded as a
useful approach to brief psychotherapy and approximately
two-thirds of suitable patients are reported as showing
a satisfactory response. Three-fourths (76%) of the
physicians believe that psychotherapy is an effective form
of treatment and most (85%) believe it has a useful place
in the practice of internal medicine. Preference generally
is for brief treatment and for a therapeutic approach
emphasizing activity. (Journal summary).

242.   Castelnuovo-Tedesco, P., Decreasing the
        length of psychotherapy: Theoretical
        and practical aspects of the problem, in,
        Arieti, S., (ed.), The world biennial of
        psychiatry and psychotherapy, New York,
        Basic Books, 1970.

The author describes brief psychotherapy as a multidimensional process, of which duration of treatment is but
one defining facet, although it bears upon the depth, intensity, goals, and methods of treatment. In a section on
fundamental issues of brief therapy, he examines range of
goals, temporal focus, analysis of resistance, analysis of
transference reactions, and working through. In a discussion of brief therapy techniques, he lists eight commonly
used strategems and notes various criteria which enter into
selection of specific approaches. A significant issue is
whether the techniques are predominantly interpretive or
predominantly manipulative. Although he notes that indications and limitations of brief therapy necessarily entail
issues of treatment goals and therapist's particular
orientation toward these, he does offer a survey and
rationale of those factors which make patients more or less
accessible to brief therapy. He also examines some philosophical and practical implications of this type of treatment. (abstract by Deborah Schuller).

243.   Castelnuovo-Tedesco, P., Brief psycho-
        therapy: Technique, indications, and
        limitations, Behavioral Sciences Tape
        Library, Sigma Information, Inc., Fort
        Lee, N.J., 1972.

244.   Castelnuovo-Tedesco, P., Brief psycho-
        therapy, in, American Handbook of
        Psychiatry, Second Edition, Vol., 5,
        New York, Basic Books, 1975.

This chapter provides a concise overview of the multi-
faceted field of brief psychotherapy. The author presents
a quick history of brief therapy, defines what is encom-
passed by the term, its scope and range of goals, the

theory on which it is based, various technical strategies and tactics employed in brief therapy, and particular indications, limitations, and outcomes. He extracts principles common to the field, without minimizing the diversity of specific versions of brief therapy. (abstract by Deborah Schuller).

245. Castelnuovo-Tedesco, P., The twenty minute hour: A technic of brief psycho-therapy, Southern Medicine, 1976, 64, 33-37.

The Twenty-Minute Hour is a technic of brief, supportive psychotherapy which was developed to provide the medical resident or practitioner with a simple and dependable approach to the less complicated emotional disturbance of many patients. It consists of one or two initial inter-views, aimed at obtaining a history and then a series of approximately 10 treatment interviews, each 20 minutes in length. The physician is shown how to take a medical history that emphasizes the social context of the illness, how to develop a plan of treatment, how to begin and terminate treatment, how to use drugs as adjuncts to psychotherapy, and which types of patients are suitable for this technic. The approach to the patient is in in terms of everyday living using ordinary untutored under-standing of people and situations. The Twenty-Minute Hour is sufficiently circumscribed in its goals that it can be employed effectively by physicians inexperienced at psycho-therapy without risk of serious complications. (Journal abstract).

246. Castelnuovo-Tedesco, P., Brief psych-therapy of depression, in, Cole, J.O., et al., (eds.), Depression: Biology psychodynamics, and treatment, New York, Plenum Press, 1978.

This chapter addresses the fundamental requirements and basic steps in the brief psychotherapeutic treatment of the depressed patient. The author elaborates on criteria of selection of candidates for such therapy, and provides

a framework for understanding depressive reactions (notably
the patient's disappointment/regret, anger, guilt, and
feelings of dependency or helplessness). Therapy must
first give the patient an understanding of what is bothering
him (i.e., depression), then help him identify significant
losses and disappointments, and finally, facilitate a full
discharge of the principal feelings, especially bitterness
and regret. The author notes that these steps may be
effectively achieved in a limited number of sessions and
that even when the condition is not totally resolved
within a short period, a lifting of mood and movements
toward a more constructive approach are frequently observed.
He concludes by reaffirming the importance of the therapist's focussing on the principal reactions of disappoint-
ment (versus efforts at character reconstruction), helping
the patient to recognize his strengths, communicating in a
spontaneous back-and-forth way, and withstanding the
patient's sense of helplessness. (abstract by Deborah
Schuller).

247.   Castelnuovo-Tedesco, P., Psychotherapy
        for the nonpsychiatric physician:
        Theoretical and practical aspects of
        the twenty minute hour, in Karasu, T.B.,
        and Steinmuller, R.I., (eds.), Psychothera-
        peutic approaches in medicine, New York,
        Grune and Stratton, 1978.

Following a short review of the topic of therapy for the
non-pyschiatrist, the author explains the twenty-minute
hour, its origins, rationale, and format. He clarifies
issues which need to be considered in planning a training
program for non-psychiatrists: active mastery as a basis
for learning, problems of professional identity, common
physician attitudes towards psychotherapy, the issue of
time, level of language, existing bases of knowledge,
interpersonal skill, and the emotional climate of the
training program. (abstract by Deborah Schuller).

248.   Castelnuovo-Tedesco, P., Review of
        Davanloo, H., Basic principles and
        techniques of short-term psychotherapy,
        American Journal of Psychiatry, 1979,
        136, 251.

249.   Catanzaro, R.J., and Green W.G., WATS
       telephone therapy: New follow-up tech-
       nique for alcoholics, American Journal of
       Psychiatry, 1970, 126, 1024-1027.

The authors present the rationale and description of a
promising development in psychology - WATS telephone
therapy. In certain selected cases the formal regular use
of the telephone to conduct routine psychotherapy has many
advantages over traditional psychotherapy. They describe
the use of this method in following up alcoholics and
express the belief that a similar plan might be helpful
with other diagnostic groups such as opiate addicts,
depressives, and schizophrenics. (Journal abstract).

250.   Cattell, J.P., et al., Limited goal therapy
       in a psychiatric clinic, American Journal
       of Psychiatry, 1963, 120, 255-260.

The authors provide a description of the workings of the
Continuation Clinic (CC) at the Psychiatric Clinic of
Columbia-Presbyterian Medical Center. The CC operates one
morning/week and services subacute or chronic depressive
and schizophrenic symptomatology, with most patients
struggling with anxiety and defenses designed to deal with
anxiety. Patients are seen for 15-20 minute sessions,
once/week. Some use of medication is indicated for symptom
reduction. Even though the approach is one of brief
therapy sessions, issues wuch as transference and counter-
transference appear during the course of treatment, and
the types of games patients play are detailed. The types
of demands that such an approach requires of a therapist
are discussed, as well as a brief report of the treatment
of one patient. The clinic has processed 260 to 270
patients in the Continuation Clinic per month at the time
of the report, with positive results indicated in general
although not specifically listed.

251.   Cavallin, Hector, The advantages of brief
        psychotherapy over drugs in the treatment
        of depression, Psychiatry Digest, 1973,
        34, 41-45.

The author describes in detail a particular therapy
approach to the treatment of depressions, which includes
a highly structured, physical exercise involvement on the
part of the patient. A patient's time is regulated
throughout the day, involving a wide range of activities,
and requiring the keeping of a daily log by the patient.
The dynamic concepts which underlie such an approach are
presented as well as some of the practical advantages to
such an approach. The inclusion of family members as part
of the treatment focus is also highlighted. The advantage
of such an approach over the use of drugs in the treatment
of depression is stressed.

252.   Chafetz, M.E., The effect of a psychia-
        tric emergency service on motivation for
        psychiatric treatment, Journal of Nervous
        and Mental Disease, 1965, 140, 442-448.

The author traces the changes in patient population serviced by the Massachusetts General Hospital emergency
service. The wide range of presenting problems, age ranges
referral sources, and disposition decisions are summarized.
The approach consists of a team evaluation, treatment
planning, including family as well as the identified
patient, the involvement of community resources, specific
tailoring of the initial contact so as to maximize the
continued involvement of the patient in treatment, and
research measurements to provide feedback on the effectiveness of the program. The type of techniques used to
increase motivation are "constructive utilization of
dependency needs", rapid access of services without long
and frustrating delays, etc. The lower-social-class
patient for whom this service is primarily geared has
profited from this type of approach. Detailed characteristics of the population are presented.

253.   Chafetz, M., et al., Acute psychiatric
        services in the general hospital, I.
        Implication for psychiatry in emergency
        admissions, <u>American Journal of Psychiatry</u>,
        1966, 123, 664-670.

At Massachusetts General Hospital, visits to the psychiatric
service increased from one percent of total visits in 1952
to three percent in 1961. This probably reflects an
increase in acknowledgement of psychiatric disturbance
rather than an actual rise in its incidence. The increase
in emergency psychiatric admissions to general hospitals -
which are now often used as "the poor man's family doctor" -
has many implications for the future practice of psychiatry.
(Journal abstract).

254.   Chandler, H.M., Crisis intervention: Plan
        for therapy and family follow-up, <u>Frontiers
        of Hospital Psychiatry</u>, 1969,

255.   Chandler, H.M., Family crisis intervention,
        <u>Journal of the National Medical Association</u>,
        1972, 64, 211-216, 224.

The author describes the work of the Psychiatric System at
Grady Hospital in Atlanta. Approximately 12,000 new cases
are seen each year in a department in which a family crisis
intervention approach is used. It is based both on a
general systems approach and the theoretical formulations
of Erik Erikson. Therapy is usually done by a male and
female co-therapist team from varying disciplines. Families
are usually seen for six sessions, one of which is usually
a home visit. The family is the focus of treatment, not
one individual within it. The therapists attempt to
ascertain the nature of the precipitating crisis and are
often quite active (e.g., assignment of tasks). The major
focus is on resolving the present crisis. Three case
examples are presented to highlight the approach. Cases
dealt with at the hospital psychiatric system cover a wide
range of presenting problems, and the focus is not on
diagnosis per se, but rather on the ability of the patient(s)
to form a meaningful relationship with one of the therapists,
the availability of support outside, and the lack of active

or impulsive homocide or suicidal tendencies in the family.
The later phases of therapy are usually less active ones
for the therapists, and tend to be more of a non-directive
contact. Termination provides an opportunity to resolve
unresolved dependency needs, and usually results in some
grief reactions. Typical responses to both families and
therapists during this phase are discusssed.

256.   Chapman, J.D., Frigidity: Rapid treatment
        by reciprocal inhibition, Journal of the
        American Osteopathic Association, 1969,
        67, 871-878.

257.   Chapman, L.C., The short contact in
        casework with hospitalized neuropsy-
        chiatric patients, Smith College Studies
        in Social Work, 1950-51, 21, 141.

The author presents a research abstract of a study carried
out at a VA hospital. The average stay in the hospital for
those involved in the program was 10 days, and although
negative attitudes on the part of many of the patients were
reported, some positive results did occur. The value of
social work services and full utilization of community
resrources are mentioned.

258.   Charen, S., Brief methods of psychotherapy -
        A review, Psychiatric Quarterly, 1948, 22,
        287-301.

In one of the early overviews of methods of brief therapy,
the author discusses some of the changes in treatment
populations since the end of World War II. The emergence
of briefer forms of psychoanalysis is outlined. A brief
overview of the aims and methods of psychiatry is presented,
followed by a discussion of some of the shorter methods of
therapy which rely on psychoalanytic technique. A presentation of hypnoanalysis and drug analysis is also included.

259.   Chaskel, R., Short-term conseling: A
        major family agency service, Social Work
        Journal, 1953, 34, 20-23.

260.   Chaskel, R., Assertive casework in a
        short-term situation, Casework Papers,
        1961, N.Y., Family Service Association of
        America, 1961.

261.   Chess, S., and Lyman, M.S., One hour
        service for disturbed kids, Medical
        World News, 1968, 9, 47.

The authors report on their work at the Children's
Psychiatric Unit at Bellevue Hospital in New York City.
They report success in using a short-term treatment
approach, provided service is offered immediately without
the need for patient waiting. Their approach includes
parent guidance, changes in the child's environment, etc.,
and they report that often formal psychotherapy is not
needed.

262.   Chiles, J.A., et al., Group intake, brief
        therapy, and the use of expertise: Evolving
        changes in intake procedure, Comprehensive
        Psychiatry, 1972, 13, 489-492.

The authors describe the structural and functional changes
at a training-oriented. psychiatric clinic designed to make
the clinic more helpful to the community it serves. Teams,
consisting of three trainees and three supervisors were
formed, each team responsible for the functioning of the
clinic on an afternoon/week. A group intake format was
used, in which patients are first seen in a group, and
then after an initial orientations period in the group
lasting about 15 minutes, are individually seen one at a
time, and then returned to the continuing group intake
process. Advantages and purposes of the group intake
include the ability for patients to see that others are
suffering from similar difficulties, ability of the
therapists to compare the patient's functioning both in
group and individual contexts, and helping to realistically
orient the patient to the possible processes of group
therapy. Further, each patient is then seen in brief
therapy sessions (lasting from 15 to 45 minutes each).

The use of the supervisors during this phase is described,
covering a wide variety of possible uses of their expertise.
The increase in the number of patients who can be seen
during the year is emphasized, as well as the increased
morale of the staff, both trainees and supervisors.

263.   Chiles, J.A., and Sanger, E., The use
        of groups in brief inpatient treatment
        of adolescents, Hospital and Community
        Psychiatry, 1977, 28, 443-445.

The authors describe a short-term inpatient program for
adolescents that uses a variety of group sessions to help
them deal with their immediate problems and when necessary,
prepare them for outpatient treatment. No attempt at complete ego reconstruction is made. The program includes
family therapy and sessions on practical living skills,
such as job hunting, productive use of leisure time,
transportation, food planning, and renting and leasing.
Assertiveness techniques are taught in small groups, and
their use is encouraged on the unit, where staff attempts
to create an acceptable social environment and provide a
model for group decision-making. This program was
initiated in 1974 at the University of Washington Hospital.
The average length of stay was 26 days, the average age
of adolescents was 16, with about equal numbers of males
and females. A total of 58 adolescents were seen, with
about half diagnosed as depressed, a sixth as psychotic,
and a fifth as adolescent adjustment reaction. (Journal
abstract adapted).

264.   Claiborn, W.L., Crisis intervention and
        the trail of broken treaties, Professional
        Psychology, 1973, 4, 392-396.

The author describes and evaluates the organization
structure that he formed to respond to the emergency mental
health needs of the Indians who participated in the Trail
of Broken Treaties demonstration. He offers possible
explanations for its nonacceptance. (Journal abstract).

265. Clare, A.W., Brief psychotherapy: New approaches, Psychiatric Clinics of North America, 1979, 2, 93-109.

In recent years, a veritable melange of diffuse and poorly defined approaches, such as Gestalt therapy, emovite releases or body therapy, transactional analysis, and Erhard seminars training, have emerged. Aimed not merely at treatment but at providing a basis for individual growth, acceptance of self, a philosphical understanding of life, and a spiritual dimension to ordinary human experiences, these approaches are limited to ministering to relatively intact individuals who, while disillusioned with their lives and in search of meaning, support, and solace, are able to function adequately and independently. To date there is scant evidence that they have much to offer individuals suffering serious and incapacitating psychiatric symptoms. (Journal abstract).

266. Clark, C.C., A social systems approach to short-term psychiatric care, Perspectives in Psychiatric Care, 1972, 10, 178-182.

This article describes the value of a social systems approach versus a therapeutic approach in the daily functioning of a short-term psychiatric hospital ward. Specific examples and suggestions made as to how the nurse in such a situation can intervene effectively using a social systems apporach.

267. Clark, S.C., and Rootman, I., Street-level drug crisis intervention, Drug Forum, 1974, 3, 239-247.

The Calgary Drug Information Center is a youth oriented clinic that deals with drug related crises. Telephone and drop-in service is available 24 hours a day, seven days a week. The Center has approximately 80 non-professional volunteers and 7 paid staff members. Information about the crisis contacts made with the Drug Center is given. The Calgary Center may prove a useful model upon which to base other youth oriented drug crisis intervention facilities. Further, the drug contact form currently employed supplies useful information about the operation. Use of such a form in other street clinics could provide significant information about the nature and dimensions of drug-related problems. (Journal abstract).

268.   Clifton, P.M., and Ransom, J.W., An
        approach to working with the "placed
        child", Child Psychiatry and Human
        Development, 1975, 6, 107-117.

Three cases are presented elucidating the use of an active, short-term therapy as a primary prevention action with children who are "placed". The author emphasizes the uncertain aspects of the lives of these children, in which they are faced with placement separation, and the emotional upheavels which attend such experiences.

269.   Cloninger, C.R., Recognizing and treating
        sociopathy, Medical World News, 1975, 16,
        12-16, 18.

The author reviews nine characteristics of the antisocial personality: school problems, running away, trouble with police, poor work history, marital difficulties, repeated outbursts of rage or fighting, sexual problems, vagrancy or wanderlust, and persistent and repeated lying. A number of research studies are reviewed which have attempted to clarify the issue of etiology or sociopathy. These studies range across such diverse focusses as body physique and development, cardiovascular and automatic reactions, endocrine shifts, EEG evaluation and chromosomal studies. The studey concludes by focussing on various treatment studies, and the author concludes that for many diagnosed as sociopathic, a concrete, explicit, problem-oriented, limited and short-term therapy approach is recommended.

270.   Coddington, D.R., The use of brief
        psychotherapy in a pediatric practice,
        Journal of Pediatriacs, 1962, 60, 259-265.

The author presents four case examples to highlight the use of brief therapy techniques within a pediatric practice.

Specifically, viewing such pediatric activities as helping
a mother of a well baby express herself, preparing a child
for on operation, and counseling parents of a chronically
ill child, as forms of psychotherapy, is stressed. The value
of diagnostic evaluation as a therapeutic tool is also
emphasized. Children with psychoneurotic traits, with
anxiety as the presenting symptoms were the most frequent
problem, followed by personality disturbances (behavior
problems), followed by situations in which the major problem
lay in the pathology of the parents.

271. Coffey, E.M., et al., Brief hospital
      treatment of schizophrenia - early
      results of a multiple hospital study,
      Hospital and Community Psychiatry, 1968,
      19, 282-287.

272. Cohen, A.I., A note on brief focused
      psychotherapy, Psychotherapy: Theory,
      Research, and Practice, 1969, 6, 199-200.

The author describes a specific short-term therapy approach,
lasting 16 sessions of one hour each, in which the present
and future become the focus of treatment. The issues
related to separation in short-term therapy are discussed,
and specific strategies presented. Specifically, the use of
confrontation rather than interpretation is discussed, as
well as the active nature of such an approach.

273. Cohen, R., Principles of preventive
      mental health programs for ethnic
      minority populations: The acculturation
      of Puerto Ricans to the United States,
      American Journal of Psychiatry, 1972,
      128, 1529-1533.

The author begins by detailing the differences in values
between Puerto Rican and American social values as relates
to time, relational patterns, activity, and basic conceptualization of human nature. The implications of these
conflicts between the two value systems for mental health
intervention are then detailed. Recommendations for a

seven point program aimed at dealing with these conflicts
are presented, including a focus on issues of education,
mental health training, participations and collaboration,
consultation, intervention, delivery of service, and
research, data collection, and follow-up.

274.   Cohn, C.K., et al., A case of blood-
        illness-injury phobia treated behaviorally,
        Journal of Nervous and Mental Disease, 1976,
        162, 65-68.

A patient with a 24 year history of blood-illness-injury
phobia associated with bradycardia and syncope was treated
behaviorally. He was taught to prevent bradycardia and
resulting syncope occurring in the presence of phobic stimuli
by provoking anger in himself using appropriate imagery.
Within a few weeks, the patient was able to use the procedure successfully to prevent syncope in every day
situations. At 6 months follow-up he remained comfortable
in the presence of previously phobic stimuli and he no
longer needed to use self-induced anger to prevent synocopal
episodes. (Journal abstract).

275.   Coleman, J.V., Distinguishing between
        psychotherapy anc casework, Journal of
        Social Casework, 1949, 30, 244-251.

Coleman first acknowledges the considerable overlap in
procedures and skills between psychotherapy and casework
(e.g., skills in interviewing and in creating at atmosphere of confidence, the offer of help to people in
emotional distress, recognition of transference phenomena,
etc.). He then considers characteristics of casework as a
helping process: definition of problems as a function of
the client's situation, the caseworker's necessary background knowledge, and goals. The author then treats the
differential characteristics of psychotherapy, with
reference to indications, treatability, the concept of
"reliving", establishment of transference, goals, use of
anxiety, timing of termination, and function of insight.
He concludes that psychotherapy and casework, despite
overlapping aspects, are separate disciplines. The

existence of mutually exclusive methods, distinctive
results and aims, dissimilar problem areas, separate value
systems, philosophical presuppositions, and traditional
mythologies lead him to this conclusion. (abstract by
Deborah Schuller).

276. Coleman, J.V., Psychotherapeutic
principles in casework interviewing,
American Journal of Psychiatry, 1951,
108, 298-302.

The author presents what he considers to be the essential
and intrinsic characteristics of casework. He comments on
casework interviewing, and the traditional concerns and
goals of social work. He describes its particular
diagnostic approach, based on concepts of ego psychology
of (situational) stress reactions, and the notes the
applicability of casework to all varieties of conflict-
ridden life situations. Coleman summarizes his comments
with review of psychotherapeutic principles that have been
absorbed into casework, with specific reference to therapeutic attitude, diagnostic approach, and method of casework. He concludes that while casework evolved under the
influence of psychoanalytic concepts, it has developed its
own particular psychology and method, and that it affords
treatment to large numbers of people for whom psychiatric
help was hitherto unavailable. (abstract by Deborah
Schuller).

277. Coleman, J.V., Banter as psychotherapeutic
intervention, American Journal of Psychoanalysis, 1962, 22, 1-6.

The author presents indications and justifications for the
use of banter as a special form of intervention in therapy,
of particular importance for both patient and therapist
within the context of goal-limited psychotherapy.
Masochistic manoeuvers in which patients ambivalently reach
out for help may elicit uneasy reactions on the part of the
therapist. By dramatizing these reactions via the major
elements of banter (irony, humorous depreciation, and
impersonation), the therapist effectively and humorously

plays the part of the patient's self-abasing superego.
Within this framework of impersonation, interpretive
activity on issues of fundamental significance to the
patient can take place. The author suggests that the
experience of therapy operates accoring to principles of
the dramatic mode of presentation. The use of banter can
facilitate an integrated, holistic experience in self-
realization, which for patients in goals-limited therapy
may substitute for the intellectual exercise of insight in
the analytic sense. (abstract by Deborah Schuller).

278.   Coleman, J.V., Therapy of the
        "inaccessible" mentally ill patient,
        Mental Hygiene, 1965, 49, 581-584.

The author describes a group of patients with special
problems for the community mental health system. They are
described as individuals who are not interested in insight-
oriented, depth psychotherapy, but who are suffering from
one of a variety of difficulties. The diagnostic characteristics of such patients are described, with one case
example provided. The type of therapeutic relationship
needed in such "unmotivated" patients is a supportive one,
with specific emphasis on daily life stresses. No
significant in-depth personality changes are sought or
expected in this approach. The involvement of other
community support groups and agencies is stressed, with the
aim of helping the patient deal more effectively with his/
her daily life problems.

279.   Coleman, J.V., Research in walk-in
        psychiatric services in general hospitals,
        American Journal of Psychiatry, 1968, 124,
        1668-1673.

Emergency treatment services in the general hospitals of
urban centers have grown spectacularly in recent years,
reflecting in effect a medical care vacuum for the slum
poor. The medical and psychiatric needs of this population
are known to be great, and a unique opportunity is presented
to meet a changing pattern of medical-psychiatric demand.

To do so, the emergency service as an accident accommodation must be replaced by its development as a primary
clinic treating patients with illnesses associated with
poverty. (Journal abstract).

280.   Coleman, J.V., and Errera, P., The
        geneal hospital emergency room and its
        psychiatric problems, American Journal of
        Public Health, 1963, 53,

281.   Coleman, M.D., Emergency psychotherapy,
        Progress in Psychotherapy, 1960, 5, 78-85.

The author focusses on techniques which are frequently used
in emergency psychotherapy. Examples included are clarification, supporting defense mechanisms, interpretation,
transference and the manipulation of transference, and
social manipulation. The author reports that such
techniques have been useful in the treatment of acute
depressions, postpartum obsessional states, and in reactive
anxiety states, all of which are acute reactions to stressful events.

282.   Coleman, M.D., Problems in an emergency
        psychiatric clinic, Mental Hospitals,
        1960, 11, 26-27.

283.   Coleman, M.D., and Rosenbaum, M., The
        psychiatric walk-in clinic, The Israel
        Annals of Psychiatry and Related Disciplines,
        1963, 1, 99-106.

284.   Coleman, M.D., and Zwerling, I., The
        psychiatric emergency clinic: A flexible
        way of meeting community mental health
        needs, American Journal of Psychiatry,
        1959, 115, 980-984.

The Bronx Municipal Hospital psychiatric department provides
a 24 hour service in which all psychiatric patients entering
the hospital are seen. The focus is on early diagnosis and

treatment and immediate access. Many presenting problems
are dealt with within five sessions, and a vast majority
of patients show significant improvement. The therapy is
dynamically-oriented, of a supportive nature, and designed
to reestablish the patient's previous stability. The
types of patient symptomatology include acute neurotic or
psychotic decompensation. The authors detail a case to
highlight their approach. The use of limited EST, the
value of consultation with other agencies involved with
the patient, and the continuing treatment of chronically
ill patients are discussed. Over a period of six months,
the authors report that over 1800 patients had been seen,
and almost all were seen in brief therapy (only 151 seen
in longer term treatment). The value of such an approach
in eliminating the need for a waiting list is emphasized
as well.

285.   Collins, A., et al., The evaluation of a
        counseling center innovation, Journal of
        College Student Personnel, 1973, 14, 144-148.

The authors report on an evaluation study focussed on the
University of Maryland Counseling Center, in which an
attempt was made to eliminate the waiting list and provide
clients with therapy at the time of the request for psychological help. The authors report that when the waiting
period between the initial screening and the first counseling session was minimal, the no-show rate for therapy
was lowest. The findings point to the conclusions that
long delays in receiving treatment after it has been
requested by a client will tend to increase attrition rates.

286.   Conklin, L.T., et al., Use of groups
        during the adoptive postplacement period,
        Social Work, 1962, 7, 46-52.

The authors report on the use of groups for parents who
were adopting children. Each group met with a social
worker once/month, for one year. They focussed on a wide
range of concerns, including the couples' resistance to
on-going supervision during the first year of placement,

and their reluctance to sharing their experiences. The
value of such groups in aiding and facilitating the adjustment to a new placed child is discussed, and such groups
have now become part of the on-going daily agency practice.

287.   Conroe, R.M., et al., A systematic
        approach to brief psychological inter-
        vention in the primary care setting,
        Journal of Family Practice, 1978, 7,
        1137-1142.

Presents a systematic approach to psychological intervention that can be used by the primary care physician.
The approach specifies the sequence the physician takes
when providing therapy: (a) identify the context of the
patient's complaints, (b) assess patient's current status,
(c) develop a therapeutic plan, and (d) implement a
therapy approach. These steps are based on four current
status categories - functional, ambiguous, crisis, and
dysfunctional - that describe the patient's life situation
and serve as a gateway for planning and carrytng out
therapy. Four types of psychological intervention - short-
term therapy, structured assessment, crisis intervention,
and referral - are described, and methods for implementation are given. The advantages of the schema and a
brief critique are presented. (Journal abstract).

288.   Cooper, A.J., Disorders of sexual
        potency in the male: A Clinical and
        statistical study of some factors
        related to short-term prognosis,
        British Journal of Psychiatry, 1969,
        115, 709-719.

Out of 67 male subjects who presented in a psychiatric outpatient department with a primary disorder of potency and
who provided social, clinical, and psychological data, 49
(73%) satisfied the "treated criterion" of attending for
a minimum of 20 fortnightly interviews during one year.
43 female partners provided complementary data and co-
operated to a greater or lesser degree in treatment. The
response to therapy was comparatively poor; 39% of the
series were recovered or improved, whilst 61% were

unchanged or worse. The factors associated significantly
with a poor outcome were: premature ejaculation; insidious
onset impotence; a disorder of long duration; personality
disorder in the male; absence of motivation for therapy;
a sex drive other than heterosexual; absence of desire in
the coital situation; unwillingness or inability of the

onset impotence, a disorder of short duration, a hetero-

marital happiness in the male; a male rating of loving his
spouse; motivation for treatment; marital happiness in the
female; willingness and ability of the female to co-
operate fully in treatment; absence of personality
disorder in the female. (Journal summary).

289.   Cooper, A.J., Frigidity, treatment and
        short-term prognosis, Journal of
        Psychosomatic Research, 1970, 14, 133-147.

A total of 50 female patients who reported a primary
disorder of frigidity, were included in this study. They
attended for a minimum of 20 sessions, which was focussed
on the practical (i.e., no in-depth psychosynamic therapy
was used). The results indicated that slightly above 50%
of those treated were successful in the alleviation of the
symptom. The author reports on some of the positive
prognostic variables (e.g., shorter duration of symptom,
previous sexual responsiveness, heterosexual orientation,
etc.).

290.   Corsini, R.J., Immediate therapy, Group
        Psychotherapy, 1951, 4, 322-330.

Techniques of brief psychotherapy are presented within the
context of psychodrama. The author contends that as
problems are solved, others resolve themselves through a
process of "irradiation". Various other theoretical
concepts are presented, including the "principle of
retease", and the "principle of teleology". The value of
quick treatment, countering resistance, and producing a
rapid increase and then dissipation of anxiety.

291.   Cox, R.H., Short term counseling
        techniques, Journal of Pastoral Care,
        1972, 26, 166-171.

292.   Crabtree, L.H., and Graller, J.L.,
        Improvised short-term therapy in a
        military center, Reported anon:
        Frontiers in Hospital Psychiatry,
        1968, 5,

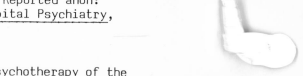

293.   Cramond, W.A., Psychotherapy of the
        dying patient, British Medical Journal,
        1970, 3, 389-393.

A number of issues are raised and discussed in this paper
on psychotherapy with a dying patient. These include
questions about whether the therapist and patient should
talk about how the patient feels about the prospect of
dying, whether the patient fears death or the process of
dying, typical reactions to loss (depression), the role of
anger in the process, issues of transference and counter-
transference, and questions of regression. Five case
examples are presented to highlight the theoretical issues
raised. Implications for the training of personnel who
will be working with dying patients are discussed.

294.   Crary, W.G., Goals and techniques of
        transitory group therapy, Hospital and
        Community Psychiatry, 1968, 19, 389-391.

An approach to brief therapy with groups whose membership
changes frequently is described. Transitory group therapy
is intended for use in psychiatric settings where the
patient's stay is brief. Concrete and general goals are
outlined. Principles for conducting such groups include
avoidance of criticism; positive response to health
behaviors; a problem-solving, reality-oriented focus on
the present; and a broad base of group participation in
discussion of group concerns. Crary discusses the advantage of this approach, which he notes is an effective
adjunctive treatment modality. (abstract by Deborah
Schuller).

295.   Crow, M.S., Preventive intervention
        through parent group education, Social
        Casework, 1967, 48, 161-165.

Parent education in small groups is effective in helping
parents with the tasks of child rearing and also in
preventing potential problems. Through it certain sources
of psychological pressure are lessened, and deficits in
the parent's feeling of self-worth and parental identity
are modified. Group support, increased perspective and
reality orientation, improved understanding of child
development and family interaction, and a broader knowledge
of alternative ways of dealing with family situations are
all important to the process, which is aimed at freeing
parents to make greater use of their capacity for healthy
parental functioning. In addition, it should be pointed
out, such groups can be planned to aim toward specific
points of stress in certain families, such as physical or
environmental handicap, or toward times of stress in the
developmental process. (Journal conclusion).

296.   Crowe, M.J., et al., Time-limited
        desensitization, implosion and shaping
        for phobic patients: a crossover study,
        Behavior Research and Therapy, 1972, 10,
        319-328.

A comparison was made of the short-term time-limited
efficacy of three forms of behaviour therapy in phobic
patients: Systematic desensitization (in imagination),
Implosion (in imagination) and Shaping, or Reinforced
Practice. A block design was used, all patients receiving
all treatments in randomized order. Improvement was
measured behaviourally and by symptom rating scales.
Differences emerged only on the behavioural measures:
Shaping was significantly superior to Desensitization,
with Implosion between the two, and not significantly
different from either. Comparison of treated with untreated phobias within subjects showed Shaping to be more
specific than the other two forms of treatment. It was
concluded that Implosion and Shaping are potentially
useful types of therapy, worthy of further study and
application. (Journal summary).

297.   Crum, R.S., Counseling rape victims,
        Journal of Pastoral Care, 1974, 28,
        112-121.

298.   Cummings, N.A., The health model as
        entree to the human services model in
        psychotherapy, The Clinical Psychologist,
        1975, 29, 19-21.

299.   Cummings, N., Prolonged (ideal) versus
        short-term (realistic) psychotherapy,
        Professional Psychology, 1977, 8, 491-501.

It is argued that not only can psychotherapy be included
economically in a prepaid insurance plan such as national
health insurance, but also that the failure to include
psychotherapy in prepaid insurance schemes would deprive
a substantial proportion of patients (with emotional as
opposed to organic etiology) of the benefits they might
enjoy under such plans. A series of studies examining the
outcomes of therapy of varying durations showed that the
cost of the psychotherapy was more than offset by the
savings in medical visits. A cost-therapeutic-effective-
ness index shows that it is not the provision of a mental
health component that determines optimal cost-therapeutic-
effectiveness but the manner in which psychotherapeutic
services are delivered. It is shown also that for the
vast majority of patients studied, innovative short-term
psychotherapy is more effective than long-term psychotherapy.
(Journal abstract).

300.   Cummings, N.A., The Kaiser-Permanente 20
        year experience with delivering prepaid
        brief psychotherapy, Paper presented at
        Oxford, England, International Society for
        Research in Psychotherapy, July, 1979.

301.   Cummings, N.A., and Follette, W.T.,
        Psychiatric services and medical
        utilization in a prepaid health plan
        setting: Part II, Medical Care, 1968,
        6, 31-41.

302.   Cummings, N.A., and Follette, W.T.
        Brief psychotherapy and medical
        utilization: An eight-year follow-up,
        in, Dorken, H., & Associates, The
        professional psychologist today: New
        developments in law, health insurance
        and health practice, San Francisco,
        Jossey-Bass, 1976.

The authors present some further clarifying research to
their original findings regarding the utilization and
impact of brief therapy contact by subscribers to a prepaid,
comprehensive medical plan. Earlier findings were that
there was no basis for the concern that an increased demand
for therapy would financially endanger the prepaid system.
Further, one therapy session was found to reduce subsequent
medical utilization by 60% over the subsequent five year
period. A 75% reduction of further medical utilization
was registered when patients received 2-8 therapy sessions
(i.e., brief therapy), as compared with matched patients
who did not. The detailed professional working relationships and disciplines involved in the plan are described.
A total of 87 patients seen in brief therapy eight years
previously were contacted, and a detailed questionnaire
administered (a total of 121 had been seen in brief therapy,
but only 87 were traceable). The results showed that
patients did recall the reason for the mental health visit,
reported that the difficulty had been resolved, and
primarily due to his/her own (i.e., the patient's) efforts.
Two critical elements in the treatment approach used were
immediate and easy access to treatment, and the absence of
a long and complicated intake interview and procedure.
Being able to meet a patient at the moment of crisis is
stressed.

303.   Cytryn, L., et al., The effectiveness of
        tranquilizing drugs plus supportive
        psychotherapy in treating behavior
        disorders in children, American Journal of
        Orthopsychiatry, 1960, 30, 113-123.

Meprobamate, prochlorperazine, or placebo was administered
to each of 83 children in a double-blind clinical trial.
Concurrent psychotherapy was offered each patient and his

mother over a 3-month period at predetermined intervals.
The children fell into four diagnostic categories: neurotic,
hyperkinetic, defective with behavior disorder, and anti-
social. Drop-out rate was gratifyingly small (7%) and
confirmed the feasibility of conducting outpatient studies
with children to evaluate psychiatric treatment. Outcome
showed no relation to the medications used in this study.
Placebo produced results equivalent to either drug. Outcome of treatment was significantly influenced by the nature
of the presenting syndrome; neurotic children showed
substantial improvement, hyperkinetic children moderate
gains, and the other two groups little or none. Toxic
reactions were mild. The lack of an untreated control
group precluded any final judgement as to the role played
by "spontaneous" improvement in the results observed.
However, the symptomatic improvement for this series of
neurotic children and their parents treated in 5 interviews
over a 3-month period together with the administration of
placebo capsules, proved to be of the same order as that
described for more intensive programe of psychotherapy.
These findings have public health implications. (Journal
summary).

304.   Dahl, A.A., et al., A presentation of
        short-term psychotherapy project at the
        Oslo University Psychiatric Clinic,
        Psychotherapy and Psychosomatics, 1978,
        29, 299-304.

The authors describe the information and research results
of a short-term university therapy clinic (mostly outpatient), based on the work of Sifneos (i.e., selection
criteria, etc.).

305.   Dakan, E., Brief psychotherapy in
        graduate education, Teachers College
        Record, 1957, 58, 248-253.

306.   Danesh, H.B., The angry group, International
        Journal of Group Psychotherapy, 1977, 27,
        59-65.

The author describes the "angry group". and specific time-
limited group therapy program for dealing with questions
of anger in group members. The aims of such a group, its
unique qualities, and the characteristics stages which
unfold are all discussed. Excluded from such groups are
psychotics and alcoholics or other drug users. Each group
consists of up to 6 members, which meets for a 6-7 week
period, once/week for 2 hours/session. Cotherapists are
involved. The specific stages include the initial reflec-
tive/evaluative stage ("How I get angry"); the middle
projective/emotive stage ("experiencing anger"); and the
final resolution state ("growing out of anger"). Throughout, the focus remains exclusively on anger, and a variety
of techniques are used (interpretation into the group
processes, Adlerian focus on life style of members, and
Transactional Analysis as a means of focussing on interpersonal realtionships).

307.   Darbonne, A.R., Crisis: A review of
        theory, practice, and research,
        Psychotherapy: Theory, Research and
        Practice, 1967, 4, 49-56.

The author summarizes a wide range of divergent literature
on crisis theory, practice, and research. A brief historical
review is presented, along with an attempt at defining
crisis and outlining the characteristics of crisis. The
relationship of crisis theory to other theoretical positions
(e.g., ego psychology, existential theory, behaviorism and
conditioning theory, etc.) is also examined. The situational,
interpersonal and family and group aspects, and the individual and psychodynamic aspects of crisis are presented and
discussed. The article contains an extensive bibliography
of 110 references.

308.   Dauber, B., et al., Abortion counseling
        and behavioral change, Family Counseling
        Perspectives, 1972, 4, 23-27.

The authors describe the abortion counseling program at
San Francisco General Hospital designed to provide support

interpretation of these resistances, and (b) the deliberate
use of non-verbal methods of communication. The therapist
reports on the work with six female schizophrenics over a
period of six months, with a total of between 15 and 25
hours per patient. Most of these patients had been
hospitalized for five years or more. The author reports
that four were discharged through normal hospital procedures, one patient was rated as improved enough for
weekend visits away from the hospital. The approach
involved the establishment of a narcissistic transference
rather than an object transference. As a result, the
patient is forced into experiencing the therapist as someone who feels and thinks as he/she does, and who understands
him/her in a very deep way, something the author postulates
these patients never had had the opportunity of experiencing when they were young children. Three cases are
presented in some detail, along with a theoretical discussion covering some of the issues raised by the approach,
including the use/misuse of tranquilizers, the importance
of the emotional atmosphere within the hospital, etc. An
attempt to explain the process of the dynamics of "joining
intervention" is made, in which the surprise seen in
patients where resistance is not confronted is equated
with the surprise seen in classical analysis when an
interpretation has been accurate and properly timed. The
value of such an approach with narcissistic patients is
stressed.

314.   Deatherage, G., The clinical use of
        "mindfulness" meditation techniques in
        short-term psychotherapy, Journal of
        Transpersonal Psychology, 1975, 7, 133-143.

The author describes some of the possible applications of
"eastern psychology" to the field of psychotherapy.
Specifically, the technique of "mindfulness" meditation
is reviewed. Its use with psychiatric clinic patients in
short-term treatment (2-12 weeks) is highlighted through
case examples. Some cautions are also expressed.

315.   Decker, B., and Stubblebine, J.M.,
        Crisis intervention and prevention of
        psychiatric disability: A follow-up
        study, American Journal pf Psychiatry,
        1972, 129, 725-729.

Two groups of young adults were followed for two and a
half years after their first psychiatric hospitalization.
The first group received traditional modes of treatment;
the second group was hospitalized after the institution of
a crisis intervention program. The authors compared the
outcomes of the two groups to test whether crisis intervention could reduce long-term hospital dependency without
producing alternate forms of psychological or social
dependency. They found that crisis intervention did reduce
hospitalization throughout the second group's follow-up
period without an increase in other indices of disability.
(Journal abstract).

316.   DeCourcy, P., The hazard of short term
        psychotherapy without assessment: A
        case history, Journal of Personality
        Assessment, 1971, 35, 285-288.

A brief battery of psychological tests (Shipley Scale,
MMPI, Rorschach) that were administered solely for training
purposes revealed the presence of a parnoid schizophrenic
psychosis that had ϙot been detected by the therapist. As
a result, the treatment modality and goals were revised
and the agency practices were modified. (Journal summary).

317.   Deeths, A., Psychodrama crisis
        intervention with delinquent male
        drug users, Group Psychotherapy, 1970,
        23, 41-44.

Deeths describes a one-session psychodrama in which she
and 12 adolescents from a residential treatment center
interacted with six adolescents who had recently returned
to using drugs. Attention was focussed on the "leader" of
the delinquents. The background of this boy and the psychodrama which unfolded are presented. (abstract by Deborah
Schuller).

318.   Deitz, P.F.D., Dynamically-oriented brief
        psychotherapy: Psychocutaneous excoriation
        syndromes, Psychosomatic Medicine, 1953, 15,
        200-242.

319.   Delaney, Jo A., et al., Crisis intervention
        and the prevention of institutionalization:
        An interrupted time series analysis,
        American Journal of Community Psychology,
        1978, 6, 35-45.

In the context of the community mental health movement in
Illinois, the evolution and development of a crisis intervention program aimed at avoiding state hospitalization
and bringing more appropriate and efficacious resources
to bear on the difficulties of the individual and/or family
is discussed. This intervention program is characterized
by a more active-seeking style of delivering mental health
services. With the novel application of interrupted
time series analyses to both the targeted and matched
nonequivalent control communities the efficacy of this more
active intervention in reducing the number of state
hospital admission diagnosed as "mentally ill" is highlighted. The cost/benefit to the taxpayer is also discussed.
(Journal abstract).

320.   de la Torre, J., The therapist tells a
        story: A technique in brief psychotherapy,
        Bulletin of the Menninger Clinic, 1972, 36,
        609-616.

The author relates a case of a patient seen for a total of
four hours in order to illustrate a typical application of
brief psychoanalytically-oriented psychotherapy. The
technique implied little use of transference, no attempt
to induce marked regression, a focus on contemporaneous
primarily conscious material, and a clear delineation of
boundaries of problems to be examined during therapy.
de la Torre stresses the importance in brief treatment of
therapist intuition, rapid diagnosis, and activity - but
also notes the risks inherent in these. His use of metaphor in the second hour of treatment afforded a greater
scope in tapping specifics of the patient's most relevant

dynamic conflict, without sacrificing the tentativeness
of an initial intervention. The metaphor was used by the
patient to work on possible solutions, while at the same
time it served as a face-saving device, permitting her to
bypass some of her resistance. He notes that this case
dealt with dynamic elements in a brief period of time,
without precluding later exploration by the patient of her
emotional problems. (abstract by Deborah Schuller).

321.   de la Torre, J., Outpatient services:
        A present perspective, Bulletin of the
        Menninger Clinic, 1973, 37, 581-597.

The author summarizes various outpatient strategies and
interventions such as brief therapy, consultation,
evaluation, follow-up, and crisis intervention. Such
services are offered at the Menninger Memorial Hospital,
and various case histories are offered illustrating the
types of interventions.

322.   de la Torre, J., Brief encounters: General
        and technical considerations, Psychiatry,
        1978, 41, 184-193.

The first part of this paper contains a review of factors
militating against greater acceptance and use of brief
therapy by long-term therapists. The author states that
brief therapy does not have to be divorced from analytic
understanding, that such a split has deleterious consequences for both long and short-term treatment. Assumptions to the effect that the lengthier the treatment, the
better, that psychoanalysis is the "best treatment", that
structural changes are precluded in brief encounter, all
need to be examined. In the second part, de la Torre
focusses critically on specific technical considerations
in the analytic use of brief therapy: activity in the
initial interview, transference, the "here and now",
neutrality, focus of work and goals of treatment, termination. Such issues incorporate the author's contention
that expressive therapeutic interaction can take place in
a few sessions, that brief therapy rooted in analytic
understanding can present more than a palliative "pat on
the back". (abstract by Deborah Schuller).

323.   de la Torre, J., Brief psychotherapy:
        Current psychoanalytic interpretations,
        Behavioral Sciences Tape Library, Sigma
        Info, Inc., 1240 Grand Ave., Leonid,
        N.J., 07605.

324.   de la Torre, J., Anxiety states and short-
        term psychotherapy, in, Phenomenology and
        Treatment of Anxiety, New York, Spectrum
        Publications, 1979.

The author distinguishes three modalities of brief psychotherapy for use in management of anxiety with psychiatric
outpatients: crisis intervention, nonspecific short-term
therapy, and specific short-term therapy. de la Torre
presents characteristics and distinct treatment objectives
of each type, together with an illustrative clinical
vignette and comments. The three modalities differ in
emphasis, scope and technique. Crisis intervention deals
with an "overloaded ego exhausted in its coping resources,
under extremely stressful circumstances. Nonspecific
short-term therapy, sometimes referred to as "anxiety-
suppressing" or "supportive", is impelled forward by a
positive transference that remains undisturbed. Such a
therapy is centered on a present conscious situation, and
aims primarily at restoration of the patient's prior level
of functioning. Specific short-term therapy is described
as the most ambitious form of short-term treatment,
requiring the establishment of a dynamic focus. Present
conflicts are relived in the transference and explored
genetically. As the patient acquires insight, psychological changes occur which may lead to concomitant
structural modification. Overlapping of these three
interventions is, according to the author, the rule rather
than the exception. (abstract by Deborah Schuller).

325.   DeLeon, G., and Mandell, W., A comparison
        of conditioning and psychotherapy in the
        treatment of functional enuresis, Journal
        of Clinical Psychology, 1966, 22, 326-330.

This study compared a form of psychotherapy-counseling
with a training device approach based upon conditioning
principles, as treatments for functional nocturnal enuresis.

The Ss were 87 male and female children ages 5 1/2 to 14
of whom 56 were assigned to conditioning, 13 to psychotherapy for 12 sessions, and 18 to an untreated control
group which was followed for 90 days. The results showed
that of the children who completed treatment, 44 of 51
(86.3%) were "cured" with the training device while 2 of
11 (18.2%) and 2 of 18 (11.1%) children "cured" in the
psychotherapy and control groups respectively. Although
relapse rates were high in the conditioning group, the
'severity' of enuresis in relapse was significantly lower
than in the pre-treatment period and the remaining time
was rapid relative to initial training. (Journal summary).

326.   Delk, J.L., and Golden, K.M., Tandem
        psychotherapy: A model for rotating
        student therapists, American Journal of
        Psychotherapy, 1975, 29, 243-253.

Student psychotherapists often spend brief periods in
clinical placements or rotations. In this article, Lewis,
L. Wolberg's model for short-term therapy is extended and
adapted for use in long-term treatment by multiple student
therapists treating patients in tandem. Techniques are
proposed to enhance continuity of therapy and smooth
changing of therapists. (Journal abstract).

327.   Dengrove, E., Behavior therapy of the
        sexual disorders, Journal of Sex Research,
        1967, 3, 49-61.

The author summarizes the range of sexual problems which
can be successfully treated in a short period of time
using behavioral therapy techniques. Specific conditions
reviewed include impotence, premature ejaculation,
frigidity, homosexuality, transvestism, exhibitionism and
others.

328.   Dengrove, E., A single-treatment method
        to stop smoking using ancillary self-
        hypnosis: Discussion, International
        Journal of Clinical and Experimental
        Hypnosis, 1970, 18, 251-256.

Dr. Spiegel's dramatic approach to smoking modification
fits the behavioral paradigm with hypnosis acting as a
catalyst. Comparison is made to behavior and suggestions
offered applying these principles to smokers not responding
to Dr. Spiegel's approach. (Journal abstract).

329.   Dengrove, E., Mechanotherapy of sexual
        disorders, Journal of Sex Research, 1971,
        7, 1-12.

The author describes in some detail a number of mechano-
therapeutic devices used in the treatment of impotence and
frigidity. Specifically, the artificial penis, a con-
stricting device, the vibrator, and the Kegel perineometer
are described. The use of these as part of a brief therapy
practice is presented. Typical patient reactions to such
devices are described.

330.   de Schazer, S., Brief therapy with couples,
        International Journal of Family Counseling,
        1978, 6, 17-30.

Presents a model for brief therapy with couples that is
based on "balance theory". This model allows the therapist to develop a cognitive map of the relationship
through the use of graphs and then to plan a specific
step-by-step approach to the therapy of a particular
couple. The couple is viewed as an interlocking system
of interdependent relationships. Case examples are used
to illustrate the use of this model in helping to change
"stuck" or dysfunctional patterns. (Journal abstract).

331.   de Shazer, S., On getting unstuck: Some
        change-initiating tactics for getting
        the family moving, Family Therapy, 1974,
        1, 19-26.

The author provides a number of case examples to illustrate
a technique of breaking into a rigid family system and
initiating change by throwing the homeostatic balance
within the family out of balance. Specific techniques
described include "the hunch-as-bombshell", "the strength
assessment task", and the use of paradoxical interventions.
Examples presented all involved a brief therapy approach.

332.   de Shazer, S., The confusion technique,
        Family Therapy, 1975, 2, 23-29.

This paper reports on a brief therapy situation that exem-
plifies the use of the confusion technique expanded to the
family therapy context. The couple's interaction pattern
shifted significantly in the eight weeks of treatment.

The confusion technique was used to force the couple to
"spontaneously" develop a mutual goal for therapy. This
goal was established in the sixth session, and the confusion
technique was dropped in response. The goal of "starting
to have a better, more satisfactory sex life for both" was
reached in two more weeks. Further improvements were left
to them--with the agreement that they could and should
return if and when the learning process ran into further
trouble. (Journal summary).

333.   de Shazer, S., Brief therapy: Two's
        company, Family Process, 1978, 17, 79-93.

de Shazer grounds some basic types of family interaction
on the principle of "odd-man-out", a typical triadic
system observable in families sufficiently disturbed to
seek therapy. This triad, consisting of an isolate and a
pair of allies, frequently implies a rigidification of
familial interaction patterns to a dysfunctional point.
The alliance may be covert or overt. The author describes
four interventions which proved effective in dealing with

this "stuck" triangle. General treatment strategy relies on the use of covert family patterns to undermine the overt, dysfunctional pattern. The therapist re-labels behavior, and attempts to persuade the family to accept a change-initiating intervention. This task must be presented to the family in understandable terms, based on the therapist's grasp of their conceptual framework. (abstract by Deborah Schuller).

334. Deutscher, M., Brief family therapy in the course of first pregnancy, A clinical note, Contemporary Psychoanalysis, 1970, 7, 21-35.

The author begins by describing the typical pattern of husband and wife reaction to a first pregnancy. Ten young middle-class couples were studied to provide an impressionistic description. They exhibited shared decision-making styles, good degrees of emotional sharing, and they had decided to have a child. Even though such a "decision" had been made, there was still some shock at the confirmation of pregnancy. The first trimester involved each couple member learning the differences between being sick and being pregnant, along with coping with shifting patterns of dependency and nurturance. The second trimester precipitated the beginnings of a sense of a new triadic family structure developing (e.g., fantasies about the coming child). The third trimester was the most difficult. The women reported being increasingly self-preoccupied, with an increasing feeling of isolation on the husband's part. Reactions pertaining to the delivery and the postpartum period were presented. The author perceives pregnancy as a time-limited, circumscribed crisis experience, and transposes the above information to a therapy context. The brief therapy focus with "pregnant couples" usually involves a searching and clarification of the changes that the pregnancy has meant for both partners. Changing roles and expectations, and emotional reactions to these are focussed on. Issues of isolation, fears of dependency in onself or in the other, and communication difficulties are all addressed. Possible involvement of extended family members where appropriate is considered. Two case histories are presented.

335.   Dewees, R.F., et al., An open service in
       a university psychiatric clinic, Mental
       Hygiene, 1961, 45, 57-64.

Fifteen years of experience in a student health service
(UC Berkeley) organized around the concept that a student
should be seen promptly on request with the focus on the
emergent conflict that brought him to the clinic has
convinced us that ego-oriented psychotherapy is useful over
a wide range of patient problems. The therapeutic transaction is not determined by the severity or chronicity of
the patient's problems but by the fact of preconscious
conflicts which can be perceived in terms of their
emotional pattern and focused in the therapeutic interaction in an adaptive or ego-oriented way. The focusing
is a mutual, flexible process within the framework of:
(1) ego-orientation and (2) time-limitation. Within these
two frames of reference, interruption and termination
should be dynamically determined and not mechanically
imposed. Administrative policies were set up to facilitate
these psychotherapeutic concepts. (Journal summary).

336.   Deyoub, P.L., and Epstein, S.J., Short-
       term hypnotherapy for the treatment of
       flight phobia: A case report, American
       Journal of Clinical Hypnosis, 1977, 19,
       251-254.

A 30-year old married female with a history of flight
phobia was treated in three sessions with Erickson's
hypnotic techniques. Treatment consisted of client
description and visualization, under hypnosis, of a future
successful flight, training in posthypnotic techniques for
self-management and dream induction. The client successfully flew cross-country immediately after treatment, and
a six months follow-up revealed that she would not
hesitate to fly again on her next vacation. The hypno-
hterapeutic techniques resulted in a successful flight in
fewer sessions than reported behavior therapy techniques;
possible reasons for the superiority of hypnotherapy in
the treatment of flight phobia were discussed. (Journal
abstract).

337.   Dickes, R.A., Brief therapy of conversion
        reactions: An in-hospital technique,
        American Journal of Psychiatry, 1974, 131,
        584-586.

The role of secondary gain in making hysterical conversions
difficult to treat is discussed. A treatment approach,
entitled a special regimen, is described, in which the
patient is initially informed of the psychological aspects
of his symptomatology. The patient is then put in complete
bed rest with bedpan, with no bathroom privileges. The
use of outside distractions such as visitors, books,
magazines, etc. was also limited. The patient was told
that as he improved (i.e., as symptomatology decreased),
such privileges would be gradually phased back in. In
addition, group therapy and the milieu of the hospital ward
itself were included in the treatment. A total of 16
patients, all male between the ages of 18 and 31 were
treated, with some given traditional treatment approaches,
and some given the special treatment regimen. A significant difference in favor of the special regimen was
reported. Further, those cases in which the symptoms had
been of short-duration prior to treatment responded to
treatment significantly better than did those of long
symptom duration. The importance of rapid treatment at
the time of onset is stressed.

338.   Didato, S.V., Delinquents in group therapy:
        Some new techniques, Adolesence, 1970, 5,
        207-222.

This article reviews some of the specialized techniques
used with 28 juvenile delinquents who were treated over a
period of slightly more than one year, in a short-term
group therapy program. Most of the patients exhibited the
psychopathic personality, and the aims of the group treatment included decreased acting out, and the development of
new more appropriate behavioral patterns. The boys ranged
in age from 11-17. Details of the psychodynamics of the
groups, as well as background information on the patients
are provided. Special attention is directed at the issue
of affect in these delinquents, and the use of the group
in the development of more appropriate affective experiences. The special role of the therapist is also discussed.

339.   Didato, S.V., Psychotechniques, New York,
        Grosset and Dunlap, (in press).

The book is a compilation of self-applied techniques which
are usually taught to patients in the consultation room.
It is a form of bibliotherapy, in that the patient reads
material and then applies it to himself/herself. The range
of techniques is based on both research and clinical
practice, and includes self-desensitization, Bootzin's
technique for alleviating insomnia, Miller and Munoz's
techniques for alleviating alcoholism, Stuart's methods of
weight reduction, and Beck's strategies for dealing with
depression.

340.   Dies, R.R., and Hess, Self-disclosure,
        time perspective and semantic differential
        changes in marathon and short-term group
        psychotherapy, Comparative Group Studies,
        1970, 1, 387-395.

This is a study which compares reactions of patients to
short-term, session-spaced group therapy versus marathon
(i.e., one session) group therapy. Three marathon and
three short-term therapy groups were formed. The short-
term therapy group met for 12 sessions, each lasting one
hour. The marathon group met for only one session,
lasting 12 hours. The results indicated that the marathon
sessions produced greater intimacy and interpersonal openness than the short-term group therapy.

341.   Dies, R.R., and Sadowsky, R., A brief
        encounter group experience and social
        relationships in a dormitory, Journal
        of Counseling Psychology, 1974, 21,
        112-115.

The investigation examined the effects of a brief encounter
group experience upon residents in a university dormitory.
Women living on three separate floors were designated
experimental subjects and provided with a group experience
designed to encourage personal interaction, while women on
two other floors were assigned to a control group. Pre-
experimental and follow-up measures administered to members

of both groups showed that experimental subjects evidenced
greater improvement in their attitudes toward the importance of "floor spirit" in their semantic differential
ratings of the social atmosphere of their floor and in the
number of peers they subsequently identified as acquain-
tances. (Journal abstract).

342.   DiLorento, A., Comparative psychotherapy:
        An experimental analysis, Aldine-Atherton,
        Chicago, 1971.

The author compares three different approaches to therapy
(systematic desensitization, rational-emotive, and client-
centered) are compared with each other and with a "placebo"
attention and control group. Critiques by some of the
leaders in each mode of therapy are also included.
Systematic desensitization was generally more effective
in reducing anxiety caused by interpersonal contacts.

343.   Dinges, N.G., and Wiegel, R.G., The
        marathon group: A review of practice
        and research, Comparative Group Studies,
        1971, 2, 339-459.

This review article spanning over 100 pages, provides a
systematic overview of the historical development of the
marathon group therapy movement, the structure and
process of such groups, their applications and variations,
the research results, including a critical evaluation, and
a discussion of the social implications of such groups.
Over 250 references are cited.

344.   Dodd, J.A., A retrospective analysis of
        variables related to duration of treatment
        in a university psychiatric clinic,
        Journal of Nervous and Mental Disease,
        1970, 151, 75-84.

A statistical analysis was performed to ascertain variables
that would differentiate patients who terminated treatment
before and after a median of four interviews, of 169 new
outpatients who were accepted for treatment during the

first 3 months of 1967 at a university psychiatric clinic.
The variables which could be cross-validated in a sample
taken from the succeeding month, consisting of 57 patients,
were as follows: those patients who were Negroes, or who
were seen by medical students, or who received no drug
prescriptions tended to terminate early without their
therapist's consent. It was found that two treatment
variables, viz., who saw the patient and drug prescription,
correctly classified 81 per cent of the cross-validation
group. The literature concerning studies of the length of
outpatient psychiatric treatment was reviewed and discussed
in reference to the finds of this study. (Journal abstract).

345.   Doeff, J.W., et al., Brief psychotherapy
        in a community mental health center,
        Pennsylvania Psychiatric Quarterly, 1966,
        6, 62-64.

346.   Doherty, E., Length of hospitalization
        on a short-term therapeutic community,
        Archives of General Psychiatry, 1976,
        33, 87-92.

Patient length of hospitalization was examined in a private
short-term therapeutic community unit using a longitudinal,
multimethod, multivariate approach, with data analyzed
separately by patient sex. Patient data were entered into
stepwise linear regression analyses for weeks 1, 2, and 4
of an average seven-week hospitalization for male and
female patients separately. Results for men were not
specifically replicated among the women. Longer-staying
men were diagnosed more frequently as "personality disorders", tended to be somewhat aloof, perceived the ward
as encouraging denial, facade, order and organization.
Among women, verbal behavior, interpersonal relations,
discontendedness with family, and other variables were
related to length of hospitalization. Shorter-staying
male and female patients tended to exhibit characteristics
at the "feminine" end of a hypothetical masculinity-
feminity continuum. Conforming, accepting behavior seemed
reinforced for all patients. (Journal abstract)

347.   Dolan, A.T., and Sheikh, A.A., Short-term
        treatment of phobia through eidetic imagery,
        American Journal of Psychotherapy, 1977,
        31, 595-604.

The authors outline in detail an innovative approach to the
treatment of phobias. They distinguish between phobias of
long-standing and those of recent origin or onset, and provide methods for dealing with each type using eidetic imagery
in a brief therapy context. Based on the original work of
the Marburg school in Germany and continuing work by Ahsen,
the authors define an eidetic as a ... "specific kind of
mental image different from the dream, daydream, guided
fantasy image, or free-association image in that it requires
rigid fixation for arousal and has near-hallucinatory vivid-
ness." A discussion of the processes by which eidetics
normally develop, their negative and positive poles, and
their meanings, somatic characteristics, and visual components are presented. A five step eidetic methodology is
delineated, involving: a) initial exploration, much like a
brief psychiatric history work-up; b) introducing the patient
to eidetics, by actively asking the patient to recall a
recent experience and attempt to visualize it in image form;
c) assembling the symptom anew in the office (clinic) by
carefully listening to the patient's psychological and
physiological descriptions of the symptom; d) using the age
projection test, and, finally, e) using eidetics to study
the precipitating events which led to the symptom itself,
stressing the positive and negative polarities of the image.
Two case studies are presented, one representing a phobia of
long-standing duration, and one of recent onset. The authors
conclude that this approach offers a middle-of-the-road
method, falling between a strict behavioristic approach to
the treatment of phobias and a classical psychoanalytic
approach.

348.   Dolber, A., et al., From symptom to
        problem in living: Family approach to
        the treatment of the hospitalized psychia-
        tric patient, Psychotherapy: Theory
        Research, and Practice, 1977, 14, 52-56.

The problem of how to provide meaningful psychotherapeutic
service in a short term hospital setting is a most
vexatious one, especially when the patient population is

of the chronic, fairly disturbed, and "revolving door"
type. The treatment modality that we have found most
effective is one that most closely approximates the Crisis
Intervention model. Our understanding of this model of
intervention is that it is most critical to elucidate a
precipitant to hospitalization, to do whatever may be
helpful to restore the psychological balance that may have
upset just prior to hospitalization, and to make detailed
plans for discharge and followup. Since the precipitant
of the crisis is often repressed or otherwise obfuscated
by the patient, we have found it essential to see family
members shortly following admission and to explore with
them any changes in life situation that might have been
sufficiently stressful to propel patient into the hospital.
Such explorative attempts are often therapeutic and almost
always lead patient and family to reconceptualize the
initial presentation of symptoms to more workable "problems
in living". While the treatment team remains organized
along fairly traditional interdisciplinary lines, our roles
tend to blend, reemerging only as needed in specific
instances. Intake interviews and family meetings are held
jointly with the various disciplines represented. Treatment and treatment planning is carried out by the entire
team. (Journal abstract).

349.   Donner, J., Short-term therapy of
        schizophrenia, in, Usdin, G., (ed.),
        Psychoneurosis and schizophrenia,
        Philadelphia, Lippincott, 1966.

350.   Donner, J., and Gamson, A., Experience
        with multifamily, time-limited out-patient
        groups at a community psychiatric clinic,
        Psychiatry, 1968, 31, 126-137.

The work of the Community Psychiatric Clinic in Bethesda
Maryland is presented. Specifically, the use of a brief,
multifamily outpatient group therapy approach in dealing
with problem teenagers ranging from 13-17 is described.
Presenting problems included truancy, underachievement,
promiscuity, shoplifting, depression, etc. The type of
orientation to this group approach given to the families
is summarized, and three phases which most of these

families exhibited in reaction to the treatment program
are presented. These included an initial withdrawn or
inactive phase on the part of the adolescents accompanied
by expressions of anger and frustration on the part of
their parents. The second phase involved the increasing
participation by the teenagers, including their expressions
of anger and frustration. The third phase involved a more
equal sharing by all participants. The authors provide a
case example delineating these stage progressions.
Involvement of other adolescent sibs is recommended, and
the value of a cocussed approach is advised. Follow-up
results indicate that there was symptomatic alleviation in
two-thirds of the adolescents in the program (20 of 30).
About one half of the families required and received more
extensive psychotherapy. A total of 16 sessions were
provided in this program of brief treatment. The overall
theoretical base of the treatment was analytic.

351.   Donovan, W.B., and Marvit, R.C., Alienation-
        reduction in brief group therapy, American
        Journal of Psychiatry, 1970, 127, 825-827.

The authors describe a controlled study of patients in
brief group therapy that was designed to determine whether
this kind of therapy reduces alienation. They found that
while alienated attitudes were not reduced, the participants
became more sociable and content; affective and behavioral,
but not attitudinal, components of alienation were affected.

352.   Dorosin, D., et al., Very brief inter-
        ventions - a pilot evaluation, Journal
        of the American College Health Association,
        1976, 24, 191-194.

The authors summarize results of a study of the effectiveness of short-term therapy at the Counseling and Psychological Services Department of Stanford University. The
center operates without waiting lists and offers a crisis-
intervention and short-term therapy to its clients.
Questionnaires were mailed to 220 clients who had completed
therapy. 118 returned them completed. Over 80% evaluated
their first brief therapy experiences as positive. Further,

those clients reporting negative responses indicated that
they had not appreciated being referred outside the center
to outside professionals for continued treatment, or that
they had been turned off by the personal characteristics
of the initial interviewer. Therapists had also rated a
large percentage of client contact as positive and helpful.

353.   Douglas, D., Post-war psychiatry in the
        army: What it teaches, American Journal
        of Psychotherapy, 1948, 2, 306-315.

Various psychiatrists discuss the advantages and disadvantages of the shorter forms of psychotherapy.

354.   Doyle, A.M., and Doriac, C., Treating
        chronic crisis bearers and their families,
        Journal of Marriage and Family Counseling,
        1978, 4, 37-42.

Presents a model for family crisis intervention, utilizing
a case history approach. The goal is extended from
restoring the crisis bearing unit to its precrisis level
of coping to a basic restructuring of maladaptive precrisis
behaviors; it is aimed at general behavior change as well
as resolution of the immediate crisis; it adapts crisis
intervention theory to intervention involving chronic
crisis bearers and their families; it eliminates the
tendency to identify 1 member of the family as the patient
without considering the impact on the other members. This
approach consists of short-term intensive treatment combined with selected traditional techniques. (Journal
abstract).

355.   Doyle, W., et al., Effects of supervision
        in the training of nonprofessional crisis-
        intervention counselors, Journal of
        Counseling Psychology, 1977, 24, 72-78.

This study evaluated three major models currently used by
crisis-intervention centers to train and supervise non-
professional counselors. Training groups included
preservice training only (PSO), preservice training and

immediate supervision (SPI). The nonprofessional counselors in each group saw actual clients of a walk-in clinic and were compared on (a) pattern and timing of interventions, (b) self-evaluations of their interview performance, and (c) client evaluations of treatment received. Analyses of intervention patterns revealed that, except for explicit empathy, the groups did not differ in frequencies of counselor statements. Across time periods, only PSI counselors' response patterns began to approximate those of experienced crisis counselors. PSI counselors rated their interview performance most positively, followed by PSD and then PSO counselors. Clients reported greatest satisfaction with treatment received from PSI counselors. These findings indicate that most of the learning by nonprofessionals occurs during ongoing supervision. The practice of relying on pretaining may promote harmful outcomes for volunteers and may account for the common problem of high staff attrition. (Journal abstract).

356. Draper, E., et al., Adaptive psychotherapy: an approach toward greater precision in the treatment of the chronically disturbed, Comprehensive Psychiatry, 1968, 9, 372-382.

The authors report on the effect of a Thursday Morning Clinic (TAC) at the University of Chicago Hospital in which over 600 patients have been seen. The treatment approach used is called, Adaptive Psychotherapy, a term originally used by Heinz Hartmann. The focus is not on intrapsychic changes on a massive scale, but rather on a minor scale focussed on specific difficulties. The attempt is to guard against any further regression and to use such things as flights into health and transference cures. There is an emphasis on reality education. The authors describe the importance of careful diagnostic workups regarding the disabling variables and then tailoring techniques to help the patient. The match between thera- pist and patient is also discussed in this context, in which the strengths of both are used in the treatment. A number of case vignettes are presented to highlight the approach.

357.   Dreiblatt, I.S., and Weatherley, D., An
       evaluation of the efficacy of brief-contact
       therapy with hospitalized psychiatric
       patients, Journal of Consulting Psychology,
       1965, 29, 513-519.

In 2 experiments, brief-contact therapy - series of very
brief, friendly, casual conversations between a staff
member and a patient - was shown to have a beneficial
effect upon the psychological status of newly admitted
psychiatric patients. In the first study, conducted with
44 recently admitted patients, a 2-week regimen of brief
contacts produced a reduction in subjective anxiety, an
increase in self-esteem, and a reduction in length of
hospitalization. More frequent contacts (6 each week)
appeared to be more effective than fewer contacts (3 each
week). A second study with 84 Ss provided further confirmation of the effectiveness of brief-contact therapy, and
demonstrated that the content discussed during the contacts
has a bearing on their efficacy. (Journal abstract).

358.   Dressler, D.M., and Nash, K.B., Project
       team organization and its application to
       crisis intervention, Community Mental
       Health Journal, 1974, 10, 156-162.

A team approach to treatment of clients in a state of
crisis is described. The team consists of mental health
specialists selected on the basis of expertise in performing tasks required by a particular client. The team leader
is designated based on skill in establishing effective
client rapport. The leader manages the team activities,
expanding or contacting the team membership according to
the needs of the client. The leader represents the team
in its interface with the sponsoring service and is
accountable to the service for completion of task assignments. The team model is applicable to various health care
systems and provides a mechanism for the training of mental
health professionals. (Journal abstract).

359.   Dressler, D.M., et al., Life stress and
        emotional crisis: The idiosyncratic
        interpretation of life events, Comprehensive
        Pyschiatry, 1976, 17, 549-55.

The authors present a conceptual model to deal with the
phases of reactions to stressful experiences. The stages
are: a) prestress life context; b) precipitating event;
c) an intrapersonal emotional state of the individual
(i.e., his/her perceptions and meaning placed on the event);
d) a behavioral response to the situation; e) the social
outcome. This model was utilized in a research project
carried out at an emergency treatment unit of a mental
health center. Forty patients were chosen randomly from
a total of 145, and were given a combination of individual,
family, group, and drug therapies in an intensive short-
term treatment facility. Patients were mostly white,
young to middle aged, and of lower to middle income levels.
Approximately three-quarters were female patients. Their
life contexts indicated few friends and many stressful
events within the year prior to their serious difficulty
and referral to the clinic. Precipitating events arose
from interpersonal activities (arguments, etc.), and all
patients experienced these events as very stressful. They
responded within a short-term period of time (usually
within 1-3 days), with many reacting in self-inflicting
(e.g., suicide attempt, inward expression of tension, etc.)
and rigid ways. Many patients had played an active role in
precipitating the crisis. Thus although this article is
not specifically about the short-term therapy approach and
its effect, it does focus on the types of patients seen in
the brief therapy unit, and the stress model used by the
professional team in dealing with these patients.

360.   Driscoll, J., et al., Training police in
        family crisis intervention, Journal of
        Applied Behavioral Science, 1973, 9, 62-82.

A program of family crisis intervention for police, adapted
from that implemented in New York City by Bard (1970), was
conducted and evaluated. Twelve officers were given five
to six hours of training, five days a week, for five days.
Officers were then assigned to regular duties. Questionnaire
responses from officers four months into the project

indicated increased understanding of family problems,
greater acceptance of them by citizens, heightened receptivity to their suggestions, a decrease in the use of
force, and an increase in overall effectiveness. Telephone
interviews showed that citizens dealt with by trained
officers, as compared to those dealt with by untrained
officers, reported greater rapport between themselves and
officers, greater involvement of officers, more satisfaction with the intervention, and an increased regard
for the police. (Journal abstract).

361.   Duckworth, G.L., A project in crisis
        intervention, Social Casework, 1967,
        48, 227-231.

A pilot project was conducted by a family agency to assess
effects of a crisis intervention approach, from the stand-
points of the agency, the caseworker, and the client.
Fifty-one cases presenting a wide range of family difficulties and types of crises, were carried in the 24 weeks
of the project. Duckworth describes procedure, selection
criteria, client characteristics, fees and disposition/
outcome. In 94% of the cases, brief intervention was
deemed sufficient. Subjective comparison of this approach
with previous policy (which entailed written applications
and a waiting period) leads the author to conclude that
the crisis intervention method offers distinct advantages.
(abstract by Deborah Schuller).

362.   Duddle, C.M., The treatment of marital
        psychosexual problems, British Journal
        of Psychiatry, 1975, 127, 169-170.

The author describes the use of a combination of brief
psychotherapy and behavioral techniques in the treatment
of marital psychosexual problems. A total of 220 cases
were reviewed. Initial separate interviews for each spouse
were arranged, followed by joint treatment. The various
types of sexual problems were listed, and an overall
treatment improvement rate of approximately 70% was
attained. Stress is placed on improving communication
between husband and wife. Such improvement leads to a
greater sense of security on the part of both partners, and
aids in the continuing improvement in the sexual areas.

363.   Dunbar, F., Technical problems in
        analysis of psychosomatic disorders
        with special reference to precision in
        short-term psychotherapy, International
        Journal of Psychoanalysis, 1952, 33,
        385-396.

In this paper the purpose has been: (1) To call attention
to the need for improving precision in short-term psychotherapy, (2) To suggest a means of selecting from among a
large group of persons in need of treatment, for whom
psychoanalysis is impossible or undesirable, those likely
to respond best to briefer methods, (3) To point out that,
in determining the treatment of choice, the psychic and
somatic components in the illness syndrome must be evaluated
not only quantitatively but also qualitatively, (4) To
illustrate the peculiar hazards inevitably encountered in
short-term treatment and the reasons why some analysts
hesitate to accept the responsibilities involved, (5) To
point out the service that skilled psychoanalysts may
render if they are willing to direct their attention to
this somewhat neglected field of research and therapy.
(Journal summary).

364.   Durbin, O.A., Effects of intensive short-
        term psychotherapy on veteran drug addicts,
        Newsletter for Research in Mental Health
        and Behavioral Sciences, 1974, 16, 25-27.

365.   Dyrud, J.E., and Rioch, M.J., Multiple
        therapy in the treatment program of a
        mental hospital, Psychiatry, 1953, 16,
        21-26.

Multiple therapy - the treatment by interview of a
psychiatric patient by more than one therapist at the same
time - is a procedure in which the goals, methods, and
accomplishments can be just as varied as in individual
therapy. Carl A. Whitaker and his associates at Emory
University have used the term chiefly for situations in
which two or more therapists begin treatment of a patient
simultaneously. In this paper 7 patients will be described
all of whom had been receiving individual intensive psycho-

therapy before the multiple therapy experiment began and
all but one of whom continued with it after the multiple
therapy was terminated.   In all but the first of these
cases there was less than seven multiple therapy interviews.
Thus we are concerned here, in the main, not with long-term
treatment, but with a type of brief therapeutic intervention
within the framework of long-term individual psychotherapy.
(Journal abstract).

366.   Eagle, M., The role of silence and
        enactment in brief psychoanalytically-
        oriented psychotherapy: A case history,
        Unpublished manuscript, Toronto, York
        University and Clarke Institute of
        Psychiatry, 1979.

The author summarizes in discussion form some of the
changes and modifications is psychoanalytic thoery and
practice as a result of briefer forms of analytic treatment.
Specifically, the role of silence and what the author refers
to as "enactment" (a particular kind of acting out) are
focussed on and explored using a detailed case history from
thrapy.   In essence, the case history illustrates that
silence on the part of the therapist can be seen as interpretation in and of itself, and that acting-out (or enactment) behavior can also be seen as playing an important
positive role in the treatment process, rather than simply
being viewed as a sign of resistance to be interpreted.
The case cited involved a 26 year old female graduate
student with a presenting problem of severe pain during
sexual intercourse, a condition present from her first
sexual encounter at 18.   The work of leading analysts
practicing briefer forms of treatment is reviewed.

367.   Eastham, K., et al., The concept of crisis,
        Canadian Psychiatric Association Journal,
        1970, 15, 463-471.

Focussing primarily on theoretical and methodological
issues, this paper reviews the existing crisis literature
in order to clarify the term "crisis" and to investigate
its heuristic value.   The authors examine specifically the

relationship between crisis and stress, discuss six overlapping conceptions of "crisis", review the characteristics
of stress and the problems in research usage of the term,
and recommend potential methodological approaches which
resolve these particular problems. They conclude that the
ambiguity of the term "crisis" has advantages in a treatment context, but its present use in research adds little
to previous usages. (abstract by Deborah Schuller).

368.   Eisenberg, L., An evaluation of psychiatric
        consultation service for a public agency,
        American Journal of Public Health, 1958, 48,
        742-749.

The most effective way to make use of the psychiatrist's
skills is today an urgent problem. This paper reports the
results in a special diagnostic clinic where the psychiatrist was a diagnostic consultant and therapy was left to
other workers. State mental hygiene clinics and psychiatric services within public agencies do draw the majority
of their patients from the lower socioeconomic strata.
Intragency communication and cooperation was stressed in
the system described here, in which a policy of diagnostic
study, short-term psychotherapy, and the use of community
resources was substituted for a previous focus on long-
term psychotherapy. The interval between referral and
intake was reduced from an average time of one year to
6-8 weeks. Further, clinical results were also positive,
and referring agencies also reported confirmatory evidence
of improvement in service. (Journal abstract and discussion
modified).

369.   Eisenberg, L., The pediatric management
        of school phobia, Journal of Pediatrics,
        1959, 55, 758-766.

The psychiatric principles underlying the effective management of school phobia by a pediatrician are outlined in
this article. Eisenberg describes the basic characteristics
of the problem - the relatively stereotyped symptom
formation in contrast to the range and complexity of underlying causes, which Eisenberg illustrates with some
vignettes. Specific treatment procedures are detailed,

beginning with a thorough diagnostic evaluation, followed
by a pediatrician's identification of major family issues
which have given rise to the symptoms. The central focus
in management is prompt return to school, in a manner which
provides adequate support to child and family. In a final
section, the author recounts results of 67 cases of school
phobia treated in his clinic over a seven year period. The
data indicate that while 90% of elementary school-age children were successfully returned to school, only 45% of
children 11 or older were returned. He suggested that the
adolescent with school phobia is not suitable for pediatric
management. Over an average follow-up period of three years,
the successes appear enduring, with no indication of symptom
substitution sufficiently large to imply that the therapeutic
emphasis outlined by the author was incorrect.

370.   Eisenberg, L., Possibilities for a
        preventive psychiatry, Pediatrics, 1962,
        30, 815-828.

The author defines and illustrates three levels of preventive psychiatry. He then discusses the issue of social
responsibility in the field of psychiatry and suggests
specific needed revisions in training to meet more fully that
responsibility. To illustrate the level of primary prevention, he examines the syndrome of deprivation, its biologic
and environmental etiological factors. He enumerates known,
if not implemented, aspects of prevention on this level.
Noting that secondary prevention has had an ameliorating
effect on certain metabolic and functional disorders, the
author relates results of his investigation which suggest
important possibilities for prevention in such areas as case
management, neurotic children, school phobics, and delinquents. Eisenberg then offers suggestions for the third level
of prevention, the minimization of disability and the pro-
motion of physical rehabilitation. He poses the question of
why psychiatrists have not been more active as public advocates for a psychiatry of prevention, and offers some possible
reasons. Lastly, he argues for major revisions in the content
and methods of psychiatric training, stressing implicitly the
dual role of the psychiatrist as professional and as citizen.
(abstract by Deborah Schuller).

371.   Eisenberg, L., et al., Effectivness of
        psychotherapy alone and in conjunction
        with placebo in the treatment of neurotic
        and hyperkinetic children, American Journal
        of Psychiatry, 1961, 117, 1088-1093.

Pediatric patients with neurotic and hyperkinetic reaction
have been treated experimentally on one of 3 schedules:
(a) brief psychotherapy, (b) brief psychotherapy plus
placebo, (c) brief psychotherapy plus perphenazine.
Analysis of the clinic response rates has led us to the
following conclusions:
1.   Children with neurotic symptomatology show a prompt and
enduring response to a brief program of psychotherapy at a
level of improvement (60-70%) that is significantly greater
than that attained by children with hyperkinetic syndromes
(15-40%).
2.   No evidence was obtained for any enhancement of the
response to brief psychotherapy from the addition of
placebo medication.
3.   We were unable to demonstrate a significant difference
between response to placebo and to perphenazine when
administered concomitantly with psychotherapy. The implications of these finds have been discussed. (Journal
summary).

372.   Eisenberg, L., Treatment for disturbed
        children: a followup study, in Mental
        Health Program Reports, PHS Publication
        #1568, NIMH, Bethesda, Md., 1967.

373.   Eisenberg, L., et al., A controlled study
        of the differential application of out-
        patient psychiatric treatment for children,
        Japanese Journal of Child Psychiatry, 1965,
        6, 125-132.

Subjects in the study reported were patients referred from
community agencies for psychiatric care. An intake
evaluation permitted a division of the subjects into two
separate populations, on the basis of a diagnosis of
hyperkinesis or neurosis. Hyperkinetic subjects were
assigned on a double-blind basis to coded medication of

placebo for an eight-week period with five return visits
to the clinic. Two-thirds of the neurotic subjects were
randomly assigned to consultation, for a total of four
clinic visits over eight weeks. The remaining neurotic
patients were assigned to brief psychotherapy after the
consultative procedure, for a total of nine clinic visits.
Data presented suggest that brief treatment is effective
for neurotic outpatients, and the use of dextroamphetamine
or methylphenidate is effective for hyperkinetic subjects.
This study points to the value of categorizing patients
into separate clinical groups as means of determining an
effective treatment program, and suggests that treatment
may be differentially-effective in different groups.
(abstract by Deborah Schuller).

   374.   Eisenberg, M., Brief psychotherapy:
           A viable possibility with adolescents,
           Psychotherapy: Theory, Research, and
           Practice, 1975, 12, 187-191.

The author presents a review of a number of therapists
practicing briefer forms of therapy with adolescents. The
aims of brief therapy are reviewed (resolution of immediate
problems), the role of the therapist is discussed (active
involvement), and the particular kind of client suited for
this type of therapy is presented (people experiencing
personality growth). Certain contraindications for the
use of short-term treatment include individuals with a
known past record of failure to cope with previous stress
earlier in life, schizophrenics. A short discussion of
the issues of whether to involve parents of adolescents in
treatment is presented. Brief therapy techniques include
critical use of the initial diagnostic process, and setting
up of a focussed set of goals, limited in their scope.
Such techniques as advice-giving, information-giving, the
issue of transference, and reality testing are reviewed.
A table containing a summary of the variety of approaches
in the field of brief therapy is provided, covering the
number of sessions each reported study used, and other
specifications to each approach (e.g., patient population,
etc.).

375.   Eisenberg, M., Short-term psychotherapy
        with a pre-adult population, Vocational
        Guidance, 1976, 12, 280-292.

A survey of the literature on short-term psychotherapy is
presented to determine the feasibility of such treatment
for secondary school, collegial, and university populations.
Five areas are covered: the goals of brief therapy, the
therapist's role, indications and contraindications for
such treatment, the potential usefulness of short-term
parental involvement, and therapeutic techniques particularly adapable to brief treatment. She includes a
table listing the number of sessions and specifications
of brief therapy as reported by 10 authors over a 17-year
period. The author concludes that brief therapy is
feasible for the populations considered. (abstract by
Deborah Schuller).

376.   Eisler, R.M., Crisis intervention in the
        family of a firesetter, Psychotherapy:
        Theory, Research, and Practice, 1972, 9,
        76-79.

The author presents a case history in which six, 2-3 hour
sessions of crisis family interventive therapy were used.
The presenting problem revolved around the firesetting
behavior of the 14 year old son. The authors conceptualized the acting out behavior in terms of disturbed
social or family relationships. The focus of treatment was
not on the behavior of the teenager per se, but on the
unresolved crises within the family. The authors present
a description of the precipitant factors, the role
relationships, and the communication patterns within the
family in question. The treatment process, with a
modification of the Satir structured family tasks, is
delineated. Some of the reasons why such a crisis-oriented
approach, based in communication and systems theory was
effective are listed, including significant positive
relationships within the family, a willingness to commit
to the treatment process, and the ability to readily
define a specific problem area.

377.   Eisler, R.M., Behavioral techniques in
        family crises, Current Psychiatric
        Therapies, 1976, 16, 255-262.

The various techniques described by Eisler have as their
aim the rapid restructuring of a family's interactive
repertoire around their present difficulties. The approach
stresses the teaching of strategies which promote adaptive
conflict resolution (e.g., increasing rates of reciprocal
positive reinforcement in crisis-prone families). Specific
techniques examined are feedback to confront a family with
their ineffective behavior, behavioral rehearsal, modeling
and role-playing, therapist coaching, and behavioral
contracts. Eisler concludes by presenting a case illustration in which some of these techniques were utilized.
(abstract by Deborah Schuller).

378.   Eisler, R.M., and Hersen, M., Behavioral
        techniques in family-oriented crisis
        intervention, Archives of General Psychiatry,
        1973, 28, 111-116.

Behavioral techniques in short-term family-oriented crisis
intervention treatment are examined within the context of
crisis theory and behavior modification. It is noted that
both approaches emphasize the importance of environmental
influences in developing and maintaining maladaptive
behaviors. Methods of restructuring discordant family
relationships through the use of particular behavioral
techniques such as feedback, modeling, behavioral rehearsal,
instructions, and behavioral contracts are outlined. Three
case studies are presented to illustrate the therapeutic
flexibility of these techniques with crisis-prone families.
Not only are families helped with presenting complaints,
but a major emphasis is placed on their learning more
successful problem solving skills that are to be implemented
in daily interactions. (Journal abstract).

379.   Eisler, R.M., and Williams, W.V.,
        A comparison of preadmission
        characteristics of patients selected
        for long-term or short-term psychiatric
        treatment, Journal of Clinical Psychology,
        1972, 28, 209-213.

First admissions to a state mental health facility who had
been assigned to either an "acute" short-stay service or a
"chronic" long-term service were compared on their previous
social adjustment and present impaired characteristics.
The major findings were that long term admissions could be
differentiated from short term admissions on the basis of
single, separated, or divorced marital status, lengthier
history of psychiatric treatment, and lower socio-economic
status.   Present impairment characteristics which differentiated long term from short term admissions were psychotic
diagnosis, involuntary admission status, unemployed status,
and under psychiatric treatment at the time of admission.
(Journal summary).

380.   Elitzur, B., In and out of Pandora's Box,
        Journal of Contemporary Psychotherapy,
        1978, 9, 151-154.

The author presents a novel approach to the short-term
treatment of phobias.   It was stimulated by the author's
son's development of a phobia after being attacked by a
large dog.   The approach used was based on similar therapeutic ideas which are implicit in children's literature,
children's T.V. programs, and folk tales.   Basically, it
involves leading the child through a story, in which there
is a catastrophe and a rescue, a process the author labels,
"in and out of Pandora's Box."

382.   Elkin, M., Short contact counseling in
        conciliation court, Social Casework,
        1962, 43, 184-190.

A form of brief marital counseling is described for couples
on the verge of separation or divorce offered by the
Conciliation Court of Los Angeles County.   The author
outlines the purpose and application procedures of the

Court, client characteristics and referral sources, the
nature of the conciliation conference, and of the formal
reconciliation agreement. The Court limits its services
to three conferences/couple, although a couple may request
further service at a later time. Since approximately two-
thirds of the clientele require continued counseling, the
Court has developed a complementary relationship with
community family casework agencies. Elkin discusses the
Court's use of authority, and the effectiveness of the
counseling services offered. The author concludes that
this program, utilizing short-term counseling, a formalized
reconciliation agreement, and the authority vested in the
Court, provides a valuable recognition of the socio-
psychological (versus purely legal) aspects of divorce.
(abstract by Deborah Schuller).

383.   Elkin, T.E., et al., Modification of
        caloric intake in anorexia nervosa: An
        experimental analysis, Psychological
        Reports, 1973, 32, 75-78.

The effects of feedback, reinforcement, and increased food
presentation on caloric intake were sequentially examined
in an experimental single-case design with an anorexia
nervosa patient. Although feedback on weight and a point-
reinforcement system for weight gains led to increased
consumption, augmenting the amount of food presented in
combination with feedback and reinforcement resulted in
the most dramatic change in caloric intake.   (Journal
summary).

384.   Ellis, A ., New approaches to psychotherapy
        techniques, (Monograph supplement), Journal
        of Clinical Psychology, 1955, 19, 246.

The author summarizes much of the literature on brief
therapy, covering its advantages, the research results
regarding effectiveness with specific patient populations,
as well as the limitations of briefer forms of treatment.
Short-term psychotherapy is included as one section in a
much larger review of various innovations in psychotherapy
techniques.

385.   Ellis, A., Outcome of employing three
        techniques of psychotherapy, Journal of
        Clinical Psychology, 1957, 13, 344-350.

Data are presented on therapeutic outcome when the same
therapist employed orthodox psychoanalysis, psychoanalytically-oriented psychotherapy, and rational psychotherapy with groups of matched clients. It was found that
individuals treated with orthodox psychoanalysis showed
little or no improvement in 50% of the cases, distinct
improvement in 37%, and considerable improvement in 13%.
Those treated with psychoanalytically-oriented therapy
showed little or no improvement in 37% of the cases,
distinct improvement in 45%, and considerable improvement
in 18%. Those treated with rational psychotherapy showed
little or no improvement in 10% of the cases, distinct
improvement in 46%, and considerable improvement in 44%.
Data are also presented on the basic irrational ideas held
by neurotic clients and their tendency to give way to more
rational replacements with therapeutic improvement.
(Journal summary).

386.   Ellis, A., Reason and emotion in
        psychotherapy, Secaucas, N.J., Lyle
        Stuart and Citadel Press, 1962.

387.   Ellis, A., et al., Growth through reason:
        Verbatim cases in rational-emotive therapy,
        Palo Alto, Science and Behavior Books, 1971.

388.   Ellis, A., and Abrahams, E., Brief
        psychotherapy in medical and health
        practice, New York, Springer Publishing
        Company, 1978.

389.   Ellis, A., and Grieger, R., (eds.),
        Handbook of rational-emotive therapy,
        New York, Springer, 1977.

390.   Elmore, J.L., and Saunders, R., Group
        encounter techniques in the short-term
        psychiatric hospital, American Journal
        of Psychotherapy, 1972, 26, 490-500.

The use, benefits, and limitations of encounter techniques
in a traditionally-oriented, private psychiatric hospital
providing intensive short-term treatment are discussed.
The authors look briefly at the concept of encounter, its
history, and the relative dearth of follow-up studies
assessing the dangers of encounter group methods. Roles
of the leader and encounter group members, the context of
the hospital, and features and techniques of a hospital
encounter group are then examined. Elmore and Saunders
note that their experience with such groups does not fully
bear out contraindications for participants by certain
categories of people (e.g., certain psychotic patients,
characterologic neurotics, persons with hysterical personality traits) cited by other authors. However the
importance of using encounter techniques with a specific
purpose in mind is stressed, as is the responsibility of
the therapist in screening group members. The authors
conclude that encounter techniques have a contributing
role to play in the treatment of actually ill patients in
the psychiatric hospital. (abstract by Deborah Schuller).

391.   Emery, M., The short contact in wartime,
        Social Casework, 1944, 25, 27-33.

The overriding atmosphere of wartime and its effects on
daily casework is discussed. The need for immediacy in
times of pressure and crisis is stressed, with the author
reporting that many problems were dealt with in one
session.

392.   Engs, R.C., and Kirk, R.H., The
        characteristics of volunteers in crisis
        intervention centers, Public Health
        Reports, 1974, 89, 459-464.

The authors report on the results of a study initiated in
Tennessee in order to ascertain the training and knowledge
levels of volunteers serving in crisis intervention centers.

The results point to the conclusions that those volunteers
who were working to help others remained on the job an
average of twice as long as those who were volunteering
because of course credit, self-growth, or experience. The
implications of this for hiring and staff turnover were
discussed.

393.   Epstein, N., Brief group therapy in a
        child guidance clinic, Social Work, 1970,
        15, 33-38.

The author reports on the brief therapy program of an
Eastern child guidance center. Parents and teens are seen
separately in groups, each lasting six sessions, while
younger children are seen individually for a limited number
of sessions. The techniques used include advice giving,
suggestions, basic education regarding parent-child
interactions and expectations. The focus remains on the
present, with little delving into marital conflicts of
parents, the assumption being that parents can act
responsibly as parents even with marital difficulties.
The author has found that the majority of families seeking
help do so because of difficulties with their first born
child. The author details the operation of the program
(i.e., some of the mechanics of operation), and the process
of therapy over the six sessions. Some tentative results
from the adolescent groups are presented, and the positive
value of a limited number of sessions is discussed. The
brief therapy program has resulted in a dramatic decrease
in the waiting list time, in positive follow-up reports
from families, and in changing orientations in the staff
perceptions of pathology.

394.   Epstein, N., Techniques of brief therapy
        with children and parents, Social Casework,
        1976, 57, 317-323.

The author presents a description of a short-term approach
with children and parents, consisting of one or two
sessions/week, over a six week period, in which the
resolution of an agreed upon highly focussed problem is
the aim. Both children and parent groups are used when

needed, with parents able to observe their children in the
group setting. The process of the therapy is described,
and contraindications for such an approach are discussed.
Severe acting out, depressed, or withdrawn children should
not be offered such treatment. Further, the younger the
child, preferably a pre-teen, the more effective the
treatment approach.

395.   Erickson, M.H., Hypnosis in medicine,
        Medical Clinics of North America, 1944,
        28, 639-651.

The author provides a description of a case treated in
three hours successfully. The patient, a woman suffering
from 14 hours of retention of urine with no organic cause,
was hypnotized. She revealed her fears, and Erickson gave
her insight into the cause of her present state, placing
emphasis on a positive context or approach. Post-hypnotic
suggestion was used. The author presents a general discussion of the value of using hypnosis in a number of
presenting difficulties.

396.   Erickson, M.H., The therapy of a
        psychosomatic headache, Journal of
        Clinical and Experimental Hypnosis,
        1953, 1, 2-6.

397.   Erickson, M.H., Special techniques of
        brief hypnotherapy, Journal of Clinical
        and Experimental Hypnosis, 1954, 2,
        109-129.

The focus of this article is on the treatment of patients
who, for a variety of reasons, have decided that comprehensive therapy is unacceptable to them. For some, their
present level of functioning and adjustment is based on the
need to continue certain maladaptive patterns. The author,
acclaimed for his unique approach to hypnotherapy, details
four methods or techniques of intentionally using the
patient's neurotic symptomatology to satisfy the patient
and meet his/her needs. The specific techniques are:

a) symptom substitution: the patient presents a situation
in which no possibility for the correction of the underlying causal factors exists, and where the hypnotherapist
substitutes another, comparable non-incapacitating symptom
which is acceptable to the patient; b) symptom transformation: in which the therapist uses the neurotic behavior
by transforming the personality purposes it originally
served, without dramatically changing the symptomatology
itself; c) symptom amelioration: in which the patient
presents the therapist with an overwhelming all-engrossing
symptom complex, and in which the therapist accepts the
entire complex of symptoms but acts to ameliorate them;
d) corrective emotional response: in which the patient
is involved in intensely emotional problems, and the therapist helps by creating an atmosphere wherein a corrective
emotional experience occurs. Specific case histories are
presented for each of these approaches, with comment
following each case. The author also includes an appendix
of 14 techniques which are variations on some mentioned in
the body of the paper.

398.   Erickson, M.H., Naturalistic techniques
        of hypnosis, American Journal of Clinical
        Hypnosis, 1958, 1, 3-8.

The author defines naturalistic hypnotherapeutic techniques
"...the acceptance of the situation encountered and the
utilization of it, without endeavouring to restructure it
psychologically...the presenting behavior of the patient
becomes a definite aid and an actual part of inducing a
trance, rather than a possible hindrance." The author
presents six case histories to illustrate such an approach.
All of the cases highlight the role of the therapist in
tailoring his/her approach to fit the conditions existing
in the sessions, rather than utilizing a specific series
of predetermined steps for inducing change through the use
of hypnosis.

399.   Erickson, M.H., Further clinical
        techniques of hypnosis: Utilization
        techniques, American Journal of Clinical
        Hypnosis, 1959, 1, 3-21.

A number of differing special techniques of hypnotic trance
induction are reported and illustrated by clinical and
experimental examples. These methods are based upon the
utilization of the subject's own attitudes, thinking,
feeling, and behavior, and aspects of the reality situation,
variously employed, as the essential components of the
trance induction procedure. In this way, they differ from
the more commonly used techniques which are based upon the
suggestion to the subject of some form of operator-selected
responsive behavior. These special techniques, while
readily adaptable to subjects in general, demonstrate
particularly the applicability of hypnosis under various
conditions of stress and to subjects seemingly not amenable
to its use. They also serve to illustrate in part some of
the fundamental psychological principles underlying hypnosis
and its induction. (Journal summary).

400.   Erickson, M.H., and Rossi, E.L.,
        Varieties of double bind, American
        Journal of Clinical Hypnosis, 1975,
        17, 143-157.

This paper begins with an autobiographical account by
Erickson of the experiences from childhood that led to his
use of the double bind in hypnosis and psychotherapy.
Erickson presents a number of examples of the use of the
double bind in everyday life and a few case studies of its
use in psychotherapy. In the second half of this paper,
Rossi summarizes the characteristics of Erickson's clinical
approach to the double bind. He outlines several varieties
of the double bind and offers an explanatory analysis of
the operation of the bouble bind in terms of Russell's
Theory of Logical Types. A clear differentiation is drawn
between Erickson's therapeutic double bind and Bateson's
schizophrenic double bind. The ethics and limitations in
the use of the double bind in psychotherapy are proposed
together with suggestions for future research. (Journal
abstract).

401.   Erlich, R.E., and Phillips, P.B., Short-
        term psychotherapy of the aviator,
        Aerospace Medicine, 1963, 34, 1046-1047.

402.   Errera, P., et al., Psychiatric care
        in a general hospital emergency room,
        Archives of General Psychiatry, 1963,
        9, 105-112.

The emergency room of the general hospital is examined as
a psychiatric resource for the community. On one such
setting where psychiatric coverage is readily available,
1,155 emergency psychiatric consultations were provided
over a 12-month period (1960-61). This study presents the
statistical data as to personal and social characteristics
of the patients seen, the timing of their visits, the
diagnoses made, and dispositions recommended. Some formulations are suggested to explain the data observed.
(Journal summary).

403.   Errera, P., et al., Length of psychotherapy,
        Archives of General Psychiatry, 1967, 17,
        454-458.

Compared two groups of patients at a university community
psychiatric clinic, one group which was in therapy from
6-10 sessions, the second group which was in therapy for
more than 21 sessions.

There were no significant differences between the two
groups on the following characteristics: age, sex, marital
status, religion, race, social class, number of previous
admissions, or diagnosis on intake.

They found that, contrary to widely held belief, there
were a number of lower-class patients who were capable of
benefitting from psychotherapy. Also, found that the
following characteristics usually associated with long
term therapy (relatively well preserved ego controls,
ability to evaluate one's past experience, and a desire to
connect the present with the past), were equally distributed
in both patient groups.

The researchers were unable to distinguish between the two therapy groups on the basis of the type of therapy approach used, outcome measures of therapy, original diagnosis, or social class factors.

404.   Everstine, D.S., et al., Emergency
        psychology: A mobile service for
        police crisis calls, Family Process,
        1977, 16, 281-292.

The authors describe an emergency 24 hour/day emergency community service which operates as a back-up to 10 northern California police departments. The focus is on home visits for families in crisis and continuity of service to that family after the initial contact. The number of sessions (lasting on the average about 2 - 2.5 hours/initial visit) ranges from two to six. The authors describe the details of the daily operating of the service. Methods used include eclectic and flexible, but a focus on tasks and problem-solving is stressed within a warm orientation. Specific examples are provided regarding the methods of initial contact, from the point of first call for help to the resolution of the crisis. Cases handled during the first year of operation of the service totaled 340 families, and the problems handled included rape, attempted or threatened homocide, attempted suicide by adolescents, assault, incest or molestation, etc. As of the data of the article, no completed suicides or homocides have been recorded for those families helped by the service. A comparison of the cost of such a service with that of an outpatient community mental health service in the same community is briefly presented.

405.   Ewalt, P.L., The crisis-treatment
        approach in a child guidance clinic,
        Social Casework, 1973, 54, 406-411.

This article proposes that within the time usually allotted to evaluation, a clinic worker be permitted the flexibility to proceed with therapeutic interventions once he has identified the salient problem. For three identified categories or patients, traditional evaluation may be ill-suited. Brief treatment during the initial contact may be

both appropriate and useful in terms of providing more
diagnostic information. Ewalt describes the brief treatment program in one child-guidance clinic, specific
administrative arrangements, and personality traits helpful
for personnel working in such a setting. She mentions the
in-service training aspects for crisis program workers and
field work training aspects for students. Lastly, results
of this program are reviewed with special reference to the
relatively high rate of continuation of treatment following
the crisis program by patients recommended for further
treatment. (abstract by Deborah Schuller).

406.   Ewing, C.P., Crisis intervention as
        psychotherapy, New York, Oxford
        University Press, 1978.

The initial section of this book presents the evolution of
crisis intervention theory covering the last four decades,
present-day status of the field, including current use,
specific programs, and a review of the outcome literature.
Issues of patient selection are also covered in detail.
A brief lcok into the future of the possible expansion of
the field of crisis intervention as psychotherapy is also
presented, along with a model for its use in clinical
practice. An extensive bibliography is included.

407.   Fallon, C., Providing relevant brief
        service to couples in marital crises,
        American Journal of Orthopsychiatry,
        1973, 43, 235-236.

The author describes a task-oriented and goal directed
eight session therapy approach for helping couples in
marital crisis. The focus of treatment is on role
expectations, types and methods of communication, and
active attempts at problem-solving. Some examples are
presented. Such an approach is not recommended for couples
in which severe pathology is evident, couples who have been
married more than 10 years, or for those couples who are
unwilling to stay together for the eight week therapy
treatment period.

408.   Faries, M., Short-term counseling at
        the college level, Journal of Counseling
        Psychology, 1955, 2, 3, 182-184.

One hundred and forty counseled freshmen were matched with
an equal number of noncounseled freshmen to determine
whether the numbers graduating from each group showed any
difference. The findings indicated that the counseled
students graduated in significantly greater numbers than
did their control-group partners who received no counseling.
The largest uncontrolled variable would appear to be the
factor of personal motivation of the counseled students.
(Journal summary).

409.   Farnsworth, B.K., et al., Implosive
        psychodrama, Psychotherapy: Theory,
        Research, and Practice, 1975, 12, 200-201.

The author provides for a combining of principles of
psychodrama and those of implosive therapy, with the
emphasis on the role of the antagonist (or therapist). In
this way originally suppressed and repressed material is
elicited as well as the experiencing of corrective
emotional reactions (new operant attempts) to counter the
negative material. The value of this type of combining of
two different approaches is called implosive psychocrama.
A brief case report is provided to illustrate the technique.

410.   Fay, A., Clinical notes on paradoxical
        therapy, Psychotherapy: Theory, Research,
        and Practice, 1976, 13, 118-123.

Fay illustrates with five cases his use of a technique in
which the therapist (or any significant other) agrees with
a patient's irrational statements, and in fact exaggerates
the distortion. Benevolently mirroring back to the patient
his "irrationality" may interrupt persistent pathological
patterns of communication if the patient can respond to
the irrationality as distorted or inappropriate. Paradoxical therapy cuts across theoretic and diagnostic
boundaries, but a personal style which includes a good
sense of humor as well as empathic concern appears helpful.

The author notes three basic objections to "absurd therapy" and responds to each. He conceives conventional and paradoxical therapy as complementary. The introduction of humor and distortion as described in the clinical material can facilitate a closer, more spontaneous relation between patient and therapist. (abstract by Deborah Schuller).

411.   Fazio, A.F., The treatment components in
        implosive therapy, Journal of Abnormal
        Psychology, 1970, 76, 211-219.

In an effort to evaluate reality-testing and supportive aspects of implosive therapy (IT) independent of the anxiety-eliciting scenes, college females with a fear of a specific insect were administered three sessions of one of three tape-recorded treatments. In two double blind experiments, Ss treated with IT were not found to improve significantly as measured by repeated overt behavioral tests. In both studies, the reality-supportive discussions were associated with significantly greater reductions in phobic behaviors than IT. The findings were related to the theoretical formulations of IT and to treatment applications. (Journal abstract).

412.   Feder, B., Limited goals in short-term
        group psychotherapy with institutionalized
        delinquent adolescent boys, International
        Journal of Group Psychotherapy, 1962, 12,
        503-507.

This article presents a controlled study designed to evaluate empirically two frequent assumptions about discussion group therapy as a treatment measure with delinquent adolescent boys, namely, that short-term group therapy promotes therapeutic readiness, and that it facilitates institutional adjustment. The sample consisted of 80 newly-admitted patients, ages 14-17. The treatment consisted of a total of 16, twice-weekly sessions, each 90 minutes long. Two hypotheses concerning increased therapeutic readiness in such boys were borne out; three hypotheses concerning facilitation of adjustment to the

institution received no support from the data. The author
suggests the need for further research into the critical
length of therapeutic contact, noting that the increased
readiness for a therapeutic process observed within two
months might represent a prelude for desired behavioral
changes over a longer time period. (abstract by Deborah
Schuller).

413.   Feirstein, A., et al., A crisis model
        for inpatient hospitalization, Current
        Psychiatric Therapies, 1971, 11, 183-190.

The authors describe the functioning of the Emergency
Treatment Unit (ETU) of the Connecticut Mental Health
Center, which provides service to individuals in crisis.
The maximum length of stay is three days. The focus is on
the present life situation with the aim of helping the
individual return to a reasonable level of functioning.
A one month outpatient concinuing service aids in the
transition from inpatient to community participant. The
techniques used are described, including time-limited
contracts, active involvement of multiple-therapist teams,
etc. The use of psychotropic drugs is considered in
situations which such administration would lead to decrease
in the target symptoms, and allow for a more rapid dealing
with the presenting problems. The patients seen were
predominantly from a lower socioeconomic background. A
follow-up research project carried out at the center
revealed a number of facts about the positive changes in
the patient population in general. One of the most
interesting findings was that 90% of those patients seen
in the program who lived with their parents had to be
rehospitalized within the next year compared to 30% for
those patients who did not reside with their parents.
Further, the type of adjustment in the community was also
studied, by use of in-depth home interviews two months
after discharge, and at the time of publication of the
article, at one year after initial contact with the service.
Positive results for those treated in the ETU versus those
treated in the more traditional way were reported.

Measures used included length of consequent hospitalization, employment record, adjustment ratings by both patients and their families, and certain cognitive measures, such as certain WAIS subscale testing. All measures point to a positive outcome.

414.   Feldman, L., Strategies and techniques
        of family therapy, American Journal of
        Psychotherapy, 1976, 30, 14-28.

A conceptual model of the strategies and techniques of family therapy is presented. Attention is drawn to the complex relationships between the family therapist's manner of relating, the strategies and techniques which he or she employ, the presenting problem or problems, the particular characteristics of the family, and the developmental phase of the family therapy process. (Journal abstract).

415.   Fell, E., Short-term treatment in a child
        guidance clinic, Journal of Jewish Communal
        Service, 1959, 36, 144-149.

416.   Fenichel, O., Brief psychotherapy, in,
        Fenichel, H., and Rapaport, D., (eds.),
        The collected papers of Otto Fenichel,
        New York, W.W. Norton, 1954.

417.   Ferber, H., et al., Training parents
        in behavior modification: Outcome of
        and problems encountered in a program
        after Patterson's work, Behavior Therapy,
        1974, 5, 415-419.

Using Patterson's method of parent training for dealing with child management problems, the authors report the results of work with seven families. Although changes were reported in three of the five families who completed the program as prescribed, a follow-up 12 months later indicated the three of four families questioned were experiencing serious difficulties with the children. The intervention program lasted a total of 10 weeks.

418.   Ferenzi, S, The further development of
        an active therapy in psychoanalysis, in,
        Further Contribution to the Therapy and
        Technique of Psychoanalysis, New York,
        Basic Books, 1951.

419.   Ferenzi, S., Contra-indications to the
        active psychoanalytic technique, in,
        Further contributions to the theory and
        techniques of psychoanalysis, New York,
        Basic Books, 1951.

420.   Ferguson, J., et al., Rapid desensitization
        of a needle phobia by participant modeling,
        Western Journal of Medicine, 1976, 124,
        174-176.

The theoretical and practical issues related to participant
modeling are presented. The case history presented involved
an individual with a needle and intravenous phobia who was
to be involved in surgery. Measures of positive therapeutic change included the patient's comfort level across
a number of dimensions. This type of approach can be
useful to alleviate a number of specific patients fears,
and accomplished within a short period of time.

421.   Finney, J.C., Therapist and patient after
        hours, American Journal of Psychotherapy,
        1975, 29, 593-602.

A patient in brief psychotherapy told of a sexual advance
made to her now by a former psychotherapist. Computer
testing predicted her motivation and behaviour accurately.
A number of related issues in professional ethics and in
dynamic psychology are discussed. Legal cases are cited.
(Journal abstract).

422.   Firestone, R.W., et al., Evaluation of
        psychotherapeutic screening for enuretic
        recruits, U.S. Armed Forces Medical
        Journal, 19   7, 20-24.

A study was conducted to evaluate the extended effectiveness of a brief intervention designed to reduce the number
of military recruits discharged for enuresis. Data
indicates a 26% reduction in number of recruits discharged
during pre- and post-experimental periods of 41 consecutive
weeks each. Firestone et al. attribute the effectiveness
of this very brief (approximately three minutes), flexible
intervention to the permissive, accepting attitude shown by
the screening interviewer, who represents a benevolent
authority figure at a critical early point in training,
during which the recruit may be highly motivated to overcome the habit. This positive motivation is reinforced by
appropriate behavioral suggestions. (abstract by Deborah
Schuller).

423.   Fisch, M., et al., Epidemiology of
        psychiatric emergencies in an urban
        health district, American Journal of
        Public Health, 1964, 54, 572-579.

Over half the people (young and middle aged adults) who
appeared for care at the psychiatric unit of a municipal
hospital from one Health District in New York presented
crisis situations requiring immediate response. The
authors conclude that a clinical psychiatric service in a
metropolitan area must be prepared to deal with a large
number of emergencies. (Journal abstract).

424.   Fisch, R., Sometimes its better for the
        right hand not to know what the left hand
        is doing, in, Papp, P., (ed.), Family
        therapy: Full length case studies, New
        York, Gardner Press, 1977.

The author presents a case in which the identified patient
was a 12 year old boy who was experiencing difficulties in
school and at home. Details of each therapy session are
included, covering a period of approximately four months,
in which a total of seven sessions were held.

425.   Fisher, S.G., Time-limited brief psycho-
        therapy: An investigation of therapeutic
        outcome at a child guidance clinic,
        Dissertation Abstracts International,
        1978, 39(1-B), 377.

426.   Fishman, J., and McCormack, J., Mental
        health without walls: community mental
        health in the ghetto, American Journal
        of Psychiatry, 1970, 126, 1461-1467.

Group activity and action-oriented therapeutic programs
without the "psychiatric" label, particularly those that
link meaningful work, compensation, education and social
competency, appear to offer great potential for use in mental
health programs in the ghetto. Intervention must be of
immediate and recognizable relevance to the pressing life
problems of youth and adults and must provide significant
incentive to change through achievement and reinforcement of
meaningful goals. Development of the program and community
and institutional supports required to sustain this change,
however, will involve many problems of, social, administrative, and institutional resistance. The professional must
be a tactful and skillful, but unrelenting, change agent.
(Journal abstract).

427.   Fitzgerald, O.R., Crisis intervention
        with open heart surgery patients,
        Dissertation Abstracts International,
        1978, 39(1-A), 127-128.

428.   Fitzgerald, R.V., Conjoint marital
        psychotherapy: An outcome and follow-
        up study, Family Process, 1969, 8,
        260-271.

Therapist rating of the results at termination and patient
ratings of their status at an everage of 2½ years after
termination of conjoint marital psychotherapy are reported
on a series of 49 couples judged to have been involved in
therapy. Comparisons were made between the results of this
study and the reported results of two outcome studies, plus

one outcome and follow-up study of individual short-term
psychotherapy, as well as with another form of conjoint
therapy and with psychoanalysis. This study and the
comparisons made seem to indicate that the conjoint
approach compares favorably with these other forms of
therapy and that certain predicted technical advantages
of conjoint therapy are valid. (Journal summary).

429.   Fitzgerald, R.V., Conjoint marital
        therapy, New York, Jason Aronson, 1973.

430.   Flomenhaft, K., et al., Avoiding
        psychiatric hospitalization, Social Work,
        1969, 14, 38-46.

In order to compare the results of outpatient family crisis
therapy with hospitalization, a clinical team from Colorado
Psychiatric Hospital treated on an outpatient basis 186
patients considered acutely in need of admission to a
psychiatric hospital. The control group consisted of 150
patients from the same population who were routinely
hospitalized. In all except 3 of the initial 36 pilot
cases, it was possible to avoid hospitalization. Family
crisis therapy has proved to be a more economical and less
stigmatizing form of psychiatric treatment than hospitalization. Its principles are outlined and the specific
participation of the clinical social worker and his role
on the crisis therapy team are described. (Journal
abstract).

431.   Flomenhaft, K., and Langsley, D.G.,
        After the crisis, Mental Hygiene, 1971,
        55, 473-477.

The authors present results of follow-up research on 186
families originally seen at the Family Treatment Unit of
the Colorado Psychiatric Hospital. Approximately 50% of
those families seen at the Treatment Unit were in need of
longer-term treatment. The authors stress the importance
of continuing and meaningful liaison with other agencies
in the community with whom patients will have continuing
contact. The value of making such referrals in person or

by phone (i.e., live), rather than by letter is advised.
Further, the importance of the Family Treatment Unit being
willing to maintain contact with the agency to whom the
family has been referred is also stressed, in that it
produces more willingness on the receiving agency's part
to deal and accept difficult patients. Several case
vignettes are presented.

432.   Follette, W.T., and Cummings, N.A.,
       Psychiatric services and medical
       utilization in a prepaid health plan
       setting, Medical Care, 1967, 5, 25-35.

433.   Follingstad, D.R., et al., Prediction of
       self-actualization in male participants
       in a group conducted by female leaders,
       Journal of Clinical Psychology, 1976, 32,
       706-712.

This study attempted to predict which male Ss would reflect
higher self-actualization scores after participation in a
16-hour marathon group conducted by a female leader team.
Twenty-five male undergraduates were assigned randomly to
one of two marathon groups or to a no-treatment control
group. The same female leader team conducted both groups
according to the same treatment format. The three predictor scales measured authoritarianism, attitudes toward
women, and need for social approval. Participants who
showed the highest self-actualization scores at the posttest and at the follow-up rated the group more effective,
scored lower in authoritarianism, and held greater agreement with profeminist attitudes. (Journal abstract).

434.   Fontane, A.S., Using family of origin
       material in short-term marriage counseling,
       Social Casework, 1979, 60, 529-537.

The use of historical material can be a helpful tool in
planned short-term marital counseling. Discussion of
family origin material is helpful because much important
material of a high degree of relevance to the present
marriage is readily accessible and less threatening than

direct discussion of some of the individuals' own fears
and pain. Relatively easy insights - making connections
between the parents' marriages and the present marriage -
result from these discussions, which gives the couples a
feeling of achievement. These insights are often general-
izable to other areas of marital conflict, and most
importantly, clarify that one's parents were people, not
just parents. This emotional understanding furthers the
separation-individuation growth processes of the partners
and renders them capable of relating together on a more
mature basis. (Journal summary).

435.   Forer, B., The therapeutic value of crisis,
        Psychological Reports, 1963, 13, 275-281.

The experience of crisis is an inevitable occurrence among
persons and groups. The process of living imposes
biological and social pressures which challenge old forms
of adaptations and necessitate psychological changes.
While the experience of personal crisis is painful, it is
essential to growth and represents both a condition of
vulnerability and the opportunity for rapid psychological
change for better or worse. An initial attempt to formulate
a psychology of crisis in terms of psychological structure
and therapeutic resolutions envisages three levels of
crises. (1) situational crises: significant disruptions
in the adaptation of a fairly effective person because of
a change in his situation; (2) crises in secondary
narcissism: disequilibrium in the form or adequacy of
the compromise between the ego and internal standards
(superego); (3) crises in primary narcissism: weakening
in the integration within the ego. Psychotherapy, like
life, can be considered a succession of instigations and
resolutions of crises with the goal of orienting clients
to seek new and varied experiences that will enable them
to change and grow. (Journal Abstract).

436.   Forizs, L., Brief intensive group-
        psychotherapy for the treatment of
        alcoholics, Psychiatric Quarterly,
        1955, 29, 43-70.

The author summarizes the work with over 1,600 patients at
the Rehabilitation Center of the North Carolina Program.

A total of 60 beds are available for a 28 day voluntary
inpatient group therapy program. Patients arrive after a
period of detoxification, and the focus of the treatment
includes physical rebuilding, education, and psychotherapy.
The advantages of group versus individual therapy are
discussed, the use of films as catalysts for group discussion is reviewed, and the encouragement of acting out
verbally in a group while sober, material that would
normally come out when intoxicated is detailed. Such a
combination of methods and the use of professionals from
a number of different disciplines enhances the positive
outcome of treatment.

437.   Foulds, et al., Marathon group: A six
        month follow-up, Journal of College
        Student Personnel, 1970, 11, 426-431.

438.   Fox, R.P., Post-combat adaptational
        problems, Compresensive Psychiatry,
        1972, 13, 435-443.

This article focusses on the types of psychological
problems encountered by returning Viet Nam American
Veterans, and a brief therapy program designed to aid them
in the transition. A total of 34 patients were seen in
brief therapy, out of a total of 106 who had been referred.
None had exhibited any previous need for psychiatric help.
Their presenting symptoms included varying combinations of
anxiety, depression, insomnia, nightmares, disciplinary
problems with the Marine Corps, and family and marital
difficulties. The treatment focus was on recent experiences and current problems in adjusting to daily life.
The short-term individual therapy lasted from 3-20 sessions,
with rapid symptom resolution during that time for almost
all of the patients. Issues raised included problems in
handling feelings of guilt, fear, or grief, as well as
anger, and fears about its expression leading to possibly
violent behavior.

439.   Fox, S.S., and Scherly, D.J., Crisis
        intervention with victims of rape, Social
        Work, 1972, 17, 37-42.

The authors report on findings related to the phases or
stages of psychological reaction to being raped. Their
work was based on working with 13 young unmarried adult
females, all of whom had exhibited previous psychological
health and records of achievement, prior to being raped.
The initial phase, acute reaction, involved emotional reactions of shock, disbelief, dismay, followed by anxiety/
fear. The importance during phase I of getting the
victim to talk about the rape is stressed by the authors.
Such things as issues of medical attention, legal service,
police involvement, notification of relatives and/or
friends, various practical items, and the sensitive reactions of the crisis worker to the emotional reactions of
the victims are all discussed, with specific practical
information provided. Phase II involves an outward adjustment, during which normal activities are resumed. During
this period victims usually speak infrequently of the rape,
and the authors encourage this shift, rather than probing
too deeply. This is followed by phase III, a period of
integration. Individuals report feeling depressed, and
have a desire to talk. The precipitants of this phase are
discussed, along with practical suggestions for crisis
workers in dealing with these issues. The critical tasks
involve working through the victim's feelings about herself
and her feelings about her attacker. The authors also
provide practical suggestions for workers who are contacted
by a rape victim for the first time who is already in phase
II or phase III.

440.   Foxx, R.M., and Azrin, N.H., Dry pants:
        A rapid method of toilet training children,
        Behaviour Research and Therapy, 1973, 11,
        435-442.

Toilet training sometimes requires considerable time. An
intensive learning procedure was devised for shortening
this training time and tested with 34 children who were
experiencing toilet training problems. The procedure had
the following major characteristics: (1) a distraction-
free environment, (2) an increased frequency of urination

by increased fluid intake, (3) continuous practice and
reinforcement of the necessary dressing skills, (4) continuous practice and reinforcement in approaching the
toilet (5) detailed and continuing instruction for each
act required in toileting (6) gradual elimination of the
need for reminders to toilet, (7) immediate detection of
accidents (8) a period of required practice in toilet-
approach after accidents as well as (9) negative reinforcement for the accident, (10) immediate detection of correct
toileting (11) immediacy of reinforcement for correct
toileting, (12) a multiple reinforcement system including
imagined social benefits as well as actual praise, hugging
and sweets, (13) continuing reinforcement for having dry
pants, (14) learning by imitation, (15) gradual reduction
of the need for immediate reinforcement and (16) post-
training attention to cleanliness. All 34 children were
trained and in an average of 4 hr; children over 26 months
old required an average of 2 hr of training. After
training, accidents decreased to a near-zero level and
remained near zero during 4 months of follow-up. The
results suggest that virtually all healthy children who
have reached 20 months of age can be toilet trained and
within a few hours. (Journal abstract summary).

441.   France, K., Evaluation of lay volunteer
        crisis telephone workers, American Journal
        of Community Psychology, 1975, 3, 197-220.

Evidence of how well lay vonunteer crisis telephone workers
are performing the three predominate roles expected of them
is reviewed. Present research suggests that trained nonprofessionals can function as helping persons, but their
effectiveness as referral agents and as technique-equipped
behavior changers is questionable. Current research needs
in the evaluation of lay volunteers are discussed in terms
of performance and evaluative procedures. (Journal
abstract).

442.   France, K., Crisis service paraprofessional:
        Expectations, evaluations, and training,
        Crisis Intervention, 1977, 8, 2-18.

443.   Frank, J.D., Treatment of the focal
        symptom: An adaptational approach,
        American Journal of Psychotherapy,
        1966, 20, 564-575.

A psychotherapeutic viewpoint has been presented that
focuses on the adaptive functions of focal symptoms. They
are viewed as more or less disguised efforts to express
certain feelings toward other persons and gain certain
responses from them. They are perpetuated primarily by
the fact that neither the patient nor the others involved
can read their meanings correctly. The goal of therapy is
to help the patient to clarify his feelings and find more
effective ways of expressing them. This requires that
therapy be focused on the patient's current transactions
with others rather than on the origins of his difficulties.
Although this therapeutic approach is not applicable to all
patients and had modest goals, it often obtains results
that compare favorably with those of more prolonged and
ambitious forms of treatment. (Journal summary).

444.   Frank, J.D., The influence of patients'
        and therapists' expectations on the
        outcome of psychotherapy, British Journal
        of Medical Psychology, 1968, 41, 349-356.

Frank reviews studies concerned with the relations of
patients' expectations to therapeutic outcome. Research
on the placebo effect has generated data suggesting that
patient response is more a function of the interaction
between his momentary state and immediate situationsl
variables (including physician expectations) than of
personality traits. A more promising approach than
placebo response studies to an investigation of expectations in relation to therapeutic outcome lies in the
direct observation and experimental manipulation of
patients' expectations. Results of such studies (conducted
by the author and othes) are presented and discussed.
Frank concludes with several tentative generalizations
which follow from his concise review of this complex issue.
(abstract by Deborah Schuller).

445.   Frank, J.D., Psychotherapy: The
        restoration of morale, American Journal
        of Psychiatry, 1974, 131, 271-274.

The author suggests that the primary function of all
psychotherapies is to combat demoralization - which
aggravates and is aggravated by psychiatric symptoms -
through restoring the patient's sense of mastery. All
psychotherapeutic rationales and rituals perform this
function despite differences in content. The author
reviews the evidence consistent with this hypothesis,
pointing out the potential implications for classification
of candidates for therapy and for research on sources on
the therapist's healing powers. (Journal abstract).

446.   Frank, J.D., Therapeutic components of
        psychotherapy: A 25 year progress
        report of research, Journal of Nervous
        and Mental Disease, 1974, 159, 325-342.

This paper summarizes the experiments of the John Hopkins
Psychotherapy Research Unit on brief psychotherapy of
psychiatric outpatients. Major findings were that the
beneficial results of psychotherapy include two components,
activation of patients' expectations and learning of social
skills; that psychiatric outpatients showed a marked
decrease of symptoms in response to placebo, the degree
of response depending on the interaction between the
patient's momentary state at a particular time and the
situation; that an interview preparing patients for
therapy led to more appropriate behavior in therapy and
greater clinical improvement; that emotional arousal by
inhalation of ether or adrenalin increases attitude change
in response to the therapist's suggestions; that therapeutic improvement which the patient attributes to his own
efforts is more enduring than that attributed to a pill;
and that there is a significant interaction between
whether a patient sees himself as controlled by or in
control of his environment and his response to these therapeutic conditions. Data are summarized concerning factors
related to these therapeutic conditions. Data are summarized concerning factors related to remaining treatment and
to short term improvement. Aspects of the long term course
of psychiatric outpatients revealed by 5-and 10-year
follow-up studies are reviewed. (Journal abstract).

447.   Frank, J.D., et al., Why patients leave
        psychotherapy, Archives of Neurology and
        Psychiatry, 1957, 77, 283-299.

Study of the 91 psychiatric outpatients, in conjunction
with a review of relevant literature, leads to the following tentative generalizations with respect to factors
determining whether or not a patient will stay in psychotherapy.
Attributes of the patient which are positively related to
remaining in treatment are class, education, and occupation,
fluctuating illness with manifest anxiety, readiness to
communicate distress and personal liabilities, influence-
ability, social integrity, and perseverance. With respect
to the treatment situation, its relation to the patient's
life situation, aspects of treatment itself, and attributes
of the therapist influence whether or not a patient will
stay. Some of the factors which determine whether a
patient will remain in treatment may differ from those
determining whether improvement in patients who do remain.
(Journal summary).

448.   Frank, J.D., et al., Patient's expectancies
        and relearning as factors determining
        improvement in psychotherapy, in, Stollak,
        G.E., et al., (eds.), Psychotherapy research:
        Selected readings, Chicago, Rand McNally &
        Co., 1966.

449.   Frank, J.D., et al., The effective ingredients
        of successful psychotherapy, New York, Brunner/
        Mazel, 1978.

450.   Frankel, A.S., Treatment of multisymptomatic
        phobic by a self-directed, self-reinforced
        imagery technique: A case study, Journal
        of Abnormal Psychology, 1970, 76, 496-499.

The treatment of a woman with disabling fears of earthquakes, sexuality, and enclosed places is reported. The
treatment was a variation of implosive therapy in which the
client was encouraged to imagine herself experiencing

sequences of images involving her fears. The imagery
sequence ended only when she imagined the feared experience
terminating. A 6-mo. follow-up found her functioning
without any of the fears she reported in treatment and
without the occurrence of any new fears. (Journal
abstract).

    451.   Frankel, A.S., Implosive therapy: a
                critical review, Psychotherapy: Theory,
                Research, and Practice, 1972, 9, 251-255.

Noting the paucity of well-controlled studies of implosive
therapy, Frankel reviews IT research literature and discusses some difficulties which exist. Problems of selection
and definition of "phobic" subjects (e.g. usually college
students admitting to a fear of snakes or spiders) lead to
questions about the validity of analogue studies. The
variable of the therapist (training and performance) has
not been sufficiently measured; and frequently experimenter
bias has not been adequately controlled. Conceptual and
methodological ambiguities are evident in IT data which can
more plausibly be explained by factors other than the
specific effectiveness of the technique. A final problem
area examined by Frankel is the potential of covert sensitization to create conditioned avoidance responses to
formerly neutral stimuli. The author briefly discusses a
variation of IT, developed in part to minimize the possibility of creating new phobias. (abstract by Deboral
Schuller).

    452.   Frankel, F.H., The effects of brief
                hypnotherapy in a series of psychosomatic
                problems, Psychotherapy and Psychosomatics,
                1973, 22, 269-275.

The use of hypnosis on its own or in association with other
treatment procedures produced improvement, subjectively
and/or objectively, in 17 of a series of 50 patients
suffering from a variety of psychosomatic problems. All 50
patients were tested for trance capacity. When this was
present to any reasonable degree, the patients were immediately instructed in how to induce the trance themselves

and, thereby, achieve muscular relaxation and altered
perception in the various organ systems. They were told
to exercise three or four times per day for a few minutes.
The 17 successful patients were interviewed for a total of
one to six times. Patients able to experience and induce
the trance state also gained in self-confidence and
optimism. (Journal abstract).

453.   Frankel, F.H., Hypnosis: Trance as a
        coping mechanism, New York, Plenum
        Publishing, 1976.

454.   Frankel, F.H., Chafetz, M.E., and Blane,
        H.T., Treatment of psychosocial crises
        in the emergency service of a general
        hospital, Journal of the American Medical
        Association, 1966, 195, 626-628.

Emergency facilities in metropolitan general hospitals
have been facing increasing demands in recent years with
a corresponding increase in the number of patients with
psychosocial crises. A flexible and multidisciplinary
approach to these problems is considered to be the most
effective means of handling them and of applying principles
of crisis intervention. The ranks of the flexible and
assiduous practicing general psychiatrists are the
obviously desirable sources of the senior personnel required. (Journal abstract).

455.   Frankl, V.E., Paradoxical intention, a
        logotherapeutic technique, American
        Journal of Psychotherapy, 1960, 14,
        520-535.

In the frame of Logotherapy of Existential Analysis
(Existenzanalyse), a specific technique has been developed
to handle obsessive, compulsive, and phobic conditions.
This procedure, called Paradoxical Intention, is based on
the fact that a certain amount of pathogenesis in phobias
and obsessive-compulsive neuroses is due to the increase
of anxieties and compulsions that is caused by the

endeavour to avoid or fight them. Paradoxical Intention consists in a reversal of the patient's attitude toward his symptom, and enables him to detach himself from his neurosis. This technique mobilizes what is called in Logotherapeutic terms the Psychonoetic Antagonism, i.e., the specifically human capacity for self-detachment. Paradoxical Intention lends itself particularly as a useful tool in short-term therapy, especially in cases with an underlying anticipatory anxiety mechanism. (Journal summary).

456.   Frankl, V.E., Logotherapy and esistential analysis, a review, American Journal of Psychotherapy, 1966, 20, 252-260.

According to existential analysis (Existenzanalyse) which underlies logotherapy, there are two specifically human phenomena, the "capacity of self-transcendence" and the "capacity of self-detachment." They are mobilized by two logotherapeutic techniques, "de-reflection" and "paradoxical intention," respectively. Both lend themselves particularly to the short-term treatment of sexual as well as obsessive-compulsive and phobic neuroses, especially in cases in which the anticipatory anxiety mechanism is involved. It is the contention of some authors that in existential psychiatry, logotherapy is the only school which has evolved psychotherapeutic techniques. (Journal abstract).

457.   Frankl, V., Paradoxical intention and dereflection, Psychotherapy: Theory, Research, and Practice, 1975, 12, 226-237.

This article contains a series of clinical vignettes gathered from a number of different therapists all of whom used the techniques of paradoxical intention and dereflection. Examples of the successful use of such techniques in brief therapy cover phobias, obsessions and compulsions, and neurotic sexual difficulties. The relationship between these techniques and those of other therapy approaches (e.g., flooding, implosion, anxiety-provoking, etc.) is also explored, and parallels drawn.

458.   Frazier, S.H., The status of brief
        psychotherapy, American Journal of
        Psychiatry, 1965, 122, 205.

In this very short article, Frazier comments on the
increasing importance of brief therapy as a treatment
vehicle. He notes that empiric studies continue to afford
greater precision in the application of specific brief
techniques and prediction of outcome. He affirms that
increased diagnostic understanding and the ability to
formulate a plan of therapy lead naturally to the administration of treatment--whatever the specific format.
Frazier contends that the range of problems and types of
patients for which brief therapy is effective will be
determined through experimental learning. (abstract by
Deborah Schuller).

459.   Frederick, C., and Farberow, N., Group
        psychotherapy with suicidal persons:
        Comparison with standard group methods,
        International Journal of Social Psychiatry,
        1970, 2, 103-111.

The authors present a conceptual model for viewing the
structures and aims, of therapy groups. They categorize
group methods into: a) special problem groups (e.g.,
suicide attempters, stutterers, physically handicapped,
etc.); b) discussion groups (e.g., Alcoholics Anonymous
meetings, etc.); d) insight-oriented groups (various
analytic groups, sensitivity training, etc.). The similarities and differences across these types of groups are
presented and discussed. Items singled out include age of
members, sex, diagnostic mix within the group, therapist
age, training, and method of functioning, and the specific
techniques, including the amount of time the groups meet.
Special problem and discussion groups are seen as
essentially short-term in nature, while insight-oriented
groups tend to be long-term. The value of a group therapy
approach for self-destructive individuals is also discussed.

460.   Freed, H., Narcosynthesis for the civilian
        neurosis, Psychiatric Quarterly, 1944, 20,
        54-55.

Reports on the use of barbiturates to induce narcosis and
thus decrease the length of psychotherapy. A total of 12
patients were involved. The results point to the production of strong affect, which aids in the shortened treatment. The synthesis of memories, fantasies, and ideational
material is critical. The resistances must also be
confronted in the patient in an active way.

461.   Freedman, D.R., Counseling engaged couples
        in small groups, Social Work, 1965, 10,
        36-42.

The author reports on an on-going service for self-referred
engaged couples. A short-term (6-10 session) Slavson-
oriented group approach was used. No specific evaluation
measures were used, but clients reported positive sense
from the experience. Some screening was done in order to
form the groups, and specific focus for discussion was
decided upon.

462.   Freud, S., (1893-1895), Katharina
        (Standard Edition, Vol. 2), Studies
        in hysteria, London, Hogarth Press, 1955.

This is a case presentation by Sigmund Freud in which the
treatment lasted only a few hours. The patient, Katharina,
a female patient in her late teens, was suffering from
fears related to facing the world of sexuality for the
first time.

463.   Freudenberger, H.J., New psychotherapy
        approaches with teenagers in a new world,
        Psychotherapy: Theory, Research and
        Practice, 1971, 8, 38-43.

The author presents his personal experienced in setting up
and running a free clinic for teenagers (The St. Mark's
Free Clinic) in the East Village of New York City. The

changes necessary in providing counseling services to an
adolescent population are reviewed, including the need for
short-term approaches. The range of reasons that teens
seek help at the clinic is summarized, along with a
number of examples.

464.   Friedman, D.E., A new technique for the
        systematic desensitization of phobic
        patients, Behaviour Research and Therapy,
        1966, 4, 139-140.

A desensitizing technique is described using methohexitone
sodium in 25 cases of phobic anxiety. No untoward effects
were encountered and preliminary results have been
extremely encouraging. (Journal summary).

465.   Friedman, D.E., et al., Treatment of
        phobic patients by systematic desensi-
        tization, Lancet, 1967, 1, 470-472.

Twenty phobic patients were treated by a new technique of
systematic desensitization based on the use of intravenous
methohexitone sodium to produce relaxation and to counter
anxiety. At the end of treatment all patients showed
striking improvement. By the time of follow-up, at least
6 months after the end of the treatment, 15 of the 18
patients who were re-examined continued to show striking
improvement. The results compare favourably with those
achieved by other workers using different methods. Moreover, the new technique is more economical in terms of
treatment-time; and it has certain theoretical advantages
over other treatments. On the basis of these results
systematic desensitization using methohexitone sodium is
suggested as the treatment of choice for phobic symptoms.
(Journal summary).

466.   Friedman, D.E., A synthetic approach to
        the treatment of anxiety, Psychiatry,
        1972, 35, 336-344.

The author emphasizes the value of brief therapy in which
both behavior therapy and dynamic brief therapy approaches
are used. Specific psychoanalytic techniques are used in

the initial stages (e.g., free association; dream interpretation; interpretation of transference). Systematic
desensitization is also used in focussing on the symptom
of anxiety, so that a two pronged approach aimed at
alleviation of the symptom and an understanding of its
meaning is accomplished. Examples of such an approach in
discussion form are presented for agoraphobic-claustro-
phobic syndrome and frigidity.

467.   Friedman, H.J., Patient expectancy and
        symptom reduction, Archives of General
        Psychiatry, 1963, 9, 61-67.

A group of 43 predominantly neurotic, psychiatric American
and English outpatients were studied. Patients reporting
marked relief of discomfort tended to have high levels of
expectancy significantly more often than did those reporting little improvement; the partial correlation coefficient
between expected and reported reduction of symptom intensity was at the level of significance (0.05); reduction
in reported symptom intensity occurred significantly more
often when a reduction was expected than when it was not
expected. Symptoms commonly associated with anxiety and
depressive states were most affected by the patient's
expectations that they would be helped. These findings
suggest that expectancy of help is activated at the first
patient-physician contact and may be an important determinant of symptom reduction in neurotic outpatients.

468.   Friedman, I., et al., Changes in
        symptomatology associated with short-
        term psychiatric hospitalization,
        Journal of Clinical Psychology, 1972,
        28, 385-390.

The authors reports on a research study in which the focus
was on the nature of symptomatology related to hospitalization, and how it changes over the course of hospitalization. The subject population consisted of 840 patients
who had been followed up over the course of their stay, an
average of 44 days. The predominant patient diagnostic
group were psychotics. The Brief Psychiatric Rating Scale,

a 16 item questionnaire was used to monitor changes in symptomatology. The results indicate that a brief hospitalization period does have a large effect on the rated level of patient symptomatology. The authors also report on some residual symptomatology in patients at discharge.

469.   Friedman, J.H., Short-term psychotherapy
        of "phobia of travel", American Journal
        of Psychotherapy, 1950, 4, 259-278.

The author reviews the findings of treating 50 patients (18 males, 32 females) all of whom were suffering from the fear of travel. Excluded from the population were those with a fear of travel by air or water. Included were those fearful of travel by subway, bus, street car, and the fear of leaving home. These patients, each seen in individual private therapy, were diagnosed as either obsessivecompulsive (N=11) or as suffering from anxiety neurosis (N=39). Many of them also exhibited other symptoms (e.g., conversion and hypochrondriacal symptoms), some of whom required further therapy for other difficulties. For most, there was no awareness of a specific precipitation event, although many did the cause to a previous frightening experience. Many case examples are provided to elucidate the unique treatment process of each patient. Techniques such as interpretation, persuasion, and suggestion were employed. The findings include: a) the longer a patient has been unable to travel via a particular vehicle, the worse the prognosis; b) good prognosis existed for those patients whose phobias has lasted less than a year prior to treatment; d) the age of onset of the phobia was not related to outcome measures; d) those patients who gained the most from treatment were those who required the least number of sessions. (Treatment lasting more than a year with two sessions/week had worse chance of positive outcome).

470.   Frings, J., What about brief services? -
        A report of a study of short-term cases,
        Social Casework, 1951, 32, 236-241.

The author reports on the results of a study of 349 cases receiving short-term treatment in an outpatient family agency. Requests for help ranged from interpersonal difficulties to financial problems (e.g., housing concerns, etc.). Most of the families were seen for a small number of sessions. The few families who continued to recontact the agency for help also gained. External judges' ratings on the sample were done to determine whether there was agreement between the original case worker's decision regarding the type of treatment offered and received versus an uninvolved clinical judgement. Reasons for agreement and disagreement between case worker and independent judge are presented and discussed. The implications for the training and practice of professionals doing brief therapy in a family agency are presented.

471.   Frohman, B.S., Brief psychotherapy,
        Philadelphia, Lea and Febiger, 1948.

472.   Fuerst, R.A., Problems of short time
        psychotherapy, American Journal of
        Orthopsychiatry, 1938, 8, 260-264.

In one of the earlier articles on short-term therapy, the author distinguishes between the suggestive therapies and those using an analytic base. It is the author's position that shorter therapies are effective for a limited type of psychological disturbances, and only produce temporary results. The types of pathology which are recommended for brief therapy are the hysterical types, as well as those patients for whom a longer psychoanalytic involvement is impossible either because of practical concerns or patient motivation. The author concludes by stressing the need for more specific short-term techniques and research to determine the limited value of such an approach in specific cases.

473.   Fulchiero, C.F., Evaluation of a
        therapeutic paradox technique in brief
        psychotherapy, Dissertation Abstracts
        International, 1976, 36, 8B, 4153.

474.   Galdston, R., and Hughes, M.C., Pediatric
        hospitalization as crisis intervention,
        American Journal of Psychiatry, 1972, 129,
        721-725.

The authors describe a follow-up clinic for pediatric
patients who have been hospitalized; an attempt is made to
transform the acute crisis of hospitalization into a therapeutic relationship aimed at ameliorating intrapsychic and
intra-family problems. This approach has been successful
both with patients with demonstrable organic disease and
those without such disease. (Journal abstract).

475.   Garfield, S.L., and Affleck, D.C., An
        appraisal of duration of stay in out-
        patient psychotherapy, Journal of Nervous
        and Mental Disease, 1959, 129, 492-498.

The authors present method and results of a study to determine possible variables associated with duration of stay
in an adult outpatient clinic. Closed cases (135) who
received a minimum of one therapeutic interview after the
intake procedure form the basis of this study. Number of
interviews was analysed for possible correlation with sex,
age, level of education, psychiatric diagnosis, and
previous psychiatric hospitalization of patient. Age was
the only variable to approach significance. Two further
analyses examined length of psychotherapy relative to
therapist ratings of improvement and to source of termination (i.e. patient- or therapist-initiated)--both as a
function of patients' previous psychiatric hospitalization.
Garfield and Affleck discuss their data, with particular
attention to factors which may account for some variance
between their findings and those of other studies. The
authors conclude that appraisal of the problem of reducing
drop-out rates is at least somewhat specific to the
individual clinic setting and its selection policies.
Further areas for research are suggested. (abstract by
Deborah Schuller).

476.   Garfield, S.L., and Kurtz, M., Evaluation
        of treatment and related procedures in
        1,216 cases referred to a mental hygiene
        clinic, Psychiatric Quarterly, 1952, 26,
        414-424.

The records of 1,216 cases referred to a V.A. mental
hygiene clinic were analyzed for purposes of appraising
treatment and related matters. Analysis of the data
revealed that 32 per cent of the persons referred were not
offered treatment for a variety of reasons. Of the remaining patients, 27 per cent refused to undertake treatment
although it was offered to them. An alysis of those
accepting treatment showed that the median length of treatment fell between six and seven interviews, with approximately two-thirds of the cases receiving less than 10
interviews. In almost two-thirds of the cases, the treatment was terminated by the veteran, himself. Evaluations
of treatment were provided by the therapist in only one-
quarter of the cases treated. Generally, improvement was
noted in over three-quarters of these cases. While there
was a tendency for a relatively greater frequency of
improvements to be related to length of treatment, over
one-half of the cases judged to be improved received less
than 10 interviews.

The foregoing results were discussed and compared with
comparable findings in other studies. Particularly noted,
was the rather high incidence of improvement with very
brief psychotherapy. The inadequacy of current evaluative
reports was discussed with particular emphasis on the
ambiguity and subjectivity of existing findings. The need
for more rigorous and meaningful appraisals of psychotherapy
was emphasized, along with some suggestions for improving
research efforts in this area. (Journal summary).

477.   Garner, H.H., A confrontation technique
        used in psychotherapy, American Journal
        of Psychotherapy, 1959, 13, 18-34.

This paper attempts to ground the use of a confrontation
technique in an internally consistent analytically-oriented
theoretical system. Orthodox analytic theory is reviewed,
particularly as they relate to issues of treatment procedures, impediments to improvement, invariable assumptions

in situation and treatment, and expected effects of
analytic therapy. The various modifications towards
greater therapist acitvity are also reviewed, with
reference to the work of Freud, Ferenczi, and Alexander
and French. Factors which motivate patients to seek
therapy are discussed, as are the reasons why poor adaptive
responses are difficult to change. The factors which make
for better adaptation and integration are also presented.
Within the context of such adaptive factors, the author
presents a procedure and rationale for a confrontation
technique, along with two case histories to illustrate the
technique. (abstract by Deborah Schuller).

478. Garner, H.H., A nascent somatic delusion
treated psychotherapeutically by confrontation technique, Journal of Clinical and
Experimental Psychopathology, 1959, 20,
135-143.

479. Garner, H.H., A confrontation technique
used in psychotherapy, Progress in
Psychotherapy, 1960, 5, 94-98.

The author presents a particular type of technique (confrontation) in the form of a specific type of question
directed to the patient ("What do you think of what I
said?") This question follows from any one of a number of
statements initially made by the therapist (prohibitive
statement, permissive statement, or adaptive statement).
A specific case example is presented, and the value of
such a technique discussed. One of the applications of
such an approach is in goal-limited therapy.

480. Garner, H.H., A confrontation technic
used in psychotherapy, Comprehensive
Psychiatry, 1960, 1, 201-211.

The author presents the theoretical background to and uses
of a confrontation therapy technique. It consists of the
presentation to a patient of a repeated statement, "What
do you think about what I told you?". It forces the

patient to continually re-evaluate his/her perceptions.
Basically three types of confrontation statement categories
listed: a) a prohibitive statement "You must never, under
any circumstances..." b) an expressive statement: "It
would be better if ..." d) an adaptive statement involving
a mature value orientation: "I want you to continue to work
at your job". Once a particular confrontation statement
is devised for a particular patient, it is repeated at
various times, followed by the initial question listed
about ("What do you think of what I just told you?"). The
author presents a number of different patients for whom
such a technique is appropriate, with case examples to
highlight each type.

481.   Garner, H,H,, Interventions in psycho-
        therapy and the confrontation interview,
        American Journal of Psychoanalysis, 1962,
        22, 47-58.

The various types of elements in the therapeutic communication process are reviewed. These include asking
questions, reassurance, advice, suggestions, clarification,
interpretation, persuasion, commanding, or forbidding, and
exclamations. The importance of understanding both verbal
and non-verbal aspects of therapeutic communications is
stressed. A discussion of the what, why, and how of
therapeutic intervention is presented. Specifically, the
use of a confrontation, problem-solving technique is
discussed, the main aim of which is to overcome resistance.
Various methods of wording statements are presented,
followed by the question: "What do you think of what I
told you?". Such an approach ultimately leads to an
integration on the part of the patient.

482.   Garner, H.H., Confrontation technique in
        psychotherapy: Some existential impli-
        cations, Journal of Existential Psychiatry,
        1962, 2, 393-408.

483. Garner, H.H., The confrontation technique,
      Current Psychiatric Therapies, 1963, 3,
      57-67.

Garner describes 10 types of interventions into which a
therapist's verbal and explicit expressions tend to fall:
questioning, reassurance, suggestion, clarification,
interpretation, persuasion/controlling statement, exclamations, cliches, and passivity. He notes three interpretive contexts through which the patient tends to view
the intervention: a) as the repetition of an earlier life
experience, with therapist as parent and patient as child;
b) as a relatively neutral exchange between equals, or,
c) as an educational effort aimed at increasing the
patient's facility for acquiring new information. The
author then outlines the technique and rationale of a
confrontation approach. Although it originally evolved
out of a psychoanalytically-oriented framework, this
technique can be used with a variety of therapeutic
approaches. This technique tends to focus the integrative
task for the patient, by inviting the patient to work out
a solution to his conflicts via the question: "What do
you think about what I told you?" The statement selected
usually highlights a critical area of conflict, and may be
classes as prohibitive, expressive or permissive, or
adaptive. Once the statement is formulated, it is repeatedly used throughout treatment. (abstract by Deborah
Schuller).

484. Garner, H.H., Brief psychotherapy,
      International Journal of Neuropsychiatry,
      1965, 1, 616-622.

485. Garner, H.H., Psychotherapy and the
      confrontation technique theory, British
      Journal of Medical Psychology, 1966, 39,
      131.

Garner seeks in the first half of this paper to extra-
polate a theoretic common ground for psychotherapy. He
discusses briefly basic principles shared by all the
psychotherapies, as articulated by Hoch (1955). The
author then summarizes central therapeutic principles and

effects as formulated by different schools--e.g. psychoanalytic, biodynamic, conditioning theories, perceptual
and learning theory, etc. In the latter portion, Garner
outlines theoretic and practical considerations of the
confrontation problem-solving technique. This technique,
applicable within a broad spectrum of therapeutic
approaches, evolved from within the framework of psychodynamically-oriented therapy. In developing reasons for
its efficacy, Garner initially examines factors which
contribute to the persistence of maladaptive responses;
then suggests nine factors contained within the confrontation technique which contribute to better integrated,
adaptive behaviors. (abstract by Deborah Schuller).

486.   Garner, H.H., The confrontation problem-
        solving technique: Developing a psycho-
        therapeutic focus, American Journal of
        Psychotherapy, 1970, 24, 27-48.

The author begins by defining the essence of the confrontation problem-solving approach in therapy. It consists
of the presentation of a statement by the therapist,
followed immediately by a question posed to the patient.
The initial therapist treatment is frequently designed to
stun or shock the patient, in an attempt to overcome
resistance. The therapist statement will vary according
to the unique characteristics and presenting style of the
patient. The therapist question which immediately follows
is usually phrased in the following terms: "What do you
think or feel about what I told you?" The statements by
the therapist are also designed to narrow the focus on the
session so that the patient/client can begin working on
something specific.Many examples of the types of confrontation statements which can be made are presented. The
question is designed to force the client to either explore,
affirm, or disprove the original statement and set of
assumptions which underlie the client's presentation of
him/herself. The importance of a working alliance with
the client is stressed within the context of the confrontation problem-solving approach.

487.   Garner, H.H., Brief psychotherapy and the
        confrontation approach, <u>Psychosomatics</u>,
        1970, 11, 319-325.

Garner describes how the confrontation technique can be
utilized by the non-specialist in brief psychotherapy
based on 10 minute sessions. After the initial history
and thorough evaluation, the physician outlines a specific
treatment arrangement with the patient. In succeeding
sessions, the physician practices selective inattention to
the patient's physical symptoms, and selective attention
to his present life events and emotionally disturbing
circumstances. Nine interventions which can be used in
the 10 minute visit are discussed. The remainder of the
article focusses on the problem-solving psychotherapy of
confrontation - the specific method and rationale, expected
patient reaction, and probable effect. The aim of this
approach is to highlight those fixed attitudes or maladaptive processes which have become largely habitual, and
through the confrontation to encourage the patient to re-
appraise them critically. (abstract by Deborah Schuller).

488.   Garner, H.H., <u>Psychotherapy: confron-
        tation problem-solving technique</u>, W.H.
        Green, St. Louis, Mo., 1970.

489.   Garner, H.H., The confrontation problem-
        solving technique: applicability to
        Adlerian psychotherapy, <u>Journal of
        Individual Psychology</u>, 1972, 28, 248-259.

Garner reviews essential elements of confrontation
technique and key principles of Individual Psychology;
then illustrates the applicability of confrontation to
Adlerian therapy. Emphasis on interpersonal versus intrapsychic components, the purposiveness of neuroses, and the
dynamics of inferiority-superiority are three aspects of
Individual Psychology described by the author. He discusses possible reactions of patient to therapist (i.e.,
compliance, non-compliance, or problem-solving through
critical appraisal); and then compares an Adlerian confrontation ("What would you do if you were well?") with his

specific technique of asking "What do you think and feel
about what I told you?". He notes that although the
Adlerian technique has similar implications, its use and
therapeutic value are different. In a final section, he
illustrates the use of confrontation within therapeutic
foci frequently chosen by Adlerian therapists. (abstract
by Deborah Schuller).

490.   Garner, H.H., and Waldman, I., The
        confrontation technique as used in the
        treatment of adolescent schizophrenia,
        American Journal of Psychotherapy, 1963,
        17, 240-253.

This article summarizes the confrontation technique and its
successful application in the treatment of an adolescent
schizophrenic breakdown. The technique fosters problem-
solving, and focusses on the uncovering, resolution, and
integration of the source of rage or anxiety which
frequently underlies the schizophrenic process. Confrontation consists of a strongly worded statement to the
patient, followed by the question: "What do you think of
what I told you?" This statement delineates a core
conflict or a critical precipitating factor in the acute
breakdown. The technique uses analytic concepts
(repression, transference, psychotic defenses). The focus
is maintained on selected areas of conflict, and is therefore amenable to research. A case history is detailed to
highlight the use and usefulness of the approach.
(abstract by Deborah Scbuller).

491.   Garrigan, J.J., and Bambrick, A.F., Short-
        term family therapy with emotionally dis-
        turbed children, Journal of Marriage and
        Family Counseling, 1975, 1, 379-385.

This report focusses on a brief treatment approach with
white, middle class intact families whose sons were
enrolled in classes for the emotionally disturbed. Variety
of methods used, including videotape, audiotape, role-
playing, etc. The results showed significant gains in
family adjustment, as reported by the parents, with the
teachers reporting no significant changes in the children's
behavior in the classroom.

492.   Gass, M., Comparison of time-limited and
        time-unlimited therapy related to self-
        concept change, adjustment change, problem
        resolution, and premature termination,
        Dissertation Abstracts International, 1975
        36, 75-20, 246.

493.   Gazda, G., and Ohlsen, M., The effects of
        short-term group counseling on prospective
        counselors, Personnel and Guidance Journal,
        1961, 39, 634-638.

Gazda and Ohlsen present method and results of a study to
assess the effects of short-term group counseling on
prospective counselors. Thirty-four subjects comprised
four experimental groups who met twice-weekly for one-hour
sessions over seven weeks. Strict statistical interpretation of results suggests that such counseling is generally
not effective in improving the emotional health of essentially normal individuals--although significant positive
changes in manifest needs were noted. The authors suggest,
however, on the basis of six- and fourteen-month follow-up
data, that a more optimistic conclusion is warranted when
trends in the data are examined in conjunction with clients'
impressions of the value of brief counseling. (abstract
by Deborah Schuller).

494.   Gazda, G.M., et al., The use of a modified
        marathon in conjunction with group
        counseling in short-term treatment of
        alcoholics, Rehabilitation Counseling
        Bulletin, 1971, 15, 97-105.

The addition of a modified marathon group counseling
experience to an ongoing counseling treatment approach in
the rehabilitation of alcoholics was described. Two
conclusions were drawn from the application of the modified
marathon to a short-term (in-patient) treatment center.
First, the modified marathon had the advantages of "holding"
alcoholics for treatment once they were sober; and secondly,

it enhanced the quality of typical group counseling and therapy treatment. In the short treatment time available, the counseling or therapy was intensified. Alcoholics had more opportunity for involvement in a rehabilitation program and more opportunity for positive behavioral changes. (Journal summary).

495.   Gelder, M.G., and Marks, I.M., Desensitization and phobias, a crossover study, British Journal of Psychiatry, 1968, 114, 323-328.

Of the 16 phobic patients who had group therapy in a previous investigation, 7 had not improved 6 months after treatment ended. These 7 patients were desensitized. On average, phonias improved about three times as much in the 4 months' desensitization as they had done in the previous two years. Changes in other symptoms were less striking. Another case received both group therapy and desensitization. Detailed assessment of the changes after each treatment showed that desensitization effected an immediate improvement on the phobias treated in the session. Although some of this was lost by the next week, this improvement accumulated gradually week by week and was significantly greater than that seen in group therapy. The findings are discussed in relation to the indications for desensitization. (Journal summary).

496.   Gelder, M.G., et al., Desensitization in the treatment of phobic states: A controlled inquiry, British Journal of Psychiatry, 1967, 113, 53-73.

A prospective trial is described of desensitization and two forms of psychotherapy is phonic patients. Sixteen received desensitization in imagination, 16 group psychotherapy and 10 individual psychotherapy. Groups were well matched on clinical and other variables. Desensitization lasted, on the average, 9 months. Individual psychotherapy was limited to a year, and group psychotherapy to 18 months. All treatments were carried out once a week. Results were compared over two years through treatment and follow-up.

Desensitization produced more patients whose symptoms improved at the end of treatment and follow-up. Symptoms improved faster with desensitization than with psychotherapy. After 6 months, desensitization patients had changed significantly more than others, but this difference diminished later, as patients in psychotherapy went on improving slowly. Greater and more rapid improvement occurred in work and leisure with desensitization. Desensitization and group therapy produced equal changes in relationships with other people, but with desensitization this occurred only after symptoms had changed, with group therapy it took place also in the absence of symptom change. There was no evidence for "symptom substitution". Patients who did badly with either treatment tended to be agrophobic, to be older at treatment, and to have more obsessional symptoms and more neurotic symptoms. Both treatments can contribute in different ways to the treatment of phobic patients; neither can be relied on for all patients, and some patients may need both. (Journal summary).

497.   Geller, J.A., Reaching the battering
        husband, Social Work with Groups, 1978,
        1, 27-37.

This paper presents a descriptive account of a social service project involving a new client population - battering husbands. The short-term group is the treatment of choice. The focus is on helping the group members acknowledge their spouse-directed violence as a problem and finds alternative methods for dealing with their anger. The paper describes this group process, presents a graphic picture of the battering husbands, and sheds light on the women and why they stay. Suggestions are made for offering viable service to this population as well as delineating area for exploration regarding spouse abuse. (Journal abstract).

498.   Gelso, C.J., et al., Exploration of a
        research program on time-limited therapy,
        Research Report #9-78, Counseling Center,
        University of Maryland, College Park, Md.,
        1978.

This research report presents in its entirety the symposium
of the same title given at the 86th Annual Convention of
the American Psychological Association. The report contains
four different investigations on various aspects of time-
limited counseling. Issues covered are: a) Comparison of
therapies of different durations: A long-term follow-up
study; b) must clients get what they expect: Expectancies
and satisfaction revisited; `c) The process of time-limited
therapy; and, d) Counselor expectancies and goals in time-
limited and time-unlimited therapy.

499.   Gendlin, E.T., and Shlien, J.M., Immediacy
        in time attitudes before and after time-
        limited psychotherapy, Journal of Clinical
        Psychology, 1961, 17, 69-72.

The authors used a time attitude questionnaire to measure
changes in reported immediacy of experiencing and success
in therapy. A total of 45 clients were used, in which a
time-limited, one-to-one Rogerian therapy approach was
offered. The results indicated that there were high
correlations between immediacy scores and success after
therapy, but not before.

500.   Gentry, D., Directive therapy techniques
        in the treatment of migraine headaches:
        A case study, Psychotherapy: Theory,
        Research and Practice, 1973, 10, 308-311.

Directive therapy techniques rooted in hypnosis and the
work of Milton Erickson were used to rid a 26-year old
female of migraine headaches. Gentry summarizes the goals
and course of each of the 11 one-hour, weekly sessions
which comprised the treatment. Therapy is focussed on the
woman's present circumstances and the functional use of
her symptoms to gain defining control in her relationship

with another person. According to the theory of directive
therapy, treatment success is due to the therapist's
gaining control of the patient's symptoms (including
resistance), thereby defeating the original purpose of
the symptomatic behavior. Twelve-month follow-up indicates
no return of the patient's headaches. (abstract by
Deborah Schuller).

501.   Gentry, D.L., The treatment of premature
        ejaculation through brief therapy,
        Psychotherapy: Theory, Research, and
        Practice, 1978, 15, 32-34.

Reports on the successful resolution of premature ejaculation in a 37-yr-old patient through brief therapy.
Treatment was based on communication and systems theory
and employed interventions specifically designed to bring
about rapid change in the symptomatic behavior. Treatment
emphasized behavioral change rather than intellectual
insight. (Journal abstract).

502.   Gershman, L., Case conference: A
        transvestite fantasy treated by thought-
        stopping, covert sensitization and
        aversive shock, Journal of Behavior
        Therapy and Experimental Psychiatry,
        1970, 1, 153-161.

The subject of this case conference is a 22-year-old
college senior with a transvestite fantasy whose origin
dated back to preschool days. It was successfully treated
in six sessions using the behavioral techniques of thought-
stopping, covert sensitization and aversive shock. Questions
concerning goals, procedures, timing of approaches, and
practical issues are discussed. (Journal abstract).

503.   Gerson, S., and Bassuk, E., Psychiatric
        emergencies; An overview, American
        Journal of Psychiatry, 1980, 137, 1-11.

The psychiatric emergency ward has become a primary entry
point into the network of mental health services for
people who need help coping with their problems of living.

It is also the only source of treatment for many
chronically ill patients living in the community. The
authors critically review the literature on emergency
psychiatric services, focusing on ways these services are
used, the atmosphere in the emergency room, and the determinants of disposition decision making. On the basis of
their research, they suggest a model for emergency services
that includes evaluation of the patient's and his or her
community's resources and competence and minimizes subtle
diagnostic considerations. (Journal abstract).

504.   Gerz, H.O., The treatment of the phobic
        and the obsessive-compulsive patient
        using paradoxical intention sec: Viktor
        Frankl, Journal of Neuropsychiatry, 1962,
        3, 375-387.

Characteristics of phobic neuroses are reviewed, including
stress on the anticipatory anxiety involved (e.g., fear of
panicking etc.), and the vicious cyclical aspects of such
anxiety. The underlying principles involved in paradoxical
intention are discussed. The patient is asked to provide
developmental information regarding his/her past history.
Then the therapist explains the principles of paradoxical
intention as well as presenting some case histories of past
successes in using the technique. The patient is instructed
to try and consciously make the symptom(s) worse. A number
of trials are tried in the office, or whereever the fear
expresses itself (e.g., at patient's home). The usual
number of therapy sessions varies with the severity of the
presentation symptoms and the duration of these symptoms.
Therapy last from 4-12 sessions for symptoms of shorter
duration, to 6-12 months for symptoms of longer duration.
The need to repeat the use of Paradoxical Intention is
stressed because the initial success may be followed by a
reappearance of the symptom due to the patient ceasing to
use Paradoxical Intention too early. The author recommends
the use of such a technique in the treatment of phobic and
obsessive-compulsive neuroses. Seven case examples are
provided. The approach is based on work with 24 phobic
and obsessive-compulsive patients, and this non-analytic
approach was highly successful in removing the symptomatic
behavior.

505. Gerz, H.O., Experience with the logotherapeutic technique of paradoxical
intention in the treatment of phobic
and obsessive-compulsive patients,
American Journal of Psychiatry, 1966,
123, 548-553.

The author reports that of 51 patients treated during a
6 year period by the logotherapeutic technique of paradoxical intention (which he describes, citing case
histories), almost 90% recovered or made considerable
improvement. He notes that the technique is intended to
supplement dynamic therapy, not replace it; drugs are also
often used. (Journal abstract).

506. Getz, W., et al., Fundamentals of crisis
counseling, Lexington, Mass., Heath, 1974.

507. Gilbert, A., An experient in brief
treatment of parents, Social Work, 1960,
5, 91-98.

The author reports on a combination of drug treatment and
supportive psychotherapy for the servicing of children
with behavior disorders. Spread over a period of 11 weeks,
five sessions each lasting 2.5-3.5 hours, were held.
Children were seen sparately while parents were also seen.
A total of 100 children and their families were involved.
Specific case material is offered to illustrate some of
the types of problems faced and the approaches used.
Measures of behavior at home and school were used as
indices of progress. Close to 80% of the children showed
some improvement, with about half of 100 showing marked
symptom decrease. A follow-up found the gains maintained.
The author stresses the use of a focal history taking
procedure and an active, specific helping approach.

508. Giles, S.L., Separate and combined effects
of biofeedback training and brief individual
psychotherapy in the treatment of gastro-
intestinal disorders, Dissertation Abstracts
International, 1978, 39(5-B). 2495.

509.   Gillis, J.S., and Jessor, R., Effects
        of brief psychotherapy on belief in
        internal control: An exploratory
        study, Psychotherapy: Theory, Research,
        and Practice, 1970, 7, 135-137.

The authors link an interpretation of psychological
maladjustment as alienation with the concept of internal-
external control. They hypothesized that successful
psychotherapy would imply a decreased sense of alienation,
or an increased belief in internal control. Method and
results of a study to assess this hypothesis are presented.
Subjects were 29 inpatients of a Veteran's Administration
hospital, of whom 13 received individual and/or group
therapy (for nine to eleven sessions) and 16 did not.
Results on an internal-external control inventory indicate
a significant shift in the direction of greater internal
control for the nine patients of the treatment group rated
as "improved" after therapy. (abstract by Deborah Schuller).

510.   Gillman, R.D., Brief psychotherapy:
        A psychoanalytic view, American Journal
        of Psychiatry, 1965, 122, 601-611.

The author presents concepts in brief psychotherapy from a
psychoanalytic perspective. A short historical view,
including early work by Freud, Fenichel, Alexander, Stone,
and others, is reviewed. The major principles of brief
analytic therapy are covered, which include a limited,
specific setting of goals, focus on the present, the use of
positive transference, high levels of motivation in the
patient, early interpretation of transference manifestations in the patients, and interpretation of feeling
regarding termination of treatment. Those chosen for such
an approach had reported seeing themselves as functioning
in a satisfactory manner prior to their difficulty, and in
whom the therapists viewed promoting regression in the
patient as counter-productive. In a discussion, the author
summarizes the work of a number of analysts who attempt to
explain and understand the changes that occur as a result
of brief contacts (terms used include spontaneous cures,
positive-adjustment promoting experiences, changes in

perceptual capacity, resumption of the learning process
etc.) Seven different cases are presented, in which the
author highlights both what was accomplished in each case
as well as what was not accomplished.

511.   Gitelson, M., The critical moment in
        psychotherapy, Bulletin of the Menninger
        Clinic, 1942, 6, 183-189.

A case history is presented of a young married woman who
had suffered a severe blow to her self-esteem, and had
been diagnosed as a schizophrenic psychotic by another
professional who had recommended that she be given shock
treatments. The author describes a total of nine psychotherapy interviews which resulted in marked improvement
without the need for ECT. A specific active approach,
involving the use of direct advice, making contact with
her in an equal-to-equal way, the release of anger and
resentment held in, the staying away from specifically
sensitive areas protected well by certain defenses, etc.
is detailed. The main aim of such an approach was to
rehabilitate the patient socially so that she would be able
to return to her previously postive and useful level of
functioning. A final follow-up report approximately one
year after therapy termination indicated that the patient
was maintaining her gains. The timing of various techniques, including suggestion, persuasion, or re-education,
is stressed in the article. The patient's role in this
critical timing involves his/her readiness for change.

512.   Glass, A.J., Principles of combat
        psychiatry, Military Medicine, 1955,
        117, 27-33.

The author elucidates certain operational principles of
field psychiatry. He examines the current view of the
etiology of psychological combat disorders, factors
determining symptomatic manifestations, and the suggestive
effects of terminology applied to psychiatric casualties.
He notes the essential purposiveness of non-effective
behavior, and how it is shaped by pressures from both the
combat situation and combat group. Three basic principles

are reviewed. Decentralization, which stresses bringing
psychiatry to the field, rather than evacuating casualties
to hospital facilities, has a number of demonstrated
advantages. Expectancy, which concerns the attitudes
displayed toward acute psychiatric casualties, must be
strongly oriented to recovery and return to duty. (The
author notes difficulties in such an orientation for
medical officers, particularly those away from the combat
zone). The necessity of brief, simplified methods of
treatment is the third principle. Despite the inherent
difficulty of treatment which must enable a person to
withstand conditions similar to those which disabled him,
some optimism may be warranted in that immediately prior
to breakdown, effective behavior was maintained. The
objective of brief therapy is thus the restoration of
previous competency. Techniques include ventilation,
suggestion, and reassurance, directed primarily toward the
present (combat) situation. (abstract by Deborah Schuller).

513.   Glasscote, R.M., et al., The psychiatric
        emergency - A study of patterns of
        service. Joint Information of the APA
        and the National Association for Mental
        Health, Washington, D.C., 1966.

514.   Glasscote, R., and Fishman, M.E.,
        Mental health on the campus: A field
        study, Washington, D.C., American
        Psychiatric Association, 1973.

515.   Glick, I.D., Short-term intensive
        psychiatric hospital treatment: Which
        treatment and for whom? Journal of
        the National Association of Private
        Psychiatric Hospitals, 1977, 9, 8-11.

516. Glick, I.D., et al., Short vs. long
hospitalization. A prospective
controlled study. I: The preliminary
results of a one year followup study of
schizophrenics, Archives of General
Psychiatry, 1974, 30, 363-369.

Although inpatient hospitalization ov very short duration
for schizophrenia is currently a widely prevalent treatment approach in the United States, there are few controlled studies of such treatment. Furthermore, there are
no controlled studies comparing short-term (21-28 days)
with long-term (90-120 days) inpatient treatment. This
study has been designed to try to answer, in part, the
following questions: What is the relative clinical cost-
effectiveness of short-term hospitalization as an alternative to long-term hospitalization for schizophrenic
patients in need of hospital care and for whom both types
of treatment are judged clinically feasible? (Journal
abstract).

517. Glick, I.D., et al., Short vs. long
hospitalization: A controlled study.
III: Inpatient results for non-
schizoprenics, Archives of General
Psychiatry, 1976, 33, 78-83.

A controlled, prospective, two-year follow-up study
examined the relative effectiveness of short-term vs.
long-term psychiatric hospitalization. Results of the
inpatient phase for a sample of 74 nonschicophrenic
patients are reported here. About four weeks after
admission the patients hospitalized for a short stay were
discharged, and at that time were functioning better than
the patients in the long-stay group. When the patients
hospitalized for a long stay were discharged, three to
four months after admission, they were then functioning as
well as, but not noticeably better than, the patients in
the short-stay group had been at their earlier time of
discharge. Patients with affective disorders were more
impaired at admission and improved more than patients with
other diagnoses, regardless of length of stay. (Journal
abstract).

518.   Glick, I.D., et al., Short vs. long
        hospitalization: A prospective
        controlled study. IV: One year follow-
        up for schizophrenic patients, American
        Journal of Psychiatry, 1976, 133, 509-514.

The authors compared treatments results for 141 schizophrenic patients randomly assigned to short-term or long-
term hospitalization. Test results indicated that the
long-term group was functioning significantly better one
year after admission according to global measures only.
The authors caution that the differences between the two
groups, although statistically reliable, were modest and
may have been confounded by the amount of psychotherapy
the patients received after hospitalization. Although
there appears to be a general advantage to the long-term
approach, further work will be needed to identify patient
subgroups for whom this more expensive treatment is cost
effective. (Journal abstract).

519.   Glick, I.D., et al., Short vs. long
        hospitalization: A prospective
        controlled study. V: One year follow-
        up results for nonschizophrenic patients,
        American Journal of Psychiatry, 1976,
        133, 515-517.

The authors studied the effect of long-term versus short-
term hospitalization on a group of 74 patients with the
diagnoses of affective disorder, neurosis and personality
disorder, and hysterical personality one year after their
admission to the hospital. Although they had found in an
earlier study that short-term patients seemed to integrate
more rapidly in the hospital, the results reported in this
study showed no statistically reliable differences between
the long-term and short-term groups. In contrast to the
authors' results for schizophrenic patients, their findings
for nonschizophrenic patients do not support extended
hospitalization. (Journal abstract).

520.   Glick, R.A., et al., (eds.), Psychiatric
        emergencies, New York, Grune and Stratton,
        1976.

521.   Glicken, M.D., A rational approach to
        short term counseling, Journal of
        Psychiatric Nursing and Mental Health
        Services, 1968, 6, 336-338.

The author offers some practical guidelines for the
practice of medical social work in a general hospital.
The problem of limited time in the hospital makes the
longer-term psychotherapy approach impractical. The
approach recommended and detailed is based on the rational
approach of Albert Ellis.

522.   Gliedman, L.H., et al., Reduction of
        symptoms by pharmacologically inert
        substances and by short-term psychotherapy,
        Archives of Neurology and Psychiatry, 1958,
        79, 345-351.

A total of five studies involving response to placebos in
psychiatric patients are reported. The similarity of
symptom reduction attained by this means and by short-term
psychotherapy is noted. The nature of symptoms relieved
is related to Beecher's concept of the "reaction or
processing component of suffering" (i.e., preponderance of
anxiety and depression in the reactor groups, as well as
the greater tendency for psychic symptoms to show relief
than for somatic ones). A few variables related to
placebo response are indicated. The complexity of the so-
called placebo effect in a psychiatric setting is elaborated. (Journal summary).

523.   Gluck, M.R., Psychological intervention
        with pre-school age plastic surgery
        patients and their families, Journal of
        Pediatric Psychology, 1977, 2, 23-25.

The clinical child psychologist has unique opportunities to
serve in pediatric health facilities. This is by virtue
of the psychologist's multifaceted background of developmental knowledge and clinical skills. This paper reports
2 clinical interventions relying on both clinical expertise
and familiarity with appropriate research data. The child

patients (4- and 5-yr old boys) and their parents were
provided with psychological support during crises in
their lives associated with massive reconstructive facial
surgery needed by the children. (Journal abstract).

524.   Godbole, A., and Falk, M., Confrontation-
        problem solving therapy in the treatment
        of confusion and delirious states,
        Gerontologist, 1972, 12, 151-154.

The need for brief psychotherapeutic interventions in the
treatment of physically ill patients is obvious, since
factors such as motivation for recovery, a capacity for
sensible care of the body, and willingness to cooperate
with the physician, as well as other psychological
functions, play a crucial role in recovery from illness.
The role of these factors in the production and perpetu-
ation of a clinical syndrome of delirium and confusion
and its management by confrontation-problem-solving
therapy (Garner) is discussed with three case studies.
This presentation is part of a more extensive study
carried out for evaluation of effectiveness of brief
psychotherapies in the treatment of emotional reactions
to physical illness. Developing similar but specific
methods of psychiatric treatment which can be used by a
general practitioner or an internist is clearly the future
need, if comprehensive treatment is to be the goal.
(Journal abstract).

525.   Godbole, A., and Verinis, J.S., Brief
        psychotherapy in the treatment of
        emotional disorders in physically ill
        geriatric patients, Gerontologist, 1974,
        14, 143-138.

A controlled study of the effectiveness of brief psychotherapy in the treatment of emotional reactions to acute
and chronic physical illness is attempted here. The
subjects included 61 aged and physically ill patients in
a short-term Rehabilitation Hospital. The results of the
study indicate statistically significant benefits in the

use of psychotherapy. To meet the particular needs of
these patients, "confrontation-problem-solving" technique
of psychotherapy is found to be especially effective,
although a more sophisticated and elborate study is
recommended. (Journal abstract).

526.   Goin, M., et al., Therapy congruent with
       class-linked expectations, Archives of
       General Psychiatry, 1965, 13, 133-137.

Two hundred and fifty applicants to the Psychiatric Outpatient Clinic of the Los Angeles County General Hospital
were given a questionnaire to learn what they hoped to
have in the way of treatment. 52% wanted to solve their
problems by talking about their feelings and past life.
Only 14% wanted medication and the remaining 34% wanted
advice. Of the 86 patients who wanted advice, 40 were in
our study and had the opporuntity to complete 10 sessions
designated as our treatment period. These 40 patients
were mainly from the lowest socioeconomic ranges wherein
the majority fell in class IV and V of Hollingshead's two-
factor indix. Only two patients fell in class III and
none were of classes I and II. Three-fourths of the
patients terminated therapy without notifying the doctor
after an average of 4 visits. The fact that 61% of our
patients expected ten or fewer visits might explain such
noncompletion of the 10 sessions. Of the patients given
advice, 72% reported improvement and of those given no
advice 57% said they had improved. Ten patients stayed
for 10 visits, 6 had been given congruent therapy and
four had been given noncongruent therapy, and all of these
individuals felt that they improved. (Journal summary).

527.   Golan, N., When is a client in crisis?
       Social Casework, 1969, 50, 389-394.

The author presents the assumption that the treatment of
clients when they are in crisis, provided the treatment is
rational and purposefully focussed, will be more effective
than a longer term treatment offered at a point far
removed timewise from the crisis precipitants. She
summarizes the four identifications of a crisis, including

the hazardous event, the vulnerable state, the precipitating factor, and the disequilibrium or state of active
crisis. The author also provides a detailed model for the
initial intake interview, using a crisis intervention base
for the structure of the interview.

528.   Golan, N., Short-term crisis intervention:
        An approach to serving children and their
        families, Child Welfare, 1971, 50 101-107.

With a focus on children and families, the author presents
a practical approach of using crisis intervention in a
selective way. The author focusses on two aspects of
crisis intervention, namely, how to identify elements of a
crisis, and how to translate these elements into methods
of producing change.

529.   Golan, N., Treatment in crisis situations,
        New York, The Free Press, 1978.

Written by one of the leaders in crisis intervention in
the field of social work, Dr. Golan's book provides an in-
depth overview of a wide variety of human experiences
which involve the element of stress and crisis. The text
includes a theoretical framework on crisis intervention,
broadly drawing from a number of mental health services
professions. This is followed by a series of chapters on
the practical aspects of providing such services, from
initial client contact to termination. The importance of
rapid assessment, active involvement, and the use of
community resources and support systems are all highlighted.
The final section of the book provides a detailed view of
three such crises, covering natural or man-made disasters,
developmental and transitional crises, and situational
crises. The book concludes with an overview and look at
the future, and an extensive current bibliography.

530.   Goldber, C., Termination - a meaningful
        pseudodilemma in psychotherapy, Psycho-
        therapy: Theory, Research, and Practice,
        1975, 12, 341-343.

In a general article about therapy and the issue of time,
the author states that he deals with the issue of termi-

nation as the major goal of therapy, and starts this focus from the very beginning of treatment. He suggests making the length of treatment explicit, not vague and uncertain. In essence, he states that the main goals of therapy are to deal with the realities of life, and one of the major realities of life is its finiteness. Therapy should reflect this aspect.

531. Golden. L.H., et al., Crisis intervention for cardiac outpatients, Medical Insight, 1972, 4, 18-23.

The authors present an overview of a program for helping the cardiac patient better adapt to his life situation. All the subjects were males who exhibited high levels of anxiety, hyper-reactivity to stress, excessive dependence on the physician, and various family difficulties. A multidisciplinary team was used and various aspects, from the physical issues involved to the psychological adaptation of each man were treated. Specific outcome measures included number of noncardiac complaints, sleeping patterns, appetite levels, cardiac concern on the part of the patient, and general measures of sense of health or illness. All measures showed positive improvement, and the staff felt that brief therapy of this nature was of major benefit. Indication for longer term therapy in specific cases was also noted.

532. Goldensohn, S.S., et al., The delivery of mental health services to children in a prepaid medical care program, American Journal of Psychiatry, 1971, 127, 1357-1362.

A New York prepaid group practice plan offered mental health services to children under 15 during a 24 month demonstration period. On an annualized rate basis, the psychiatric consultation rate was 12.6 per 1000 enrollees and the treatment start rate was 8.6 per 1000. The average number of services per patient during the first 12 months was 14.5. Among the children receiving treatment, 39 percent had another family member who was also in treatment. (Journal abstract).

533.   Goldfarb, A.I., and Sheps, J., Psychotherapy
        of the aged III. Brief therapy of inter-
        related psychological and somatic disorders,
        Psychosomatic Medicine, 1954, 16, 209-219.

This paper constitutes a preliminary report on the use of
a technique of brief psychotherapy in behavior disorders
of aged residents of a Home in whom the interrelation of
social and sexual maladjustments with somatic disease led
to a need for psychiatric treatment. In these patients
psychological factors and overreaction with fear and rage
complicated the diagnosis and treatment. The behavior
disorders in our patients appeared to be maladaptive efforts,
arising out of a sense of helplessness and fear, to gain
pleasure by dominance of parent surrogates. Therapy made
use of the patient's delegation of power to the psychiatrist
to prove an illusion that the latter was master and his
powers were available to them. Such a transaction was
pleasurable for the patient so long as the illusion was
maintained. In certain types of psychotherapy wherein the
psychiatrist may believe himself acting as a friendly advisor,
counselor, or supportive figure, the success of treatment
actually rests on the patient's secret and somewhat contemp-
tuous conviction that he has tricked and overpowered the
doctor. This conviction he masks for himself as well as the
doctor. Unless the doctor is endowed with a magical mantle
of power such a victory is hollow, meaningless and therapeutically valueless; the aged sick encountered here invari-
ably viewed the doctor as such a magical figure. (Journal
summary).

534.   Goldfarb, A.I., and Turner, H., Psycho-
        therapy of aged persons: II. Utilization
        and effectiveness of "brief" therapy,
        American Journal of Psychiatry, 1953, 109,
        916-921.

This article is a report on a study of brief supportive
therapy for 75 aged persons, ranging from 63-91 years in
age, with the majority between 80 and 90 years old. The
authors present a description of the deficits in homeostatic, sensory, effector, and cortical-integrative
functioning within this group. The psychological stages

in loss of self-esteem are also reported. The treatment
program consisted of brief, 15 minute sessions, spread
over a period variable period of time. The focus was on a
supportive, parent-child type of relationship, in which
the patients received emotional gratification for their
needs. The entire staff of the home for the aged where
the study was conducted were involved and informed of the
treatment process. A description of the operation of the
therapy approach is provided. The results of the study
are presented for various diagnostic categories in terms
of improved, stabilized, and unimproved ratings. The
treatment approach was relatively ineffective for those
patients diagnoses as psychotic, but highly effective for
a number of others.

535.   Goldsmith, W., and Zeitlin, M., Crisis
        therapy for disaster victims, Exchange,
        1973, 1, 3-7.

536.   Gomes-Schwartz, B., Effective ingredients
        in psychotherapy: Prediction of outcome
        from process variables, Journal of
        Consulting and Clinical Psychology, 1978,
        46, 1023-1035.

This study was designed to examine the impact of (a)
exploration of the psychodynamic roots of patients'
conflicts; (b) warmth and friendliness of the therapist
offered relationship, and (c) positiveness of patients'
attitudes toward working in therapy on the outcome of
brief therapy with 35 college males exhibiting symptoms of
depression, anxiety, and social introversion. Analyses of
process ratings for audiotaped segments from four sessions
through the course of therapy revealed that the activities
of therapists of differing theoretical orientations and of
professional versus untrained, "inherently helpful" therapists could be distinguished. Although patients' attitudes
toward the therapist and patient involvement in the
therapy process did not differ as a function of the type
of therapist, the process dimension that most consistently
predicted therapy outcome was patient involvement.
Exploratory processes and therapist-offered relationship
had a lesser influence on outcome. (Journal abstract).

537.   Gonen, J.Y., The use of psychodrama
        combined with videotape playback on an
        inpatient floor, Psychiatry, 1971, 34,
        198-213.

This is a report on the application of psychodrama and role-
playing to the treatment of short-term hospitalized patients
whose average length of stay was about three weeks. The
program involved one 1-hour session/week which all patients
were urged to attend and which was videotaped and shown to
patients on the TV screen four hours later. The TV camera
was introduced from the start as part of the overall technique, and it was located in the audience during each
session. A day later the videotape was shown to staff
members for comments and suggestions. As recommended by
Parish, immediately before each session staff members met to
plan the session. After each session a meeting was held to
discuss the results.

As the program progressed, a wealth of ideas and impressions
was accumulated by the participating staff members. These
impressions related to such diverse issues as the cultish
reputation of psychodrama, the therapeutic rationale of
this technique, group-centered and protagonist-centered
psychodrama, the effect of the videotape playback, the ease
with which patients with certain ego lacunae adopted and
discarded role and the ambivalent reaction of staff members
toward psychodrama. This report presents some of the conclusions reached by the staff. (Journal abstract).

538.   Goodstein, L.D., and Crites, J.O., Brief
        counseling with poor college risks,
        Journal of Counseling Psychology, 1961,
        8, 318-321.

The present study evaluated the effects of individual
vocational-educational counseling on the academic achievement of a group of probationery, low-ability college
freshmen. There were 19 students in the Counseled group,
7 in the Noncontacted Control group. After adjustments
were made by covariance techniques for differences in
intellectual ability between the three groups, the GPA
of the Noncontacted Control group was significantly higher

than that of the other two groups for successive summer
and fall semesters. These results were attributed to a
statistical artifact produced by the use of scores from
the extreme lower end of the college ability continuum.
There was no evidence that vocational-educational counseling, as it is usually conducted, leads to greater
academic achievement by low ability college students. The
implication of the findings were briefly discussed.
(Journal summary).

539.   Goolishian, H.A. A brief psychotherapy
        program for disturbed adolescents,
        American Journal of Orthopsychiatry,
        1962, 32, 142-148.

A family approach called Multiple Impact Brief Therapy is
presented in detail, based on the assumption that contained
within most families is the ability for rapid change based
on strengths of many of its members. The author summarizes
the preliminary findings of the work of the Youth Development Project of the University of Texas. The treatment
team, consisting of psychiatry, psychology, and social
work, works intensively with one family for a period of
2-3 days, 6-8 hours/day. The sequence of interviews
(individual, joint, overlapping etc.) and the aims of each
step of the structure are delineated. The ways in which
the major family dynamics are ascertained and shared with
teh family, and the methods by which specific new ways of
interacting are tried are presented. A few very short
cases are presented. The success of such an approach is
hinted, at, with a promise of future reporting of the
results of a more rigorous research outcome study. The
advantages of such an appraoch are included, encompassing
positive aspects for the families, therapists, and
therapists-in-training, who are also included as part of
the team.

540.   Gordon, R.H., Efficacy of a group crisis-
        counseling program for men who accompany
        women seeking abortion, American Journal of
        Community Psychology, 1978, 6, 239-246.

This study investigated the effect of a group crisis-
counseling session on the anxiety level and attitudes of

males who accompanied women seeking legal abortions.
Twenty-three companion males participated in one 2-hour
counseling session. Each session was comprised of three
to seven men. Twenty-three other men, who served as
control subjects, remained in the waiting room of the
abortion clinic and did not participate in a counseling
session. All subjects completed the Spielberger State-
Trait Anxiety Inventory (STAI) and four other attitudinal
measures based on the semantic differential. These were
filled out by all subjects when they first arrived at the
clinic and again approximately 2 hours later. Results
from both the STAI and the other attitudinal measures
indicated that State anxiety (A-State) decreased and
attitudes towards abortion concepts generally were more
positive for men in the group which received crisis
counseling. (Journal abstract).

541.   Gordon, R.H., and Kilpatrick, C.A.,
        A program of group counseling for men
        who accompany women seeking legal
        abortions, Community Mental Health
        Journal, 1977, 13, 291-295.

Counseling in legal abortions have previously focused only
on the women who seek such abortions and has neglected
their partners. A program of group counseling for these
men was developed at an abortion clinic. The program was
influenced by two major theoretical approaches: crisis
intervention and group psychotherapy. The purpose of this
paper is to propose a foundation for further similar
interventions by presenting the approach and conclusions
reached from developing the present program. (Journal
abstract).

542.   Gottschalk, L.A., Bibliotherapy as an
        adjuvant in psychotherapy, American
        Journal of Psychiatry, 1948, 104, 632-637.

The author describes a method of therapy which involves
the patient reading a selected type of book in order to
help with a given problem. The article describes how
such a procedure works, the types of patients who gain

from such an approach, subdivided into children and
adolescents, and adults. Specific case examples are
provided to further elucidate this approach. A representative bibliography suitable for such an approach is
provided.

543.   Gottschalk, L.A., An introductory
        outline of a short method of psycho-
        therapy, Journal of Nervous and
        Mental Disease, 1949, 110, 315-335.

In this detailed article, the author describes some of the
practical issues involved in shorter-term treatment
approaches. The article is meant for students in the
mental health field, and is not offered as a comprehensive
view, but one which covers a great many of the important
practical considerations. The author lists those patient
characteristics which have been found to relate to positive
outcome in brief therapy. A great deal of emphasis in this
article is placed on the assessment (initial interview)
phase of treatment. The nature of the presenting problem
and the patient's perception of this are critical.
History-taking is also detailed. The stages of formulation
of the dynamics of the situation and of feedback of this
information to the patient are explained, along with issues
of proper preparation of the patient for psychotherapy.
Methods of beginning interviews and of keeping them
running smoothly are offered, along with suggestions for
dealing effectively with emotional outbursts, resistance,
and dependency. Rules for making interpretations are
provided. This shift in therapist style from the first
interview to the middle stages and termination phases of
treatment is also discussed. Specific behavioristic
methods for extinguishing undesired behavior and for the
enhancement of desired behaviors are also presented. Such
information is tailored for students who are working with
minor personality disorders.

544.   Gottschalk, L.A., et al., Prediction and
        evaluation of outcome in an emergency
        brief psychotherapy clinic, Journal of
        Nervous and Mental Disease, 1967, 144,
        77-96.

This study reports the results of a preliminary project
involving a brief, emergency therapy clinic. A maximum of
six sessions, lasting between 25-50 minutes each were
offered. The details of the team structure and the
research instruments used are presented. Measures included
verbal behavior scales, a psychiatric morbidity scale, a
therapist attitude inventory, and a rating of social class.
Significant positive changes in a large percentage of the
patients were reported both immediately following termination of therapy and at a later follow-up point. The
more severely disturbed patients were still the more severe
at the end of therapy when compared with initially less-
severe patients, although the more severely disturbed
changed more during therapy. Lower class patients improved
more than upper class patients, and reasons for this were
presented. Therapists preferred those patients who
initially appeared less debilitated functionally, but no
significant relationship was found between how much a
therapist originally liked a patient and how much that
patient improved. A significantly higher drop-out rate
was found for younger patients.

545.   Gottschalk, L.A., et al., The Laguna
        Beach experiment as a community approach
        to family counselling for drug abuse
        problems in youth, Comprehensive Psychiatry,
        1970, 11, 226-234.

The authors describe the development of a drug abuse center
for youth and their parents--initial goals, professional
staff, setting, and general procedure. In the second year
of operation, format was altered to limit attendance at
each clinic session to groups of six families seen for
eight consecutive weekly sessions. Although no formal
records were kept, the authors present frequently noted
characteristics of the center's clients. A questionnaire

designed to evaluate effectiveness was submitted to 29
family members before and after the eight-week attendance
period. The findings are summarized. Gottschalk, et al.,
briefly review typical steps in group process, and conclude
with a general consideration of the value, limitations,
and feasibility of drug abuse centers for yours.
(abstract by Deborah Schuller).

546.   Gottschalk, L.A., et al., A study of
        prediction and outcome in a mental
        health crisis clinic, American Journal
        of Psychiatry, 1973, 130, 1107-1111.

Sixty-eight patients who came voluntarily to a crisis
intervention clinic were randomly assigned to one of two
groups. Those in the first group received immediate intervention therapy while those in the second group were put
on a waiting list. By the end of six weeks (and after
minor changes in the makeup of the groups were taken into
account) there was no significant difference in the psychiatric morbidity scores of the two groups; both had improved.
The authors used a variety of pretreatment and posttreatment measures and found that the best predictor of a
patient's condition at the end of six weeks was his pre-
treatment psychiatric morbidity score. The authors
conclude that individuals vary in both their reactions to
life crises and their therapeutic needs and that the
central issue may not be the recovery itself, but the
difficulty and pain with which it is achieved. (Journal
abstract).

547.   Gould, E., and Glick, I.D., The effects
        of family presence and brief family
        intervention on global outcome for
        hospitalized schizophrenic patients,
        Family Process, 1977, 16, 603-510.

The authors report a study which compared global outcome
measures for 141 schizophrenic inpatients by 1) presence
of a family, and 2) amount and/or kind of family intervention. Design, subjects, therapeutic setting, treatment
program, and evaluation instruments are described; and

results presented. The data suggest that the presence of
a patient's family during the period of hospitalization is
related to more functional, less symptomatic post-hospital
behavior. Although results are inconclusive, family
therapy in addition to family presence does not appear to
correlate with improved outcome. Gould and Glick briefly
compare their findings with other studies, and suggest
areas for further investigation. (abstract by Deborah
Schuller).

548.   Goz, R., Women patients and women
        therapists: Some issues that come up
        in therapy, International Journal of
        Psychoanalytic Psychotherapy, 1973, 2,
        298-319.

One emphasis of the current women's liberation movement is
in the notion that women should rely more on women rather
than on men. This idea, which is expressed by some women
patients who request women therapists, is used as a point
of departure for a discussion of some clinical instances
in which such a combination of patient and therapist may
have been particularly useful for the progress of treatment. It is important to stress that the advantages
accrued were specifically in the context of short-term
psychotherapy, with its limited goals, that may be
especially enhanced by distinctive attributes and activities
of the therapist. In long-term psychotherapy the sex of
the therapist is not necessarily an issue. Nevertheless,
this discussion is relevant in general to the oft-heard
statement, "This patient needs a woman therapist." The
problem of when a woman is contraindicated for a woman
patient is not discussed. (Journal abstract).

549.   Graham, S.R., Patient evaluation of the
        effectiveness of limited psychoanalytically-
        oriented psychotherapy, Psychological
        Reports, 1958, 4, 231-234.

96 adults who were neurotic or psychotic rated themselves,
and 44 children were rated by their parents on a 5-point
scale of improvement from worse to almost completely cured.
Reported degrees of improvement were not significantly

different from children evaluated by their parents and adults who evaluated themselves. Both adult neurotics and child neurotics reported statistically significant degrees of improvement as the number of hours in therapy increased whereas adult psychotics did not. Adult neurotics showed significant improvement when seen twice a week as compared with those who were seen only once a week. On the other hand, adult psychotics appeared to be worse off when seen twice a week as compared with those who were seen only once a week. It is therefore concluded that limited psychoanalytically-oriented therapy is an effective tool in an out-patient lcinic, although some reservations must be made as to its utility with psychotics. (Journal summary).

550.   Grayson, H., (ed.), Short-term approaches to psychotherapy, New York, Human Sciences Press, 1979.

551.   Grayson, R.S., The psychiatric emergency clinic: Implications for community mental health, in, Casework Papers, New York, Family Service Association of America, 1961.

552.   Greenbaum, C.W., et al., The military psychologist during wartime: A model based on action research and crisis intervention, Journal of Applied Behavioral Science, 1977, 13, 7-21.

This paper present a model for the application of organization development, action research, and group-oriented crisis intervention by field psychologists with army units during wartime. It is suggested that military social psychology must utilize all three approaches to gain maximum effectiveness. The model is based on experience gained by the Military Psychology Unit of the Israel Defence Forces before, during, and after the Yom Kippur War of 1973. The basic assumptions underlying the model suggest that the following factors improve the functioning

of the unit being served and promote the well-being of
the individual soldiers in it: reliable feedback on the
state of the unit to its officers; problem-related crisis
intervention by psychologists with soldiers and officers
related to experience in stress situations; and instruction
to officers on handling of problems concerning morals,
anxiety, and interpersonal relations. (Journal abstract).

553.   Greenberg, R., Anti-expectation techniques
        in psychotherapy, Psychotherapy: Theory,
        Research, and Practice, 1973, 10, 145-148.

Greenberg illustrates with two case examples a technique
which may be employed either to deal directly with symptoms,
or to circumvent resistance, thereby facilitating therapy
within any conceptual framework. Anti-expectation techniques consist of the therapist's aligning himself with a
resistant patient's negative comments, while echoing and
exaggerating those views which the patient expects the
therapist to refute or oppose. In his discussion, the
author stresses that anti-expectation techniques comprise
only one facet of therapy; that they do not substitute for
a thorough theoretical understanding of a case. Greenberg
employed these techniques only within the context of an
established therapeutic relationship, in which alternative
means of diminishing resistance had been tried; and when
he had appraised as unlikely the probability that such
techniques would precipitate harmful behaviors. The author
supports his contention that anti-expectation techniques
are consistent with ideas from a broad spectrum of psychotherapies. (abstract by Deborah Schuller).

554.   Greenblatt, M., et al., The prevention of
        hospitalization: Report on the Community
        Extension Service of the Massachusetts
        Mental Health Clinic, Boston, Mass., New
        York, Grune and Stratton, 1963.

555.   Greenspan, S.I., and Mannino, F.V., A
         model for brief intervention with couples
         based on projective identification,
         American Journal of Psychiatry, 1974, 131,
         1103-1106.

Projective identification is a mechanism that has been
described by many observers from different perspectives in
a variety of settings. It has been most frequently associated with rather disturbed families as an interpersonal
mechanism involved in distorted perceptions, identifications, and communication. The authors illustrate how
this mechanism manifests itself in couples with relatively
intact, although neurotic, personality organizations and
how it interferes with their capacity to resolve problems
and experience joint interpersonal growth. They suggest
that a short-term treatment approach with such couples may
usefully organize itself around the identification and
correction of perceptual distortions involved in projective
identification. (Journal abstract).

556.   Greenspan, S.I., et al., A psycho-
         dynamically oriented group training
         program for early childhood care givers,
         American Journal of Psychiatry, 1977,
         134, 1104-1108.

A training program for enhancing the care-giving qualities
of child-care workers was developed and implemented through
semistructured groups for family day-care mothers. The
authors describe the theoretical orientation, program
goals, and the outcome for trainees and trainers. Most
impressive was the group rocess and content, which indicated
the effectiveness of a psychodynamically oriented program
for care givers - people who ordinarily would not be
expected to integrate such an experience successfully. A
total of seven sessions were held. (Journal abstract
modified).

557.   Greist, J.H., et al., Running as a
        treatment for depression, Comprehensive
        Psychiatry, 1978, 20, 41-54.

This study describes the results of a program of running
as a treatment for depression as compared with both time-
limited psychotherapy and time-unlimited psychotherapy.
The results reported indicate that running was at least as
effective in the treatment of depression when compared to
time-limited and time-unlimited treatment, for the alleviation of the symptoms of depression. Some of the dangers
of an improperly managed running program as well as alternative interpretations of the results are discussed.

558.   Grimaldi, K.E., and Lichenstein, E., Hot,
        smoky air as an aversive stimulus in the
        treatment of smoking, Behaviour Research
        and Therapy, 1969, 7, 275-282.

Twenty-nine smokers were assigned to one of three groups:
contingent punishment, non-contingent punishment, and
attention-placebo. The contingent punishment group had
hot, smoky air blown in their faces as they smoked. The
non-contingent group had fresh air blown in their faces
while they smoked and received the hot, smoky air while
they were not smoking. The control group went through the
same procedures as the contingent group except that they
received no smoke. All Ss were seen for 7 treatment
sessions spaced over three weeks and were followed up one
month later. There were 10 trials (cigarettes) per session.
A three-way analysis of variance using the number of
cigarettes smoked before, during, and after treatment
showed a significant trials effect but no treatment effect
or trials X treatment interaction. A rise in smoking rates
was noted at follow-up period, but smoking rates were still
significantly lower than baseline. Trial duration and
ratings of trial unpleasantness were not related to treatment success. The results of this study considered with
previous use of aversive procedures indicates that contingent punishment is of limited value in the control of
smoking. (Journal summary).

559.   Grinker, R., Brief psychotherapy in war
         neuroses, Brief Psychotherapy Council
         Proceedings, 1944, 2, 6-19.

560.   Grinker, R.R., Brief psychotherapy in
         psychosomatic problems, Psychosomatic
         Medicine, 1947, 9, 98-103.

The author begins with a presentation of four major
theoretical formulations in the field of psychosomatic
medicine, which have not necessarily been borne out by
experience. More specifically, the results of work in this
field indicate the following conclusions: a) the amount
of stress is not significant in the development of
pathology and symptomatology (i.e., the amount needed to
produce breakdown will vary from individual to individual);
b) the type of stress that will produce such a deterioration
cannot be predicted for any given individual; 3) an acute
psychosomatic syndrome is not always the result of a single,
nonexpressed emotion or need; and d) changes in the tissue
morphology are not always related to time course of the
symptomatic process. Further, it has become clear that
the dysfunction is the result of the breakdown of normal
channels of emotional communication, and does not represent
the conflict itself. The author concludes with a case
example, illustrating the use of brief psychotherapy in the
treatment of a 22 year old serviceman, hospilized because
of severe attacks of abdominal pain and diarrhea.

561.   Grinker, R.R., and Speigel, J.P.,
         Management of neuropsychiatric
         casualties in the zone of combat,
         Manual of military neuropsychiatry,
         Philadelphia, W.B. Saunders, 1944.

562.   Grinker, R.R., and Spiegel, J.P., Brief
         psychotherapy in war neuroses, Psycho-
         somatic Medicine, 1944, 6, 123-131.

Among a number of techniques used, the authors detail the
use of narcoanalysis to help alleviate war neuroses.

Soldiers were able to relive their traumatic battle
experiences, and together with an explanation of the
behavior, were able to be restored to health. The intense
emotions were released under the influence of the drug and
under the control of the therapist.

563.   Gross, R.B., Supportive therapy for the
        depressed college student, Psychotherapy:
        Theory, Research, and Practice, 1968, 5,
        262-267.

This paper employes Hartman's notion of loss or impairment
of secondary ego automomy to examine the common and
difficult problem of depression in college students.   After
a brief description of theoretical considerations, Gross
examines orienting therapeutic concepts derived from
psychoanalytic ego-psychology: the dynamics of depression,
and the goals of supportive, anti-depressive therapy.   She
reviews Hollan's anti-depressive regimen for patients and
then adapts this short-term treatment for use with the
depressed student client - noting specific characteristics
of the initial contact and the nature of subsequent
sessions. Effectively, the therapist functions as the
client's ego until autonomy is restored. Frequent contact
and telephone access to the therapist are therefore
important. (abstract by Deborah Schuller).

564.   Gross, W.F., and DeRidder, L.M.,
        Significant movement in comparatively
        short-term counseling, Journal of
        Counseling Psychology, 1966, 13, 98-99.

The authors describe a short-term, one-to-one therapy
program for 8 clients, presenting problems ranging widely.
All clients were seen at a university counseling center,
with the mean age of the group being 19.2, and the total
number of sessions ranging from 7-18 (mean=10.1).   There
were four male clients, four female clients. Each client's
perception of his counselor's congruence, empathy, un-
conditionality and level of regard was obtained by a
relationship inventory. The Gendlin-Tomlinson Experiencing
Scale was also applied to taped excerpts from the second

and next to last interviews of each client to measure
amount of movement. (1) Significant movement in the predicted direction occurred in each client; (2) clients
whose EXP ratings were high early in counseling manifested
significantly more movement than those having low ratings;
(3) congruence, empathy, and unconditional regard correlated significantly with movement. Significant and
measureable movement of the kind described by Rogers does
take place in comparatively short-term counseling cases.
(Journal abstract and discussion adapted).

565.   Grotjahn, M., A survey of brief psycho-
        therapy research of the Institute for
        Psychoanalysis in Chicago, Proceedings
        of the Council for Research on Brief
        Psychotherapy, 1942.

566.   Grotjahn, M., Discussion remarks to
        Franz Alexander's: The evolution and
        present trend of psychoanalysis, 5th
        Volume, Proceedings of the First World
        Congress of Psychiatry, Paris, Hermann
        and Co., Editeurs, 1952.

567.   Gruen, W., Effects of brief psychotherapy
        during the hospitalization period on the
        recovery process in heart attacks,
        Journal of Consulting and Clinical
        Psychology, 1975, 43, 223-232.

Seventy patients with a first heart attack were randomized
into a treatment or a control group. Treated patients were
seen almost every day during hospitalization for psychotherapy to facilitate coping and to unearth psychological
resources and hidden strengths. Data collected ton all
patients showed the following significant differences in
favor of the treated: days in intensive care and in the
hospital; development of supraventricular arrhythmias and
congestive heart failure; nurses' observations of weakness;

physician report of depression; self-report of surgency;
social affection and vigor; presence of either extreme
anxiety or extreme lack of anxiety; and residual fears,
as well as inability to return to normal activity at a 4-
month follow-up. Mechanisms to explain these results are
offered, including action of catecholamines, mobilization
of psychological energy and active coping to counteract
the "sick role", and feedback of information to provide a
more accurate and wide-angled cognitive map. Recommendations are made for systematic application of this treatment with hospital patients. (Journal abstract).

568.   Grumet, G.W., Telephone therapy: A
        review and case report, American Journal
        of Orthopsychiatry, 1979, 49, 574-584.

The impact of the telephone upon practice of medicine and
psychiatry is reviewed. As an exclusively auditor medium,
the telephone conveys meaningful vocal information while
screening out visual and other stimuli. It is suggested
that some highly anxious and unstable individuals, who
find psychotherapy too threatening, may benefit from telephone contact with a therapist. An illustrative case of
telephone therapy is presented. (Journal abstract).

569.   Guido, J.A., and Payne, D.H., 72-hour
        psychiatric detention: Clinical
        observation and treatment in a county
        general hospital, Archives of General
        Psychiatry, 1967, 16, 233-238.

A 72-hour psychiatric detention center is described. The
center serves emergency needs ob observation and detention,
and some short-term treatment where indicated. A total of
8,264 patients who were seen in this facility over a three
year period were part of the data presented in this paper.
The largest group of patients had presented psychotic,
severe depression, and/or suicidal symptomatology. Pre-
disposing, precipitating, aggravating, and contributory
factors of the sample are described. The types of personal,
family, and community complications which typically arise

in treatment settings of this type are described. The
therapy was tailored for the individual patient, in that
biological, psychological, drug, and environmental
therapies were used in various combinations.

570.   Guinan, J.F., and Foulds, M.L., The
        marathon group: Facilitator of personal
        growth? Journal of Counseling Psychology,
        1970, 17, 145-149.

The present study is a report of changes on the scales of
the Personal Orientation Inventory (POI), a measure of
positive mental health, following a weekend marathon group
experience. Pretest and posttest results indicated
significant changes in the mean scores of an experiental
group on the following scales: Inner-Direction, Feeling
Reactivity, Spontaneity, Self-Acceptance, Acceptance of
Aggression, Capacity for Intimate Contact. There were no
significant changes for a control group. Differences were
found between those who volunteered for the group experience
and those from the same population who volunteered "to be
in an experiment." The results were discussed with
reference to a number of hypotheses that are in need of
testing. (Journal abstract).

571.   Guinan, J.F., et al., Do the changes
        last? A Six-month follow-up of a
        marathon group, Small Group Behavior,
        1973, 4, 177-180.

The authors describe the follow-up results from 14 college
students who had participated in a 24 hour marathon group.
This article reports on the fact that most of the participants report lasting changes as a result of the marathon
group experience (e.g., changes in self-acceptance,
increases in self-understanding and confidence on onself).
The value of such experiences are briefly discussed.

572.   Gurian, B.S., The psychiatric house
        call, American Journal of Psychiatry,
        1978, 135, 592-593.

Although caregivers in many disciplines have provided home
visits as part of their services, psychiatrists have rarely
made house calls. The author discusses some of the
practical and emotional issues that have traditionally
caused both patient and psychiatrist sufficient discomfort
to limit this model of therapeutic intervention. Special
emphasis is made in support of the psychiatric house call
for elderly persons. (Journal abstract).

573.   Gutheil, E., Basic outline of the active
        psychoanalytic technique, Psychoanalytic
        Review, 1933, 20, 53-72.

The author describes various modifications to Freudian
analytic principles as grounded in Stekel's active method
for shortening the length of analysis. Gutheil examines
some fundamental principles of active analysis, a number of
which explicitly follow Freud although with a slightly
different emphasis on aspects of the transference and
resistance. The author strongly urges shorter, more active
analyses, and "blames" two factors for the length of
orthodox analytic treatment: the deliberate passivity of
the therapist in collecting material from the patient; and
the fact that patients consciously prepare reports for the
sessions. He outlines according to the active method, the
gathering of the case history, interpretation, and other
"active encroachments", such as the giving of advice.
Gutheil warns against lay analysis, and describes the
necessary qualifications of the active analyst. The author
maintains that orthodox analysis is dangerous when used
with children or psychotics; but active methods can be
adapted in such cases. He concludes the paper (first
presented in 1931), with his perception of the future of
psychoanalysis, namely, the application of active methods
within a more time-limited framework. (abstract by
Deborah Schuller).

574.   Gutheil, E., Psychoanalysis and brief
        psychotherapy, Journal of Clinical
        Psychopathology and Psychotherapy,
        1944-45, 6, 207-230.

575.   Gutheil, E., Proceedings of the
        Association for the Advancement of
        Psychotherapy, American Journal of
        Psychotherapy, 1948, 2, 675-680.

In a post-war article, the author present a discussion of
the controversy over briefer versus longer term therapy
approaches. He indicates that shorter forms of therapy
are not anti-psychoanalytic in nature, as evidenced by the
work of Stekel. He also announced the formation of the
Council of Brief Psychotherapy to begin to meet the increasing needs for proper training in the shorter methods
of therapy.

576.   Guttman, E.S., Research Report # 36:
        Effects of short-term psychiatric
        treatment on boys in two California
        Youth Authority Institutions, California
        Youth Authority, December, 1963.

577.   Hadley, S.W., and Strupp, H.H.,
        Contemporary views of negative effects
        in psychotherapy, Archives of General
        Psychiatry, 1976, 33, 1291-1302.

As part of a larger investigation into negative effects in
psychotherapy, we conducted a survey of researchers and
practitioners in psychotherapy. We now present an integrated account of the consensus of these experts on the
following issues: (1) Is there a problem of negative
effects? (a) What constitutes a negative effect? (3) What
factors are prominently associated with negative effects?
There was an overwhelming affirmation of the reality of
negative effects amount the respondents. Furthermore,
they urged negative effects be subjected to systematic
research scrutiny, a strategy made more feasible by the

identifying criteria and possible causative factors cited
by these experts (e.g., exacerbation of presenting
symptoms, or the appearance of new symptoms). It is
suggested that there is a need for research into therapeutic actions and psychotherapy outcomes in general, with
special reference to negative effects. (Journal abstract
modified).

578.   Haley, J., Control in brief psychotherapy,
        Archives of General Psychiatry, 1961, 4,
        139-153.

The author presents an overview of the work of hypnotherapist Dr. Milton Erickson, as part of a discussion of
the issues of control in brief therapy. Some of the basic
characteristics of brief therapy are presented, such as
active, directive approaches designed to accomplish
specific, limited goals. A detailed discussion of the
initial interview along with examples of Dr. Erickson's
techniques are presented. Specific techniques of directing the patient and symptom utilization are highlighted.
Further, the author presents the essentials of the hypnotic
relationship as a model for psychotherapy, with a major
focus on the interpersonal or interactional aspects of
symptomatology. The major aim is to place the patient in
a position wherein he/she can no longer continue to use
the symptoms developed.

579.   Haley, J., Strategies of psychotherapy,
        New York, Grune and Stratton, 1963.

580.   Haley, J., (ed.), Advanced techniques of
        hypnosis and therapy: Seledted papers of
        Milton H. Erickson, M.D., New York, Grune
        and Stratton, 1967.

This is a book of collected articles authored by Dr. Milton
Erickson, known for his non-traditional methods of hypnosis
and brief therapy approach. A total of 36 articles are
presented.

581.   Haley, J., Uncommon therapy: The
        psychiatric techniques of Milton
        Erickson, New York, Grune and Stratton,
        1969.

The author presents a detailed summary of the work of Dr.
Milton Erickson, whose brief therapy techniques have
revolutionized the field of hypnosis. Dr. Erickson has
specialized in methods of inducing trance, including the
use of non-formal trance induction. In this book, Haley
surveys the strategic therapy approach used by Erickson,
and proceeds to provide examples throughout the remainder
of the book as to its usefulness across the life span.

582.   Haley, J., Strategic therapy when a child
        is presented as the problem, Journal of
        the American Academy of Child Psychiatry,
        1973, 12, 641-659.

The author characterizes families with problems as
suffering from overintense involvements across generational
lines (e.g., mother-son, mother-daughter, father-daughter,
etc.), in which cross-generational dyads are formed with
one adult excluded. Within this conceptualization, the
major aim of treatment is to realign the generations,
allowing for disengagement across generations. The author
then describes three alternative methods of dealing with
families in which the child is the presenting problem.
The type of families described are middle class, two-parent
families, in which the child exhibits severe, clearly
defined problems, not of a psychotic nature. Ways of using
the peripheral, excluded adult as means of intervening on
the pathological family interaction are described, with a
case example (dog phobia) to help elucidate the theoretical
issues. Ways of breaking up the dyad alliance within the
family are also presented, along with a case of enuresis
to illustrate the method. Finally, methods of using the
parents as a way of intervening on the family system are
described, accompanied by a case of encopresis. All
examples involved a brief period of treatment (up to 10
sessions).

583.   Hallsten, E.A., Adolescent anorexia
        nervosa treated by desensitization,
        Behaviour Research and Therapy, 1965,
        3, 87-91.

A case of pathological food avoidance in a 12-year-old
female is described in terms of learning theory principles.
A relevant behavioral treatment was immediately successful
in resolving the disorder and re-establishing normal
eating habits. Follow-up five months after termination
of treatment indicated that neither relapse nor symptom
had occurred. (Journal summary).

584.   Halpern, H., Crisis theory: A definitional
        study, Community Mental Health Journal,
        973, 9, 342-349.

The author reports on the results of a study designed to
develop a test of crisis behavior, and by so doing to
increase the clarity of the definition of the term crisis.
A cognitive model of crisis was utilized, and the statistical results presented. More specifically, four different
crisis conditions were used: a) divorce; b) students in
personal crisis; c) newly admitted patients to a public
health institution; d) individuals in process of bereavement. Based on clinical descriptions of behaviors
observed in crises (using the work of a number of contributors such as Caplan, Rapaport, and Miller and Iscoe)
60 personal statements were constructed, grouped into
clusters of 10 for analysis purposes. Each statement
reflected one aspect of crisis. Among the groups were
the following: 1) feelings of tiredness of exhaustion;
2) feelings of helplessness; 3) feelings of inadequacy;
4) feelings of confusion; 5) physical symptoms; 6) feelings
of anxiety; 7) disorganization in work functioning; 8)
family disorganization; 9) social relationship disorganization; 10) social activity disorganization. Two
hypothesis were tested and supported by the findings:
a) Crisis behavior will occur significantly more frequently
among individuals in crisis as opposed to those not in
crisis; b) There will be a negative correlation between
defensiveness and crisis (i.e., individuals more open to

change during periods of crisis). Further, no significant
differences were found between the various crisis groups
(4), indicating a significant amount of communality in
the behavior of people in crisis situations.

585.   Halpern, H.A., et al., A systems-crisis
        approach to family treatment, Journal of
        Marital and Family Therapy, 1979,   ,
        87-94 (April).

This paper presents a model which integrates a wide range
of possible interventions using family treatment and
provides a method of differential decision making with
regard to the intervention to be used in a given case.
The model uses an ecological perspective and draws on
concepts from general systems theory and crisis theory.
A number of case examples are provided to demonstrate how
the model has been applied in a clinical setting.
(Journal abstract).

586.   Hampe, E., et al., Phobic children one
        and two years posttreatment, Journal of
        Abnormal Psychology, 1973, 82, 446-453.

Sixty-two phobic children were followed up one and two
years after termination of treatment or waiting period.
Eighty percent were either symptom free or significantly
improved, and only 7% had a severe phobia. Successfully
treated children tended to remain symptom free and to be
free from other deviant behaviors as well. Time-limited
therapy of two months duration is effective for about 60%
of phobic children. Sixty percent of the failures at
termination continued to receive treatment and most were
symptom free two years later. After two years, the effects
of the original psychotherapy and reciprocal inhibition
therapy no longer were related to outcome. However, age,
status at the end of treatment, and time were related to
outcome. Results are discussed in terms of the nature of
child phobia and implications for research of the treatment of child phobia. (Journal abstract modified).

587.   Hand, I., and Lamontagne, Y., L'intention
        paradoxale et techniques comportementales
        similaires en psychotherapie a court terms,
        Canadian Psychiatric Association Journal,
        1974, 19, 501-507.

The logotherapeutic technique of paradoxical intention and
behavior therapy techniques use almost identical ways in
treating patients with phobias, obsessions and other
anxiety states. These consist of confronting the patient
with his anxiety and/or avoidance (ritual), eliciting
situations, discouraging overreaction to symptoms and
encouraging alternative activities. Patients learn
different ways of coping during the confrontation (exposure)
trials, and therapist also use a variety of ways to motivate the patients. Frankl has claimed for many years that
humor is a particularly helpful device to motivate patients
for such a treatment and to get them to do the exercises
properly. It was found in a group experiment with behavior
therapy for agoraphobics that patients used humor spontaneously as one of their coping mechanisms. The use of
humor as an auxiliary in paradoxical intention and behavior
therapy techniques is therefore reconsidered, with particular emphasis on Frankl's theoretical framework.
(Journal summary).

588.   Hanfmann, E., Productive brief encounters:
        Crisis and consultation, in Hanfmann, E.,
        Effective therapy for college students,
        San Francisco, Jossey-Bass, 1978.

This chapter describes a number of brief therapy encounters
in a university setting. Most of the cases lasted from
one-four sessions, and most of the students involved
indicated that they had achieved the goals they had
intended working on. The range of interventions was wide,
including information giving, interceding with university
authorities around specific issues, and crisis management.
Some of the presenting problems were quite serious.
Specific case examples are provided.

589.   Hanfmann, E., Negative brief encounters:
        Dropping out, in, Hanfmann, E., Effective
        therapy for college students, San Francisco,
        Jossey-Bass, 1978.

This chapter continues a description of a number of brief
encounters at a university counseling center, which produced negative or non-follow-through therapy results.
Issues of time constraints, lack of proper initial communication or service delayed are discussed as possible contributors to premature therapy termination or lack of
initiation of treatment. The chapter provides a number of
case histories and examples of negative brief therapy
encounters.

590.   Hankoff, L.D., Emergency psychiatric treat-
        ment: A handbook of secondary prevention,
        Springfield, Ill., C.C. Thomas, 1969.

591.   Hankoff, L.D., et al., A program of crisis
        intervention in the emergency medical
        setting, American Journal of Psychiatry,
        1974, 131, 47-50.

The general hospital emergency room provides an excellent
opportunity for the conduct of crisis intervention toward
a goal of primary psychiatric prevention. The authors
describe the development of a collaborative program
involving psychiatric staff as consultants and emergency
room nurses as crisis intervention counselors. Patients
were readily located and engaged, nurses effectively
conducted counseling, and families often reported benefit
from their contact with the nurses. (Journal abstract).

592.   Hansell, N., et al., Decision counseling
        method: Expanding coping at crisis-in-
        transit, Archives of General Psychiatry,
        1970, 22, 462-467.

Decision counseling centers upon clarity in the cognitive
structuring of the world by persons in crisis. It can
facilitate radical improvement in social and decision

skills during the heat of crisis. The method involves an
inventory of the problem, of possible responses, design
of a decision model, and expects competent action. The
method can be used in inpatient, outpatient, and home-
care settings and works with seriously troubled persons.
Convening the pertinent members of the family and social
network into the effort appears to focus on solutions to
problems and reduces focus on sickness and symptoms.
Because the method promotes maturation of life-problem
skills, it enhances the dignity of individuals and the
growth opportunity at crisis-in-transit. (Journal summary).

593.   Hare, M.K., Shortened treatment in a
        child guidance clinic: The results
        in 119 cases, British Journal of
        Psychiatry, 1966, 112, 613-616.

This study evaluates a shortened method of treatment in
119 consecutive cases attending a Child Guidance Clinic.
Treatment was carried out by the psychiatrist alone. The
average number of attendance per case was 6.3 and the
median number of months under treatment was 3.8. A follow-
up assessment was made about two years after discharge.
Adequate information was obtained on 95% of the cases. At
discharge, 49% of cases were recovered, and 23% improved.
At follow-up, 75% were recovered and 24% improved. Outcome was better in girls than boys and in older than
younger children. Outcome was best in neurotic cases,
worst in conduct disorders. The improvement rates compare
favourably with those of other studies. They add evidence
that short methods of treatment at Child Guidance Clinics
are as effective as longer, conventional methods. Some
disadvantages of the longer methods are noted. (Journal
summary).

594.   Hare-Mustin, R., Treatment of temper
        tantrums by paradoxical intervention
        Family Process, 1975, 14, 481-486.

In the present case, a paradoxical intervention was employed
in the treatment of a 4-year-old boy for temper tantrums.

Temper tantrums, which had been a daily occurrence, disappeared entirely after the second session. A follow-up
at nine months indicated there had been no further
tantrums. (Journal abstract).

595.   Hare-Mustin, R., Paradoxical tasks
        in family therapy: Who can resist,
        Psychotherapy: Theory, Research, and
        Practice, 1976, 13, 128-130.

Hare-Mustin defines paradoxical tasks and presents five
clinical vignettes to illustrate how apparently absurd
tasks can effect change within a family system. Paradoxical tasks require that an individual continue and
even exaggerate his usual (maladaptive) behavior. Thus,
any resistance on the part of the client produces change
in the desired direction. Within family therapy, tasks
frequently focus on parental complaints about a child.
Imposing tasks of an absurd nature (e.g., requiring the
disturbing behavior) breaks up the family's usual ways of
behaving and perceiving, and facilitates a degree of
detachment from the problem as previously defined.
(abstract by Deborah Schuller).

596.   Harris, C.W., A study of patients'
        perceptions of their experiences with
        short-term therapy, Smith College
        Studies in Social Work, 1973, 44, 44-45.

This is a summary of a master's thesis research project,
in which a group of 20 patients who had undergone short-
term therapy were interviewed to ascertain their perceptions about the process. The patients were from lower
socioeconomic group, and variables such as age, sex,
educational level, and nature of the presenting problem
bore no relationship to the rating of treatment outcome.
The value of such a short-term approach in community
mental health centers is discussed.

597.   Harris, D.H., et al., Brief psycho-
         therapy and enuresis, Journal of
         Consulting Psychology, 1955, 19, 246.

The authors report on a study with Navy recruits. The
hypothesis tested was that "a significant reduction of
admissions to the psychiatric observation ward in which
enuresis is a factor will result if, during the regular
screening procedure, enuretics receive brief psychotherapy
combining recognition and acceptance of their problem with
specific suggestions for overcoming the habit." A total
of 200 subjects were involved, ranging in age from 17-27.
One hundred were assigned to the control group, 100 to the
experimental group. The findings indicate that therapy
was instrumental in significantly reducing the number of
ward admissions.

598.   Harris, M.R., et al., Precipitating
         stress: An approach to brief therapy,
         American Journal of Psychotherapy, 1963,
         17, 465-471.

The authors report on their findings in dealing with 43
therapy applicants at an outpatient department of a neuropsychiatric institute. All patients were seen within 24
hours of the request for help, something the authors stress
as critical in their therapy approach. The main goal was
to clarify and resolve the precipitating stress, by the
working through of the conflict derivatives which were
instrumental in disrupting the previous level of functioning of the patient. Most patients were reported to have
not been consciously aware of the precipitating stress,
and the goal of the therapy was to aid in the identification of the precipitating stress. The focus was mainly
on the present, with some use of past history material
when it relates to the present situation. Two case
histories are used to highlight essentials of the approach,
which the authors postulate is appropriate for all patients
seeking psychiatric assistance. One advantage of such an
approach is that if often helps patients to clarify their
own motivation for longer term treatment.

599.   Harris, M.R., et al., An approach to
        short-term psychotherapy, <u>Mind</u>, 1964,
        2, 198-206.

The authors provide a short summary of some of the major
aspects of the Precipitating Stress Project of the Langley-
Porter Outpatient Department, started in 1958. The focus
was on delineating the factors which precipitated patients'
seeking help, and evolved into a focus for short-term
therapy for most of those who sought help. Issues of a
specific focus, getting help at the time of crisis, a
detailed exploration of the reasons for seeking help, and
the types of stressors are all discussed in the article.
Such precipitators as threat of a loss of a love-relation-
ship, difficulty with a previous mental health professional,
a surge of unmanageable impulses, etc. are detailed. A
case report is presented to highlight the type of working
through which occurred in the project. The active involvement of the therapist is also detailed. Issues of termination are discussed, including referral of a selected few
patients for longer term therapy. (e.g., for those
patients where the focus in short-term therapy continued
to widen rather than remain focussed and narrow). The
value of short-term therapy even for those who continued
on in longer term therapy was stressed, with shorter
term approaches helping to prepare the patient more
effectively.

600.   Harris, R.E., and Christiansen, C.,
        Prediction of response to brief psycho-
        therapy, <u>Journal of Psychology</u>, 1946,
        21, 269-284.

Measures of personality, (MMPI and Rorschach), were
administered to 53 patients suffering from delayed convalescence from physical disease or injury. The test
findings were compared with clinical ratings of outcome
after the patients were exposed to brief psychotherapy.
Both techniques showed differences between the patients
responding to well and poorly to therapy. Analysis of
both techniques led to hypotheses stated in terms of ego
strength, sub-clinical psychotic trends, or a factor of
stability-modifiability in the personality. (Journal
summary).

601.   Hartley, D.E., Therapeutic alliance
        and the success of brief individual
        psychotherapy, Dissertation Abstracts
        International, 1978, 39, 2985-2986.

602.   Haskell, D., et al., Time-limited
        psychotherapy for whom? Archives of
        General Psychiatry, 1969, 21, 546-552.

43 outpatients were studied for change after 12 weeks in
a time-limited (TL) psychotherapy program. The group as
a whole changed significantly on 5 measures of depression,
anxiety, and overall improvement. Relationships between
patient characteristics and treatment outcome were tested
in order to isolate predictors of improvement. The best
predictor of patient response was a Terminator-Remainer
test which indicated that patients classified as likely to
terminate conventional time-unlimited treatment actually
improved most in TL therapy. Other factors relating
positively to improvement were referral by a physician, no
prior treatment, short duration of illness, few somatic
complaints, and high score on the Bass Social Acquiesence
Scale. Students tended to report less improvement in
themselves and therapists tended to report less improvement
in hostile patients. The principal interpretation
suggested by the pattern of results is that the type of
patient who responds to TL therapy differs markedly from
the type who responds to long-term therapy. An approach
is offered for improving prediction of outcome and for
further studies to test the effectiveness of different
methods of psychotherapy. (Journal summary).

603.   Hauck, P.A., Short-term therapy with
        Rational-Emotive Therapy, Tulsa,
        Oklahoma, Affective House Cassette Tape
        Set, 1978.

604.   Hauck, P.A., Brief counseling with RET,
        Philadelphia, The Westminster Press, 1980.

The author describes in detail and with the use of clinical
examples how the principles of Rational-Emotive Therapy
can be used to effectively deal with a wide range of
presenting problems, and within a very few number of
sessions.

605.   Hausman, W., and Rioch, D. McK, Military
        psychiatry: A prototype of social and
        preventive psychiatry in the United States,
        Archives of General Psychiatry, 1967, 16,
        727-739.

In this paper we have attempted to summarize the history
of the development of the concepts of preventive and
social psychiatry insofar as they have been pioneered
since the first World War in military psychiatry. The
cardinal principles of military psychiatry, immediacy,
proximity, and expectancy, were established as the basis
for new techniques for the management of cases of combat
neurosis by Salmon in World War I, and were rediscovered
and reimplemented prior to the end of World War II by Army
psychiatrists. Glass' contributions in the latter campaign,
in Korea, and in establishing, documenting, and dissemin-
ating the principles and techniques of community psychiatry
since those combat periods, also have been described. The
principles of immediacy, proximity, and expectancy have
been further elaborated and extended into their non-
military applications, and Bushard's descriptions of the
terms concurrence and commitment, originally defined in
relationship to the military environment only, have been
broadened in context in order to demonstrate their
application to the larger discipline of social and
preventive psychiatry. (Journal summary).

606.   Hawkins, D., et al., Brief psychotherapy
        with medical students, Journal of
        Psychiatric Education, 1978, 2, 62-67.

Analyzed the relationships between psychopathology
presented by 12 medical students and success in brief
psychotherapy. Success in psychotherapy was related to

inward-directed pathology (neuroses), regardless of
severity. The findings suggest that when brief psychotherapy is offered to medical students, they will avail
themselves of the opportunity and those with inward-
directed pathology can achieve significant clinical benefit
in a short time. Those with outward-directed pathology
(character disorders) may need to be prepared for entering
long-term psychotherapy. (Journal abstract).

607.   Haywood, C.H., Emergency, crisis and
        stress services for rape victims, Crisis
        Intervention, 1975, 6, 43-48.

The author describes an interdisciplinary approached used
which conceptualizes victims of rape as a heterogeneous
group, and develops a range of services for them. The
author describes the differences between emergency treatment, crisis intervention, and stress moderation.

608.   Heiberg, A., Indications for psychotherapy
        in a psychiatric clinic population: A
        survey, Psychotherapy and Psychosomatics,
        1975, 26, 156-166.

As a part of larger project to differentiate the therapies
for inpatients in a psychiatric clinic, we have made a
half year's survey of the patients' needs for short-term
dynamic psychotherapy. Our findings point to less than
10% of the inpatients being able to profit from this kind
of therapy. These findings and their implications are
discussed briefly. (Journal abstract).

609.   Heiberg, A., et al., Short term dynamic
        psychotherapy: Three models of treatment,
        Psychotherapy and Psychosomatics, 1975,
        26, 229-236.

The method, patient selection criteria, and case histories
for three different brief therapy modalities are presented.
The approaches used by Malan, Sifneos, and Leewan and
Mulvey are described. The qualitative and quantitative
similarities and differences among the three approaches
are looked at.

610.   Heiberg, A., The main lines of the
        short-term psychotherapy project in
        Oslo, Psychotherapy and Psychosomatics,
        1978, 29, 309-311.

Results from 46 patients who were treated at the Oslo
University Psychiatric Clinic are reported. The approach
used was focused, insight-oriented, short-term, and rooted
in psychoanalytic theory. The aims of treatment are not
simply symptom relief, but deeper characterological change.
A specific case of a 38 year old housewife suffering from
anxiety attacks and heart palpitations, is used to detail
the process of this type of treatment. The author
emphasizes the need to stick to the therapeutic focus, and
the necessity to interpret the transference early in treatment.

611.   Heilbrun, A.B., Prediction of continuing
        client contact in a brief-treatment campus
        mental health agency, Psychological Reports,
        1978, 42, 481-482.

Confirmed the ability of the Counseling Readiness Scales
to predict the number of sessions spent in short-term
counseling or brief psychotherapy within a university
mental health service. Highly ready clients spent more
time in both than those low on readiness. Significant
positive correlations between number of sessions and rated
improvement of clients within both short-term modes of
treatment suggest the practical utility of measurement of
readiness. (Journal abstract).

612.   Heilig, S.M., et al., The role of non-
        professional volunteers in a suicide
        prevention center, Community Mental
        Health Journal, 1968, 4, 287-295.

The procedures in the selection training, and supervision
of 10 nonprofessional volunteers, to provide direct
therapeutic crisis services to patients in a Suicide
Prevention Center (Los Angeles) are described. One year's
experience indicates a high degree of proficiency achieved
by the volunteer in handling of suicidal crises? The

volunteers' reactions to the program are reported. Significant problems for the agency emerged in reference to
precipitous increase in size of staff communications, and
for the volunteer, in stimulation of problems of identity
and self-concept. The comments are limited to agency
situations involving the use of nonprofessional volunteers
in regular collaboration with a professional staff. Other
models, such as entirely volunteer staffed groups, must
be evaluated separately. (Journal abstract).

613.   Heinicke, C.M., and Strassman, L.H.,
        Toward more effective research on child
        psychotherapy, Journal of the American
        Academy of Child Psychiatry, 1975, 14,
        561-588.

The authors first review research results and interpretations based on an "inadequate" question: Does psychotherapy do any good? Variables which require further
careful study are then examined: e.g., frequency of
session, duration of treatment, therapist-child matching,
and the nature of parental impact. The authors describe
the types of studies which can lead to firm conclusions,
and cite two such studies. Directions for future research
are also presented. (abstract by Deborah Schuller).

614.   Hendin, H., Growing up dead: Student
        suicide, American Journal of Psychotherapy,
        1975, 29, 327-338.

College students who had made serious suicide attempts
were studied in detail. Short-term therapy was administered in most cases and long-term therapy in some. The
study indicates the ways in which death has become a way
of life for these students - an integral, ongoing part of
their adaptation.   It traces the origins of this
adaptation in a family relationship that the students
perceived as requiring their emotional extinction. These
students are tied to their parents in a kind of death knot
and have become overly suicidal when life - coming to
college, graduating, becoming seriously involved with

another person - threatens to unravel this knot.   The study
also explores some of the psychological changes contributing to the increasing number of young suicides.   It deals
with the special problems involved in the treatment of the
severely suicidal young person.   (Journal summary).

615.   Hendin, H., Student suicide: death as a
        life style, Journal of Nervous and Mental
        Disease, 1975, 160, 204-219.

This is a study of the psychology of college students who
are seriously suicidal.   Fifty college students who had
made suicide attempts were studied in detail over a 5-year
period.   Short-term therapy was administered in most cases
and long term therapy in some.   Psychological tests (WAIS,
Rorschach, TAT, Sentence Completion, Figure Drawing, and
Word Association) were performed and used as an independent
check on the data derived from interviews.   The study
indicates the way in which death has become a way of life
for these students - an integral, ongoing part of their
adaptation.   It traces the origin of this adaptation in a
family relationship that the students perceived as
requiring their emotional extinction.   These students are
tied to their parents in a kind of death knot and have
become overtly suicidal when life - coming to college,
graduating, becoming seriously involved with another person
- threatens to unravel this knot.   (Journal abstract).

616.   Hendricks, J., Transactional analysis
        and the police: Family disputes,
        Journal of Police Science and
        Administration, 1977, 5, 416-420.

This article describes how the principles of TA can be
applied to situations in which police are called in to
handle family disputes.   The basic concepts of TA (parent,
child, adult) are reviewed, and the specific games which
families that require police intervention usually play are
presented (e.g., Wooden Leg, Uproar, and Courtroom).
Specific techniques are offered to deal with these games,
which can significantly decrease the length of time needed
during each police intervention, and which would also lead
to a decrease in the frequency of repeat calls.

617.   Henry, S.E., and Kilmann, P.R., Student
        counseling groups in senior high school
        settings: An evaluation of outcome,
        Journal of School Psychology, 1979,
        17, 27-46.

This paper reviewed the studies which evaluated counseling
groups in senior high school settings. A methodological
evaluation was conducted within four areas: subjects,
counselors, treatment, and outcome criteria. The studies
were reviewed according to the type of outcome measure:
achievement, attitude and personality, behavioral, and
vocational. Three levels of voluntariness (voluntary,
semivoluntary, and nonvoluntary) were examined in relation
to outcome. Subjects who were free to volunteer for the
group experience achieved greater gains than subjects who
were coerced into participation. Overall, behavioral and
directive groups achieved greater success than nondirective
or client-centered groups. The time spent on topics
relating to treatment goals appeared to be an important
factor for success. Future researchers should assess the
effects of treatment on each participant instead of relying
upon group mean changes. (Journal summary).

618.   Henry, W.E., and Shlien, J.M., Affective
        complexity and psychotherapy: Some
        comparisons of time-limited and un-
        limited treatment, Journal of Projective
        Techniques, 1958, 22, 153-162.

A rationale has been presented in which the assumed
relationship between simplicity and personal adjustment is
questioned and an alternative concept of effective complexity suggested. This concept has been adapted to a
scoring based upon the Thematic Apperception Test, and an
application to a comparison of long unlimited and brief
time-limited therapies presented. The TAT scores of
affective complexity are found to differ markedly at the
follow up period between limited and unlimited cases. The
TAT scores, different from other measures available on
these cases, show a marked decline in affect differentiation
in the brief, time-limited cases. A variety of possible
explanations are suggested. It seems possible that the
TAT scores have reflected a particular resistance to the
arbitrary limits aspects of the treatment. (Journal summary).

619.   Herr, J.J., and Weakland, J.H.,
        Counseling elders and their families,
        New York, Springer, 1979.

This text provides a detailed description of a brief interactional intervention approach in dealing with problems of
aging.

620.   Herz, M.I., et al., Brief hospitalization
        of patients with families: Initial results,
        American Journal of Psychiatry, 1975, 132,
        413-418.

A total of 175 newly admitted inpatients who lived with
families were randomly assigned to three treatment groups:
standard inpatient care (discharge at the therapist's
discretion), brief hospitalization (one week or less),
with transitional day care available, and brief hospitalization without day care. Outpatient aftercare was offered
to all patients. The three groups showed no significant
differences as to amount of improvement in levels of
psychopathology at 3 and 12 weeks, but the briefly hospitalized patients were able to resume their vocational roles
sooner. There were no significant differences among the
groups in readmission rates. (Journal abstract).

621.   Heyder, D.W., A contribution to overcoming
        the problem of waiting lists, American
        Journal of Orthopsychiatry, 1965, 35,
        772-778.

Attitudes toward and psychodynamics of waiting lists are
discussed. The literature is reviewed. Organizational
changes, procedures of intake, reduction of treatment time,
the multiplying effect of consultation to social agencies
are outlined with suggestions for the use of volunteers.
The future challenge and means of meeting it close the
paper. (Journal abstract).

622.   Hickman, M.E., and Baldwin, B.A.,
        Use of programmed instruction to
        improve communication in marriage,
        Family Coordinator, 1971, 20, 121-125.

The authors report on two different approaches to helping
couples who have reached conciliation court. The first
approach is a communication-focussed counseling program,
the second a taped programmed instruction. A total of 20
couples were involved in the study, 10 in each group. A
Semantic Differential Test was used to measure attitudes
towards the relationship and a tabulation was made of the
number of reconciliations. The programmed instruction
group showed no significant changes, while there were
significant changes as measured by the instruments for the
therapy group.

623.   Hill, R., Generic factors of families
        under stress, Social Casework, 1958,
        39, 139-150, and 179-182.

The author presents a conceptual framework for looking at
families in crisis. Included in the article is a discussion of a classification of stressor events, factors
which make for crisis-proneness, adjustments to crises,
types of families which are best equipped to face difficulties, as well as implications of these issues for
professional practice and agency policy.

624.   Hill, S., Twelve-Hour psychotherapy,
        Canadian Nurse, 1976, 72, 30-31, 34.

The author, using the principles advocated by Mann, presents
two case histories to illustrate the value of short-term
therapy, limited to 12 sessions. The patient presentation
of difficulty with independence-dependence conflict, low
esteem, and difficulties related to grief are particularly
appropriate to a brief therapy. Severe, deep-seated
psychopathology does not lend itself to short-term therapy
in the opinion of the author. Stressed re procedure for
brief therapy are accurate diagnostic work-up, collaborative

effort on the part of patient and therapist, and a specific
focus in terms of agreed upon goals. Improvement as a
result of such a brief approach was reported in both
patients presented.

625.   Himler, L.E., Psychiatric treatment:
        brief psychotherapy procedures for the
        industrial physician, in, Nolan, R.,
        Industrial Mental Health and Employee
        Counseling, New York, Behavioral
        Publications, 1973.

Brief therapy in industrial settings is reviewed, and
specific techniques used discussed: nondirective questioning; reassurance; confession; referral; follow-up. The
emphasis is on emotional reeducation for the individual
worker.

626.   Hirschowitz, R.G., Crisis theory: a
        reformulation, Psychiatric Annals, 1973,
        3, 33-47.

This article provides an introduction to crisis theory.
Issues of life change, a description of the crisis state,
the sequence of crisis, and descriptions of healthy and
unhealthy coping with crises are presented.

627.   Hitchcock, J.M., Crisis intervention:
        The pebble in the pool, American Journal
        of Nursing, 1973, 73, 1388-1390.

The author presents concepts and principles of crisis
intervention in the context of the nursing profession.
Seen as a problem-solving process, various stages are
described, including assessment (precipitating factors,
previous stability and methods of coping, etc.), planning
specific intervention activities, and anticipatory
planning and evaluation. A case history, involving a 20
year old male experiencing a maturational crisis is
described. A total of one, 2-hour session was offered the
patient. The therapist focussed on issues of loss and of
reestablishing a previous level of adequate functioning.

The active role of the therapist, and the stress placed
on the patient's strengths are highlighted.

628.   Hobbs, N., Insight in short-term
         psychotherapy, American Psychologist,
         1949, 4, 273.

Although insight is a central concept in psychotherapy,
its function in the therapeutic process is ambiguous.
Insight is presumed to be a precursor to change in behavior.
However, experience in therapy indicates that change may
occur without insight and insight does not necessarily
produce change. The ambiguity may arise from the arbitrary
designation of some client statements as insightful and
others as not-insightful, as viewed by the psychologist.
To the client, it is probable that all statements which
represent his attempts to solve a problem are equally insightful. To him, they are all reasonable hypotheses for
guiding behavior. Understanding of the role of insight
may be increased by defining the ways in which symbols are
related to behavior. It is suggested that the efficacy
of a symbol is a function of its perceived utility in
preserving the individual's sense of control over his
world. Effective therapy would then be contingent upon
the use of symbols that have immediate meaningfulness to
the client, which he can employ in the solution of problems
as he perceives them at the time when the symbols are
required. Efforts to promote insight may retard therapy
by introducing symbols having little relevance to the
situation as perceived by the client. Therapy which
focuses on aiding the client to explore important life
relationships, utilizing primary symbols pertinent to
these relationships (and not the psychologist's abstrac-
tions or insights) is likely to be most effective in
promoting change. Insights may then emerge as symptoms of
changes that have already occurred. (Journal abstract).

629. Hoch, P.H., Present status of narco-
diagnosis and therapy, Journal of Nervous
and Mental Disease, 1946, 103, 248-259.

Presents the use of narco-therapy with reluctant, quiet
patients for whom traditional psychotherapy had been
unsuccessful. A quicker transference was accomplished
when compared to traditional therapy. The author outlines
the use of suggestion and cathartic processes as part of
the overall treatment approach.

630. Hodgson, R.J., and Rachman, S.,
An experimental investigation of the
implosion technique, Behavior Research
and Therapy, 1970, 8, 21-27.

An experiment was designed to test the hypothesis that a
prolonged implosion session leads first to a reduction in
emotional reactivity and then to extinction (or desensitization) during subsequent presentation of the phobic
stimuli. An attempt was made to reduce emotional reactivity, in snake-phobic girls, by using horrific images
which were unrelated to the phobia. A 30-min. session of
horrific images was followed either immediately (Group 2)
or after 24 hr. (Group 3) by a 10-min. session imagining
phobic images. It was found that Group 2 condition
produced desensitization and the Group 3 condition
produced sensitization. This effect was significant at
the 5 percent level. Three other groups were included in
the design. These were implosion, horror only and control.
We failed to replicate the dramatic implosion effects
previously obtained, and possible reasons for this failure
are given. (Journal summary).

631. Hoehn-Saric, R., Evaluation of
psychiatric training in the emergency
room, Comprehensive Psychiatry, 1977,
18, 585-589.

Records of 233 patients evaluated by psychiatric residents
in the Emergency Room and subsequently re-evaluated by
senior psychiatrists in the Acute Treatment Clinic were
examined for gross discrepancies in diagnosis, mental

status, prescribed medication, and appropriate disposition
of outpatients to a crisis clinic. The work in the
Emergency Room was rated satisfactory in 90% of the cases.
Length of training heightened the agreement between residents and senior staff on the mental status examination,
the diagnosis, and to a lesser extent, the medication.
There was no relationship between length of training and
the agreement about the disposition. This was probably
due to the lack of follow-up of the patients by the residents who had seen them in the Emergency Room. It was
concluded that for optimal training purposes the Emergency
Room experience should be combined with work in a crisis
clinic where residents continue to treat patients whom
they have referred from the Emergency Room. (Journal
abstract).

632.   Hoehn-Saric, R., et al., Systematic
        preparation of patients for psychotherapy,
        I. Effects on therapy behavior and out-
        come, Journal of Psychiatric Research,
        1964, 2, 267-281.

Our hypothesis was that an appropriate introduction to
psychotherapy in form of a Role Induction Interview (RII)
would improve therapy behavior, attendance and outcome in
suitable, psychologically unsophisticated psychoneurotic
patients. The sample comprised 40 psychoneurotic patients
between the ages of 18 and 55. 20 patients were prepared
with an RII and 20 patients served as controls. They were
offered therapy one hour, once a week for 4 months, with
some variation at the therapist's discretion, by 4 senior
psychiatric residents who had no knowledge of the purpose
of the experiment. The experimental group exhibited
better therapy behavior than the control group on 5 of the
7 measures. These differences reached significance for 3
of those 5 measures: the experimental group scored better
on the Therapy Behavior Scale in the third therapy session,
it had better attendance rate and therapists rated the
experimental group more favorably with respect to establishing and maintaining therapeutic relationship. The
experimental group showed a more favorable outcome on 5 of
the 8 outcome measures. Three of those five favored the

experimental group at a significant level: therapist's
rating of improvement, patient's rating of mean target
symptom improvement and social effectiveness ratings.   It
was concluded that RII had a favourable effect on certain
aspects of patients' therapy behavior and improvement, and
properly used, could be a valuable tool in psychotherapy.
(Journal summary).

633.   Hoehn-Saric, R., et al., Focused
        attitude change in neurotic patients,
        Journal of Nervous and Mental Disease,
        1968, 147, 124-133.

The study aimed at developing a method which would permit
a quantifiable evaluation of the effect of emotional and
cognitive manipulations of clinically relevant attitudes
in psychoneurotic patients.   Several outpatients were
exposed to suggestions on one low and three high arousal
therapy sessions.   The high arousal condition was facilitated by ether.   Before and after the sessions the patients
rated, on Osgoode's Semantic Differential, concepts which
were directly, tangentially or not related to the attitude
which was to be changed by the suggestion.   Those concepts
on which the suggestions were focused changed significantly
more than the tangential and nonrelated concepts.   The
change in the focal concept during the therapy sessions
was partially preserved between sessions, leading to a
step-by-step shift of the attitude in the desired direction.
The effectiveness of the suggestion in the high arousal
condition was greater than in the low arousal session.
The significance of this result was discussed.   (Journal
summary).

634.   Hoehn-Saric, R., et al., Prognosis in
        psychoneurotic patients, American
        Journal of Psychotherapy, 1969, 23,
        252-259.

A large number of follow-up studies are in agreement that
approximately two-thirds of psychoneurotic patients improve
over time.   There is less agreement about the characteristics which permit prediction in individual patients.   This
paper describes two studies.   In Study 1, 40 outpatients

received four months of psychotherapy. Neither diagnosis,
severity of symptoms, or type of presenting complaints
were related to short-term change. There was a positive
relationship between outcome and the ratings of "attractiveness as a psychiatric patient", a global judgement which
was influenced by patient's personality, assets, and
ability to relate. "Attractive" patients not only improved
more than those rated "unattractive" but also demonstrated
a greater ability to learn from therapeutic intervention.
Ratings of prognosis by the evaluating psychiatrist were
significantly correlated to independent ratings of the
therapist but did not predict the outcome accurately.   In
Study 2, the admission histories of former outpatients who
returned for a 10-year follow-up were examined. Long-term
changes were related to patient's premorbid personality
and to the presence of stress at the onset of illness,
occupational history, social isolation, and domestic
situation did not differentiate the most-improved from the
least-improved patients. The significance of the results
was discussed. (Journal summary).

    635.   Hoehn-Saric, R., et al., Arousal and
            attitude change in neurotic patients,
            Archives of General Psychiatry, 1972,
            26, 51-56.

An earlier study demonstrated that psychoneurotic patients
aroused by ether inhalation showed significant shifts in
selected concepts in response to persuasive communications
given by a prestigious person under dramatic circumstances.
The present study aimed to separate effects of ether
arousal from other factors in the situation. Twenty
patients received as part of their psychotherapy two
special sessions identical with those of the previous
study. One half were aroused by ether inhalation and one
half were kept in a state of low arousal through pre-
medication with chlorpromazine. Short-term attitude
changes, measured by Osgood's Semantic Differential, were
comparable for both groups during the first session but
were significantly greater for the aroused group during
the subsequent session, indicating that in influencing
patients, persuasive circumstances were less effective
alone than when combined with arousal. (Journal abstract).

636. Hoehn-Saric, R., et al., Attitude change and attribution of arousal in psychotherapy, Journal of Nervous and Mental Disease, 1974, 159, 234-243.

Earlier studies demonstrated that psychoneurotic patients aroused and confused by ether inhalation showed significantly greater responses to persuasive communications than patients in a state of low arousal. The present study explored: a) the effect of arousal without confusion on patients' suggestibility; and b) the role of attribution of the source of arousal on the acceptance of the communication. Forty-two patients were divided into three groups. An adrenalin inhalant served as the arousing substance. Two groups received as part of their therapy three adrenalin arousal sessions during which a persuasive communication was given. One group was informed, i.e., knew that they were receiving an arousing inhalant; the second group did not know that the inhalant was arousing; the third group served as a control group and received a pharmacologically inert inhalant. Short-term attitude change, measured on Osgood's semantic differential, was identical in the informed and uninformed adrenalin group. Thus, not knowing the source of arousal did not heighten patient's readiness to accept an apparently clarifying explanation and therefore did not increase his suggestibility. However, the combined adrenalin groups showed a regular response pattern to the intervention significantly more frequently than the control group. They also showed significantly more directional attitude change in the second experimental session than the control group. Although one has to conclude that adrenalin arousal had some effect on patients' suggestibility, the ratings of therapist performance and patient response suggest rather complex interactions. At the end of the study the adrenalin patients, but not the control group, exhibited increased cardiac lability to focal topics which had been discussed under adrenalin arousal in previous sessions. This finding suggests that some form of association may have occurred between the focal topic and the emotional response. (Journal abstract).

637.   Hoffman, D.L., and Remmel, M.L.,
         Uncovering the precipitant in crisis
         intervention, Social Casework, 1975,
         56, 259-267.

The authors discuss rationale, theory, and method of a
model of crisis psychotherapy developed by one family
agency. This therapy, which attempts to blend psychoanalytic theory of personality with Caplan's crisis theory,
stresses the importance of clarifying the "precipitant"--
the thought or feeling aroused by the precipitating event.
Conceptualizing the client's presenting complaint as a
type of solution (albeit unsatisfactory) to a more
fundamental underlying conflict is another key notion in
this model. Hoffman and Remmel treat in some detail tasks
and procedural considerations of three distince therapeutic phases. Clinical material is interwoven into the
discussion. The authors describe benefits which have
accrued to clients and to the clinic as a result of
offering this form of crisis psychotherapy. (abstract by
Deborah Schuller).

638.   Hogan, R.A., Implosive therapy in short-
         term treatment of psychotics, Psychotherapy:
         Theory, Research, and Practice, 1966, 3,
         25-32.

Implosive therapy, its theoretical foundation and clinical
techniques supplemented by illustrative case histories,
are presented in conjunction with the results of empirical
research. 26 experimental and 24 control subjects, treated
by implosive and traditional methods of psychotherapy
respectively and equated for degree of initial disturbance
on the MMPI were evaluated after short-term treatment and
upon one year follow-up. The experimental subjects
(implosively treated) showed significant shifts away from
pathology, improved on 5 MMPI scales, and were significantly
successful (.02) in terms of release from a state hospital
setting. (Journal summary).

639. Hogan, R.A., The implosive technique,
Behavior Research and Therapy, 1968,
6, 423-432.

A brief history of the implosion technique is followed by
an illustrative case-history. A detailed description of
the method is provided. (Journal abstract).

640. Hogan, R.A., and Kirchner, J.H.,
Preliminary report of the extinction of
learned fears via short-term implosive
therapy, Journal of Abnormal Psychology,
1967, 72, 106-109.

In this study, the effectiveness of short-term implosive
therapy was tested. 43 Ss with an ascertained fear of
rats were divided into an experimental and a control group.
The experimental Ss were treated by implosion; whereas the
controls were exposed to relaxing cues. All therapy was
conducted in 1 session. A posttest which consisted of
picking up a rat was the criterion for success of the
therapy. The behavior of the experimental group was significantly different (chi-square, p < .001) from that of
the control group on the posttest. The utility of short-
term implosion was demonstrated. (Journal abstract).

641. Hogan, R.A., and Kirchner, J.H., Implosive,
eclectic verbal and bibliotherapy in the
treatment of fears of snakes, Behaviour
Research and Therapy, 1968, 6, 167-171.

Thirty co-eds with ascertained fears of snakes were exposed
to an implosive, eclectic verbal or bibliotherapy session.
Ten Ss were in each group. For a S to be judged a success
at the conclusion of the session, she had to pick up a
3 1/2 ft. king snake. There were significant differences
(0.05 level) between Ss who had implosive therapy and those
who had bibliotherapy on the post test. No significant
differences were found between the implosive and eclectic
verbal Ss on this post test. Subject who failed to pick
up the snake were subsequently imploded. 66.6% of them
later lifted up the animal. Results of this study were
compared with those of previous research on implosion.
(Journal summary).

642.   Holland, C.J., Elimination of the parents
        of fire-setting behavior in a 17-year old
        boy, Behaviour Research and Therapy, 1969,
        7, 135-137.

The author reports a case of a persistent fire-setting
behavioral pattern of two years duration in a seven year
old boy. The behavioral technique used involved positive
reinforcement and the possibility of punishment-by-loss as
implemented by the parents of the boy. The fire-setting
behavior was eliminated by the end of the fifth week of
treatment, and information gathered over an eight month
follow-up period indicated no recurrence of the symptomatic
behavior.

643.   Holland, C.J., An interview guide for
        behavioural counseling with parents,
        Behavior Therapy, 1970, 1, 70-79.

A 21-step interview guide is discussed as an aid for
counselors in teaching parents to apply operant techniques
to the problems they are experiencing with their children.
The guide provides an analysis of the information required
for a behavioural assessment of the problem and for choice
of modification techniques. It may also serve the purpose
of providing a standardized interview format for use in
research projects. (Journal abstract).

644.   Holland, C.J., Directive parental
        counseling: The parents' manual,
        Behavior Therapy, 1976, 7, 123-127.

A 30-point manual to train parents as agents of intervention for remediating the problems of their children was
developed to allow a counselor in a group setting to gather
systematically the information necessary to bring about
behavior change, and to teach the parents to make the
necessary interventions. (Journal abstract).

645. Holland, C.J., A token economy system for home-based behavior modification, Canada's Mental Health, 1977, 25, 17-19.

The following article is a detailed description and rationale for a token economy system that has been used successfully by a wide range of parents employing a home-based behavior modification procedure to remediate the problem behaviors of their children. (Journal abstract).

646. Holland, C.J., et al., The student nurse as a therapeutic consultant, International Journal of Nursing Studies, 1978, 15, 153-157.

During the past decade parents have been taught to act as the primary agents of change for the problem behaviours of their children, which formerly often necessitated treatment by the professional. Although this extension of therapeutic services is still in its earlier stages of development and is awaiting much needed research, it promises to become one of the most significant developments in applied mental health in the latter part of the 20th century. Concurrent with this development is an attempt to train parapsychotherapeutic specialists to assume the role of primary consultants for the home-based programs of the parent-therapist. This article describes one such program, Directive Parental Counseling and its implementation by student nurses. (Journal introduction).

647. Hollensbe, S.M., Script enactment as a technique for brief psychotherapy, Dissertation Abstracts International, 1976, 36, 8B, 4160.

648. Hood-Williams, J., The results of psychotherapy with children, Journal of Consulting Psychology, 1960, 24, 84-89.

This article presents an evaluative survey of a number of outcome studies on the effectiveness of psychotherapy with children. Criticism is leveled at the many studies

which do not state the length of time of treatment provided,
as well as the many studies which neglect to inform the
reader of the professional level of the child-therapist.
A total of 18 studies were reviewed. Conflicting results
are reported regarding the relationship between length of
treatment and success, although the author concludes that
there is a general positive relationship between length of
treatment. Many of the confounding research factors which
make definitive conclusions impossible are reviewed and
discussed.

649.   Horowitz, M.J., and Kaltreider, N.B.,
         Brief psychotherapy of stress response
         syndromes, in, Karasu, T.B., and Bellak, L.,
         (eds.), Specialized techniques in individual
         psychotherapy, New York, Brunner/Mazel, 1980.

The authors describe stress response syndromes, and detail
goals and techniques of a brief, analytically-oriented
psychotherapy which affords both symptom relief and
restoration of ongoing personal development. Phases of
response to a stressful life event, with normal pathological
variations, are reviewed. Horowitz and Kaltreider elucidate
in depth a variety of technical considerations--including
goals, treatment pattern, the nature of the therapeutic
relationship, information processing issues, necessity of
realignment of therapeutic focus as treatment proceeds,
recognition of habitual control operations and therapeutic
counteractants, and termination. Clinical material is
provided which illustrates both the syndrome and the application of brief therapy as delineated in this chapter.
(abstract by Deborah Schuller).

650.   Hotkins, A.S., et al., An interview
         group therapy program for the waiting-
         list problem, Social Work, 1958, 3, 29-34.

The authors describe their efforts to confront the
perennial problem of a long waiting list at a small child
guidance clinic. A "Waiting List Group", an educational
group therapy for parents, was established to meet for
twelve weekly sessions of one and one-half hours each.
Primary objectives included relief of stress induced by

the long period of waiting; collection of diagnostic
material and clinical observations to shorten the time
later required for intake; and the "weeding out" and
referral to other agencies of ineligible children. The
authors present particular features of the group method
and process. Clinical material from the group is inter-
spersed in the discussion of findings. Hotkins, et al.
conclude that some relief, though possibly temporary, was
verbally noted by participants. Valuable diagnostic
material was obtained which made possible a more realistic
assessment of the actual eligibility of families waiting
for clinic services. The authors stress the necessity of
exploring means of reaching parents and children new on
waiting lists. (abstract by Deborah Schuller).

651.   Howard, H.S., Of "gimmicks and gadgets"
        in brief psychotherapy, Delaware Journal
        of Medicine, 1965, 37, 265-267.

652.   Hoyt, M., Aspects of termination in
        time-limited brief psychotherapy,
        Psychiatry, 1979, 42, 208-219.

The author presents a theoretical review of the use of a
time-limited model and its impact on the therapy process.
This is followed by a detailed case report, of a 69 year
old female patient, in good physical health, presenting
with depression. The patient had lost her husband five
months previous to her seeking therapy, and also had strong
unresolved feelings about his affair which she had found
out about long before his death. The therapy issues are
detailed for each session, with transcripts of exchanges
provided. The discussion revolves around the appropriateness of such an approach for this patient, including a
discussion of her age and its role in therapy.

653.   Huffine, C., and Craig, T., Social factors
        in the utilization of an urban psychiatric
        emergency service, Archives of General
        Psychiatry, 1974, 30, 249-255.

Admissions to the psychiatric emergency service of an inner-
city university hospital are analyzed from two perspectives:

(1) Characteristics of patients and the areas in which
they reside are described with focus directed toward social
characteristics found to be associated with high admission
rates. (2) The ways in which a hospital, by virtue of its
organizational structure, might contribute to misuse of
its emergency facilities by patients are explored. Based
on both modes of analysis, suggestions are offered for
ways in which services may be altered to more effectively
meet the treatment needs of inner-city populations.
(Journal abstract).

654.   Hulse, W.C., et al., On the spot psycho-
        therapy in a children's institution,
        Psychiatric Quarterly Supplement, 1954,
        28, 121-130.

One of the earlier reports of brief therapy with children
in a large institution. Teenagers between the ages of
12-16 were involved in a psychodynamic five session group
psychotherapy because of anti-social behavior on the teenagers part. Individual treatment was also made available
in those situations where it seemed warranted. Results
were extremely positive, in that much of the anti-social
behavior was stopped. The author stresses the difficulties
inherent in instituting such a brief therapy approach when
the training and professional preferences of the staff do
not fit such a view therapy.

655.   Hunt, G.M., and Azrin, N.H., A community-
        reinforcement approach to alcoholism,
        Behaviour Research and Therapy, 1973,
        11, 91-104.

Several theoretical approaches to alcoholism exist. An
operant reinforcement approach was used in the present
study to develop a new procedure that rearranged community
reinforcers such as the job, family and social relations
of the alcoholic such that drinking produced a time-out
from a high density of reinforcement. The results showed
that the alcoholics who received this Community-Reinforcement counseling drank less, worked more, spent more time
with their families and out of institutions that did a
matched control group of alcoholics who did not receive

these procedures. This new approach appears to be an
effective method of reducing alcoholism. An analysis in
reinforcement terms is presented of the etiology, epidemiology, and treatment of alcoholism.

656.   Hutten, J.M., Short-term contracts,
       III. Some clinical illustrations,
       Social Work Today, 1975, 6, 538-541.

Five case studies are presented to highlight the usefulness
of brief family therapy. Each case presents a different
aspect related to presenting problem e.g., one case in
which brevity of therapy was necessitated by external
factors; one in which client wished limited involvement;
cases in which crises in the families (death) precipitated
their reaching out for help.

657.   Hutten, J.M., Short-term contracts, IV.
       Techniques - how and why to use them,
       Social Work Today, 1976, 6, 614-619.

Specific case histories are presented which highlight the
various techniques used in brief therapy. The danger of
inappropriate use of these approaches is discussed, and
the issue of therapist training is looked at.

658.   Ichikawa, A., Observations of college
       students in acute distress, Student
       Medicine, 1961, 10,

The author presents a description of a number of students
who seek help from a university mental health clinic based
on problems of acute situational stress. Three case
histories are presented which highlight some of the issues
raised, illustrating the focus on aiding the student to
utilize and develop resources within the university
environment. The emphasis is on short-term intervention
with the aim being the development of ego-enhancement
mechanisms. The approach taken is remedial and supportive.

659.   Illing, H.A., Short-contact group
        psychotherapy, International Journal
        of Group Psychotherapy, 1952, 2, 377-382.

The author presents a report on the use of short-term
group therapy in a military setting, initiated because of
heavy patient load. Specific examples are provided, with
the author somewhat unconvinced of the long lasting effects
of such an approach.

660.   Imber, S.D., Short-term group therapy,
        American Psychologist, 1953, 8, 371-372.

The purpose of this investigation was: (a) to demonstrate
certain benefits of short-term group psychotherapy for
psychotic patients, (b) to compare nondirective and
directive therapy with respect to therapeutic progress
and certain aspects of the process of therapy, and (c) to
determine whether benefits are more dependent on therapeutic techniques, therapist personality, or their interaction.

The Ss were 36 male patients in a neuropsychiatric hospital.
Each was assigned to one of four experimental groups or to
one of two control groups. Each group consisted of six
patients. Two experimental groups received nondirective
group therapy and two received directive (or lecture) group
therapy. All groups met for ten sessions over a five-week
span. The control groups met for an identical number of
sessions to read and discuss literature; they were led by
an experienced librarian.

FINDINGS: (a) Short-term group psychotherapy produced
improvement in attitude toward the self and other people,
outlook regarding the future, feeling state, and appreci-
ation of self-continuity. (b) Reading and literary
discussion groups did not bring about therapeutic gains.
(c) There were no consistent differences between non-
directive and directive therapy. (d) Successful treatment
did not depend only on the therapist or only on the kind
of therapeutic approach used. Both therapists in the
investigation produced patient gains, but neither therapist
was equally effective with both techniques. (Journal
abstract).

661.   Imber, S.D., et al., Improvement and
        amount of therapeutic contact: An
        alternative to use of no treatment
        controls in psychotherapy, Journal of
        Consulting Psychology, 1957, 21, 309-315.

The unavailability of nontreatment control groups to test
the efficacy of psychotherapy and dissatisfaction with the
use of dropout and wait-list groups as substitute procedures, has prompted the use of an alternative experimental design. This design requires the precise statement
of hypotheses relative to the presence or absence of an
assumed significant element of treatment and the consequent
changes in patients. Adopting this scheme, the present
study specified that patients having fewer and briefer
sessions of psychotherapy will show significantly less
improvement than patients with more and longer sessions,
over the same period of time. Fifty-four psychiatric
patients were assigned at random to three psychiatrists,
each of whom treated an equal number of patients in group
therapy and two different forms of individual therapy. In
one of these latter forms, the patients were able to have
only one-half as many psychotherapy sessions and the
sessions lasted only one-half as long as patients in the
other two forms. Over a six-month experimental period the
patients with restricted therapeutic contact showed less
improvement on the criterion of change used. The significance of amount of therapeutic contact is discussed.
(Journal summary).

662.   Imber, S.D., et al., Suggestibility,
        social class, and the acceptance of
        psychotherapy, in, Goldstein, A.P., and
        Dean, S.J., (eds.), Investigation of
        psychotherapy: Commentaries and readings,
        New York, John Wiley and Sons, 1966.

663.   Imber, S.D., et al., A ten-year follow-up
          study of treated psychiatric outpatients,
          in, Leese, S. (ed.), An evaluation of the
          results of the psychotherapies, Springfield,
          Ill., C.C. Thomas, 1968.

The author reports on a follow-up study done 10 years
following treatment. A brief psychotherapy program had
been completed by 34 psychoneurotic patients, who were
contacted 10 years following the termination of treatment.
Measures covered areas such as social ineffectiveness and
discomfort, as well as a number of other dimensions.
Results indicated that over the 10 year period, improvement
followed a negatively accelerated function. Those who
gained from treatment exhibited those gains within the
first two years of the program. Clients who had improved
were able to identify reasons for the improvement; those
who did not change positively, were unable to explain
their conditions.

664.   Imber, S.D., et al., Time-focussed
          role induction, Journal of Nervous
          and Mental Disease, 1970, 150, 27-30.

Of the several possible components of a role induction
interview this investigation examined "hope for improvement", defining it in terms of a 4-week period when
improvement could be expected. The hypothesis was that
patients induced to expect improvement after 4 weeks of
psychotherapy will report greater change at that point
than other patients, whose expectations extend to a 4-month
period. 14 psychoneurotic patients who appeared not to
hold fixed time expectations regarding their rate of
improvement, as revealed in a screening interview, were
included in the study. All patients were administered a
series of mock physiological tests; half of them were
informed that the "tests" revealed they would experience
improvement by the 4th week of psychotherapy and the
remainder that improvement would be a gradual process over
the 4-month psychotherapy period. All patients received
a standard role induction interview and were assigned to
one of four psychotherapists who saw patients weekly. In
addition to several scales for measuring the outcome of
treatment, a relief expectancy questionnaire was administered prior to and immediately following the mock session.

Outcome measures revealed no difference between the
experimental and control groups at either the 4-week or
termination points and the questionnaire findings demonstrated failure of time induction to produce anticipated
shifts even immediately after that procedure. It is
concluded that patients have quite definite prior expectations with respect to improvement, and these are not
easily manipulated. The 4-week expectancy we sought to
induce may be too abbreviated even for clinically naive
patients. Also, the isolation of time for experimental
emphasis may do violence to role induction as an integral
process, and the effect may be dissolved in the surround
of the many other principles presented in a general role
induction procedure. (Journal abstract).

665.   Imber, S.D., et al., Uses and abuses of
        the brief intervention group, International
        Journal of Group Psychotherapy, 1979, 29,
        39-49.

The experiences reported here took place at the Western
Psychiatric Institute and Clinic, in Pittsburgh, a major
university medical center. The groups are open, but each
participant is requested to commit him/herself to six
sessions. The major functions of such immediate access
brief therapy groups are: a) the relief of stress;
b) crisis intervention; c) exploration of resources and
problem resolution; d) as a possible screening device for
longer-term therapy; e) diagnostic observation, f) patient
selection for other forms of treatment as a result of
observing patient in short-term therapy; g) a bridge, "wait-
list" function, in which the group provides interim support
prior to a lengthier therapy; and, h) as an opportunity
for student interns to gain valuable practical experience.
The authors briefly discuss some of the technical issues
that arise in running such groups, including such issues
as the activity level of the therapist, how to deal with
the open-endedness of the groups, the critical importance
of the orientation interview prior to joining the group,
etc. The authors also briefly outline some of the possible
abuses of the brief intervention group therapy.

666.   Ingham, Ruth, E., and Allgeyer, Jean, M.,
        Early access to clinic treatment, <u>Hospital
        & Community Psychiatry</u>, Dec., 1968, 387-
        388.

This very brief article describes an intake plan instituted
in 1965 to cimplify and speed the process of application
to an outpatient clinic in Los Angeles County. Based upon
a recognition of the value of immediate attention, and the
belief that diagnosis and treatment can proceed contem-
poraneously, the authors' principle goals were provision
of easy access to services and reduction of staff time
required. Ingham and Allgeyer discuss specific steps in
implementing these goals, including more hours for telephone screening interviews, revision of schedules for
office interviews, setting aside one day per week for
intake interviews, use of mimeographed outlines as guides
for those interviews, etc. Two years after implementation
of the new procedure, without any additional staff, the
number of patients in treatment increased by 25 per cent.
(abstract by Deborah Schuller).

667.   Jakcson, B.T., A case of voyeurism treated
        by counter conditioning, <u>Behaviour Research
        and Therapy</u>, 1969, 7, 133-134.

This very brief report presents a case study of a 20 yr.
old, single male who was self-referred to a mental health
clinic. In the initial interviews, he admitted to active
voyeurism. The behavior was explained to the patient in
learning theory terms, and a hierarchy of excitation was
established. A counterconditioning procedure was instituted, and successful elimination of the behavior occurred.
A total of eight sessions were needed for this change to
occur. A follow-up nine months later revealed that the
behavior had not reappeared. A brief discussion of the
results is presented.

668.   Jacob, T., et al., A follow-up treatment
        terminators and remainers with long-term
        and short-term symptom duration, Psycho-
        therapy: Theory, Research and Practice,
        1972, 9, 139-142.

The authors report on a study in which 100 children who
had been seen in therapy at a child guidance center were
recontacted between one and two years after termination
in order to compare those with long-standing symptomatology
and those with symptoms of short duration (less than six
months). Significant differences were obtained which
distinguished improvement ratings between: a) remainers
in therapy with long-term symptoms versus remainers in
therapy with short-term symptoms (remainers with short-term
symptoms rated more improved); b) terminators with short-
term symptoms rated more improved than terminators with
long-term symptoms. The overall conclusion was that short-
term stress may be altered by factors other than formal
psychotherapy, whereas that was not found to be the case in
situations where long-term stress had occurred. Further,
those patients who had terminated therapy but who had
exhibited long-term symptoms sought additional treatment
significantly more often that did terminators with short-
term symptoms within a two year period following the
original termination of treatment. Finally, those parents
of children with short-term symptoms who terminated
reported that treatment was significantly more helpful to
them than did parents of children with long-term symptoms
who had terminated treatment. Suggestions for future
research are provided.

669.   Jacobs, D., et al., Preparation for
        treatment of the disadvantaged patient:
        effects on disposition and outcome,
        American Journal of Orthopsychiatry,
        1972, 42, 666-674.

Effects of a brief orientation of lower-class patients to
the initial psychiatric interview, and a similar preparation of psychiatric residents, were compared to control
patients and residents not differentially prepared.

Findings relating to disposition and outcome support the
authors' contention that reduction of social distance has
salutary effects in making psychotherapy more accessible
to disadvantaged patients. Significance of these findings
for operation of a walk-in clinic serving a lower-class
population are discussed.

   670.   Jacobs, L.I., Marital sex therapy,
          Current Psychiatric Therapies, 1975,
          15, 205-212.

The article begins with a short introduction to marital
dynamics. The treatment approaches used in marital sex
therapy are reviewed, including educational dimensions,
instructional dimensions (sensate focus, squeeze technique,
desensitization imagery, etc.), and the interpretive
aspects. The author reviews treatment approaches to
specific sexual dysfunctions, including impotence, orgasmic
dysfunctions in the wife, ejaculatory incompetence, premature ejaculation.

   671.   Jacobs, L.I., The impotent king:
          Secondary impotence refractory to brief
          sex therapy, American Journal of Psycho-
          therapy, 1977, 31, 97-104.

The article describes the common characteristics of 6 cases
of secondary impotence that failed to respond to a 15-week
marital sex therapy program. The existence of a grandoise
self-concept in the husband and the increased reluctance
of the wives to pay tribute to them without receiving any
satisfaction of their own emotional needs are instrumental
in triggering and maintaining the erectile problem.
Pathological self-esteem operations in their relationship
are analyzed. Other forms of impotence, in which the new
sex therapy techniques are effective are delineated and
contrasted with the impotent-king syndrome. A successfully
resolved case of this syndrome, in which the husband's
homosexual activity was a complicating factor, is presented.
The alterations in therapy technique used here have implications for other treatment approaches for the impotent-
king syndrome. (Journal summary).

672.   Jacobson, G.F., Crisis theory and
        treatment strategy: Some sociocultural
        and psychodynamic considerations, Journal
        of Nervous and Mental Disease, 1965, 141,
        209-218.

The author describes the work of the Benjamin Rush Center
in Los Angeles, in which a walk-in psychiatric service is
offered, available to anyone 17 1/2 years or older.   The
treatment consists of a focus on crisis resolution, with a
maximum of six sessions (one hour/session).   The center
attracted a larger proportion of lower socio-economic
patients, and the author provides a number of clinical
findings as a result of working with this population.
Some of the critical differences in therapist and client
cultural and psychodynamic differences are highlighted,
and the value of a crisis-oriented brief treatment model
in overcoming many of these differences is discussed.
The type of therapist and client expectations are also
discussed as they relate to the process of therapy.   The
focus on crisis intervention is viewed as a focus on a
universal aspect of all human experience, whatever the
cultural or racial backgrounds of the individuals involved -
namely, all human beings must face and overcome various
crises and stresses in their lives.   Further, it was found
that the process of crisis resolution (i.e., the stages
or steps involved) were also universal.   Data indicate
that there were no statistically significant relationships
found between social class and variables related to therapy
process (e.g., number of visits, percentage treated, rate
of improvement).   These results are directly attributable
to the structure of the clinic program, and are in contra-
diction to previous work reported in the field.   The value
of such an approach is also seen in its ability to motivate
those who need to seek longer-term treatment.   The problem
of a shortage of competent therapists to provide such a
service is also discussed.

673.   Jacobson, G.F., Some psychoanalytic
        considerations regarding crisis therapy,
        Psychoanalytic Review, 1967, 54, 649-654.

The focus of this paper is on the use of psychoanalytic
principles in the use of crisis intervention.   The Benjamin
Rush Center for Problems of Living in Los Angeles was the

treatment setting for approximately 3,000 patients, ages
17 1/2 and older. The upper limit of six therapy sessions
was set, with a variety of mental health professionals
offering treatment. After a short review of the major
tenets of crisis theory, the treatment stages and therapist
activities are presented, including dynamic problem formulation and recapitulation to the patient. The emphasis is
on the ego-adaptive capabilities of the patient, with focus
placed on the present crisis and not on regressive infantile
conflicts that may be connected to the present crisis.
Repeated use is made of interpretation of the patient's
dependent needs and desires. Over two-thirds of the
patients seen were rated as improved, with a number reporting significant insight even in the brief time allotted to
the treatment process. One case example is provided.

674.   Jacobson, G., The briefest psychiatric
        encounter - acute effects of evaluation,
        Archives of General Psychiatry, 1968, 18,
        718-724.

The effects of a psychiatric evaluation, a brief, dynamic,
interpersonal encounter, is examined by comparing the month
before and the month following a two-interview clinic
evaluation. The patient in this study tended to see their
difficulties as residing in themselves rather than pro-
jecting them outward. Many presented soon after an
important loss and many hoped for direct help from the
evaluation itself. The test population as a whole showed
an overall alleviation of anxiety but not depression. A
subgroup was outlined who were apparently able to use the
evaluation as ultra-brief therapy. They reported a
distinct improvement in affect, interpersonal relations,
and job satisfaction, as well as positive feelings toward
their evaluation experience and a feeling that they had
derived specific gains from that experience. The gains
they described had elements similar to those described in
successful short-term therapy. Another group, smaller in
size, showed opposite characteristics. This study suggests
that systematic attention be given not only to the diagnostic function of the evaluation but to its therapeutic
potential as well. (Journal summary).

675.   Jacobson, G.F., Crisis intervention from
        the viewpoint of the mental health
        professional, Pastoral Psychology, 1970,
        21, 21-28.

676.   Jacobson, G.F., Emergency service in
        community mental health: problems and
        promises, American Journal of Public
        Health, 1974, 64, 124-128.

The author summarizes some of the factors which have
impeded the development of emergency services, such as the
low status of such services in the eyes of senior staff,
reflected in low pay for individuals providing such
services. The author also contends that underlying this
view is a lack of clarity in defining the nature of emergency services and in providing a meaningful theoretical
framework for such services. He distinguishes three types
of emergency services: a) suicide prevention; b) evaluation
and referral programs; c) crisis intervention programs.
A discussion of each of these and how they differ from the
other two is presented. The importance and value of
supervision in such work is stressed. The major emphasis
in this article is on the connection between crisis theory
and the practice of crisis intervention.

677.   Jacobson, G.F., Programs and techniques
        of crisis intervention in Caplan, G.,
        (ed.), American handbook of psychiatry,
        Vol. II, New York, Basic Books, 1974.

Jacobson introduces this chapter by defining crisis intervention programs, crisis theory, and crisis intervention
techniques. He then elaborates on each of these major
areas, basing much of his presentation on experience
gathered at the Benjamin Rush centers in Los Angeles.
Goals and rationale, organization models, and special
difficulties inherent in crisis intervention programs are
discussed. He examines origins (with special mention of
psychoanalysis and social work/sociology) and major
principles of crisis theory, as well as Caplan's conceptualization of crisis phenomena. The author reviews
crisis intervention techniques currently used by mental

health professionals.   Interventions on the individual,
family, and group level are presented.   Jacobson concludes
with a brief consideration of social class in relation to
crisis intervention, various outcome studies, and current
frontiers of this rapidly expanding field.   (abstract by
Deborah Schuller).

   678.   Jacobson, G.F., Therapy: Crisis
           intervention, in Resnick, H.L.P., and
           Hathorne, B.C., (eds.), Teaching outlines
           in crisis in suicide studies and crisis
           intervention, Bowie, Maryland, The Charles
           Press Publishers, Inc., 1974.

   679.   Jacobson, G.F., Crisis-Oriented Therapy,
           Psychiatric Clinics of North America,
           April, 1979, 2, 39-54.

Crisis-oriented treatment is a promising approach to the
definitive resolution of crises arising as a result of
changing life events which have disrupted a previous
equilibrium.   Based on crisis theory, the therapeutic
modality involves a relative de-emphasis on pathology as
such and a focus on clear identification of the chain of
events which has led to the crisis, first by the therapist
and eventually by both therapist and patient.   A major
goal of crisis treatment is a shared understanding of
hazardous events and their sequellae at a level of awareness which is appropriate to the ego structure of the
patient.   Along with the cognitive formulation, crisis
treatment provides for the expression of appropriate affect
and for the joint formulation by patient and therapist of
coping strategies to deal with the newly defined problem.
Referral for longer-term treatment, if required at all,
should occur only at the end of crisis therapy.   (Journal
summary and conclusion).

680.   Jacobson, G.F., and Portuges, S.H., Marital
        separation and divorce: assessment of an
        preventive considerations for crisis inter-
        vention, in Parad, R.P. (ed.), Emergency
        and disaster management, Bowie, Maryland,
        The Charles Press Publishers, Inc., 1976.

The authors discuss preventive intervention strategies for
persons in various stages of marital dissolution. Clinical
experiences and a consideration of the process of marital
disruption are also presented. Jacobson and Portuges
stress that the process by which the relationship is ended
determines the subsequent psychological performance of
separated or divorced individuals. Thus the role of the
crisis intervenor to facilitate more adaptive resolutions
to the emotional hazards inherent in a threatened marriage.
Approaches to management and potential outcomes are surveyed for the following crises: active threat (external
or internal) of marital dissolution; recent separation and/
or divorce; post-divorce crises; and remarriage. (abstract
by Deborah Schuller).

681.   Jacobson, G.F., et al., Generic and
        individual approaches to crisis inter-
        vention, American Journal of Public Health,
        1968, 58, 338-343.

The authors summarize briefly the work at the Benjamin
Rush Center, which provides immediate access, brief
psychiatric therapy approach to anyone over 17 1/2 years
of age. Treatment is problem-oriented, carried by a
mental health team (psychiatry, psychology, psychiatric
social work). A summary of the characteristics of crisis
is presented, reviewing the work of Caplan and Lindemann.
Two approaches to crisis intervention are described, the
generic and the individual approaches. The generic
approach assumes that for each crisis there are specific
identifiable stages or processes which will result in either
adaptive or maladaptive reactions on the part of an
individual. Examples of such a focus include delineating
the stages involves in grieving the loss of someone
significant in a person's life. The second approach, the
individual focus, differs from the generic in that specific

intrapsychic and interpersonal factors are assessed and
focussed on. The uniqueness of the individual's circumstances become the focus. The use of para-professional
personnel is stressed in the first type of approach while
the use of skilled professional personnel is stressed in
the second approach. Two case examples are provided highlighting the two methods.

682.   Jacobson, G.F., et al., The scope and
        practice of an early-access brief
        treatment psychiatric center, American
        Journal of Psychiatry, 1965, 121, 1176-
        1182.

The Benjamin Rush Center was organized as a walk-in clinic
to provide brief (up to 6 visits) and ready-access treatment, with resolution of acute crises with the goal of
restoration of functioning. In the first 19 months of
operation 776 patients were seen, at about the rate of 500
a year, perhaps twice the number that could have been
served with similar staff in clinics offering more
customary service. Research monitoring of Rush Center
operations revealed the following: i) service was provided
for a wide range of cases; ii) Rush Center patients are
genuinely in need of psychiatric assistance; iii) some
acute personal crisis, accompanied by identifiable precipitating events, were found in three-fourths of the
patients; iv) more than 40% of patients saw a therapist
4 more times; v) whatever the number of visits, 85% of
patients received treatment from the very first session,
a number being referred for further psychotherapeutic
attention. A variety of treatment modes are emoted
including adjunctive pharmacotherapy. Emphasis is on
clarification and definition of the precipitating event,
restoring the patient's problem-solving capacity, and
putting him in touch with warded off feelings. These
techniques require the development of new skills. Two-
thirds of patients are viewed by therapists as having
improved as a consequence of Rush Center treatment.
(Journal summary and conclusions).

683.   Jeffrey, W.D., et al., Schizophrenia:
        treatment in therapeutic community,
        New York State Journal of Medicine,
        1976, 76, 384-390.

Through the use of clinical examples from a hospital
treatment setting, the author explores the various facets
of treatment of schizophrenics. The value of a brief
therapy model within a milieu context is emphasized.

684.   Jenni, M.A., and Wollersheim, J.P.,
        Cognitive therapy, stress management
        training, and the Type A behavior
        pattern, Cognitive Therapy and Research,
        1979, 3, 61-73.

The effectiveness of two treatments for reducing stress
associated with the Type A behavior pattern was evaluated.
One treatment, Stress Management Training, was a replication of a previously reported treatment. The Cognitive
Therapy treatment, based on the principles of rational-
emotive therapy, was designed specifically for this study.
Both treatment groups were compared with a waiting list
control group on several self-report and physiological
measures. For subjects who initially had the highest
degree of Type A characteristics, Cognitive Therapy was
more effective than Stress Management Training or no
treatment in reducing self-perceived levels of Type A
behavior. Both treatments reduced self-reported anxiety
levels, and were more effective than no treatment. Neither
treatment reduced subjects' cholesterol levels or blood
pressure. (Journal abstract).

685.   Johnson, D.H., Counselor expectancies
        and goals in time-limited and time-
        unlimited counseling, Dissertation
        Abstracts International, 1979, 39(9-B),
        4582-4583.

686.   Johnson, D.H., and Gelso, C.J., The
        effectiveness of time limits in counseling
        and psychotherapy: A critical review,
        Research Report #5-79, Counseling Center,
        University of Maryland, College Park, Md.,
        1979.

To combat lengthy treatment and correspondingly long
waiting lists, many counseling centers and other mental
health agencies have begun to experiment with treatment
in which definite time limits are initially and explicitly
set. The present paper offers a critical review of
research on the effectiveness of such procedures. Time-
limited therapy (TLT) seems to be qualitatively different
from brief counseling in which no specific limit is established. Studies evaluating TLT are classified according
to source of measurement and time of measurement, factors
which appear crucial to conclusions about the comparative
effects of TLT vs. time-unlimited treatment. In general,
TLT emerges as a helpful way of setting a client's change
process in motion, a process which is then continued by
time outside counseling. Implications of the literature
for the use and study of TLT are discussed.

687.   Johnson, J., Psychiatric emergencies in
        the community, Comprehensive Psychiatry,
        1969, 10, 275-284.

One hundred ninety-four psychiatric emergencies were
referred either directly to the hospital psychiatrists or
to the local mental welfare service over a period of 3
months in an area committed to community care (England).
46% required immediate admission and constituted 53% of all
psychiatric admissions. Mental welfare emergencies were
largely re-referred psychotics while emergencies to the
hospital psychiatrists mainly related to incidents of self-
poisoning and self-injury. One-third of the emergencies
to the mental welfare service were treated with immediate
help of the local psychiatrist. Suggestions are made about
the use of walk-in clinics to prevent psychiatric emergencies and the role of the mental welfare office in such
clinics. (Journal summary).

688.   Johnson, R.L., and Chatowsky, A.P., Game
        theory and short-term group counseling,
        Personnel and Guidance Journal, 1969,
        47, 758-761.

The search for effective approaches to short-term group
counseling in a Navy brig focused on Transactional Analysis
and game theory, which seemed interesting to prisoners as
well as readily comprehensible and productive of insight.
Along with a summary of game theory, this discussion
presents a description of some common games in their military forms as they appeared in the brig groups. Advantages
and difficulties associated with using game theory with
"unmotivated clients" are noted. (Journal abstract).

689.   Johnson, R.W., Number of interviews,
        diagnosis, and success of counseling,
        Journal of Counseling Psychology, 1965,
        12, 248-251.

Two client samples from the University of Missouri Testing
and Counseling Service were divided according to diagnostic
categories. Each sample was examined in three ways:
(1) The combined categories were tested to determine if a
relationship existed between success and number of interviews. (2) The diagnostic categories were distributed
separately by number of interviews. (3) The successes for
both categories were compared in terms of number of interviews. Significant relationships were found between
numbers of interviews and success for emotional problems
but not for combined diagnosis or for vocational problems.
Also, a "failure" zone was found for the emotional problems.
The authors conclude that the results point to the fact
that success in treatment and length of treatment are
probably intimately tied to the type of problem the patient
presents and is struggling with (i.e., diagnosis).
(adapted journal abstract).

690.   Jones, M., and Polak, P., Crisis and
        confrontation, British Journal of
        Psychiatry, 1968, 114, 169-174.

The authors describe a procedure to deal with hospital
crisis situations either in staff members or in patients

through the use of face-to-face confrontations. The model
consists of 5 basic principles: a) Face-to-face confrontations: This is to be done as close as possible to the
moment of crisis, and should involve all of the significant
participants in the crisis; b) Strong skilled leadership:
This involves knowledge of the importance of timing of
confrontations as well as an understanding of the contributions of the participants; c) Open communication: It is
the responsibility of the leader to select a setting where
confrontations can be made in a safe way, without the fear
of reprisal for having shared one's feelings; d)Appropriate
level of feelings: The leader must help the participants
to express their feelings in such a way that the feelings
are neither too overwhelming or too tempered. Both kinds
of situations will not produce the needed change; e) Attitudes of participants conducive to growth: There must be
genuine desire on the part of the participants for change.
Two case examples are provided, one of a patient and his
family, the other of a staff crisis within the hospital.
The overall approach used is to view learning as a social
process, in which two-way communication is stressed.

691.   Jones, W., The A-B-C method of crisis
        management, Mental Hygiene, 1968, 52,
        87-89.

The author presents a conceptual model for dealing with
crises, in which three basic principles are follows:
A- achievement of contact with the individual in crisis;
B- boiling the problem down to its central issue(s);
C- coping effectively and actively through an emphasis on
the client's strengths and resources.

692.   Julian, A., and Kilmann, P.R., Group
        treatment of juvenile delinquents: A
        review of the outcome literature,
        International Journal of Group Psycho-
        therapy, 1979, 29, 3-37.

This paper has reviewed 32 studies which evaluated group
treatment of juvenile delinquents. A methodological
evaluation was conducted within five areas: time periods,
subjects, therapists, treatment, and outcome measures. A

considerable number of methodological problems were found, most notably in regard to the failure to specify the characteristics of treatment and the lack of follow-up evaluation of the delinquents' adjustment to the outside community. The studies were reviewed within four outcome categories: personality and attitude measures, behavioral measures, recidivism measures, achievement and intelligence measures. Positive results were obtained on less than one-third of all measures in all outcome categories. Overall, behavioral and modeling groups appeared the most effective, although these groups did not facilitate change on recidivism measures. Closed milieu group treatment seemed superior to open milieu group treatment across therapy, discussion, and behavioral groups. Future studies should: (a) specify subject and therapist characteristics, (b) conduct a multidimensional assessment of outcome, and (c) examine the effectiveness of different treatments with different etiological types of delinquents. (Journal summary).

693.   Julius, E.K., Family sculpting: A
        pilot program for a schizophrenic group,
        Journal of Marriage and Family Counseling,
        1978, 4, 19-24.

Describes a pilot program of brief group therapy that utilized nonverbal sculpting techniques as the central therapeutic modality. Family sculpting provided a structural format for the patients to organize perceptions of self and family within specific contexts, to experience these perceptions in action, and employ them in resolving family conflicts. Two case examples are presented of the technique. (Journal abstract).

694.   Kaffman, M., Short-term family therapy,
        Family Process, 1963, 2, 216-234.

The author reports on the use of a short-term family therapy approach at two clinics in Israel. A total of 70 cases referred to these treatment facilities were included in this report. The focus on family interation and evaluation of family dynamics, with a wide variety of therapeutic techniques used. The author outlines the

criteria for inclusion in the brief therapy program, and
acknowledges that the guidelines were violated in that more
severe pathology was included in the sample than had been
originally decided upon. The process of history-taking,
(including parents alone, child alone, family together,
etc.) over a 2-2 1/2 hour period is described. This is
followed by an assignment of a single therapist to the
family. The flexibility of the therapy sessions in terms
of the participants involved within each session is described, with clinical examples used to highlight to points
made. A report of a follow-up research project on these
families and their children revealed at six months post-
termination that over 75% reported significant improvement
as shown by the total disappearance of the symptoms which
brought the family into treatment in the first place.

695.   Kahn, M., and Baker, B., Desensitization
        with minimal therapist contact, Journal
        of Abnormal Psychology, 1968, 73, 198-200.

Phobic Ss were randomly assigned to 1 or 2 treatment groups:
(1) a "conventional desensitization" group, which was
treated by a therapist in the laboratory, or (2) a "do-it-
yourself" group, which carried out the desensitization
process at home. For the latter, the only therapist
contact was an initial interview and a weekly progress-
check phone call. According to Ss' reports of success,
both groups did equally well. These results are discussed
with respect to the relative importance of relationship
and content in the therapeutic process. (Journal abstract).

696.   Kalis, B.L., Restoring emotional balance
        as a goal in psychotherapy, Paper presented
        at the 15th Annual Psychiatric Social Work
        Institute, San Francisco, 1961.

Kalis explores various theoretic considerations for one
type of goal-limited psychotherapy. Issues relevant to
the underlying conceptual framework and to the formulation
of treatment goals are elaborated. An essential notion is
that a call for help represents a breakdown of an individual's adaptive emotional balance between intrapsychic and

external forces. Prompt attention to this disruption of
equilibrium, with particular emphasis on the unique personal meaning of the crisis for the individual concerned,
and, especially, the stresses precipitating the application
for help, can help restore emotional balance. This approach
assumes that precipitating stress evokes and at the same
time is derived from the applicant's core conflicts; thus,
the patient is not fully conscious of the actual factors
behind his request for help. Lastly, the author focuses
on process issues related to the dimension of time with
regard to the occurrence of precipitating stress; time
required for identification and resolution of stress in
the therapeutic transaction; time between the application
for help and the initial interview; and time required for
the emergence of data confirming the relationship between
precipitating stress and core conflicts. Some factors
affecting these processes are mentioned. Kalis includes
two case examples to illustrate her discussion. (abstract
by Deborah Schuller).

697.   Kalis, B.L., The continuum of crisis,
        Paper presented at Symposium on Crisis
        Intervention and Cokmunity Mental Health,
        Annual Meeting of Western Psychological
        Association, Long Beach, 1966.

Kalis discusses some theoretical issues and implications
regarding crisis. Although intellectual consideration is
generally accorded the interaction of intrapsychic and
environmental factors in the origin and termination of a
crisis state, too often therapeutic interventions are a
function of the intervening agent rather than the demands
of the situation. She argues that the field of community
mental health is uniquely situated so as to attend to both
internal and external variables. But she notes that the
definition of such variables is contingent upon the social
system in question--e.g. the individual, a family, a
population at risk, etc. Further, intervention at one
level will have reverberations at other levels.Thus, the
crisis consultant must be attentive to the full range of
contexts in which he contemplates intervention, and to the

variety of social systems which may be affected. To illustrate the need for a shifting conception of the meaning
and resolution of crisis, the author presents a hypothetical work day of a community psychologist. (abstract
by Deborah Schuller).

   698.   Kalis, B.L., Crisis theory: Its relevance
           for community psychology and directions
           for development, in, Adelson, D., and
           Kalis, B.L. (eds.), Community Psychology
           and Mental Health: Perspectives and
           Challenges, Scranton, Pa., Chandler
           Publishing Co., 1970.

This chapter first examines areas of definitional concensus
and divergency with regards to crisis theory; then analyzes
the present status of crisis theory and its conceptual
relevance to the concerns embodied in community mental
health. The analysis proceeds along nine dimensions
originated by Chapman for the analysis of disaster theories.
These nine continua are implication, situational reference,
systematic unity, comprehensiveness, temporal extension,
spatial extension, manipulability of variables, and evolu-
tionism. The author places crisis theory along each
dimension or an adaptation thereof - e.g,, Chapman's
spatial extension can be translated two ways in crisis
theory: to refer to the magnitude of hazardous events
appropriate to the definition of crisis, or to refer to
the locus of crisis reactions. In her conclusion, Kalis
reviews three general heuristic questions which a thorough
conceptual model of community mental health must attempt
to answer, and recapitulates the current status of crisis
theory using Chapman's paradigm. (abstract by Deborah
Schuller).

   698a.   Kalis, B.L., Single session crisis
           intervention symposium discussion,
           Paper presented at the Annual
           Convention of the American Psycho-
           logical Association, Honolulu, 1972.

The author highlights some general themes which emerged
from a series of papers on single session crisis intervention and its applicability to police work. The model

and training program outlined in the papers concerns
specialized techniques for intervention with families or
groups in crisis. She notes that application of this
model points explicitly to the role of the police as part
of the network of community mental health resources; while
it confronts directly the need for an increased level of
problem-solving skills in all the service professions.
Kalis cites the potential of the program for specific
tailoring to other communities and other professions.
(abstract by Deborah Schuller).

  699.   Kalis, B.L., et al., Precipitating stress
          as a focus in psychotherapy, Archives of
          General Psychiatry, 1961, 5, 219-228.

The authors address the issue of why patients come for
help. They postulate the concept of precipitating stress,
in which stress moves an individual from a previous stable
state to one of emotional disequilibrium. This instability
reactivates a previous psychic conflict, and the origin=
ating stressful event and the original conflict interact
to moving the individual to seek help. Forty patients
seen at the Langley-Porter Outpatient Department were
interviewed in depth specifically about what brought them
to therapy at the time they requested help. The ways an
interviewer can ascertain the answers to this question are
outlined in the article. Further, the various categories
of precipitating stress are summarized, including object
loss or threat of loss, "bind with previous source of
professional help", responses to identification with
another person (internal reaction rather than external
event), "surge of unmanageable impulses", "threat to
current adjustment". Examples are provided for each category of precipitating stress. The value of focussing on
precipitating stress and of working through with the
patient the meaning of the stress is discussed. The
importance of immediate access, brief intervention is also
reviewed.

700.   Kanas, N., et al., Response to catastrephe:
        A case study, Diseases of the Nervous
        System, 1977, 38, 625-627.

The occurrence of a sudden overwhelming stress may throw a
previously well-ordered life into turmoil. An understanding of the characteristic pattern of response to
stress has led to a treatment approach aimed at resolution
of the symptomatology by helping the patient integrate the
painful event into his life experience. This paper focuses
on the treatment of a young woman coping with three consecutive events: the murder of her lover, a gunshot wound
she received from her father, and the death of her father
in a suicide action. The reestablishment of equilibrium
in her own fragmented life through a stress-oriented
therapy provides a clear case example of this form of brief
therapy. (Journal introduction).

701.   Kandel, H.J., Paradoxical intention:
        An empirical investigation, Dissertation
        Abstracts International, 1978, 38(12-A),
        7152.

702.   Kandel, H.J., et al., Flooding or
        systematic exposure in the treatment of
        extreme social withdrawal in children,
        Journal of Behavior Therapy and Experi-
        mental Psychiatry, 1977, 8, 75-81.

Several children provided social stimuli for treating the
extreme social withdrawal of two young boys, one treated
by flooding, the other by systematic exposure. To assess
the effectiveness of the treatment procedures, within-
subject designs were used, consisting of multiple baselines
across settings. The results showed that when flooding was
introduced in the first setting for the first child, a
dramatic increase in interaction from 0 to 60% resulted,
with an accompanying decrease in self-talk from 70 to 20%.
These behavioral changes did not occur in the second
setting until flooding was introduced, when interaction
increased from 10 to 40% and self-talk decreased from 85

to 20%. Similar results were obtained with systematic
exposure in the second child. Follow-ups of 5 months in
the first child and 9 months in the second indicated that
the therapeutic gains were maintained. Thus, in treating
anxiety related problems in children in their natural
environment either flooding or systematic exposure can be
effective. (Journal abstract).

703.   Kaplan, D.M., A concept of acute
        situational disorder, Social Work,
        1962, 7, 15-23.

Kaplan briefly reviews current conceptualizations of casework problems and offers a critique of the conception of
the "Environmental problem"--one major category of the
environmental-individual classification dichotomy.
Grounding his work on Lindemann's study of bereavement
reactions, Kaplan defines the conditions which constitute
"acute situational problems", and suggests that many
problems now labeled as "Environmental" are in fact
examples of the former. Acute situational problems are
conceptualized as analogous to acute disturbances within
the disease theory of somatic medicine. An acute emotional
disorder need not arise from an established chronic disease,
but may be precipitated by an individual's attempt to cope
with a threatening psychological event for which, initially,
he has inadequate resources. After elaboration of this
concept of acute situational problems, Kaplan examines
implications for casework typology, treatment, and prevention. (abstract by Deborah Schuller).

704.   Kaplan, D.M., Observation of crisis
        theory and practice, Social Casework,
        1968, 49, 515-155.

The author reports on efforts to deal with a woman's
emotional reaction of ambivalence to the birth of a premature baby. Individual therapy totalling five sessions
was used, with successful outcome reported.

705.   Kaplan, H.S., The new sex therapy,
        New York, Brunner/Mazel, 1974.

705a.   Kaplan, H.S., Sex therapy: An overview,
        in, Ard, B. (ed.), Handbook of Marriage
        Counseling, Palo Alto, Science and
        Behavior Books, 1976.

In this overview article, a leader in the field of sex
therapy focusses attention on three issues: a) what is
sex therapy? b) how effective is it? c) have the successes
of sex therapies invalidated psychoanalytic theory? She
defines sex therapy as goal-limited, aimed at the relief of
a patient's sexual symptom, in which prescribed sexual
experiences (exercises) are combined with psychotherapy.
Termination occurs when the patient's symptom has been
eliminated and when the assumption can be made that sexual
functioning is relatively stable and permanent. The various
types of treatment formats used in sex therapy are reviewed
briefly. The lack of tightly controlled studies is raised
as a difficulty in the area, but some trends are summarized
from uncontrolled, outcome studies. Generally, one can
expect about an 80% cure rate with short-term intensive,
active, experientially-oriented therapy, in which both
partners are actively involved. The author also reports,
that generally, the positive effects of such treatment are
limited to the patient's sexual functioning. No change in
the psychodynamic make-up of each partner after successful
completion of sex therapy sessions has been reported with
some frequency, although some major positive changes and
some major negative changes have also been reported.
Finally, the author concludes that psychoanalytic theory
and sex therapy are not in opposition, for they tend to
intervene at different levels and appear to be appropriate
for different presenting problems.

706.   Kapp, R.A., and Weiss, S.D., An inter-
        disciplinary, crisis-oriented graduate
        training program within a student health
        service mental health clinic, Journal of
        the American College Association, 1975,
        23, 340-344.

We have described the goals, history and structure of our
interdisciplinary training program in crisis intervention
which involves five academic departments: Psychiatry,
Clinical Psychology, Psychiatric Nursing, Psychiatric
Social Work, and Rehabilitation Counseling. The trainees
in this program receive specialized training in crisis-
intervention and brief-focal psychotherapy. Active supervision, direct observation, interdisciplinary teams, and
cotherapy constitute the major aspects of our model of
supervision. The specific skills that our trainees seem
to acquire from the program include diagnostic skills, the
ability to establish rapport quickly, the ability to conceptualize and implement a plan of action, and familiarity
with a wide array of techniques. We concluded by evaluating
the advantages of the training program in terms of needs
met and cost-benefit factors, as well as pointing out some
specific problems we have encountered. (Journal summary).

707.   Kardener, S.H., A methodologic approach
        to crisis therapy, American Journal of
        Psychotherapy, 1975, 29, 4-13.

The author provides a brief history on short-term psychotherapy, citing work by Freud, Ferenzi, Rank, Grinker and
Spiegel, and Lindemann, and Lindemann and Caplan. A
mthodology is presented focussed on determining what caused
the patient to seek therapy at a given time. This methodology is based on categorizing life events and experiences
into the work-school world, the familial world, the social
world, and the intrapsychic world of the patient. The
author stresses the mutually agreed-upon and attainable
goal-setting nature of brief therapy. The wide range of
techniques that a short-term therapist must use are
discussed (e.g., environmental manipulation, family therapy,
conditioning, hypnotherapy, psychodynamically-oriented
therapy, etc.). Four case histories are provided to
illustrate many of the points made.

708.   Karon, B.P., The resolution of acute
        schizophrenic reactions: A contribution
        to the development of non-classical psycho-
        therapeutic techniques, Psychotherapy:
        Theory, Research, and Practice, 1963, 1,
        27-43.

The basic element of a brief, apparently effective,
psychoanalytic therapy for acute schizophrenic reaction is
presented. The therapeutic devices which are aimed specifically at rapidly resolving the acute symptoms are also
described. These are to establish emotional contact as
quickly as possible, build differentiation between thoughts
and actions, wishes and reality, and to unearth unconscious
problems as possible. The therapist must continually aim
at decreasing the patients feelings of anxiety, guilt, sin,
and unworthiness. (Journal abstract).

709.   Karon, B.P., Suicidal tendency as the
        wish to hurt someone else, and resulting
        treatment technique, Journal of Individual
        Psychology, 1964, 20, 206-212.

Suicide has been described as the result of a specific
fantasy that killing onself is an effective aggressive
retaliation. Direct dramatic denial of the effectiveness
of suicide as a technique of retaliation, when combined
with a warm therapeutic relationship that arouses in the
patient a hope which cannot be realized in death, suffices
to end the suicidal danger. Several illustrative cases
are presented. (Journal summary).

710.   Karon, B.P., and Vandenbos, G.R.,
        Psychotherapeutic technique and the
        economically poor patient, Psychotherapy:
        Theory, Research, and Practice, 1977, 14,
        169-180.

Psychotherapy with the poor patient is no different from
good psychotherapy with anyone. The intertwining of
reality and psychodynamics must be dealt with in all its
complexity. The therapist must also educate the patient
as to what therapy is all about, and why it should be
helpful. When appropriate , crisis intervention, or

repeated crisis intervention, can be as effective as continuous therapy. Whether to help the patient adapt to
being lower class or to escape, is ideology, not therapy.
The therapist must help the patient evaluate the alternatives in the light of his reality and psychodynamics,
and then to act. (Journal abstract modified).

711.   Karp, H.N., and Karls, J.M., Combining
        crisis therapy and mental health con-
        sultation, Archives of General Psychiatry,
        1966, 14, 536-542.

One year of experience in a new community mental health
program has been described, using an ortho-team approach
of a psychiatrist, clinical psychologist, and psychiatric
social workers. Crisis-oriented psychotherapy and mental
health consultation have been used as the primary services.
The success in treating large numbers of patients for
short-term therapy, using other agencies for identification,
referral, and follow-up, is described. This approach,
using the same staff members to participate in both the
mental health consultation and crisis therapy aspects of
the program simultaneously, merits consideration in setting
up similar community mental health programs elsewhere.
Three cases are described, in which this approach worked
successfully to treat the patients, preclude hospitalization, and enable close follow-up. Further research on
such combined methods appears indicated. (Journal summary).

712.   Karpman, B., "Blitz" psychotherapy,
        Medical Annals of the District of
        Columbia, 1942, 11, 291-296.

The author presents a method of brief therapy in which the
therapist constantly intrudes or intervenes on the free
associations of the patient, and works actively with the
patient. The therapist often requires that the patient
write out his/her life history, and then bases specific
questions on the history. Homework is also given, in the
form of a question for the patient to answer by the next
visit. From time to time, the therapist will summarize in
writing the patient's problem. The use of bibliotherapy
focussed on readings in psychotherapy and psychodynamics

is also utilized. Karpman stresses that the patient
should only receive enough insight to handle his/her life
problems, with the implication that too much insight can
be harmful at times. The therapist also can bring in
someone related to the patient (e.g., husband or wife), in
cases where the patient refuses to co-operate.

713.   Karson, S., Group psychotherapy with
        latency age boys, International Journal
        of Group Psychotherapy, 1965, 15, 81-89.

A time-limited group program with "acting-out" and neurotic
boys has been described in which mothers and latency age
children are treated separately for about six months on a
one-a-week basis. Such short-term group therapy seems to
be especially effective with children in reducing guilt,
impulsive excitability, and neurotic symptomatology, and
in increasing masculine identification, frustration
tolerance, and especially, self-esteem. The program
appears to hold much promise as a treatment method for
parents and children, as well as being a technique for
providing training in group therapy. (Journal summary).

714.   Kartha, M., and Ertel, I.J., Short-term
        therapy for mothers of leukemic children,
        Clinical Pediatrics, 1976, 51, 803-806.

715.   Katz, A.J., et al., Change in inter-
        actions as a measure of effectiveness
        in short-term family therapy, Family
        Therapy, 1975, 2, 31-56.

The authors report in detail a study to determine whether
family interaction changes as a result of short-term (four
sessions) family therapy. After a brief review of relevant
outcome literature, methodological considerations and
research goals are discussed. The study utilized the
Family Interaction Scales of Riskin and Faunce to measure
changes in the communication process between and among
family members (17 families in total). Methodology and
results are carefully outlined. Katz, et al. interpret
their data as it pertained to families who sought and

received clinical help, families who sought but had not yet received help, and families who had not sought assistance. This study indicates that family therapy does effectively enhance family interactions. Social policy implications deriving from this finding are briefly discussed. The authors conclude with specific recommendations for future research. (abstract by Deborah Schuller).

716.   Keilson, M., Time limited vs. unlimited
        therapy in a university counseling center,
        Dissertation Abstracts International, 1974,
        34, 11-B, 5862.

717.   Keilson, M.V., et al., the effectiveness
        of time-limited counseling in a university
        counseling center, Research Report #5-78,
        Counseling Center, University of Maryland,
        College Park, Md., 1978.

This study investigated the effects of eight-session time-limited counseling on clients' self concepts. Forty-two students seeking personal counseling at the university counseling center were randomly assigned to either time-limited, time-unlimited, or control groups, after screening with the MMPI to eliminate the most severely disturbed clients. The Bills Index of Adjustment and Values was administered before and after counseling. Results of a two-way repeated measures analysis indicated significant improvement in both time-limited and unlimited counseling groups, but not for the controls. The two treatment groups did not differ in improvement. A two and one-half year follow-up of 18 of the former clients suggested that treatment gains were maintained, and were equivalent for thos receiving time-limited and open-ended counseling. (author abstract).

718.   Keilson, M.V., et al., The effectiveness
        of time-limited psychotherapy in a
        university counseling center, Journal of
        Clinical Psychology, 1979, 35, 631-636.

Investigated the effects of eight-session, time-limited therapy on clients' self-concepts. Forty-two students who

sought psychotherapy or personal counseling at the
university counseling center were assigned randomly to
either time-limited, time-unlimited, or control groups
after screening with the MMPI to eliminate the most
severely disturbed clients. The Bills Index of Adjustment
and Values were administered pre- and post-therapy.
Results of a two-way repeated measures analysis indicated
significant improvement in both time-limited and unlimited
groups, but not in the controls. The two treatment groups
did not differ in improvement. A 2½ year follow-up of 18
of the former clients suggested that treatment gains were
maintained and were equivalent for those who received
time-limited and open-ended therapy. (Journal abstract).

    719.   Kellner, R., and Sheffield, B.F.,
            The relief of distress following
            attendance at a clinic, British
            Journal of Psychiatry, 1971, 118,
            195-198.

Twenty new neurotic out-patients whose symptoms had lasted
for more than six months were selected. They were told
that they had to wait for treatment (first waiting period).
After this waiting period, anxious and depressed patients
(N=10) had three sessions of abreactions followed by a
second waiting period, then three sessions of interpretive
psychotherapy utilizing tape recordings from the abreactions,
followed by a third waiting period. Patients who had
psychophysiological symptoms who believed that they
auffered from a phsycial illness (N=10) had a physical
examination and physical investigations. After being told
that they were physically health, they had one session of
explanatory therapy, followed by a second waiting period.
Fifteen patients completed the study. A significant
decrease in the Symptom Rating Test scores occurred in
each group during the first waiting period before treatment, but not during the other waiting periods. The
results are in accord with the findings of others that
there is a marked initial decrease of distress scores in
neurotic patients following attendance at a clinic without
treatment. (Journal summary).

720.   Kennedy, W.A., School phobia: Rapid
        treatment of fifty cases, Journal of
        Abnormal Psychology, 1965, 70, 285-285.

The two major competing professional points of view
regarding the etiology and treatment of school phobias are
presented, namely, the psychoanalytic and behavioristic
view points. Type I phobias (the neurotic crisis) and
Type II phobias (the way of life) are distinguished from
each other on a 10 item scale. The Human Development
Clinic of Florida State University treated 50 cases of
Type I school phobia. The major characteristics of such
a phobia include first episode of illness when referred,
appears on Mondays following illness previous Thursday or
Friday, acute onset, more prevalent in younger school aged
children, expressed anxiety about death, mother's physical
health in question for the phobic child, basic positive
communication between parents and good adjustment of parents
in most areas, father competitive with mother in household
chores, parents relatively easy to work with. All 50 cases
of this type I school phobia had complete remission of
symptoms at termination and at follow-up. The specific
treatment approach is detailed, including good professional
public relations (i.e., with schools, etc.), avoidance of
emphasis of somatic complaints, forced school attendance,
structured therapy interviews with parents, brief interviews with the child, and follow-up

721.   Kerns, E., Planned short-term treatment,
        a new service to adolescents, Social
        Casework, 1970, 51, 340-346.

This article focusses on the work of an outpatient
adolescent service, in which the modality of treatment was
planned short-term therapy. The clinic located in the
Cleveland area, provides service to any, 12-21 years old
and their parents. The focus is on contracting around
specific problems and renegotiating contracts as needed.
The minimizing of the development of dependency on the
part of the client and focus on problem solving are
stressed. The details of the processes of diagnosis,
treatment, and termination are discussed and highlighted
through the use of two case histories. The difficulties

staff members go through in shifting to this type of treatment approach are delineated. The staff at this service
have found that the psychiatric diagnosis per se does not
enter into the determination of whether a particular
client would benefit from planned short-term treatment.
The criteria for selection of PSTT is based on the kind
of goal a client acceptable to client and therapist, the
level of positive factors (intrapsychic, external) in the
adolescent's life which could be used in problem-solving,
and the skill and confidence of the therapist.

  722.   Kassler, D.R., and Glick, I.D., Brief
         family therapy, Psychiatric Clinics of
         North America, 1979, 2, 75-48.

Brief family therapy may include weekend marathon "growth"
groups, two to six session crisis-intervention approaches,
or sector treatment of a particular aspect of family interactions for up to several months. The emphasis in these
formats is different, and the format chosen depends to a
large extent on the nature of the problems as well as the
therapist's stylistic preferences and flexibility.
(Journal abstract).

  723.   Keyes, B.L., et al., Psychiatry in the
         general hospital, American Journal of
         Psychotherapy, 1949, 3, 90-95.

The brief therapy approach as practiced at Jefferson
Memorial Hospital was presented. The average therapy
duration was five-six days. The advantages of such a
service within the context of a general hospital were
presented, especially for neuroses, psychosomatic disease,
and developing stages of schizophrenia.

  724.   Kiev, A., Psychotherapeutic strategies
         in the management of depressed and
         suicidal patients, American Journal of
         Psychotherapy, 1975, 29, 345-354.

This paper examines the Crisis Intervention Therapy
developed by Dr. Kiev's Cornell Program, for the management
of depressed and suicidal patients. Combining chemotherapy

with supportive psychotherapy, he emphasizes the acquisition of Life Strategy Skills, using motivational audiotaped material. The therapeutic rationale is also explored
and related to the explosive and unpredictable interpersonal world of suicidal patients and attitudes of
patients and significant others toward the sick role.
(Journal abstract).

725.   Kiev, A., Crisis intervention and suicide
       presention, in Scheidman, E.C. (Ed.),
       Suicidology: Contemporary developments,
       New York, Grune and Stratton, 1976.

After situating suicidal behavior as a major health problem
in the United States, Kiev begins his examination of a
number of critical factors associated with suicide risk
and its management. He implicitly emphasizes the necessity
of considering thd dialectic between the patient and his
social environment, and particularly his relationship with
significant others, at all points of therapeutic intervention. The author treats in detail evaluation of
suicidal potential, and the identification of life stresses
which may be exacerbated by suicidal preoccupation. He
discusses treatment of depression, especially as applied
by one suicide prevention clinic; and presents method and
findings of one study which demonstrated the value of
chemotherapy as part of an overall treatment of potentially
suicidal patients. Antidepressant drugs are one important
early component of the approach of this clinic. Once a
degree of symptom relief is obtained, assessment of the
patient's problems can more easily be made. Kiev elaborates on phases of treatment which have as their objective
prevention of further crises. Lastly, the author considers
the question of duration of treatment and disposition.
(abstract by Deborah Schuller).

726.   Killeen, M.R., and Jacobs, C.L. Brief
       group therapy with women students,
       Social Casework, 1976, 21, 521-522.

This article describes a brief group therapy program for
women students at the Mental Health Division of the
University of Georgia Health Services. The types of

presenting issues are discussed, such as depression, disruptions in heterosexual relationships, difficulties with
authority, problems with assertiveness, etc. The active
role of the therapists was discussed. Clinical impressions
indicate improvement in communication patterns as a result
of participation in the brief group therapy, especially
improvement between the women and their mothers. A total
of 40 women have participated in the program.

727.   Kilmann, P.R., and Auerbach, S.M.,
        Effects of marathon group therapy on
        trait and state anxiety, Journal of
        Consulting and Clinical Psychology,
        1974, 42, 607-612.

This study evaluated the effects of marathon group therapy
on anxiety. The subjects were 84 institutionalized female
narcotic drug addits. Combining all groups of subjects
(directive therapy, nondirective therapy, control), state
anxiety (A-State) declined significantly from pretherapy
to posttherapy, with the two therapy groups showing a far
greater decline than the control group. Trait anxiety
(A-Trait)was unchanged from pretherapy to posttherapy when
the scores for all groups were combined. However, there
was a significant interaction between type of therapy and
periods. Subjects receiving nondirective therapy declined
in A-Trait, directive therapy subjects increased, and
control subjects showed virtually no change in A-Trait.
The results were interpreted as supporting Spielberger's
notion that trait anxiety reflects a dispositional tendency to respond with anxiety in ego-threat situations and
as suggesting that personality trait measures may be more
relevant outcome indicators than measures in transitory
mood states in marathon therapy research. (Journal
abstract).

728.   Kilmann, P.R., et al., Effects of a
        marathon group on self-actualization and
        attitudes toward women, Journal of Clinical
        Psychology, 1976, 32, 154-157.

This study investigated the impact of a 16-hour marathon
session on levels of self-actualization and attitudes
toward women both 1 day and 5 weeks after the group

experience. Female undergraduates were assigned randomly
to one of two marathon groups or to a no-treatment control
group. Ss in both marathon groups experienced a significant shift toward increased independence or self-supported-
ness on both posttests. However, differential group effect
was found from separate comparisons of each marathon group
with tte control group on pre- post shifts in attitudes
toward women: Ss in one marathon group reflected significantly greater agreement with profeminist attitudes on the
first posttest and experienced an even greater shift in
that direction on the second posttest, while Ss in the
other marathon group did not differ signficantly from the
control Ss on either posttest. (Journal summary).

729. Kilmann, P.R., et al., The impact of
effective education on elementary school
underachievers, Psychology in the Schools,
1979, 16, 217-223.

This study examined the impact of affective education on
elementary school underacnievers who either were referred
by their teachers for behavior problems or were randomly
selected for treatment. Sixty-three students in the
fourth through sixth grades participated in nine counseling
groups that met once a week for 15 weeks. Seventy-seven
underachievers responded to the measures at the same time
intervals as the experimental subjects, but received no
treatment. The experimental subjects showed a significantly greater increase in reading skills, and described
themselves as more warmhearted, more emotionally stable,
more venturesome, and more vigorous after the group
experience than did their control counterparts. (Journal
abstract).

730. Kilmann, P.R., et al., Marathon versus
weekly encounter-group treatment on
self-actualization: Two years later,
Group and Organizational Studies, 1978,
3, 483-488.

This study investigates the comparative ability of a
marathon and a weekly encounter group to produce gains in
self-actualization. The subjects were twenty-three under-

graduates who volunteered for each of the experiences.
The marathon group was conducted for 16 relatively continuous hours. The weekly group met for two hours, twice
weekly, for four weeks - a total of 16 hours. Both the
treatment groups, conducted by the same leader, received
the same sequence of group exercises. A significant
group effect indicated that both groups increased their
self-actualization scores from the pretest. No significant differences were found between the two experimental
groups on self-actualization or perceived adjustment to
life events over the two-year follow-up. No significant
group differences were found on participants' retrospective ratings of short-term and long-term group effects.
Among other issues, the possibility that certain treatment
goals may be selectively influenced by one time format
over the other is discussed. (Journal abstract).

731.   Kilmann, P.R., and Sotile, W.M., The
        effects of structured and unstructured
        leader roles on internal and external
        group participants, Journal of Clinical
        Psychology, 1976, 32, 848-856.

This study assessed the impact of structured and unstructured leader roles on measures of outcome for Ss who
differed on the pretest dimension "locus of control."
On the basis of their pretest locus of control scores, Ss
were assigned to a structured or an unstructured marathon
group. The treatment in the two 16-hour marathon consisted of a defined series of exercises; the only difference between the two groups was the degree of leader
control over member participation. As predicted, internal
Ss in the unstructured group rated the leader and the
group more positively than did the external Ss, while the
reverse responsivity occurred in the structured group.
Significant Locus of Control X Treatment interactions
indicated that internal and external Ss reflected
differential shifts in general anxiety general depression,
and locus of control as a function of treatment. The
relationship between changes in self-actualization and
locus of control and changes in conflict-handling styles
and negative affects differed as a function of locus of

control and treatment condition. The overall results
coupled with prior findings tentatively support the
appropriateness of an unstructured leader role for internal
scorers and a structured leader role for external scorers.
(Journal abstract).

732.   Kilmann, P.R., and Sotile, W.M., The
        marathon encounter group: A review of
        the outcome literature, Psychological
        Bulletin, 1976, 83, 827-850.

Forty-five investigations of the marathon encounter group
are systematically evaluated. Comparisons of the studies
are made within sections on time format, subjects, leaders,
treatment, testing periods, and outcome criteria. All but
six studies used "normal" college volunteers as subjects.
Some positive results are found in varied aspects of
personal or social functioning, although the group effects
seem to be temporary. The methodological shortcomings are
considerable. The superiority of the marathon encounter
group over traditional spaced group treatment is not
established, and the treatment methods most effective in
the extended session still need to be identified. Critical
limitations of the studies indicated that further investigations of variables predictive of desired outcomes should
use treatment and control groups, defined treatment formats,
multiple outcome criteria, and comprehensive follow-up
investigations. (Journal abstract).

733.   Kimbro, E.L., et al., A multiple family
        group approach to some problems of
        adolescence, International Journal of
        Group Psychotherapy, 1967, 17, 18-24.

The authors present a description of a unique multiple
family, short-term group therapy program for the treatment
of problems of adolescence. Three families and their
problem teenager are seen in group therapy. Two types of
presenting problems were reported, those involving underachievement in high school and those involving delinquency.
The groups are set up so that there is a homogeneity of

presenting problem within each group. The advantages of
such a structure are reviewed. The patterns which emerged
during the process of therapy are described, and the
differences between families of underachievers and delinquents are presented. The specific goals and roles of the
therapist are also described in detail.

734.   Kinston, W., and Bentovim, A., Brief
        focal family therapy when the child is
        the referred patient - II. Methodology
        and results, Journal of Child Psychology
        and Psychiatry, 1978, 19, 119-143.

The experience of a workshop set up within a Department of
Child Psychiatry to foster family therapy and to develop
a brief focal technique is described. Details are provided
of the first 29 cases. Twenty-two families engaged in
therapy and the referred child in 19 (87%) of these cases.
Family change was measured using a methodology developed
by Malan to assess psychodynamic change in individuals and
problems in adapting it are discussed. Eleven (50%) of
the engaged families improved. The pattern of child and
family improvement supported the theory that a symptomatic
child can be a manifestation of family pathology. A
contraindication to the brief focal approach is past or
present formal mental illness in a parent. Marital disturbance was frequently covert: this affected the therapeutic plan but was not related to outcome. (Journal
summary).

735.   Kirshner, L., and Kaplan, N., Conversion
        as a manifestation of crisis in the life
        situation: A report of seven cases of
        ataxia and paralysis of the lower
        extremities, Comprehensive Psychiatry,
        1970, 11, 61-66.

The authors report on seven cases whose presenting problems
were either leg paralysis and/or ataxia, seen in short-term
therapy by a psychiatric staff. The article described the
specific personality characteristics of each patient, and
the present-oriented focus of therapy. The results
indicate that four patients produced a rapid, full
recovery. One patient improved slightly.

736.   Kissel, S., Mothers and therapists
        evaluate long-term and short-term child
        therapy, Journal of Clinical Psychology,
        1974, 30, 296-299.

Mothers and therapists evaluated the effectiveness of
clinic services; 186 cases of children seen foe either
short- or long-term psychotherapy were surveyed 6 years
after termination. Mothers found the service significantly
more beneficial than would have been predicted on the basis
of therapists' ratings alone, which in the past comprised
the major measure of improvement in psychotherapy. While
the type of service, number of sessions, or duration of
service were not related to mothers' evaluation of effectiveness, the therapist felt that that children had to be
seen in long-term psychotherapy for a greater number of
sessions and for a longer period of time to be considered
improved. The findings strongly suggest that therapists
have a built-in bias when it comes to evaluating effectiveness of psychotherapy. Parents overwhelmingly stated that
symptomatic relief in their children and improved parenting
were the benefits that they derived from their involvement
with the clinic. (Journal abstract).

737.   Klein, N.C., et al., Impact of family
        systems intervention on recidivism and
        sibling delinquency: A model of primary
        prevention and program evaluation,
        Journal of Consulting and Clinical
        Psychology, 1977, 45, 469-474.

Eighty-six families of delinquents were randomly assigned
to one of four treatment conditions: no treatment controls,
a client-oriented family approach, an eclectic-dynamic
approach, and a behaviorally oriented short-term systems
approach. A program evaluation model focusing on tertiary,
secondary, and primary prevention effects of intervention
was developed. Three levels of evaluation were performed:
Process changes in family interaction at the termination
of treatment (tertiary prevention); recidivism rates of
identified delinquents 6-18 months following treatment
(secondary prevention); and rate of sibling contact with
the court 2½-3½ years following intervention (primary
prevention). The family systems approach, when compared

to the other conditions, produced significant improvements
in process measures and a significant reduction in recidivism. To evaluate the primary prevention impact, juvenile
court records were examined to obtain rates of court
referrals for siblings of initially referred delinquents.
Results indicated that only 20% of families in the treatment condition had subsequent court contacts for siblings,
compared to a 40% rate for no-treatment controls and 59%
and 63% rates for the alternative treatment conditions
(p   001). (Journal abstract).

738.   Koegler, R.R., Brief-contact therapy and
        drugs in outpatient treatment, in, Wayne,
        G.J., and Moegler, R.R. (eds.), Emergency
        psychiatry and brief therapy, Boston,
        Little, Brown, 1966.

739.   Koegler, R.R., et al., A psychiatric clinic
        evaluates brief-contact therapy, Mental
        Hospitals, 1964, 15, 564-570.

A five year controlled, double-blind study of the effects
of tranquilizing drugs on nonpsychotic female outpatients
was conducted by the UCLA Neuropsychiatric Institute. The
results indicated fairly uniform average improvement among
five groups treated, respectively, with psychotherapy,
meprobamate, prochlorperazine, phenobarbital, or placebo.
Furthermore, patients treated in five- to 15-minute interviews in conjunction with "mild or innocuous medication"
did as well as those receiving hour-long, weekly sessions
over an extended period of time. This study helped overcome staff resistance to brief supportive treatment and
the use of drugs for selected patients. To provide this
type of treatment, a special program (The General Psychiatric Clinic) was instituted whereby residents treat three
patients per hour, one half-day each week with brief
contact therapy, often supplemented by psychotropic medication. Improvement has been noted in a wide range of
patients. Three case histories are presented. (abstract
by Deborah Schuller).

740.   Koenig, K.P., and Masters, J., Experimental
        treatment of habitual smoking, Behaviour
        Research and Therapy, 1964, 3, 235-243.

Habitual cigarette smoking in 42 Ss was used as model of
problem behaviour to which 3 different therapies were
applied by therapists. Two of the therapies were based on
techniques associated with "behaviour therapy" while a
third consisted of supportive counselling. The experiment
was designed to test the effects of different therapists
as well as different therapies. Amount of change in smoking behaviour was significantly related to therapists but
unrelated to the particular therapy administered. Ss were
significantly effective predictors of their own level of
success. Relatively successful Ss tended to evaluate the
therapists to whom they were assigned more negatively than
did unsuccessful Ss. (Journal summary).

741.   Kogan, L.S., The short-term case in a
        family agency, Parts I, II, and III,
        Social Casework, 1957, 38, 231-238,
        269-302, 366-374.

This three part article reports on a study designed to
delve into a number of different dimensions related to
short-term therapy. A total of 195 cases involving over
90 different therapists are summarized. The duration of
therapy lasted from one-five sessions. The author reports
that certain variables collected in the initial intake
interview turned out to be predictive of whether a patient
would stay in therapy for the entire number of specified
sessions or whether they would drop out prematurely. A
large percentage of the cases (72%) were one interview
only. About two third of these were agreed upon one-
interview-closings, about one third unplanned terminations.
Clients who terminated prematurely were more likely to have
presented a greater resistance to and lower motivation for
therapy and solving their problems. Those in both groups
were rated as having been helped, but those who remained
were rated as having gained more.

742.   Konick, D.S., et al., Change in
        symptomatology associated with short-
        term psychiatric hospitalization, Journal
        of Clinical Psychology, 1972, 28, 385-390.

The impact of short-term hospitalization on symptoms of
psychopathology was examined in a study of 840 patients
who had been rated on the BPRS (Brief Psychiatric Rating
Scale) by psychiatrists at the time of admission and at
discharge. Although the group of patients improved significantly in all areas of symptomatology, those symptoms
that characterized the group at admission were still
present at discharge. When the data were examined ward
by ward, it was found that the patients on all hospital
wards improved and that some wards were slightly more
effective than others. (Journal summary).

743.   Konick, D., et al., Changes in nurses'
        ratings of hospital adjustment associated
        with short-term hospitalization, Journal
        of Clinical Psychology, 1972, 28, 579-580.

The authors present the results of a large scale evaluation
project at a psychiatric in-patient hospital, in which
nurses were asked to rate the changes in close to 1,200
patients who received short-term treatment. The Nurses
Observation Scale for Inpatient Evaluation (NOSIE-30) was
used, and filled out at admission, after three days, and
three days prior to discharge. The results indicated a
positive effect in many areas of functioning, and provide
further support for the short-term hospital treatment.
The average length of stay in the hospital was 44 days,
and over half the patients treated were diagnosed psychotic.

744.   Korner, H., Abolishing the waiting list
        in a mental health center, American
        Journal of Psychiatry, 1964, 120, 1097-
        1100.

Since 1961, the Black Hawk County Mental Health Center
(Waterloo, Iowa) has functioned without a waiting list for
diagnosis, consultation or treatment. A previous waiting

list of 210 patients was worked up quickly, by adopting a
clinical and administrative approach which differs from
the method traditionally used by most mental health centers.
These clinical-administrative tools are descroned, and the
thinking behind each change is detailed. (Journal
summary).

745.   Koss, M.P., Length of psychotherapy
        for clients seen in private practice,
        Journal of Consulting and Clinical
        Psychology, 1979, 47, 210-212.

Length of treatment for all clients (N=100) seen for psychotherapy during 1975 by 7 therapists in a private
practice psychological clinic was examined to determine the
relative frequenty of long-term (more than 25 sessions) vs
short-term (less than 25 sessions). Clients were young,
middle class, intelligent, and mildly to moderately disturbed. The median length of treatment was 8 sessions.
Fully 80% of the clients had left treatment before receiving 25 sessions. This finding mirrors the trend for public
treatment settings. Results reaffirm the necessity of
further research and development of short-term treatment
techniques designed to effectively utilize the brief time
even private patients spend in psychotherapy. (Journal
abstract).

746.   Kotkov, B., Technique and explanatory
        concepts of short-term group psychotherapy,
        Journal of Clinical Psychopathology, 1949,
        10, 304-316.

Kotkov describes technique and underlying concepts of
short-term group therapy as practised with white male
veterans suffering from emotional disabilities. The group
meets once to twice weekly for one and one-half hours over
a period of 16 sessions. Most members are carried in
parallel individual psychotherapy as well. Methodological
considerations examined include composition of the group,
selection of patients, reasons for referral, and nine
specific features of the therapy process. In a succeeding
section, the author treats objectives, the relative

influence of "group climate" versus content of material
discussed by the group, the role of group therapist, and
five therapeutic effects which occur as a function of the
group setting. (abstract by Deborah Schuller).

747.   Kraft, I.A., Brief group psychotherapy,
        Psychiatric Clinics of North America,
        1979, 2, 85-92.

This modality differs from group psychotherapy primarily
in the length of time a patient spends in the group. Brief
group psychotherapy has value for specifically designed
groups with varied purposes and make-up. A review of the
literature suggests that brief group psychotherapy has
value for inpatient adolescents, and, on an outpatient
basis, for individuals or parents of children with chronic
diseases. (Journal abstract).

748.   Kriegman, G., and Wright, H.B., Brief
        psychotherapy with enuretics in the army,
        American Journal of Psychiatry, 1947, 104,
        255-258.

The authors report on a treatment program for dealing with
soldiers who were enuretic. The study eliminated those
soldiers for whom treatment was made impossible by virtue
of such factors as mental deficiency, etc. A wide variety
of treatment techniques and approaches were used, including
hypnosis, re-educative methods, simple supportive procedures, etc. The treatment was spread over a four month
period, with approximately five sessions per patient. The
cessation of enuresis was the criterion of successful
treatment. A total of 25 patients participated in the
study, and of these, 16 were reported to have ceased the
enuretic behavior, four showed some movement toward
cessation, with five failures reported. A follow-up was
included as part of the study, but only 19 cases were
reviewed. The enuretic behavior did recur in a number of
cases.

749. Krimmel, H., and Falkey, D.B., Short-
term treatment of alcoholics, Social Work,
1962, 7, 102-107.

The authors report on a study in which short-term treatment focussed on stopping drinking of alcoholic beverages
in confirmed alcoholics was used. A multi-disciplinary
professional team treated a number of alcoholics and
reported a success rate of about 35%. They also indicate
that their brief therapy approach worked best with alcoholics who had retained family connections and resources,
who themselves sought treatment (usually following a
disturbing bout with alcohol), or those who were willing
and ready to begin to face reality.

750. Kris, E.B., Intensive short-term therapy
in a day care facility for control of
recurrent psychotic symptoms, American
Journal of Psychiatry, 1959, 115, 1027-
1028.

The author reports on efforts to decrease the relapse rate
of patients, formerly hospitalized, by attempting to treat
them in a day care, outpatient basis. Medication was used
along with occupational therapy, and social work backup
for various family difficulties.

751. Kris, E.B., Intensive short-term treatment
in a day-care facility for the prevention
of rehospitalization of patients in the
community showing recurrence of psychotic
symptoms, Psychiatric Quarterly, 1964,
34, 83-88.

A combination of treatment approaches was reported on in
this study in order to decrease the need for rehospitalization of psychotic patients. A functional measure of
outcome was used, consisting of whether the patient
returned to their previously held job, or whether they
obtained a new job, or whether they were able to successfully return to their household duties. Of the original
26 patients, 23 were reported improved. The approach used,

although utilizing a number of methods of treatment,
placed heavy emphasis on drug treatment. The author
concludes that such an approach can be of great value in
keeping psychotic patients out of the hospital, and with
continued treatment and support can help them to lead
reasonably functional lives.

752.   Kritzer, H., and Langsley, D.C.,
        Training for emergency psychiatric care,
        Journal of Medical Education, 1967, 42,
        1111-1115.

Assignment to an emergency psychiatric service can be a
meaningful experience for a psychiatric resident by
providing him with the opportunity to deal with acute
stress, clarify crises, and make rapid decisions with
regard to treatment. The operation of the Emergency
Psychiatric Service of the Colorado Psychopathic Hospital
is described, as is its emphasis on the teaching of these
skills. This unit has halved the percentage of patients
formerly thought to require hospitalization and has made
immediately available to patients the crisis-oriented
treatment which has been useful in avoiding chronic mental
illness and social disability. (Journal summary).

753.   Kritzer, H., and Pittman, F.S., Overnight
        psychiatric care in a general hospital
        emergency room, Hospital and Community
        Psychiatry, 1968, 19, 303-306.

The authors briefly review tabulated results of types of
patients who utilized the overnight service of an emergency
room over a two-month period in 1965, of whom 13 per cent
(the third largest category) were considered primarily
psychiatric cases. Of these patients, more than 60 per
cent were discharged directly from the emergency room after
an average stay of 16.5 hours. Kritzer and Pittman present
four cases to illustrate the variety of services which are
afforded by such an overnight service--e.g. evaluation,
brief therapy, environmental manipulation, family support,
treatment and resolution of an acute psychosis. Lastly,
the advantages of an emergency room over a mental hospital

for emergency psychiatric care are adumbrated--some of
which include less stigma, faster treatment, and less
tendency by the patient to seek rehospitalization as a
solution to subsequent problems. (abstract by Deboral
Schuller).

754.   Kroger, W.S., Hypnotherapy for intractable
        post-surgical hiccups, American Journal of
        Clinical Hypnosis, 1969, 12, 1-4.

A case of intractable hiccups successfully treated by
hypnosis over the telephone is reported. The patient was
one whom the hypnotherapist had never met. Hypnosis, self-
hypnosis, posthypnotic suggestion and autosuggestions,
taught on the first session, were used as positive, conditioning reinforcement procedures. There was almost a
prompt and dramatic cessation of the hiccups. The patient
received brief psychotherapy directed toward the symptoms
and the characterological level. (Journal abstract).

755.   Kuehn, J.K., and Kuehn, J.L., Conspiracy
        of silence: psychiatric counseling with
        students at high risk for academic failure,
        American Journal of Psychiatry, 1975, 132,
        1207-1209.

The authors examined the academic records and counseling
histories of 132 freshman students at a state university
who sought psychiatric counseling. They found that most
students with poor previous academic performance were not
helped academically by brief (crisis intervention) psychiatric counseling. They also found that many counselors
resisted confronting such students with their academic
inadequacies. (Journal abstract).

756.   Kurtz, H., and Davidson, S., Psychic
        trauma in an Israeli child: Relation-
        ship to environmental security, American
        Journal of Psychotherapy, 1974, 28, 438-
        444.

This paper describes the etiology, dynamics and therapy of
a case of somnabulism in an eleven-year-old child who

underwent a trauma following the injury of his father in
an Israeli security operation. Implications of this case
for the theory of "constructive trauma" are discussed.
(Journal abstract).

757.   Kusnetzoff, J.C., Communication theory
        and brief psychotherapy: Its application
        to therapy of children and adolescents,
        American Journal of Psychoanalysis, 1974,
        34, 141-149.

The author stresses techniques of brief psychotherapy and
their application to working with problem children and
adolescents. Specifically, the characteristics of brief
therapy stressed are its active nature for both therapist
and patient, with the main focus on the superego. The
problem child or teen is viewed within the context of a
problem family or group, and suggestions for including the
family in on-going treatment are given. More specifically,
communication theory and aspects of metacommunication are
reviewed and discussed within the context of brief therapy.
The meaning of a family identifying a child as "sick" (and
itself as not sick), the use of paradoxical communication,
as well as specific points for dealing with adolescents
are presented.

758.   L'Abate, L., and Weeks, G., A bibliography
        of paradoxical methods in psychotherapy of
        family systems, Family Process, 1978, 17,
        95-98.

Provides a listing of 90 references pertaining to the use
of paradoxical methods in family therapy.

759.   LaFerriere, L., and Calsyn, R., Goal
        attainment scaling: An effective
        treatment technique in short-term
        therapy, American Journal of Community
        Psychology, 1978, 6, 271-282.

Compared the outcome of short-term therapy of 34 clients
who established therapy goals with their therapists and 31
clients with whom no formalized goal setting occurred.

When compared to control clients, clients receiving Goal
Attainment Scaling (GAS) had significantly (a) more positive outcomes as measured by posttests of anxiety, self-
exteem, and depression, (b) higher ratings of their own
change as a result of therapy, (c) higher rating of their
own motivation to change. Therapists perceived GAS clients
to have changed more as a result of therapy but not to have
been more motivated to change than controls. (Journal
abstract).

760.   Lamb, C.W., Telephone therapy: Some
        common errors and fallacies, Voices:
        The Art and Science of Psychotherapy,
        1969-70, 5, 42-46.

This paper presents some of the recurrent difficulties
experienced and observed by the author in training volunteers for "telephone therapy" with callers to a suicide
prevention and crisis service (Erie County, N.Y.). The
"therapist" is warned against a number of potential traps,
such as the pressure for instant answers, the fear of
being manipulated, the need to achieve closure and provide
ultimate answers, and the tendency to rely too heavily
upon referrals. The author is convinced that a great deal
of truly therapeutic work can be done on the phone with
persons in crisis, and that such services are valuable as
more than mental health clearing-houses or stop-gap
measures. (Journal summary).

761.   Lambert, M.J., Characteristics of patients
        and their relationship to outcome in brief
        psychotherapy, Psychiatric Clinics of North
        America, 1979, 2, 111-123.

Among the more important factors affecting outcome in all
forms of psychotherapy are variables relating to the
patient himself: diagnosis, severity of maladjustment,
personality traits, motivational states, demographic
characteristics, expectations about therapy, etc. While
it is difficult to bring order into this diverse list,
several conclusions can be drawn from research done since

the 1940's. These findings and their implications for
psychotherapy in general precede a more specific discussion
of characteristics of patients and brief psychotherapy.
(Journal abstract).

762.   Lambley, P., The dangers of therapy
        wihtout assessment: A case study,
        Journal of Personality Assessment,
        1974, 38, 263-265.

The dangers of embarking on a course of short-term therapy
without proper assessment are elucidated through a case
presentation of a psychotic patient, not originally perceived as such by the therapist.

763.   Landgarten, H., et al., Art therapy as
        a modality for crisis intervention,
        Clinical Social Work Journal, 1978,
        6, 221-229.

Ten days after the Symbionese Liberation Army's "shoot-
out" in Los Angeles in 1974, the Cedar-Sinai Medical
enter, Department of Family Child Psychiatry, Thalians
Community Mental Health Center, sent a crisis team of 3
psychotherapists to a school in the Black community. The
psychotherapists used art therapy with a 3rd grade classroom of 21 Black children. The team's procedure helped
the children ventilate their reactions to the frightening
event that occurred in their neighbourhood. This paper
describes the art therapy techniques and the children's
pictorial and verbal expressions accompanied by the psychological aspects of their responses. (Journal abstract).

764.   Lang, J., Planned short-term treatment
        in a family agency, Social Casework,
        1974, 55, 369-374.

The author summarizes the use of Quick Response Units at
the Jewish Family Service in New York. They are involved
in crisis intervention and planned brief therapy. The
service offered is up to six weeks. The factors used in
determinining whether an individual or family could benefit

from the use of this service is based on worker expectations and goals of treatment than on specific diagnostic categories. The diagnostic label does not take into account the specific precipitating factor(s), client's level of motivation and discomfort, methods the client used in the past for coping with crises, and the obstacles which would impede a successful resolution of the problem (internal and external). The effect of time limits on both patient and therapist are discussed, and the issue of termination is dealt with specifically. Two case histories illustrate the points raised.

765.   Lang, P.J., and Lazovik, A.D., Experimental
        desensitization of a phobia, Journal of
        Abnormal and Social Psychology, 1963, 66,
        519-525.

24 snake phobic Ss participated in an experimental investigation of systematic desensitization therapy. Ss who experienced desensitization showed a greater reduction in phobic behavior (as measured by avoidance behavior in the presence of the phobic object and self-ratings) than did nonparticipating controls. Ss tended to hold or increase therapy gains at a 6-month follow-up evaluation, and gave no evidence of symptom substitution. (Journal abstract).

766.   Lang, P.J., et al., Desensitization,
        suggestibility and pseudopsychotherapy,
        Journal of Abnormal Psychology, 1965,
        70, 395-402.

44 snake phobic Ss participated in laboratory experiments assessing the degree of fear change associated with systematic desensitization, no treatment, placebo treatment, and the trait of suggestibility. Desensitization Ss showed significantly greater fear reduction than controls, while placebo Ss change no more than did untreated Ss. Successful desensitization was relatively independent of suggestibility. Desensitization of specific fears generalized positively to other fears, and among desensitizations Ss, degree of fear change could be predicted from measurable aspects of therapy process. (Journal abstract).

767.   Langsley, D.G., Crisis intervention,
        American Journal of Psychiatry, 1972,
        129, 734-736.

768.   Langsley, D.G., Crisis intervention
        and communication, in, Ostwald, P.,
        (ed.), Human communication, New York,
        Grune and Stratton, 1977.

769.   Langsley, D.G., Three models of family
        therapy: Prevention, crisis intervention,
        and rehabilitation, Journal of Clinical
        Psychiatry, 1978, 39, 792-796.

Models of intervention at a family level are described as
preventive, crisis intervention, or rehabilitative. The
preventive intervention model suggests that certain
stresses produce family disorganization and individual
family members may regress to symptoms of disease. Family
dysfunction could be avoided through identification of high
risk groups and intervention at developmental milestones.
The data on early intervention with children has produced
the most promising results. Crisis intervention, the
second model, suggests that early identification and prompt
intervention may avoid the development of more serious
disorganization. The rehabilitation model is focused on
changing long term patterns of maladaptive behavior. It
includes the homeostasis model, the conflict resolution
model and other approaches to long-term family therapy.
(Journal abstract).

770.   Langsley, D.G., Family crisis therapy,
        in, Herink, R., (ed.), Psychotherapy
        handbook, New York, Jason Aronson, 1978.

771.   Langsley, D.G., Crisis intervention:
        Managing stress-induced personal and
        family emergencies, Behavioral Medicine,
        1978, 31-37 (May).

772.   Langsley, D.G., Brief psychotherapy,
        Journal of Continuing Medical Education,
        1978, 17-28. (December).

773.   Langsley, D.G., et al., Clinical pastoral
        training in an emergency psychiatric
        service, Journal of Religion and Health,
        1967, 6, 99-105.

774.   Langsley, D.G., et al., Adolescence and
        family crisis, Canadian Psychiatric
        Association Journal, 1968, 13, 125-133.

Like the individual, the family may be better understood
from a developmental point of view. It has different
tasks and problems at various stages of its existence.
The family with adolescent children faces a change in
composition (loss of children and the responsibility of
helping these children become adults). This threat may
produce a family crisis and individual members may react
to the specific conflicts in a manner which depends on
their previous problems. The family member who becomes
a 'patient' may be the teenager or a parent. A family
crisis therapy approach permits tension reduction within
the group, improves functioning on the part of the
'patient' and permits the family to work out a more
adaptive solution. (Journal summary).

775.   Langsley, D., et al., The treatment of
        families in crisis, Grune and Stratton,
        N.Y., 1968.

776.   Langsley, D.G., et al., Family crisis
        therapy - results and implications,
        Family Process, 1968, 7, 145-158.

The authors report a study which compares outcome results
of inpatient with outpatient treatment, for a similar
population. One hundred-fifty patients for whom hospitalization was requested were randomly assigned to experimental (outpatient) or control (inpatient) groups. No

significant differences existed on any of 15 areas of
comparison for the two groups. The type of treatment
received by each is summarized. Hospitalization was
avoided in all experimental cases; and six-month follow-up
data reveal that re-hospitalization rate among controls
was as high as hospitalization rate among experimentals.
Further, on instruments measuring social adjustment and
levels of functioning and recompensation, the experimental
group was found to be at least as healthy as the control
at three and at six months following the end of treatment.
The authors conclude with a discussion of theoretic and
practical implications of their data. (abstract by
Deborah Schuller).

777.   Langsley, D.G., et al., Followup
        evaluation of family crisis therapy,
        American Journao of Orthopyschiatry,
        1969, 39, 753-759.

Six-month followup evaluations of 150 family crisis therapy
cases and 150 hospital treatment cases demonstrate that
those treated as outpatients do as well as the hospital
cases. Social functioning is maintained equally in both
groups. Patients are less likely to be rehospitalized if
admission was avoided initially. (Journal abstract).

778.   Langsley, D.G., et al., Family crises
        in schizophrenics and other mental
        patients, Journal of Nervous and Mental
        Disease, 1969, 149, 270-276.

This paper reports the development of an instrument which
quantifies events which may lead to crisis with the family,
and the management of such crises. The study of 50
families which included a schizophrenic patient and of 50
which included a nonschizophrenic mental patient (in each
group, half were treated by outpatient family crisis
therapy and half by hospitalization) demonstrates a
difference between the schizoprehnic and nonschizophrenic
groups. The nonschizophrenics become more efficient at
dealing with crises and are more able to interact within

the family to work out problems. The psychopathology of
the family as well as that of the patient contributes to
less efficient crisis management and problem solving.
(Journal abstract).

779.   Langsley, D.G., et al., Avoiding mental
        hospital admission: A follow-up study,
        American Journal of Psychiatry, 1971,
        127, 1391-1394.

Three hundred patients requiring immediate hospitalization
were randomly assigned to outpatient family crisis therapy
(FCT) or were admitted to a university psychiatric hospital. Post-treatment follow-up showed patients treated
without admission were less likely to be hospitalized after
treatment and that their hospitalization was significantly
shorter. At both 6 and 18 months, FCT patients were doing
as well as the hospitalized patients on two measures of
social adaptation and were managing crises more efficiently.
(Journal abstract).

780.   Langsley, D.G., and Yarvis, R.M.,
        Evaluation of crisis intervention,
        Current Psychiatric Therapies, 1975,
        15, 247-252.

The article begins with a short summary of the development
of crisis intervention. The authors then review some of
the more salient evaluation studies on crisis intervention,
the aims of such studies, and the general findings. The
types of approaches used in crisis intervention work are
also reviewed, with strikingly similar approaches used by
a diversity of professionals in the field (e.g., eclectic
approach and orientation of therapists, aim of restoration
of patient's previous level of functioning, etc.). The
authors conclude with a discussion of the types of studies
which need to be done.

781.   Langsley, D.G., and Yarvis, R.M., Crisis
        intervention prevents hospitalization, in,
        Parad, H.J., et al., Emergency and disaster
        management, Bowie, Md., Charles Press, 1976.

782.   Lantz, J.F., and Werk, K., Short-term
        casework: A rational-emotive approach,
        Child Welfare, 1976, 55, 29-38.

Time-limited psychotherapy is the focus of this article,
in which the theoretical orientation used is a rational-
emotive approach, based on the work of Ellis. Within such
a framework, four distinct stages are delineated:
a) Contract stage (assessment and feedback of assessment);
b) intellectual insight stage (teaching client how to
analyze and understand affect); c) practice stage (client
encouraged to discover and analyze the thoughts behind
the dysfunctional affect, including use of Rational Self-
analysis Form); and, d) termination (stress placed on
client continuing to do own work using framework to
address future difficulties). The authors also include
a discussion of some of the indications and contraindications for the use of such a brief therapy approach, and
a case illustration highlights many of the points raised.

783.   Lau, H., and Cooper, S., A night in
        crisis, Psychiatry, 1973, 36, 23-36.

The authors describe eight patients seen by Lau in the
course of one night's work in a crisis clinic. A discussion follows each case presentation. The writers
examine the conceptual principles underlying the therapeutic interventions and their application to crisis
theory; significant differences between crisis work and
long-term therapy; and system considerations--e.g. the
impact on case management of the value placed on crisis
work by the psychiatric center, the interrelation between
various services within such a center, and the relation of
a crisis service to other community agencies. (abstract
by Deborah Schuller).

784.   Laughlin, J., and Bressler, R., A family
        agency program for heavily indebted
        families, Social Casework, 1971, 52,
        617-626.

The authors provide figures to support their contention
that the number of families suffering from severe indebtedness is reaching epidemic proportions. The social work

profession, according to the writers, has generally
ignored the pervasiveness of this problem, despite its
implications for family disruption and breakdown. Laughlin
and Bressler describe one agency's approach to a deb-
counseling service. Their approach premises that family
counseling must accompany financial counseling; that if
underlying emotional problems are ignored, families will
again incur major debts or be confronted with other types
of problems. After an initial intake interview, the counselor usually sees a family   to eight times, while,
concurrently, a non-professional volunteer assists the
family in budgeting and in handling creditors. The training program for these volunteers is described and several
case examples illustrate the manner in which this service
operates. The authors conclude with implications of this
program and the problem it confronts--stressing the
feasibility of adapting this approach to other family
agencies, and the need for a reorientation to the issue of
indebtedness. (abstract by Deborah Schuller).

785.   LaVietes, R.L., Crisis intervention
       for ghetto children: contraindications
       and alternative considerations, American
       Journal of Orthopsychiatry, 1974, 44,
       720-727.

Clinicians and administrators have emphasized crisis intervention as a means of extending services and reducing
costs. This paper asserts that ghetto children, because
of their multiple deprivations, complex problems, and
family structures, are particularly unsuitable for short-
term contacts. Modalities other than crisis intervention
are indicated as alternatives to long-term child treatment.
(Journal abstract).

786.   Lazare, E., The psychiatric examination
       in the walk-in clinic, Archives of
       General Psychiatry, 1976, 33, 96-102.

Rapid assessment for decision making is a major goal of
the initial psychiatric interview in walk-in clinics,
emergency psychiatric services, and the ambulatory services
of community mental health centers. To accomplish this

task, the clinician must learn to elicit specific data
to confirm or refute clinical hypotheses rather than gather
complete history. This report, in formulating a hypothesis generating and testing approach for the initial
psychiatric examination, proposes 16 hypotheses that
organize the clinical data necessary to help the clinician
make efficient use of limited time, guard him from coming
to premature closure in the collection of data, and provide
a stimulus for the exploration of relevant but neglected
clinical questions. (Journal abstract).

787.   Lazare, A., et al., The walk-in patient
       as a "customer": A key dimension in
       evaluation and treatment, American Journal
       of Orthopsychiatry, 1972, 42, 872-883.

The authors provide a discussion of the differences between
a professional-client relationship based on trust and the
buyer-seller relationship of caveat emptor (buyer beware).
They argue that often the patient's dominant or primary
request changes during the course of treatment, a reflection of either progress or regression. When the initial
request was appropriately handled by the therapist, progress
occurred; when it was not, regression resulted. Varying
the quality and quantity of therapist response in relation
to the initial client (customer) request is detailed and
stressed.

788.   Lazare, A., et al., Disposition decisions
       in a walk-in clinic, American Journal of
       Orthopsychiatry, 1976, 46, 503-509.

The success of a walk-in clinic in providing care without
regard to social and diagnostic factors is measured in a
study of 391 patients. Results indicate that acceptance
or nonacceptance into the clinic system were unrelated to
social class and diagnosis, although these factors did
influence referrals to specific clinic resources.
(Journal abstract).

789.   Lazarus, A.A., Group therapy of phobic
        disorders by systematic desensitization,
        Journal of Abnormal and Social Psychology,
        1961, 63, 504-510.

Wolpe's technique of systematic desensitization based on
relaxation was adapted to the treatment of phobic disorders in groups. Of the 18 subjects who were treated by
direct group densensitization, 13 recovered in a mean of
20.4 sessions. Follow-up inquiries after an average of
9.05 months revealed that 3 of the subjects had relapsed.
With a more traditional form of interpretive group psychotherapy applied to 17 subjects, after a mean of 22 therapeutic meetings, it was found that only 2 patients were
symptom-free. Both these patients attended groups in which
relaxation was employed as an adjunct to the interpretive
procedures. The 15 subjects who were not symptoms-free
after interpretive group therapy were then treated by
group desensitization. After a mean of 10.1 sessions, 10
of them recovered. The very much shorter time required to
effect a recovery by desensitization in those patients who
had previously received interpretive therapy suggests that
the therapeutic relationship and additional nonspecific
factors may have facilitated the reciprocal inhibition of
neurotic anxieties motivating the phobic symptoms. There
is some basis for the idea that therapists of every persuasion could helpfully employ systematic desensitization
as an adjunct to their traditional techniques in the
management of phobic disorders. (Journal summary).

790.   Lazarus, A.A., The treatment of chronic
        frigidity by systematic desensitization,
        Journal of Nervous and Mental Disease,
        1963, 136, 272-278.

An account of various cases suffering from persistent
frigidity precedes a discussion of the application of
Wolpe's technique of systematic desensitization therapy.
By employing this psychotherapeutic procedure, nine of 16
recalcitrant cases of frigidity were discharged as
"sexually adjusted" after a mean of 28.7 sessions. Follow-
up inquiries strongly suggested the durability of this

method and supported the conclusion that desensitization
is the method of choice in those instances where specific
anxieties underly patient's frigid responses. (Journal
summary).

791.   Lazarus, A.A., The results of behavior
        therapy in 126 cases of severe neurosis,
        Behavior Research and Therapy, 1963, 1,
        69-79.

this paper deals with the outcome of behaviour therapy
on 126 patients who were selected from the writer's
clinical records on the basis of neurotic severity and
complexity. A brief resume of certain psychodiagnostic
procedures precedes a discussion of the main therapeutic
rationale. The principal therapeutic techniques (with
certain innovations) are briefly outlined. Some of the
pitfalls in evaluating the effects of treatment are mentioned and an attempt is made to achieve greater clarity
and objectivity by means of rating scales coupled with
stringent criteria for 'therapeutic recovery'. On this
basis, it was found that out of a total of 408 patients
treated by the writer, 321 individuals (i.e. 78 per cent)
appeared to derive definite and constructive benefit. Of
the 126 patients, most of whom chould be described as
'extremely neurotic', 61.9 per cent were rated as 'markedly
improved or 'completely recovered' in a mean of 14.07
sessions. Some of the possible reasons for therapeutic
failure are then outlined, and finally follow-up information over a mean of 2.15 years is given. (Journal
abstract).

792.   Lazarus, A.A., Behavior therapy,
        incomplete treatment and symptom
        substitution, Journal of Nervous and
        Mental Disease, 1965, 140, 80-86.

The author presents a theoretical discussion of the roots
of behavior therapy, specifically with regard to the
origins of neurotic symptoms, and in particular with
regard to anxiety and obsessive-compulsive disorders. A
few case examples are presented to highlight the material.

793.   Lazarus, A.A., Behaviour rehearsal vs.
        non-directive therapy with advice in
        effecting behaviour change, Behaviour
        Research and Therapy, 1966, 4, 209-212

An objective clinical appraisal of behaviour rehearsal
(a systematic role-playing therapeutic procedure) is
described. This approach was compared with two other
techniques, direct advice and non-directive reflection-
interpretation, in the management of specific interpersonal problems. Behaviour rehearsal was shown to be
almost twice as effective as direct advice and the non-
directive treatment procedure fared worst of all.
(Journal summary).

794.   Lazarus, A.A., Learning theory and
        treatment of depression, Behaviour
        Research and Therapy, 1968, 6, 83-89.

Difficulties in defining and measuring "depression"
operationally have led behavior therapists largely to
ignore the subject. This paper describes several
operational factors which lend themselves to more objective assessment and therapeutic maneuvers. Within this
context, S-R analyses can presumably lead to effective
and specific treatment procedures. Three treatment techniques are described (time projection with positive
reinforcement, affective expression, and behavioral
deprivation). (Journal abstract).

795.   Lazarus, A.A., Behavior therapy in
        groups, in, Gazda, G.M. (ed.), Basic
        approaches to group psychotherapy and
        group counseling, Springfield, C.C. Thomas,
        1968.

796.   Lazarus, A.A., Behavior therapy and beyond,
        New York, McGraw-Hill, 1971.

797.   Lazarus, A.A. (ed.), Clinical behavior
        therapy, New York, Brunner/Mazel, 1971.

798.   Lazarus, A.A., Multimodal behavior
        therapy in groups, in, Gazda, G.M. (ed.),
        Basic approaches to group psychotherapy,
        and group counselling, 2nd Edition,
        Springfield, C.C. Thomas, 1975.

799.   Lazarus, A.A., Multimodal behavior
        therapy, New York, Springer, 1976.

800.   Lazarus, A.A., and Abramovitz, A.,
        The use of "emotive imagery" in the
        treatment of children's phobias, Journal
        of Mental Science, 1962, 108, 191-195.

A Recriprocal Inhibition technique for the treatment of
children's phobias is presented which consists essentially
of an adaptation of Wolpe's method of "systematic desensitization".   Instead of inducing muscular relaxation as the
anxiety-inhibiting response, certain emotion-arousing
situations are presented to the child's imagination.   The
emotions induced are assumed, like relaxation, to have
autonomic effects which are incompatible with anxiety.
This technique, which the authors have provisionally
labelled "emotive imagery" was applied to nine phobic
children whose ages ranged from 7-14 years.   Seven children
recovered in a mean of 3.3 sessions and follow-up enquiries
up to 12 months later revealed no relapses or symptom
substitution.   An outstanding feature of this pediatric
technique is the extraordinary rapidity with which
remission occurs.   (Journal summary).

801.   Lazarus, A.A., and Wilson, G.T., Behavior
        modification: Clinical and experimental
        perspectives, in, Wolman, B. (ed.),
        Treatment methods of mental disorders:
        A handbook for practitioners, New York,
        Van Nostrand Rheinhold Co., 1976.

802.   Lazarus, A.A., et al., Classical and
        operant factors in the treatment of a
        school phobia, Journal of Abnormal
        Psychology, 1965, 70, 225-229.

To the best of our knowledge, this report is the 1st to
recognize the advantages of employing both classical and
operant conditioning procedures in the treatment of a
neurotic case. A model which appears to have heuristic
value was developed: When avoidance behavior is motivated
by high levels of anxiety, classical counterconditioning
techniques are called for; when anxiety is minimal, and
avoidance behavior is seemingly maintained by various
secondary reinforcers, operant strategies should be applied.
Furthermore, this paper indicates that the practice of
interchanging therapists not only failed to disrupt or
impede therapeutic progress but had certain distinct
advantages. (Journal abstract).

803.   Leaverton, D.R., et al., Brief therapy
        for monocular hysterical blindness in
        childhood, Child Psychiatry and Human
        Development, 1977, 7, 254-263.

A case report of monocular blindness, a rare form of
childhood conversion reaction, is presented. A brief
description of the treatment is included, which utilized
a team approach and short-term management. An attempt is
made to compare this patient's motivation with other cases
of conversion reactions and to identify a possible dynamic
mechanism for monocular hysterical blindness. (Journal
abstract).

804.   LeBaron, G.I., Ideomotor signalling
        in brief psychotherapy, American Journal
        of Clinical Hypnosis, 1962, 5, 81-91.

This report attempts to define a modern hypnotic technique
applicable within the framework of brief psychotherapy,
psychodynamically based, and utilizing a limited dis-
sociation to focus ego functions within the limits of the
patient's ego strength. This technique is referred to as
ideomotor signalling and involves the structuring of

dissociated finger movements. The participation of the
patient's ego operations and the minimizing of regressive
transference is emphasized. It is postulated that an
alter ego system makes possible the patient's participant
observation in his own psychological processes. The
technique is not offered as a radical approach to character
problems but as a facilitant in dealing with critical
resistances. (Journal summary).

805.   Lecker, S. et al., Brief intervention:
       A pilot walk-in clinic in suburban
       churches, Canadian Psychiatric Association
       Journal, 1971, 16, 141-146.

Results of a 12-month pilot study of the usefulness and
viability of a roving, walk-in clinic serving an upper-
middle class suburb are presented. The authors indicate
goals and rationale behind this type of crisis-intervention
program. Two sample case histories illustrate the nature
of problems seen by the clinic. Referral source, age of
patient, type of problem, and type of intervention are
broken down according to patients' previous contact with
psychiatric treatment. Lecker, et al. discuss implications of their data, concluding that this format is
effective in facilitating the early delivery of mental
health care to a population-at-risk not reached by other
means. (abstract by Deborah Schuller).

806.   LeCron, L.M., and Bordeaux, J., A
       system of brief hypoanalysis, in,
       LeCron, L.M., and Bordeaux, J.,
       Hypnotism Today, N. Hollywood,
       California, Wilshire Book Company, 1976.

Through the use of examples, the authors provide an overview of the use of hypnoanalysis to shorten the length of
therapy. The value of not having the patient overly
dependent upon the therapist, especially as it relates to
the issues of termination is discussed.

807.   Leeman, C.P., and Mulvey, C.H., Brief
       psychotherapy of the dependent personality:
       Specific techniques, Psychotherapy and
       Psychosomatics, 1975, 25, 36-42.

Brief psychotherapy, structured specifically for patients
with chronic difficulties with dependency, is described.
A time-limited approach focussed primarily on the patient's
relationships other than with the therapist, and aimed at
the patient's taking responsibility for behavior change
(not simply insight) was used. The therapist communicated
the strengths of each patient in treatment, encouraging
them to use these resources. A total of six patients from
the outpatient psychiatric clinic of Beth Israel Hospital
in Boston were involved in this treatment. They were seen
once per week, for three-seven months, depending upon the
particular patient. All patients were white, between the
ages of 31 and 44. Four of the six had had previous
psychiatric treatment (range: 16 months to 10 years).
Major presenting symptoms included anxiety, phobias,
depression, and none presented circumscribed symptoms.
They were pervasively dissatisfied with their lot in life.
At termination and two-and-a-half years after termination,
evaluation measures were implemented to assess the effects
of the treatment. Four of the six patients had made
significant improvement across measures of behavior, self-
esteem, and general levels of satisfaction. One patient
improved with some further brief treatment, and one
remained unchanged. Specific case material is presented
to highlight the structure of the program as it unfolded
in individual treatment. A short discussion is also
presented distinguishtng this type of approach from crisis
intervention and from short-term anxiety-provoking psychotherapy (STAFF- Sifneos). This approach de-emphasized the
examination of transference. Further, patients selected
in this approach did not meet the selection criteria set
by Sifneos for STAPP.

808.   Lehrman, N.S., Follow-up of brief and
       prolonged psychiatric hospitalization,
       Comprehensive Psychiatry, 1961, 4, 333-340.

Comparison of published results of follow-up studies of
psychiatric hospital populations reveals that briefness of
hospital stay, a factor determined by hospital policy

rather than by the illness of the individual patient,
seems to be the outstanding factor associated with good
results. In general, the longer the hospital stay, the
poorer the results. The presence of in-patient psychotherapy as measured in this study, has, if anything, a
negative effect on outcome. In the schizophrenics groups
studied, no clear-cut relationship was demonstrable
between duration of hospitalization and eventual outcome,
although this paper has compared only three psychotherapeutically treated hospital groups with corresponding
groups in the New York State Hospital system. If these
conclusions are valid, it might be in order to consider
ending long-term psychotherapeutic hospitalization, as well
as attempting to shorten markedly psychiatric hospitalization in general. Hospitalization in itself may at
times be harmful to psychiatric patients, and the longer
they are exposed to the hospital, the more adversely they
sometimes seem to be affected. (Journal summary and
conclusion).

809.   Lehrman, N.S., The joint interview:
        An aid to psychotherapy and family
        stability, American Journal of
        Psychotherapy, 1963, 17, 83-93.

The joint interview, in which husband and wife are seen
together, and the interaction between them observed and
defined, can sometimes be of value in resolving both intra-
familial disputes and impasses in therapy. A technique
for studying and treating this interaction is described
from both a theoretical and clinical viewpoint. The
active, vigorous, and precise role required of the therapist in the joint interview, which deals directly with the
"interpersonal relationship," is contrasted with the more
passive attitude of classic psychoanalysis and much of
contemporary psychotherapy. It is suggested that such a
more active type of relationship-oriented technique can
sometimes accomplish considerably more in a given time
than the usual more passive, individually oriented methods.
It may also be significantly helpful in the more conventional psychotherapies. (Journal summary).

810.   Leiblum, S.R., et al., Group treatment
        format: Mixed sexual dysfunction,
        Archives of Sexual Behavior, 1976, 5,
        313-322.

This study reports the rationale and results of a ten-
session group composed of six couples with mixed sexual
dysfunctions. Dysfunctions included premature ejaculation,
primary and situational orgasmic dysfunctions, situational
impotence, and incompatible sex drives. A variety of pre-
treatment behavioral and attitudinal measures were
administered, including a Life History Questionnaire,
Sexual Assessment Inventory, Marital Adjustment Scale, and
Sexual Interaction Inventory. Post group measures revealed
marked increases in marital satisfaction, orgasmic attainment, ejaculatory control, and enhanced self-acceptance,
particularly for females (SSS changes). The consistency
between outcome measures was also a noteworthy finding.
The results suggest increased use of mixed short-term
groups, particularly when cost-effectiveness accountability
is important. One contraindication for such groups is,
however, severe marital discord, as evidenced by the Locke-
Wallace means scores of 80 or less. (Journal abstract).

811.   Leiblum, S.R., and Kopel, S.A.,
        Screening and prognosis in sex therapy:
        To treat or not to treat, Behavior
        Therapy, 1977, 8, 480-486.

Success in sex therapy may be obtained with individuals
typically considered poor prognostic risks. The following
case study reports successful outcome with a middle-aged
couple displaying an unstable and unsatisfying marital
relationship, a chronic sexual dysfunction (primary
orgasmic dysfunction and premature ejaculation), and a
rigid religious belief system. The use of several
innovative treatment interventions is noted, particularly
the assistance of a Roman Catholic priest. The article
concludes with a plea for open-mindedness when screening
potential clients considering the present state of
knowledge and empirical research in sexual counselling.
(Journal abstract).

812.   Leiblum, S.R., and Rosen, R.C., The
        sexual-enhancement week-end workshop:
        Assets and limitations, in, Cook, M.,
        and Wilson, G. (eds.), Love and attrac-
        tion, New York, Permagon Press, 1979.

Two separate sexual-enhancement weekend workshops for
sexually dysfunctional couples were conducted, and results
compared with those obtained from a 10-week, 20-hour group
treatment with other dysfunctional couples. This article
presents method (screening criteria, assessment instruments, content schedule of the weekend program, goals) and
results. In a discussion, the authors note that the workshop appears effective in improving couple communication,
increasing marital satisfaction, and restructuring sexual
attitudes. Problems seemingly not amenable to this type
of brief treatment are described. Leiblum and Rosen
conclude that specific dysfunctions are more effectively
treated with intensive group therapy, but that the weekend
workshop is of benefit for some couples. (abstract by
Deborah Schuller).

813.   Leibovich, M.A., Short-term insight
        psychotherapy for hysterical
        personalities, Psychotherapy and
        Psychosomatics, 1974, 24, 67-78.

The different stages of the therapeutic process of short-
term insight psychotherapy for hysterical disorders is
described. This method is found useful to help in the
emotional maturation of these patients who, despite the
fact that they do not appear to have major psychological
problems, suffer a great deal and deprive themselves from
achieving gratifying relationships. It is felt that the
planning of the overall strategy before it begins is
important, as well as the structuring of the therapeutic
process in well delineated stages. A strict criteria for
patient selection and the therapist's technique are
emphasized. A clinical case serves as illustration.
(Journal abstract).

814.   Leisher, A.R., Applicant receiving
        brief service in a family agency, Smith
        College Studies in Social Work, 1949, 20,
        137-139.

The author reports in abstract form on thesis research
focussed on patients who received only one interview at a
family agency. The range of presenting problems included
financial concerns, physical difficulties, or traumatic
family situations. The group consisted of 101 patients,
and these individuals were contrasted with a group which
had been seen at the agency approximately 15 years
previous. A number of patients who had been seen during
this one interview were referred to other sources of
assistance, and a follow-up indicated that many of them
had in fact followed through with the referral. The
value of such a brief, one interview session is discussed.

815.   Lemere, F., Brief psychotherapy,
        Psychosomatics, 1968, 9, 81-83.

The technique of brief therapy consists of 15 to 30 minute
interviews once a week or less, for as long as necessary
to help the patient. This may be for a few weeks in simple
cases to a lifetime in seriously handicapped patients where
prolonged maintenance is required. The advantages of
brief psychotherapy are obvious. More patients can be
cared for more economically and on a more realistic basis.
There are advantages in greater flexibility, lessened
dependency on the therapist, greater opportunity for the
patient to work through his own problems with the
physician's help and less emphasis on unhealthy introspection and self-analysis. (Journal summary).

816.   Lemkau, P., and Crocetti, G., The
        Amsterdam municipal psychiatric service,
        American Journal of Psychiatry, 1961, 11,
        779-783.

The ideology, practices, and therapeutic rationale of one
comprehensive mental hygiene service are discussed, based
on visits to that service by a psychiatrist and two
sociologists. Three overlapping programs are examined:
post-care, pre-care, and emergency services. Crucial to

post-care are medical supervision, housing, and employment.
This program was extended to include outpatients awaiting
hospitalization, and termed the pre-care program. Based
on the recognition that these two programs constituted a
24 hour responsibility, a psychiatric emergency service
was organized. The authors discuss the theoretical under-
pinnings of the Amsterdam Service: a) acceptance of long-
term management responsibility; b) direct manipulation of
patients' social environment to minimize consequences of
their illnesses; and, c) a flexible conception of "institution" as a set of social practices and patterns of
behavior. (abstract by Deborah Schuller).

817.   Lemon, E.C., and Goldstein, The use
        of time limits in planned brief
        casework, Social Casework, 1978, 59,
        588-596.

Structuring casework in such a way that termination date
is known at the outset of treatment offers advantages in
work with passive or compliant adults whose submissive
stance arises from unresolved dependency issues. The major
therapeutic focus in such brief interventions is upon the
casework relationship and its implicit transference
components. The authors describe their approach (which
uses 12 interviews of 50 minutes each, scheduled on a
weekly basis), as well as criteria of selection of
potential clients. Case material chosen to highlight the
effects of time limits on the worker-client relationship
is presented. Special attention is given the process of
terminatton, which, the authors note, is frequently
experienced as a threat since the termination date was not
jointly reached by worker and client. The authors examine
the optimal role of the social worker during this sensitive
phase of the casework. (abstract by Deborah Schuller).

818.   LeShan, L., and LeShan, E., Psychotherapy
        and the patient with a limited life span,
        Psychiatry, 1961, 24, 318-323.

The authors affirm the potential of psychotherapy to fulfill important needs of the dying patient. They stress the
need to explore the patient's value system and philosophy.

The question of the worth of such therapy, given the
limited number of therapists, is posed. To respond, the
authors note the difference in approach to treatment of a
person with limited life expectancy between clinical
medicine and psychotherapy. Various reasons for general
avoidance of the dying person by psychotherapists are
explored, with implications suggested regarding the basic
goals and values of psychotherapy. (abstract by Deborah
Schuller).

  819.   Lessman, S., and Mollick, L.R., Group
          treatment of epileptics, Health and
          Social Work, 1978, 3, 105-121.

In most cases epilepsy need not be a major handicap to the
individual. However, epileptic patients usually have a
variety of psychosocial problems, largely because of the
pressures and frustrations with which they are often confronted in society and at home. An interdisciplinary
approach to the health care of epileptics in which short-
term group treatment was a primary component is described.
The treatment was felt to be particularly effective with
adult patients because it: (a) helped to foster their
view of themselves as indpendently functioning adults,
(b) provided a system in which patients were able to
experient with new behavior or relationships, (c) provided
support from peers, and (d) prevented patients from
becoming overly dependent on treatment by using a time-
limited framework. (10-15 weeks). (Journal summary).

  820.   Lester, D., and Brockopp, G.W., (eds.),
          Crisis intervention and counseling by
          telephone, Springfield, Ill., C.C.
          Thomas, 1973.

This edited book of readings is divided into a number of
sections: the various types of emergency telephone
services, issues related to crisis intervention and
counseling in which the telephone is the medium of exchange
of information, issues related to problem callers, evaluation of such services, etc.

821.   Lester, E.P., Brief Psychotherapies in
        child psychiatry, Canadian Psychiatric
        Journal, 1968, 13, 301-309.

The author presents four stages in the process of brief
therapy with children and their families. They include:
a) first contact with the therapist; b) establishing the
nature of the presenting problem; c) promoting insight in
both the child and parents; and, d) termination. Two case
histories are used to highlight these stages. The importance of assessing the child's ability to enter into
therapy without serious arrests or fixations, or
regressions, as well as the importance of assessing the
flexibility of the overall family is discussed. Both
assessments play a critical role in deciding whether or
not a family should be included in a brief therapy program.
A list of the types of presenting problems which would be
amenable to brief therapy (e.g., eating difficulties,
sleeping, play inhibitions, neurotic but not character-
logic acting out, etc.) are presented. Those which would
be contraindicated for brief therapy would include
characterological disorders, development retardation,
multiple phobias developed over a long period of time, etc.

822.   Leuner, H., Guided affective imagery:
        A method of intensive psychotherapy,
        American Journal of Psychotherapy,
        1969, 23, 4-22.

Guided Affective Imagery (GAI) is a method of intensive
psychotherapy which can be used in conjunction with any
theoretical view of personality dynamics that acknowledges
subconscious motivation, the significance of symbols,
resistance, and the therapeutic importance of mobilization
of affect. Under suggestions of relaxation, the recumbent
patient is encouraged to daydream on specific themes which
are offered by the therapist. The daydream process
typically takes on an autonomous direction. It evokes
intense latent feelings that are relevant to the patient's
problems. Techniques for the guiding and transformation
of imagery lead to desirable changes in both affect and
attitudes toward life situations. GAI has been applied
successfully to patients with neuroses, psychosomatic
disturbances, and borderline states. It does not seem

useful with either full-blown psychotics or with addicts.
Therapists who are psychoanalytically trained and who are
skilled in dream interpretation will find this method
congenial. An abbreviated form is especially useful for
training student therapists. GAI is suitable for short-
term psychotherapy. Also, it is less dependent on the
patient's ability accurately to verbalize his attitudes
than conventional methods. (Journal summary).

823.   Levene, H., et al., A training and
        research program in brief psychotherapy,
        American Journal of Psychotherapy, 1972,
        26, 90-100.

We have described the development of a university program
that successfully combined an open service to a catchment
area, interdisciplinary teaching and supervision in
theories and practice of brief psychotherapy, and a co-
ordinated research effort designed to evaluate the methods
and effects of different approaches to brief pyschotherapy.
Teaching programs were developed in psychoanalytic, jungian,
behavioral, and eclectic group approaches to therapy.
Patients were admitted to each program on an unselected
basis. All interviews were tape recorded. Comparison
data were collected on a sample of patients who had brief
contact for intake-evaluation purposes only. We evaluated
outcome by means of therapist and patient self-ratings on
a five-point scale covering seven areas of possible change
in functioning. A six-to twelve-month telephone follow-up
of treated patients was conducted. Results indicated that
a significantly higher proportion of patients in brief
were rated improved than patients who had brief contact
for intake-evaluation only. No significant differences at
termination or follow-up emerged from a comparison of the
different treatment approaches. Therapeutic styles
associated with different theoretical orientation were
identical. (Journal summary).

824.   Leventhal, T., and Weinberger, G.,
        Evaluation of a large-scale brief therapy
        program for children, American Journal
        of Orthopsychiatry, 1975, 45, 119-133.

This article is a report on experiences of treating
children and adolescents up to 18 years of age at the
Children's Psychiatric Center in central New Jersey. The
approach involved brief therapy spread over a six week
period, in a one therapist/family setup. The treatment
philosophy consists of viewing clients as having problems
in living, with the focus on the self, self-expectations
and perceptions. Specific problem areas are delineated
and worked on, with the involvement of the entire family,
with the aim to help families gain more control over their
lives. A total of over 1,700 families are reported on.
The findings of the research included: a small number of
drop-outs from treatment, about a 10% readmission rate
over a four year follow-up period, brief therapy most
effective with less pathological cases, therapists become
less pathology oriented (i.e., more focussed on strengths
and potentials of families); compared with control group,
parents in therapy group reported a significant decrease
in the number of problems, with a continuing high level of
parent satisfaction with the treatment offered. The
authors discuss the overall efficiency and effectiveness
of the program in terms of lowered withdrawal rates, an
increase in the volume of patients seen, and the value of
not separating the diagnostic and treatment phases of
therapy.

825.   Levine, R.A., A short story on the long
        waiting list, Social Work, 1963, 8, 20-22.

The dramatic changes in structure and function of the
Henry Street Settlement Mental Hygiene Clinic begun in
1961 are detailed. The long waiting list was abolished
through the streamlining of both intake and treatment.
Time limits were placed on certain patients' therapy, when
specific conditions were met (e.g., clear, limited goals,
active involvement of both therapist and patient, patient
goals rather than therapist goals as the center of treatment). The range of short-term treatment approaches used
is summarized, and the often beneficial results for clients
reported.

826.   Levine, S.V., The inner city: Setting,
        subgroups, psychopathology, and service,
        American Journal of Orthopsychiatry,
        1971, 41, 168-177.

A large pediatric hospital in downtown Toronto served as
the site of an immediate psychiatric clinic. Distinct
subgroups appeared among the patients along clinical,
ethnic, and socio-economic lines, necessitating differing
modes of intervention. While the problems of providing
mental health services in this major Canadian city are
many and complex, the city has not experienced the same
degree of inner deterioration and violences seen in many
cities in the United States. (Journal abstract).

827.   Levis, D.J., Implosive therapy: A
        critical analysis of Morganstern's
        review, Psychological Bulletin, 1974,
        81, 155-158.

The purpose of the present article was to provide a
critique of Marganstern's recently published review of
implosive therapy and "flooding" literature. The following
conclusions were reached: (a) the majority of negative
results published by investigators using implosive therapy
analogue subjects occurred with taped presentations which
violate the implosive therapy procedure in two important
ways; (b) at the analogue level only one published study
was found to provide negative results which used an actual
therapist; (c) all patient therapy studies cited reported
that an implosive therapy or flooding procedure was found
to be effective; (d) only one study using a live therapist
reported that a systematic desensitization procedure more
effective than implosive therapy; and (e) whether it was
the implosive therapy technique per se that produced the
positive findings is still unclear. (Journal abstract).

828.   Levis, D.J., and Carrera, R.N., Effects
        of 10 hours of implosive therapy in the
        treatment of patients, Journal of Abnormal
        Psychology, 1967, 72, 504-508.

The present report, investigating the effectiveness of
implosive therapy (IT) with outpatients, mainly was

designed as an exploratory study to determine the feasibility and value of more effective evaluations of this new
behavioral therapy. 40 patients were divided into 1
experimental and 3 control groups. Only the IT group
showed a consistent trend shift away from psychopathology
as measured by MMPI. Some evidence is presented that the
changes in this group are not due to the number of
sessions, to skills and personal qualities of the therapists independent of the treatment technique, to the
termination of treatment, or to effects resulting from the
commitment to and expectation of professional treatment.
(Journal abstract).

829.   Levit, H.I., Marital crisis intervention:
       Hypnosis in impotence/frigidity cases,
       American Journal of Clinical Hypnosis,
       1971, 14, 56-60.

The author presents three case histories to highlight a
hypnotherapy approach to impotence/fridigity. The
theoretical basis for such an approach is also presented,
in which issues of denial, depression, guilt, and repressed
anger are highlighted. Hypnotherapy was used to shorten
the length of treatment by allowing for the rapid coming
to awareness of much of the repressed emotional under-
current.

830.   Levit, H.I., Depression, back pain,
       and hypnosis, American Journal of
       Clinical Hypnosis, 1973, 15, 266-272.

This brief article presents a case in which severe back
pain masked an unconscious, serious depression. The course
of successful treatment over three hypnotherapy sessions
is described. The author believes this case typifies a
syndrome in which "disproportionate" pain is a defense
against underlying anxiety and hostility. The case demonstrates the therapeutic value of hypnosis in such situations, as well as pointing to potential problems in
treating such forms of somatization. In conclusion, Levit
raises the issue of the need for psychological evaluation

of surgical candidates (and treatment where necessary) in order to reduce the rate of surgical intervention and to increase the rate of surgical successes. (abstract by Deborah Schuller).

831. Levy, R.A., Six-session therapy, Hospital and Community Psychiatry, 1966, 17, 340-343.

The author describes the course of psychodynamically-oriented brief therapy with patients seen in a crisis-oriented mental health clinic for a maximum of six session each. Factors believed to have led to a high success rate in treating severely disturbed patients without recourse to hospitalization include the following: positive attitudes of the treatment team who attempt to utilize the strengths of the patients and their families; use of psychotropic drugs; environmental manipulation; active and immediate family casework; and, where necessary, co-operation with other community agencies. The psychotherapy is designed to enable the patient to recognize his feelings, and to acquire healthier coping mechanisms. The author concludes that a well-defined program of crisis therapy in the community reduces markedly the need for hospitalization of emotionally-disturbed individuals. (abstract by Deborah Schuller).

832. Lewin, K., A brief psychotherapy method, Pennsylvania Medical Journal, 1965, 68, 43-48.

833. Lewin, K.K., A method of brief psycho-therapy, Psychiatric Quarterly, 1966, 40, 482-489.

The author presents details of a psychoanalytically-oriented approach to brief therapy, in which an active, immediate series of interpretations are used, focussed on issues of negative transference and anxiety around separation. The critical importance of the initial session is stressed and discussed, especially in terms of decisions around the appropriateness of brief therapy for

a given client. If the therapist is able to quickly
understand the nature of the conflicts the patient is
presenting, and if the patient is willing and able to use
interpretations in the first interview, the indications
are for brief therapy. An early emotional response to an
interpretation is a positive prognostic indicator for
brief therapy outcome. The author reports improved levels
of functioning in clients as a result of brief therapy,
but the reports are clinical rather than statistical.
The work was done at the Staunton Clinic of the Department
of Psychiatry at the University of Pittsburg School of
Medicine.

834.   Lewin, K.K., Brief encounters: Brief
        psychotherapy, St. Louis, W.H. Green,
        Inc., 1970.

The approach presented in this book is rooted in psychoanalytic theory with two major deviations from the more
traditional analytic position. The author places a
different emphasis on female psychosexual development, and
highlights the role of the conscience while playing down
the role of instinct. Further, the methodology of therapy
is markedly different as well. The approach is based on
a) both therapist and patient agreeing to a specific
structure in advance; b) a very active involvement on the
therapist's part, focussed primarily on the self-punishment
patient behavior; c) early interpretation of manifested
transference; d) active restructuring by the therapist
from session to session in order to establish and maintain
continuity; e) specific away-from-the-session "homework"
as the prime responsibility of the patient; f) therapist
allowing the patient to use his (therapist's) less
punitive conscience through interaction with the therapist.
The book presents a comprehensive review of theory and
practice, including a focus on intake and diagnostic work,
the treatment process, and termination. Case material is
presented to elucidate the approach.

835.   Lewinsohn, P.M., and Shaw, D.A., Feedback
       about interpersonal behavior change: A
       case study in the treatment of depression,
       Psychotherapy and Psychosomatics, 1969,
       17, 82-88.

This case study describes the brief but intensive treatment of a young woman who complained of feeling depressed
and had numerous somatic complaints. Interactional data
based upon home observations and rating played an important
part in the treatment. Observing the patient's behavior
in her home was useful in that it: (1) very quickly and
powerfully focussed the case as an interactional problem;
(2) provided the therapists with specific behavioral
information to be used in the treatment process; and
(3) represented a methodology for evaluating behavior
change. (Journal summary).

836.   Lewinsohn, P.M., et al., Behavioral
       treatment of depression, in, Davidson, O.,
       (ed.), The behavioral management of anxiety,
       depression, and pain, New York, Brunner/
       Mazel, 1976.

The authors offer an in-depth account of depression and
behavioral methods of combatting it. Lewinsohn, et al.,
analyse the term "depression" to provide a heuristic
framework for future research and clinical practice.
Various behaviors which depressed persons manifest and the
criteria of depression which the authors have utilized in
their own studies (e.g., selected MMPI scales and Grinker
interview ratings) are described. Measurement of the level
of depression is based on interview rating scales, self-
report measures, and behavioral observation. Assessment
of suicidal risk is discussed, and a functional analysis
of depressive phenomena presented. A central tenet in the
authors' model posits that a reduction in the rate of
response contingent positive reinforcement is a critical
antecedent to dysphoria. This concept underlies the treatment paradigm employed. Various components considered
include intake procedure, use of home observation, establishment of goals, three-month time limit, and contingencies
motivating subjects to continue anti-depression treatment
programs. The remainder of this paper concerns therapeutic

interventions into those aspects of a depressed person's functioning which appear most significant--i.e. engagement in pleasant activities; social behavior; covert and overt verbal behavior; and sleep difficulties. In concluding, the authors briefly examine some extensions and other applications of their conceptualization of depression and its management. (abstract by Deborah Schuller).

837.   Lewis, A.B., Brief psychotherapy in the
        hospital setting: Techniques and goals,
        Psychiatric Quarterly, 1973, 47, 341-352.

Contrary to the current vogue, the author argues that brief hospitalization should provide considerable psychotherapy in order to prepare the patient for long-term outpatient care. This preparation should concentrate on: (1) clarifying the history so as to stimulate motivation, (2) resolving the problems which precipitated hospitalization, (3) utilizing hospital services to restructure ego defects, (4) helping the patient to achieve control over suicidal, addictive, and other forms of destructive behavior, and (5) instructing him in the "ground rules" for psychotherapy. If these goals are kept firmly in mind, a short hospitalization can do more than treat acute psychoses with somatic therapies. It can initiate a long-term treatment process in the community with the prospect of achieving significant behavioral change. (Journal abstract).

838.   Lewis, J., and Mider, P.A., Effects of
        leadership style on content and work
        styles of short-term therapy groups,
        Journal of Counseling Psychology, 1973,
        20, 137-141.

Ninety-two patients in a short-term psychiatric facility were exposed to 20 group sessions under two leadership conditions; cognitive and experimental. Cognitive leaders encouraged discussion of topics, goals, and purposes of hospitalization, while experimental leaders focussed on expression of feeling and thoughts and on immediate (in-group) interpersonal relationships. Two judges using the Hill interaction Matrix rating device independently scored

each session according to the context and work styles of
the therapy groups.   Interrater reliabilities ranged from
.78 to .95 for the four quadrants of the instrument.
Groups in the experimental condition were significantly
more member and work centered than groups in the cognitive
condition.   The results supported the implication that an
experiential leadership style possesses greater potential
for member-related discussion (content) and member-centered
interaction (work).   (Journal abstract).

839.   Lewis, M.S., et al., The course and
        duration of crisis, Journal of Consulting
        and Clinical Psychology, 1979, 47, 128-134.

Crisis theory rests in part on the assumption that specific
psychological changes accompany the crisis state and that
adaptation to a crisis occurs within 6 to 8 weeks after
onset.   To verify these assertions, psychological tests
were administered to a crisis group composed of patients
undergoing surgery for cancer and to a comparison group
composed of patients undergoing surgery for less serious
illnesses.   The test included measures of anxiety, self-
esteem, depression, perceived locus of control, and a
general measure of crisis.   Tests were administered four
times, first on the night before surgery and thereafter at
3-week intervals.   Results indicated significant psychological changes only in the crisis group, in which feelings
of helplessness preceded the appearance of depression and
lowered self-esteem.   Contrary to present theory, the
duration of crisis was found to be greater than 6 weeks
but less than 7 months.   (Journal abstract).

840.   Liberman, B.I., et al., Patterns of change
        in treated psychoneurotic patients: A
        five-year follow-up investigation of the
        systematic preparation of patients for
        psychotherapy, Journal of Consulting and
        Clinical Psychology, 1972, 38, 36-41.

Neurotic outpatients were evaluated five years after
participating in a psychotherapy study at the Henry Phipps
Psychiatric Clinic.   Measures of improvement and of current
mental status were compared to the results obtained in the

original study. It was found that differences between the
experimental groups obtained immediately following treatment disappeared after five years. Nevertheless, all
patients exhibited significantly greater improvement after
five years than they did immediately following treatment.
These results parallel those obtained by a previous five-
year follow-up which was based on a similar patient sample.
The nature and effect of differential treatment over long
periods of time was discussed in terms of differential
patient attrition, criteria of successful psychotherapy,
and the influence of nonspecific factors in psychotherapy.
(Journal abstract).

841.   Liberman, R., Behavioral approaches to
        family and couple therapy, American
        Journal of Orthopsychiatry, 1970, 40,
        106-118.

The author reviews some of the theory and terminology of
behavioral therapy. The diagnostic workup consists of a
behavioral or functional analysis of a family's problems.
Specifically focussed on is determining which behavior is
maladaptive, which allows each member of the family to
delineate the types of changes he/she would like to see in
others and in themselves. The specific goals are then set
out, and the types of factors which have been maintaining
the problem behavior are analyzed. Specific strategies
are chosen to alter the chosen behavior(s). The types of
behavioral techniques used by the therapist are discussed,
such as shaping, role playing, behavioral rehearsal, etc.
Three case examples are presented which highlight the
above-mentioned issues. The use of outside supports (e.g.,
community services) is also recommended where appropriate.

842.   Lick, J.R., and Bootzin, R.R., Expectancy,
        demand characteristics and contact desensi-
        tization in behavior change, Behavior
        Therapy, 1970, 1, 176-183.

Contact desensitization, attention placebo, and instructions
to simulate the effects of attention placebo were compared
in their ability to alleviate fear of rats in college
students under brief group therapy conditions. These

results were: (a) contact desensitization was highly
effective and superior to groups controlling for expectancy
and demand characteristics and to a no-treatment group:
(b) although not performing as well as Ss receiving contact
desensitization, role playing Ss effectively simulated
improvement on the behavioral approach test: and (c) the
expectancy manipulation did not result in significant
improvement. (Journal abstract).

843.   Lind, E., From false-self to true-self:
        a case in brief psychotherapy, British
        Journal of Medical Psychology, 1973,
        46, 381-389.

The author presents a case history of the treatment of a
23 year old patient, treated within the context of a brief
psychoanalytic model. The presenting symptoms of the
patient were depression and possible psychosis. The
changes which occurred over the course of 19 therapy
sessions are detailed. The context within which treatment
was accomplished, namely a hospital setting which provided
a safe place for the patient to temporarily be, was also
stressed in evaluating the positive outcome. A six month
follow-up indicates that the gains have been maintained.

844.   Lindemann, E., Symptomatology and
        management of acute grief, American
        Journal of Psychiatry, 1944, 101, 141-148.

This classic paper summarizes the findings from experiences
gained in working with survivors and families of victims
of a major disaster, the Coconut Grove fire. The symptomatology of those experiencing acute grief is presented
(marked sighing respiration; feelings of lack of strength,
exhaustion; digestive difficulties; sense of unreality,
emotional distance from others; feelings of guilt;
irritability, restlessness, disorganization of activity;
preoccupation with image of the deceased). The normal
course of grief reactions is described (grief work),
covering a period of four-six weeks. The author also
describes morbid or abnormal grief reaction (delay of
grief reaction; distorted reactions) with case examples
and suggestions for therapy. Prognostic indicators are

also presented (e.g., greater severity of reaction in
obsessive make-up, history of depression; mothers who have
lost young children, etc.). The critical issue is the
intensity (positive or negative) of the involvement between
the patients and the deceased prior to the death. A short
section on anticipatory grief reactions (reaction to
impending or feared separation) is also presented.

845.   Lindemann, E., The meaning of crisis in
        individuals and family living, Teachers
        College Record, 1956, 57, 310-315.

846.   Lindner, R.M. Hypnoanalysis as psycho-
        therapy, Diseases of the Nervous System,

The author describes a shortened therapy technique in
which psychoanalysis is combined with hypnosis. Free
association is used, and hypnosis is introduced whenever
the patient produces resistance in order to reveal the
cause of the resistance. Further hypnosis is used at the
end of therapy to dissolve the transference situation.

847.   Litman, R.E., Emergency response to
        potential suicide, Journal of the Michigan
        Medical Society, 1963, 62, 68-72.

848.   Litman, R.E., Acutely suicidal patients:
        Management in general medical practice,
        California Medicine, 1966, 104, 168-174.

Suicidal crises are best understood as late stages in the
progressive breakdown of adaptational behavior in emotionally exhausted patients. The premonitory symptoms of
suicide include verbal communications, suicide attempts,
symptomatic actions, depression, treatment failure,
excessive emotional reactions to specific disease states
and panic reactions. In treating suicidal patients, the
physician should maintain his medical attitude. The
patients need emergency medical care including appropriate
drugs. Free communication between patient and physician
is very important. This may take some extra time.

Patients benefit from emergency psychological support and
stimulation toward constructive action. Family, friends,
and community agencies should be mobilized to aid the
patient. For seriously suicidal patients, consultation is
recommended, and treatment in hospital is advisable.
(Journal abstract modified).

849.   Litman, R.E., Principles of crisis
        intervention and emergency care, in,
        Resnik, H., and Ruben, H., (eds.),
        Emergency care: The management of
        Mental health crises, Bowie, Md.,
        The Charles Press, 1974.

850.   Litman, R.E., et al., Suicide-
        prevention telephone service, Journal
        of the American Medical Association,
        1965, 192, 21-25.

Suicide is a serious public health problem. Recognizing
this, many communities have initiated antisuicide programs.
This communication describes the rationale, operation, and
experiences of a suicide-prevention telephone service which
functions nights, weekends, and holidays to supplement an
active daytime, crisis-oriented, brief-therapy clinic.
During the first year, 1,607 calls were received.
Approximately two thirds of the patients concerned were
somen. Wednesday was the busiest night. Nearly one fifth
of the calls involved persons with high suicide poten-
tiality. A suicide attempt has been made recently by 22%.
There was a history of one or more previous psychiatric
contacts for 45% of the patients. Acute depressive
reaction was the most frequent diagnosis. (Journal
abstract).

851.   Lobitz, W.C., and LoPiccolo, J., New
        methods in the behavioral treatment of
        sexual dysfunction, Journal of Behavior
        Therapy and Experimental Psychiatry, 1972,
        3, 265-271.

For 3 yrs. we have been treating couples for a variety of
sexual dysfunctions ranging from primary orgasmic

dysfunction (frigidity) in females to premature ejaculation
and erectile failure in males. An "orthodox" behavioral
treatment program emphasizing in vivo desensitization has
been supplemented by several clinical methods either
adapted from psychotherapies or newly introduced. A
systematic masturbation program, in combination with
erotic fantasy and literature, enhances sexual responding.
Role-playing orgasmic response disinhibits female orgasm.
Therapist self-disclosure reduces client inhibition and
anxiety and models an open acceptance of sexuality. Daily
client records provide data on ongoing client sexual
behavior. A refundable penalty fee deposit heightens
client motivation. Clients plan their own treatment for
the final stages and the months following therapy.
Clinical examples and outcome statistics are given.
(Journal summary).

   852.   London, L.S., Hypnosis, hypno-analysis,
           and narcoanalysis, American Journal of
           Psychotherapy, 1947, 1, 443-447.

This article presents the use of hypnotherapy as a way of
shortening the duration of therapy. Case examples are
provided, which focus on the issue of alcoholism (e.g.,
chronic alcoholism, periodic alcoholism), fainting and
constipation, cardiac neurosis, insomnia, paranoid condition, sexual psychopathy, anxiety neurosis related to
racial complex, impotence, and anxiety neurosis. The cases
were followed-up for a period of two years, and with the
exception of two minor relapses, gains were maintained.

   853.   Longaker, W.D., Psychiatric emergencies
           in industry, New York State Journal of
           Medicine, 1971, 71, 2069-2072.

Some general approaches to psychiatric emergencies in
occupational medicine are given. Emphasis is placed on
training personnel, both medical and management, to deal
with these situations. It is also important to set up a
preventive program, with the support of the organizational
structure of the industrial complex and the effort of the
physicians, to minimize the frequency of and degrees of
severity of the occurrence of psychiatric emergencies.
(Journal abstract).

854.   Lord, E., Two sets of Rorschach records
obtained before and after brief psychotherapy, Journal of Consulting Psychology,
1950, 14, 134-139.

Lord presents Rorschach test records obtained on one male
and one female subject six months after termination of a
half-year of therapy. The author summarizes the problems
of the subjects at the time of the first Rorschach test
(prior to initiation of therapy), and their behavior, with
reference to those problems, one year later. The before-
and-after Rorschach records are analyzed four different
ways, and the results presented. Both subjects' data
reflect some basic, unchanged personality factors. However, both sets of data also indicate that certain
negatively-weighted factors disappeared from the records,
while certain positively-weighted factors emerged. Lord
infers that the Rorschach test does indeed reflect both
constant and altered personality components. From this
study, she derives six hypotheses concerning basic personality stability and change in relation to successful
outcome in brief therapy. (abstract by Deborah Schuller).

855.   Lorion, R.P., Socioeconomic status and
traditional treatment approaches reconsidered, Psychological Bulletin,
1973, 79, 263-270.

In view of scarce mental health services and previous
research with traditional therapies, innovative treatment
approaches are employed increasingly with low-income
patients. Pertinent data must be carefully considered
lest the present trend produce separate and unequal
services for various social groups. While socioeconomic
status appears to be a significant correlate of acceptance
for, and duration of, individual psychotherapy, it does
not relate to treatment outcome. Clarification of this
discrepancy requires a more precise identification of the
social groups comprising the "lower-classes"; a clearer
understanding of the environmental demands faced by such
patients; and an objective assessment of specific socioeconomic status factors that may, or may not, exclude a
given patient from a given treatment. Resolution of such
issues is necessary for a realistic allocation of available
mental health services (Journal abstract).

856.   Lorion, R.P., Patient and therapist
        variables in the treatment of low income
        patients, Psychological Bulletin, 1974,
        81, 344-354.

Because negative results for Class IV and Class V clients
appear early in treatment, therapist and patient variables
operative during that period require careful attention.
For example, attrition rates and outcome data have been
found to relate directly to therapists' attitudes toward
treating low-income patients. Dealing with their negative
attitudes through educational or supervisory procedures
reduces negative outcomes, yet techniques for doing so
require more systematic evaluation than is currently
available. The course of treatment is also critically
shaped by the patients' attitudes and expectations concerning therapy. Despite extensive theorizing about the
more inappropriate expectations held by low-income
patients, few actual differences among social groups have
been observed. All social classes share expectancies
about the nature and duration of treatment. Attempts to
adjust the goals and the format of therapy to reflect more
accurately patient needs, expectations, and reality-
problems produce marked reductions in attrition rates.
Furthermore, behavioral and time-limited procedures serve
as useful examples of alternative treatment procedures
that can be effectively adjusted to low-income mental
health needs. (Journal abstract).

857.   Lorr, M., Relation of treatment frequency
        and duration to psychotherapeutic outcome,
        in, Strupp, H.H., and Laborsky, L., (eds.),
        Research in Psychotherapy, II, Washington,
        D.C., American Psychological Association,
        1962.

858.   Lorr, M., et al., Frequency of treatment
        and change in psychotherapy, Journal of
        Abnormal and Social Psychology, 1962,
        64, 281-292.

The authors report in detail a controlled study to test
the hypothesis that gains resulting from individual
psychotherapy increase with the number of treatment

interviews received over fixed time intervals. Study
design, setting, sample, treatment, and characteristics of
therapists, as well as measures used by patients, therapists, and social workers to evaluate change, and method
of analysis are presented. Subjects were 133 male outpatients (of seven Veterans Administration clinics),
assigned to one of three different treatment schedules:
twice-weekly, once-weekly, and once biweekly. Evaluations
of status were made immediately prior to initiation of
treatment, and again at the end of 16 weeks and 32 weeks
of psychotherapy for patients remaining in the study. The
differential effects of treatment frequency and treatment
gains are reported. At both measurement times, the
research hypothesis did not receive support, although a
one-year follow-up which retested 102 of the original
sample yielded interesting results. In their discussion
and summary, the authors comment on related studies,
contingent variables, and the issue of treatment gains,
treatment frequency and duration. (abstract by Deborah
Schuller).

859.   Lowry, F., Case work principles for
        guiding the worker in contacts of short
        duration, Social Service Review, 1948,
        22, 234-239.

Lowry briefly summarizes 10 problems which confront the
caseworker who must serve a client within a time-limited
frame. She then formulates six general principles (pertaining essentially to the evaluation process) which enable
the worker to make more effective use of the time available.
She concludes that sound case-work services can be
delivered within contacts of short duration, but that
special skills are required of the caseworker. (abstract
by Deborah Schuller).

860.   Lowry, F., the caseworker in short contact
        services, Social Work, 1957, 2, 52-56.

The author first examines psychological pressures which
may be experienced by the caseworker as a function of his
knowledge of time restrictions. Anxiety generated by time
limits may result in overly directive or too narrowly-

focused interviews. It may distort clarity of thinking
and lead to uneconomical haste and a sense of frustration.
Short contact services also require a special set of interviewing and diagnostic skills. Lowry summarizes these,
and concludes that the limits of time need not limit the
quality of services offered. (abstract by Deborah
Schuller).

   861.   Lowry, F.H., and Winbrob, P.M.,
          Psychiatric emergencies at Expo '67,
          Canadian Psychiatric Association Journal,
          1969, 14, 47-52.

The authors describe the results and their experiences as
providers of psychiatric emergency service at Expo '67, in
Montreal. They report the relatively small numbers of
individuals needing such service, with most such requests
coming at the end of the Exposition, reflecting feelings
of depression and loss.

   862.   Luborsky, L., and Singer, B., Comparative
          studies of psychotherapies: Is it true
          that everyone has won and all must have
          prizes? Archives of General Psychiatry,
          1975, 32, 995-1008.

Tallies were made of outcomes of all reasonably controlled
comparisons of psychotherapies with each other and with
other treatments. For comparisons of psychotherapy with
each other, most studies found insignificant differences
in proportions of patients who improved (though most
patients benefitted). This "tie score effect" did not
apply to psychotherapies vs psychopharmacotherapies
compared singly - psychopharmacotherapies did better.
Combined treatments often did better than single treatments. Among comparisons, only two specially beneficial
matches between type of patient and type of treatment were
found. Our explanations for the usual tie score effect
emphasize the common components among psychotherapies,
especially the helping relationship with a therapist.
However, we believe the research does not justify the
conclusion that we should randomly assign patients to

treatments--research results are usually based on amount
of improvement, "amount" may not disclose differences in
quality of improvement from each treatment. (Journal
abstract).

863.   Luborsky, L., et al., Factors
        influencing the outcome of psycho-
        therapy: A review of quantitative
        literature, Psychological Bulletin,
        1971, 75, 145-185.

864.   Ludwig, A.M., and Levine, J., A
        controlled comparison of five brief
        treatment techniques employing LSD,
        hypnosis, and psychotherapy, American
        Journal of Psychotherapy, 1965, 19,
        417-435.

This study was designed to compare in a controlled manner
the therapeutic efficacy of hypnodelic therapy (LSD +
hypnosis + psychotherapy) with four other treatment
techniques employing various combinations of these
variables. 70 post-narcotic drug addict inpatients (40
amles, 30 females) were assigned to one of five treatment
conditions. The Psychiatric Evaluation Profile (PEP) a
questionnaire instrument designed by the authors to evaluate psychopathology and attitudes concerning "self-concept"
and "coping" was employed to measure the effects of each
therapeutic procedure at two weeks and two months following
the single therapy session. When treatment conditions were
evaluated separately, each group of patients showed significant therapeutic improvement, regardless of type of
therapy, at the two month post-therapy time period.
However, when the five treatment conditions were compared
to one another, both at the two-week and two-month post-
therapy evaluations, hypnodelic therapy led to significantly
greater improvements than any other technique. The authors
offer some possible explanations for the mechanism of
therapeutic action of hypnodelic therapy.   (Journal
summary).

864a.   MacGregor, R., Multiple impact psycho-
        therapy with families, Family Process,
        1962, 1, 15-29.

MacGregor reports on the clinical development and technique of an outpatient treatment method for families with
problem adolescents. "Multiple Impact Therapy" premises
the potential of brief therapy to mobilize self-rehabili-
tating family processes. It is in essence an expanded
version of intake which entails staff team conferences
with each other and with family members, on an individual
and group basis. Half a week is devoted by the orthopsychiatric team to one family. Procedures of each day
are detailed. MacGregor presents preliminary results of
follow-up data obtained on 55 families treated by MIT.
The data suggest that this treatment method results in
benefits comparable to those derived from established
intensive methods. Variations in frequency of follow-up
and its therapeutic effect are briefly discussed, as well
as diagnostic classifications used in the study. The
author concludes with clinical observations and a discussion of the implications of the data. (abstract by
Deborah Schuller).

865.   MacGregor, R., et al., Multiple impact
        therapy with families, New York, McGraw-
        Hill, 1961.

866.   Machler, T.J., Pinnochio in treatment of
        school phobia, Bulletin of the Menninger
        Clinic, 1965, 29, 212-219.

This paper is based upon experience with a single parent,
and reports a diagnostic and therapeutic method utilizing
hand puppets and the Pinnochio theme in the brief treatment of a ten-year old girl with a school phobia. The
method and treatment were used adjunctively with other
forms of play therapy and case work with the parents.
This method cannot be regarded as applicable for all
children with school phobia. It is an effective technique
that allows the child a nonthreatening way to explore,
develop, and express his fantasies, and to discharge the
feelings associated with his fantasies. (Journal introduction).

867. Mackay, J., The use of brief psychotherapy with children, Canadian
Psychiatric Association Journal,
1967, 12, 269-278.

The author begins by reviewing the small number of articles
focussed exclusively on brief therapy with children,
followed by the beginnings of a frame of reference for
such treatment. The length, nature of the process, the
focus on symptom-cure versus personality growth, and
techniques are discussed. The question of parent involvement is discussed, along with management questions and
indications for and contra-indications against the use of
brief therapy with children. The author also summarizes
the findings of others doing research in the field of brief
child therapy. The critical issue of parent motivation is
highlighted.

868. Mackey, R.A., Crisis theory: Its
development and relevance to social
casework practice, Family Life
Coordinator, 1968, 17, 165-173.

This paper examines the concept of crisis as a clinical
frame of reference for psychotherapeutic intervention.
After a theoretical discussion of the concept, clinical
material is presented and then analyzed within the frame
of reference. Implications are drawn both in terms of
material itself and for casework programs. (Journal
abstract).

869. MacKenzie, K.R., The eclectic approach
to the treatment of phobias, American
Journal of Psychiatry, 1973, 130,
1103-1106.

A patient with air travel phobia was treated by a variety
of therapeutic techniques. Initially, intensive reciprocal
inhibition similar to implosion therapy was used, with
concomitant supportive psychotherapy. Then psychodynamically oriented short-term therapy was introduced to
achieve more lasting results. The author suggests that

rather than establishing a dogmatic position in terms of
selected technique, the therapist should take a truly
eclectic approach within the unfolding treatment of a
single patient. (Journal abstract).

870.   MacLeod, J.A., and Middleman, F., The
        Wednesday Afternoon Clinic: a supportive
        care program, Archieves of General
        Psychiatry, 1962, 6, 56-65.

Many seriously disturbed patients are unable to make use
of the usual individual psychotherapy where treatment
arrangements encourage the development of intensive one to
one relationships. This paper reports on a clinic which
offers supportive psychotherapy with the treatment arrangements fostering the development of a relationship with the
clinic and with a number of helpful people rather than
with one therapist. The report presents evidence which
suggests that the treatment arrangements in this supportive
care clinic are especially appropriate for the group of
severely disturbed patients served. This group of patients
is apparently attending the clinic more frequently and
over a longer period of time than was the experience when
the usual individual psychotherapy was planned. (Journal
summary).

871.   MacLeod, J.A., and Tinnin, L.W., Special
        service project: A solution to problems
        of early access, brief psychotherapy,
        Archives of General Psychiatry, 1966,
        15, 190-197.

Attempted to divide brief therapy patients according to
the precipitating event which contributed most to the
patient's problems. They presented the following categories: a) Loss, such as death, divorce, job loss, etc.;
b) Disturbance in critical interpersonal relationships;
c) Pregnancy-related experiences; d) Demands of a new role,
such as job, marriage, school, etc.; e) Traumatic illness
or injury to the patient.

872. Maher, B.A., and Katkovsky, W., The
efficacy of brief clinical procedures
in alleviating children's problems,
Journal of Individual Psychology,
1961, 17, 205-211.

Children treated in a psychological clinic by brief
methods designed to change parental attitudes were compared
with children who did not receive help. The follow-up
investigation utilized a questionnaire addressed to
parents and covered cases seen from one to five years
previously. The criterion for estimating improvement was
the same as that used for deciding that there was a problem·
in the first place - namely, the opinion of the parents.
Based on the parents' estimates the conclusion emerges that
treatment is significantly effective in producing improvement in the referral problem. (Journal summary).

873. Maizlish, I.L., Group psychotherapy of
husband-wife couples in a child guidance
clinic, Group Psychotherapy, 1957, 10,
169-180.

The author initiated psychotherapy groups which required
the participation of both spouses. He relates his experience with a total of 17 couples, comprising four groups
which met weekly, for one and a half hours, over 12 to
15 weeks. Each group was led by male and female co-
therapists. Selection procedure, characteristics of the
couples and children referred to the clinic, therapeutic
aims and activities, and group process are described. He
illustrates changes which occurred as a result of treatment by focusing on the experience of two couples.
Maizlish concludes that group therapy with both husband
and wife appears effective, then draws additional infer-
ences from the experience. (abstract by Deborah Schuller).

874. Maizlish, I.L., and Hurley, J.R.
Attitude changes of hushands and wives
in time-limited group psychotherapy,
Psychiatric Quarterly Supplement,
1963, 37, 230-249.

An experimental program of time-limited psychotherapy with
small groups of husband-wife couples, originally referred

to clinic facilities for the adjustment problems of their
children, is described. A total of 16 couples were
involved, with the majority of the parents from middle
or lower socioeconomic classes. The program lasted a
total of 13 weeks, each weekly meeting being 1 1/2 hours
in length. Distinctive characteristics of this approach
include no direct treatment of the child in most cases,
full participation of the husband, a minimization of
dependency upon professional psychotherapists, and the
relative brevity of professional intervention. Response
changes among the participants were studied through
administering an original attitude-questionnaire before
and after group therapy. Comparison of pre- versus post-
therapy response disclosed highly reliable evidence of PA
gains (parent-attitude) among the therapy participants,
with the husbands gaining as much as did their wives. A
similar study of the incidence of response shifts among
parents enrolled in a conventional college child psychology
course revealed virtually no evidence of PA gains concomitant with this period of academic instruction by either
the students or their spouses, although the demographic
characteristics of the control group do not match those
of the group couples treatment sample. A number of
specific case examples are given, along with a description
of the process and issues occurring during the group
therapy. (Journal abstract adapted).

875.   Malamud, W., Brief psychotherapy in
        medical practice, Medical Clinics of
        North America, 1948, 32, 1195-1206.

Malamud addresses physicians in his presentation of some
general goals and methods of brief psychotherapy. In his
discussion of goals, he comments on the need to understand
psychological factors in relation to physical illness,
establishment of a physician-patient relationship conducive to therapy, eradication of factors causing the
symptoms, and emancipation from the therapeutic relationship. Various techniques of brief therapy are mentioned
under the headings of exploration, emotional participation,
and maturation and emancipation. He notes contributions
available to the physician from the allied disciplines of
social work and clinical psychology. (abstract by
Deborah Schuller).

876.   Malan, D.H., A study of brief psycho-
        therapy, C.C. Thomas, Springfield, Ill.,
        1963.

The author ranges over a wide area of concerns in the
field of brief therapy. Specifically he discusses the
key factors which combine for successful therapy on a
short-term basis. Factors include an active focal approach
focussed on a patient's major conflict, the issue of involvement on the therapist's part, the issue of negative transference in brief therapy and how it should be dealt with,
views about how to deal with issues of termination, and
the special status of issues of termination in briefer
forms of therapy, assessing the patient's capacity to
grieve, etc. He also discusses the reasons why therapy
over the years has gradually gotten longer and longer.

877.   Malan, D.H., The outcome problem in
        psychotherapy research, Archives of
        General Psychiatry, 1973, 29, 719-729.

This paper is an attempt to summarize aspects of the
history of psychotherapy research, with special reference
to dynamic psychotherapy, during the past 20 years. A
prominent feature has been the inability to demonstrate
that psychotherapy is effective; another has been the lack
of impact on clinical practice. A thorough review of the
literature suggests that evidence for the effectiveness
of psychotherapy, and even of dynamic psychotherapy, is
stronger than is generally supposed. Recent studies,
based on outcome criteria that do justice to the complexity
of psychodynamic change, have begun to heal the split
between research and practice and offer renewed hope for
the future. (Journal abstract).

878.   Malan, D.H., Therapeutic factors in
        analytically-oriented brief psycho-
        therapy, in, Gosling, R., Support,
        Innovation, and Autonomy, London,
        Tavistock, 1973.

879.   Malan, D.H., Psychoanalytic brief
        psychotherapy and scientific method,
        in, Bannister, D., (ed.), Issues and
        approaches in the psychological therapies,
        London, Wiley, 1976.

880.   Malan, D.H., A study of brief psychotherapy,
        New York, Plenum Rosetta Medical Publi-
        cations, 1976.

881.   Malan, D.H., The frontier of brief psycho-
        therapy: An example of the convergence of
        research and clinical practice, New York,
        Plenum Medical Book Co., 1976.

The author presents impressive research evidence to refute
the notion that brief therapy should be viewed only as a
supportive, goal-limited approach. Malan surveys the
major principles of dynamically-oriented brief therapy,
the types of clients most suited to such an approach,
specific techniques used, and specific assessment of outcome. He points out that brief dynamic psychotherapy
contains all of the essential elements of psychoanalysis.
He further demonstrates that such an approach is valuable
with the more severely disturbed and chronically ill. The
research is based on a large sample and rigorous methodology. The results indicate that a brief dynamically-
oriented therapy can produce longer lasting and in-depth
personality changes in specifically selected patients.
He presents the details of 12 cases to elucidate his
findings.

882.   Malan, D.H., Toward the validation of
        dynamic psychotherapy, New York, Plenum
        Press, 1976.

883.   Malan, D.H., Individual psychotherapy
        and the science of psychodynamics,
        Boston, Butterworths, 1979.

884.   Malan, D.H., et al., Psychodynamic
        changes in untreated neurotic patients,
        Archives of General Psychiatry, 1975,
        32, 110-127.

This work is part of a study of 45 neurotic patients who
were seen for consultation at the Tavistock Clinic but
who never received treatment, and who, by the time they
were asked to come for a follow-up, had never been interviewed by a psychiatrist more than twice in their whole
lives. In a previous report, we described 13 patients
who were at least "improved" on purely symptomatic criteria
but whom we did not regard as improved on dynamic criteria.
Here we describe 11 patients who were judged to be improved
on dynamic criteria. These patients are of extraordinary
interest, providing not only direct evidence of therapeutic mechanisms in everyday life - an answer to a
question posed by Strupp and Bergin in 1969 - but also,
quite unexpectedly, evidence about the therapeutic effects
of single interviews. (Journal abstract).

885.   Malouf, R., and Alexander, J. Family
        crisis intervention: A model and
        technique of training, in, Hardy, R.E.,
        and Cull, J.C., (eds.), Therapeutic needs
        of the family, Springfield, Illinois,
        C.C. Thomas, 1974.

886.   Mandel, H.P., "Judo" and psychotherapy:
        Incidents from a case report, Voices:
        The Art and Science of Psychotherapy,
        1975, 11, 66-70.

The author describes the use of a particular therapeutic
technique, rooted in "judo" principles, which can dramatically shorten the length of time needed to make meaningful
contact with a resistive patient. A case example is used
to illustrate the technique.

887.   Mandel, H.P., and Cooper, I.J.,
        Paradoxical intention and hypnosis in
        brief psychotherapy: A case report,
        Ontario Psychologist, 1980, 12, 6-12.

This article contains a short review of the historical
factors which have led to the gradual increase in the
use and popularity of briefer forms of treatment, followed
by a case history in which the techniques of paradoxical
intention and hypnosis were used.

888.   Mandel, H.P., and Uebner, J., "If you
        never chance for fear of losing...",
        Personnel and Guidance Journal, 1971,
        50, 192-197.

This article, written by both therapist and client, contains a description of a brief therapy of an underachieving
university student. The client's poetry is included to
highlight the essence of the changes he experienced during
treatment.

889.   Mandel, H.P., et al., Personality change
        and achievement change as a function of
        psychodiagnosis, Journal of Counseling
        Psychology, 1968, 15, 500-515.

This research article reports on the findings of a brief
therapy approach with underachieving university students.
A particular technique, including confrontation and
reality-testing, was used and found to be successful for
one particular type of underachiever.

890.   Mandel, H.P., et al., Reaching
        emotionally disturbed children: "Judo"
        principles in remedial education, American
        Journal of Orthopsychiatry, 1975, 45, 867-
        874.

This article surveys the issue of control in various
systems of therapy, and highlights the use of a particular
approach rooted in "judo" principles as one method of
producing needed changes in a short-term treatment context
with teenagers.

891.   Mandell, A.J., The fifteen minute hour,
        Disease of the Nervous System, 1961,
        22, 559-562.

Mandell describes an ultra brief therapeutic form which
may prove useful, in selected cases, for therapists or
outpatient psychiatric clinics experiencing shortages of
available therapeutic time. He discusses patient selection, technical considerations, and difficulties encountered in this treatment format. The author describes the
process of the initial hour-long intake interview, and the
first fifteen-minute session. Thereafter, therapeutic
maneuvers are dictated according to five general themes,
which Mandell briefly reviews: emphasis of patient's
strengths; reinforcement of defenses; making unchangeable
pathology ego syntonic; leaving unexplored the positive
transference; and role playing for therapeutic effect
within the transference. Within three or four brief interviews, the therapist will be able to assess whether this
type of therapy is helpful to a patient. (abstract by
Deborah Schuller).

892.   Mann, J., The specific limitation of time
        in psychotherapy, Seminars in Psychiatry,
        1969, 1, 375-379.

The author describes a particular type of brief psychotherapy. He delineates its structure, purpose, and the
processes which unfold within this structure. The total
number of sessions is 12, which does not vary from patient
to patient. The timing of the sessions will vary somewhat,
but the total always remains the same. Further, the
specific termination date is agreed upon at the beginning
of therapy. Within this structure, therapy progresses
through an initial phase, middle phase, and termination
phase. The characteristics of each phase are discussed,
and the role of the therapist throughout is delineated.
The major focus remains the issue of separation, and the
meaning of such in the patient's life. The issue of
selection of patients for such an approach and of the
training of therapists within this model are also briefly
discussed.

893.   Mann, J., Time limited psychotherapy,
        Cambridge, Mass., Harvard University
        Press, 1973.

894.   Mannino, F.V., and Greenspan, S.I.,
        Projection and misperception in couples
        treatment, Journal of Marriage and
        Family Counseling, 1976,   , 139-143.

Projective identification is discussed as an interpersonal
mechanism involved in distortions of perceptions and
communications. Several case illustrations are presented
to show how this mechanism manifests itself, in relatively
healthy, though neurotic, couples. A treatment approach
based on correction of the perceptual distortions is
suggested as a model for short-term counseling with such
couples. (Journal abstract).

895.   Margolis, P.M., and Andre, J.M. The
        treatment of a psychiatric emergency in
        a university hospital setting, Michigan
        Medicine, 1968, 67, 1227-1229.

One of the responsibilities of a University Hospital is
the evaluation and appropriate management of psychiatric
emergencies. A conceptual model of an "ideal" emergency
program is presented, and a structural format for dealing
with emergencies is outlined. The structure includes:
a telephone service, a walk-in service, a crisis intervention clinic, a consultation service, and a flexible use
of inpatient beds. The implications of the service-
training-research triumvirate is discussed here in the
context of the residency program. (Journal abstract).

896.   Maris, R., and Connor, H.E., Do crisis
        services work? A follow-up of a
        psychiatric outpatient sample, Journal
        of Health and Social Behavior, 1973,
        14, 311-322.

This study reports on the results of a one year follow-up
of various therapy approaches used with 200 outpatient
psychiatric patients seen at a hospital emergency unit.

The aim of the study was to answer questions frequently
posed by critics of crisis services: a) What measures of
changes were used? b) What about medication effects?
c) Which specific treatments were most effective? d) Once
crises are resolved, do new emotional problems crop up to
take their place? The specific measures used in this
study are spelled out in detail. The results show no
significant improvement differences between those patients
on medication and those not on medication. Further, there
were no differential effects among the various drugs used.
The authors caution about premature conclusions, based on
small sample cell size may may have contributed statis-
ticallt to the results. They did report that the larger
the dosage used, the greater the extent of reported
improvement. There were no significant differences between
patients seen in individual versus group therapy regarding
improvement. Noticeable improvement began to appear in
those patients who had three-four months of treatment, and
there was a significant relationship between duration of
treatment and improvement, up to one year. Further, treatment outcomes reflect some redistribution of symptoms over
the year. Patients report being less depressed, less
likely to have major problems or complaints, and get along
better with others, but they do report more work and
financial problems, with increases in irritability.
Cautions in the interpretation and generalizability of the
data are presented.

897.   Markowitz, M., and Kadis, A.L., Short-
        term analytic treatment of married couples
        in a group by a therapist couple, in, Sager,
        C.J., and Kaplan, H.S., (eds.), Progress in
        in group and family therapy, New York,
        Brunner/Mazel, 1972.

898.   Marks, I.M., and Gelder, M.G.,
        A controlled retrospective study of
        behaviour therapy in phobic patients,
        British Journal of Psychiatry, 1965,
        111, 561-573.

Thirty-two phobic patients are reported who received
behaviour therapy. They were divided into 21 with agora-
phobia and 11 others with animal and social phobias.

Matched controls, not treated by behaviour therapy, were
found for all but one. Behaviour therapy patients had
graded practical retraining. Behaviour therapy was longer,
more frequent and took more sessions than treatments
received by the control patients. Agoraphobic patients
who had behaviour therapy did slightly better than controls
at the end of treatment, but this was related to more
frequent and longer treatment. The groups did not differ
in general condition. The improvement rate of 55-60%
during treatment of both groups of agoraphobic patients
masked considerable residual disability at the end of
treatment and a year later. There was no evidence that a
particular kind of patient responded better to behaviour
Patients with other phobias who had behaviour therapy did
much better than controls but some had relapsed a year
later. Symptom substitution did not appear during or after
behaviour therapy. In complex agoraphobias, behaviour
therapy on the lines of graded practical retraining was
not particuarly useful. In other phobias behaviour
therapy produced a useful short-term improvement which
diminished with time. (Journal summary).

   899.   Marks, I.M., et al., Hypnosis and
           desensitization for phobias, a controlled
           prospective trial, British Journal of
           Psychiatry, 1968, 114, 263-274.

The effects of systematic desensitization were compared
with those of hypnosis in 28 phobic out-patients.
Originally, two groups of 14 patients each received one
treatment in twelve weekly sessions. After a 6 weeks'
delay unimproved patients then had twelve sessions of the
alternative procedure in a cross-over design. Both treatment produced significant improvement in phobias. Most
patients were left with some residual disability at the
end of each treatment. (Journal summary modified).

   900.   Marmor, J., New directions in psycho-
           analytic theory and therapy, in,
           Marmor, J., (ed.) Modern psychoanalysis:
           New direction and perspectives, New York,
           Basic Books, 1968.

901.   Marmor, J., Short-term dynamic psycho-
       therapy, American Journal of Psychiatry,
       1979, 136, 149-155.

Describes short-term dynamic psychotherapy as rooted in
psychoanalytic theory. The historical background of brief
psychotherapy is traced, focusing on the contributions of
Freud, S. Ferenczi, O. Rank, and F. Alexander and T. French,
and a synthesis of contemporary views is presented.
Selection criteria for patients who can benefit from short-
term therapy and techniques used are discussed. Similarities to and differences from crisis intervention techniques
are pointed out. It is suggested that the future trend
is toward shorter-term therapies, but given the present
state of psychiatric knowledge, long-term therapy will
still be necessary for many patients. (Journal abstract).

902.   Marmor, J., Current trends in psycho-
       therapy, in, Davanloo, H. (ed.), Short-
       term dynamic psychotherapy, New York,
       Spectrum Publication, 1978.

In this chapter, Marmor surveys the historical developments in the dynamic therapies, group therapies, behavior
therapies, and sensate-emotive approaches (e.g,, T-groups).

903.   Marmor, J., Historical aspects of short-
       term dynamic psychotherapy, Psychiatric
       Clinics of North America, 1979, 2, 3-9.

Short-term psychodynamic techniques based on psychoanalytic
theory constitute innovative techniques and approaches
that open the way to new objectives and potentialities for
psychoanalytic psychotherapy. They constitute a historical
trend of the first magnitude and point to one of the major
directions in which the rational psychotherapies of the
future will be moving. (Journal abstract).

904.   Marmor, J., Recent trends in psycho-
        therapy, American Journal of Psychiatry,
        1980, 137, 409-416.

The author briefly reviews and tentatively categorizes a
number of psychotherapeutic techniques that have emerged
in recent decades, particularly those which fall under
the rubric of the human potential movement. He asks and
endeavours to answer four major questions with regard to
these therapies: 1) What is the meaning of their rise
and popularity? 2) Do they help, and if so, how? 3) Do
they present any dangers? d) What relevance and meaning
do they have for more contentional psychotherapies? He
also discusses some of the cognitive therapies and the
common denominators in all psychotherapies. (Journal
abstract).

905.   Marquis, J.N., Orgasmic reconditioning:
        Changing sexual object choice through
        controlling masturbation fantasies,
        Journal of Behavior Therapy and
        Experimental Psychiatry, 1970, 1, 263-271.

Sexual responses can become attached to formerly neutral
stimuli by pairing them with masturbation. The history of
using this model to explain perversions and to modify
choice of sexual object is discussed along with theoretical
considerations. A procedure for eliminating perversions
through careful programming of masturbation fantasies is
described and results for fourteen cases are given.
(Journal summary).

906.   Marrone, R.L., et al., A short duration
        group treatment of smoking behavior by
        stimulus saturation, Behaviour Research
        and Therapy, 1970, 8, 347-352.

Two saturation procedures of different lengths were
administered to Ss who desired to quit smoking. Ss chain-
smoked for either 20 hr (group E_1) or 10 hr (E_2). Total
abstinence was the main dependent measure. Both groups
experienced relatively equal success on a short-term basis.
Long-term abstinence was noted for group E_1 only. Sixty
percent of the E_1 Ss were not smoking 4 months after
treatment. (Journal summary).

907.   Marshall, C.D., The indigenous nurse
        as community crisis intervener, Seminars
        in Psychiatry, 1971, 3, 264-270.

We have demonstrated that there is a natural tirage which
screens clients prior to arrival at the doors of the
mental health worker. The role of the professional
should be to increase the effectiveness of the tirage
systems since the need for care by the professional sig-
nifies failure of the customary channels of assistance.
We have identified only one of these channels and are
deeply impressed with the degree of pathology with which
they deal and the imaginative resourcefulness of the nurse
crisis intervener or gatekeeper. (Journal summary).

908.   Martin, B., Family interaction associated
        with child disturbance: assessment and
        modification, Psychotherapy: Theory,
        Research, and Practice, 1967, 4, 30-35.

The author reports on some preliminary research involving
four families, in which each family had been referred
because of a behavior problem and underachieving son. The
sons ranged in age from 8-11, and were in grades four,
five, or six. A behavioral approach, set up in an experimental format, was used both to assess the family interaction among the three participants (mother, father, and
son), as well as to begin the process of behavior modification. Two main theoretical concepts used were cue
strength and reinforcement. The degree of indirect blame,
direct blame, self-blaming, non-blaming description of the
situation, and non-blaming of one's own feelings were used
as categories for independent ratings. Over the course of
the six treatment sessions, the families showed a greater
proportionate decrease in blaming scores than those of the
control group. The behavior of the children at school
also showed signs of improvement when compared with those
in the control group. No follow-up was done to ascertain
the length of time these changes were maintained.

909.   Martin, B., Brief family intervention:
        Effectiveness and importance of including
        the father, Journal of Consulting and
        Clinical Psychology, 1977, 45, 1002-1010.

A brief family intervention consisting of training in
conflict resolution and contingency management was given
to families reporting high rates of parent-child problems
of long duration. Families were randomly assigned to a
father-included treatment, father-not-included treatment,
and a wait-control group. Preintervention, postinter-
vention, and 6-month follow-up assessments were made daily
by telephone calls and by interview. Families receiving
the treatment procedures showed significantly greater
reductions in rates of problem behaviors at postinter-
vention than did the wait-control group and these changes
were maintained at follow-up. Improvement in mother-child
problems was the same whether fathers were included or
not. Families receiving a telephone monitoring procedure,
designed to prevent relapses during the 6-month follow-up
period, were not significantly different at follow-up
from families not receiving this procedure. The implications of these findings for a strong systems view of
families and family therapy are discussed. (Journal
abstract).

910.   Martin, C.V., and Alvord, J.R., Long
        term effects of intensive short-term
        treatment of the character and behavior
        disorder, Corrective Psychiatry and
        Journal of Social Therapy, 1966, 12,
        433-442.

The present study was initiated to determine the degree of
adjustment of some 348 persons discharged from the military
over a two year period. The mean age of the sample was
19.7 years, and of the original 348 subjects, a total of
135 completed all questionnaire and test materials. The
focus of the treatment was short-term, with character
behavior disorder personality types included as patients.
Those receiving treatment showed sufficient improvement
in scales of adjustment to lead the researchers to conclude
that the brief therapy approach used was beneficial.
Details of the program are included.

911.   Marziali, E.A., and Sullivan, J.M.,
        Methodological issues in the content
        analysis of brief psychotherapy,
        British Journal of Medical Psychology,
        in press.

This is a report of a study which extended D. Malan's
methodology for examining three factors typically present
in the interpretive work of brief psychotherapy. In his
work, the higher incidence of two factors (transference-
parent link) were found to correlate with a favourable
outcome. In this study operational definitions for
defense, anxiety, and impulse, the conflict factors associated with interpretive work, were developed and tested
on Malan's original data. All cases were rated on six
factors (Malan's original person-factors plus the additional
conflict factors) and their interlinkages. In the 22 cases
the rating scheme applied to more than 95% of all interpretations. Malan's findings were replicated. Problems
in deriving this complex rating scheme were delineated and
directions for future work were outlined. (Journal
abstract).

912.   Masserman, J.H., Historical-comparative
        and experimental roots of short-term
        therapy, in, Wolberg, L.R., (ed.),
        Short-term psychotherapy, New York,
        Grune and Stratton, 1965.

913.   Master, W.H., and Johnson, V.E., Human
        sexual inadequacy, Boston, Little/Brown,
        1970.

The two pioneers in the field of research and treatment of
sexual dysfunctions provide the results of the work at
their clinic in St. Louis. Their approach involves a two
week treatment program. The results are based on 510
dysfunctional couples. They report an 80% cure rate, with
a relapse rate after a five year follow-up of 5%. The
authors report some differing outcome results depending
upon the presenting dysfunctional syndromes. Specific
treatment techniques are also presented in detail.

914.   Mattsson, A., et al., Child psychiatric
        emergencies, <u>Archives of General Psychiatry,</u>
        1967, 17, 584-592.

A study of 170 child psychiatric emergencies seen over a
two-year period in a university hospital setting (Western
Reserve University) is presented. Demographic, clinical,
diagnostic, and follow-up data on the emergencies were
examined. Most of the demographic and clinical data
could be compared with those of a randomly selected group
of regular clinic intakes not considered emergencies.
Many significant differences between the two groups were
found to be particularly striking along the sex and age
variables. The follow-up information regarding the
children and their families seen for emergency evaluation
highlighted some deficiencies in the staff's handling of
families in crisis; it also confirmed the impression of
often longstanding and serious psychopathology among these
children and their families. The findings allow a discussion of a definition of a child psychiatric emergency,
and the formulation of several criteria for an effective
child psychiatric emergency service program. (Journal
summary).

915.   McCall, R.J., Group therapy with obese
        women with varying MMPI profiles,
        <u>Journal of Clinical Psychology,</u> 1974,
        30, 466-470.

Obese women who were participating in short-term group
therapy that was oriented toward development of self-
control techniques showed improvement post-therapeutically
in personality profile and in capacity to lose weight.
This small but reliable dual effect is most striking for
those who originally show the most deviant MMPI profiles.
(Journal summary).

916.   McCardel, J., and Murray, E.J., Non-
        specific factors in weekend encounter
        groups, <u>Journal of Consulting and
        Clinical Psychology,</u> 1974, 42, 337-345.

A weekend encounter experience was arranged for three
groups varying in techniques used from highly structured,

exercise-oriented to nonstructured basic discussion.   In
comparison with an at-home control group, the three
encounter groups showed significant improvement on self-
report measures but did not differ among themselves to
any great extent.   On the other hand, the encounter groups
did not differ substantially from an on-site control group
whose participants were led to believe they were also in
an encounter group but were given only recreational
activities.   Behavioral and sociometric measures, with one
minor exception, showed that the three encounter groups
and the on-site control group were virtually indistin-
guishable.   It was concluded that the favorable outcomes
of encounter groups reported in the literature may be
accounted for by nonspecific therapeutic factors such as
expectancy of favorable outcome, group enthusiasm, and the
reactive nature of outcome measures.   (Journal abstract).

917.   McClure, D., and Schrier, H., Preventive
        counseling with parents of young children,
        Social Work, 1956, 1, 68-80.

This article describes a project in preventive mental
health at the Family Counseling Service of the Child
Association of America.   The theoretical bases lie in concepts of normal development, in the parent-child interaction, and in the idea of selective aid via short-term
counseling.   The techniques used include advice, clarification, listening, interpretation etc.   Criteria for
selection to treatment include: a) parent: relatively
intact ego-functioning, ability to learn and focus;
b) parent-child: temporary imbalance in relationship, and
potentially gratifying; c) child: problems of onset, acute,
not multiple, age-adequate, not yet internalized.   The
counseling process is conceptualized into a tri-level
process.   Level I: focus on offering reassurance and
understanding; Level II: Focus on clarifying parent-child
interaction around specific problem area; Level III:
focus on clarifying distortions in parent attitude which
have caused problem and black its resolution.   A number
of examples are presented to elucidate these process
levels.   No systematic follow-up of cases had been done
at the time of the reporting of the article.

918.   McCombie, S.L., Characteristics of rape
        victims seen in crisis intervention,
        Smith College Studies in Social Work,
        1976, 46, 137-158.

McCombie reports on an exploratory study to establish a
preliminary data base on rape victims seen in the first
year of a rape crisis intervention program. Prior
research, program setting and method of data collection
are outlined. The author presents characteristics of the
victims studied, of whom the majority were middle-class,
white women, between the ages of 15 and 25. McCombie
characterizes the assaults with regards to a number of
variables--e.g. circumstances leading to the attack,
including location and time; persons present; prior
relationship with the assailant; presence of weapons;
nature of the assault; interaction accompanying the assault,
etc. Victims' feelings and behavior during and after the
incident are described. The author concludes with a discussion of implications for clinical intervention and
future research. (abstract by Deborah Schuller).

919.   McCombie, S.L., et al., Development of
        a medical rape crisis intervention
        program, American Journal of Psychiatry,
        1976, 133, 418-421.

The Rape Crisis Intervention Program at Beth Israel
Hospital utilizes volunteer multidisciplinary counseling
teams drawn from psychiatry, social work, psychology, and
nursing staffs. The premise of the program is that early
crisis intervention can prevent later development of
psychological disturbances in victims. Counselors accompanying victims throughout emergency room procedures:
follow-up begins 48 hours after the initial contact and
continues at regular intervals for at least a year. The
authors discuss the problems of implementation, which
include staff resistance, funding questions, and varying
levels of counseling sophistication, and describe how
these difficulties have been handled in their program.
They note that this program is becoming a resource center
for the community. (Journal abstract).

920. McConaghy, N., Aversive therapy of
homosexuality: Measures of efficacy,
American Journal of Psychiatry, 1971,
127, 1221-1224.

The author describes three investigations that attempted
to give objective evidence of the value of several types
of aversion therapy in the treatment of homosexuality.
The results were favorable but they showed little difference in the efficacy of the various aversion therapies.
The findings did suggest, however, that aversion therapy
does not act by setting up conditioned reflexes, as is
generally supposed. (Journal abstract).

921. McCord, E., Treatment in short-time
contacts, The Family, 1931, 12, 191-193.

This article is a brief report of the work of a committee
which studied various aspects of short-term treatment, as
part of the work of the Philadelphia Chapter of the
American Association of Social Workers. Among the valuable
aspects of short-term treatment were the sense of release
a client may feel, a sense of sharing, being able to place
the problem in a new perspective, and renewed hope leading
from this to continue to tackle the problem. The role of
the therapist is also discussed, including the active
involvement aspect of such a role.

922. McCord, J., and Packwood, W., Crisis
centers and hotlines: A survey,
Personnel and Guidance Journal, 1973,

Crisis centers and hotlines are relatively new approaches
to the nation's growing concern for mental health problems.
In order to provide information for those beginning a
center, 253 centers were surveyed regarding five major
aspects of crisis center operations: screening procedures
for telephone listener-counselor applicants, training
procedures, services offered, types of calls received,
and financing. Resources for further information and for
better communication among centers are identified.
(Journal abstract).

923.   McGee, R.K., Toward a new image for
        suicide and crisis intervention,
        Crisis Intervention, 1970, 2, 62-63.

924.   McGee, T.F., Some basic considerations
        in crisis intervention, Community
        Mental Health Journal, 1968, 4, 319-325.

In an effort to add greater understanding to the concept
of crisis intervention, it is proposed that emotional
crisis be placed on a continuum ranging from normal
developmental crises to psychiatric emergencies. If
emotional crises are placed on such a continuum, reasons
behind crisis intervention are clarified as are the roles
of direct treatment and consultation. Along with such
clarification it is suggested that a variety of viewpoints
of an emotional crisis should be considered in its assessment. This in turn results in a more pragmatic and comprehensive orientation for a community mental health
center to effectively assist people in crisis. (Journal
abstract).

925.   McGee, T.F., and Meyer, W., Time-
        limited group psychotherapy: A
        comparison with schizophrenic
        patients, Comparative Group Studies,
        1971, 2, 71-84.

This study compares the effects of time-limited and time-
unlimited group psychotherapy on a schizophrenic population.
Subjects in this study were closely matched on demographic
variables, and other conditions of treatment were held
constant. Differencies between the two groups of subjects
treated in the respective types of group psychotherapy are
explored and discussed. Implications and the effects of
time-limited and time-unlimited psychotherapy groups with
schizophrenic patients are examined. (Journal summary).

926. McGuire, M.T., The process of short-
term insight psychotherapy, Journal of
Nervous and Mental Disease, 1965, 141,
83-94.

The author provides a brief overview of the contributions
to the field of brief therapy of Alexander and Sifneos,
and discusses some of the differences between longer-term
and shorter-term therapies, as well as some of the differences between supportive and short-term therapy. Four
critical variables related to the success or failure of
brief therapy are presented and discussed. These are
issues of positive transference, transference neurosis,
experience bias, and increased symptomatology. A four
phase model is also detailed, including a perceptual
ordering, a perceptual reordering, a transference interpretation, and an integration and termination phase. Two
cases are provided to help elucidate the theoretical and
practical points presented.

927. McGuire, M.T., The process of short-
term insight psychotherapy: II. Content,
expectations, and structure, Journal of
Nervous and Mental Disease, 1965, 141,
219-230.

In a companion article to the previous article, the author
provides a brief restatement of some of the principles
mentioned. He then proceeds to detail some of the fantasies patients bring with them, which emerge when they
are told that they will be seen in brief therapy. All
are related to the patient's concept of past, present,
and future (i.e., to their concepts of time), and the
author elucidates the implications of these fantasies and
perceptions for therapy. The process of therapy in its
briefer form is further described and a case history is
presented.

928. McGuire, M.T., The instruction nature of
short-term insight psychotherapy, American
Journal of Psychotherapy, 1968, 22, 218-231.

Short-term, insight psychotherapy is viewed as a way of
teaching problem solving. The argument runs as follows:

This type of therapy is set up to teach problem solving
methods; the problems are internal, not external; the
measure of successful treatment is the use of methods
learned in treatment to solve extra-therapy conflicts.
There are two main difficulties in attempting to do this.
First, getting the patient to recognize that an internal
problem is the cause of the difficulty. Second to teach
him methods of solution which may be carried away from
treatment. Considerations about the sequential nature of
instruction and views of instruction by the psychologist,
Jerome Bruner, provide the framework in which these issues
are discussed. (Journal summary).

929.   McGuire, M.T., and Sifneos, P.E., Problem
        solving in psychotherapy, Psychiatric
        Quarterly, 1970, 44, 667-673.

The authors present a discussion of a model of problem-
solving in brief therapy. They provide a four part conceptual scheme, consisting of ends, means, conditions, and
response, in order to better understand the process of
brief therapy. The advantages of such a model for both
the therapist and client are presented, as well as some
research findings pertaining to the natural sequencing
versus logical sequencing of the elements of the model in
therapy. Strong support is reported for allowing patients
to follow the natural rather than the logical sequencing
approach.

930.   McKinnon, K.M., A clinical evaluation
        of the method of direct analysis in
        the treatment of psychosis, Journal of
        Clinical Psychology, 1959, 15, 80-96.

Direct analysis in the treatment of psychosis has been
described with emphasis on the psychological rationale
underlying this method as compared with psychoanalysis in
the treatment of neurosis. It is believed that a successful resolution of the psychic conflicts in psychosis occurs
through the process of working with the patient's transference symptoms and his resistances. To this extent
direct analysis is similar to psychoanalysis. However,
the intensity of the transference and the resistances in

psychosis, as a result of diminished ego functioning, require methods of treatment that are radically different from the method of psychoanlaysis. The various methods utilized by Rosen in successfully generating emotional and verbal interaction with psychotic patients have been described and documented with brief excerpts from treatment sessions. For the purpose of conveying the total effectiveness of direct analysis, consecutive treatment sessions, during a two month period in the case of one psychotic patient, were summarized. Probably the most significant consequences of Rosen's method are that it has been successful with patients who have presented the severest form of psycnotic regression; and that the duration of time required for treatment is relatively short as compared with many of the methods of psychotherapy adapted to psychosis heretofore reported in the literature. (Journal summary).

931.   McKitrick, D.S., and Gelso, C.J.,
        Initial client expectancies in time-
        limited counseling, Journal of Counseling
        Psychology, 1978, 25, 246-249.

This experiment assessed the effects on initial expectancies of whether counseling was time-limited (12 sessions), of the interaction of time limits with the chronicity of the client's problem, and of the rationale given for time limits (time limits effective/appropriate vs. long waiting list). Eighty female college students were asked to place themselves into the role of a client they saw interacting with a counselor on film. Pre- and postfilm written material manipulated the independent variables. It was found that subjects in the chronic (vs. acute) problem condition had the most negative expectancies for the counseling relationship and outcome when the counseling was time-limited (vs. unlimited). While the rationale for time limits did not affect the primary dependent variables, post hoc analyses of subjects' essay responses indicated that the waiting-list rationale stimulated more negative expectancies than the time-limits-effective/appropriate rationale. Contrary to predictions, time limits did not affect subjects' expectancies for client activity and responsibility and for counselor activity. (Journal abstract).

932.   McMullen, S., and Rosen, R.C., Self-
        administered masturbation training in
        the treatment of primary orgasmic
        dysfunction, Journal of Consulting and
        Clinical Psychology, 1979, 47, 912-918.

Sixty nonorgasmic women participated in a clinical outcome
study of sexual dysfunction. Subjects included an equal
number of married and single women. After initial
screening, the subjects were randomly divided into three
groups of equal size (n=20): (a) videotape modeling,
(b) written instructions, and (c) waiting list control.
Both treatment procedures involved a 6-week, self-
administered masturbation-training program. After the
pretest interview, treatment was carried out without direct
contact with the experimenter. Of the subjects receiving
treatment, 60% became orgasmic by the end of the treatment
period. Four additional married subjects became orgasmic
by the time of the 1-year follow-up. For those who failed
to transfer orgasmic capacity to coital intercourse, the
role of partner dysfunction is discussed. Although no
significant differences were found between the videotaped
modeling condition and the written instructions group, the
overall effectiveness of the treatment compares favorably
with other treatment programs. With respect to cost-
benefit assessment, however, the self-administered treatment is clearly superior. (Journal abstract).

933.   McNair, D.M., A season for brevity,
        Seminars in Psychiatry, 1969, 1, 411-431.

This article examines research issues and offers interpretations of current findings concerning three brief
outpatient treatment methods: time-limited psychotherapy,
treatment with anti-anxiety drugs, and behavior therapy.
The author suggests in his introduction that the 1952
proposals of Edwards and Cronbach provide a convenient
evaluative frame of reference for the studies cited in
this review, most of which are prediction and outcome
experiments. McNair supports his conclusion that outcome
studies of time-limited therapy are at least suggestive,
and predictor studies only tentative and preliminary. He
then examines evidence for the effectiveness of three mild
anti-anxiety agents, and illustrates one direction for

future psychopharmacological research by describing a series of studies in which a particular drug-personality interaction appeared consistently. In a section on behavior therapy, five treatment procedures are outlined, and a critical review of some clinical research on one of those techniques (desensitization) is presented. Several weaknesses of current desensitization research are summarized. The author concludes that all three brief treatment methods are at present inadequately documented by solid research evidence. (abstract by Deborah Schuller).

934. McPherson, S.B., and Samuels, C.R., Teaching behavioral methods to parents, Social Casework, 1971, 52, 148-153.

The authors employed a didactic method in conjunction with a programmed text in their group work with four sets of parents whose children exhibited acting-out, aggressive, or hyperkinetic behavior. Evaluation procedures, group membership, and the process of the meetings are described. Outcome is examined both from parental and therapist viewpoints. McPherson and Samuels conclude that their behaviorally-grounded project has limited success with families; that it increases readiness for other therapeutic interventions. (abstract by Deborah Schuller).

935. Meerloo, J.A., Emergency psychotherapy and mental first aid, Journal of Nervous and Mental Disease, 1955, 124, 535-545.

Emergency methods of psychotherapy are not only urgent in times of mass catastrophe, but can be used in acute psychosomatic ailments, in acute psychoses and in the many psychotraumatic accidents and acute frights of life. The urgency and didactic value of emergency psychotherapy and mental first aid are stressed. Examples are given of different emergency techniques: 1) First aid in panic and catastrophe; 2) Hypnocatharsis with autohypnosis is a time-saving device; 3) First aid hypnocatharsis to be used as a device for solitary treatment but also for mass treatments; 4) Attention is asked for the prolonged initial interview with its immediate cathartic action. These

methods are recommended for use in various mental health
clinics, where lack of time, lack of money, or lack of
intellectual comprehension prevents the patient from
undergoing long-term psychotherapeutic exploration.
(Journal resume).

936.   Meichenbaum, D., Cognitive behavior
        modification, New York, Plenum
        Publishing, 1977.

937.   Mendelsohn, R., Critical factors in
        short-term psychotherapy: A summary,
        Bulletin of the Menninger Clinic, 1978,
        42, 122-149.

Brief psychotherapy is defined here as any dynamically-
oriented therapy which continues up to a one year time
period, with a frequency of 1-2 sessions/week. Specific
factors which are important in these briefer forms of
treatment are discussed in some detail. These include:
a) active attention on the therapist's part, focusing, the
use of active methods and techniques (confrontation, clarification and reflection, commands and advice, the use of
role-playing, actively changing the frequency of interviews, using anxiety-provoking questions, and the specific
setting of time limits). A clinical example is provided
of a seven session brief dynamically-oriented therapy with
a 27 year old single female patient. The theoretical
issues presented earlier in the article are then reviewed
with particular reference to the case material. The author
concludes with a discussion of the limitations of such an
approach and contraindications for its use. The importance
of the diagnostic skill of those providing short-term
therapies is stressed.

938.   Merrill, S., and Cary, G.L., Dream
        analysis in brief psychotherapy,
        American Journal of Psychotherapy,
        1975, 29, 185-193.

Dream analysis in brief psychotherapy relieves symptoms
and reduces acting out by facilitating patient participation through helping him experience disowned feelings.

Transference remains generalized and is easily displaced.
Dream interpretations are based on readily assimilated and
currently meaningful experience. Dependency is avoided by
a therapeutic interaction which emphasizes the patient's
part in creating conflict and experiencing symptoms rather
than emphasizing his helplessness. Interpreting dreams
close to the manifest level catalyzes their meaningful
relevance to current experience both inside and outside
therapy, creating a transitional phase of self-awareness
and self-acceptance. The patient reported on in this
article was a university student. (Journal summary
adapted).

939. Messer, S.B., and Lehrer, P.M., Short-
term groups with female welfare clients
in a job-training program, Professional
Psychology, 1976, 7, 352-358.

The authors describe a work incentive program which
attempts to meet medical, economic, and psychological needs
of very low-income persons, primarily single mothers on
welfare. Two-hour, bi-weekly group sessions with a psychological consultant appear catalytic to the exploration and
modification of emotional conflicts and maladaptive behavior. They outline common problems and themes expressed
by these women. The authors aim to achieve the following
goals in leading such groups: identification of persons
needing and able to benefit from further psychological
help; brief treatment within the group of certain emotional
problems; education by example regarding the role of mental
health professionals; providing factual information on
such topics as childbearing, sex, and emotional disorders.
Based on their experience with 35 different groups, the
authors suggest that treatment of the emotional problems
of very low socioeconomic status clients should encompass
two aspects: psychotherapy, and intervention addressed to
social and economic problems. (abstract by Deborah
Schuller).

940.   Meyer, E., et al., Contractually time-
        limited psychotherapy in an outpatient
        psychosomatic clinic, American Journal
        of Psychiatry, 1967, 124 (suppl.), 57-68.

The study reported here was done between 1963-65, with a
total of 176 patients seen in an outpatient, contractually-
limited (10 sessions) therapy program at the Psychiatric
Liaison Service of the Johns Hopkins Hospital. About 80%
of the sample were from the lower socioeconomic levels.
The results indicate that patients who dropped out of
therapy did not differ from those who remained in therapy
on the basis of age, sex, race, social class, marital
status, psychiatric diagnosis, or duration of presenting
symptoms. Patients with Catholic backgrounds, high school
graduates, and patients referred from outside the hospital
tended to complete therapy more often than others. Those
patients who had originally sought therapy because of
presenting psychological problems tended to complete
therapy more than those who sought help because of presenting physical problems. The results are taken as support
for the view that patients from lower socioeconomic levels
can be motivated to actively participate in a structured
time-limited psychotherapeutic experience.

941.   Migler, B., and Wolpe, J., Automated
        self-sensitization: a case report,
        Behaviour Research and Therapy, 1967,
        5, 133-135.

This case history details the behavioral treatment
(systematic desensitization) of a patient with a public
speaking phobia. The apparatus used is described, as well
as the treatment steps involved. A total of seven therapy
sessions were needed to eliminate the fear. An eight month
follow-up showed no public speaking anxiety or avoidance
of public speaking.

942. Miller, A.L., Treatment of a child with
Gilles de la Tourette's Syndrome, Journal
of Behavior Therapy and Experimental
Psychiatry, 1970, 1, 319-321.

The author describes an individual case of Gilles de la
Tourette's Syndrome in a five year old child, which was
treated by using a behavior modification approach, in
which non-performance of the undesirable behavior was rewarded. Details of the case are presented, including the
use of the child's parents and teacher. The child had
exhibited the beginning of the "barking" noises two years
earlier, and had developed accompanying frequent eye
blinking, facial grimaces, jerking, neck twisting. No
organic involvement was found upon appropriate testing.
The step-by-step treatment is described, and the successful
conclusion points to the ability to treat such a case on
an outpatient basis in the home.

943. Miller, F.T., and Mazade, N.A., Crisis
intervention services in comprehensive
community mental health centers in the
United States, Proceedings of the 9th
International Congress on Suicide
Prevention and Crisis Intervention,
1978, 273-284.

944. Miller, L.C., Short-term therapy with
adolescents, American Journal of
Psychiatry, 1959, 29, 772-779.

The author summarizes his clinical findings gathered over
an eight year period in treating middle and upper class
adolescent boys of above average intelligence and interest
in academic achievement. The main focus is on the developing teenager's ego identity, using the conceptualization
formulated by Erik Erikson. There are four conditions
which block or hinder the normal development of an ego
identity, and they are discussed by the author. a) Failures
in coping with previous developmental problems, b) accidental or motivated exposure to overwhelming tension-
producing situations; c) failure in the area of values,
and, d) withdrawal from societal structures which facilitate

identity formation. The author provides examples for each
of these conditions. The value of using outside resources
as part of the on-going treatment process (i.e., boys
groups, etc.). The issue of termination is raised in the
context of brief treatment.

945.   Miller, L.C., Southfields: Evaluation
        of a short-term inpatient treatment
        center for delinquents, Crime and
        Delinquency, 1970, 305-316.

Southfields, a Kentucky replication of Highfields, a New
Jersey program for the treatment of delinquents, was
evaluated for four successive years to determine whether
the Highfields program could be effectively applied to
another, widely different part of the country. Recidivism
rates for 191 boys admitted to Southfields during that
period were compared with rates for two similar groups,
one put on probation and the other sent to Kentucky
Village, a correctional institution. Boys were assigned
to treatment on the basis of the court's judgement but the
study attempted to match groups on major variables.
Recidivism rates were also compared with Highfields
recidivism rates. Statistical tests showed that Southfields
obtained results similar to, if not better than, Highfields'
and better than Kentucky Village's. However, the success
of the probation group was on a par with the Southfields
graduate group. Psychometric measures were unable to
specify either which boys would complete the Southfields
program or which would resume delinquent behavior once
released from the institution. All evidence suggests that
Southfields works as both a screening and a remedial procedure, helping some boys while screening out others
either for return to the community or for further custodial
care. Critical incident observations indicate that the
treatment sprocess is too complex for current measures of
personality to be effective in predicting which candidate
will successfully complete the Southfields program. The
study concluded that Southfields should be the second
stage in a three-stage remedial program, probation being
the first and the state correctional institution the third.
(Journal abstract).

946. Miller, L.C., et al., Comparison of
reciprocal inhibition, psychotherapy,
and waiting list control for phobic
children, Journal of Abnormal Psychology,
1972, 79, 269-279.

Sixty-seven phobic children, ages 6-15, were randomly
assigned to a 2 X 3 factorial, repeated-measures, covariate
design which included two male therapists and three time-
limited treatments: reciprocal inhibition, psychotherapy,
and waiting list control. Following 24 sessions or 3-mo.
and at 6 week follow-up, Ss were reassessed by an independent evaluator and by parents. Results indicated a significant effect due to time and child's age. Clinical
evaluation, using initial scores as the covariate, showed
no effects of treatment or therapist. Parents reported
treatment effects for both target fear and general fear
behavior. Therapies were equally efficient, and all treatment effects were achieved with phobic children aged 6-10.
(Journal abstract).

947. Miller, W.B., A psychiatric emergency
service and some treatment concepts,
American Journal of Psychiatry, 1968,
124, 924-933.

The author describes the operations of a psychiatric
emergency service in a university hospital during a six-
month period. He discusses the importance of the social
environment in both the development and the therapeutic
resolution of a psychiatric emergency. Five cases are
discussed which exemplify the work that the emergency
psychiatrist can do with the patient and his ecological
group during the emertency stage of contact. (Journal
abstract).

948. Minuchin, S., Conflict-resolution
family therapy, Psychiatry, 1965,
28, 278-286.

Novel approaches developed at the Wittwyck School for boys
are described. Families involved at this school have
produced delinquent children, and are usually from a lower
socio-economic background. They are characterized by

aggression, helplessness, abandonment, and need for
nurturance. Interactional patterns tend to be focussed
on the here and now, with very few skills to deal effectively with conflicts. Work with a total of 60 families
has led to the development of new, active techniques
focussed on helping the families to develop conflict
resolution skills. The therapist actively frames the
interactions between family members around specified issues
(which have consistently produced conflict) and directs
those family members not directly involved to observe,
introspect and comment on their own reactions and their
perceptions of the observed interactions. This allows for
some "distance" to develop, permitting a beginning awareness into the nature and quality of the difficulties.
Many of the families had been in more traditional forms of
family therapy for lengthy periods of time prior to
becoming involved in this conflict-resolution family
therapy, an approach which shortens the length of treatment.

949.   Minuchin S., and Mantalvo, B.,
        Techniques for working with
        disorganized low socioeconomic
        families, American Journal of
        Orthopsychiatry, 1967, 37, 880-887.

The authors detail some of the structural changes they
have found effective in working with highly disorganized
families of low socioeconomic background. The conscious
manipulation of family subgroups (i.e., working with some
members at one point, and regrouping at another point) has
led to a heightening of the affective experiences in these
families and has allowed for a clearer learning of how
changes can be made by each family member. Examples are
cited in which the authors show how the language of
aggression in these families is often interpreted by
members as just that, and not an expression of concern,
which it often really is. Allowing for the separation of
family members within the context of on-going therapy
allows for the reperception of this issue and others
(e.g., tenderness versus being a sucker), so that unrewarding behavior patterns are changed. The separation
also allows for discrete rather than diffuse issues to be

focussed on, which increases the probability of positive outcome. The authors also described the use of exaggeration on the part of the therapist as a therapeutic strategy for encouraging emotional-cognitive reorganization and the emergence of new interactional patterns. They also point to the therapist needing to close the gap between his/her style of communication and that of the family in therapy, and specific examples are also presented to highlight this point. The authors close by postulating that their approach may be useful in dealing with all disorganized families, not just those from lower socioeconomic levels.

950.   Minuchin, S., et al., A project to teach learning skills to disturbed, delinquent children, American Journal of Orthopsychiatry, 1967, 37, 558-567.

Patterns of communication in low socioeconomic families which produce acting-out children were analyzed, implications for learning discussed, and an experimental "game" curriculum for teaching formal elements of communication was designed and tested in ten sessions over five weeks with six disturbed delinquent children. (Journal abstract).

951.   Mitchell, H.C., Short term therapy for the psychiatric patient, Diseases of the Nervous System, 1972, 33, 781-782.

This study summarizes the results of a short-term treatment approach for psychiatric inpatients. Drug therapy was a part of the approach, and results show that there were distinct advantages to the patients, staff, and hospital in the shortened hospitalization needed. The average length of stay was 2.5 weeks, with 15% being readmitted within one month. Approximately 70% of the patients remained out of hospital for over three months, and a follow-up one year later showed that none of these had been readmitted. The major drugs used were Thorazine and Mellaril.

952.   Mitchell, K.R., and Orr, F.E., Note on
        the treatment of heterosexual anxiety
        using short-term massed desensitization,
        Psychological Reports, 1974, 35, 1093-
        1094.

Data from traditional and short-term desensitization
procedures (ns=7.8) showed decreased anxiety associated
with paper-and-pencil measures of heterosexual interactions but the two desensitization groups were not significantly different nor did a relaxation and no-treatment
group (ns=9.5) differ in reports.   (Journal summary).

953.   Mittelmann, B., Briefer psychotherapy
        in psychosomatic disorders of children
        and adolescents, Nervous Child, 1950,
        8, 291-300.

Three types of psychosomatic disorders of mild or moderate
intensity may be amenable to briefer psychotherapy, at
times combined with drug therapy: (a) easily reversible
disturbances of organ function, e.g. vomiting.   (b) disorders with grosser organ pathology, e.g., asthma. (c)
disorders with a well-defined primary organic pathology,
e.g., adiposogenital dystrophy (correctable) or diabetes
(not fully correctable), fused with psychogenic disturbances.   The psychotherapeutic measures include (a)
mediation between child and parent of controversial rules
of conduct; (b) advice to the parent on how to handle the
child in a recent conflict situation; (c) play sessions,
with the child's general knowledge of the reasons for his
coming to treatment; (d) discussion of focussed problems,
and, (c) correction of the environment.   Specific case
examples are provided to highlight the points raised.
(Journal summary adapted).

954.   Moleski, R., and Rosi, D.J., Comparative
        psychotherapy: Rational-emotive versus
        systematic desensitization in the treat-
        ment of stuttering, Journal of Consulting
        Psychology, 1976, 44, 309-311.

The study involved a total of 20 patients, 15 male and
five female with an average age of 28, all of whom

suffered from stuttering. Treatment approaches involved
rational-emotive, systematic desensitization, and no treatment control groups. A total of eight intensive therapy
sessions per subject were provided. Assessment measures
were taken prior to and following completion of the treatment, and one month after the termination of treatment.
The results indicated that overall rational-emotive
therapy was more effective than systematic desensitization
in reducing stuttering, and systematic desensitization was
more effective than the control group. The authors
recommend a cognitive-behavioral approach in the treatment
of stuttering problems, rather than the more traditional
behavioral approach.

955.   Mone, L.C., Short-term group psycho-
        therapy with postcardiac patients,
        International Journal of Group
        Psychotherapy, 1970, 20, 99-108.

A report is presented about the effectiveness of a short-
term group therapy program for male and female cardiac
patients. A total of 10, 90-minute sessions were held,
with a patient sample of 14. The content of the sessions
is presented in to form of major issues or themes which
emerged. Included were such issues as fear of death,
feelings about overexertion from sexual activity, feelings
of helplessness, and abandonment by someone significant.
Results of the group experience included decreases in
anxiety levels, and lessening of depression. The value of
using a short-term group therapy approach as part of the
rehabilitation program for post-cardiac patients is
stressed.

956.   Montgomery, A., and Montgomery D.,
        Contractual psychotherapy: Guidelines
        and strategies for change, Psychotherapy:
        Theory, Research, and Practice, 1975, 12,
        348-352.

This paper focuses on therapeutic contracts to specify the
long- and short-term goals of treatment. The authors discuss advantages of contractual treatment and propose
guidelines for negotiation and implementation of a workable

contract.   Contracts are negotiated to delineate clearly
the responsibilities of both therapist and client; thus,
they provide safeguards for both parties, while increasing
the efficiency of therapeutic time.   Once a general therapeutic objective has been formulated in a contract, and
specific problem behaviors have been identified, the
therapist attempts to foster an attitude conducive to
change.   Three approaches to dealing with client resistance, as based on the work of Schiff, Haley, and Perls,
are described.   After the "proper" attitude toward change
is observed, the therapist translates client goals into a
series of graduated steps.   The authors stress that
attitudinal and emotional elements, as well as behavioral,
are inherent in change.   (abstract by Deborah Schuller).

957.   Morganstern, K.P., Implosive therapy
        and flooding procedures: a critical
        review, Psychological Bulletin, 1973,
        79, 318-334.

After a brief explanation of implosive theory and technique,
the case reports and experimental investigations of
implosive therapy and flooding procedures with human
subjects are critically reviewed.   Much of the research
has produced confusing and contradictory results and these
findings are discussed in terms of response rehearsed in
therapy, exposure time, and cognitive factors.   However,
since a majority of the experimental reports are so badly
confounded, interpretation of the literature is exceedingly
difficult.   It is concluded that there is, at present, no
convincing evidence of the effectiveness of implosion or
flooding with human subjects nor is there any evidence
that the techniques are superior to systematic desensitization.   In addition, the theoretical basis of implosion
therapy appears to be unsupported.   Finally, serious
realistic and ethical questions are raised in regard to
the desirability of the clinical use of implosive procedures.   (Journal abstract).

958.   Morganstern, K.P., Issues in implosive
        therapy: Reply to Levis, Psychological
        Bulletin, 1974, 81, 380-382.

Levis' critique of Morganstern's review on implosion and
flooding, although containing a few points of agreement,
consisted mainly of unsupported or contradictory challenges.
More importantly, Levis' arguments did not alter the major
conclusions reached by Morganstern, namely: (a) There
exists, at present, no convincing evidence of the efficacy
of implosive therapy or flooding nor of the superiority
by either of these techniques to systematic desensitization.
(b) There are serious ethical questions concerning the
clinical application of the implosive therapy procedures.
(Journal abstract).

959.   Morley, W.E., Treatment of the patient
        in crisis, Western Medicine, 1965, 3,
        77-87.

Morley briefly discusses the issue of psychiatric hospitalization, then examines crisis-oriented outpatient treatment as an alternative. History and theory of crisis
treatment (based on the Lindemann-Caplan conceptual framework) are presented. The author describes general
operating characteristics of the Benjamin Rush Center, the
nature of the patient population seen there, and techniques
of the consultation (underlying attitudes and specific
methodology). Lastly, a case history illustrates the
style and type of intervention typical of the Center.
(abstract by Deborah Schuller).

960.   Morley, W.E., Theory of crisis
        intervention, Pastoral Psychology,
        1970, (April).

Morley touches briefly on reasons why knowledge of crisis
intervention technique is appropriate and valuable for
clergy. He discusses history and theory of crisis intervention as grounded on the work of Lindemann and Caplan.
He describes four different levels of intervention, each
succeeding level subsuming former levels in terms of
increased potential effectiveness and requisite therapeutic
knowledge. Morley believes the trained clergyman capable

of third level crisis intervention (the "generic" approach)
which implies a thorough understanding of crisis in
general terms, of specific crises, and types of effective
interventions. Finally, to illustrate the leverage for
change offered by crisis, the author presents a case
history treated on the fourth level. (abstract by
Deborah Schuller).

961.   Morley, W.E., and Brown, V.B., The crisis
        intervention group: A natural mating or
        a marriage of convenience? Psychotherapy:
        Theory, Research, and Practice, 1969, 6,
        30-36.

This article presents a summary of the use of a crisis-
interventton group therapy program initiated in 1966 at
the Benjamin Rush Center, Venice branch, a division of the
Los Angeles Psychiatric Service. The service was offered
to lower income blue collar patients, ages 13 1/2 years
and up. Serious suicidal or homocidal risks at intake,
severe psychosis which would be too disruptive of group
process, and inability of the patient to speak English
were used to exclude patients from this program. The
authors compare crisis group therapy with traditional
group therapy, and conclude that there are advantages and
disadvantages. There is also a comparison of group crisis
versus individual crisis intervention, with the pros and
cons of each discussed. Excerpts from three consecutive
groups sessions are presented, along with detailed background on the various group members.

962.   Morley, W., et al., Paradigms of
        intervention, Journal of Pyschiatric
        Nursing, 1967, 5, 531-544.

The rationale for the position of a psychiatric nurse as a
consultant in crisis intervention at the Benjamin Rush
Center in Los Angeles has been discussed. A paradigm of
the nurses' relationships in crisis intervention consultation has been depicted. Techniques of crisis intervention have been discussed in detail and illustrated with a
clinical case study. (Journal summary).

963. Morrice, J.K., Emergency psychiatry, British Journal of Psychiatry, 1968, 114, 485-491.

Psychiatric hospitals are providing an increasingly wide range of services, and at the same time evolving new concepts regarding their treatment roles and practices. The present revolution in American psychiatry, it is suggested, has lessons for Britain at this period of development. Not least is the emphasis on emergency services. Social factors as precipitants of a patient's admission to hospital are examined with reference to both Britain and the U.S.A. It is concluded that methods of crisis intervention have much to offer in dealing with the mental needs of a community, and may often provide an alternative to hospitalization. Such a development in treatment demands a fresh deployment of resources and a changing role for the psychiatrist. Emergency psychiatry and community psychiatric services go hand-in-hand and derive naturally from therapeutic community ideals. (Journal summary).

964. Morrice, J.K.W., Crisis intervention: Studies in community care, Oxford, Permagon Press, 1976.

965. Morris, B., Crisis intervention in a public welfare agency, Social Casework, 1968, 49, 612-617.

The author reports on the work of the Special Family Counseling Unit of the Department of Social Services of the City of New York. This unit provided social casework to families in acute need at the time of the application for social welfare benefits. The focus included an exploration of the nature of the precipitating stress. The families exhibited anxiety and depression, and many had been paralyzed by major and sudden changes in their precarious life situations. Specific help was given families who were in danger of break-up and to unwed adolescent mothers. Of a total of 50 cases evaluated, about half indicated that they had received help and had

gained from the service. About 25% entered short-term
therapy, lasting about three months. The changes in staff
were also noted, including the realization of the importance of early intervention in family crises.

966.   Morrison, G.C., Therapeutic intervention
        in a child psychiatry emergency service,
        Journal of the American Academy of Child
        Psychiatry, 1969, 8, 542-558.

The author summarizes the establishment of a psychiatric
emergency service for children and their families at the
Central Psychiatric Clinic of Cincinnati. The average age
of the children was 12, and a review of the first 100
families seen is presented. The initial interview consisted of a team of diagnostic with all significant family
members present. Specific focus is on the nature of the
presenting problem and previous methods of coping. Number
of interviews ranged from one-eight, with an average
between three and four. Schools refusals, suicide attempts
or threats comprised the greatest number of referrals.
Case histories of the above presenting problems are
presented, as well as examples of problems of fire-setting
and promiscuity. Stress is placed in the service on rapid
access to treatment and flexible treatment schedules to
accommodate the families.

967.   Morrison, G.C. (ed.), Emergencies in
        child psychiatry, Springfield, Ill.,
        C.C. Thomas, 1975.

968.   Morrison, G.C., and Collier, J.G.,
        Family treatment approachesto
        suicidal children and adolescents,
        Journal of the American Academy of
        Child Psychiatry, 1969, 8, 140-153.

This paper is a report of the clinical experience in an
outpatient child psychiatric emergency service of treatment with families in which children were referred because
of a suicide attempt or threat. Attempted or threatened
suicide by a child or adolescent was understood as a

serious symptom of acute emotional distress which reflected
long-standing problems within the family. In 76% of the
families we saw, the event which precipitated the child's
suicide threat or attempt was an important loss or separation, or the anniversary of such a loss, through death,
illness, marital separation, hospitalization, or household
move of a parent or parent surrogate. We saw the family
promptly in an interview. The crisis episode was used to
effect increased openness of family communication and
therapeutic movement within the family system. A homogeneous group of families were seen through the study.
They presented a history of long-standing problems and
symptoms in the individual family members. They seemed to
make little connection between past events and the current
crisis. They requested help only around a crisis
situation and stayed involved with the therapeutic team
only until the current crisis was alleviated. The number
of interviews ranged from one to eight, but for most a
planned termination occurred after three or four interviews.
(Journal summary).

969.   Morrison, J.K., The family heritage:
        Dysfunctional constructs and roles,
        International Journal of Family
        Counseling, 1977, 5, 54-58.

970.   Morrison, J.K., Successful grieving:
        Changing personal constructs through
        mental imagery, Journal of Mental
        Imagery, 1978, 2, 63-68.

Mental imagery techniques, in combination with other psychotherapeutic interventions, can facilitate the grieving
process when such techniques are used to reconstruct death-
related events (death, wake, funeral, burial). Such re-
constructions evoke a variety of strong feelings which
prompt clients to integrate conflicting constructs about
the deceased and to clarify their role in the family
system. The personal construct theory of George Kelly is
used to explain how imagery techniques can often lead to
a successful completion of the grieving process. (Journal
abstract).

971.   Morrison, J.K., Emotive-reconstructive
        psychotherapy: Changing constructs by
        means of mental imagery, in Sheikh, A.A.,
        and Sahffer, J.T. (eds.), The potential
        of fantasy and imagination, New York,
        Brandon House, 1979.

Morrison outlines theoretical assumptions on which emotive-
reconstructive therapy (ERT) is grounded, as well as
clinical techniques employed. Key concepts concerning
stress, memory, and early childhood experiences are combined in ERT theory. On an operational level, ERT is
comprised of two phases. The emotive phase attempts to
recreate, physiologically and psychologically, stressful
events of early childhood. Three basic mental imagery
techniques are employed toward this end. In the second
phase, the client effects a reconstruction or reconceptual-
ization of his life by acquiring a more complex construct
system. Morrison briefly presents some case illustrations,
and describes characteristics, advantages, and special
applications of this approach. He includes data on the
effectiveness of ERT. (abstract by Deborah Schuller).

972.   Morrison, J.K., and Cometa, M.S.,
        Emotive-reconstruction psychotherapy:
        A short-term approach, American Journal
        of Psychotherapy, 1977, 31, 294-301.

Emotive-reconstructive therapy, a short-term approach to
psychotherapy, is based on a cognitive model of personality
and incorporates the notion of intrapersonal variations in
the level of RAS arousal. Within the context of this
model, a person is viewed as an active organism, constantly
engaged in the process of monitoring and interpreting
experiences in order to maintain an orderly view of the
world, and concomitantly, an optimal, nonstressful level
of arousal. By means of selective hyperventilation and a
concentrated focus on the sensorial context, an emotive-
reconstructive therapist encourages clients to recall and
reexperience developmentally early stress events. Such
techniques often lead to a reconstruing of self and significant others, which in turn facilitates the adoption of
more productive life roles. With certain clients, this
therapy can promote rapid personality and behavior change.

Specific case material is included, and ancillary therapy techniques are also used (e.g., Gestalt-like techniques, verbal confrontation, direct role playing, etc.). Most therapy cases need only 15 sessions for successful treatment. Some of the advantages of ERT are presented. (Journal summary adapted).

973.   Morrison, J.K., and Teta, D.C.,
        Simplified use of the semantic
        differential to measure psychotherapy
        outcome, Journal of Clinical Psychology,
        1978, 34, 75-1753.

To initially establish the validity and utility of a simplified use of the Semantic Differential to measure psychotherapy outcome, 14 clients were administered, before and after 15 sessions of individual psychotherapy, the Semantic Differential and a symptom checklist. As predicted, results indicated that change of clients' self-constructs in a positive direction was associated with symptom reduction. Implications for psychotherapy research are discussed. (Journal abstract).

974.   Morton, R.B., An experiment in brief
        psychotherapy, Psychological Monographs,
        1955, 69, No. 386.

975.   Moss, S.C., Brief successful psycho-
        therapy of a chronic phobic reaction,
        Journal of Abnormal and Social Psychology,
        1960, 60, 266-270.

This is a report of the brief successful treatment of a phobic reactions in which the patient's repressive defenses were penetrated, leading to a simple convincing demonstration of the childhood learning of the phobic response and its subsequent ramifications. A symbolic fantasy procedure, tailored to the patient's unique personality dynamics, was then instituted in order to consolidate the obtained insights and further desensitize the patient to the fear-provoking stimuli. Primary reliance was placed on several innovations in hypnotherapeutic technique. (Journal introduction).

976   Moss, S.C., et al., an additional study
        in hysteria: The case of Alice M.,
        International Journal of Clinical and
        Experimental Hypnosis, 1962, 10, 59-74.

A highly detailed account of the psychotherapy of one
female hysteric - a treatment failure - is the stimulant
for discussion of the genetics and dynamics of this
nosology. The patient's symptomatology includes feelings
of unreality, seizures, an embryo dual personality, and
frigidity. Hypnosis revealed the experimental basis for
these sytptoms and associated adjustment difficulties.
The dynamics bear a remarkable resemblance to those
advanced by Freud and Breuer, though issue is taken with
several fundamental psychoanalytic concepts. The Discussion deals largely with the phenomenology of the female
hysteric. It is concluded that the seemingly favorable
prognosis of the hysteric is illusionary if the goal is
characterologic changes. (Journal abstract).

977.   Moss, S.C., Crisis-oriented hypnotherapy,
        in Gordon, J. (ed.), Handbook on clinical
        and experimental hypnosis, New York,
        MacMillan Co., 1967.

978.   Moss, S.C., Black rover, come over: The
        hypnosymbolic treatment of a phobia,
        (with audio tape), Urbana, Ill.,
        University of Illinois Press, 1970.

979.   Moss, S.C., The hypnosymbolic treatment
        of a case of conversion hysteria: a
        treatment failure, Philadelphia,
        American Academic of Psychotherapists
        Tape Library, 1970.

980.   Moss, S.C., Treatment of a recurrent
        nightmare by hypnosymbolism, American
        Journal of Clinical Hypnosis, 1973,
        16, 23-30.

This case is an example of the use of hypnosis in relief
of nightmares associated with a traumatic neurosis. The
presence of the precipitating incident of three years'
duration was followed by recurrent anxiety dreams symbol-
izing the situation, which in turn allegedly led to extensive drug taking. The treatment objective was to eliminate
the disturbing dreams, which hopefully would lead to a
decrease or elimination of the drug habit. As will be
evident, the effect on the drug practice was left ambiguous;
however, there is provided evidence that it is possible to
extinguish a troublesome symptom (i.e., the nightmare)
through a combination of brief counseling and hypnosymbolism.
(Journal abstract).

981.   Moss, S.C., Hypnosymbolic psychotherapy,
        Fort Lee, N.J., Behavioral Sciences Tape
        Library, 1973.

982.   Moss, S.C., Hypnotherapy to resolve a
        recurrent nightmare, American Society
        of Clinical Hypnosis, (tape), 1973.

983.   Mountney, G., et al., Psychiatric
        emergencies in an urban borough,
        British Medical Journal, 1961, 1,
        498-500.

The authors present an analysis of emergency phone calls
made to social workers in a community after regular work
hours, over a period of one year. The most frequent users
of the service were men and women between the ages of 40
and 49 years. Further, most callers had longer standing
problems rather than problems of an acute nature.

984.   Mozdzierz, G., et al., The paradox in
         psychotherapy: An Adlerian perspective,
         Journal of Individual Psychology, 1976,
         32, 169-184.

The authors consider Adler's conception of paradoxical
strategy to be the touchstone of the Adlerian approach to
understanding the patient. Both the therapeutic relationship and specific treatment techniques contain dialectical/
paradoxical elements. Mozdzierz, et al. examine the
dynamics of the paradox under six basic headings. Twelve
non-exclusive meanings or functions of the paradox are
then delineated according to intended effect on the
patient--. "neutralizing" (primary paradox); "tranquilizing"
(permission, postponement, prohibition); or "energizing/
challenging" (prediction, proportionality, persuasion,
pro-social redefinition, prescription, practice, pedagogism,
and provocation). The authors specify that the paradox be
implemented only within the context of a caring relationship, in which the therapist thoroughly understands the
patient's goals. (abstract by Deborah Schuller).

985.   Muench, G.A., An investigation of the
         efficacy of time-limited psychotherapy,
         Journal of Counseling Psychology, 1965,
         124, 294-299.

The author reports on a research project initiated in
order to help solve the problem of long waiting lists at
a university counseling center. A total of 105 clients
were used, divided into three groups: a) short-term
therapy, defined as 1-7 sessions with normal termination
in that time; b) time-limited therapy, defined a 8-19
sessions with pre-arranged termination date; c) long-term
therapy, defined as 20 or more sessions, normally terminated. Measures used included the Rotter Sentence Completion
Test and Maslow's Security-Insecurity Inventory. The
results indicated that both short-term therapy and time-
limited therapy were found to be significantly more effective than long-term therapy. These differences were not
due to the degree of illness within the groups prior to
treatment nor were they due to the differences in skills
of the therapists involved in the research. Some of the
possible implications of the findings, as well as cautions
regarding possible interpretations are presented.

986.   Muench, G.A., and Schumacher, R., A
        clinical experiment with rotational time
        limited psychotherapy, Psychotherapy:
        Theory, Research, and Practice, 1968,
        5, 81-84.

This study reports on the results of three different time-
limited approaches to therapy. The differences in approach
were not related to different theoretical positions, but
to differences in structure of therapy. More specifically,
the first group of students, the control group, were
offered 12 individual therapy sessions, with the same
therapist. The second group of students were offered six
therapy sessions with one therapist and the reamining six
sessions with three different therapists, and the final
group were offered six sessions with three different therapists and the final six sessions with the same therapist.
Various instruments were used, including the MMPI, Mooney
Problem Checklist, and the Rotter Sentence Completion Test.
Pre measures, post sixth session measures, and post total
treatment measures were obtained. No statistically significant results were reported between the rotational
groups. The authors conclude with a discussion of a number
of client-therapist relationship issues. A total of 15
students participated in the study, five in the control
group, six in each of the rotational groups.

987.   Muller, J., et al., Acute psychiatric
        services in the general hospital: III.
        Statistical survey, American Journal of
        Psychiatry, 1967, 124, 46-56.

The authors provide an overview of knowledge of acute
psychiatric services as they function within a general
hospital setting. The focus on trying to help a patient
during a critical brief period of vulnerability is stressed.
The value of brief, effective intervention on increasing
the probability continued, longer term therapeutic follow-
through by patients is also mentioned.

988.   Munjack, D.J., Short-term behavioral
        treatment and applications to sexual
        dysfunction, Psychiatric Clinics of
        North America, 1979, 2, 55-73.

A case of sexual dysfunction is used to illustrate
behavioral analysis of a problem and then the implementation of such anxiety-reducing interventions as cognitive
restructuring, systematic desensitization, and assertive
training. (author abstract).

989.   Munro, J.N., and Bach, T.R., Effect of
        time-limited counseling on client change,
        Journal of Counseling Psychology, 1975,
        22, 395-398.

Twenty-four clients seeking help from a counseling center
for emotional of personal-social problems were randomly
assigned to one of two treatment conditions: time-limited
or undetermined-time counseling. Pre- and post-counseling
measures were obtained relating to client status and problems. Findings indicated signficant improvement in terms
of self-acceptance and increased dependence as well as on
various other self-report statements for clients in the
time-limited group over a period of 8 weeks. In addition,
clients' and counselors' assessment of improvement in both
groups were significantly related. Implications of findings in terms of use of time-limited counseling in a time-
limited environment, for example, college counseling
centers, are discussed. (Journal abstract).

990.   Murphy, W.F., A comparison of psycho-
        analysis with dynamic psychotherapies,
        Journal of Nervous and Mental Disease,
        1958, 126, 441-450.

There are definite theoretical and technical differences
between classical psychoanalysis and the majority of the
dynamic psychotherapies. The possibility of a confusion
between the two has been enhanced by modifications of the
psychoanalytic technique for the purpose of treating
certain types of cases, and by the vagueness, lack of a

clinically well-substantiated theory, and a general
looseness of technique on the part of the dynamic psychotherapies. General and specific differences between
these two types of psychotherapy have been described
(e.g., issues of neutrality, focus on symptom removal or
reduction, etc.). (Journal summary modified).

991.   Murphy, W.F., and Weinreb, J.,
        Problems in teaching short-term
        psychotherapy, Journal of Nervous
        and Mental Disease, 1948, 9, 38-42.

992.   Murray, E.R., and Smitson, W.S., Brief
        treatment of parents in a military
        setting, Social Work, 1963, 7, 57-64.

The authors describe a program operated from within the
psychiatric unit of a military general hospital. Team
treatment which focuses on the parents of families in
crisis provides for a maximum of four 30-minute sessions
following the initial intake interview. In a seven-month
period, 87 children and their parents were seen. Procedure
of intake and treatment interviews, and the nature of
adjunctive weekly evening classes for parents are outlined.
Two case vignettes illustrate the emphasis of the program--
e.g., beliefs in the importance of behavioral change prior
to attitudinal, focus on the father's role in the family,
and to therapeutic support of parents. Follow-up
questionnaires and clinic assessment suggest that significant positive changes occurred following brief treatment
for three-quarters of the families treated. Murray and
Smitson conclude that time-limited, highly focused treatment of parents is of value to the majority of families.
(abstract by Deborah Schuller).

993.   Muzekari, L.H., The induction process:
        A method of choice in institutional
        transfer, Journal of Nervous and Mental
        Disease, 1970, 150, 419-422.

An induction process was developed to reduce anxieties
aroused by transfer from a custodial to a therapeutic
milieu. Muzekari describes this process, consisting of

16 biweekly sessions begun two weeks prior to transfer.
He discusses data gathered over a two-year period which
permit comparison of the effects of gradual versus abrupt
intrainstitutional transfer. Unexpectedly, instances of
acute "transfer trauma" within three months of the move
were comparable for both groups of patients (approximately
nine per cent). However, the less intense concept of
"transfer anxiety" may be the more typical response of the
chronic psychotic faced with new surroundings. Analysis
of the data supports the notion that the gradual induction
procedure facilitates anxiety reduction and increases
involvement in the interpersonal aspects of treatment--
particularly in instances of great divergence between the
old and the new institution. (abstract by Deborah
Schuller).

    994.   Muzekari, L.H., et al., Self-experimental
            treatment in chronic schizophrenics,
            Journal of Nervous and Mental Disease,
            1973, 157, 420-427.

Two 6-week self-experimental programs deemed to effect
direct modification of the self-concept and improve
psychiatric adjustment of the chronic schizophrenic were
developed and implemented. The results revealed that
self-experiential treatment did not result in a positive
change in self-concept and psychiatric adjustment when
compared with social interaction treatment which served as
a control condition. The findings also indicated that the
manner in which videotape feedback is presented is a
crucial determinant in assessing its effect upon the
individual. It was suggested that consideration should be
directed toward helping the patient initially deal with
his perceptions and feelings as generated by self-confron-
tation procedures. Subsequent efforts could then be
directed toward restructuring his self-perceptions in
accord with reality. (Journal abstract).

995.   Myerhoff, H.L., et al., Emotionality
       in marathon and traditional psycho-
       therapy, groups, Psychotherapy: Theory,
       Research, and Practice, 1970, 7, 33-36.

The authors report a study to test two hypotheses from
clinical impressions: 1) more intense emotional variability
will be observed in a marathon versus a traditional psychotherapy group; and, 2) group cohesion (as measured by
attendance rates and the desire to continue group treatment after the experimental period) will be greater in the
marathon than in the traditional group. Volunteer subjects
were seventeen psychiatric inpatients, half of whom were
diagnosed schizophrenic. Eight experimental subjects
completed three, six-hour therapy sessions; and nine controls
received three two-hour sessions per week for three weeks.
Procedure and instruments are described. Analysis of the
data suggests that the more intense emotionality believed
characteristic of marathon groups is represented by a
generally increased occurrence and variability in the
expression of negative emotional states. In both groups,
a regular, steady expression of positive response was noted.
The second hypothesis was generally corroborated. In their
discussion, the authors speculate on reasons for the
increased rate of negative response observed in the marathon group; and note limitations on the generalizability
of the data. (abstract by Deborah Schuller).

996.   Myers, J.K., and Auld, F., Some
       variables related to outcome of
       psychotherapy, Journal of Clinical
       Psychology, 1955, 11, 51-54.

We have presented evidence to support the following two
hypotheses: (1) Length of psychotherapy is related to the
manner in which treatment is terminated, and, (2) Experience
and training of the therapist are related to treatment outcome. Specifically, we found that the longer the duration
of contact and the greater the training and experience of
the therapist, the higher the patient's chance of being
discharged from treatment as improved. Whether these
results would hold for other clinics or other definitions
of outcome of therapy is not known. This must be determined by other studies. A total of 63 cases were used in
this study. (Journal summary adapted).

997.   Nash, E.H., et al., Systematic
        preparation of patients for short-
        term psychotherapy, II. Relation to
        characteristics of patient, therapist,
        and the psychotherapeutic process,
        Journal of Nervous and Mental Disease,
        1965, 140, 374-383.

The major focus of this study was to examine the effects
of the setting of specific expectations for patients as
they were being prepared for therapy on therapy outcome
measures. A total of 40 patients and four therapists were
included in the study, with ten patients/therapist. Prior
to the beginning of therapy, a patient was seen by a research psychiatriast for a screening and evaluation. This
was followed by a Role Induction Interview based on Orne's
Anticipation Socialization procedure for those Ss in the
experimental group. A range of rating scales were used
both at the beginning of the process and throughout treatment, including a four month rating from the beginning of
the treatment. The results indicated that the creation of
specific expectations in the process of preparing patients
for upcoming therapy does increase the probability for
improved outcome. Further, a number of variables were
found to affect the various expectations produced. Patient
attractiveness was found to be involved, for those patients
rated as attractive at the outset of therapy tended to do
better in therapy. The greater the amount of therapist
experience was also found to increase the chances for
successful therapy outcome. The higher the patient expectations, the greater the amount of improvement. Further,
the attitudes of the therapists to the overall research
project also were influential in the outcome. The authors
provide a discussion of some of the issues in role induction
procedure with the aim of increasing its effectiveness.
The work was carried out at the Psychiatry Department, Johns
Hopkins University School of Medicine.

998.   Nathan, P.E., et al., Experimental
        analysis of a brief psychotherapy
        relationship, American Journal of
        Orthopsychiatry, 1968, 38, 482-492.

The operant procedure Televised Reciprocal Analysis of
Conjugate Communications - (TRACCOM) was used to perform

the experimental analysis of a brief psychotherapy relationship between a psychiatrist and his patient. Though the
operant responding of both paralleled their subjective
evaluations of the relationship, the therapist also showed
dramatic changes in operant behavior following the suicide
of a psychiatric resident supervisor. (Journal abstract).

999.   Natterson, J., and Grotjahn, M.,
        Responsive action in psychotherapy,
        American Journal of Psychiatry, 1965,
        122, 140-143.

The term "responsive action" is used to characterize the
therapist's reaction to a client's unconscious needs. It
is characterized by spontaneous and accurate homing in on
a patient's unconscious messages. Two cases are presented
to illustrate this technique. The use of such an approach
in crisis situations, or in situations where therapy appears
to be bogged down is recommended. The authors indicate
that if such a move on the therapist's part is accurate
and sensitively presented, the client will show a new surge
of movement and willingness to work.

1000.   Neale, D.H., Behavior therapy and
        encopresis in children, Behaviour
        Research and Therapy, 1963, 1, 139-149.

A method of treating encopresis based on learning theory is
described. It entails the following steps: 1) Accurate
diagnosis of the physiological derangement; 2) Correction
of the derangement; 3) Accurate diagnosis of the behavioral
aetiology of the encopresis; 4) If the conditioned avoidance
drive is not excessive, then instrumental conditioning will
be adequate and the regime as described may be instituted.
The child is taken to the lavatory 4 times/day, to sit
until a motion is passed or 5 minutes has elapsed. If a
motion is passed he is congratulated and given an appropriate reward. If his pants are soiled, he is given clean
ones. No punishments of any sort are given for dirty
pants and no rewards for clean ones. Once the child is
clean he should be rewarded intermittently for successful
bowel actions for several months. If the conditioned
avoidance reaction is excessive, then a programme to reduce

this must be devised. This method has been applied to 4
cases of longstanding psychogenic encopresis resistant to
other methods. There was rapid success in 3 cases and in
the case which failed this is attributable to faulty
application of learning theory rather than defects in the
approach. It is concluded that learning theory can usefully be applied to encopresis but methods can be further
refined. (Journal summary).

    1001.   Nebl, N., Essential elements in short-
              term treatment, Social Casework, 1971,
              52, 377-381.

The article begins with an introduction to the development
of short-term treatment programs in various centers in
North America. The work of Mid-Missouri Mental Health
Center, the author's professional location, is summarized
as it shifted from a more conventionally-oriented therapy
center with longer term treatment and waiting lists, to a
briefer, more immediately accessible treatment facility.
The work of Drs. Stella Chess and Margaret Lyman, at the
Children's Psychiatric Unit of Bellevue Hospital in New
York, Dr. Manuel Straker, in the Psychiatry Department of
the Montreal General Hospital, and Robert Shaw et al. of
the Madeleine Borg Child Guidance Institute of New York
is reviewed. From these the author presents three major
factors as critical to the success of short-term treatment
appraoches with children: a) Immediacy of treatment; b)
environmental manipulated; c) use of community resources
as part of the treatment plan. Further, the clarity of
the contract with parents is discussed and emphasized.

    1002.   Nebl, N., and Watt, R., Parents'
              perceptions of short-term psychiatric
              evaluation, Journal of Operational
              Psychiatry, 1970, 1, 38-41.

The authors report on the findings of a large research
project carried out at the Mid-Missouri Mental Health
Center. They found that they were able to see a significantly greater number of families using a brief therapy
approach, that the families were following treatment

recommendation at a rate equal to or greater than those
families in more conventional therapy. Brief treatment
was not found to be related to a large number of demographic variables.

1003.   Negele, R.A., A study of the effective-
         ness of brief time limited psychotherapy
         with children and their parents,
         Dissertation Abstracts International,
         1976, 36, 8B, 4172.

1004.   Neiger, S., Some new approaches in
         treating the anorgasmic woman,
         Canadian Family Physician, 1971, May,
         52-56.

The focus of this article is on those women who are experiencing a decreased or absent ability to achieve an orgasm.
The author presents two of the major views held in the
field today regarding the etiology of such conditions,
namely, evolutionary theory and a social/conditioning
learning model. Specific approaches to dealing with this
problem are presented, including manual and oral stimulation,
self-stimulation, the use of vibrators (both external and
internal), behavioral techniques such as systematic desensitization. The author claims that such methods, used
singly or in some combination, will bring about orgasm in
about 90% of anorgasmic women who are motivated for treatment. The author also details the characteristics of those
women who fall into the remaining 10%, in which they appear
to exhibit a complete lack of interest in sex or have a
direct aversion to the sex act itself. These women usually
do not come for treatment on their own, but because of
pressure from their husbands. The article concludes with
a short discussion of the role of orgasm in the larger
framework of sexual activity, and within the still larger
framework of an on-going couple relationship.

1005.   Neiger, S., Short-term treatment
         methods for delaying ejaculation,
         Canadian Family Physician, 1972,
         March.

This article summarizes, and describes in some detail, a
number of short-term methods (both individually and in
combination) for delaying premature ejaculation in sexually
vigorous men. Such individuals exhibit a health libido,
erection, ejaculation, and orgasm, but have difficulty in
the timing of these responses. Some of the reasons for
such difficulty are discussed, including such issues as
inability or unwillingness to exert control, overanxiousness
to please, fear of failure, etc. Non-intercourse sex techniques are described (hand-genital and mouth-genital),
methods of reducing inner stimulation, reducing outer
stimulation, reducing innter receptivity (e.g., concentrat-
ing on an absorbing non-sexual image; "cooling-off period":
use of nembutal or seconal, or mellaril - CNS decrease in
receptivity), reducing outer receptivity (lubricants,
condoms, the squeeze technique), and systematic desensitization (e.g., the sensate focus technique). The importance of the quality of the relationship between partners
is highlighted.

1006.   Nelson, Z.P., and Mowry, D.D.,
         Contracting in crisis intervention,
         Community Mental Health Journal,
         1976, 12, 37-43.

The use of contracts in the social services is an important
area that needs to be looked at. This paper is concerned
specifically with the use of contracts in one particular
part of social services: crisis intervention. Contracts
that define the working relationship between the client
and mental health counselor can be beneficial for both when
they attempt to solve the problems that contributed to the
crisis situation. There are five benefits to be gained
from the use of contracts in crisis intervention and they
are briefly discussed (definition of the role relationships,
providing a model for future contact; definition of the
problems, responsibilities, decisions for both counselor
and client; setting time limitations; control of symptomatology; avoiding stigmatizing labels of deviance.)
(Journal abstract adapted).

1007.   Neu, C., et al., Measuring the inter-
        ventions used in the short-term inter-
        personal psychotherapy of depression,
        American Journal of Orthopsychiatry,
        1978, 48, 629-636.

Describes a method for measuring the interventions employed
by psychotherapists in the short-term interpersonal treatment of depressive disorders. The psychotherapy techniques
(descriptive, reflective, and affective response) are
described, and the methodology for measuring these techniques is presented. These are illustrated with the finding
of the collaborative Boston-New Haven project. The patients
in this study (32 moderately severely depressed persons
ated 20-65 yrs.) were imrpoved significantly by the end of
16 weeks. (Journal abstract).

1008.   Newman, M.B., and San Martino, M.,
        Therapeutic intervention in a
        community child psychiatric clinic,
        Journal of Child Psychiatry, 1969,
        8, 692-710.

The authors describe, through extensive use of case example
material, the functioning of the Mystic Valley Children's
Clinic, in Lexington, Massachusetts. Six detailed cases
are presented illustrating a range of children with varying presenting problems (e.g., stealing and vandalism,
violent behavior against sibs, reactions to death in the
family, severe headaches with no organic basis, uncontroll-
able sneezing attacks, etc.). The aim was to understand
and meet each family at the level at which the family was
willing to become involved in the therapy process, to use
the strengths of the families, etc. The changes indicated
were of a limited nature, but of benefit to both parents
and children.

1009.   Newton, J.R., Considerations for the
        psychotherapeutic techniques of symptom
        scheduling, Psychotherapy: Theory,
        Research and Practice, 1968, 5, 95-103.

Using the term symptom scheduling to include such diverse
labels as negative practice, therapeutic paradoxical

intention, reactive inhibition, the author provides a series of principles relating to any approach which involves the control by the therapist of a patient's symptoms. The principles are presented in three groups, one focussed on the symptom itself, one on the structure in therapy for symptom scheduling, and the final group of principles related to the therapist. The author suggests choosing an expandable, current, interpersonal, and stressful symptom. The same ingredients are listed for the structures needed, plus the need to explain the rationale to the patient, the use of humor, the specificity of instructions, within-session timing of the presentation of the symptom scheduling instructions, the use of office exercises and patient associates. With regard to the therapist variable related to principles of symptom scheduling, the need for patience, understanding the symptom, the nature of treatment goals when using symptom scheduling, and the type of active, directive, and at time authoritative approach needed, as well as the value of follow-up questioning on the part of the therapist are all highlighted. Examples from clinical material are used often throughout the article to provide quick highlights of the principles presented. The value of symptom scheduling as a technique, and not a theory of therapy, is stressed, as well as the non-verbal advantages of such an approach.

1010.   Newton, J.R., Therapeutic paradoxes, paradoxical intentions, and negative practice, American Journal of Psycho-therapy, 1968, 22, 68-81.

The psychotherapeutic technique of symptom scheduling was reviewed according to three different theoretical positions: Haley's therapeutic paradox, Frankl's paradoxical intention, and Dunlap's negative practice. Two different experimental groups were formed by giving instructions, consistent with the therapeutic paradox or negative, to 20 volunteer patients who then were seen for 10 sessions of individual psycho-therapy. Symptom scheduling was done several times in both groups. While the patients showed some positive changes, there were no significant differences according to experimental group membership. The implications of this finding for the theory of the therapeutic paradox, in particular,

are pointed out. The results are also inspected from the
viewpoint of the different methods of data collection and
the presence of method-specific variance is discussed.
(Journal summary).

1011.   Newton, J.R., and Stein, L.I., Implosive
        therapy in alcoholism: Comparison with
        brief psychotherapy, Quarterly Journal
        of Studies on Alcohol, 1974, 35, 1256-
        1265.

The authors report on a study of 61 male alcoholic patients
treated in one of three therapy programs immediately following detoxification: (a) 25 days of inpatient, milieu
therapy (N=29); (b) Inpatient therapy and brief therapy
(N=16); (c) Inpatient therapy and implosive therapy (N=16).
Follow-up data was collected five times during the year
following termination. The results indicate that adding
implosive or brief therapy to a milieu therapy program for
male alcoholics does not significantly improve the results
of the milieu program alone. Future reports will detail
the follow-up results.

1012.   Nichols, M.P., Outcome of brief
        psychotherapy, Journal of Consulting
        and Clinical Psychology, 1974, 42,
        403-410.

The present study evaluated the impact of catharsis on the
outcome of brief psychotherapy. A group of University
Health Service patients was treated with emotive psychotherapy and compared with another group, treated with
insight-oriented analytic therapy. Outcome data consisted
of change on the MMPI scales of Depression, Psychasthenia,
and Schizophrenia; change in comfort with affect, measured
by Hamsher's Test of Emotional Styles; ratings of change
in personal satisfaction; and progress toward behaviorally
defined goals. The emotive group experienced significantly
more catharsis, and high-catharsis patients changed significantly more on behavioral goals and showed a trend
toward greater improvement in general satisfaction. The
findings confirmed the effectiveness of emotive psycho-

therapy in producing catharsis and tended to validate the
hypothesis that catharsis leads to therapeutic improvement.
(Journal abstract).

    1013.   Nichols, M.P., and Reifler, C.B.,
                 The study of brief psychotherapy in
                 a college health setting, Journal
                 of the American College Health
                 Association, 1973, 22, 128-133.

This article discusses the design difficulties in doing
therapy outcome research. Issues such as research versus
the smooth running of the health center are discussed. A
research study, in progress, is used to illustrate some of
the discussion points.

    1014.   Nigl, A.J., and Weiss, S.D., Effects
                 of presenting symptom and therapist
                 orientation on treatment outcome:
                 A follow-up study of brief therapy
                 with college students, Journal of the
                 American College Health Association,
                 1976, 24, 203-207.

A pilot study of outcome of brief therapy with college
students is reported. Subjective self-reports from clients
seen at a university mental health facility (N=45) form
the basis of the study. Effects of treatment were investigated according to treatment type (eclectic, psychoanalytic,
or behavioral) and symptom group type (anxiety-depression,
interpersonal problems, or academic difficulties).
Additional analyses were performed on other variables (new
symptoms, improvement, acquisition of coping skills, frequency of other help seeking behavior, and negative changes)
with treatment group and symptom type as main factors.
Results are presented and discussed. For all combinations
of primary symptoms and treatment type, post-ratings of
symptom intensity were significantly lower than preratings;
however, 69% of subjects felt they had not acquired skills
for dealing with future problems. Some directions for
future research to improve delivery of mental health
services to a university population are proposed.
(abstract by Deborah Schuller).

1015.   Nilsen, J.A., Immediate treatment
        expedites hospital release, Hospital
        and Community Psychiatry, 1969, 20,
        36-38.

1016.   Norkus, A., Sex of therapist as a
        variable in short-term therapy with
        female college students, Dissertation
        Abstracts International, 1976, 36,
        12-B, Pt 1, 6361-62.

1017.   Normand, W., et al., The acceptance
        of the psychiatric walk-in clinic in
        a highly deprived community, American
        Journal of Psychiatry, 1963, 120,
        533-539.

A major problem exists concerning the use of psychiatric
facilities by people in economically deprived areas. It
is suggested that the walk-in clinic may be a means of
meeting this need; however, studies have indicated that
people from such an area would be unlikely to make use of
such a facility on a voluntary basis. The present study
analyzed the intake data on 682 patients seen during a
6-month period in a walk-in clinic servicing such a deprived area. The data collected show that: i) the patient
group as a whole was of low socioenconomic level; ii) the
rate of self-referral in this group was 16%; iii) 46% of
the patients presented their problems in psychological
terms; iv) the self-referred group did not differ markedly
from a clinic-referred group on a series of social variables.
It is concluded that even without a community educational
program, the walk-in clinic did make contact with a significant number of residents of this deprived area.
(Journal summary).

1018.   Normand, W.C., et al., A systematic
        approach to brief therapy for patients
        from a low socioeconomic community,
        Community Mental Health Journal, 1967,
        6, 349-354.

1019.   Normand, W.C., et al., Brief group
         therapy to facilitate the use of
         mental health services by Spanish
         speaking patients, American Journal
         of Orthopsychiatry, 1974, 44, 37-42.

The authors describe the functioning of an outpatient
clinic in the East Harlem area of New York City. The aim
of the service is to provide immediate intensive short-
term treatment with Spanish-speaking staff for those Puerto
Ricans in need. The types of problems presented by this
patient population are discussed, including loneliness,
depression, unhappiness, and specific psychosomatic complaints, marital difficulties, relationship difficulties
with others, and in a high proportion of the children seen,
drug related difficulties. Other problems related to
housing conditions. A group therapy experience is described
which provided a culturally accepting environment in their
own language, with the focus on the present and future.
The group leader was also able to provide concrete information about community resources which the participants
were unaware of, which often produced alleviation of
specific complaints and problems. These experiences
resulted in a significant increase in the number of
sessions attended, and number of referrals for various
forms of alternative service which were successful. The
value of such a group experience in preparing patients
for further treatment is emphasized.

1020.   Notman, M.T., and Zinberg, N.E.,
         Functions of a short-term therapy
         program: Problems of the maintenance
         of quality, Archives of General
         Psychiatry, 1969, 20, 403-407.

The authors highlight conflicts arising between priorities
related to patient care and those related to excellence
of psychiatric training--conflicts which particularly
jeopardize the quality of short-term psychotherapy programs.
Notman and Zinberg attribute in part the increasing conflict
between service and training functions to the great emphasis
within community mental health on reaching large numbers
of people, and the ensuing press for brief treatment programs. The authors describe pressures and impediments to

the maintenance of quality as experienced by four different groups: the hospital or clinic administration, program supervisors, residents or trainees, and patients. The authors caution that unless hospital personnel remain constantly alert to the problems outlined here, not only is the quality of short-term therapy programs undermined, but also, brief treatment may begin to be perceived as a "dumping ground" for patients considered ill-suited to "real" therapy. (abstract by Deborah Schuller).

1021.   Nuland, W., A single-treatment method
         to stop smoking using ancillary self-
         hypnosis: Discussion, International
         Journal of Clinical and Experimental
         Hypnosis, 1970, 18, 257-260.

The implications of Dr. Spiegel's findings with a standard-ized single-session technique are discussed. Despite the inevitable tentativeness of conclusions--since somewhat less than half of the patients answered a follow-up questionnaire--the results are encouraging. The question is raised whether those patients who did not respond to treatment initially might respond to an analogous, although superficially dissimilar, approach with another effective therapist. (Journal abstract).

1022.   Oberleder, M., Crisis therapy in mental
         breakdown of the aging, Gerontologist,
         1970, 10, 111-114.

Life crises had precipitated institutionalization in all cases in a random selection of state hospital patients, whose "senile" symptoms were successfully treated during a 6 months' period of therapy based upon crisis theory. Twelve patients, average age 76.4 years, all having diag-noses of chronic brain syndrome or arteriosclerosis with psychosis, were exposed to an intensive treatment and practical action program geared toward discharge and expedited by staff, family, and community collaboration. The post-hospital adjustment of the discharged patients offers an opportunity for study of the recovery potential of the so-called "hopelessly deteriorated" elderly person.

The present study offers alternative interpretations of
symptoms commonly attributed to organic impairment and
suggest some preventive and treatment approaches. (Journal
abstract).

1023.   Oberman, E., The use of time-limited
         relationship therapy with borderline
         patients, Smith College Studies in
         in Social Work, 1966-67, 37, 127-141.

Based on the work with two adult patients, the author
provides details of a psychodynamically-oriented time-
limited approach to dealing with borderline individuals.
The treatment structure was individual, covering a total
of 12 interviews, the number being agreed upon at the onset of treatment. The case studies presented show how a
focus was developed over the course of treatment, based on
current life difficulty, and how the patients were encouraged to activate themselves toward meaningful action. The
therapist rated each patient's change at the end of treatment, and both patients were rated as improved.

1024.   O'Connor, J., and Stern, L., Results
         of treatment in functioning sexual
         disorders, New York State Journal of
         Medicine, 1972, 72, 1927-1934.

The authors report on the results of a two year study at
the Columbia Psychoanalytic Clinic, in which patients
presenting sexual symptoms were divided into two treatment
groups. One was provided with psychoanalytically-oriented
psychotherapy, the other with psychoanalysis. Based on
the ratings of the treating therapists, and with a total
sample of 96 patients, an overall 66% (male and female
combined) reported cure or improvement of sexual symptoms
after two years of therapy or analysis.

1025.   Ohlmeier, D., et al., Psychoanalytic
        group interview and short-term group
        psychotherapy with post-myocardial
        infarction patients, Psychiatria
        Clinica, 1963, 6, 240-249.

Within the framework of a research project on psychodynamic
personality factors and psychotherapeutic possibilities in
the after-treatment of post-myocardial infarction patients
also group-analytic methods are used. The therapeutic
relevance of group-analysis is described, and a clinical
survey of the development of a short-term group process is
given. A new diagnostic approach, i.e., the 'psychoanalytic group interview' as an instrument of psychodynamic
research, is introduced. The protocol of each tape-
recorded group session was evaluated according to a 'system-
atiszized description' using a number of formal categories
('configurations'). Strong oral-symbiotic needs, characterized specifically by needs to incorporate human objects
in order to gain 'enormous strength and fitness' could be
observed. A deep fear of loss of identity and a strong
tendency to depersonalize the 'addition-like' introjected
(transference-)object were apparent. Defence mechanisms
of rationalisation, denial, and identification with the
aggressor seem to be specific. The ego-structure, especially the group-functions of the ego in patients with myocardial infarction are characterized by these personality
traits. Further investigations are necessary. (Journal
abstract).

1026.   Oldz, J.S., The effects of a time limited
        and non-time limited mode of counseling
        on producing therapeutic change, Disser-
        tation Abstracts International, 1975, 36..

1027.   Oppenheimer, J.R., Use of crisis inter-
        vention in casework with the cancer
        patient and his family, Social Work,
        1967, 12, 44-52.

Cancer, an emotionally charged illness, can be expected to
precipitate a state of crisis for most patients and their
families. An understanding of crisis theory and the

phenomena that occur during a state of crisis are basic to
the social worker's approach to the problems the cancer
patient presents. The techniques for intervention and
change are focused on (1) helping the patient or family
develop conscious awareness of their problem, (a) assessing their total situation, and (3) enabling them to make
a new use of their existing ego-adaptive techniques or to
develop new and more effective mechanisms. (Journal
abstract).

1028.   Oradei, D., and Waite, N., Group
         psychotherapy with stroke patients
         during the immediate recovery phase,
         American Journal of Orthopsychiatry,
         1974, 44, 386-395.

Daily group therapy sessions were held with hospital patients recovering from strokes. This paper discusses the
psychosocial issues that were presented by the group
members, and describes the impact of group sessions on
patients, staff, and ward milieu.

1029.   Orange, A.J., A note on brief psycho-
         therapy, International Journal of Group
         Psychotherapy, 1956, 5, 80-83.

The author presents the view that short-term group therapy
should be tried when a longer term treatment is not possible.
The author also suggests the use of co-therapists, and an
active therapeutic orientation.

1030.   O'Regan, J.B., A psychiatric emergency
         service: A preliminary report, Canadian
         Medical Association Journal, 1965, 93,
         691-695.

An emergency service for psychiatric patients was organized
in a general hospital owing to the increasing need for such
a service. Its main functions have been to screen cases,
to offer short-term treatment, and to provide immediate
consultation facilities to general practitioners and clinical
experience to students, interns, and residents. Of 133
patients, 40% were diagnosed as psychotic and 35% as

neurotic. The commonest present symptoms were anxiety and depression. Approximately 40% were treated by the staff of the emergency service, 40% were sent back to the general practitioner for treatment, and 20% were transferred to a mental hospital. It is concluded that this type of service can provide immediate and effective consultation and treatment for psychiatric emergencies, and is a very useful teaching facility, especially for students and physicians not intending to specialize in psychiatry. (Journal abstract).

1031.   Ornstein, P.H., and Ornstein, A.O.,
        Focal psychotherapy: its potential
        impact on psychotherapeutic practice
        of medicine, Psychiatry in Medicine,
        1972, 3, 311-325.

A condensed illustration of a complete treatment process of "focal psychotherapy" is presented to contrast the specificity of this form of psychotherapy with nonspecific approaches. A two-year follow-up illustrates the meaning of specificity. The relationship of therapeutic results to the focal interventions is reflected in the patient's own views of his accomplishments in therapy. The theory and techniques of focal psychotherapy were originally worked out by Balint and his co-workers. The case example presented here is the basis of discussion showing how focal psychotherapy can help re-conceptualize and add precision to the theory, techniques and processes of both short- and long-term psychoanalytic psychotherapy. Such increased precision in intervention and focal aims could help leaders and general practitioner training groups to better achieve their collaborative tasks. (Journal abstract).

1032.   Orovan, S.K., Patients help plan
        nursing care, Canadian Nurse, 1972,
        68, 46-48.

In a Brief Therapy Unit of a Montreal Hospital patients were given the opportunity to participate in planning their own care. The results show that patients who participated in the project responded more readily to nursing efforts on their behalf.

1033.   Osberg, J.W., Initial impressions of
         the use of short-term family group
         conferences in a community mental
         health clinic, Family Process, 1962,
         1, 236-244.

Osberg presents clinical impressions based on short-term
group conferences with 15 families. Goals and process of
intake and diagnostic interviews, as well as therapy
sessions, are summarized. Sharpened communication within
the family is an ultimate goal. The most immediate and
attainable goal, according to the author, is that of helping a family clarify its purpose in obtaining clinic help.
Osberg outlines recurrent patterns observed in the family
sessions--the seeking of therapeutic allies by individual
members, and family attempts to manipulate each other,
while adopting a passive, help-seeking stance with staff.
He presents a case example of a family seen for nine joint,
one-hour conferences, extended over one year. Nature of
staff response to this joint problem-solving approach, its
advantages and disadvantages, are briefly described. (For
a more detailed, later report on this study, see Shellow,
et al., "Family Group Therapy in Retrospect: Four Years
& Sixty Families".). (abstract by Deborah Schuller).

1034.   Oxley, G.B., A life-model approach
         to change, Social Casework, 1971, 52,
         627-633.

This approach to treatment is based upon the ways in which
growth and positive change occur in life. Research findings
verify that which we know; namely, many persons experience
constructive change in life without therapeutic intervention.
The major ways in which natural change occurs are (1)
maturation, (2) interaction, (3) action, (4) learning, and
(5) crisis resolution. Treatment interventions must be
selected to facilitate the natural change processes. This
treatment approach implies confidence in the client to
grow and to increase his control over his own life experience. It is generally short term but open ended. The
concept of action as a way in which positive change can be
enhanced in treatment was selected to specific discussion.
Action has therapeutic value when it occurs within the
interview and encounter and when the interview stimulates
a client to action in his own environment. (Journal summary).

1035.   Oxley, G.B., Short-term therapy with
         student couples, Social Casework,
         1973, 54, 216-223.

The author describes a short-term therapy approach successfully used with 10 student couples at a university counseling center. Treatment offered was immediate and problem
focussed, with a total of six sessions/couple. Conjoint
interviews were held, using the Virginia Satir model. The
couples had been married for between 1 1/2 to three years.
Five had children. From a diagnostic viewpoint, all individuals were either neurotic, mild character disorder,
or normal. The types of difficulties they presented
included communication problems, sexual difficulties, role
confusion, problems with intimacy and alienation, etc. The
types of questions asked by the therapist and the goals
behind those question areas are specified: a) Focus on
presenting problem; b) dynamic history of relationship;
d)dynamic history of the families of origin; d) ongoing
focus on communication. The dynamics of change are discussed in terms of issues of understanding and insight,
transference and countertransference, therapist modeling,
and experiential learning. Critical importance is placed
on the nature of mutual goals in contracting with a couple,
and emphasis on the active involvement of each couple member,
without placing total responsibility on the therapist for
change.

1036.   Palazzoli, M.S., Self starvation:
         From the intrapsychic to the trans-
         personal approach to anorexia nervosa,
         London, Chaucer Publishing, 1974.

The author details an approach to the treatment of anorexia
nervosa in which family therapy is used. The treatment
approach is rooted in communication theory, general systems
theory, and cybernetics. Rather than focus on the individual exhibititing the anorexia, the entire family is viewed
as a symptom in which the symptom plays a significant role.
Active interventions are used to produce rapid and lasting
changes in these families. The techniques used, and case
material are contained in this work of the Milan Center for
Family Studies, in Italy.

1037.   Palazzoli, M., et al., The treatment
         of children through the brief therapy
         of their parents, Family Process, 1974,
         429-442.

This is a report on the successful resolution of behavior
problems (encopresis and anorexia, respectively) in two
small children through the brief therapy of their parents.
Treatment was based on general systems theory and the cyber-
netic model and employed interventions designed specifically
to bring about rapid change in family interactions.   The
course of the treatments, as well as the technical problems
arising out of such rapid changes, are discussed.   (Journal
abstract).

1038.   Palazzoli, M.S., et al., Paradox and
         counterparadox: A new model in the
         therapy of the family in schizophrenic
         transaction, New York, Aronson, 1978.

The authors present the work of the Milan Center for Family
Studies, in Italy, in which 15 families were treated by
novel techniques of brief therapy. Five of the families
had children who exhibited psychotic symptoms, and 10 who
had young adults who had been diagnosed as schizophrenic.
The major theoretical concepts include a focus on patterns
of communication within the family, as well as devising
specific prescriptions which will allow for the transition
from pathology. Systems theory, cybernetics, and issues
of human communication patterns are all used in the understanding and manipulation of the pathological patterns.
A large number of examples are provided to highlight the
theoretical material.

1039.   Pannor, R., and Nerlove, E.A., Fostering
         understanding between adolescents and
         adoptive parents through group experi-
         ences, Child Welfare, 1977, 56, 537-545.

The authors present a summary of a short-term educational
group experience involving adoptive parents and adopted
children. The children and parents were seen separately
initially for four sessions, and then brought together.

A number of issues were raised in the initial individual meetings, including questions about sealed records. The joint session then involved dealing with some of these issues.

1040.   Papp, P., Brief therapy with couples groups, in Guerin, P.J., (ed.), Family Therapy, New York, Gardner Press, 1976.

The author describes a focussed, task-oriented (including homework), planned strategy approach aimed at producing accelerated change in couples in short-term group therapy. The aim is to reverse or change the self-defeating cyclical transactions. Techniques used and described include family choreography (derived from family sculpturing), prescribed tasks, and a group setting. The philosophical context for such an approach lies in the belief that: a) people induce change by beginning to behave or act differently than they had previously; b) change can be produced quickly; c) these changes can be long lasting; d) the therapist expectations about change and the rate of change have a profound impact on the results of therapy in this short-term context. The specific process of therapy is outlined, with case examples. A total of 12 sessions are held, with four couples/group.

1041.   Parad, H.J., The use of time-limited crisis intervention in community mental health programing, Social Service Review, 1966, 10, 275-282.

The author briefly discusses the concept of community mental health (pre-care; under-care; after-care) and the concept of crisis. A review of a selected number of such programs is presented, including the Wellesley Human Relations Service (established in 1948 by Dr. Erich Lindemann), the Albert Einstein College of Medicine Municipal Hospital Center, the Massachusetts General Hospital in Boston (with their therapy approach for dealing with high-density urban mental health problems); a multiple-impact therapy approach in Texas designed for the needs of adolescents and their families in a rural environment, the Langley-Porter preceipitating stress project in San Francisco, the Jewish Board of Guardians service to children

and their parents, and various family agencies including
the Cleveland Family Service Association and the Community
Service Society of New York. The author concludes with an
overview of the common themes inherent in all of these
diverse treatment programs. These are: a) The use of the
time dimension, reducing waiting lists; b) immediate accessibility of service; c) flexible treatment schedule, with
higher frequency of immediate contact during initial stages
of crisis; d) consultation to community and other family
support personnel; e) use of positive transference, active
techniques, focus on concrete goals and results; f) effective follow-up and referral.

1042.   Parad, H.J., (ed.), Crisis Intervention,
         Selected Readings, Family Service Associ-
         ation of America, New York, 1967.

This edited books of readings is divided into four main
sections: selections dealing with the theoretical issues
associated with crisis intervention, a review of some of
the more common maturational and situational crises,
specific clinical applications, and the measurement of
various crisis phenomena.

1043.   Parad, H.J., and Caplan, G., A framework
         for studying families in crisis, Social
         Work, 1960, 5, 16-21.

1044.   Parad, H.J., and Miller, R.R., (eds.),
         Ego-oriented casework: Problems and
         Perspectives, New York, Family Service
         Association of America, 1963.

1045.   Parad, H.J., and Parad, L.G., A study
         of crisis-oriented planned short-term
         treatment: Part I, Social Casework,
         1968, 49, 346-355.

This article is the first of a two part article. It provides the results of a national research survey focussed
on crisis-oriented, planned short-term treatment (PSTT)

with agencies associated with two national associations,
the Family Service Association of America (FSAA), and the
American Association of Psychiatric Clinics for Children
(AAPCC). A total of over 1,600 patient treatments were
used, covering a wide range of socioeconomic conditions
and therapist orientation. The results indicate the success
of brief forms of therapy in close to 70% of the cases. No
improvement was reported in 30%. Some of the differences
between the FSAA and the AAPCC agencies in terms of treatment variables were reported. The usual number of sessions
for PSST was 12.

   1046.   Parad, L.G., Short-term treatment: An
            overview of historical trend, issues,
            and potentials, Smith College Studies
            in Social Work, 1971, 41, 119-146.

The author provides a detailed overview of the many aspects
of changing agency function and changing agency treatment
goals which have emerged as a result of an increasing focus
on short-term casework and therapy. Among the factors in
this resurgence are: a) financial limitations both for
the client and agency; b) emphasis on ego psychology;
c) emergency of behavior modification techniques; d) existential focus on the here and now problems and their
solutions; e) an increasing literature on crisis theory
and technique; f) increasing number of research studies
indicating the effectiveness of shorter-term therapies. A
history of the kinds of services from the 1930's to the
present is provided, within the context of short-term
treatment. The impact of functionalism in the 1930's, the
dramatic need for social services following the war, and
the beginning awareness among mental health professionals
of the high drop out rate from treatment of a large segment
of the population in the 1950's, have all combined to influence the directions toward shorter-term treatment
approaches. The results of outcome studies over a 40 year
period are summarized. The need for more in depth research
on the process of brief therapy is mentioned, a type of
research which goes beyond mere outcome measures of success
or failure in brief treatment.

1047.   Parad, L.G., and Parad, H.J., A study
         of crisis-oriented planned short-term
         treatment, Part II, Social Casework,
         1968, 49, 418-426.

In this second of two reports, the authors summarize and
discuss the research findings of 1656 cases of planned
short-term treatment (PSTT). Part I consisted of a description of the background and methodology of the study.
The findings are presented in terms of: a) case disposition
and outcome, for which it was found that a greater percentage of clients rated themselves as improved (75%) than
therapists' ratings of client improvement (66%); b) crisis
factors, including a description of the theoretical basis
and variations from this in actual practice of short-term
therapy, along with a detailed series of findings pertaining
to the types of crises which precipitated the reaching out
for help; (no consistent association between outcome and
precipitating event, crisis, or timing of treatment in
relation to the event was found, and reasons for this are
discussed); c) a clinical description of various characteristics of the cases, including presenting problem, level
of ego functioning, diagnosis, intrafamily functioning and
family relationship to the outside community, and ability
to adapt to stress; d) client reaction to information about
PSTT, in which it was found that clients who had been informed about PSTT were less likely to drop out of therapy
against therapist advice; e) positive relationship between
therapist prognosis and percentage of improved cases at
termination (i.e., as therapist rating of prognosis became
more optimostic, proportion of improved cases increased
for each outcome variable); f) some evidence for underlying
personality change even though the focus of treatment was
on restoring level of functioning. Differences in sub-
samples (in terms of treatment setting) are also presented.

1048.   Paradis, A.P., Brief outpatient group
         psychotherapy with older patients in
         the treatment of age related problems,
         Dissertation Abstracts International,
         1973, 34, 6B, 2947-48.

1049.   Parker, L., et al., Short-term family
         therapy: An intake catalyst for group
         treatment of adolescent girls, in,
         Wolberg, L.W., and Aronson, M.L., (eds.),
         Group Therapy 1977, An Overview, New York,
         Grune and Stratton, 1978.

1050.   Parks, A.H., Short-term casework in a
         medical setting, Social Work, 1963, 8,
         89-94.

Using two case studies, the author presents a discussion
of the use of one-five sessions, each lasting about one
hour, for the treatment of various presenting problems.
The advantages and disadvantages of brief therapy are discussed.

1051.   Parsons, B.V., and Alexander, J.F.,
         Short-term faimily intervention: A
         therapy outcome study, Journal of
         Consulting and Clinical Psychology,
         1973, 41, 195-201.

Based on a matching-to-sample philosophy, modification of
the destructive communication patterns of delinquent
families are attempted by systematically shaping behavior
characteristic of adaptive family systems (increased reciprocity, greater activity, and increased clarity). Based
on direct observation of family interaction in a discussion
talk, the results indicated a significant change in the
four interaction measures, while two indexes of questionnaire agreement remained unchanged. The utilization of a
rigorous experimental design that controlled for pretest
sensitization, maturation, and nonspecific professional
attention demonstrated that these changes did not occur as
a function of extraneous variables. The need for rigorous
process research regarding the characteristics of specific
target populations coupled with equally sound outcome research that can then evaluate change within these populations is emphasized by the findings of this study.
(Journal abstract).

1052.   Pasewark, R.A., and Albers, D.A., Crisis
         intervention: Theory in search of a
         program, Social Work, 1972, 17, 70-77.

The author begins this article by summarizing the assumptions about the nature of human crises. Among these are
the notion that a crisis is not a pathological experience,
that it is temporary, that the course of crisis consists
of specific, characteristic stages (as described by Lindemann and others), that the individual in crisis is particularly open to help and change, etc. Various typical crises
are described, including specific stages of crisis (event
occurs, which is then perceived by the individual and a
meaning is placed on it, which is then followed by a period
of disorganization, followed by a period of reorganization,
followed by a request for help). Characteristics of those
who appear to cope well with crises are presented, particularly as they pertain to families. Details relating to
primary and secondary prevention are briefly summarized.

1053.   Patrick, J.D., and Wander, R.S.,
         Treatment of the adolescent crisis
         patient, Psychotherapy: Theory,
         Research, and Practice, 1974, 11,
         246-249.

The authors combine crisis theory and a knowledge of the
adolescent in crisis in order to conceptualize a treatment
approach for such adolescents. Crisis theory is combined
with psychoanalytic principles of development, along with
an approach in which the parents are involved in therapy.
Among the unique characteristics of such adolescents is
the emphasis on the present, and the therapeutic approach
is likewise focussed on currrent concerns including both
conscious and unconscious material. A case illustration
is provided.

1054.   Patterson, G.R., Retraining of
         aggressive boys by their parents,
         Journal of the Canadian Psychiatric
         Association, 1974, 19, 142-158.

The author presents an extensive overview of studies done
in the area. Further, the article presents the results of

a research project in which 27 families who had problem
and behaviorally aggressive latency aged boys were trained
in behavior modification techniques. The results showed
that upon termination of the program, independent raters
produced significant positive changes for targeted behavior,
but that at follow-up one year later showed only slight
improvement in the children's targeted negative behavior.
The positive changes in parent symptoms being reported
maintained its improved rating over the course of the year
following termination of treatment. A detailed presentation of problems and issues related to behavioral coding
and rating is included.

1055.   Patterson, G.R., et al., A behaviour
         modification technique for the hyper-
         active child, Behaviour Research and
         Therapy, 1965, 2, 217-226.

This paper describes a procedure for the conditioning of
attending behaviour in a brain -injured hyperactive boy.
Observations of the behaviour of two hyperactive children
were made in the classroom setting. These observations
were made from an observation booth adjoining the classroom and provided data on the frequency of occurrence of
the following high rate responses: walking, talking, distraction, "wiggling". Each child was observed for a minimum
of 10 minutes a day, four days a week. Following several
weeks of baseline observation, the conditioning procedure
was begun with the experimental subject. The conditioning
trials took place in the classroom setting. During each
time interval in which one of the high rate responses did
not occur, S received an auditory stimulus (secondary reinforcer). This auditory stimulus had previous been paired
with the delivery of candy and pennies. The stimulus was
dispensed by a radio device which activated an earphone
worn by the subject. At the end of each conditioning trial,
S received what ever candy or pennies he had "earned".
The data show that the control subject showed no significant
change in the frequency of occurrence of the high rate
responses during the three month period. The experimental
subject showed a significant decrease in non-attending
behaviour. This reduction was maintained over a four week
extinction period. (Journal summary).

1056.   Patterson, G.R., and Reid, J.B., Inter-
         vention for families of aggressive boys:
         a replication study, Behaviour Research
         and Therapy, 1973, 11, 383-394.

Using the Patterson behavioral parent training program,
the authors report results of a study in which overall 61%
reduction in targeted behaviors occurred. An average of
approximately 30 hours treatment/family was needed to produce changes which on follow-up were for the most part
sustained.

1057.   Patterson, V., Brief psychotherapy, in,
         Ostwald, P., (ed.), Communication and
         social interaction - clinical and
         therapeutic aspects of human behavior,
         New York, Grune and Stratton, 1977.

Patterson offers a general description of one brief therapy
service, training program, and research project run by a
university teaching center. She relates findings and
impressions from various phases of the study--including
mention of demographic and diagnostic characteristics of
patients; outcome for brief therapy patients versus those
seen for intake-evaluation only; comparison of outcome as
a function of brief therapeutic approach (especially, psychodynamic versus behavioral); interaction between style
of therapy and personality of therapist; administrative
stance necessary for maintenance of a brief therapy program;
and selection criteria for patients. She concludes with a
discussion of the advantages of a brief therapy program,
with reference to patient service, clinical training, and
research opportunities. (abstract by Deborah Schuller).

1058.   Patterson, V., et al., Treatment and
         training outcomes with two time-limited
         therapies, Archives of General Psychiatry,
         1971, 25, 161-167.

This study was designed to compare two different forms of
brief therapy, namely, brief behavior therapy and brief
psychoanalytic psychotherapy. Both forms were given to an
unselected client sample by mental health trainees. Aside
from the outcome measures studied, the trainees' personality

in its relation to theoretical orientation preferences and
therapy outcome measures was studied. The authors defined
brief behavior as directive and oriented toward the change
of specific behavior. Behavioral prescriptions were often
used (homework), and assertive training was included at
times. The brief psychoanalytic approach stressed the
building of a relationship in which clients were encouraged
to explore within themselves with the aim of gaining some
insight into themselves. Techniques used included many of
those used in longer term psychoanalysis. The overall
framework used in both approaches parallels the work of
Malan and his empirically-derived conclusions about brief
therapy. The results indicate that: a) Dropping out of
treatment was more related to therapist experience rather
than patient demographic or diagnostic variables; b) Patients treated by brief behavior therapy rated themselves as
significantly more improved than those patients treated in
a psychoanalytically-oriented brief therapy model; c) No
significant differences in outcome measures were obtained,
however, at a three month follow-up; d) Positive attitudes
expressed toward a behavior therapy approach by the therapist was a predictor of negative attitudes on the part of
the therapist for the brief psychoanalytic approach;
e) Therapist personality variables associated with a preference for psychoanalytic therapy included such terms as
self-assured, controlled, psychologically complex individuals, with a concern for the inner life of others. Variables associated with a preference for behavior therapy
included active, task-oriented rather than person-oriented,
etc.; f) Behavior therapy was seen as faster, more active,
simpler, rational. Psychoanalytic was seen as slower, less
active, intuitive, orthodox, and more complex; g) There
were no differences in outcome across therapist-trainees.
The implications, drawbacks, and possible interpretation
of some of the findings were presented.

1059.   Patterson, V., and O'Sullivan, M., Three
         perspectives on brief psychotherapy,
         American Journal of Psychotherapy, 1974,
         28, 265-277.

Shortening the length of psychotherapy is one way in which
the discrepancy between supply and demand in mental health
services may be reduced. Brief therapeutic approaches

developed from three different theoretical orientations
are described: crisis intervention, brief behavior therapy,
and brief psychoanalytically oriented psychotherapy. The
three approaches are compared with reference to conceptualization of the problem and techniques of treatment as
applied to a clinical case excerpt. Differences and common-
alities are discussed. (Journal abstract).

1060.   Patterson, V., et al., A one year follow
         up study of two forms of brief psycho-
         therapy, American Journal of Psychotherapy,
         1977, 31, 76-82.

This paper reports on a one-year follow-up of patients
treated in a comparison study of two forms of time-limited
psychotherapy: behavioral and psychoanalytically oriented.
Of an original 55 patients who completed brief therapy
contracts, 20 patients could be located and consented to
come in for interview and rating-scale evaluation. Results
of the follow-up revealed that patients saw themselves at
one-year follow-up as improved over their status at three-
months follow-up but less so than at the termination of the
brief therapy. No significant difference was found in the
status of patients who had had either form of therapy. A
rather large percentage (60%) of the patients had had intervening therapy. It was noted from records at the beginning
of brief therapy that approximately 60% of the patients
had had prior therapy. These figures concur with reports
in the literature in suggesting that patients tend to seek
repeated therapeutic contacts. (Journal summary).

1061.   Patterson, V., and O'Sullivan, M.,
         Training films on, Six approaches to
         brief psychotherapy, University of
         California at San Francisco Audio-
         Visual Center, 1978.

These tapes demonstrate the approaches used in brief psychotherapy by a number of different therapists using different
theoretical orientations. All work was carried out at the
Langley-Porter Neuropsychiatric Institute. Among the
approaches presented are brief analytic, brief Jungian,
behavior modifications, etc.

1062.   Paul, G.L., Two years follow-up of
         systematic desensitization in therapy
         groups, Journal of Abnormal Psychology,
         1966, 71, 124-135.

1063.   Paul, G.L., Insight versus desensi-
         tization in psychotherapy, Stanford,
         Stanford University Press, 1966.

1064.   Paul, G.L., Insight versus desensi-
         tization two years after termination,
         Journal of Consulting Psychology, 1967,
         31, 333-348.

A test battery assessing specific and general treatment
effects was readministered to Ss previously assessed before
treatment, after treatment, and at a 6-wk. follow-up from
groups undergoing individual programs of (a) modified systematic desensitization, (b) insight-oriented psychotherapy,
(c) attention-placebo treatment, and (d) no treatment.
Higher return rates were obtained than in any previous long-
term follow-up, revealing maintenance of improvement found
earlier for interpersonal performance anxiety. Systematic
desensitization resulted in the greatest significant improvement (85%), followed by insight-oriented psychotherapy and
attention placebo (50% each), and untreated controls (22%).
Changes were relaible, predictable, and showed evidence of
further generalization. No evidence of relapse or symptom
substitution was obtained, although they were specifically
sought. Methodological problems of follow-up studies are
also discussed. (Journal abstract).

1065.   Paul, G.L., and Shannon, D.T., Treatment
         of anxiety through systematic desensi-
         tization in therapy groups, Journal of
         Abnormal Psychology, 1966, 71, 124-135.

The effects of short-term treatment by modified systematic
desensitization in time-limited intensive therapy groups
were evaluated in a matched groups design. 10 chronically
anxious college males, treated by the group method, were
evaluated on the basis of personality and anxiety scales

against an "own-control" period and 4 equated groups of 10
Ss each. 1 group served as an untreated control for evaluating extra-treatment effects on college grade-point average
(GPS), as an objective, public criterion. Ss in the remaining groups received 1 of the following individual treatments: systematic desensitization, insight-oriented psychotherapy, or an attention-placebo treatment. The group
produced several significant improvements, suggesting the
combined group desensitization offers an efficient and
effective treatment for social-evaluative anxiety.
(Journal absract).

    1066.   Paul, L., Crisis intervention, Mental
             Hygiene, 1966, 50, 141-145.

A summary of the work and conceptualizations of Lindemann
and Caplan is presented. The four phases Caplan described
are briefly reviewed, including implications of the process: i.e., a small intervention at a moment of greatest
crisis can produce major change quickly which could be long
lasting. Strategies for dealing with pent-up grief are
detailed, including identifying the precipitating event,
uncovering the defensive reactions used, and conveying
these to the client in an appropriate way. Two case illustrations are presented, along with issues in the therapeutic relationship (equality of social power; presence of
the therapist; confirmation of the being of the client).
The typical pattern of normal grieving is outlined, with
its main characteristic of preoccupation on the client's
part with the deceased. Abnormal grief reactions are also
described, all of which involve a lack of preoccupation
with the deceased.

    1067.   Paul, L., Treatment techniques in a
             walk-in clinic, Hospital and Community
             Psychiatry, 1966, 17, 49-51.

The author describes the functioning of the Benjamin Bush
Center for Problems in Living, which opened in 1962 in Los
Angeles. Therapist qualities for working successfully in
such a brief therapy center are presented, including such
characteristics as resourcefulness, spontaneity, directness.
The author also describes a number of techniques used by

the staff in the daily treatment. The aim of the center
is to help individuals return to their previous level of
functioning within a relatively short period of time. The
approach is a focussed one, uncovering the major conflict,
and working to get the patient to begin working on solutions
to the problem. Techniques such as interpretation, instruction, confrontation, focussing on behavior rather than
causes, and encouragement of feelings are used. Gestalt
techniques, and the use of drugs are also utilized at times.
The value of a limited number of sessions (six) is seen in
limiting the amount of dependence on the therapist, and on
forcing the patient to rely on internal resources to solve
problems.

1068.   Peck, H.B., and Kaplan, S., Crisis
         theory and therapeutic change in small
         groups: Some implications for community
         mental health programs, International
         Journal of Group Psychotherapy, 1966,
         16, 135-149.

The authors present a small groups approach with case
examples, based on a crisis theory model of change. Issues
related to individual treatment versus group treatment,
manifest versus latent content, chronic versus acute conditions, as well as other issues are presented and discussed. A systems approach is suggested in dealing with
crises, and the small groups approach allows the therapists
to see the interpersonal, systems issues occur much as they
are occurring in the lives of the patients.

1069.   Peck, H.B., et al., Prevention treatment
         and social action: a strategy of inter-
         vention in a disadvantaged urban area,
         American Journal of Orthopsychiatry,
         1966, 36, 57-69.

An effective community mental health program for urban disadvantaged areas requires techniques derived from social
action as well as the more traditional services. The use
of small group approaches and staffing of neighbourhood
storefront centers with nonprofessionals are examples of
innovative programs designed to bring about substantial

changes in the community's mental health status. This
paper describes the initial stages of such a program,
located in a severely impoverished area of the South Bronx,
and operating out of the Lincoln Hospital, and connected
with the Albert Einstein College of Medicine. (Journal
abstract adapted).

1070.   Penick, S.B., et al., Short-term acute
         psychiatric care: A follow-up study,
         American Journal of Psychiatry, 1971,
         127, 1626-1630.

Every fourth patient from the total of 1,571 patients admitted to the Carrier Clinic during 1967 (with a mean
hospital stay of 25 days) was followed up 2.5 years later.
Ninety percent of the study group, whether or not they had
been rehospitalized in the interim, gave evidence of adequate social functioning. A relatively small number were
regularly followed by physicians; these tended to be sicker
and had a higher readmission rate than the rest of the
study group. (Journal abstract).

1071.   Perlman, H.H., Social casework: A
         problem-solving process, Chicago,
         University of Chicago Press, 1957.

Among other issues raised, the author points out that often
in brief therapy a presenting problem to-be-solved is super-
imposed upon a more basic problem, and therapist must be
aware that the solution of each type of problem demands a
different treatment approach.

1072.   Phillips, E.L., Parent-child psycho-
         therapy: A follow-up study comparing
         two techniques, Journal of Psychology,
         1960, 49, 195-202.

The author describes a series of experiments done to assess
the value of a short-term method of non-depth therapy with
children and their parents. The structure of this approach
involves the immediate initiaton of therapy in the first
session, with children and parents seen for half of the
time allotted for each case (i.e., 50% parent, 50% child

sessions). Sessions are set up no more frequently than
twice per month, the child's teacher is involved as a part
of the information pool and is informed of the focus of
treatment and requested to provide feedback about the child
in school. Specific common sense explanations and instructions are given to parents in dealing with their children,
and the focus is on maintaining a realistic structure by
the parents for the children. The usual number of sessions
is 10, spread over a five-six month period. Homework
assignments are an important part of the program. In comparisons with children and families seen in a depth-therapy,
those seen in non-depth therapy consistently report better
results. The savings of time is discussed in relation to
community mental health work, and strong support for such
brief forms of treatment stressed.

1073.   Phillips, E.L., Social skills instruction
         as adjunctive/alternative to psychotherapy,
         NATO Conference on Social Skills, Leuven,
         Belgium, June, 1979.

The author reviews the literature for support of the use of
social skills training in a broad range of situations where
behavior change is desired - e.g., with hospitalized psychotics, rehabilitation and job-seeking candidates, and
young adults with developmental problems. Psychotherapy
may play little or no role in the application of social
skills instruction to such groups. Phillips contends that
this type of intervention can serve as an adjunct, or even
an alternative to psychotherapy. Citing therapists' notions
and theories of anxiety as the primary resistance to incorporation of social skills training within verbal psychotherapies, he proposes conceptualizing anxiety as a by-
product of an approach-avoidance conflict in conjunction
with social skills deficits. He then demonstrates how
skills training could be as applicable to regular psychotherapy candidates as to other groups. He cites the need
for a "social curriculum" to switch the emphasis from
remedial to preventive aspects of skills training.
(abstract by Deborah Schuller).

1074.   Phillips, E.L., Some principles governing
         therapist behavior in short-term psycho-
         therapy, American Psychological Associ-
         ation Annual Meeting, Sept., 1979.

Positing the therapist as a collection of independent variables and the patient as a collection of dependent,
Phillips states 13 points which together constitute an
augmented therapist role and slant the therapy towards
short-term results. The therapist can, for example, set
therapeutic time limits with the patient at the outset;
communicate the limitations of therapy and its problem-
solving focus; locate relevant therapeutic variables in the
interaction between patient and environment; and develop
rules which the patient can use both in and outside of
therapy. Phillips conceives therapy as teaching social
skills competencies. Behavior change is considered pivotal.
This is effected in part by elucidating the meaning of conflict, rather than by focusing on anxiety, per se. Phillips
affirms that these principles are not incompatible with
qualities proferred by humanistic psychologists, but that
such qualities (e.g., warmth, acceptance, etc.) function
primarily as reinforcers contingent upon a patient's
actions--not as ends in themselves. Brief therapy should
be grounded in a coherent conceptual system in order to
avoid becoming a "patchwork of techniques". The author
suggests that short-term therapy be posited on an analysis
of behavior which explicitly acknowledges some of the foregoing principles. Finally, he advocates short-term intervention as, minimally, a trial therapy which should precede
any lengthier intervention. (abstract by Deborah Schuller).

1075.   Phillips, E.L., and Adams, N.M.,
         Multiple approaches to short-term
         psychotherapy, American Psychologist,
         1964, 19, 475.

This paper reports on the effectiveness of 3 approaches to
short-term psychotherapy (N=22), as evaluated by psychometric and behavioral indices (grades). The same evaluations
were applied to a no-formal-therapy group (N=8). Therapeutic approaches were: Non-directive Group, Structured
(Directive) Group, and Individual Writing Therapy. Follow-
up results indicate some reliable psychometric changes (6

months after therapy ended) and generally reliable behavioral
changes (1 year or 2 semesters after therapy), suggesting
the effectiveness of short-term psychotherapy methods over
no formal therapy, as shown by specific measures. (Journal
abstract).

1076.   Phillips, E.L., and Johnston, S.H.,
         Theoretical and clinical aspects of
         short-term parent-child psychotherapy,
         Psychiatry, 1954, 17, 267-275.

This is a report on the comparison of the effectiveness of
short-term (10 sessions) treatment versus longer term treatment for parents and their children. The work was done at
two outpatient child guidance clinics in the Washington,
D.C. area. The theoretical basis for the short-term approach
is taken from the work of a number of contributors in the
field of psychology. The focus of treatment was on the
child's pattern of interaction in the family, and not on an
in-depth long term retrospective self-examination. Sixteen
parents and their problem children were provided short-term
therapy (parent and child seen individually), and 14 parents
and their children were seen in longer term, traditional
therapy. Each parent couple and child were seen individually. The importance of structuring both the therapy process and educating parents in structuring for their children
in a way which was different from the ways they had previously tried were stressed. The focus was on behavior change.
A one year follow-up post-termination revealed, in which
rating of improvement by both parents and therapists were
obtained. The results clearly show that briefer therapy
was superior to the longer term approach. Two specific
cases are presented to highlight the qualitative aspects of
the treatment approach.

1077.   Phillips, E.L., and Wiener, D.N., Short-
         term psychotherapy and structured behavior
         change, New York, McGraw-Hill, 1966.

1078.   Pillay, A.P., Common sense therapy of
         male sex disorders, International Journal
         of Sexology, 1950, 4, 19-22.

The author focusses on an approach to reducing the receptivity of the mind to sexual stimulation by shifting the focus
away from the sexually stimulating object. In males with
premature ejaculation as the presenting problem, the author
recommends that the patient concentrate on breathing. It
requires the patient, at the moment of approaching orgasm,
to take a deep breath and hold it for a moment prior to
exhaling it. Such an approach borrows on a principle known
for centuries, and the principle can be found in many ancient
Oriental love books.

1079.   Pillay, A.P., Common sense therapy of
         male sex disorders, International
         Journal of Sexology, 1952, 6, 15-20.

1080.   Pine, I., et al., Experiences with short-
         term group psychotherapy, International
         Journal of Group Psychotherapy, 1958, 8,
         276-284.

This article is a description of a short-term therapy program which was part of a larger milieu therapy psychiatric
hospital treatment program. Patients met in both individual
and group therapy, as well as recreation and occupation
therapy. Each brief therapy group lasted from 8-12 weeks,
with two, one hour sessions/week. The processes occuring
over the course of the brief treatment are detailed, including the initial griping sessions, attacks on the therapist, the emergence of general and personal psychological
problems of individual patients, the beginnings of struggle
and resolution of specific issues, and the issues around
termination. Changes in attitude toward mental illness on
the part of the patients are discussed. Specific issues
related to short-term treatment are presented, including
questions about patient motivation, dependence-independence
struggle, and adjustment to the hospital setting.

1081.   Pinsky, J.J., Chronic, intractable,
         benign pain: A syndrome and its
         treatment with intensive short-term
         group psychotherapy, Journal of Human
         Stress, 1978, 4, 17-21.

There is sufficient reason to classify some ongoing pain
problems as syndromes. Patients who suffer with chronic,
intractable pain syndromes (CIBPS) have truly functional
biopsychosocial disorders. There is no longer any current
pathophysiology operative, and the pain syndrome persists
with its psychosocially perpetuating and disrupting features.
An intense group psychotherapy approach in the therapeutic
milieu of a medical-surgical setting fosters and evokes
affect expression and understanding. This encourages the
formation of cognitive patterns that are therapeutically
useful in that they extend coping abilities and, hence,
diminish the pain and suffering experience and life problems
attendance to it. (Journal abstract).

1082.   Pion, R., and Annon, J., The office
         management of sexual problems: Brief
         therapy approaches, Journal of Reproduc-
         tive Medicine, 1975, 15, 127-143.

This paper presents a four-level treatment approach to
management of sexual problems, and considers, from within
a social learning context, a variety of sexual learning
modules other than traditional patient-therapist verbal
encounters. The first three levels of the P-LI-SS-IT model
constitute successively more complex levels of brief therapy.
The authors detail method and limitations of each of these
three stages: Permission, Limited Information, and Specific
Suggestions. Each succeeding level may be applied if the
physician has the requisite setting, skills, and experience
--and if further therapy appears necessary. The reader is
referred elsewhere for a behavioral approach to intensive
treatment of sexual problems, the fourth level. Pion, et
al., discuss a study designed to test three hypotheses
investigating the use of observational learning procesures
(e.g., a series of six cassette videotapes) as a strategy
for increasing certain sexual behaviors, and effecting more
favorable attitudes towards the same. Results are presented

and discussed. The authors include guidelines for taking
a "sexual problem history", and samples of various questionnaires and taped messages which have proved useful in their
work. (abstract by Deborah Schuller).

1083.   Pittman, F.S., Managing acute psychiatric
         emergencies: Defining the family crisis,
         in Block, D.A., (ed.), Techniques of
         family psychotherapy, New York, Grune and
         Stratton, 1973.

The author presents seven steps involved in providing crisis
intervention services. 1) Immediate intervention, which
helps to decrease symptoms through supportive presence;
2) Problem definition, involving understanding the nature
of the crisis; 3) Helping client focus rather than bringing
up old conflicts; 4) Beginning of alleviation of acute symptoms; 5) Helping patient explore possible solutions; 6) Working to overcome natural resistances to proposed change;
7) Termination. These steps are presented in the context
of family treatment.

1084.   Pittman F.S., et al., Family therapy as
         an alternative to hospitalization, APA
         Psychiatric Research Reports, 1966, #20,
         188-195.

1085.   Pittman, F.S., et al., Crisis family
         therapy, Current Psychiatric Therapies,
         1966, 6, 187-196.

The authors present results of working with 50 families at
the Family Treatment Unit at Colorado Psychopathic Hospital
on an outpatient, brief therapy approach. A description of
the mental health team is provided, as well details of the
types of techniques and focus the team uses. A major
emphasis is on the involvement of the entire family and on
the issue of each person's responsibility within the family.
Structures include assignment of specific tasks for all
members of the family, use of medications, involvement of

outside support agencies of individuals, home visits, etc.
The writings and ideas of Berne and Haley are mentioned as
being relevant to some aspects of treatment, especially
with regard to the difficult or uncooperative patient or
family. Two specific case histories are presented. Of the
original 50 families treated, 42 avoided hospitalization.
The average hospital stay for the six families who needed
to have one of their members hospitalized was 17 days. The
remaining two cases were referred elsewhere for long term
treatment. Ten of the families recontacted the agency
after termination in order to deal with new crises. Some
members of 75% of the families was referred for longer term
therapy. The authors specifically focus on suicide as a
presenting problem and discuss how a focus on issues of
responsibility underlie their approach.

1086.   Pittman, F.S., et al., Work and school
         phobias: A family approach to treatment,
         American Journal of Psychiatry, 1968,
         124, 1535-1541.

The authors describe the syndrome of work phobia, which is
not a classical phobia but separation anxiety associated
with leaving home to go to work. Differentiated from work
inhibition (any chronic, diffuse disturbance of performance
due to a variety of nonspecific conflicts) and success
neurosis (specifically due to an unconscious fear of punishment for achieving), work phobia is considered to be the
adult form of school phobia. It occurs most often in former
school phobics and, like school phobics, responds to helping
the wife or mother to firmly allow the man to separate.
The authors feel that such crisis family therapy is more
successful than long-term individual therapy in the treatment of this syndrome. 11 randomly chosen cases of work
phobia are the focus of this paper, of which 5 were treated
in short-term conjoint family therapy. 6 were treated in
long term individual therapy. A case report is presented.
(Journal abstract adapted).

1087.   Pittman, F.S., et al., Therapy techniques
         of the family treatment unit, in, Haley, J.,
         (ed.), Changing families, New York, Grune
         and Stratton, 1971.

The authors describe the work of the Family Treatment Unit
at Colorado Psychiatric Hospital. The approach is structured
to provide patients with immediate access to treatment, formulation of the presenting problem in family crisis terms,
a maintenance of focus on the presenting problem (i.e.,
current crisis), use of medication where indicated, the
assignment of tasks, the use of negotiation of role conflicts
within the family unit, and continuing support for future
crises. A total of 186 patients who normally would have
been hospitalized, were treated within this structure. Of
that total, 87.5% did not need hospitalization. Case examples are provided.

1088.   Polak, P., Social systems intervention,
         Archives of General Psychiatry, 1971,
         25, 110-117.

I have outlined the techniques of social systems assessment
and intervention developed as a result of intervening directly in the problems of the immediate social environment
of over 1,600 routine psychiatric patients. The techniques
are based on an application of therapeutic community principles to real life settings outside the hospital. Concepts
of leadership , role, structure, and patterns of communication and reinforcement apply equally well to the social
system of a childless marriage couple and to the neighbourhood in which they live. The assessment of a social system
should lead to an understanding of its structure and functioning, and external precipitants of its disturbance and
the conflicts internal to the system. (Journal abstract).

1089.   Polke, P., Short-term therapeutic work
         with a ten year old girl, Journal of
         Child Psychotherapy, 1973, 3, 61-70.

In this paper, Polke relates her work over five weekly
sessions with a 10-year old child suffering from insomnia
and a fear of ghosts. The author describes the themes which
emerged in the course of treatment, as well as the processes

which occurred. These were presumably influenced by the
therapist's and patient's knowledge of the small number of
interviews possible. In a Postscript, Polke briefly summarizes three more sessions which took place at the child's
request after a four-month break. The author comments on
characteristics of the patient which were favourable to
short-term therapy; and concludes by justifying the particular techniques used to effect a reduction of anxiety
and confusion in the child. (abstract by Deborah Schuller).

1090.   Porter, R.A., Crisis intervention and
         social work models, Community Mental
         Health Journal, 1966, 2, 13-17.

The author reports on a community mental health consultation
crisis intervention model, used in working with teachers.
Specific case material is presented and characteristics of
cases which are best suited to such an approach are highlighted. The theoretical concept of intervention originally
presented by Caplan is discussed.

1091.   Posin, H.I., Approaches to brief psycho-
         therapy in a university health service,
         Seminars in Psychiatry, 1969, 1, 399-404.

The author summarizes his experiences of working at two
university health services for approximately 15 years. The
focus of the treatment offered is on restoration of a previous equibilibrium or homeostasis; personality reorganization is not the aim. The value of a detailed life history
is stressed. The importance of the first interview is also
discussed, and the specific role of the therapist is outlined. Three case histories are presented to highlight the
approach used.

1092.   Potter, H.C., and Stanton, G.T., Money
         management and mental health, American
         Journal of Psychotherapy, 1970, 24,
         79-91.

Pathopsychologic attitudes toward money, often found among
those suffering from emotional disturbances, may cause
serious financial problems that need to be relieved before

the individuals can function effectively. While the psychiatric literature indicates some awareness of money attitudes,
it gives no precedent for money therapy. The authors'
experiences indicate that money therapy has great promise.
It is a form of short-term situational therapy that can
enable the patient to manage his money effectively and thereby
be relieved of considerable worry and tension arising from
mismanagement. As the patient achieves simple money goals
through group therapy, his ego is strengthened and his social
adjustment improved, giving complementary support to psychotherapy. It is hoped that others will use the suggestions
for money therapy as a springboard for extensive experimentation and development in this area. (Journal summary).

   1093.   Potts, F., Relief of an anxiety state by
            a single psychodrama session, Group
            Psychotherapy, 1958, 11, 330-331.

The author reports a single case history of a married female
in her early 30's, with neurotic presenting symptomatology.
The psychodrama approach used consisted of one hour of
therapy, followed by a one hour audience discussion period.
An immediate decrease in symptom anxiety was reported. She
was ready to make some major decisions in her life, including
a divorce. The value of both the therapist and the audience
is discussed, in providing a more complete coverage of the
many facets of the woman's problem.

   1094.   Pretzel, P.W., The clergy man's role in
            crisis counseling, in, Clinebell, H.J.,
            (ed.), Community mental health: The
            role of the church and temple, New York,
            Abingdon Press, 1970.

   1095.   Prins, D., Improvement and regression
            in stutterers following short-term
            intensive therapy, Journal of Speech
            and Hearing Disorders, 1970, 35, 123-134.

The author presents a description of a summer camp experience
for stutterers, ages 9-21. A total of 94 male stutterers
were involved in an eight week treatment and social environ-

ment program within a camp setting. The focus was on the
interpersonal difficulties and self-perceptions of the
subjects, and a reinforcement theory formed the conceptual
basis for both understanding the behavior and for its treatment. Follow-up data were collected from six months to
3.5 years after the camping-treatment experience. Dramatic
improvement was reported, but also regression. Explanations
for this pattern were offered. One factor which remained
stable over time, having increased dramatically as a result
of the program was in the area of morale. Results of the
research have produced changes in the treatment program.

1096.   Proceedings of the Brief Psychotherapy
         Council, Chicago Institute for Psycho-
         analysis, Chicago, 1942, 1944, 1946, 1948.

1097.   Proskauer, S., Some technical issues in
         time-limited psychotherapy in children,
         Journal of the American Academy of Child
         Psychiatry, 1969, 8, 154-169.

Realities of training and increasing demands for service in
child psychiatric facilities necessitate time-limited
therapeutic interventions. A useful distinction can be made
between an incomplete fragment of long-term therapy spanning
several months and an equal period of time-limited therapy
designed specifically for the short-term situation. Three
issues of technique which help to establish this distinction
have been discussed: (1) Definition of a focus of treatment
by therapist and child together through symbolic play;
(2) Use of the therapist's insight more as a guide to
developing the optimal relationship with each child then as
a basis for direct interpretation to him, and; (3) Management of termination as the most pressing reality and potentially the most fruitful issue in the time-limited situation.
Specific case examples are provided to highlight each of
these issues. (Journal summary adapted).

1098.   Prugh, D.G., and Brody, B., Brief
         relationship therapy in the military
         setting, American Journal of Ortho-
         psychiatry, 1946, 16, 707-721.

This is a clinical article on the types of problems and
approaches seen in a military setting. Presenting symptoms
include anxiety states, conversions or psychosomatic reactions, etc., all subsumed under the heading, "war neuroses". The authors stress the value of a brief empathic
approach. Clinical issues which relate specifically to the
practice of therapy in a military setting are discussed,
and two examples are presented. Clinical impressions
suggested gains from the use of such an approach.

1099.   Pumpian-Mindlin, E., Considerations in
         the selection of patients for short-
         term psychotherapy, American Journal
         of Psychotherapy, 1953, 7, 641-652.

In one of the earlier articles in the field, the author
skillfully summarizes the criteria for short-term therapy,
its techniques, goals, and determination of its point of
termination. Under criteria for short-term therapy are
included the following: a) Not dependent upon severity of
psychopathology of patient, but on "ego strength" or "ego
crystallization" as it is characterized in this article;
the ways of determining the extent of this in a patient is
also discussed. b) Level of genuine concern on the patient's
part for change. c) Level of discrepancy between patient's
fantasies and actual reality situation. d) Patient's ability
to tolerate past and present trauma/frustration, etc.
d) Adequacy of patient's relationships, past and present,
especially including parents, sibs, marital partners, etc.
f) Patient's current environmental situation; i.e., level
of environmental stability and reasonable flexibility.
Under techniques of brief therapy, the author includes
focussing on the present, the level of directness and
activity of the therapist, the emphasis on the postive, the
de-emphasizing of the transference relationship, use of
interpretation in more general terms and in terms of the
pre-conscious rather than unconscious, the use of self-
concept. In terms of goals, the importance of both patient
and therapist being willing to accept improvement rather

than "cure" is stressed. Further, termination is defined
as that point at which the therapist concludes that he/she
can no longer deal with the immediate presenting problem
without beginning to deal with many of the underlying,
deeper aspects of the individual's past (shift from interpersonal and present, to intrapersonal and past).

1100.   Puryear, D.A., Helping people in
         crisis: A Practical family-oriented
         approach to effective crisis inter-
         vention, San Francisco, Jossey-Bass,
         1979.

Details the steps from first contact, through assessment,
intervention strategies, process of intervention, to termination. Contains many clinical case examples.

1101.   Rabin, M.C., The relative efficacy of
         three short-term therapy analogues in
         the reduction of anxiety, Dissertation
         Abstracts International, 1976, 37,
         (5-B), 2522.

1102.   Rabkin, R. Strategic psychotherapy:
         Brief and symptomatic treatment, New
         York, Basic Books Inc., 1977.

The author presents a review of the assumptions underlying
a brief, active, symptom-relief orientation to psychotherapy.
The roles of therapist and client are outlined. Such techniques as hypnosis, relaxation, reverse psychology, symptom
substitution, transfer, group work, are discussed in detail.
Issues of termination are also discussed.

1103.   Rachman, S., Studies in desensi-
         tization. I: The separate effects
         of relaxation and desensitization,
         Behaviour Research and Therapy, 1965.
         3, 245-251.

The purpose of the study was to investigate the separate
effects of desensitization and relaxation in Wolpe's

technique of "systematic desensitization". Four small
groups of spider-phobic, normal subjects were allocated to
the following treatments: desensitization with relaxation,
desensitization without relaxation, relaxation only, no-
treatment controls. The effects of treatment were assessed
by subjective reports, avoidance tests and fear estimates.
Marked reductions in fear were obtained only in the desensi-
tization-with-relaxation group and it was concluded that
the combined effects of relaxation and desensitization are
greater than their separate effects. (Journal summary).

1104.   Rachman, S., Studies in desensitization,
         II. Flooding, Behaviour Research and
         Therapy, 1966, 4, 1-6.

The purpose of the study was to investigate the effectiveness of "flooding" as a technique for reducing fear. Three
normal S's who were spider-phobic were given 10 sessions
of flooding treatment in which they were exposed to intensely
disturbed imaginal stimuli involving spiders. Although
strong emotional reactions were provoked by this procedure
it did not produce a reduction in fear of the phobic object.
The results obtained from the Ss in the flooding group were
compared with earlier findings and it was found that they
did not differ from the No-Treatment Control S's. The
results obtained with S's who received desensitization
under relaxation were seen to be superior to those of the
Flooding and Control groups. (Journal summary).

1105.   Rachman, S., and Costello, C.G., The
         etiology and treatment of children's
         phobias: a review, American Journal
         of Psychiatry, 1961, 118, 97-105.

The authors focus on two major theoretical influences on
the field of psychiatry and psychology, namely, psychoanalytic theory and behavioral theories. Basic assumptions
embedded in psychoanalytic theory are reviewed, including
issues of clinical evidence, elaboration by analysts of
evidence presented by the patient, the use of suggestion,
inversions and non-acceptance of patient material by the

analyst. Specific details of the behavioral treatment of
phobias are presented, along with a behavioral reinterpre-
tation of the psychoanalytic cases. The authors conclude
that there are probably elements of each approach embedded
in the other.

1106.   Rada, R., et al., A therapeutic waiting
         area experience for patients with chronic
         psychiatric illnesses, Comprehensive
         Psychiatry, 1964, 54, 191-192.

The authors describe a limited treatment approach with
chronic (borderline and ambulatory) psychotic patients.
Therapy sessions usually are 15 to 30 minutes in duration,
with backup from environmental manipulation and the use of
medication. The structure and atmosphere in the waiting
room area of the clinic are described.

1107.   Rada, R., et al., An outpatient setting
         for treating chronically ill psychiatric
         patients, American Journal of Psychiatry,
         1969, 126, 789-795.

The relative neglect of the chronically ill psychiatric
patient in community mental health planning emphasizes the
need for new treatment methods and resources. This paper
presents an eight-year experimental application of psychoanalytic principles in an outpatient clinic with a form of
therapy (termed "adaptive psychotherapy") specifically
designed for the treatment of the chronically ill psychiatric
patient. The advantages of thic clinic for the training of
mental health professionals are also discussed. (Journal
abstract).

1108.   Rado, S., The relationship of short-
         term psychotherapy to developmental
         stages of maturation and stages of
         treatment behavior, in, Wolberg, L.,
         (ed.), Short term psychotherapy, New
         York, Grune and Stratton, 1965.

1109.   Radwan, R., and Davidson, S., Short-
term treatment in a general hospital
following a suicide attempt, Hospital
and Community Psychiatry, 1977, 28,
537-538.

The authors discuss the value of short-term psychiatric
treatment in the nonpsychiatric wards of a general hospital
for patients who attempt suicide. During 1974 a total of
124 such patients were seen in the emergency room of Meir
General Hospital in Kfar Saba, Israel. Following an initial
psychiatric examination, 110 of the patients were admitted
to the internal medicine or surgical wards. After further
observation 30% were transferred to psychiatric hospitals,
and the rest were treated in the general hospital's nonpsychiatric wards for an average of 3 days. There were no
suicide attempts during hospitalization. The authors emphasize the usefulness of a short hospitalization to separate
the patient from his traumatic home environment until his
return to it becomes feasible. (Journal abstract).

1110.   Rahe, R.H., et al., Group therapy in
the outpatient management of post-
myocardial infarction patients,
Psychiatry in Medicine, 1973, 4, 77-88.

A controlled experiment of the utility of group therapy
(total 6 sessions) as an adjunct to the medical outpatient
management of patients following myocardial infarction has
been in progress for nearly a year. The long-range purpose
of the experiment is to assess the possible benefits of
group therapy experience in terms of subjects' job rehabilitation rates, angina pectoris prevalence, nitroglycerin use,
rehospitalization for coronary heart disease, as well as
reinfarction and mortality rates-compared to those for
control subjects. The early results from the group therapy
experience, however, have provided important information
and are reported here to illustrate the psychological
physiology of the rehabilitation process and emphasize
patients' special needs, too often ignored during their
convalescence. (Journal abstract).

1111.   Rahe, R., et al., Brief group therapy
         following myocardial infarction: An
         eighteen month follow up of a controlled
         trial, International Journal of Psychiatry
         in Medicine, 1975, 6, 349-358.

Sixty post-myocardial infarction (MI) subjects have been
followed for up to eighteen months' time following their MI.
Thirty-eight of these subjects completed a brief series of
four to six group therapy sessions during their early rehabilitation phase; the others received no group therapy.
Both groups were placed on otherwise identical schedules of
outpatient follow-up. Group therapy patients have, to date,
experienced significantly fewer cardiac complications than
controls. Only one death has occurred, and that one patient
was in the control group. A coronary heart disease teaching
evaluation questionnaire was given to a sample of group
therapy patients, a sample of controls, and a comparison
group of men without MI. Following their group therapy
sessions, these men demonstrated significantly greater
knowledge of their disease and its optimal rehabilitation
than did the control or comparison subjects. Control
patients' questionnaire results proved to be significantly
different from those of the comparison group. (Journal
abstract).

1112.   Rahe, R.H., et al., Brief group therapy
         in myocardial infarction rehabilitation:
         Three to four-year follow-up of a con-
         trolled trial, Psychosomatic Medicine,
         1979, 41, 1229-1242.

A trial of brief group therapy as part of a rehabilitation
program for postmyocardial infarction (MI) patients was
carried out. Forty-four patients surviving their first MI
were randomly allocated to either group therapy or control
group status and were followed over 4 years. An additional
group of 17 patients were referred for post-MI group therapy
sessions after the termination of the controlled experiment
and were followed for 3 years. Patients who received group
therapy had significantly less follow-up coronary morbidity
and mortality, and returned to work at significant higher
percentages than control patients. Although neither group
therapy nor control group patients meaningfully altered

conventional coronary risk factors, group therapy patients
(in the controlled trial) successfully altered selected
coronary-prone behaviors. Educational information regarding the physiological and psychological aspects of coronary
heart disease, presented in the group therapy sessions, was
forgotten over follow-up. It is concluded that the supportive aspects of the group therapy experience played the
most important role in determining the rehabilitation
advantages seen for treatment patients. (Journal abstract).

1113.   Raphling, D.L., and Lion, J., Patients
         with repeated admissions to a psychiatric
         emergency service, Community Mental Health
         Journal, 1970, 6, 313-318.

Psychiatric emergency treatment units traditionally care
for patients with acute psychological crises and are not
ordinarily concerned with providing long term follow-up
treatment. Nevertheless, a significant percentage of
patients continues to utilize emergency treatment services
repeatedly rather than become involved in other more definitive and durable treatment programs. These patients, as
well as the nature of their intermittent and recurrent
emergency treatment contacts, are described. It is postulated that psychiatric treatment on an emergency basis may
be an effective mode of treatment for those patients who
are prone to recurrent crises and are unable to establish
more stable treatment relations. (Journal abstract).

1114.   Rapoport, L., Working with families
         in crisis: An exploration in pre-
         ventive intervention, Social Work,
         1962, 7, 48-56.

Rapoport discusses theoretic and practical considerations
of preventive intervention with families considered to be
in crisis due to the birth of a premature infant. Crisis
theory and theories of prevention as formulated in the
field of public health serve as underlying frames of
reference. After a brief summary of characteristics of
crisis, the author reviews Caplan's description of the
psychological tasks facing the mother of a premature baby.

Rapoport then presents three case histories to illustrate a range of responses to such a crisis. She classifies the preventive work undertaken with these families according to three broad categories. These include maintaining an explicit focus on the crisis; offering basic information with regards to child care and development; and creating bridges to community resources. (abstract by Deborah Schuller).

1115. Rapoport, L., The state of crisis: Some theoretical considerations, Social Service Review, 1962, 36, 211-217.

The author summarizes the theoretical concepts which underlie the concept of a crisis state. The work of Erikson, Lindemann and Caplan, Tyhurst, Bowlby and others is presented. Factors which can produce states of crisis are discussed (e.g., hazardous event posing some threat; inability to respond with adequate coping mechanisms, etc.). The characteristics of a crisis state are also delineated, including its temporal limits, phases or stages, and various coping mechanisms, both healthy and maladaptive. The implications for professional practice are surveyed, including need to clarify the precipitating causes of the presenting problem, use of community resources, both interpersonal and institutional, etc. The susceptibility of a family or individual in crisis to positive help and change is highlighted.

1116. Rapoport, L., Crisis-oriented short-term casework, Social Service Review, 1967, 41, 31-43.

Rapoport situates short-term casework within the framework of crisis theory, and formulates implications for treatment and theory. She first notes theoretical fallacies and myths which impede creative thinking about brief intervention; then reviews central concepts of "crisis theory". Brief treatment is distinguished from other treatment modalities on the basis of several parameters other than the time element--e.g., need for acceptance of limited goals, a high degree of focusing in the treatment, communication addressed to specific aspects of the ego. Techniques especially useful in brief treatment of people in states of crisis are reviewed. Finally, the author examines theoretical implications with regard to diagnosis, therapeutic relationship, motivation, change-inducing forces, and self-determination. The author states that many aspects of traditional casework theory bear directly on brief treatment, but other concepts should be re-evaluated for their relevance to this newer treatment approach. (abstract by Deborah Schuller).

1117. Rashkis, S.R., Short-term psychotherapy of a patient with anorexia nervosa, Journal National Association of Private Psychiatric Hospitals, 1974, 6, 17-26.

Therapy of a young girl began when she had to be hospitalized because of a dangerous weight loss related to anorexia nervosa. Short-term therapy was used, both in the form of individual and family sessions, which interrupted the self-destructive choices she had been making.

1118. Raskin, D.E., and Klein, Z.E., Losing a symptom through keeping it: A review of paradoxical treatment techniques and rationale, Archives of General Psychiatry, 1976, 33, 548-555.

The therapeutic technique of symptom prescription has been used by practitioners from a variety of clinical schools. This article reviews techniques based on learning theory, symptom redefinition, paradoxical intention, and directive therapy, among other approaches. A conceptual framework for understanding these various approaches is offered, utilizing data from psychoanalysis, learning theory, and interpersonal communication theory. (Journal abstract).

1119. Rawlings, E.I., and Gauron, E.F., Responders and non-responders to an accelerated, time-limited group: A case history, Perspectives in Psychiatric Care, 1973, 11, 65-69.

Work done at the University of Iowa Hospital is reported. Inpatient, closed-membership, brief psychotherapy groups were set up with a highly structured approach by therapists. Group membership was limited to eight members, and three therapists, with a total of 10 sessions over a five week period. Therapists were asked to rate each member independently at the conclusion of treatment as to whether the patient improved markedly, was slightly improved, or had shown no improvement. It is reported as the authors' clinical experience that those patients who do not improve in a brief accelerated group therapy experience also tend to show little improvement when provided with another form of therapy of a longer term nature. The authors suggest the use of such time-limited groups as a screening device.

1120.   Reed, L.S., et al., Health insurance and psychiatric care: Utilization and cost, Washington, D.C., American Psychiatric Association, 1972.

1121.   Regan, P.F., Brief psychotherapy of depression, American Journal of Psychiatry, 1965, 122, 28-32.

In this article, the author summarizes the value of using tactics in the treatment of depression. The value of such tactics includes the clarity it forces on the treatment process, the opportunities for research given this clarity, and the verification of various theoretical positions within the field regarding the nature and etiology of depression. A number of tactical approaches to depression are presented, including short case history material. Tactics include protecting the patient as change occurs in therapy, use of an initial detailed exploration of the many aspects of the patient's life, the interruption of the patient's tendency to ruminate, the inclusion of a physical therapy program, the focus on changing the patient's attitude, and the use of community resources as an adjunct to the treatment process.

1122.   Reibel, S., and Herz, M.I., Limitations of brief hospital treatment, American Journal of Psychiatry, 1976, 133, 518-521.

A total of 175 newly admitted inpatients who lived with their families were randomly assigned to three treatment

groups: standard inpatient care and brief hospitalization
with and without transitional day care. Case reports of 6
of the 9 patients considered "study failures" illustrate
that effective postdischarge adaptation is limited by the
patients' degree of impairment as well as the family and
community capacity to accept him. Although rapid return
to the community is beneficial to many patients, rigid
adherence to this policy is neither wise nor clinically
effective. (Journal abstract).

1123.   Reid, W.J., Characteristics of casework
         in intervention, Welfare in Review,
         1967, 5, 11-19.

1124.   Reid, W.J., A test of a task-centered
         approach, Social Work, 1975, 20, 3-9.

Reid reports a controlled study to assess the efficacy of
a particular type of task-centered treatment. He summarizes
the set of interventions which comprise the Task Implementation Sequence (TIS), then clearly describes method and
design of the experiment. Use of TIS with a particular
task was hypothesized to contribute significantly to the
client's progress in carrying out that task. Thirty-two
cases were assigned to experimental or control conditions.
Reid presents findings derived from analyses of achievement
ratings, the nature of the task assigned, specific interventions used, etc. The results indicate that clients can
be helped to carry out specific tasks through a concentrated
preparatory program given with the casework interview. In
addition to the experimental variable, the classification of
the task as unique or repetitive appears related to outcome.
TIS appears particularly effective in assisting clients on
one-time tasks. The author discusses implications of the
data. (abstract by Deborah Schuller).

1125.   Reid, W.J., and Epstein, L., Task
         Centered Casework, New York, Columbia
         University Press, 1972.

1126.   Reid, W., and Shyne, A., Brief and
         extended casework, Columbia University
         Press, N.Y., 1969.

1127.   Reik, L.E., Short-term hospital treat-
         ment of mental illness: A historical
         perspective, Mental Hygiene, 1957, 41,
         74-81

Reik compares the present trend toward short-term physical
treatment of emotional disturbance with the more psychological orientation propounded in the 19th Century, focusing
particularly on the ideas of Isaac Ray, Reik constructs his
comparison around four common arguments advanced today (as
in the past) against specialized mental hospitals: a) the
popular prejudice against such hospitals; b) the persistent
belief in the efficacy of short-term physical treatment in
curing mental illness; c) the "excessive" expense entailed
in treatment in a mental hospital; d) the belief that a
general hospital environment is superior to that afforded
by a hospital specializing in psychiatric treatment. On
the basis of his consideration of these arguments, the
author outlines some inherent limitations of the general
hospital psychiatric unit in which the goal must be absolute
control over the patient. He advocates continued attention
to the psychological (versus technological or purely physical) components of psychiatric care. (abstract by Deborah
Schuller).

1128.   Reitz, W.E., and Keil, W.E., Behavioral
         treatment of an exhibitionist, Journal
         of Behavior Therapy and Experimental
         Psychiatry, 1971, 14, 67-69.

Behavioral treatment of a long-standing (25 years) case of
exhibitionism is described. Treatment involved having the
patient exhibit himself under office conditions witnessed
by nurses. He reacted with shame, guilt, and embarrassment.
After 19 months, the patient has not again exhibited himself.
(Journal summary).

1129.   Renshaw, D.C., Psychiatric emergencies
         of childhood and adolescence, Illinois
         Medical Journal, 1973, 143, 353-357.

This report summarizes the typical emergencies of a psychiatric nature which children and teens produce. The
criteria for effective handling of these crises are:
a) immediate evaluation of child and family; b) clarifying
precipitating factors for the family; c) partnership involvement with parents for concrete guidelines form prompt
alleviation of the child's difficulty; d) access to hospital
facilities for a limited number of these children; e) effective use of community resources.

1130.   Resnick, H.L.P., and Hathorne, B.C., (eds.),
         Teaching outlines in crisis in suicide
         studies and crisis intervention, Bowie,
         Maryland, The Charles Press Publishers,
         Inc., 1974.

1131.   Resnick, H., and Reuben, H., (eds.),
         Emergency psychiatric care: The manage-
         ment of mental health crises, Bowie,
         Maryland, Charles Press, 1975.

1132.   Reynolds, B., An experiment in short
         contact interviewing, Smith College
         Studies in Social Work, 1932, 3, 1-133.

Reynolds first describes the method and underlying concepts
of an experiment in which she interviewed applicants to the
New York Children's Aid Society, Department of Boarding
Homes. The author summarizes characteristics of the
applicants interviewed by her over the period of November,
1931 through March, 1932, and their reasons for seeking
help. She then discusses the difficulty of assessing an
applicant in a single contact. Four processes used by the
social worker in the interviews were selected for study:
observation, use of the "sample situation", application of
social norms as evaluation criteria, and the use of psychiatric concepts. Having carefully delineated the background
of the study, Reynolds presents "in their original form in

order to show the writer's immediate impressions and her
method of recording them" 25 case records, with her observations on each. Twelve of these cases were applicants who
desired to board foster children for the agency; 13 applicants who sought to place their children in foster homes.
The author conceives the function of casework as the development of an individual's "fullest possible capacity for self-
maintenance in a social group". Reynolds concludes from
her study that the most important issue in any contact, but
particularly the first, is the safeguarding of the client's
autonomy--e.g., by setting the "keynote of the client's
participation and responsibility on as high a level as he
is capable of at the time." Apart from the theoretic
contributions to short-contact interviewing methods, Reynolds
offers in the case records an interesting close-up of problems prevalent in that era. (abstract by Deborah Schuller).

1133.   Reynolds, B., and MacGregor, M.L.,
         Collected papers on relationships in
         short-contact interviewing, N.Y.,
         National Travelers Aid and Transient
         Services, 1934.

1134.   Rhine, M.W., and Mayerson, P., Crisis
         hospitalization within a psychiatric
         emergency service, American Journal
         of Psychiatry, 1971, 127, 1386-1391.

The authors describe the expansion of an emergency psychiatric service to include the use of short-term hospitalization as an integral part of crisis therapy. Experience
during the first year of operation, when 200 patients were
treated, is summarized. The authors believe that a small
hospital unit, integrated within an emergency psychiatric
service, can greatly enhance the scope and efficacy of
crisis intervention. (Journal abstract).

1135.   Rhodes, S.L., Short-term groups of
         latency age children in a school
         setting, International Journal of
         Group Psychotherapy, 1973, 23,
         204-216.

An experimental program of short-term group therapy was
carried out in an elementary school setting with latency-
aged children. The therapists utilized a conventional
verbal treatment model. The children demonstrated an
ability to share their difficulties, to explore feelings
related to their problems, and to make limited attitudinal
and behavioral changes. The group provided an opportunity
for the development of socially adaptive behavior. The
therapeutic interventions were directive and geared to modifying behavior through the interpretation of ego conflicts
and the introduction of alternative ways of behaving. Treatment techniques were directed to the solidification of ego
development so necessary for the latency-age child to proceed
to more advanced psychosexual stages. This program grew out
of the conviction that existing modalities can be expanded
to teet the needs of the growing number of children for whom
preventive and ameliorative treatment is indicated.
(Journal summary).

1136.   Richardson, F., and Suinn, R.M., A
         comparison of traditional systematic
         desensitization, accelerated massed
         desensitization, and anxiety management
         training in the treatment of mathematics
         anxiety, Behavior Therapy, 1973, 4, 212-
         218.

Mathematics anxiety in 20 university students was treated
by traditional systematic desensitization and accelerated
massed desensitization (AMD). The traditional group was
exposed to all items of an 8-item mathematics anxiety
hierarchy in nine treatment sessions over 3 weeks. The
accelerated (AMD) group was exposed to the three highest
items in a single, massed treatment session. Results on a
self-rating scale showed significant equivalent improvement
for both groups following therapy. The treatment groups'
improvement on a performance measure approached, but did
not reach significance as compared with no-treatment

controls. The results were compared with those obtained previously in another study using a similar population and the same measures, by anxiety management control (AMT), another short-term approach introduced recently by the authors. (Journal abstract).

1137. Richardson, R.C., and Suinn, R.M., Effects of two-short-term desensitization methods in the treatment of test anxiety, Journal of Counseling Psychology, 1974, 21, 457-458.

A total fo 44 undergraduate students who volunteered to participate in a test anxiety program were assigned randomly to one of four groups: a) Traditional desensitization group, involving six, one hour sessions spread over a two week period, involving a standard test anxiety hierarchy. b) Accelerated massed desensitization, involving a one hour training session of relaxation followed one week later by a two hour massed desensitization session utilizing the top three items of the same hierarchy. c) A program in anxiety management training group, involving a one hour relaxation training and two hour treatment sessions. d) Control group, which received no treatment. All three treatment programs significantly decreased anxiety levels when compared with the control group. The differences among the results for each of the three treatment groups are presented, and the possible uses of these different approaches are discussed.

1138. Ritchie, A., Multiple impact therapy: An experiment, Social Work, 1960, 5, 16-21.

The author describes an approach called Multiple Impact Therapy, used and research at the Neuropsychiatric Department of the University of Texas Medical Branch, Galveston, as part of a Youth Development Project. It consists of a short-term (average two days), intensive treatment of families in crisis by a clinic team made up of members from various mental health professions. The approach is based on the assumption that while under a crisis situation, individuals and families are more susceptible to possible alternative ways of dealing with their lives. The author

describes in detail the daily routines involved in MTT.
Families seen present a wide range of problems, such as
chronic runaways, school phobias, homosexual behavior,
other sexual deviations, etc. A total of 12 families
originally seen in this program were part of an on-going
program evaluation, with six month follow-up done. A
larger study included a total of 26 families. The value of
such an approach both for treatment and teaching functions
was discussed.

1139.   Robinson, C., and Suinn, R.M., Group
        desensitization of a phobia in massed
        sessions, Behaviour Research and Therapy,
        1969, 7, 317-321.

The authors report on a study in which 20 female students
were treated in a group desensitization procedure in order
to help diminish or eliminate their fear of spiders. A
total of five sessions were needed (all completed in a five
day period). Positive changes in self-ratings of fear, as
well as actual spider-approach behavior were reported,
supporting the notion that such treatment can be carried
out in a group format with a standardized anxiety hierarchy.

1140.   Robinson, C., et al., The office
        management of sexual problems: Brief
        therapy approaches, Journal of Repro-
        ductive Medicine, 1975, 15, 127-144.

1141.   Rochman, J., and Hindley, M., A
        bibliography relating to crisis theory,
        including material on life stress
        situations, Harvard: Laboratory of
        Community Psychiatry, 1969.

1142.   Rockwell, W.J., et al., Individual versus
         group: Brief treatment outcome in a uni-
         versity mental health service, Journal of
         the American College Health Association,
         1976, 24, 186-190.

During portions of two academic years, all students presenting themselves to a university mental health service were
evaluated as potential candidates for three brief treatment
modalities: 3-session individual psychotherapy, 12-session
psychotherapy, and 10-session group psychotherapy. One of
the modalities was recommended on a random basis to 33.3%
of the students evaluated and 22% completed pretreatment
and end-of-treatment testing.

There was no statistically significant differences on outcome measures among the three modalities.

One finding is that use of brief group treatments is not a
generally applicable device for managing students or for
conserving staff time. The findings do suggest procedures
which should combine effective management of a substantial
percentage of students with some savings of staff time.

An incidental finding that students consistently rate their
anxiety and depression higher than do their therapists is
discussed as a potential source of misunderstanding.
(Journal summary).

1143.   Rosen, J.N., The treatment of
         schizophrenic psychosis by direct
         analytic therapy, Psychiatric
         Quarterly, 1946, 20, 3-25.

The author describes in great detail the use of direct
analytic therapy in the treatment of psychotic patients.
The total number of patients treated was 37, all of whom
had been diagnosed as deteriorating schizophrenics. A table
containing the demographic characteristics at intake of these
patients is presented, along with the results of direct analytic therapy. Most patients were successfully treated from
a few days to a number of months, with data on follow-up
showing maintenance of improved state. A detailed case
history is also provided covering the process of the treatment.

1144.   Rosen, J.N., The treatment of schize-
         phrenic psychosis by direct analytic
         therapy, Psychiatric Quarterly, 1947,
         21, 3-37.

The author describes in great detail the background information on 37 cases of schizophrenia, who were treated
successfully using the Direct Anatytic Therapy approach
developed by Rosen. The range of time necessary to effect
positive change in these patients was varied, from a few
days to a few years, with most being treated within a relatively short time period.

1145.   Rosen, J., Direct psychoanalytic
         psychotherapy, Chicago, University
         of Chicago Press, 1950.

1146.   Rosen, R.C., and Schnapp, B.J., The
         use of a specific behavioral technique
         (thought-stopping) in the context of
         conjoint couples therapy: A case
         report, Behavior Therapy, 1974, 5,
         261-264.

This case illustrates the possible rapprochement between a
family therapy and behavioral approach in couples therapy.
To maintain the emphasis on dyadic communication, however,
techniques such as thought-stopping need to be used in a
somewhat modified form. The couple treated had their sym-
biotic relationship severely disrupted by the wife's short-
term affair with another man. After an initial period of
crisis intervention, therapy was impeded by the husband's
obsessional involvement in the minute details of his wife's
meetings with the other man. Thought-stopping was introduced as a new communication skill, by means of which the
couple could exercise control over such destructive interactions. Only three sessions were necessary to bring the
obsession under control, and therapy was terminated after
a total of 12 sessions. Follow-up eight months after termination indicated maintenance of therapeutic gains.
(Journal abstract).

1147.   Rosenbaum, C.P., Events of early and
         brief therapy, Archives of General
         Psychiatry, 1964, 10, 506-512.

Through the use of 12 brief clinical examples, the author
provides a detailed discussion of the factors which facilitate the early alleviation of symptoms and the choice of
ending therapy in a satisfyingly few number of sessions.
Factors such as the therapist's attitude and techniques are
shown to influence the duration of therapy. The author also
discusses some of the possible mechanisms by which symptoms
are relieved, what usually or typically occurs with patient's
presenting complaints as therapy progresses, and what directions to take when symptoms do change. The value of pur-
suing the issue of why a patient has chosen a particular
time to seek therapy, of an active, flexible approach, of
allowing patients to clearly define their own needs and
goals, of being willing to be used as a transference object,
and developing attitudes in the therapist which will allow
for earlier terminations are all presented and stressed.
The kinds of therapist attitudes which may contribute to
the prolonging of therapy are discussed, including values
internalized as part of one's training, the need to establish
a viable private practice, etc.

1148.   Rosenbaum, C.P., and Beebe, J.E.,
         Psychiatric treatment: Crisis, clinic,
         and consultation, New York, McGraw-Hill,
         1975.

1149.   Rosenberg, B.N., Planned short-term
         treatment in developmental crises,
         Social Casework, 1975, 56, 195-204.

The author summarizes some of the clinical findings in using
planned short-term therapy (PSTT) at the Quick Response Unit
of Jewish Family Service in New York. The characteristics
of PSTT are discussed, including the issue of time and its
usage in therapy, the focus of the initial interview on
actively engaging the client and on formulating and sharing
tentative hypotheses about the nature of the problem with
the client, the focus on the present and on a specific

problem area, issues of termination (with recapitulation of
therapy process), and follow-up. Erik Erikson's epigenetic
model of psychosocial development is used as a theoretical
base, as well as crisis and stress theory, systems theory,
etc. Three specific cases are presented.

1150.   Rosenberg, S., et al., Factors related
         to improvement in brief psychotherapy,
         in, Less, S. (ed.), An evaluation of the
         results of the psychotherapies, Spring-
         field, Ill., Charles C. Thomas, 1968.

1151.   Rosenblatt, B., A young boy's reaction
         to the death of his sister: A report
         based on brief psychotherapy, Journal
         of the American Academy of Child
         Psychiatry, 1969, 8, 321-335.

The details of a brief therapy experience experience with
a 5½ year old boy who had lost his sister through her death
six months prior to treatment are described. The family
background and composition and the child's reactions to
four therapy sessions is presented in great detail. Issues
such as specific techniques used to deal with the child's
religious ideas, the effect of the grief reaction, and
issues of prevention are all discussed.

1152.   Rosenblum, B., The single interview case,
         Jewish Social Service Quarterly, 1952,
         28, 257-265.

1153.   Rosenman, S., Brief psychotherapy and
         criteria of success, Journal of General
         Psychology, 1957, 57, 273-287.

Rosenman presents an ostensibly "successful" case--a 24-
year old woman seen twice-weekly over eight months--to
raise questions about the validity of therapeutic techniques and research studies which accent at face value a
patient's positive verbal statements regarding the efficacy
of treatment. The author supports his contention that the

brief therapist may be especially susceptible to using superficial approbation at the close of treatment as a measure of success. The author stresses the need for para-digmatic descriptions of brief therapy cases. Such descriptions would facilitate an understanding of major modes of interaction between given types of patients' long-term schemata, on one hand, and the therapist and the thera-peutic situation, on the other. This in turn would permit the formulation of hypotheses to assess and explain reported improvements for specified personality types. (abstract by Deborah Schuller).

1154. Rosenthal, A.J., and Levine, S.V.,
Brief psychotherapy with children:
A preliminary report, American Journal
of Psychiatry, 1970, 127, 646-651.

In this report of the preliminary findings, the authors summarize the results of a research project focussed on brief therapy with children. The study was carried out in a child psychiatry outpatient clinic in a university medical center. Excluded from the study were children with obvious psychosis, mental retardation (10 less than 75), children older the 13 years, and anyone who had had psychiatric treatment within the last year. Thirty-three patients were given brief therapy, 35 long term therapy. Parents, therapists, teachers were involved in completing various research instruments at various points in the treatment program and at follow-up. Types of presenting problems included school refusal, aca-demic problems, night terrors, aggressive acting-out be-havior, hyperactivity, asocial behavior, enuresis, etc. Of those given brief therapy, 76% were judged definitely or markedly improved. Those in the long term therapy had a 79% improvement rate. The average length of treatment for brief therapy was 8.1 weeks, for the long term group 53.5 weeks. Those families who did not improve in brief therapy had children with severe symptoms and exhibited marital discord, maternal deprivation, or psychopathology in one or both parents, all of a severe nature. The results indicate that brief therapy can be effective over a wide range of childhood pathology. Some of the characteristics of the brief therapy sessions are discussed (e.g., focus, structure, therapeutic pressure, etc.).

1155.   Rosenthal, A.J., and Levine, S.V., Brief
         psychotherapy with children: Process of
         therapy, American Journal of Psychiatry,
         1971, 128, 141-146.

This article is a follow-up report on a previously reported
study, focussing on therapeutic methods used in the brief
therapy program.   The authors discuss the effect of time
limits on families (i.e., therapeutic pressure, increased
involvement of family members, including homework, etc.),
the focus of treatment and its goals (here and now orientation), issues of rapport between therapist and family,
and questions concerning termination.   Therapists were active
and directive, often stressing the positive strengths of the
child and/or the family, and helping them utilize these
strengths.   A case history is provided.

1156.   Rosenthal, A.J., Brief focussed psycho-
         therapy with children and adolescents,
         in, Noshpitz, J. (ed.), Basic handbook
         of child psychiatry, New York, Basic
         Books, 1980.

1157.   Rosenthal, A.J., Brief psychotherapy,
         in, Skolivar, G.P., et al., (eds.),
         Treatment of emotional disorders in
         children and adolescents, New York,
         Spectrum Publications, 1980.

1158.   Rosenthal, D., and Frank, J.D., The
         fate of psychiatric clinic outpatients
         assigned to psychotherapy, Journal of
         Nervous and Mental Disease, 1958, 127,
         330-343.

Insight-based psychotherapies seem to be less effective
with psychiatric clinic outpatients than with patients in
some other types of setting, even though psychiatrists
mostly refer for psychotherapy those clinic patients whom
they deem most likely to benefit from such treatment, viz.,
young , psychoneurotic patients with relatively higher
socio-economic status and education who are relatively

better oriented and motivated toward receiving such treatment. In a study done at the Henry Phipps Psychiatric
Clinic, approximately one of every three patients referred
for psychotherapy failed to accept it when it became available, even though he had previously agreed to try it. Those
of lower social class and motivation were least likely to
accept it or to remain in psychotherapy once they tried it,
but generally obtained as much benefit from it as those of
higher social class and motivation. Three of every four
patients who began psychotherapy terminated without discussing this step with their therapists. Approximately half
of all patients had five or less hours therapy and about six
of ten were discharged as unimproved. Other clinics report
similar experiences. It is pointed out that insight-oriented
forms of psychotherapy may not be the best ones for psychiatric clinic outpatients and that the time may be at hand for
wider experimenting with other kinds of psychotherapy which
have shown evidence of being adaptable with success to a
clinic outpatient population. (Journal summary).

1159.   Rosenthal, H.R., Psychotherapy for the
         dying, American Journal of Psychotherapy,
         1957, 11, 626-633.

The focus in this article is on issues in therapy with
individuals who know that they are going to die because of
some terminal, incurable illness. The value of therapy for
such an individual is discussed, including less irrationality on the therapist's part than is often the case with
family members or friends of the patient. The therapist
should encourage the patient to discuss his fears rather
than forgetting them. Patient fears usually include re-
jection, abandonment, guilt, etc. Various typical kinds of
concerns raised by the dying include questions about one's
life (the unfulfilled self), fear of loss of power, fear of
death versus creative activity. Case examples are provided,
and specific techniques are reviewed.

1160.   Rosenthal, H.R., Emergency psychotherapy:
         A crucial need, Psychoanalytic Review,
         1965, 52, 446-459.

The author relates her experience in administering ana-
lytically-based emergency psychotherapy after trauma to

illustrate the value of this type of intervention. She
describes indications, theoretical considerations (Freud
and Fenichel), behavioral responses to trauma, general and
specific fears evoked by such an event. Goals and technique
of treatment are elaborated, and a variety of cases presented. Rosenthal concludes that emergency psychotherapy
affords some immediate relief of effects of trauma; that it
can prevent neurotic post-traumatic reactions, or, in certain
instances, result in savings of time in follow-up therapy
through the uncovering of crucial material during the
emergency interview. (abstract by Deborah Schuller).

1161.   Roth, R.M., et al., Massed time limit
         therapy, Psychotherapy: Theory, Research,
         and Practice, 1969, 6, 54-56.

Roth, et al. briefly outline their Developmental Theory of
Psychotherapy, which posits as the key therapeutic agent
the "interactional flow" in the therapist-patient relationship. Massed Time Limit Therapy attempts to utilize the
concept of time limits, without undermining the intensity
of the interaction. To effect this goal, a time limit is
set, but the sessions are offered consecutively--i.e., a 10
session time limit becomes one 10-hour session. The authors
present an exploratory study (based on one case) to investigate the feasibility of this approach. They postulated
that significant personality change (as measured by self and
ideal self Q-sort, and a self-administered form of the (TAT)
would result from a single 10-hour therapy session. Procedure and results are described. Self-ideal correlation
coefficients did increase significantly after therapy.
Furthermore, the third post-therapy correlation (eight weeks
after therapy) was significantly higher than the first post-
therapy measure (one week after therapy). Therapist and
client comments, dictated at the conclusion of the session,
are included. (abstract by Deborah Schuller).

1162.   Rothenberg, S., Brief psychodynamically
         oriented therapy, Psychosomatic Medicine,
         1955, 17, 455-457.

The author presents a technique for successfully dealing
with severe psychosomatic disorders complicating organic
ailments. It consists of giving an incisive and unexpected

brief interpretation of the unconscious meaning and aim of
the symptom. The therapist points out the paradoxical
character of the symptom and the danger involved in continuing to manifest the symptom. Specific case examples
are provided to explain this approach. Two cases are
focussed on patients with hiccups, the third example of a
patient suffering from psychological reactions to a serious
heart attack.

1163.   Rowland, S.J., Ego-directive psycho-
          therapy in limited treatment, Social
          Casework, 1975, 56, 543-553.

The author describes an ego-focussed brief therapy approach,
aimed at re-establishing a previous level of functioning,
and involving the active and directive role of the therapist.
Through the use of one case example, the major characteristics of such an approach are described and discussed. These
include a focus on the plea for help by the patient, issues
of availability and workability on the patient's part (i.e.,
issues of motivation), the establishment of a contract,
issues of time and its effective use (e.g., setting of time
and frequency of sessions), the use of anxiety (either
increasing it or decreasing it).

1164.   Rubinstein, D., Rehospitalization
          versus family crisis, American Journal
          of Psychiatry, 1972, 129, 715-720.

The Temple Follow-up at the Eastern Pennsylvania Psychiatric
Institute has provided a team approach to crisis intervention
with the goal of preventing or shortening rehospitalization
for former inpatients. In this pilot year we have been able
to establish that, through mobilizing family support, we
can encourage and sustain the successful resolution of a
patient crisis without resorting to hospitalization. We
have been able to observe some constructive changes in
family systems as we prevented "scapegoating" or the exclusion of family members in an emergency situation. We
have demonstrated that family "closeness" can provide support
instead of conflict and were able to use this to implement
healthier relationships. A by-product of our work has been

the development of the concept that a family can and should
share responsibility for the patient's treatment. Although
we can identify areas for the improvement and needed expansion of this approach, these preliminary results indicate
that the continued use of the crisis team will provide a
constructive base for preventive psychiatric care. (Journal
summary).

1165.   Rubinstein, D., Family crisis intervention
         as an alternative to rehospitalization, in,
         Maserman, J. (ed.), Current Psychiatric
         Therapies, Grune and Stratton, 1974.

Rubinstein outlines a program to prevent or reduce duration
of rehospitalization among former inpatients. He discusses
various signals of impending crisis amoung formerly hospitalized patients, and notes that the anxiety frequently engen-
dered by a patient's return to his family affords maximum
leverage in preventive work. The composition of the crisis
team and treatment techniques utilized under this program
are outlined. A home visit by a psychiatric nurse is often
the initial contact with the patient and his family.
Observations made at this time aid in the development of
further treatment strategies. These explicitly acknowledge
the importance of the family system with respect to the
identified patient's ability to function. Two case illustrations are presented. Rubinstein briefly considers some
problems areas for the service--particularly the pervasive
view, held by families and staff, of the hospital as a
"haven". He summarizes results of a six-month pilot study
which strongly suggest the effectiveness of this program
in reducing rehospitalization rates. (abstract by Deborah
Schuller).

1166.   Rusk, T.N., Opportunity and technique
         in crisis psychiatry, Comprehensive
         Psychiatry, 1971, 12, 249-263.

The author describes specific techniques used in crisis
intervention, and relates these to theory. The moment of
crisis for the individual is seen as a critical opportunity
for rapid change, with the therapist helping the patient
attain an independent course of action. Thus the guideline

is presented that the therapist should do for the patient
that which the patient cannot do for themselves, but no
more! Some of the advantages of dealing with people in
crisis (e.g., increased opportunity for rapid change due
to increased vulnerability) and disadvantages (e.g., limited
information and time constraints) are discussed. Use of
affective release, fostering maturity, focussing on current
life problems and unsatisfied needs created by the crisis,
providing a consensual formulation so that the patient can
understand what has happened, thus decreasing anxiety, the
use of feedback, and emphasizing the positive, are all
examples of such tactics.

1167.   Rusk, T.N., and Edwards, B.J.,
         Psychiatric emergencies, in Warner,
         C.G. (ed.), Emergency care: Assessment
         and intervention, St. Louis, C.V. Mosby
         Co., 1978.

This chapter covers a broad range of issues related to
psychiatric emergencies. The concept of crisis is discussed, and general principles of management of crises are
reviewed, including both assessment and treatment, and
therapy tactics. Examples of specific emergency situations
and their management are also presented (e.g., suicidal
behavior, anxiety and panic situations, aggressive and
bizarre behavior, alcohol and other drug related emergencies,
organic brain syndromes, self-mutilating patients, uncooperative patients, etc.). The active involvement of the therapist is highlighted, with the aim of restoring a previous
level of functioning and stability.

1168.   Rusk, T.N., and Gerner, R.H., A study of
         the process of emergency psychotherapy,
         American Journal of Psychiatry, 1972,
         128, 882-886.

The authors studied the relationship between the amount of
therapist talk time during crisis session interviews and
the relief of distress in 38 emergency room patients. They
found that in the sessions judged as successful the therapists talked significantly less in the first one third of

the interviews and significantly more in the last third
and had larger increases in the amount of talk time from
the first to the last third. (Journal abstract).

1169.   Ryle, A., The focus in brief interpretive
         psychotherapy: Dilemmas, traps and snags
         as target problems, British Journal of
         Psychiatry, 1979, 134, 46-54.

The need for a focus for brief interpretive psychotherapy
is considered and a new approach is suggested. In this
method, the ways in which the patient's construction of
himself and his relationships are related to this problem
are identified and expressed in the form of dilemmas, traps,
and snags. It is suggested that these formulations represent
an appropriate level of abstraction, allowing patient and
therapist to share provisional hypotheses about the goals of
therapy and offering the basis for a method of measuring how
far these goals are achieved. (Journal abstract).

1170.   Sabin, J., Case reports of the Massa-
         chusetts Mental Health Center: VI -
         short-term therapy of impotence and
         anxiety, Psychiatric Opinion, 1968,
         5, 38-42.

The author provides a description of a five session individual psychotherapy experience with a 23 year old single male
whose presenting complaints were anxiety and impotency. A
one year follow-up is reported.

1171.   Sacks, M.H., et al., Crisis and emergency
         in the psychiatric ward, Comprehensive
         Psychiatry, 1974, 15, 79-85.

The authors offer a conceptual model that facilitates recognition and management of crisis and emergency on a psychiatric ward. Emphasis is placed on aspects of the group
structure, rather than upon the individual who may precipitate the emergency. The model premises overt and covert
tasks. The overt task of a unit is generally defined as
treatment of patients; but the authors note that unacknowl-
edged, covert tasks often exert powerful antitherapeutic

effects. If these covert tasks sufficiently undermine the
primary task of treatment, a ward may be considered to be
in a crisis state. Sacks, et al. present an example in
which resolution of a ward emergency entailed recognition
of an ongoing ward crisis. Stresses which tend to sabotage
the work task are briefly examined. The authors then describe signs indicative of a crisis state--e.g., disorganization, lack of cohesiveness, boundary losses, loss of
role definition, appearance of covert leaders, displacement
of hostility through stereotyping, etc. The authors conclude by discussing various steps which maximize the recognition and resolution of ward crises--thereby minimizing
the potential for an emergency. (abstract by Deborah
Schuller).

    1172.   Sadock, B., and Gould, R.E., A preliminary
             report on short-term group psychotherapy
             on an acute adolescent male service,
             International Journal of Group Psycho-
             therapy, 1964, 15, 465-473.

Group therapy was begun on a short-term basis on the male
adolescent service at Bellevue Hospital to augment its
therapeutic program. The nature of the group was transient
throughout the four months this study was in progress, but
the rapid turnover of patients presented no major obstacle
to the over-all functioning of the group. The status of
the group in the total ward situation was unique and carried
with it increased prestige. It was found that the therapist
must function in a nonpunitive and noncritical manner. At
the same time he must set limits on the behavior of the
group as a whole. In addition, the goal-directed therapist
activity is essential. A group image with which the members
identified was formed around the therapist, with each of the
members contributing to it. This group image was one of the
most potent therapeutic forces in group. The group experience was of help to the patient going on for further psychiatric treatment. For many, this was their first encounter
with a psychiatrist, and the over-all positive response
enabled them to relate more effectively with future therapists. (Journal summary).

1173.   Sadock, B., et al., Short-term group
         psychotherapy in a psychiatric walk-in
         clinic, American Journal of Orthopsy-
         chiatry, 1968, 28, 724-732.

The authors report on a brief group therapy program at a
walk-in psychiatric clinic at the New York Medical College-
Metropolitan Hospital Center. Sessions were held once/week,
for a total of 10 sessions, although a number of patients
attended fewer than the total number of sessions. Membership in the group was open-ended, in that new members were
added as the 10 week limit came for others. The total
sample was 28 patients, who were both socially and economically deprived. Broad guidelines were used for patient
selection for this program, exclusions limited to individuals
with paranoid ideation. Cotherapists were used, consisting
of a psychiatrist and psychiatric social worker. The advantages of such a team is discussed. The average number of
sessions attended was five. All patients who attended the
entire 10 sessions were rated as improved (therapist and
patient judgements), and of those who attended less than
10 sessions, 44% were rated as improved. The treatment
techniques used are discussed, two case histories presented.

1174.   Safer, D.J., Family therapy for children
         with behavior disorders, Family Process,
         1966, 5, 243-255.

Over a two year period, short-term family therapy was
attempted with 29 children who presented with behavior
problem. All of the cases were selected because at the
diagnostic staff conference they were considered either
unmotivated or unacceptable for individual psychotherapy.
The early treatment approach aimed at the following:
interrupting repetitive, unrewarding parent-child conflict
patterns; supporting the parents to more adequately structure and enforce the major rules of the home; and encouraging
self-reliant social behavior by the child. Conjoint sessions
focussed on the practical results of behavior. To further
the treatment, the therapist actively intervened as an
educator, a manipulator, and as a temporary structuring
member of the family. After conflictive family interaction
lessened, the therapy focus shifted to supporting the positive aspects of identification between the child and the

parent of the same sex. Independent socialization by the
previously negatively involved parent was also supported.
As a result of therapeutic involvement, forty percent of
the patients showed marked improvement. Thus, treatment
for the seemingly unmotivated with behavior problems can
yield positive results. (Journal summary).

1175.   Safirstein, S.L., Psychiatric aftercare
         in a general hospital: Some basic
         principles and their implications for
         community psychiatry, Psychiatric
         Quarterly, 1968, 42, 751-758.

Ever-increasing numbers of aftercare patients in the Department of Psychiatry of The Mount Sinai Hospital of New York,
led to a revision of the philosophy and a reorganization of
the services of aftercare. The functional approach rather
than change in personality makeup was emphasized as a
criterion for improvement. The reliance on the charismatic
aspects of the hospital (institutional transference) was
sufficient to maintain the patient's functioning in the
community. The knowledge that should he require help, he
would receive it in the aftercare clinic reinforced his
confidence in the hospital. Family therapy was begun with
selected cases as a further step toward the patient's
staying and functioning in the community. Aftercare is
viewed as an integral part of the continuum of care of the
patient. These changes not only permitted a higher discharge rate, but also laid the groundwork for aftercare to
become a part of community psychiatry with its important
preventive implication. (Journal summary modified).

1176.   Safirstein, S.L., The clinging patient -
         a serious management problem, Canadian
         Psychiatric Association Journal, 1972,
         17, 221-225.

A psychotherapeutic approach in which restoration of function
is the main goal is suggested. This approach advocates non-
interference with the compulsive need to cling by facilitating relationships on the outside where the patient can
fulfill this need and by structuring a brief therapeutic
relationship, forming and maintaining an institutional

type of transference interminably. This is supportive
without the patient having to be in active treatment. The
doctor-patient relationship is the instrument of healing
which allows the patient to function when his pattern of
clinging is being undermined by events in life. The method
of treatment is unrelated to the cause of the problem.
(Journal conclusion).

> 1177.   Safirstein, S.L., Psychotherapy for
>   geriatric patients, New York State
>   Journal of Medicine, 1972, 72,
>   2743-2748.

The author presents short summaries covering a total of 10
cases of therapy with older patients. Of the 10, three
needed to continue in longer term therapy, but seven were
able to benefit from a brief therapy experience. Such short-
term treatment of the elderly focussed on a goal-directed
approach, using a psychodynamic viewpoint, and involved
extensive use of the patient's own resources.

> 1178.   Safirstein, S.L., What can the medical
>   practitioner do for patients recently
>   discharged from mental hospitals?
>   Psychosomatics, 1974, 15, 160-163.

I hope to have demonstrated that the medical practitioner
is suited and qualified to responsibly care for and treat
patients with a history of admissions to a mental hospital.
The availability and accessibility of psychiatric consultation is necessary, especially when the practitioner is
relatively inexperienced. The medical model and the medical
tradition are such that they allow rather easily the incorporation of such patients into any medical practice.
Superficial, supportive psychotherapy is no obstacle because
any practitioner is familiar with it. (Journal summary
modified).

1179.   Sanders, S., An exploration of
         utilization techniques in short-
         term hypnotherapy, American Journal
         of Clinical Hypnosis, 1977, 20,
         76-79.

The purpose of this paper is to explore Erickson's concept
of utilization in short term hypnotherapy with two clients
who had unsuccessful psychotherapy. The resistant patient
is described as a person who has lost hope and is imposing
that loss onto the therapist. A description of the major
therapeutic intervention is presented and related to the
importance of (1) hope that things can be different and
(2) the therapist's responsibility for demonstrating that
change is possible. (Journal abstract).

1180.   Sanders, S., Creative problem-solving
         and psychotherapy, International Journal
         of Clinical and Experimental Hypnosis,
         1978, 26, 15-21.

The techniques described comprise a creative problem-solving
approach to short-term individual psychotherapy which appears
effective in conjunction with hypnosis. The techniques
include describing and visualizing the client's problem,
imagining alternatives reactions, dreaming about new
solutions, and trying the solutions in real life. The
method is illustrated by 2 clinical examples. The discussion
focuses on a comparison of the techniques used with individuals versus with small groups, the fostering of regression
in the service of the ego, and the redirection of attention
from the physically out of control to the recognition of the
possibility of obtaining control. This shift of attention
fosters active coping on the part of the client. (Journal
abstract).

1181.   Sang, D.M., Re-establishing communication
         between parents and their young children
         following a disruptive life crisis,
         Journal of Clinical Child Psychology,
         1979, 8, 52-55.

The author presents a particular therapeutic technique which
is recommended as an approach for parents and their children

who are experiencing common life crises. The value of a
direct approach, and of the importance of dealing with the
needs of both parents and their children are stressed.
Types of questions raised by children are examined through
the use of case material. Included are examples of the
preverbal child as well.

1182.   Sarvis, M.A., et al., A concept of
         ego-oriented psychotherapy, Psychiatry,
         1959, 22, 277-287.

This paper reports our efforts to formulate a flexible,
relatively time-limited, ego-oriented psychotherapy.
Although, the settings in which we have developed this
concept, philosophical and expedient motives--for example,
responsibility to a large, relatively fixed patient population with equal rights to service--have been important,
we do not feel that this type of ego-oriented psychotherapy
is a method of desperation, but rather one of choice for a
wide range of patients. (Journal abstract).

1183.   Satloff, A., and Worby, C.M., The
         psychiatric emergency service:
         Mirror of change, American Journal
         of Psychiatry, 1970, 126, 1628-1632.

The authors compared the population contacting a psychiatric
emergency service in 1958 with that contacting it in 1968.
Among the most striking findings were the shift to a younger
age group being treated, the lower rate of referral to inpatient care, and an increase in patient load that greatly
exceeded the area population increase. The implications
of the findings for the planning of an adequate network of
community mental health facilities are discussed.

1184.   Satterfield, W.C., Short-term group
         therapy for people in crisis, Hospital
         and Community Psychiatry, 1977, 28,
         539-541.

The author describes a short-term group therapy program
that he believes is more effective than the traditional one-
to-one approach for people in crisis. The group focusses
on the problems of one member at a time and helps him
examine his role, identity, and value system, the significant people in his community, and his ability to appreciate
the positive things that exist within himself. Short-term
goal-setting, self-evaluation, and written homework assignments are used to teach the client a new process that can
help him look at his life positively and accept defeats and
failures as a part of the growth process. (Journal abstract).

1185.   Saucier, J.F., Brief psychotherapy in
         periods of crisis: Preliminary notes,
         Canadian Psychiatric Association Journal,
         1968, 13, 243-248.

In an article written in French with an English summary,
the author describes a brief therapy program (six sessions)
at the Notre-Dame Hospital in Montreal. The crisis oriented
approach is detailed on a session to session basis across
the total of six sessions.

1186.   Saul, L.J., On the value of one or two
         interviews, Psychoanalytic Quarterly,
         1951, 20, 613-616.

A case history of a woman suffering chronically from severe
hypochondriasis, seen two times with a three week interval
between visits, is presented. The patient gained insight
into the dynamics underlying her symptom, and thus acquired
increased confidence in her ability to handle future difficulties. One year later, these gains appear to have been
maintained. The author affirms that "if the case is suitable, and if the analytic interpretation is accurate and
sharply focused upon the central issues", two interviews
can be of therapeutic value. (abstract by Deborah Schuller).

1187.   Saul, L.J., Brief therapy in a case
         of Torticollis, Samiska, 1953, 7,
         139-141.

1188.   Schafer, R., The termination of brief
         psychoanalytic psychotherapy, Inter-
         national Journal of Psychoanalytic
         Psychotherapy, 1973, 2, 135-148.

Some essential aspect of brief psychoanalytic psychotherapy
are described, including changes it may bring about and
critical problems that develop around the issue of termination. These problems imply narcissistic aspirations and
perspectives on life itself, which shap transference,
counter-transference, resistance, and regression. Especially emphasized is the reduction of radical discontinuities,
both cross-sectional and longitudinal, in one's knowledge
about abd tolerance of onself - a reduction which implies
reduced hopelessness. These changes are part of the
patient's enlarged view of the extent and nature of his
problems and of his activity in apparent passivity. This
enlarged view develops particularly out of scrutinizing
difficulties in the therapeutic relationship, especially
resistance, and understanding them as repetitions of chronic
life problems. In conclusion, some questions are raised
about validation and the applicability of behavioral science
concepts and methods in a field whose proper methods, data,
and conclusions are those of historical understanding.
(Journal abstract).

1189.   Scherz, F.H., Maturational crises and
         parent-child interaction, Social
         Casework, 1971, 52, 362-369.

The author highlights three universal tasks of a psychological nature, and relates these to crises which arise in
the life cycle within a family context. The universal
psychological tasks include independence/dependence,
intimacy/distance, emotional separation/interdependence or
connectedness.. A general description of crises is presented, and specific transitional family life crises are
delineated. These include adjustments related to marriage,
birth of a first child, child's first strivings for autonomy

(focussed on toilet training issues) separation issues
(focussed around first school year, adolescent conflicts
and the family, the leaving of children from home to seek
their own adulthood and the crises for the marriage of the
parents, and the problems associated with advancing years).
The critical issue of communication within the family
through all of these maturational crises is highlighted,
along with suggestions for case workers.

1190.   Schilder, P., Psychotherapy, New York,
         W.W. Norton, 1938.

Presents material in favor of a brief form of psychotherapy.
The author uses an initial discussion of symptoms with the
patient, followed by free association and dream interpretation. The therapist then presents to the patient a synthesis of the patient's conflicts by reconstructing the
patient's life within a given context of the therapist's
understanding of the major conflicts. The author emphasizes
the skill needed for such a process, and suggests that
beginning therapists will not have developed such expertise.
As in the longer therapies, the therapist uses the transference developed in the treatment process with the aim of
dissolving it toward the end of treatment. He reports that
the average length of this treatment was approximately 30
sessions. Symptom relief usually occurred within the first
10-15 hours, but relapses also appeared. By explaining the
reasons for such relapses, the author indicated that the
gains made were usually maintained. Hypnosis was also used.
A major focus involved emphasizing the need for the patient
to formulate his own life plans, and in this regard the
meaning of transference was clearly explained to each patient
with the aim of aiding in the development of independence in
the patient. The author believed that the overall goal of
brief therapy was the "cure" (i.e. alleviation) of symptoms.

1191.   Schmideberg, M., Short-analytic therapy,
         Nervous Child, 1950, 8, 281-290.

The author, originally trained as a classical analyst,
reports on a number of cases in which a briefer, analytic
therapy achieved positive and for the most part lasting

results (some patients followed up as much as 10 years after
termination). The focus of the technique is on conscious
personality and strengths of the patient, time-focussed on
the present reality and emotions of the patient, and using
a more active and directive approach. The use of early
improvements of patients in brief therapy is highlighted
and their importance discussed.

1192.   Schoenberg, B., and Carr, A.C., An
         investigation of criteria for brief
         psychotherapy of neurodermatitis,
         Psychosomatic Medicine, 1963, 25,
         253-263.

Neurodermatitis patients were treated in brief psychotherapy,
following a specific method of treatment designed to encourage and reinforce the expression of hostility toward contemporary life conflicts. Significant differences were
found between those who were successfully treated and those
who were not. Of those investigated factors related to outcome, two (intensity of overt hostility as inferred from
initial interviews and hostile-content responses on the
Rorschach test) showed significant differences, although
not in the predicted direction. Such factors as inferred
motivation for treatment, likelihood of dangerous acting
out, verbal resources, and the likelihood of a psychotic
decompensation did not appear to be related to outcome.
There was no evidence of significant symptom substitution
or of dangerous acting out in the course of treatment.
Results support the hypotheses that patients with neurodermatitis can be treated in brief therapy with successful
remission of their symptoms and that patients who do not
improve or who discontinue the prescribed form of treatment
differ significantly from those who complete is successfully.
(Journal abstract).

1193.   Schonfield, J., et al., Patient-therapist
         convergence and measure of improvement in
         short-term psychotherapy, Psychotherapy:
         Theory, Research, and Practice, 1969, 6,
         267-272.

The authors reports on a study in which the relationship
between similarity of therapist/patient opinions and

improvement in therapy was the focus. Five experienced
psychiatrists were the therapists and a total of 32 patients
participated in one-to-one, one session/week for 15 weeks.
The results indicate that those patients who viewed themselves as most changed in a positive way also had the
greatest amount of similarity between their opinions and
those of their therapists.

1194.   Schonfield, J., and Donner, L., Student
         psychotherapists' speciality choices
         and changes in their perceptions of
         self and patients, Journal of Medical
         Education, 1972, 47, 645-651.

The researchers classified 44 medical students into tech-
nique-oriented and patient-oriented groups. Their perceptions of themselves and their patients prior to and immediately following their involvement as therapists in a brief
psychotherapy clinic were measured. No significant differences in opinions of psychotherapy were obtained between
the two medical student groups, either prior to or following
therapy, nor was there any significant difference in the
perceived degree of success between the two groups. A
Semantic Differential Scale was used to evaluate therapist
perceptions of their clients, and some significant differences were obtained. The issue of the active physician/
passive patient relationship was discussed as it relates
to the experiences of the students in this study.

1195.   Schulberg, H.C., and Sheldon, A., The
         probability of crisis and strategies
         for preventive intervention, Archives
         of General Psychiatry, 1968, 18,
         552-558.

The authors present a discussion on the characteristics of
crisis situations. They include such things as how the
individual perceives environmentally-produced stress, the
stress itself, the clinical syndrome of crisis, (e.g.,
signs of inner tension, unpleasant affect, disorganization
of function), and transitional life stage crises (e.g.,
adolescence, marriage, pregnancy, mid-life crises, etc.).

A probability formulation of crisis is proposed based on 3
factors: the probability that a hazardous event will occur;
the probability that an individual will be exposed to this
event; and the individual's vulnerability to this event.
Based upon this formulation, strategies for intervention
can be selected according to the predictability and frequency
of the hazardous efent or personal vulnerability or both.
A variety of anticipatory and participatory intervention
techniques are reviewed and initial guidelines are suggested
for their selection in averting crisis. (Journal summary
adapted).

    1196.   Schulman, J.L., One visit psychotherapy
             with children, Progress in Psychotherapy,
             1960, 5, 86-93.

The author presents a summary of brief therapy (one session)
work done with 20 children and their families. None of the
parents were psychotic, although they did exhibit varying
degrees of neurosis. None were involved in a complete
marital breakdown, although many of the couples were experiencing marital difficulty. The presenting problems of the
children ranged widely, and included suicide attempts, and
encopresis. Critical for acceptance into this program was
an assessment as to whether the child's symptoms had become
part of the personality, or were still a reaction to a
family situation (i.e., whether the symptoms were fixed and
rigidly part of the child's personality). Those children
for whom this had in fact occurred, were excluded from the
program. The specific structure of the one session, (three
hours) is described, which included the following five-step
format: a) greeting of parents and child; b) history-taking
from patents; c) individual focus on the child for diagnostic
purposes; d) overview and feedback presentation to parents
only; and, e) overview and feedback to child and parents.
A follow-up visit was also arranged usually occuring six
months after the initial contact. Of the 20 children, 15
had shown satisfactory improvement (alleviation of symptoms
and improvement in family relationships). A case is presented to elucidate the type of program described.

1197.   Schwartz, D.A., Therapeutic intervention
in crisis, International Psychiatry
Clinics, 1969, 6, 297-315.

In this paper, Schwartz employs the term "crisis" in its
broadest sense, as a frequent occurrence in the human
experience. Crisis is defined as temporary disruption of
equilibrium produced by external or intrapsychic stress,
which may result in psychiatric symptoms. Crisis is subjectively perceived, in relation to a person's sense of
ability to cope with the stressful situation. Thus,
implicitly, crisis may be conceived as a "nodal point", at
which individuals either learn more adaptive coping
behaviors or retreat and avoid growth. Following his discussion of the nature of crisis and its consequences,
Schwartz examines rationale for intervention into the crisis
process. He offers that the measure of the desirability of
intervention is tied proportionately to the differential
between growth that would occur with unaided resolution and
that which would result from professionally-assisted resolution. General ground rules of crisis intervention and
resolution are explored--whether to intervene, at what
point, how, for how long. Schwartz briefly discusses some
difficulties inherent in the practice of crisis intervention,
then focuses on mental health consultation as a related
technique. He concludes by considering the future of crisis
intervention within the framework of soaring demand for
mental health services. (abstract by Deborah Schuller).

1198.   Schwartz, D.A., et al., Community
psychiatry and emergency service,
American Journal of Psychiatry, 1972,
129, 710-715.

The authors report on a study comparing those patients who
were seen only once over a 4 month period versus those who
were seen more than once. The total sample surveyed was
552 patients, who were treated at an emergency unit of a
large medical center. It was found that patients with
personality disorders including those suffering from
alcohol and other drug problems, used the service more
frequently and needed to be hospitalized more often. Those
with situational crises usually only needed one visit, with
no hospitalization. The average length of stay was 34
hours. (Journal abstract).

1199.   Schwartz, M.D., Situation/transition
         groups: A conceptualization and review,
         American Journal of Orthopsychiatry,
         1975, 45, 744-755.

Small discussion-education groups moderated by a trained
leader have been used in a variety of settings for the
mutual assistance of individuals who share some stressful
life situation. This paper reviews the literature on a
broad range of such groups, and finds they have common
characteristics, modes of function, and problems of leadership. The situation group is seen as being an important
primary preventive approach for both mental and physical
health problems. (Journal abstract).

1200.   Schwartz, M.D., and Errera, P.,
         Psychiatric care in a general hospital
         emergency room, II. Diagnostic features,
         Archives of General Psychiatry, 1963, 9,
         113-121.

The diagnostic characteristics of patients seen by psychiatrists in the emergency room of a general hospital over a
year's time were presented. The group of patients was
found to differ from reported psychiatric outpatient clinic
populations in a number of respects. Some explanations and
implications of these differences were discussed. Comment
was made about problems concerning the psychiatric nomen-
clature which arose during the study. (Journal summary).

1201.   Schwartz, S.L., A review of crisis
         intervention programs, Psychiatric
         Quarterly, 1971, 45, 498-508.

The author describes three types of crises: a) psychiatric
emergencies; b) accidental crises; c) developmental crises.
The general characteristics of all crises are described,
including the stages of crises. General principles of
therapy related to helping individuals in crisis are reviewed
(e.g., fact finding, setting up manageable goals, etc.). An
overview of primary prevention programs is provided, in
which professional help is provided to those individuals
experiencing a developmental or accidental crisis. Secondary prevention programs are also summarized, with the main

goal of restoring functioning and minimizing disability.
Methods used to avoid hospitalization are described (e.g.,
walk-in clinics, home visits, telephone hot-lines, and
family intervention programs), and methods used to shorten
the length of hospital stays are also discussed. Some
research findings regarding the operation of these types of
programs is offered, with positive results highlighted.

1202.   Schwarz, C.J., and Tyhurst, J.S., An
         emergency psychiatric service in a
         general hospital, Canadian Medical
         Association Journal, 1964, 90,
         1260-1264.

The same extensive range of general hospital facilities
should be allocated to emergency psychiatric illness as are
available for other medical conditions. During the study
herein reported, for every three medical consultations in
the emergency ward of a large general hospital, two psychiatric consultations were requested. Over a two-year period
when 24-hour coverage by psychiatric consultants was
instituted, such assessments increased from 148 to 340
(during the first four months of each year); the increase
in police referrals was outstanding, rising from 16 to 105.
The general wards of the hospital assumed greater responsibility for further medical treatment, while committal to
the mental hospital declined. Many more psychiatric patients
could have been treated in the general hospital if facilities
had been available. The development of an emergency psychiatric service is not an easy process and co-ordination with
other psychiatric resources is required. Residents in
training face situations in the emergency ward which are not
encountered in any other aspect of their clinical experience.
(Journal abstract).

1203.   Seagull, A.A., Must the deeply disturbed
         have long-term treatment? Psychotherapy:
         Theory, Research, and Practice, 1966, 3,
         36-42.

A single case history is presented by the author. A two
session client-centered approach was used in dealing with
a couple in therapy. The treatment allowed both members

to indicate that each had wanted a divorce, a fact which
they had not shared with each other. Agreement was reached
between them to move toward a divorce. The focus was on
resolving the crisis between the husband and wife, and not
on alleviating or eliminating the wife's bizarre behavior.

1204.   Seibovich, M.A., Short-term insight
         psychotherapy for hysterical person-
         alities, Psychotherapy and Psycho-
         somatics, 1974, 24, 67-78.

The focus here is on the phases of brief, insight-oriented
therapy for personality disorders. One of the presenting
characteristics of such patients is the seeming lack of
major psychological problems. Yet they tend to alienate
themselves from others in personal relationships and tend
to suffer from such isolation. The value of planning
specific strategies for therapy with such individuals is
detailed along with the importance of clearly and explicitly
demarcating the stages of therapy. The criteria used to
select patients for a brief insight therapy and specific
techniques used are presented, and highlighted with material
from a case history.

1205.   Seitz, P.F.D., Dynamically oriented
         brief psychotherapy in psycho-cutaneous
         excoriation syndromes, Psychosomatic
         Medicine, 1953, 15, 200-213.

An experimental, dynamically-oriented brief psychotherapeutic method was investigated in 25 patients with psycho-
cutaneous-excoriation syndromes. The experimental psychotherapeutic procedure was directive rather than non-directive,
and was focussed upon those dynamic factors which were
postulated in advance to be significant for psychocutaneous
excoriation syndromes. The results obtained with this method
are presented and discussed. The method appears to present
certain potential advantages for several immediate problems.
Although "symptomatic cure" was achieved in a substantial
percentage of patients with this brief psychotherapeutic
method, a relatively large number of patients discontinued
treatment before it was completed; the results were complicated in other cases by the development of temporary undesir-

able character traits; in still other cases, relapse of the cutaneous disorder occurred in association with gradual return of masochistic defenses against hostile-aggressive impulses; and temporary, therapeutically-induced aggravation of the cutaneous disorder became serious enough to require hospitalization in one case. For the present, this brief psychotherapeutic method should be considered an experimental procedure, the clinical applicability of which must await further refinement and investigative trial. (Journal summary).

1206.   Selinger, D., and Barcai, A., Brief
         family therapy may lead to deep per-
         sonality change, American Journal of
         Psychotherapy, 1977, 31, 302-309.

Symptom release, behavior change, improved functioning at work and in society, concomitant with change in "man figure" drawings, were accidentally discovered during brief therapy involving a 15 1/2 year old boy with a falsetto voice. He and his family were treated by crisis intervention, and the follow-up lasted about 9 months. These findings are used to support the contentions that: (1) the direction of the overall ego integration may closely coincide with alterations in "man figure" drawings; and (2) a depth impact on personality may result from brief family therapy. (Journal summary).

1207.   Semrad, E.V., et al., Brief psychotherapy,
         American Journal of Psychotherapy, 1966,
         20, 579-598.

The authors present an overview of the various types of patients they have found have been helped by brief psychotherapy, and how each type should be dealt with. Specifically they divide up these patients into those exhibiting narcissistic regressions, affective regressions, and neurotic regressions, documenting the types of issues and difficulties which arise in dealing with each type of patient in therapy of short-duration. Issues of assessment, are also carefully reviewed. The essence of brief therapy is defined as helping the patient define more clearly the obstacle in their present life situation, and helping to solve such a present-oriented difficulty.

1208.   Serrano, A.C., and Gibson, G., Mental
         health services to the Mexican-American
         community in San Antonia, Texas, American
         Journal of Public Health, 1973, 63, 1055-
         1057.

The authors discuss problems of providing mental health
services to the Mexican-Americans who comprise 40 per cent
of the population in one Texas county. Serrano and Gibson
describe specific changes in philosophy and procedure
implemented to close the gap between the Mexican-American
community and existing institutions. A case vignette
illustrates the type of "cultural awareness" by the helping
agency which has facilitated work with this group. The
authors suggest that the role of the mental health professional be conceived as mediating consultant and facili-
tator--with a decreasing emphasis on the more traditional
role as "therapist". (abstract by Deborah Schuller).

1209.   Shafii, M., Short term psychotherapy in
         adult school phobia: A transcultural
         perspective, International Journal of
         Psychoanalytic Psychotherapy, 1974, 3,
         166-177.

This is a report of the presence of school phobia in four
adults. These patients, who were either graduate or undergraduate students between ages of 19 and 28, manifested
symptoms commonly associated with school phobia, such as
an irrational dread of going to school, acute anxiety and
psychophysiological reactions in the form of headache,
nausea, diarrhea, chest pain and stomach ache. Two of these
patients were foreign students. School phobia in adults is
conceptualized as a reactivation of an earlier but untreated
childhood school phobia. From a genetic point of view, it
is related to an unresolved and ambivalent mother-child
relationship during the separation-individuation phase of
child development. The need for recognition and immediate
therapeutic intervention is stressed. Short-term psychotherapeutic treatment and crisis intervention methods of
helping the patient start school immediately are discussed.
(Journal abstract).

1210.   Shafii, M., et al., The development of
         acute short-term inpatient child
         psychiatric setting: A pediatric-
         psychiatric model, American Journal of
         Psychiatry, 1979, 136, 427-429.

Describes the establishment of a unit for children that
emphasizes the integration of the pediatric model of acute,
short-term inpatient care with the psychological and
developmental perspective of the psychiatric model. Of the
145 children admitted during the first year, more than 33%
manifested aggressive or hyperactive behavior and 25%
depression or suicidal behavior. 85% were discharged to
their homes or previous residences after an average length
of stay of 24 days. It is suggested that similar units
established in children's hospitals or general hospitals
could help meet the urgent need for acute inpatient psychiatric care of children in this country. (Journal abstract).

1211.   Shapiro, S.H., Preventive analysis
         following a trauma: a 4 1/2 year old
         girl witnesses a stillbirth, Psycho-
         analytic Study of the Child, 1973, 28,
         249-255.

An account of the treatment of a 4 1/2 year-old girl has
been presented. The goal of therapy was to prevent the
traumatic effects of having witnessed a stillbirth at home.
The rationale for a prompt brief psychoanalytic treatment
prior to the resolution of the child's oedipal phase was
discussed. The methodology of such an approach relied upon
analytic insights into the developmental process. The
necessity for close cooperation and involvement of the mother
of the preschool child in the treatment process was amply
corroborated. The technique aimed at fostering verbalization
and identification of affects to facilitate ego mastery over
the traumatic events. The traumatic episode was reconstruc-
ted and connections between masturbation guilt and hospitalization were disrupted. Sexual information was given about
the birth process and procreation to help Linda assimilate
appropriately what she had seen. The apparent successful
outcome, as seen in a 10-year follow-up, encourages the use
of such an approach as an example of an abbreviated psychoanalytic therapy suitable for use in preventing the effects
of trauma on the developing personality. (Journal summary).

1212.   Shaw, P., A study of social problems
         in a group of young women treated with
         brief psychotherapy, British Journal
         of Medical Psychology, 1977, 50,
         155-161.

A total of nine young women were seen in a relatively short-
term treatment. Presenting problems included seven with
overt depression and two with phobic anxiety accompanied by
some depression. The therapy process uncovered the fathers'
reactions to their daughters adolescence, and the subsequent
social problems with men which developed in these women.

1213.   Shaw, R., et al., A short-term treatment
         program in a child guidance clinic,
         Social Work, 1968, 13, 81-90.

At the Madeleine Borg Child Guidance Institute, New York
City, 227 families were treated in a short-term program with
contact limited to a maximum of 12 sessions. The results
demonstrate that with proper case selection, short-term
treatment is an efficacious type of intervention that produces durable benefits. The results emphasize the importance
of crisis, school phobia, short duration of symptoms, total
family participation and readiness for change as criteria
for selection of clients most likely to benefit from short-
term treatment. Moreover, diagnoses of neurosis and inhibition of aggression were associated with higher rates of
improvement. This mode of treatment does not seem well
suited for the aggressive child. (Journal abstract and
summary adapted).

1214.   Sheeley, W.F., Short term psychiatric
         therapy, Psychocomatics, 1961, 2,
         122-126.

Sheeley presents several general guidelines for the nonpsychiatric physician who wishes to practise brief psychotherapy with selected patients. Preparations for short
term therapy include detailed medical and psychiatric workups. Having arrived at a psychiatric diagnosis, the
physician formulates explicit therapeutic goals, and treatment methods most likely to effect these. The author
enumerates possible goals and some specific treatments

available to the physician. Sheeley does suggest that whenever possible, acute psychiatric cases be treated in the
community rather than the institution. Treatment begins
with an exploration with the patient of his present life
situation. Planned environmental manipulation may then be
carried out to improve patient-environment interactions.
Sheeley discusses other resources available to the physician:
a working arrangement with a psychiatrist as an adjunctive
therapist; psychotropic drugs; and post-graduate courses to
enlarge psychiatric skills. (abstract by Deborah Schuller).

1215.   Sheikh, A.A., Eidetic psychotherapy,
         in, Singer, J.L., and Pope, K.S. (eds.),
         The power of human imagination, New York,
         Plenum Publishing, 1978.

This chapter reviews the work of a number of practitioners
and researchers of eidetic psychotherapy. Issues covered
include the classification of mental images, after-images,
eidetic images, memory images, imagination images, Ahsen's
ISM eidetic image (image, somatic pattern, and meaning),
eidetics and electrically-evoked recollection, diagnostic
and therapy procedures, etc. A case history is provided to
highlight many of the issues raised. The value of such an
approach as one method of brief therapy is stressed, especially in psychosomatic conditions which have not yielded to
verbal and/or behavioral therapies. Its use in individual
and group therapy, and in self-analysis and self-education
is also reviewed.

1216.   Sheikh, A.A., and Panagiotou, N.C.,
         Use of mental imagery in psychotherapy:
         A critical review, Perceptual and Motor
         Skills, 1975, 41, 555-585.

The paper presents arguments in favor of the use of mental
imagery for therapeutic purposes. Several existing imagery
approaches to psychotherapy are critically examined and
suggestions for future inquiry are offered. The intimate
relation between imagery and the effective-somatic process
is stressed. (Journal summary).

1217.   Shellow, R.S., et al., Family group
         therapy in retrospect: A review of
         four years and 60 families, Family
         Process, 1963, 2, 52-67.

Shellow, et al. first state central assumptions which under-
lay the decision of one community mental health clinic to
treat families as a unit. After a brief description of the
clinic staff and therapy, the authors present a systematic
review of the characteristics of 60 families selected for
Family Group Therapy: referral source, residence and socioeconomic features, family composition, ordinal position
within the family of the child referred to the clinic as
the "patient", and the nature of the presenting problem.
The authors note a tendency for therapists to select Family
Group treatment candidates from among families who arrive at
the clinic via an eldest child, who is likely to be having
achievement and performance problems in junior high school.
Treatment tends to be of a short-term nature, with an
average of four to six sessions. Duration to stay is
examined as a function of therapist experience, primary
presenting problem, and residential propinquity. Termination
data on 46 families are reported. Lastly, Shellow, et al.
discuss various uses of this format. The interaction of
community, clinic, and the family is a focal point of much
of the analysis reported in this paper. (abstract by
Deborah Schuller).

1218.   Shields, L., Crisis intervention:
         Implications for the nurse, Journal
         of Psychiatric Nursing and Mental
         Health Services, 1975, 13, 37-42.

The author provides an onverview of the work and conceptual
models used at the Benjamin Rush Center in Culver City,
California. She first reviews Caplan's four stage model of
crisis, and then presents a four step model for problem
solving (assessing the problem, planning the intervention,
intervening, and evaluating the results). Further, she
discusses a hierarchy of levels of intervention (environmental manipulation, general support, generic approach,
individual intervention) which can be instituted at whatever
level appears appropriate for a given patient or family.
Examples of the type of intervention across the four levels
of the hierarchy are provided.

1219.   Shipley, R.H., Effect of a pregroup
        collective project on the cohesive-
        ness on inpatient therapy groups,
        Psychological Reports, 1977, 41, 79-85.

An attempt was made to increase the cohesion of inpatient
therapy groups by having the group members work collectively
on a creative art project immediately prior to their second
therapy session. Ten short-term inpatient psychotherapy
groups, having 6 to 8 members each, were randomly assigned
either to this collective project or to an individual project on which group members worked individually on a similar
art project. In the therapy session which followed, groups
on the collective project showed a significant decrease in
physical distance between group members relative to a baseline therapy session and relative to groups on the individual
project. Groups on the collective project also scored significantly higher on a cohesion questionnaire than those in
the individual project. The questionnaire and intermember
distance measures of group cohesion correlated highly (0.72).
Intermember distance returned to baseline during a follow-
up therapy session. No differences in the frequency of
three types of verbal behavior were found during therapy.
Collective art projects may be used to increase cohesion in
short-term groups. Further exploration of intermember
distance as a measure of group cohesion was suggested.
(Journal summary).

1220.   Shlien, J.M., Time-limited psychotherapy:
        An experimental investigation of practical
        values and theoretical implications,
        Journal of Counseling Psychology, 1957, 4,
        318-322.

Shlien offers a research paradigm to test effects of time
limits on the therapeutic process and outcome, as well as
some preliminary analysis of data. He situates the experiment against two different "problems", practical and
theoretical. A trend toward longer cases and a demand for
service which exceeds available supply constitute the
practical problem. The theoretical problem concerns on-
going, controversial speculation regarding the consequences
of termination. Shlien summarizes the views of some
theoreticians (Freud, Rank, Taft, and Rogers) on this issue.

The research design employed by the author uses four groups of clients, receiving a different total number of therapy sessions, twice-weekly--two groups on a time-limited and two groups on a time-unlimited basis. Shlien notes various measurement criteria utilized during the four testing periods, spaced at 10-week intervals. Preliminary analysis of outcome of the briefer (20 interviews) time-limited cases compares favorably with results of longer, unlimited therapy. (abstract by Deborah Schuller).

1221.   Shlien, J.M., Comparison of results
         with different forms of psychotherapy,
         American Journal of Psychotherapy, 1964,
         18 (suppl.), 15-22.

The author provides the results of a study in which three treatment approaches were monitored in terms of effects on self-esteem of the clients, as measured by a self-ideal correlation. The therapy groups involved two short-term, maximum of 20 sessions approaches, one involving a client-centered, the other an Adlerian focus. The third group was an unlimited client-centered one, and a control group was also involved. The average length of time for the client-centered, unlimited group was 37 sessions. The two time-limited groups were statistically indistguishable from each other in terms of outcome. Further, the significant gains seen in these two groups were maintained at follow-up. These positive changes occurred in approximately half the time of the unlimited therapy group. The further accelerated characteristics seen in the first seven sessions of the time-limited groups are generally predictive of only the most successful patients in the time-limited group. The author concludes that although client-centered and Adlerian thera- pies are quite dissimilar, it is possible that the imposition of time limits on both produces some common effect.

1222.   Shlien, J.M. Cross-theoretical criteria
         in time-limited therapy, in, 6th Inter-
         national Congress of Psychotherapy,
         Selected Lectures, London, 1964, Basel/
         New York, S. Karger, 1965, 118-126.

Brief psychotherapy is investigated in a context of time limits developed from the "end setting" theory of Otto Rank.

It is first investigated in an experiment with Rogerian
therapy, shown to be effective and efficient, then repeated
in a comparison of Rogerian and Adlerian therapy. Outcomes
in both are positive. The outcome measure, a self-denial
Q-sort correlation, shows similarities between the two
therapies. Since there are probably differences as well,
results are discussed in terms of "level of abstraction".
It is suggested that future studies be carried out at a
high level of sophistication but a low level of abstraction
in order to differentiate therapies in terms of their
intensely personal meaning. (Journal summary).

1223.   Shlien, J.M., Mosak, H.H., and
         Driekurs, R., Effect of time limited:
         A comparison of two psychotherapies,
         Journal of Counseling Psychology, 1962,
         9, 31-35.

This is a brief report, with intentions of expanded reporting at some later date, of the results of setting a time
limit of a maximum of 20 sessions for two types of therapy,
client-centered and Adlerian. A control group was also used.
The therapy change measure used was the self-ideal correlations. The results indicate that both therapeutic approaches
in a time-limited structure produced increases is S-I
correlation, but that neither reached the level of the
normal control group. Further, time-limited therapy is
shown to have produced accelerated results, irrespective of
the theoretical orientation used.

1224.   Shrader, W.K., and Beckenstein, L.,
         Reality-oriented group therapy,
         Hospital and Community Psychiatry,
         1966, 17, 239-240.

The authors consider reality-oriented group psychotherapy
to be more suitable in the setting of a large psychiatric
hospital than the traditional intensive, psychodynamic
approach. Various factors which support this conclusion
are discussed. Key concepts and techniques of reality-
oriented treatment, therapist requirements, and indications

are presented. Shrader and Beckenstein believe that the
goals of reality-oriented therapy, although less ambitious
than those of traditional group work, are consistent with
the goals of a mental hospital--e.g., resocialization and
remotivation. (abstract by Deborah Schuller).

   1225.   Shrader, W.K., et al., A didactic
            approach to structure in short-term
            group therapy, American Journal of
            Orthopsychiatry, 1969, 39, 493-497.

The authors present a description of a short-term group
therapy program for five couples who were experiencing
difficulties with their oldest (first born) child. Each
couple was seen individually once prior to the group therapy,
for assessment purposes, and once after the five group
sessions, for summing up. A co-therapist approach was used,
with a didactic combined with a free interaction group proc-
cess model used. Written summary of major research findings
on first-borns was provided each couple during the final
session, emphasizing the overanxious, overexpectant parental syndrome exhibited by many parents of first born.
Preliminary findings indicate that there was a definite
improvement in the children's adjustment, both from quantitative measures such a problem checklist and from qualitative measures (clinical impressions).

   1226.   Shulman, B.H., The use of dramatic
            confrontation in group psychotherapy,
            Psychiatric Quarterly, 1962, 36,
            (Suppl. Part I), 93-99.

The author continues to present material previously published, on the use of a confrontation technique in group
therapy. The technique consists of all members of the
group discussing the behavior of one of the members, trying
to determine that patient's "private goal" for his behavior.
The group is then instructed, with the consent of the
patient, to respond to the patient's behavior in an
exaggerated way attempting to meet the needs which the
patient has shown to have. The author provides a number of

case examples to illustrate the approach. The author
suggests that the term "midas Technique" be used as a label
for this approach. The value of using such an approach, as
a way of getting a wedge opened into the patient's defensive
system is discussed, as opposed to the more traditional
methods of analysis and interpretation. The effect of such
an approach is presented, including showing the patient
that the group is aware of his secret, that they will even
try to help him get his secret needs met, which tend to
inhibit the behavior (the ploys on the patient's part are
no longer necessary if the group is providing what the ploys
were designed to achieve). Cautions in the use of such a
technique are presented (e.g., using it to help a member,
not discipline or humiliate him, a sense of humor, etc.).

1227.   Shulman, B.H., Confrontation techniques
         in Adlerian psychotherapy, Journal of
         Individual Psychology, 1971, 27,
         167-175.

The author details the use of confrontation techniques in
therapy by providing a brief historical overview of the
development of such techniques. Confrontation is defined
as "any reasonable therapeutic technique which brings the
client face to face with an issue in a manner calculated to
provoke an immediate response." The use of such techniques
in Adlerian therapy is detailed. Specific techniques are
presented including confrontation of the client's subjective
feelings, mistaken beliefs and/or attitudes, exposing the
client's private logic and private goals, confrontation of
the client's self-destructive behavior, exploring alternatives to present action, examining the future, etc. The
context of an active therapy is stressed for such techniques.

1228.   Shulman, B.H., Confrontation techniques,
         Journal of Individual Psychology, 1972,
         28, 177-183.

The author provides similar focus as in his previous
article, but highlights the issues with new case examples.
A discussion of the differences between confrontation and
interpretation as techniques is presented. Confrontation
requires the patient to focus and respond immediately.

Interpretation allows the patient to ponder or not respond
at times. The types of confrontations, and examples of
each are provided, among which are confrontation of mood
states and feelings, hidden reasons, biased perception and
private logic, private goals, mottos, immediate behavior,
responsibility for others, self-defeating behavior, etc.
Confrontations allow for exploration of alternatives, for
the taking on of responsibility for change, and for looking
into the future.

1229.   Shyne, A., What research tell us about
         short-term cases in family agencies,
         Social Casework, 1951, 32, 236-241.

In one of the early overviews of short-term treatment
research results in family agencies, the author summarizes
the findings from eight studies. Characteristics of short-
term cases in these agencies are presented, which highlight
the wide range in research and treatment focus and methodology. Specifically focussed on are those cases where
treatment consists of one session. Three types of such
cases are presented: a) clients who successfully gain
enough in the initial and only interview, so that further
treatment is unnecessary; b) those clients who are referred
to other treatment or information sources; c) those who are
presumed to need further treatment sessions, but who decide
not to follow through with further treatment. A discussion
of each of these is included.

1230.   Shyne, A., An experimental study of
         casework methods, Social Casework, 1965,
         46, 535-541.

Shyne sketches the outlines of a four-year study undertaken
to examine: a) the relative effectiveness of several
different methods and procedures of providing casework
service to families; and b) variations in the content of
treatment practice according to the method employed. The
three sets of treatment variables include supportive versus
modifying methods; short-term versus continued service; and
individual-client versus multiple-client interviews. These
three variables constitute eight different service patterns,
to which 160 cases will be evenly and randomly assigned.

Tape-recorded research interviews occur at intake, at case closing, and six months after closing to provide data on any changes in client functioning. The author describes the response of program staff and clients to this study; and notes that initial experience strongly suggests the feasibility of undertaking experimental research in social casework. (abstract by Deborah Schuller).

1231.   Shyne, A., and Kogan, L., The short-
         term case in the family agency, New York,
         Family Association of America, 1957.

1232.   Sifneos, P.E., Phobic patient with
         dyspnea: Short-term psychotherapy,
         American Practitioner, 1958, 9, 947-952.

The author reports on a single case study of a student in his late 20's presenting with phobias and dyspnea. The work was carried out at the Massachusetts General Hospital. A total of eight therapy sessions, spread over a two month period were needed to produce positive outcome. Positive transference was used as a key to therapeutic change. By the end of therapy and at follow-up, the presenting phobic symptoms and dyspnea had essentially disappeared.

1233.   Sifneos, P.E., Preventive psychiatric
         work with mothers, Mental Hygiene,
         1959, 143, 230-236.

The author summarizes work done with 50 mothers who had brought children in because of behavior problems. Both mother and child were seen separately, for four-five inter-views spread over not more than three months. The results pointed to the conclusion that when the mothers gained as a result of their therapy contact, their children also changed in positive ways. Specific case histories are presented.

1234.   Sifneos, P.E., A concept of emotional
         crisis, Mental Hygiene, 1960, 44,
         169-179.

The author summarizes some of the clinical findings in
working with over 100 upper-middle class individuals through
the facilities of a community mental health center. Five
case histories are given to provide a sense of the range
of presenting problems. The author further provides a
series of statements in an attempt to develop a theoretical
framework for studying individuals in crisis. Stress is
defined as precipitating painful emotions in an individual
(e.g., anxiety, fear, anger). Each individual then attempts
to cope with the situation, and if unsuccessful, the emotional reactions are heightened and an emotional crisis
develops. Additional stresses, either from internal or
external sources, may produce serious adverse effects and
reactions. The author stresses the value of being flexible,
ability to utilize a variety of resources, and an individual's commitment and willingness to solve the emotional
crisis as critical factors related to successful resolution.

1235.   Sifneos, P.E., Dynamic psychotherapy in
         a psychiatric clinic, in, Masserman, J.,
         (ed.), Current Psychiatric Therapies,
         New York, Grune and Stratton, 1961,
         168-175.

Sifneos reports observations of 50 patients who received
short-term dynamic psychotherapy. Six criteria used in
selection of suitable candidates are described; and several
representative cases presented. Short-term dynamic therapy
focuses upon a circumscribed area of emotional conflict,
and avoids areas of conflict involving the more primitive
aspects of character structure. The therapist subtly encourages the development of a positive transference in
order to establish a therapeutic alliance, and to facilitate
a patient's understanding of his emotional conflicts in
relation to the symptoms. The author's follow-up data on
21 patients suggest that, while only moderate symptom
relief was reported, the psychotherapy process was perceived
as a "unique" or "unusual" learning experience. Restoration
of the patient's self-esteem, and the ability to deal with

an emotional crisis which previously had been unmanageable
were also reported. Finally, patients' expectations of
changes to be effected through therapy appeared to have
become less exaggerated and more realistic. In a discussion,
Sifneos reiterates characteristics of individuals for whom
short-term therapy may be an ideal treatment mode. He distinguishes "transference" from "transference neurosis",
and cautions against the development of the latter in
ostensibly brief treatment. (abstract by Deborah Schuller).

1236.   Sifneos, P.E., Seven years' experience
         with short-term dynamic psychotherapy,
         in, Selected Lectures, 6th International
         Congress of Psychotherapy, London, 1964,
         Basel/New York, S. Karger, 1965, 127-135.

1237.   Sifneos, P.E., Crisis psychotherapy, in,
         Masserman, J., (ed.), Current Psychiatric
         Therapies, New York, Grune and Stratton,
         1966.

The author provides two examples of brief therapy, focussed
on two female patients in their 20's. The active involvement on the therapist's part in the early phase of therapy
is stressed as part of a process of ascertaining the
patient's life situation and appropriateness for brief
therapy. The partnership aspects of brief therapy, in which
the process is seen as a joint endeavour on the part of
therapist and patient is also stressed. The major focus
is on helping the patient to understand the development of
the emotional crisis which precipitated the request for
therapy, and once that is accomplished a shift should occur
in which the patient is encouraged to actively begin solving
the difficulty. Anticipating similar future difficulties
is also part of the approach, as part of an educational
approach to dealing with crises.

1238.   Sifneos, P.E., Psychoanalytically-
          oriented short-term dynamic or anxiety-
          provoking psychotherapy for mild
          obsessional neuroses, Psychiatric
          Quarterly, 1966, 40, 271-282.

One of the leaders in the field of brief therapy, Dr. Sifneos
summarizes some of the work done at the Psychiatry Clinic of
the Massachusetts General Hospital with patients exhibiting
acute obsessive-compulsive symptoms. Such patients have
originally shown a fairly good adjustment, prior to some
precipitating emotional crisis. Their defenses appeared
flexible, were well motivated for therapy, with above-
average intelligence, and with prior histories of reasonable
human relationships, which was evident by their ability to
connect meaningfully and show some affect during the initial
screening interview. A number of specific case histories
are presented to highlight the types of patients described
above, as well as to elucidate some of the techniques used
in brief therapy. Such techniques included the early utilization of early transference, prior to the development of
transference neurosis, a focus on unresolved conflict areas,
but with an active avoidance of characterological issues, a
repeated uncovering by the therapist of the patient's
ambivalence in transference situations, and as the patient
shows signs of interpretive learning or re-education, the
movement on the therapist's part toward termination. Although no statistical data are provided, clinical follow-up
indicates that patients' attitudes towards their symptoms
do change as a result of brief therapy, even when the actual
symptoms have not been totally alleviated. Further, an
increase in patient self-esteem and less suffering from
their symptoms is also reported, even though no basic
characterological changes have occurred.

1239.   Sifneos, P.E., Two different kinds of
          psychotherapy of short duration,
          American Journal of Pyschiatry, 1967,
          1967, 123, 1069-1074.

One of the major contributors in the field provides a
detailed breakdown of two different approaches to brief
therapy, one labelled anxiety-provoking, the other labelled
anxiety-suppressive. Dr. Sifneos provides a framework for

studying each type, namely, the type of patient selected
for each approach, the requirements and techniques used in
each, and the type of follow-up findings for each. Case
material is used to highlight the points made. Briefly,
anxiety-provoking therapy is used with patients exhibiting
a specific, focalized problem. Anxiety-suppressive therapy
is used with seriously disturbed, recently decompensated
patients. The author also describes a crisis intervention
and a crisis support approach under each of the respective
two methods mentioned above.

1240.   Sifneos, P.E., Motivation for psycho-
        therapy of short duration, Proceedings
        of the 4th World Congress of Psychiatry,
        Madrid, 1966, Excerpta Medica, Amsterdam,
        Part III, 1968.

1241.   Sifneos, P.E., "The motivational process":
        A selection and prognostic criterion for
        psychotherapy of short duration,
        Psychiatric Quarterly, 1968, 42, 271-279.

Author reviews briefly the two major different kinds of
brief therapy- anxiety-provoking (dynamic) and anxiety-
suppressive (supportive) therapy. Anxiety-provoking
approach is offered to patients with well defined neurotic
difficulties who meet various criteria. One of these
criteria is the individual's level of motivation. Seven
criteria are used to estimate motivation: ability to see
one's symptoms as psychologically derived; tendency to be
willing to look inside oneself and see one's emotional
difficulties with some degree of accuracy; wanting to
actively participate in therapy; a curiosity about onself;
a willingness to alter one's present state of functioning;
realistic views of the probable outcome of psychotherapy;
desire to make reasonable sacrifices, such as changing one's
schedule to meet appointment for therapy. Results of Dr.
Sifneos' work point to the following conclusion: Patients
who are evaluated as showing a high level of motivation
when they first appear for therapy usually end up profiting
from their experiences in brief psychotherapy, while those
patients who are low in the level of motivation do not.

1242.   Sifneos, P.E., Learning to solve
         emotional problems: A controlled
         study of short-term anxiety-provoking
         psychotherapy, in, Porter, R., (ed.),
         The Role of Learning in Psychotherapy,
         London, Churchill, 1968.

The results of a study of 28 patients seen on an outpatient
basis are presented in this chapter. The type of approach
used is "anxiety-provoking" therapy in which the partnership between therapist and patient is stressed. Such a
therapy approach emphasizes specified and limited focus, and
the heightening of anxiety in order to move the patient more
rapidly toward a solution of the presenting problem. The
28 patients selected for such a treatment plan were above
average in intelligence, rated as motivated for treatment
based on a number of criteria, and fairly realistic in their
judgement of the possible outcome of therapy. Patients were
encouraged to learn various problem-solving approaches.
Independent judge rated patients prior to the beginning of
therapy and at termination, as well as rating a control
group along the same dimensions. The results indicated
that patients felt better about themselves and had learned
a number of things which were important to them, even though
they had not experienced a dramatic reduction in their
symptoms.

1243.   Sifneos, P.E., Short-term anxiety-
         provoking psychotherapy: An emotional
         problem-solving technique, Seminars in
         Psychiatry, 1969, 1, 389-398.

Sifneos describes his experience in applying one specific
form of therapy to a specified group of patients--i.e.,
individuals who are fairly well integrated psychologically,
but who present "well circumscribed" neurotic symptoms
which interfere with functioning. He lists criteria used
in the selection of candidates suitable for short-term,
anxiety-provoking psychotherapy. Motivation for change via
psychotherapy is one important prognostic criterion which
subsumes seven additional criteria. Requirements and
technique of this form of treatment are concisely summarized.
Short-term, anxiety-provoking therapy is based on psychoanalytic concepts. It entails definition of an underlying

emotional problem. Positive transference is employed as
the primary therapeutic tool; and anxiety is deliberately
generated to stimulate the patient to examine previously
avoided areas of conflict. Therapy ends early--in part to
avoid the development and ensuing complications of a transference neurosis. Sifneos describes results of this form
of therapy, as shown in the majority of patients on whom
follow-up data exist; and presents a clinical case to illustrate treatment and outcome. He concludes with a summary
of a more systematic study to evaluate outcome of this type
of brief therapy. (abstract by Deborah Schuller).

   1244.   Sifneos, P.E., Learning to solve emotional
            problems: a controlled study of short-
            term anxiety-provoking psychotherapy, in,
            R. Porter (ed.), The Role of learning in
            psychotherapy, International Psychiatry
            Clinics, Vol. 6, No. 1, Boston: Little
            Brown, 1969.

   1245.   Sifneos, P.E., Change in patient's moti-
            vation for psychotherapy, American Journal
            of Psychiatry, 1971, 128, 718-722.

In dynamic psychotherapy diagnostic and prognostic criteria
are necessary in order to determine the kind of therapy best
suited to a patient's idiosyncratic needs. Linked with these
needs, and thus one important criterion, is a patient's
motivation for change rather than for relief of symptoms.
In order to assess this motivation, the author used a seven-
point scale across seven items (ability to recognize that
symptoms are psychological; introspection and honesty in
reporting about self; willingness to participate actively
in treatment; active curiosity about self; desire to change;
expectations of results; willingness to make reasonable
sacrifices). Of 42 patients evaluated over eight treatment
sessions, only nine patients' motivation for change decreased.
(Journal abstract modified).

1246.   Sifneos, P.E., Short-term psychotherapy
         and emotional crisis, Harvard University
         Press, Cambridge, Mass., 1972.

The author summarizes the findings of a number of years of
practicing and researching brief therapies. He indicates
the criteria for patient selection for short-term therapy:
a) above average intelligence; b) at least one meaningful
relationship; c) ability to show emotion during interview;
d) ability to focus on a specific complaint; e) motivation
toward change. Specific case histories are presented.
Follow-up work was done by independent raters and the results
are positive.

1247.   Sifneos, P.E., Confrontation in short-
         term, anxiety-provoking psychotherapy,
         in, Adler, G., and Myerson, P., (eds.),
         Confrontation in Psychotherapy, Science
         House, 1973.

Using five guidelines for the selection of patients for
brief, anxiety-provoking therapy, the author discusses the
use of the technique of confrontation as part of this
approach. The selection guidelines are related to the
assessment of the patient's psychological strengths. In
this approach, anxiety is precipitated and increased rather
than suppressed. Such tactics inevitably produce psychic
pain for the patient, and the therapist must be confident
that the patient is capable of withstanding this pain. A
few case examples are presented, with actual exchanges, to
illustrate this approach. The author places emphasis on
the value of confrontation in helping patients learn to
solve their own problems during as well as after treatment.
The confrontation is based on the therapist pointing out
various paradoxical and incongruous aspects of a patient's
patterns and verbal statements. If properly timed, such
therapist confrontations can have positive therapeutic
effects.

1248.   Sifneos, P.E., An overview of a psychiatric
        clinic population, American Journal of
        Psychiatry, 1973, 130, 1033-1035.

The approach of short-term anxiety-provoking psychotherapy
(STAPP) developed by the author is the focus of this paper.
More specifically, the method by which the staff of the
Psychiatric Clinic of the Beth Israel Hospital in Boston
select patients for such an approach is described. Among
the criteria for selection are ability of the patient to
present a circumscribed problem, evidence of a previously
meaningful human relationship, an above-average level of
intelligence, a reasonable level of motivation for therapy
as measured by seven criteria, assessment of the patient's
self-esteem, ability to understand him/herself, and ability
to solve his/her problems. The form used by Clinic Staff is
presented, summarizing the issues raised in the paper.

1249.   Sifneos, P.E., Criteria for psychothera-
        peutic outcome, Psychotherapy and Psycho-
        somatics, 1975, 26, 49-58.

In an attempt to investigate the results of a variety of
psychotherapies offered in the psychiatric clinic of the
Beth Israel Hospital, we have used twelve outcome criteria
for improvement. Findings on 53 patients treated by 14
therapists are presented, and a tentative comparison is
made between a homogeneous group of patients who received
short-term and long-term psychotherapies. Although a somewhat higher percentage of the long-term patients obtained
symptomatic improvement compared to the short-term ones,
impressive changes in motivation for change, self-esteem
and interpersonal relations seem to have taken place in the
short-term psychotherapy group. (Journal abstract).

1250.   Sifneos, P.E., A research study of short-
        term anxiety provoking psychotherapy,
        Panel presentation of 9th International
        Congress of Psychotherapy, 1974, Oslo,
        Norway, in, Psychotherapy and Psychosomatics,
        Basel/New York, S. Karger, 1975.

1251.   Sifneos, P.E., Program report on research
         in the Psykiatrisk Klinnikk, University of
         Oslo, Panel presentation of 9th Inter-
         national Congress of Psychotherapy, 1974,
         Oslo, Norway, in, Psychotherapy and
         Psychosomatics, Basel/New York, S. Karger,
         1975.

1252.   Sifneos, P.E., Motivation for change:
         A prognostic guide for successful
         psychotherapy, Psychotherapy and
         Psychosomatics, 1978, 29, 293-298.

This paper reports observations on 53 "moderately disturbed"
patients, 17 of whom were treated with short-term psychotherapy (other than anxiety-provoking), and 36 with long-
term dynamic therapy. Outcome, based on 12 therapist-rated
criteria, is examined in relation to the patient's "movi-
vation for change", as assessed on a seven-point scale.
Sifneos present pre-evaluation and post-therapy motivation
scores for both long- and short-term therapy groups, on the
basis of therapeutic outcome. Of the 36 patients who received long-term treatment, "very" or "moderately" successful
results were observed in 18 cases. Of these, 14 had "good
to excellent" motivation prior to therapy, and 15 showed
this after termination. Fourteen of the 17 short-term
patients had "very to moderately" successful results. Of
these 14, nine had "good to excellent" motivation scores in
pre-evaluation; and eight had such a rating after terminating. No one in the successfully-treated short-term group
was rated as unmotivated during the pre-evaluation. The
author concludes that motivation for change is an important
prognostic criterion for assessing likelihood of therapeutic success. (abstract by Deborah Schuller).

1253.   Sifneos, P.E., Short-term anxiety-
         provoking psychotherapy, in, Davanloo, H.,
         (ed.), Short-term dynamic psychotherapy,
         New York, Spectrum Publications, 1978.

In this chapter, the author describes the criteria for
selection of patients for STAPP (Short-term Anxiety-Provoking
Psychotherapy), the variety of techniques used with such an

approach, and the research and evaluation results that derive from treating certain patients. Specifically, mildly neurotic patients who exhibit a circumscribed presenting problem are recommended for such an approach.

1254. Sifneos, P.E., Evaluation criteria for selection of patients, in, Davanloo, H., (ed.), Short-term dynamic psychotherapy, New York, Spectrum Publications, 1978.

The author summarizes the major criteria for selection of patients for Short-term Anxiety Provoking Psychotherapy. These include the ability on the patient's part to present a circumscribed main problem, to be able to demonstrate that he/she has had a history of at least one meaningful or positive human relationship in the past, and is able to show such a capacity in the initial interview, above average intelligence and some psychological sophistication, and who is reasonably motivated for therapy (as measured by specific criteria).

1255. Sifneos, P.E., The case of the Italian housewife, in, Davanloo, H., (ed.), Short-term dynamic psychotherapy, New York, Spectrum Publications, 1978.

1256. Sifneos, P.E., The case of the college student, in, Davanloo, H., (ed.), Short-term dynamic psychotherapy, New York, Spectrum Publications, 1978.

1257. Sifneos, P.E., The case of the woman in the Tower of London, in, Davanloo, H., (ed.), Short-term dynamic psychotherapy, New York, Spectrum Publications, 1978.

1258.   Sifneos, P.E., Principles of technique
         in short-term anxiety provoking psycho-
         therapy, in, Davanloo, H. (ed.), Short-
         term dynamic psychotherapy, New York,
         Spectrum Publications, 1978.

Dr. Sifneos summarizes the techical approach used in Short-
term Anxiety Provoking Psychotherapy. Specifically, the
therapist maintains a focus on a circumscribed presenting
problem, using the oedipal conflict as the dynamic conceptualization. Connecting present patient experiences with
those of the past is done using the transference which is
quickly developed in the therapy. Based on the initial
selection procedures, the patients accepted into STAPP are
expected to be capable of experiencing a fair amount of
anxiety in therapy. Further, issues which would shift the
focus tend to be ignored by the therapist. Practically,
therapy is set up on a one-to-one basis, for 45 minutes per
session, and the treatment is terminated when there is a
resolution of the selected problem.

1259.   Sifneos, P.E., Techniques of short-term
         anxiety provoking psychotherapy I -
         The case of the man with the facade, in,
         Davanloo, H. (ed.), Short-term dynamic
         psychotherapy, New York, Spectrum
         Publications, 1978.

1260.   Sifneos, P.E., Techniques of short-term
         anxiety provoking psychotherapy II-The
         case of the woman with the prostitution
         fantasy, in, Davanloo, H., (ed.), Short-
         term dynamic psychotherapy, New York,
         Spectrum Publications, 1978.

1261.   Sifneos, P.E., Teaching and supervision
         of STAPP, in, Davanloo, H., (ed.), Short-
         term dynamic psychotherapy, New York,
         Spectrum Publications, 1978.

Dr. Sifneos discusses the range of characteristics required
of a therapist using STAPP (e.g., ability to form a therapeutic alliance with the patient; ability to use postive

transference; ability to use confrontation; clarification, and the skill needed in asking questions which will provoke anxiety; the need to avoid getting side-tracked from the main focus, etc.). The selection and supervision of trainees is reviewed, and an example is provided to highlight the material.

1262.   Sifneos, P.E., Short-term dynamic psycho-
         therapy: Evaluation and technique, New
         York, Plenum Medical Book Company, 1979.

The author presents detailed information regarding a brief therapy approach labelled STAPP (Short-term anxiety provoking psychotherapy), used primarily with patients whose underlying difficulties are Oedipal or triangular. Typical presenting symptoms include anxiety either by itself or in conjunction with other symptoms, phobias with obsessive thoughts, grief reactions, mild depressions, and interpersonal difficulties. The text includes a detailed account of the initial inter-views (history taking and reformulation of the patient's problems), and the selection criteria for inclusion in STAPP. The process of therapy is broken down into various phases including the opening and early phases, and height of therapy, and the closing or termination phases. The teach-ing of this approach to trainees is briefly discussed as well as research findings. A complete case history and therapy progress session by session is provided in an appendix (11 therapy sessions and follow-up). Throughout the text, examples are provided of therapeutic exchanges between therapist and patient. The number of sessions in STAPP varies with each patient, but rarely exceeds 20 inter-views. The theoretical orientation is psychoanalytic. A clear, interesting presentation of STAPP by its founder.

1263.   Signell, K.A., The crisis of unwed
         motherhood: A consultation approach,
         Community Mental Health Journal, 1969,
         5, 305-314.

Unwed motherhood, particularly for the teenager, constitutes a series of subcrises: confrontation with the pregnancy, exclusion from school, physical changes, social isolation and interpersonal conflict, delivery, and caring for an

infant. This paper describes the role which a mental health
consultant can take in regard to interagency programs, and
education. Specific consultation interventions, within the
framework of crisis theory, are discussed for helping caregivers enable teenagers cope with these subscrises.
(Journal abstract).

1264.   Silk, S., The use of videotape in brief
         joint marital therapy, American Journal
         of Psychotherapy, 1972, 26, 419-424.

The value of using videotape recording in brief marital
therapy is presented. Through the use of case studies, the
author illustrates various methods of and variations in the
use of VTR. The stark objective reality of a VTR is one of
the most powerful reasons for its use to highlight marital
miscommunication.

1265.   Silverman, H., A technique of brief
         psychotherapy of a child disorder,
         Journal of Clinical Child Psychology,
         1974, 3, 39-40.

Silverman presents a case history to illustrate one technique of brief therapy of a child disorder. A mother
experiencing chronic difficulty with an eight-year old child
over issues of the child's need for autonomy was seen for
a total of five interviews. Most of the therapeutic work,
according to the author, occurred in the first session. The
author's technique consists of asking the parent to keep a
record of the child's "disturbing" behavior, to relinquish
usual attempts to control the child, and to praise behavior
of which the parent approves. This technique addresses at
face value the presenting symptom, but more intensive therapy
is not precluded if this approach is not sufficient in itself. Silverman briefly discusses several advantages of
this method. (abstract by Deborah Schuller).

1266.   Silverman, W.H., Planning for crisis
        intervention with community health
        concepts, Psychotherapy: Theory,
        Research, and Practice, 1977, 14,
        293-297.

Planning and implementing crisis intervention services can
be aided by using concepts and principles of community
mental health. A definition of crisis is proposed which
entails the interrelationship of antecedent stress events
and consequent responses. Stress events and available
resources are classified in order to define more clearly
and inclusively crisis and effective intervention. Several
concepts and principles of community mental health including
the public health model, systems theory, and an ecological
perspective are employed to discuss the planning, execution,
and evaluation of crisis intervention services. Examples
of both effective and ineffective planning and intervention
are offered. (Journal abstract).

1267.   Simmons, J.Q., The psychiatric emergency
        in adolescence, International Psychiatry
        Clinics, 1966, 3, 37-51.

1268.   Simon, W., and Chevlin, M.R., Brief
        psychotherapy - a hospital program
        with participation of the social
        worker, Mental Hygiene, 1949, 33,
        401-410.

Four different methods of psychotherapy are distinguished:
Meyer's direct approach, Rogers' non-directive approach,
Freudian psychoanalysis, and the brief psychotherapy of
Alexander and French. The authors describe this latter
form of therapy as practised in one Veterans Administration
hospital: procedure, therapeutic emphasis, technique, and
indications. Advantages of a hospital over an office setting
are suggested. Simon and Chevlin then treat in some detail
the therapeutic role of the psychiatric social worker on the
clinical team, stressing that the social worker's involvement
as a therapist supplements and enriches traditional social
work functions rather than replacing them. (abstract by
Deborah Schuller).

1269.   Simon, W., et al., A controlled study
         of the short-term differential treat-
         ment of schizophrenia, American Journal
         of Psychiatry, 1958, 114, 1077-1086.

The authors report on a short-term treatment research
project for 80 schizophrenic patients who had no previously
reported psychotic symptomatology. Four treatment approaches
were used: a) clinical judgement: in which a patient was
administered any of a number of treatments which were deemed
good psychiatric treatment methods for the given presenting
problems (could include ECT, insulin therapy, psychotherapy,
other drugs, etc.); b) chlorpromazine; c) reserpine; and
d) hospital routine. The specific dosages of each drug was
presented in the article, along with a detailed diagnostic
breakdown, using material from psychiatric interviews and
standard psychological instruments (e.g., MMPI). The
duration of treatment was 30 days, using a variety of mental
health professionals. An independent research team rated
levels of improvement. Approximately 37% were rated as
unimproved, with the remaining patients being rated as showing at least some improvement. The clinical judgement group
(i.e., group a) had the most favorable treatment outcomes.
The authors conclude against the premature abandoning of
some of the more traditional and accepted modes of treatment
for schizophrenia (as shown by the clinical judgement group),
and also point out the relative difficulty in treating
schizoprenia. Chlorpromazine treatment came closest to the
results of group a (clinical judgement, combination of treatments). Rapid onset and short duration of symptoms was predictive of success in therapy, confirming previous results.

1270.   Skodol, A.E., et al., Crisis in psycho-
         therapy: Principles of emergency
         consultation and intervention, American
         Journal of Orthopsychiatry, 1979, 49,
         585-597.

A surprisingly large number of visits to a crisis intervention service are made by patients engaged in ongoing
psychotherapy elsewhere. Data are presented from patients
and their therapist that support the concept of a psychotherapy crisis as a major precipitant of such visits. A

typology for the therapy crisis is elaborated and guidelines
for the crisis worker's assessment and intervention are
suggested. (Journal abstract).

   1271.   Skynner, A.C.R., School phobia: a
            reappraisal, British Journal of Medicine
            and Psychology, 1974, 47, 1-16.

The previous literature on school phobia has tended to
emphasize the defect in mother-child relationship, and to
neglect a crucial failure of the father to loosen the
original exclusive mutual attachment between mother and
child. An approach is described which makes use of a conjoint family technique to achieve this aim, in which issues
of authority and control appear to be central and where the
crucial event is the confrontation and weakening of phanta-
sies of omnipotence in the child and its parents. (Journal
summary).

   1272.   Slaby, A.E., et al., Handbook of
            psychiatric emergencies, Flushing, N.Y.,
            Medical Examination Publishing Co., 1975.

   1273.   Sloane, R.B., The converging paths of
            behavior therapy and psychotherapy,
            American Journal of Psychiatry, 1969,
            125, 877-885.

Three disparate psychotherapeutic approaches - psycho-
analytical, behavioral, and Rogerian - are shown to have
more likenesses than differences. The relationship between
patient and therapist and the conversational content are
common. Techniques such as interpretation, counterconditioning (reciprocal inhibition), and the use of withholding of reward work in similar ways, despite different
labels and rationales. Dictionary constructs of the past
have done little to bridge differing theoretical assumptions;
this has served to obscure understanding of common modalities.
(Journal abstract).

1274.   Sloane, R.B., Behavior therapy and
         psychotherapy: Integration or dis-
         integration, American Journal of
         Psychotherapy, 1969, 23, 473-481.

The apparent diversity in behavior therapy and insight
psychotherapy has obscured the similarities between the two.
Psychotherapy adheres to a medical model in which the "cause"
of the symptoms is sought. Once the "cause" is removed, the
symptoms subside. In contrast, behavior therapy follows the
psychologic model of attempting to alter behavior or "symptoms" with less interest in the "cause", which is loosely
ascribed to aberrant learning. Nevertheless, the two
approaches make use of common psychologic processes which
are well understood within a social psychologic framework
as a psychoanalytic one. Moreover, techniques of therapy
are often independent of theory. (Journal summary modified).

1275.   Sloane, R.B., and Staples, F.R., (eds.),
         Brief psychotherapy, Psychiatric Clinics
         of North America, 1979, 2, 1-2.

In this foreword, the authors provide a brief introduction
to a collection of articles on brief therapy which they as
editors have chosen.

1276.   Sloane, R.B., et al., Role preparation
         and expectation of improvement in
         psychotherapy, Journal of Nervous and
         Mental Disease, 1970, 150, 18-26.

Thirty-six psychoneurotic patients were randomly assigned to
four groups, who received different indoctrinations from a
research psychiatrist. 1) The first group was assigned to
a psychotherapist without further explanation. 2) Those
in the second group were told firmly that they should feel
and function better after 4 months of psychotherapy. 3) The
third group had the process of psychotherapy explained to
them by means of Orne's anticipatory socialization interview (a didactic rationale why the patient should discuss
his past life). 4) The fourth group had the process of
psychotherapy explained and, in addition, were told firmly
that they should expect to feel and function better in a

months of psychotherapy. The therapists were unaware of
the purpose of the study. At the end of treatment the
patients who received an explanation of psychotherapy
improved slightly but significantly more than those who did
not receive it. There was no significant difference in
symptomatic change or attendance in the groups. Suggestion
that they would feel better in 4 months had no effect on
outcome. Moreover, patients who received this suggestion
were rated as less likeable by the therapists. (Journal
abstract adapted).

    1277.   Sloane, R.B., et al., Short-term
            analytically oriented psychotherapy
            versus behavior therapy, American
            Journal of Psychiatry, 1975, 132,
            373-377.

Ninety-four outpatients with anxiety neurosis or personality
disorder were randomly assigned to four months waiting list,
behavior therapy, or psychodynamically oriented therapy.
The target symptoms of all three groups improved significantly, but the two treated groups improved equally well
and significantly more than those on the waiting list.
There were no significant differences among the groups in
work or social adjustment; however, the patients who received
behavior therapy had a significant overall improvement at
four months. One year and two years after initial assessment,
all groups were found to be equally and significantly improved. (Journal abstract).

    1278.   Sloane, R.B., et al., Short-term
            psychodynamically-oriented psychotherapy
            versus behavior therapy, Cambridge,
            Mass., Harvard University Press, 1975.

    1279.   Sloane, R.B., et al., Patient
            characteristics and outcome in psycho-
            therapy and behavior therapy, Journal
            of Consulting and Clinical Psychology,
            1976, 44, 330-339.

Ninety-four psychoneurotic or personality disordered patients
received 4 months of analytically-oriented psychotherapy,

behavior therapy, or waiting list treatment. Neither active treatment was more effective than the other with any type of symptom (including affective ones), although both were more consistently effective than the waiting list. With psychotherapy, relatively greater success was associated with less overall pathology on the MMPI and higher socioeconomic status. Psychotherapy was least effective with patients who scored high on the Hysteria and Psychopathic Deviate scales. There was also a strong but nonsignificant trend for more improvement in psychotherapy patients who were younger, female, married, later born, more intelligent, and from smaller families. In contrast, behavior therapy was more effective with those who scored high on the Hysteria and Mania scales and seemed to be effective with a broader range of patients. (Journal abstract).

1280.   Sloane, R.B., et al., Patients' attitudes
         toward behavior therapy and psychotherapy,
         American Journal of Psychiatry, 1977, 134,
         134-137.

A questionnaire survey of 50 patients treated by behavior therapy or short-term, analytically oriented psychotherapy revealed that both groups, as well as those patients who improved the most, placed a high value on insight, the patient-therapist relationship, catharsis, and trust. The findings suggest that behavior therapy patients tend to place more emphasis than do their therapists on factors that have traditionally been thought important in analytic psychotherapy. (Journal abstract).

1281.   Small, L., Crisis therapy: Theory and
         method, in, Goldman, G.G., and Milman,
         D.S., (eds.), Innovations in psychotherapy,
         Springfield, Ill., C.C. Thomas, 1971.

1282.   Small, L., The briefer therapies, Revised
         Edition, New York, Brunner/Mazel, 1979.

This is the second edition of a text covering a very wide range of approaches and techniques in the field of briefer therapies. A bibliography of over 500 references is also included, in this detailed text.

1283.   Smith, E.M., Counseling for women who
seek abortions, Social Work, 1972,
17, 62-68.

Using a crisis intervention model, the author summarizes
the work of counseling servuce agency which provided
professional counseling for 46, 19-21 year old single,
white women students who had sought abortions. The average
number of sessions was three, with a range of one-six. A
counselor not involved in the counseling process did a
follow-up and found no signs of decreased or impaired
functioning on the part of the women who had received
counseling. All clients reported on the importance of having
received the counseling at a critical point in their lives.
The author provides the reader with a practical framework
for dealing with such clients.

1284.   Smith, L.L., Crisis intervention theory
and practice: A source book, Washington,
D.C., University Press, 1975.

1285.   Smith, L.L., A general model of crisis
intervention, Clinical Social Work
Journal, 1976, 4, 162-171.

This article presents a general model of crisis intervention
designed to be used in most practice settings. The model
is a synthesis of what has previously been written about
crisis intervention theory and practice along with the
author's own contributions. The various definitions of
what constitutes a crisis and the stage of a crisis reaction
are discussed. In the beginning phases of crisis treatment
it is suggested that the clinician should complete six tasks,
one of which is identifying with the client and precipitating event that led to the crisis. As the treatment
process continues it is suggested that the clinician should
complete six tasks, one of which is designing psychological
and behavioral tasks that will reduce stress and help the
client resolve the crisis. Finally, the termination process
is reviewed. (Journal abstract).

1286.   Smith, L.L., A review of crisis inter-
        vention theory, Social Casework, 1978,
        59, 396-405.

The author provides a review of crisis intervention. He
begins with a definition of crisis, as presented by a
number of leading contributors in the field. Next the
stages of crisis are detailed, along with the types of
crises which occur in everyday life. The article concludes
with a focus on treatment; initial phases of treatment are
discussed, followed by the assessment phase, and review of
some of the more frequently used strategies. The difficulties of doing research in this field is also presented,
and some suggestions provided.

1287.   Smith, R.C., Planned short-term treatment
        in a mental health clinic, Dissertation
        Abstracts International, 1978, 39(3-A),
        1845-1846.

1288.   Snaith, R.P., and Jacobson, S., The
        observation ward and the psychiatric
        emergency, British Journal of Psychiatry,
        1965, 111, 18-26.

The authors describe the functioning of the Brighton
Observation Ward (England), with the assumption that the
types of demands made on an observation ward are similar
to those made on a short-term treatment unit. The Ward is
a psychiatric emergency ward, and the admission rates,
reasons for admission, other patient characteristics, etc.
are presented. The average length of stay was five days.
Such a unit could evolve into a brief therapy unit, and
continue to fulfill its emergency role.

1289.   Socarides, C.W., On the usefulness of
        extremely brief psychanalytic contacts,
        Psychoanalytic Review, 1954, 4, 340-346.

The author presents a detailed case history of a female
military officer and the short-term treatment process
totalling five sessions (two follow-up at two and six

months post termination). The value of a brief analytic
intervention is stressed. Questions about the differences
between short term analytic therapy and long term psychoanalysis are discussed, with a focus on symptom alleviation
versus personality change.

1290.   Sokol, R.J., A short-term technique of
         psychotherapy for psychotic depressive
         reactions, International Journal of
         Psychoanalytic Psychotherapy, 1973, 2,
         101-111.

This article describes a successful technique for the short-
term psychotherapy of psychotic depressive reactions, in
which the therapist assumes the position of the patient's
id impulses and sadistically attacks the lost object.
Three clinical cases exemplify the technique, which is
derived from psychoanalytic theory. The effects of the
technique on the patient, the therapist, and the transactional process are detailed, along with dynamic considerations. (Journal abstract).

1291.   Sollod, R.W., and Kaplan, H.S., The new
         sex therapy: An integration of behavioral,
         psychodynamic, and interpersonal approach,
         in, Claghorn, J.L., (ed.), Successful
         psychotherapy, New York, Brunner/Mazel,
         1976.

1292.   Solymon, L., and Miller, S., Reciprocal
         inhibition by aversion relief in the
         treatment of phobias, Behaviour Research
         and Therapy, 1967, 5, 313-324.

The treatment reported is a combination of Wolpeian reciprocal inhibition and aversion-relief therapies. The relief
following termination of electric shock was substitued for
Jacobsonian relaxation in the reciprocal inhibition of
anxiety. Photographs of phobic objects and tape recordings
of narrated phobic experiences were utilized in treating
seven phobic patients and one ticqueur. Six of the seven

phobic tatients were free of phobic fears, without symptom
substitution, at time of follow-up. Theoretical implications
and research possibilities of the treatment are discussed.
(Journal summary).

1293.   Solyom, L., et al., Evaluation of a
         new treatment paradigm for phobias,
         Canadian Psychiatric Association Journal,
         1969, 14, 3-9.

Forty phobic patients were treated with reciprocal inhibition
by aversion relief. The development and modifications of
this technique are described. The patients were divided into
two groups, agoraphobic and non agoraphobic and the symptomatology was assessed in psychiatric interview and on various
psychological questionnaires and rating scales, before and
after treatment. The mean age of the agoraphobic patients
was higher, their illness lengthier, their anxiety score
higher and their fears more numerous. They had an average
of 28.5 half-hour treatment sessions while the non-agoraphobic patients had 23.6. The majority of patients were
followed for a mean period of 9.9 months for agoraphobics
and 14.8 months for non-agoraphobics. The results indicate
that 75% of agoraphobic patients and 89% of non-agoraphobic
patients were rated recovered or much improved at termination of therapy, and at follow-up, 63% of agoraphobic
patients and 75% of non-agoraphobic patients were rated
recovered or much improved. Differences between the two
groups and factors important to the treatment paradigm are
discussed. (Journal summary).

1294.   Solyom, L., et al., A comparative study
         of aversion relief and systematic desensi-
         tization in the treatment of phobias,
         British Journal of Psychiatry, 1971, 119,
         299-303.

Twenty phobic patients, divided equally into two matched
groups, were treated with either aversion relief or systematic desensitization. Improvements were measured by a
combination of psychiatrists' ratings, psychometric tests,
and self-assessments of phobias, neurotic symptoms and
social adjustment. Both groups showed significant benefit

after 12 hours of treatment. Improvement rates were similar
for both therapies, and increased in each case after a
further nine hours of treatment. Improvement was more
pronounced in phobias, less in other neurotic symptoms and
negligible in social adjustment. Careful assessment of
untreated fears was made to test for symptom substitution.
On the contrary, both groups showed a generalization of
effect paralleling the decrease in intensity of the main
phobia. In addition a study correlating 36 variables with
the outcome of treatment suggested prognostic indicators
for each treatment. (Journal summary).

1295. Solyom, L., Behaviour therapy versus
       drug therapy in the treatment of phobic
       neurosis, Canadian Psychiatric Association
       Journal, 1973, 18, 25-32.

The author reports on a study designed to evaluate the
efficacy of a combination of therapy approaches in the
treatment of phobias. A total of 50 patients, divided into
matched groups were used. Five different treatment groups
were used. These were: (a) Aversion therapy (AR); (b)
Systematic desensitization (SD); (c) Flooding (F); (d)
Phenelzine combined with brief psychotherapy (P-BP); and,
(e) Placebo combined with brief psychotherapy (PI-BP). The
brief therapy consisted of 12 hours over a three month
period. The results indicate that the most rapid effect
was seen in the group that had brief therapy combined with
the drug (P-BP). However, improvement was due to the
effect of the drug, and when the drug was no longer administered, all patients in this group relapsed. Those patients
in the behaviour therapy groups maintained their gains over
a two year follow-up period. The author suggests that drug
be used in the initial phases of treatment, to produce
changes and thus increase the motivational level of patients,
but that behaviour therapies be used to maintain these gains,
with further drug therapy unnecessary.

1296.   Solyom, L., et al., Paradoxical
         intention in the treatment of obsessive
         thoughts: A pilot study, Comprehensive
         Psychiatry, 1972, 13, 291-297.

The authors discuss theoretical and research considerations
underlying their decision to use paradoxical intention in
the treatment of obsessive neurosis. A study was designed
to investigate the effectiveness of this approach. Four
men and six women, all considered chronically ill, and all
previously treated by psychotherapy and drug therapy, comprised the experiental group. Each patient served as his
own control, in that two symptoms of approximately equal
significance to the patient were selected; and paradoxical
intention applied to only one of the obsessive thoughts.
Each patient was seen weekly for one hour, over a six week
period. The authors present in table form characteristics
of each patient (including course and duration of illness,
symptomatology, and scores on three instruments), as well
as target and control symptom, and degree of change following
treatment. Results indicate a diminution or elimination of
the target symptom in five of the 10 patients; no change
for three (two subjects could not apply the technique
systematically). Solyom, et al. discuss their data, possible
reasons for the observed changes, and advantages of this
treatment mode. (abstract by Deborah Schuller).

1297.   Soper, P.H., and L'Abate, L., Paradox
         as a therapeutic technique: A review,
         International Journal of Family Counseling,
         1977, 5, 10-21.

This article presents an overview of the range and uses of
paradox in therapy. Areas covered include the use of the
double bind in therapy, prescribing symptoms and reframing,
the assignments of tasks, the value of written instructions,
the use of paradoxical intention, paradoxical procedures in
hypnosis, as well as other approaches which uses paradox
(e.g., John Rosen's Direct Analysis). The authors also
include a short section on the underlying reasons why such
procedures are effective. Over 75 references are included.

1298.   Specter, G.A., and Claiborn, W.L.,
         Crisis intervention, New York,
         Behavioral Publications, 1973.

1299.   Speers, R.W., Brief psychotherapy with
         college women: technique and criteria
         for selection, American Journal of
         Orthopsychiatry, 1962, 32, 434-444.

A total of 68 female college students were initially interviewed by a consulting psychiatrist at a college counseling
center. Of the original 45 were accepted for treatment
using a brief therapy model. The approach consisted of
focussing on the presenting conflict, determination of the
underlying drive and the defense used by the patient to
minimize the drive, the interpretation by the therapist of
the defenses, allowing for a conscious recognition on the
patient's part. The therapist conceptualized the presenting
symptoms in terms of defensive breakdown against such drives
as dependency, sexuality, and hostility. Specific case
examples are provided to highlight the points made. Most
of those seen in brief therapy were in conflict because of
a present life situation difficulty or because of normal
adjustment reactions. Those with more serious pathological
defenses were referred for longer term therapy.

1300.   Sperling, M., Analytic first aid in
         school phobias, Psychoanalytic Quarterly,
         1961, 30, 504-518.

This article summarizes the work of the author using an
analytic orientation to deal with children with school
phobias. A total of 58 children, ranging in ages from
2-16 years were used as a basis for the conclusions and
clinical observations presented. Main characteristics of
phobic children are described, including the underlying
dynamics within the family. Stressed are the child's often
open concerns about death, separation, etc. Defensive
mechanisms which enter into the formation of a phobia are
discussed, including externalization, displacement, and
projection. The importance of dealing with a child in the
acute or early phases of a phobia development is stressed.

The method of treatment consists of reconstructing the
events preceding the and dynamically related to the emergence of the phobic behavior. This is followed by interpretation to the child of the unconscious connections which
lead to the phobic behavior. Three case histories are
presented highlighting the value of such an approach in
dealing with acute school phobias.

1301.   Spiegel, D.E., and Sperber, Z., Clinical
         experiment in short-term family therapy,
         American Journal of Orthopsychiatry,
         1967, 37, 278-279.

This is a short summary of a panel presented at the annual
American Orthopsychiatric Association conference. The
report focussed on the results of setting up short-term
therapy (six sessions) for seven families (father and mother
both present, and no signs of psychotic symptoms). Case
illustrations are presented of this experiment carried out
at Cedars-Sinai Medical Center in Los Angeles.

1302.   Spiegel, H., A single treatment method to
         stop smoking using ancillary self-hypnosis,
         International Journal of Clinical and
         Experimental Hypnosis, 1970, 18, 235-250.

This report discusses the first 615 patient-smokers who
have been treated with a single 45-minute session of psychotherapy reinforced with hypnosis. Technique of treatment,
including rationale of approach, induction procedure,
assessment of hypnotizability, and training instructions
to stop smoking are presented in detail. 6-month follow-up
study results are discussed. Of 271 (44%) patients who
returned a questionnaire, 121 (20%) hard-core smokers (who
had repeatedly tried and failed to stop smoking before)
were able to stop for at least 6 months. Another 120 (20%)
persons reduced their smoking to varying degrees. These
results of a 1-session treatment compare favorably with,
and often are significantly better than, other longer-term
methods reported in the literature. They suggest that every
habitual smoker who is motivated to stop be exposed to the
impact of this procedure, or its equivalent, so that at
least 1 of 5 smokers can be salvaged. (Journal abstract).

1303.   Spiegel, H., Termination of smoking by
         a single treatment, Archives of Environ-
         mental Health, 1970, 20, 736-742.

The author describes in detail, a specific hypnotherapy
method for the treatment of patients wishing to stop
smoking. The entire procedure is explained, practiced,
and demonstrated within a 45 minute session, in which the
patient can continue a self-hypnosis procedure at home or
at the office repeatedly throughout the day (each self-
hypnosis session lasts 20 seconds, done 10 times/day).
The emphasis is not on stopping smoking per se, but on the
choice to protect the body from the poison of cigarette
smoke, on the need to respect and protect the body. One
hundred and twenty-one hard core smokers had given up
smoking as a result of this one session hypnotherapy
approach, and continued to maintain this gain at a six
month follow-up. Another 120 subjects decreased their
smoking frequency, 29 showed no change, and another 344
subjects were yet to be followed-up. The value of this
procedure, presented in detail in the article, for at least
20% of those wishing to stop smoking, is stressed.

1304.   Spiegel, H., and Spiegel, D., Trance
         and clinical treatment: Clinical uses
         of hypnosis, New York, Basic Books, 1978.

The text presents a major attempt to delineate the theory
and practice of psychotherapy employing hypnosis. The
majority of the treatment strategies described involve
only one session, as the patient learns to use self-hypnosis
to further reinforce the treatment. Tests of hypnotizability
are used as a guide in selecting long-term therapies most
suitable for specific patients. Examples of short-term
hypnosis include the treatment of smoking and phobias.

1305.   Spoerl, O., Treatment patterns in prepaid
         psychiatric care, American Journal of
         Psychiatry, 1974, 131, 56-59.

The author describes the evolution and current functioning
of a mental health service in an HMO (health maintenance
organization) that serves more than 175,000 members in the

Seattle metropolitan area. A cohort of 159 patients was
followed for 18 months to investigate referral patterns,
categories or presenting problems, diagnostic impressions,
treatment modalities, and patterns of utilization. The
advantages and problems of the prepayment system vis-a-vis
psychiatric care are discussed. (Journal abstract).

1306.   Spoerl, R.H., Abstract: Single session
        psychotherapy, Diseases of the Nervous
        System, 1975, 36, 283-285.

The paper takes a look at the special opportunities which
present themselves to patient and psychotherapist in the
initial interview. Citing two case examples, the paper
suggests that it is possible to have a therapeutic impact
and to reach sufficient closure during a single interview
with certain types of clinical problems. (Journal abstract).

1307.   Springe, M.P., Work with adolescents:
        Brief psychotherapy with a limited aim,
        Journal of Child Psychotherapy, 1968,
        2, 31-37.

Springe describes brief therapy as conducted in one London
clinic which specializes in work with youth between the
agres of 14 and 22. The psychoanalytically-trained staff
differentiate three overlapping stages of adolescence,
each with characteristic defence mechanisms. Duration of
the phases and the defences used provide valuable diagnostic
pointers. The author articulates goals of treatment, and
characteristics of adolescents who respond well to brief
interventions directed towards increased insight. Three
case histories are presented to illustrate different types
of adolescent conflicts. (abstract by Deborah Schuller).

1308.   Stampfl, T.G., and Levis, D.J.,
        Essentials of implosive therapy: A
        learning-theory-based psychodynamic
        behavioral therapy, Journal of Abnormal
        Psychology, 1967, 72, 496-503.

A learning-theory-based method of psychotherapy (implosive
therapy), which integrates psychodynamics concepts into its

theoretical model and leads to a new technique of treatment
is described. The authors present results of laboratory
experimentation, focus on experimental extinction procedures,
and detail the therapy procedure. Avoidance serial cue
hierarchy, symptom-contingent cues, and hypothesized sequential cues are all outlined in the procedure. The technique
has been applied to a wide variety of psychopathology with
apparent success. Treatment time ranges from 1 to 30, 1
hour sessions with marked changes in symptomatology usually
occurring within 1-15 implosive sessions. (Journal abstract
adapted).

1309.   Stampfl, T.G., and Levis, D., Phobic
         patients: Treatment with the learning
         theory approach of implosive therapy,
         Voices: The Art and Science of
         Psychotherapy, 1967, 3, 23-27.

1310.   Stampfl, T.G., and Levis, D.J., Implosive
         therapy - a behavioral therapy? Behavior
         Research and Therapy, 1968, 6, 31-36.

Despite differences in technique and theory, most approaches
which are given the label "behavioral therapy" seem to have
in common the following three characteristics: (1) An
emphasis placed on the direct treatment of the symptom;
(2) A strong tendency to reject the concepts and rationale
of traditional psychodynamic approaches, and (3) The adherence to learning or conditioning models of symptom origin
and modification. The present paper deals with the question
as to whether implosive therapy should be considered a
behavioral therapy since only the third characteristic
stated above can be ascribed directly to it. A brief outline of the theory and treatment procedure of IT (Implosive
Therapy) is given along with how this position relates to
the above points. It is concluded that the first two of
the above characteristics are superficial and that the third
should be the sole determinant of whether a position should
be labelled a "behavioral therapy". (Journal summary).

1311.   Standal, S.W., and van der Veen, F.,
         Length of therapy in relation to
         counselor estimates of personal
         integration and other case variables,
         Journal of Consulting Psychology, 1957,
         21, 1-9.

The research reported here focussed on the degree of personal
integration, movement toward life adjustment, over-all
success, and several other variables based on therapist
judgements in 73 clients who had been seen in two or more
therapy sessions in which a client-centered approach was
used. The findings indicated that change in personal integration was positively related to the length of treatment,
and that this variable was more highly related to treatment
length than other variables in the study.

1312.   Staples, F.R., Relationship and technique
         in brief therapy, Psychiatric Clinics of
         North America, 1979, 2, 139-155.

Current theoretical formulations of psychotherapy and
empirical research studies both suggest that the quality of
the relationship may be more important to the success of
treatment than specific techniques associated with any form
of psychotherapy. Studies which have attempted to assess
the role of specific techniques associated with different
therapies are discussed, as well as an approach which has
attempted to determine what processes are common to all forms
of effective psychotherapy. (Journal abstract).

1313.   Staples, F.R., et al., Process and
         outcome in psychotherapy and behavior
         therapy, Journal of Consulting and
         Clinical Psychology, 1976, 44, 340-350.

Three behavior therapists and three analytically oriented
psychotherapists treated a total of 60 neurotic outpatients
for 4 months. Measures of Rogers-Truax factors, nonlexical
speech characteristics, therapist informational specificity,
and a content analysis of therapist activity were taken from
recordings of the fifth interview. Therapists rated their
feelings toward their patients, and patients completed the

Relationship Questionnaire and the Lorr Inventory. In
psychotherapy, patients who were most liked by their therapists and those with greater total speech time showed
greatest symptomatic improvement. Patients who used longer
average speech durations improved most in both treatments.
It was concluded that improvement was more a function of
patient characteristics than of specific therapist interventions. (Journal abstract).

1314.   Stein, C., Hypnotic projection in brief
         psychotherapy, American Journal of
         Clinical Hypnosis, 1972, 14, 143-155.

Specific hypnotic procedures are detailed, with the use of
case study material. Such rapid trance induction techniques
as the clock-telegram game, the T.V. videotaped instant
replay, the Christmas tree projection, the blackboard projection procedure, and the author's own exit-speedometer
technique are explained. The value of such approaches
across a wide variety of clinical situations is discussed.
The kind of emotional reactions produced by such techniques
are also discussed, with some suggestions for the control of
overwhelmingly traumatic reactions.

1315.   Stein, C., Brief hypnotherapy for
         conversion cephalgia (repression head-
         ache), American Journal of Clinical
         Hypnosis, 1975, 17, 198-201.

Stein relates a single hypnotherapy session with a man
suffering from a frontal headache. This headache most
troubled the patient when he would attempt to go into a
deep hypnotic trance in order to uncover the cause of the
headache. The details of this treatment, which took place
on an impromptu basis among a group of physicians, are
recounted. (abstract by Deborah Schuller).

1316.   Stein, E., and MacLeod, J., Brief
         psychotherapy in physical illness,
         Current Psychiatric Therapies, 1969,
         9, 79-85.

The general techniques of short-term psychotherapy are:
keeping treatment goals limited with an aim of symptom
relief or restoration to a previous level of functioning;
instituting early treatment; focusing a precipitating stress,
and flexibility regarding frequency of visits. Great emphasis is placed on early formulation of the clinical material.
The first session is looked upon as both diagnostic and
therapeutic in purpose. Emphasis is placed on the medical
aspects of the illness causing psychic disequilibrium, and
a careful history is taken of the illness or surgery involved, looking carefully for the emotion-laden points or
cognitive misunderstandings. Several recurrent themes also
have been found useful: (1) Focus on denial as the primary
defense; (2) close attention to the narcissistic injury and
(3) emphasis upon the patient's cognitive understanding of
the illness, with particular search for cognitive misper-
ceptions or cognitive blocks, which must be detected and
dealt with. (Journal summary).

1317.   Stein, E., et al., Brief psychotherapy
         of psychiatric reactions to physical
         illness, American Journal of Psychiatry,
         1969, 125, 1040-1047.

Physical illness of trauma often leads to psychiatric complications sufficiently complex to require psychotherapeutic intervention. The authors have found brief psychotherapy to be especially suitable in such cases. They
emphasize three techniques they have found to be useful:
a) a focus upon denial as the primary defense; 2) attention
to the narcissistic injury which is so frequently created
by the illness or trauma; and 3) exploration of the patient's
cognitive understanding of the illness, with a particular
search for cognitive blocks that retard recovery until
detected. A case report is presented to illustrate these
techniques. (Journal abstract).

1318.   Stein, J., et al., Emotional reaction
         to illness responds to brief psycho-
         therapy, Reported anon, Frontiers of
         Hospital Psychiatry, 1967, 4, 15.

1319.   Stekel, H., Short-term psychotherapy
         of a case of conversion hysteria,
         American Journal of Psychotherapy,
         1953, 7, 302-309.

The author presents a detailed, session-by-session account
of the short-term therapy of a 34 year old single male,
whose presenting problems revolved around somatic complaints
(difficulty breathing and swallowing, etc.). A total of
25 sessions were held, one session/week. An active method
of analysis was used. The patient wished for the removal
of his symptoms, with little interest in uncovering much
of the unconscious material connected to their emergence.
The treatment was successful in this sense, and no further
treatment has been requested by the subject two years
following termination.

1320.   Stekel, H., Successful short-term
         treatment of psychosomatic disease,
         American Journal of Psychotherapy,
         1954, 8, 719-722.

The author reports on a successful short-term analytically-
oriented therapy of a 27 year old single female engaged to
be married, who complained of headaches, depressions,
feelings of pain in her vagina and generalized sensations
of pins and needles, especially when she was with her fiance.
A detailed history is presented, including material from
sessions. A total of 23 sessions, once/week were held.
A follow-up covering a two year post-therapy revealed that
the improvement had been maintained. The subject had been
married, was happy, had given birth and was delighted with
her child.

1321.   Sterba, R., A case of brief psychotherapy
         by Sigmund Freud, Psychoanalytic Review,
         1951, 38, 75-80.

This article summarizes some of the details of a case of
brief therapy in which Freud was the therapist and Bruno
Walter, the famous conductor, was the patient. Extensive
material from Bruno Walter's book, Theme and Variations,
is presented which highlights from the patient's viewpoint
some of the critical aspects of the therapy with Freud.
Among the critical issues in such an approach were Freud's
sincerity and decisiveness in his advice to Walter which
allowed for the development of trust, Freud's determination
that the disequilibrium in Walter was only slight and that
the patient's ego strength was sufficient that only six
sessions were needed for successful treatment. The use of
distraction, and suggestion are highlighted. The article
provides some perspective on the analytic contributions of
Freud, which are often seen as focussed only on long term
treatment.

1322.   Stern, M.D., The recognition and
         management of psychiatric emergencies,
         Medical Clinic of North America, 1957,
         41, 817-829.

Stern surveys diagnosis and management of a variety of
psychiatric emergencies, including depressions and suicidal
threats, excitements (acute intoxication, delirium, acute
alcoholic hallucinosis), schizophrenic reactions, panic
states, acute hysteria, as well as assaults, antisocial
activity, and drug-induced states. Adverting to the potential anxiety evoked in encountering such emergencies, he
emphasizes the necessity of a realistic approach to the
dangers inherent in the situation. Physician responsibility
both to the patient and his community is implicitly stressed
in the author's discussion. (abstract by Deborah Schuller).

1323.   Stevenson, I., and Wolpe, J., Recovery
         from sexual deviations through overcoming
         non-sexual neurotic responses, American
         Journal of Psychiatry, 1960, 116, 737-742.

Three cases of sexual deviation are reported in which a
return to normal heterosexual behavior followed the development of assertive behavior on the part of the patients.
follow-up inquiries 3 to 6 years later showed that the
patients had maintained their improvements. In these
patients the sexual deviations were determined by anxiety
that did not have a sexual origin. The processes of their
therapy are discussed, and also, more briefly, the therapy
of those cases in which anxiety is specifically attached to
sexual stimuli. The recoveries in these patients were not
related to recall of repressed memories of traumatic events
or the working out of specific sexual conflicts. The alter-
ation of sexual behavior did not lead to the occurrence of
other symptoms or other undesirable side effects. The
processes whereby stimuli of anxiety lose their capacity to
arouse anxiety are discussed and it is suggested that the
concept of "repressed emotion" has hindered an understanding
of the processes of recovery from psychoneuroses with and
without psychotherapy. (Journal summary).

1324.   Stewart, H., Six months, fixed term,
         once weekly psychotherapy: A report, on
         20 cases with follow-up, British Journal
         of Psychiatry, 1972, 121, 425-435.

The work reported here, done in Great Britain, involved
setting therapy at one session/week, spread over a six month
period for a selected group of patients. Specifically,
only patients who fit the following criteria were included:
a) motivation to understand presenting problem as internally
connected; b) sufficient intelligence to be able to use
understanding; d) must be able to continue gainful employment, (including being a housewife); d) relationships with
people of both sexes must not have been too disturbed prior
to entering treatment; e) must not exhibit too many extreme
personality characteristics; f) must have been able to use
simple interpretations used in the initial interview;
g) judgement on diagnostician's part that plan offered

would be suitable to patient interviewed. The technique of
free association was used to provide material for interpretation, clarification, and working through. Issue of
transference was dealt with directly. Always present in
the sessions was the issue of termination. Each case is
described in terms of the presenting problem, view of family
background material, a tentative hypothesis as to the underlying nature of the individual's difficulty, results as
stated by patient and follow-up. Further, the specific
comments provided by patients were included to provide an
overview of the kinds of changes and types of problems in
this sample. Those cases which showed little or no change
tended to have had the most disturbed personalities at the
start of treatment. Further, chronicity of a symptom is not
a predictor of an individual's response to brief therapy.
Finally, the author reports that for those patients who had
shown some improvement by the end of the six month period,
a continuation was reported at follow-up. Thus it appears
that therapeutic processes at work at termination continued
after that point.

1325.   Stewart, H., and Cole, S., Emerging
         concepts for briefer psychotherapy:
         A review, Psychological Reports, 1968,
         22, 619-629.

The authors summarize over 30 studies in the field of brief
therapy. Short-term therapy is defined as less than six
months duration. There is a wide range in the types of
clients chosen for brief therapy, as well as the number of
sessions offered. The common characteristics across the
studies cited include the active role of the therapist,
quick diagnostic process flowing immediately into treatment,
the setting of explicit time limits, focussing on the present,
decreasing the encouragement of dependency, and focussing on
the strengths and growth potentials of the clients. Session
length varied from five minutes to 2.5 hours, and from one
session to 40 sessions over a six month period. The type
of training needed to do brief therapy is discussed, with
stress placed on therapists who already have experience
doing longer term therapy (i.e., experienced), ability to
use their intuition (i.e., risk), willingness to make termination occur (i.e., set limits and follow through),

belief in the value of shorter therapies, etc. There
appears to be little evidence suggesting that a lot of
emotional distress is a deterent to client selection for
brief therapy, and many practitioners report working with
severely disturbed as well as the less disturbed.

1326.   Stieper, D.R., and Weiner, D.N., The
         problem of interminability in outpatient
         psychotherapy, Journal of Consulting
         Psychology, 1959, 23, 237-242.

Sixty-six patients were divided into four groups, according
to the amount of time spent in therapy. Two groups were
described as "long-term," and two as "short-term."

Follow-up psychometric findings revealed insignificant
differences among the groups initially similar, suggesting
that length of time in therapy does not correlate with
improvement.

Two samples of therapists indicated that the great majority
of long-term patients were being seen by a small minority
of the therapists. A likely reason appears to be failure
on the part of "long-term" therapists to adequately formulate therapy goals, and to impersonalize the therapeutic
relationship. (Journal summary).

1327.   Stierlin, H., Short-term versus long-
         term psychotherapy in the light of a
         general theory of human relationships,
         British Journal of Medicinal Psychology,
         1968, 41, 357-367.

This article addresses the issue of whether brief therapy,
whatever the particular theoretical orientation of the
therapist, can produce meaningful and lasting change for
the client. The author uses a general conceptualization
drawn from an analysis of human relationships to address
the question. Any relationship can be conceptualized into
the contributions made by individual, social, and systematic
factors. Further, each relationship can be analyzed on five
dimensions: a) moment-duration; b) sameness-difference;
c) stimulation-stabilization; d) gratification-frustration;
d) closeness-distance. The author focusses on the first

dimension only, namely, moment-duration. In essence, he is
focussing on various factors related to the meaning of time
in human relationships, and translating these into the
therapeutic relationship. (e.g., questions of timing,
memories and anticipations, etc.). Such a perspective
allows for the explanation of changes as a result of brief
therapeutic contact. The work of Malan is used in explaining
the underlying processes which occur in successful brief
therapy, including a focussed, active approach, time limits
producing a tension of involvement, issues of termination,
interpersonal climate, and the therapist's enthusiasm. The
author concludes that given these considerations, meaningful
personality change is possible within a brief therapeutic
encounter.

   1328.   Stoller, F.S., Accelerated interaction:
           A time-limited approach based on the
           brief intensive group, International
           Journal of Group Psychotherapy, 1968,
           18, 220-235.

Accelerated interaction is a new approach mainly characterized by continuous group interaction over several days with
a very definite time limit to the therapeutic contact. It
utilizes the urgency and independence-fostering qualities
of the time-limited contact while taking advantage of the
impact of intimate group life. Elements of the group
process emerge under continuous interaction which are
scarcely realized under most conventional circumstances
and which have profound implications for promoting social
change in people. By stressing involvement, honesty,
directness, and mutuality, the accelerated group promotes
an intense experience in living with people which opens
many possibilities for personal growth. The role of the
group leader shifts from that of commentator and technician
to that of participant who reacts in an immediate fashion.
Holding such groups in homes rather than the usual office
or clinic setting places the emphasis on personal growth
and new possibilities for living instead of correcting
defective functioning. In addition, accelerated interaction
has advantageous applications for institutional programs.
(Journal summary).

1329.   Stone, A.R., et al., The role of non-
         specific factors in short-term psycho-
         therapy, Australian Journal of Psychology,
         1966, 18, 210-217.

The authors review some of the major findings from previous
research they have conducted at the Henry Phipps Psychiatric
Clinic (outpatient), of the Johns Hopkins Hospital. The
patient populations was basically a psychoneurotic group,
60% women, between ages 18-55 years. Most were from lower
socio-economic levels. Factors focussed include: a) the
degree to which the patient is clear about the nature of
his/her own problems, and how treatment could help; b) the
degree to which the expectations of the therapist were in
agreement with those of the patient regarding the unfolding
and outcome of treatment; c) the degree to which the therapist believed that the patient could benefit from short-
term psychotherapy (i.e., appropriateness of patient for
brief therapy). The authors report that the greater the
degree of patient clarity about the nature of treatment,
the greater the chance for positive outcome. Greater congruence between therapist expectations and patient expectations was also found to correlate significantly with outcome (i.e, the greater the congruence, the more positive
the outcome). Therapist belief in the value of such short-
term treatment approaches was also correlated with outcome
(i.e., the greater the belief in the approach, the more
positive the outcome). The authors conclude by suggesting
concrete steps to be implemented using these non-specific
factors to enhance the probability of positive outcome.
Suggestions as to how to orient the patient, how to involve
outside community support, and how to better train therapists are all discussed.

1330.   Stone, L., Psychoanalysis and brief
         psychotherapy, Psychiatric Quarterly,
         1951, 20, 215-236.

The author describes a specific approach to brief therapy -
rooted in psychoanalytic theory and therapy. Specifically,
the author suggests a selection of the crucial dynamic
problem presented by the patient, a continued focus on
current reality as a context for the therapy, the fostering
of positive transference without encouraging regression,

and a relying on the spontaneous forces within each patient
which would enhance the chances for a return to positive
functioning. The type of patients for whom brief therapy
is recommended include: a) individuals for whom any long
term attempt at major revisions in their personalities or
life situations may lead to greater distress or danger,
and for whom the energy investment of longer term therapy
is not warranted; b) those for whom the presenting problem
is so slight that longer term treatment is not justified;
c) acute reactive situations, in whom the individual has
provided evidence of a reasonable adaptation prior to the
stressful situation; d) transitional states (e.g., adolescence); e) as a preparatory phase for longer term therapy
at some future point; f) certain mild chronic neuroses and
other such conditions; g) individuals who are getting a high
degree of secondary gain from their symptomatology are not
recommended for brief therapy.

1331.   Straker, M., Brief psychotherapy: A
         technique for general hospital outpatient
         psychiatry, Comprehensive Psychiatry,
         1966, 7, 39-45.

Increasing congestion in our psychiatric outpatient clinic
had resulted from rapidly increasing community demands for
service, the conflict of time demands for teaching as
opposed to patient care, and the inexperience of psychiatric
residents compounded by the fragmentation of contacts with
the patient. The latter condition has made the utilization
of the transference as a healing environment unattainable.
The results were seen in a high incidence of clinic drop-
outs, few regulated medical discharges and the tendency to
foster the development of chronic clinic attendance and
dependency on the institution itself. The re-organization
of our clinic operation and the re-alignment of personnel
and of our treatment objective has left us with the time
and the opportunity to treat selected patients with a program of brief psychotherapy of 10 to 12 sessions after the
initial evaluation has been completed. The results have
been seen in the medical discharge of large numbers of
patients after brief psychotherapy, a reduction of clinic
drop-outs, improved patient service, and an improved
learning and teaching climate in the outpatient clinic.
(Journal summary).

1332.   Straker, M., Brief psychotherapy in an
         outpatient clinic: Evolution and Evalu-
         ation, American Journal of Psychiatry,
         1968, 124, 1219-1226.

The author reports on the results of a major reogranization
of the Psychiatry Department at the Montreal General Hospital. Based on a sample of 220 adult patients, he reports
that through the use of brief therapy, including a shift in
treatment aims, the discharge rate at the unit has multiplied
five times. The number of patients who dropped out of treatment has decreased by half of what it was prior to the
program, and the staff energy level, interest, and morale
have shown marked increases. The positive changes seen in
patients at the end of treatment were maintained on a two
year follow-up study. The conclusion is presented that the
value of brief therapy for specifically selected patients
has been documented. At this clinic, it has become the
primary therapy modality. The primary goal of therapy was
not to aim for a personality reconstruction but for a
reduction or alleviation of the presenting symptoms in an
attempt to help the patient re-establish the level of functioning prior to the development of the need for professional
help. Individuals seen as appropriate for such an approach
include those exhibiting transient decompensations, due to
grief, depression, or anxiety reactions. Within this group,
patients able to develop positive transferences and with a
reasonable amount of motivation to change are considered
most appropriate.

1333.   Straker, M., A review of short-term
         psychotherapy, Diseases of the Nervous
         System, 1977, 38, 813-816.

The author reviews some of the important issues in the field
of short-term dynamic psychotherapy. The relevance of such
treatment, and a brief historical review of the major
developments are presented. The work of Freud, Alexander,
Lindemann, Caplan, Erikson, and some of the more recent
dynamically-oriented brief therapists is discussed (e.g.,
Sifneos, Malan). Comparisons are made among the various
approaches to short-term therapy in terms of frequency of
sessions, number of sessions, how transference issues are
handled, the activity level of the therapist, and the goals
of therapy.

1334.   Straker, M., Short-term dynamic psycho-
         therapy: A retrospective and perspective
         view, in, Davanloo, H., (ed.), Basic
         principles and techniques in short-term
         dynamic psychotherapy, New York, Spectrum
         Publications, 1978.

The author reviews the historical developments which led to
short-term treatment approaches, and summarizes the situations in which such brief approaches are indicated. The
major techniques used are also summarized (e.g., crisis
intervention, focus on augmenting coping responses, aiding
in the positive use of existing ego strengths, and search
for insights for further development). Various treatment
issues are discussed, with specific emphasis on the therapist-patient relationship. Results of short-term therapy
studies are reported.

1335.   Straker, M., et al., A comprehensive
         emergency psychiatric service in a
         general hospital, Canadian Psychiatric
         Association Journal, 1971, 16, 137-139.

Rapid developments in general hospital outpatient psychiatry
reflect increasing demands from the community for such
services. Combining the outpatient caseload and Emergency
Room psychiatric patients, nearly 2,500 patients per year
were under care. To provide better care a new emergency
intake service has been established, with a 72 hour limit
of stay. This is a valuable therapeutic resource, and has
made it possible to better study and treat selected acutely-
ill patients. It is also a dynamic teaching setting. The
establishment of this intensive-care unit has relieved
pressure on the existing services. Suicidal patients,
those with transient deliria and acutely disturbed patients
have been accommodated. About 20% of the casualty caseload
has been admitted to the Short Stay Service, and nearly 50%
of such patients were able to return to their homes and
community living within three days. These clinical experiences confirm the description of this unit as a "comprehensive emergency psychiatric service" in a general hospital
setting. The survival of the service is assured and
encourages the establishment of similar units in other
centers. (Journal summary).

1336.   Straker, M., et al., Assaultive
         behaviors in an institutional setting,
         Psychiatric Journal of the University
         of Ottawa, 1977, 2, 185-190.

Reviews the literature concerning violent behavior caused
by individual human variables (e.g., brain dysfunction,
mental disorders, and personality variables), interpersonal
variables, and environmental variables. The role of psychotherapy in controlling institutional violence is discussed
and hospital data, derived from a review of incidents of
patient violence, record reviews, patient and staff interviews, and soliciting patient and staff opinion, are presented. In the hospital, principles of crisis intervention
were applied to formulate a plan for managing assaultive
patients. Specific measures for both treatment and prevention were developed, including a ward for brief involuntary confinement and a new mechanism to ensure that every
patient with unresolved complaints had access to consultation. (Journal abstract).

1337.   Strassberg, D.S., et al., Successful
         outcome and number of sessions: When
         do counselors think enough is enough?
         Journal of Counseling Psychology, 1977,
         24, 477-480.

Counselors rated 166 female and 97 male clients at a university counseling center over a 3 year period on four
outcome measures. Improvement was studied as a function of
the number of weekly sessions for which clients were seen.
Results revealed that through 20 sessions there was a strong
and consistent (across all outcome measures) positive
linear relationship between treatment length and counselor-
assessed outcome. After 20 sessions, however, additional
counseling was no longer associated with further increases
in the rate of improvement. The "failure zone" reported in
some earlier studies was not observed. The implications of
these findings for clinical practice are discussed. (Journal
abstract).

1338.   Strassberg, D.S., et al., Client self-
         disclosure in short-term psychotherapy,
         Psychotherapy: Theory, Research and
         Practice, 1978, 15, 153-157.

Fourteen male and 12 female graduate student therapists saw
a total of 53 clients in individual psychotherapy for an
average of 11 sessions. Second therapy sessions were audio
tape recorded, and rated for intimacy level of client self-
disclosure during a three minute period in each quarter of
the session. Analysis of the distribution of intimate self-
disclosure by clients revealed that for female clients, a
disproportionately large amount of disclosure occurred
during the final quarter of the session. During the second
half of the therapy session, female clients engaged in more
intimate self-disclosure than male clients. Improvers,
compared to non-improvers, were more likely to be rated by
therapists as high in intimate self-disclosure. (Journal
abstract).

1339.   Stratton, J.G., Effects of crisis inter-
         vention counseling on predelinquent and
         misdemeanor juvenile offenders, Juvenile
         Justice, 1975, 26, 7-18.

1340.   Strean, H.S., and Blatt, A., Long or
         short-term therapy: Some selected
         issues, Journal of Contemporary
         Psychotherapy, 1969, 1, 115-122.

The authors examine historical and current manifestations
of the ongoing "debate" over the superiority of long or
short term methods by proponents of each. In briefly
considering indications for each form of therapy, Strean
and Blatt note that intact ego functions are one criterion
favoured by both schools. The authors quote descriptions
of short-term treatment by advocates of long-term work,
and the converse. Too frequently, the patient is forced
to adapt himself to the therapist's orientation, rather
than the therapist's modifying his treatment to meet the
patient's needs. In the absence of empirical support
demonstrating the superiority of any therapy, the authors
state that patient's needs must determine therapeutic

stance. Thus, according to Strean and Blatt, no therapy
per se is the treatment of choice. The issue of how and
where to intervene must be based on a thorough psychosocial
diagnosis which adequately assesses the patient's metapsycho-
logical system. Only then can a therapist attempt to restore equilibrium to that system. (abstract by Deborah
Schuller).

   1341.   Strickler, M., Applying crisis theory
           in a community clinic, Social Casework,
           1965, 46, 150-154.

The author provides a detailed case history to highlight the
brief therapy approach developed at the Benjamin Rush Center
for Problems of Living. It is a community-oriented, walk-
in agency in which immediate therapy intervention is offered
in order to prevent the escalation of presenting problems
into more permanent psychiatric symptoms. The aim is to re-
establish the psychological homeostatic balance present in
the patient prior to the upset in balance, and to this end,
the treatment focus is on problem solving rather than on a
direct treatment of the emotional difficulties. Therapy is
limited to six sessions, and offered to anyone over the age
of 17 1/2 years. The approach involves an active therapist
involvement geared to a conscious or pre-conscious level.
The contribution of the discipline of social work to the
field of brief therapy and crisis intervention is acknowl-
edged by the author, and the various techniques used daily
by social workers are highlighted.

   1342.   Strickler, M., Crisis intervention and
           the climacteric man, Social Casework,
           1975,   , 85-89.

Strickler presents three cases to illustrate the types of
climacteric crises to which men are susceptible, and the
viability of crisis intervention as a therapeutic vehicle
in such cases. Events which may trigger climacteric crises
include job-related disappointments, separation from the
late adolescent child, decline in sexual potency, and the
appearance of somatic symptoms associated with aging. A
common theme underlying the three presented cases is the
regression to adolescent issues and view of possibilities

for the future. The author explores the development of such
crises, the central tasks which the climacteric man must
face, and the advantages of crisis-oriented techniques in
facilitating adaptive resolution to the problem. (abstract
by Deborah Schuller).

   1343.   Strickler, M., and Allgeyer, J., The
              crisis group: A new application of
              crisis theory, Social Work, 1967, 12,
              28-32.

This article reports on a new kind of group instrument
using modern crisis theory in treatment methodology and
structural design that emerged from a 6 month pilot study
at a crisis service in Los Angeles (Benjamin Rush Center).
Crisis group treatment is different from traditional forms
of group treatment because of the special nature and process
of crisis resolution. Crisis, with its time limitations and
sense of urgency, is helped toward resolution by the limit
of six weekly visits. The universal feeling of crisis
quickly welds the group into a working unit. The focus on
a high degree of cognitive as well as emotional recognition
of the dilemma sets the stage for problem-solving. Specific
clarification and awareness of the patient's coping device
that is now failing him complete the cognitive picture.
The group functions both by prodding and stimulating the
patient into awareness that his way of coping must change
and then by supporting his efforts to try out new ways.
The therapist implements this by giving open and enthusiastic
support to the patient's efforts. Together, group and therapist generate an atmosphere of hope and trust that growth
can take place. Both work hard in a highly focused and
intensive manner and experience considerable gratification
from the ability of group members to grasp the opportunity
for change. (Journal abstract and summary).

   1344.   Strickler, M., and Bonnefil, M., Crisis
              intervention and social casework: Simi-
              larities and differences in problem-
              solving, Clinical Social Work Journal,
              1974, 2, 36-44.

The similarities and differences between the traditional
psychosocial approach to casework and that of crisis inter-

vention have been discussed with the use of illustrative
case material. It is important to recognize that while
crisis intervention is justifiably subsumed under the
generalist concept of social work theory and practice on
the basis of their striking similarities, it is necessary
for the sake of professional clarity to differentiate
between the two forms of problem-solving treatment method-
ologies in terms of goals, process, and structure. (Journal
summary).

1345.   Strickler, M., and La Sor, B., The
         concept of loss in crisis intervention,
         Mental Hygiene, 1970, 54, 301-305.

The phenomenon of loss is a fundamental issue in all crisis
situations. We therefore consider that its particular nature
be clearly defined and understood in the general and characteristic assessment process of crisis intervention treatment.
This paper has therefore ventured to delineate, define, and
illustrate three kinds of adult losses: self-esteem, sexual
role mastery, and nurturing. Case material has been utilized
to demonstrate the thesis that even though all three types
of losses are involved to some degree in every crisis situation, one of these kinds of losses appears to be predominant
and qualitatively more significant than the other two, in
the etiology of any crisis reaction. The ability to identify the pertinent kind of loss in a particular crisis
enhances the preventive goals of crisis intervention.
(Journal summary).

1346.   Strickler, M., et al., The community-
         based walk-in center: A new resource
         for groups underrepresented in outpatient
         treatment facilities, American Journal of
         Public Health, 1965, 55, 377-384.

Traditional psychiatric facilities are not geared to provide
help to many persons who need it. Others do not need the
usual services but do need a form of treatment which is only
occasionally present. This paper presents an account of a
new approach to this problem in terms of a walk-in center
(Benjamin Rush Center, Los Angeles). Characteristics of
clients and intake trends are discussed. (Journal abstract).

1347.   Strupp, H.H., A multidimensional
         analysis of technique in brief psycho-
         therapy, Psychiatry, 1957, 20, 387-397.

This one case study was designed to test the validity of
short-term treatment as an effective modality. The treatment consisted of a total of nine sessions, of individual
therapy. The patient was a woman who has been suffering
from an increasing depression. The major approach used
was insight-oriented therapy done by a psychiatrist, with a
large emphasis on re-education. Two rates, after initially
rating the taped therapy sessions independently, rated
seven sessions across a number of dimensions, including
intensity of the therapeutic interaction, the type of focus,
etc. The results supported the hypothesis of the value and
effectiveness of a brief therapy approach, given the type
of problem presented.

1348.   Strupp, H.H., Psychoanalysis, "focal
         psychotherapy" and the nature of psycho-
         therapeutic influence, Archives of General
         Psychiatry, 1975, 32, 127-135.

It has traditionally been asserted that the nature of the
therapeutic influence in psychoanalysis is qualitatively
different from that in "psychotherapy." This thesis is
considered untenable. Analysis of a case history by Balint,
Ornstein, and Balint shows evidence that therapeutic change
can be conceptualized more parsimoniously along lines other
than those traditionally preferred. The therapist establishes himself as a good parent or authority figure vis-a-vis
the patient, and within that context mediates important
lessons in nonneurotic constructive living. Given strong
motivation to seek change, the patient is won over to a
point of view different from the one that has, in essential
respects, guided his life in the past, and he has to make
these teachings his own. Analytic therapy is an education
for optimal personal freedom in the context of social living.
(Journal abstract).

1349.   Strupp, H.H., Time-limited psychotherapy:
         New research evidence, Cassette tape, New
         York, BMA Audio Cassettes, 200 Park Avenue
         South, N.Y., 10003.

1350.   Strupp, H.H., The challenge of short-
         term dynamic psychotherapy, in, Davanloo,
         H., (ed.), Basic principles and techniques
         in short-term dynamic psychotherapy, New
         York, Spectrum Publications, 1978.

The author addresses three basic questions related to brief
dynamic psychotherapy: a) What are the basic assumptions
of short-term dynamic therapy? b) What are the conditions
under which it should be used? c) How should such an approach
be evaluated as to its effectiveness?

1351.   Strupp, H.H., and Hadley, S.W., Specific
         vs nonspecific factors in psychotherapy:
         A controlled study of outcome, Archives
         of General Psychiatry, 1979, 36, 1125-
         1136.

This study explored the relative contribution of the therapist's technical skill and the qualities inherent in any
good human relationship to outcome in time-limited individual psychotherapy. Highly experienced psychotherapists
treated 15 patients drawn from a relatively homogeneous
patient population (male college students, selected primarily
on the basis of elevations on the depression, anxiety, and
social introversion scales of the MMPI). By traditional
diagnostic categories, they would be classified as neurotic
depression or anxiety reactions. Obsessional trends and
borderline personalities were common. A comparable patient
group was treated by college professors chosen for their
ability to form understanding relationships. Patients
treated by professors showed, on the average, as much improvement as patient treated by professional therapists.
Treated groups slightly exceeded the controls. Group means,
however, obscured considerable individual variability.
(Journal abstract).

1352.   Stuart, M.R., and Mackey, K.J., Defining
         differences between crisis intervention
         and short-term therapy, Hospital and
         Community Psychiatry, 1977, 28, 527-529.

Using the model of "person plus stress yields reaction,"
the authors discuss the differences between crisis intervention and short-term treatment, including psychiatric

emergencies. In emergency treatment the central focus is
on the reaction, or symptoms, while in crisis intervention
the emphasis is on the stress and its quick resolution.
In short-term treatment the focus is on the person and
exploration of behavior patterns and feelings. The authors
believe that the number of crisis cases handled by a therapist must be limited because of their exhausting nature.
(Journal abstract).

1353.   Stuart, R.B., Operant-interpersonal
         treatment for marital discord, Journal
         of Consulting and Clinical Psychology,
         1969, 33, 675-682.

Operant-interpersonal treatment of marital discord is
premised on the assumption that successful marriages can be
differentiated from unsuccessful marriages by the frequency
and range of reciprocal positive reinforcements exchanged by
both partners. Beginning with the clarification of behavior
change objectives for each partner, a four-step treatment
approach culminating in an exchange of positive responses
on a reciprocal basis is suggested. The treatment of four
couples complaining of low-rate conversational and sexual
behavior is summarized, stressing the use of a token system
as a prosthesis to facilitate the transition to increased
positive reinforcement. (Journal abstract).

1354.   Stuart, R.B., Behavioral contracting
         within the families of delinquents,
         Journal of Behavior Therapy and
         Experimental Psychiatry, 1971, 2, 1-11.

The technique of behavioral contracting is used to strengthen
the control of family and school over the behavior of delinquents. A behavioral contract is a means of scheduling the
exchange of positive reinforcements among two or more persons. The use of these contracts is predicated upon four
assumptions: (1) receipt of positive reinforcements in
interpersonal exchanges is a privilege rather than a right;
(2) effective interpersonal agreements are governed by the
norm of reciprocity; (3) the value of an interpersonal
exchange is a direct function of the range, rate and

magnitude of the positive reinforcements mediated by that
exchange; and (4) rules create freedom of interpersonal
exchanges. The use of a behavioral contract with one
delinquent girl is described and analyzed using Markovian
methods. (Journal summary).

1355.   Stuart, R.B., and Tripodi, T., Experi-
         mental evaluation of three time-
         constrained behavioral treatments for
         predelinquents and delinquents, in,
         Rubin and Brady, (eds.), Advances in
         Behavior Therapy, Vol. 4, New York,
         Academic Press, 1973.

The authors report on a study in which shorter and longer
periods of treatment were used in dealing with pre-delinquent
and delinquent teenagers. A total of 77 families were involved in a behaviorally-oriented program. No differences
were reported among the shorter term and longer term
approaches, and the authors conclude that shorter methods
produce results comparable to those seen in the longer term
approaches.

1356.   Stubblebine, J.M., and Decker, J.B., Are
         urban health centers worth it? American
         Journal of Psychiatry, 1971, 127, 908-912.

On the basis of experience in San Francisco, the authors
believe that the community mental health center offers a
viable alternative to state hospital care for the mentally
ill and is able to do this economically. The centers are
functioning well and are growing in size and in range of
tasks. However, serious problems remain, including the
challenges of drug abuse, alcoholism, and childhood mental
illness, as well as a wide range of organizational and
administrative problems. (Journal abstract).

1357.   Stubblebine, J.M., and Decker, J.B., Are
         urban mental health centers worth it?
         Part II, American Journal of Psychiatry,
         1971, 128, 480-483.

The authors examine the value of community mental health
centers, using the San Francisco system as a model. This

system shows a reduction in distant state and local hospital use, and therefore a reduction in expenditures. The changing pattern of care requires coordinated but multiple treatment options and crisis intervention. When an urban program is organized in this way, more efficient use can be made of state and county tax dollars, and expenditures can often be reduced. (Journal abstract).

1358.   Suess, J.F., Brief psychotherapy of
         compulsive personalities, Current
         Psychiatric Therapies, 1973, 13, 99-103.

Since intellectualization, isolation, ambivalence, and un-doing will be constantly used by the patient, it is the therapist's task to help the patient recognize them for what they are and help the patient to set them aside. Only then can the patient perceive the nature of his emotional life and direct his feelings and abilities in a mature fashion toward realistic goals. These changes will not occur quickly with the compulsive patient, who feels comfortable only with rigid structure and order. He resists change since change to him implies dangerous loss of control and frightening uncertainty. (Journal abstract).

1359.   Suess, J.F., Short-term psychotherapy
         with compulsive personality and the
         obsessive-compulsive neurotic, American
         Journal of Psychiatry, 1972, 129, 270-275.

This article provides a concrete series of helpful psycho-therapeutic interventions recommended when dealing with a compulsive ego pattern in a patient. A general description of such a personality includes rigidity, retentive quality, little affective material, cold, etc. Such an individual views him/herself as logically minded, when in fact thought processes are quite compartmentalized. Defenses include intellectualization. Therapists should consistently focus on a patient's feelings rather than his/her words, espec-ially as they connect to his present life situation, including the therapy session itself. This would include the therapist helping the patient by identifying specific feelings from the patient's words, voice tone, facial expressions, etc. The therapist, in fact, is providing the

patient the opportunity to experience feelings without the
negative overtones. The avoidance of theoretical or intellectual discussions is encouraged. The value of the
therapist providing less critical interpretations to the
patient then those used by the patient is stressed, and is
referred to as "letting the patient borrow the therapist's
superego". The patient's use of pseudo-insight as its
incorporation into the patient's defensive structure is
also discussed. Compulsive patients' use of what Berne
referred to as "yes, but..." strategies is also reviewed
and strategies to counteract such styles are suggested.

1360.   Suinn, R.M., The desensitization of test
         anxiety by group and individual treatment,
         Behavior Research and Therapy, 1968, 6,
         385-387.

1361.   Suinn, R.M., Short-term desensitization
         therapy, Behaviour Research and Therapy,
         1970, 8, 383-384.

The author reports on the treatment of six patients whose
presenting problem consisted of extreme anxiety focusssed
on their first graduate course. The approach used was
behavioural (desensitization, including deep muscle
relaxation) with three, one-hour sessions used. Specific
outcome measures relating to decreases in anxiety were used
and positive results reported. The author points to the
value of such treatment approach in dealing with situational
crises.

1362.   Suinn, R., Anxiety management training
         for general anxiety, in, Suinn, R., and
         Weigel, R., (eds.), The innovative
         psychological therapies, New York,
         Harper, 1975.

The author describes a technique called Anxiety Management
Training (AMT), a conditioning technique. Basically, this
approach uses instructions and cues to produce anxiety reactions, and then involves the client in the development
of competing responses (e.g., relaxation or competency).

This chapter discusses the theoretical basis of AMT, provides
a comparison with other treatment methods and models, and
surveys the research findings regarding AMT.

1363.   Suinn, R.M., and Bloom, L.J., Anxiety
         management training for pattern A
         behavior, Journal of Behavioral Medicine,
         1978, 1, 25-35.

During a 3-week period, seven subjects were treated with
Anxiety Management Training (AMT) while seven subjects
served as a wait-list control. Pattern A behaviors, measured
by the Jenkins Activity Survey (JAS), self-report of anxiety,
as measured by the Spielberger state (STAI-S) and trait
(STAI-T) anxiety inventories, and indices of blood pressure,
cholesterol, and triglycerides were obtained before and after
treatment. Results indicate that treated subjects compared
to controls showed significant reductions in the Hard-Driving
component of pattern A behavior, showed lower posttest STAI-A
and STAI-T scores, but failed to evidence a statistically
significant reduction in systolic and diastolic blood
pressure or cholesterol and triglyceride levels. The implications of these data to theoretical and practical conceptualizations of stress management are discussed. (Journal
abstract).

1364.   Suinn, R.M., and Hall, R., Marathon
         desensitization groups: an innovative
         technique, Behaviour Research and Therapy,
         1970, 8, 97-98.

The aim of this study was to determine the effectiveness of
massed desensitization treatment trials over a very short
period of time, namely 24 hours. Also, the incorporation
of videotape as part of the procedure was involved. The
subjects were university students with test-anxiety problems.
Two groups were used, one given traditional desensitization
(TD) treatment and the other marathon desensitization (MD)
treatment. A total of six clients were used, three in each
group. TD group members met three time/week for a total of
11, one hour sessions. The MD group members met on one
afternoon from 1-5 P.M., and then the next morning from
8-noon. All therapy was done by having patients watch and

listen to videotapes. A total of four relaxation tapes and seven desensitization tapes were presented. Clients in both groups showed significant decreases in their anxiety scores from pre to post testing. Further, there was no significant difference between pre-treatment anxiety scores of TD and MD groups, or between post-treatment anxiety scores of TD and MD groups. The value of shortening treatment time by the use of massed desensitization treatment is supported by these findings.

1365.   Suinn, R.M., et al., Accelerated massed desensitization: Innovation in short-term treatment, Behavior Therapy, 1970, 1, 303-311.

Mathematics anxiety in 13 Ss was treated through two short-term desensitization approaches. The marathon desensitization group exposed Ss to desensitization massed in five consecutive treatment blocks totalling 4 hr. of therapy: the accelerated massed desensitization group was desensitized to only the highest items in the hierarchy within 2 hr involving two treatment blocks. In both treatment groups, Ss were not asked to signal if anxiety was experienced during scene presentation. Results on a self-rating scale, a performance measure, and an interview showed that both groups improved significantly following therapy. In addition, the level of improvement and the level of relaxation achieved by both groups were equivalent. Implications for theory and technique were discussed. (Journal abstract).

1366.   Suinn, R., and Richardson, F., Anxiety management training: A non-specific behavior therapy program for anxiety control, Behavior Therapy, 1971, 2, 498-510.

Anxiety management training (AMT) is a conditioning procedure to reduce anxiety reactions. AMT involves the arousal of anxiety and the training of the client to react to the anxiety with relaxation or success feelings. Unlike desensitization, AMT does not use anxiety hierarchies: it is based on the theory that anxiety responses can be discriminative stimuli, and that clients can be conditioned

to respond to these cues with responses which remove these
stimuli through reciprocal inhibition.

Thirteen students were treated for mathematics anxiety by
AMT, 11 by desensitization, and compared with 119 untreated,
nonanxious control subjects. Results show significant reductions in subjective anxiety for both treatment groups
but not for the control group. The AMT group showed higher
posttherapy scores on a performance measure involving mathe-
matical computations (the DAT) than the control group; the
standard desensitization group showed a significant incre-
ment in pre- to posttherapy scores on the same instrument.
Although the treatment subjects were not seeking therapy for
examination anxiety, self-ratings on test anxiety showed
significant decrements following treatment for mathematics
anxiety.

The study reports on the theoretical foandation for AMT,
details the technique, and discusses the value of the
approach in comparison with systematic desensitization.
(Journal abstract).

    1367.   Sullivan, P.L., et al., Factors in
             length of stay and progress in psycho-
             therapy, Journal of Consulting Psychology,
             1958, 22, 1-9.

A study of the factors related to length of stay and progress in psychotherapy in a VA mental hygiene clinic was
carried out. Particular attention was given to measures of
social status and to psychological variables which might be
associated with social stress. It was found that while the
Stay and Not-stay groups did not show any distinguishable
differences on the psychological variables used (MMPI),
the demographic variables of Education and Occupational
level did differentiate the Stayers from the Non-stayers.
When patients who were rated improved in psychotherapy were
compared with those rated unimproved, patients with higher
occupational achievement and less psychopathology proved to
be more successful in treatment. (Journal conclusion).

1368.   Surman, O.S., Postnoxious desensitization:
        Some clinical notes on the combined use
        of hypnosis and systematic desensitization,
        American Journal of Clinical Hypnosis,
        1979, 22, 54-60.

This paper describes a stylized form of systematic desensitization facilitated by hypnosis. The standard graduated approach methis is modified so that each event in an established hierarchy is presented under guided imagery from a vantage point of assumed task mastery. A case report is presented along with two brief clinical vignettes to illustrate the method. The method is in keeping with a cognitive approach to psychotherapy directed toward issues of self mastery and control. It has not been previously described. No statistical comparative data are available and no claim advanced of proven superiority to other methods. (Journal abstract).

1369.   Surman, O.S., et al., Usefulness of
        psychiatric intervention in patients
        undergoing cardiac surgery, Archives
        of General Psychiatry, 1974, 30, 830-835.

Twenty patients undergoing cardiac surgery were seen one or more times by a psychiatrist who performed two functions. In a supportive fashion he cleared up any misconceptions the patient had about the forthcoming surgery and he taught him a simple autohypnotic technique. Twenty controls, matched for relevant variables, received routine preoperative care. Contrary to the report of others, a single visit by the psychiatrist did not influence the incidence of postoperative delirium, anxiety, depression, pain, or medication requirements. However, there was a trend for patients receiving a greater number of preoperative visits to have a lower incidence of detected delirium. Age was the only factor in this study that differed significantly between delirious and nondelirious patients. (Journal abstract).

1370.   Swartz, J., Time-limited brief psycho-
         therapy, Seminars in Psychiatry, 1969,
         1, 380-388.

A crucial issue in time-limited therapy is delineation of a
focus around which to work. Swartz presents three cases
treated for a maximum of 12 hours of psychotherapy in an
outpatient clinic. For each case, he discusses principles
and reasoning entailed in the choice of a particular therapeutic focus. The author concludes his paper by stating
general guidelines derived from his clinical experience in
practising time-limited therapy. The first principle per-
tains to the manner in which the therapist formulates and
presents the plan of treatment to the patient. Once the
focus is chosen, the therapist should adhere to it, unless
there is incontrovertible evidence that the initial hypothesis was inaccurate. Secondly, the therapist must culti-
vate the ability to exclude material not directly relevant
to the focus. Conversely, the therapist must actively
introduce an issue which is clear and within that focus,
even if the patient has not adverted to it explicitly. His
last guideline concerns the importance of therapist activity
in the discussion of termination. (abstract by Deborah
Schuller).

1371.   Swenson, W., and Martin, H.R., A
         description and evaluation of an out-
         patient intensive psychotherapy center,
         American Journal of Psychiatry, 1976,
         133, 1043-1046.

The intensive psychotherapy center described and evaluated
in this paper (Mayo Clinic, Rochester, MN.) is unique
because of its intensity and the fact that available treatment modalities are integrated into the program. Patients
are literally immersed in therapy on a full-time basis for
an average of 3 weeks. Assessment of the program through
the use of questionnaires completed by 335 patients at the
time of discharge showed significant improvement in their
presenting symptoms, interpersonal relationships, ability to
work, and general level of comfort. An 8-month follow-up
study of 171 patients revealed that this improvement was
retained. (Journal abstract).

1372.   Tangari, A., Family involvement in the
         treatment of a psychiatric inpatient,
         Hospital and Community Psychiatry, 1974,
         25, 792-794.

The short-term diagnostic and treatment unit at C.F. Menninger Memorial Hospital emphasizes maximum involvement of the family in the treatment process. Family members are required to accompany the patient to the preadmission interview and remain available for several days after admission. Frequent visits to the hospitalized patient are encouraged; they are followed three days a week by hour-long meetings involving several patients, their families, and staff. The meetings foster increased communication between patient and their families by providing a mutually supportive group setting in which family members can explore their feelings and ventilate their anxieties. Unit staff believe that involvement of the patient's family in treatment helps reduce the likelihood of recurrence of problems that precipitated hospitalization. (Journal abstract).

1373.   Tannenbaum, S.A., Three brief psycho-
         analyses, American Journal of Urology,
         1919, 15.

1374.   Taplin, J.R., Crisis theory, critique
         and reformulation, Community Mental
         Health Journal, 1971, 7, 13-23.

Building a "crisis theory" by using pure homeostatic notions or psychoanalytic constructs is criticized. A review of crisis observations and their implications indicates that a cognitive perspective can serve as a theoretical framework: such a perspective is sketched with representative references. It is argued that several worthwhile possibilities follow from the use of a cognitive perspective: generation of systematic knowledge about crisis; an approach to research definitions; a series of new ways of conceiving of crisis intervention; spread of effect in manpower; and a broad approach to crisis prevention. Finally, a philosophy of science not supporting the looser perspective (versus tighter theory) is offered. (Journal abstract).

1375.   Taylor, J.W., Relationship of success
         and length of psychotherapy, Journal
         of Consulting Psychology, 1956, 20, 332.

The author reports on a sample of 309 subjects who were
evaluated as to improvement in therapy by their therapists
and a consultant. The results confirmed a "failure zone"
between the 13th and 21st session (i.e., earlier reports had
found such a zone using a client centered approach). This
time a psychoanalytically-oriented approach was used. That
is, higher rates of improvement were found for those clients
who had been seen either less than 13 sessions or more than
21 sessions.

1376.   Teichman, Y., et al., Crisis intervention
         with families of servicemen missing in
         action, American Journal of Community
         Psychology, 1978, 6, 315-325.

Investigated reactions and processes in a crisis situation
as well as experiences of those who engaged in crisis intervention activities. 32 volunteers, who worked with 55
families of servicemen missing in action during the October,
1973 Mideast war, described the families' reactions to the
given situation as well as their own involvement. Reactions
to crisis and expectations from the volunteers are described
and discussed. Special scrutiny was directed as the volunteering phenomenon and at the volunteers' motivations, needs,
reactions, and conflicts. (Journal abstract).

1377.   Terhune, W.B., Phobic syndrome: Study
         of 86 patients with phobic reactions,
         Archives of Neurology and Psychiatry,
         1949, 62, 162-172.

The author describes in detail the common characteristics in
a group of 86 patients with phobic reactions. The basic
phobic personality style and make-up is presented, along
with a description of the two month treatment program. The
importance of follow-up is stressed.

1378.   Terhune, W.B., Brief psychotherapy with
         executives in industry, Progress in
         Psychotherapy, 1960, 5, 132-139.

The author describes a procedure, the "Emotional Check-up
for Executives", designed to produce benefits for the
individual and the organization the individual works in.
The specific procedures are described, including the gathering of pre-interview information, and a six-day period of
intensive investigation (psychiatric, psychological, and
physical). The findings are also presented in general terms,
and specific recommendations about such a brief therapy/
assessment are discussed.

1379.   Thomas, D.V., The relationship between
         diagnostic service and short-contact
         cases, Social Casework, 1951, 32, No. 2.

Thomas briefly examines the evolution of diagnostic services
offered by the private family agency, and the relation of
diagnosis to the short-contact case. She refers to a study
conducted by the Family Service Association of America, and
notes the extent to which concepts related to continued
treatment influence conceptualizations of short-term treatment. The author argues for a more precise definition of
terms with regards to "short-contact cases", and an enlarge-
ment of the concept of diagnostic service. (abstract by
Deborah Schuller).

1380.   Thorne, F.C., Directive psychotherapy:
         theory, practice, and social implications,
         Journal of Clinical Psychology, 1953, 9,
         267-280.

The author provides an historical background to the emergence
of scientific concepts of conflict, change, and coping. The
conceptualization of therapy as a learning process is
stressed, and major points common to all forms of directive
therapy presented. These include the role of the therapist
as educator, the setting an environment conducive for learning, the active role of the therapist in the diagnostic
process and the overseeing role in confirming that the client
has in fact taken action.

1381.   Thorpe, J.G., et al., Aversion-relief
         therapy: a new method for general
         application, Behaviour Research and
         Therapy, 1964, 2, 71-82.

A new technique named Aversion-Relief Therapy is described.
It appears to be suitable for general application in the
field of neurosis and greatly simplifies the normal requirements of the treatment situation. Cases are presented in
which the technique has been applied and the therapeutic
results are so far encouraging. Some of the theoretical
issues involved are discussed. (Journal summary).

1382.   Tiller, J.W.G., Brief family therapy
         for childhood tic syndrome, Family
         Process, 1978, 17, 217-223.

This paper reports the success of brief analytically oriented
outpatient family therapy exclusively in treating an eight-
year old girl presenting with a short history of multiple
tics involving facial, thoracic, and upper limb musculature,
with associated boarse coughing and grunting. Diagnostic
features are reviewed. No medicines were used, and the
patient remained asymptomatic nine months after ceasing
family therapy. Tentative indications for family therapy
for tiqueurs are proposed. (Journal abstract).

1383.   Timmons, F.R., Brief psychotherapy in
         an adolescent medical clinic: A case
         example, Journal of Pediatric Psychology,
         1977, 2, 138-140.

A large percentage of the patients who come to an adolescent
medical clinic manifest some degree of psychological distress; however, these patients often initially prefer to see
their problems as medical and do not seek the services of a
mental health practitioner. The case presented demonstrates
one important function which a specialist in mental health
can serve in a general medical clinic. It describes the
treatment of a 14 yr. old girl who was depressed and
suffered from feelings of depersonalization. It highlights
the point that although her symptoms were severe enough to
induce her to take a leave of absence from her positions as
vice-president of the student council and president of the

Pep Club, she had a number of strengths that enabled her to
make use of brief psychotherapy. Thus, she was well suited
for treatment in the medical setting where she presented
herself. By participating in treatment she attained some
resolution of her difficulties and remission of her symptoms
without a referral to a psychiatric clinic. (Journal
abstract).

1384.   Tolor, A., Teachers evaluation of
         children in short-term treatment with
         subprofessionals, Journal of Clinical
         Psychology, 1968, 24, 377-378.

The author presents tentative results based on a short-term
(average 4.5 months) treatment approach with 25 children,
ages 6-12. The group consisted of both male and female
students and were 2/3's Caucasian and 1/3 Black. Teachers
completed behavioral and attitudinal questionnaires, and the
results show positive changes in areas of emotional maturation, increasing sense of achievement possibilities, etc.
A follow-up research project is suggested to reconfirm the
results.

1385.   Tolor, A., The effectiveness of various
         therapeutic approaches: A study of sub-
         professional therapists, International
         Journal of Group Psychotherapy, 1970,
         20, 48-62.

A study to evaluate the efficacy of three treatment formats
as employed by nonprofessional social counselors is presented. Elementary and junior high school level, emotionally
disturbed children were seen in individual, group, or
individual combined with group, therapy. Change was evaluated on both self- and teacher-rating scales. Characteristics of the counselors, the treatment setting, demographic
characteristics of the sample, and the two instruments are
described--although the content of treatment received is
not specified. Tolor reviews the significant within- and
between-groups differences on each instrument for the two
age groups. The results suggest that group therapy only,
as applied by nonprofessionals with school children is less
effective than other treatment formats. (abstract by
Deborah Schuller).

1386.   Tompkins, H.J., Short-term therapy of
         neurosis, in, Usdin, G.L. (ed.),
         Psychoneurosis and schizophrenia,
         Philadelphia, Lippincott, 1966.

Reported on a project to ascertain the practicality of
financing a brief outpatient treatment program via pre-paid
insurance.

1387.   Topel, S.I., Of crisis, family, and
         therapist: A preliminary guide to a
         therapeutic process in a disadvantaged
         Los Angeles community, American Journal
         of Orthospychiatry, 1967, 37, 280.

The author summarizes some of the differences between the
more traditional therapist role and the quality of the
therapeutic relationship demanded in a crisis situation
with economically disadvantaged families. The specific
experiences drawn upon occurred at the South Central Los
Angeles Mental Health Service.

1388.   Townsend, G.E., Short-term casework
         with clients under stress, Social
         Casework, 1953, 34, 392-398.

The author uses case material to highlight the kinds of
experiences a social worker is confronted with in daily
work with the Travelers Aid Society. Issues such as separation, family conflict, etc. are presented.

1389.   Tracey, J., Parent guidance groups:
         Is this therapy? Journal of Psychiatric
         Nursing and Mental Health Services, 1970,
         8, 11-12.

A program of primary prevention, using short-term Group
therapy with parent couples of children with school-centered
problems has been carried on for the last three years. The
results suggest the technique may have wider applicability
in this and other settings, such as Preschool programs,
Head Start, Comprehensive Mental Health Centers and Day-Care
Centers. (Journal conclusion).

1390.   Trakas, D.A., and Lloyd, G., Emergency
         management in a short term open group,
         Comprehensive Psychiatry, 1970, 12,
         170-175.

The authors report on two group therapy approaches in dealing
with a variety of patient problems. The first group was
time limited, the second open-ended re time and number of
sessions. A measure of functioning level was administered
prior to and following treatment. The patients in short-
term therapy showed significantly greater improvement, and
less need to use drugs in their treatment. A total of 78
patients were seen within the time limited model of treatment, and 90 were seen in the unlimited group treatment
condition.

1391.   Treppa, J.S., and Fricke, L., Effects
         of a marathon group experience, Journal
         of Counseling Psychology, 1972, 19,
         466-467.

The present study examined the effects of a weekend marathon
group experience on values of self-actualization and on the
interpersonal dimension of personality. The Personal Orientation Inventory, the Minnesota Multiphasic Inventory, and
the Interpersonal Check List were administered immediately
before the marathon group, 2 days after, and 6 weeks later.
Both experimental and control subjects showed significantly
positive changes on posttest and follow-up scores. It was
concluded that it was premature to believe that the positive
effects of a marathon group experience had been adequately
demonstrated. The results were discussed with reference to
two hypotheses that are in need of testing. (Journal
abstract).

1392.   Truax, C.B., et al., Therapist empathy,
         genuineness, and warmth and patient
         therapeutic outcome, Journal of Consulting
         Psychology, 1966, 30, 395-401.

A study aimed at cross-validating previous research suggesting that the levels of the therapist's accurate empathy,
nonpossessive warmth, and genuineness were casually related
to the degree of patient improvement or deterioration. An

equal number of "good" or "poor" therapy prospects were
randomly assigned to 4 resident psychiatrists (10 patients
each) for 4 months of psychotherapy. Results tended to
confirm the importance of the 3 therapeutic conditions in
combination and of empathy and genuineness separately.
Negative findings for separate analysis of therapist's
warmth were interpreted in terms of its negative correlation
with empathy and genuineness in the present sample. On the
overall measure for all patients, therapists providing high
therapeutic conditions had 90% patient improvement while
those providing lower conditions had 50% improvement.
(Journal abstract).

1393.   Truax, C.B., et al., The therapist's
         contribution to accurate empathy, non-
         possessive warmth, and genuineness in
         psychotherapy, Journal of Clinical
         Psychology, 1966, 22, 331-334.

The present data support the previous findings indicating
that the therapeutic conditions of AE, NPW, and GEN were
primarily a function of the therapist and not the patient.
In early interviews the patient, however, does effect the
level of NPW. Some evidence indicating positive relationships between the level of these conditions occurring during
therapy and degree of psychotherapeutic outcome is currently
available, the present findings fit the casual hypothesis
suggesting the therapist determines the level of conditions
occurring in therapy which in turn determines the level of
psychotherapeutic outcome.

1394.   Tuckman, A.J., Brief psychotherapy and
         hemodialysis, Archives of General
         Psychiatry, 1970, 23, 65-69.

Recent advances in the cases of patients with end-stage
renal disease whose lives are being prolonged by hemodialsys
have led to increasing interest in the psychological aspects
of these patients. A case is presented of one of these
patients who during the evaluation phase for hemodialysis
suffered a psychotic episode. The conflicts and defenses

elaborated by this stress are explored and a discussion is presented of brief psychotherapy techniques. It is felt that brief psychotherapy is the treatment choice in many of these patients. (Journal summary).

1395.   Tuckman, A.J., Disaster and mental
         health intervention, Community Mental
         Health Journal, 1973, 9, 151-157.

The author summarizes and describes the actions of a number of mental health professionals in helping a community meet with and psychologically deal with a school bus-train collision in which a large number of high school students were involved. The type of intervention done with school personnel, hospital personnel, teachers, parents, and students is presented within the context of a model for crisis intervention. Some specific examples of the work done are presented in brief form.

1396.   Tyhurst, J.S., The role of transition
         states - including disasters - in mental
         illness, Symposium of Preventive and
         Social Psychiatry, Walter Reed Army
         Institute of Research, Washington, D.C.,
         1957.

1397.   Tyler, V.O., and Brown, D.G., The use
         of swift, brief isolation as a group
         device for institutionalized delinquents,
         Behaviour Research and Therapy, 1967, 5,
         1-9.

An attempt was made to control misbehavior around the pool table in a training school cottage. The Ss were 15 boys, ages 13-15, committed by courts. Misbehavior included the rules of the game, throwing pool cues, scuffling, kibitzing and bouncing balls on floor. In Phase I (7 weeks), misbehavior resulted in S being immediately confined in a "time-out" room for 15 min. In Phase II (13 weeks), S was verbally reprimanded. In Phase III (20 weeks) confinement was resumed. Ss cumulative records showed decreasing rates

of misbehavior during confinement condition and rapid recovery during reprimand condition. The conclusion is that
swift, brief confinement was a useful control device. The
problems of obtaining greater resistance to extinction and
also, positive generalization to other situations remain
to be studied. (Journal summary).

   1398.   Tyson, R., et al., A study of psychiatric
             emergencies: Part I: Demographic data,
             Psychiatry in Medicine, 1970, 1, 349-357.

Psychiatric emergency evaluation and treatment are an increasingly important part of current psychiatric practice.
Psychiatry residency training has been affected accordingly.
Of particular importance has been the need to characterize
the emergency population seen and to describe the changes
in this population over time. At University Hospital of
Cleveland over the past nine years the psychiatric emergency
population has doubled. There has also been a shift to a
younger age group, evidence of better motivation, reduced
incidence of hospitalization, and increased use of medications. At this hospital, Negro females constituted the
largest group and contained the highest percentage of
patients receiving medications. Possible reasons for these
findings are discussed. (Journal abstract).

   1399.   Uhlenhuth, E.H., and Duncan, D.B.,
             Subjective change with medical student
             therapists, I. Course of relief in
             psychoneurotic outpatients, Archives of
             General Psychiatry, 1968, 18, 428-438.

This is a quantitative study of certain subjective changes
occurring in 128 primarily psychoneurotic outpatients, each
interviewed weekly from one to ten times (meach of six
sessions), by a senior medical student on his clinical
clerkship in psychiatry. Each patient reported his subjective distress on a checklist of 65 symptoms every week before
his interview with the student. Measures were also taken at
the outset of treatment and at termination. The course of
symptomatic change was marked by a sharp drop between the
first two interviews, followed by a somewhat slower,
but sustained decrease over the remaining interviews. The

earlier and later course of relief also differed in other
respects. Symptoms did not recur at the last two interviews of the series. The results indicate that psychoneurotic outpatients attending a university clinic for a
brief series of interviews with senior medical students
experience symptomatic relief roughly comparable to that
provided by other forms of clinic treatment. (Journal
summary).

   1400.   Uhlenhuth , E.H., and Duncan, D.B.,
            Subjective change with medical student
            therapists, II. Some determinants of
            change in psychoneurotic outpatients,
            Archives of General Psychiatry, 1968,
            18, 532-540.

This is a quantitative study of certain subjective changes
occurring in 128 primarily psychoneurotic outpatients, each
interviewed weekly about six times by a senior medical
student on his clerkship in psychiatry. The determinants
of symptomatic change were examined in 105 patients with
complete data on 35 variables including characteristics
of the patient and characteristics of the students. The
patient's initial depression score was the most important
single determinant of change. Patients with a higher
initial level of depression improved more. The following
characteristics of the patient also contributed to relief
of symptomatic distress: 1) greater optimism at the outset
about the probable outcome of treatment; 2) a shorter waiting
period between psychiatric evaluation and the beginning of
treatment; 3) greater chronicity of the present illness.
The following characteristics of the student contributed to
the patient's relief: 1) interests similar to those of
successful psychiatrists on the Strong Vocational Interest
Blank, 2) his mother's age when he was born (the most
successful students were born to unusually young and especially to unusually old mothers). (Journal summary).

   1401.   Ullmann, L.P., and Krasner, L., (eds.),
            Case studies in behavior modification,
            New York, Holt, Rinehart, and Winston,
            1965.

1402.   Ungerleider, J.T., The psychiatric
         emergency: Analysis of six months
         experience of a university hospital's
         consultation service, Archives of
         General Psychiatry, 1960, 3, 593-601.

The Psychiatric Emergency Consultation Service at University
Hospitals has been reviewed for a 6-month period (1958-59).
Three hundred and seventy-eight psychiatric emergencies
were seen during this time. The object of the study was
to provide detailed data about the psychiatric emergency
situation and patient and to answer the following hypothetical questions: 1. Who are these patients? 2. Where do
they come from? 3. How and why do the come? Are they true
emergencies? 4. What treatment and disposition do these
patients receive? What becomes of them? (Journal summary).

1402a.   Ursano, R.J., and Dressler, D.M., Brief
         versus long term psychotherapy: A treat-
         ment decision, Journal of Nervous and
         Mental Disease, 1974, 159, 164-171.

The subject of brief psychotherapy has often been mentioned
but rarely investigated. How the practicing clinician
decides for brief vs. long term psychotherapy is relatively
unknown. This study has examined this treatment decision
in 99 cases evaluated in a community mental health center.
The treatment decision was found to be unaffected by the
sociodemographic variables of the patients, but significantly
affected by certain clinical patient-clinician interactional
and institutional variables. Results did not support the
concept of brief psychotherapy as supportive and long term
psychotherapy as explorative, but rather suggested a focal-
non-focal (multifocal) model as accounting for differences
between brief and long term psychotherapy. Implications
for an institutional referral process are discussed.
(Journal abstract).

1403.   Ursano, R.J., and Dressler, D.M., Brief
         versus long-term psychotherapy: Clinical
         attitudes and organizational design,
         Comprehensive Psychiatry, 1977, 18, 55-60.

The authors present the results of a research project based
on the attitudes of the clinical staff members at the
Connecticut Mental Health Center, in New Haven, as they
relate to the issues of brief individual and long term
individual psychotherapy. Overall, the clinicians rated
brief therapy as more effective in situational adjustment
reactions. Long term therapy was seen as more effective in
dealing with neurotic depression, neuroses, psychoses, and
personality disorders. When the individual training backgrounds, and professional affiliations of the clinicians
were broken down into sub-groups, the authors found that
nurses rated long term therapy as more effective for neurotic
depressions than did social workers, psychologists, or psychiatrists. Psychologists and psychiatrists rated long term
therapy as more effective for other neuroses over all other
clinicians, and psychiatrists saw less value in brief therapy
than did the other clinicians. The authors conclude by
suggesting that rather than viewing brief forms of therapy as
supportive and long term forms as exploratory, a more meaningful differentiation would be along focal - nonfocal (or
multifocal) lines. They further stress the value of multidisciplinary teams which would contribute to interdisciplinary cross-fertilization of biases to treatment modalities.

1404.   Vachon, M.L., and Lyall, W.A., Applying
         psychiatric techniques to patients with
         cancer, Hospital and Community Psychiatry,
         1976, 27, 582-584.

A patient with cancer frequently experiences significant
stress in adjusting to his disease. The authors felt that
cancer patients who are receiving physical care in a general
hospital may benefit from psychiatric techniques used
regularly by mental health professionals. They describe
weekly group meetings in which newly diagnosed cancer
patients talk with hospital staff, consultants from a
psychiatric institute, and more experienced cancer patients
about problems in adjustment, misconceptions about cancer,
reactions of family and friends, and problems in relating

physicians. To date approximately 2000 patients have
attended the meetings. In most cases their anxiety has
decreased as they talk with other cancer patients who have
learned to live with their disease, and as they see alternative methods for dealing with their problems. (Journal
abstract).

1405.   Vaillant, G.E., Sociopathy as a human
         process, Archives of General Psychiatry,
         1975, 32, 178-183.

The author highlights, both through a theoretical discussion
as well as case presentations, some of the striking differences between treating sociopaths in inpatient versus outpatient settings. The inpatient setting denies the socio-
path the opportunity to "run" from his/her problems, and
exposes the severity and humanity of his problems. The
emphasis on external controls is discussed, and the value
of realistic confrontation, within a supportive context
rather than a punitive context is documented. Such sociopathic characteristics as absence of anxiety, lack of motivation, inability to experience depression, are discussed
in detail and related to both personality constructs and
treatment suggestions. The value of the use of group
therapy, within a realistically oriented, confrontive context is also presented.

1406.   Vaillant, G.E., et al., Current thera-
         peutic results in schizophrenia, New
         England Journal of Medicine, 1964,
         271, 280-283.

Reported on a study which followed the progress made by 103
diagnosed schizophrenics at the Mass. Mental Health Center.
The main finding was that a large percentage of those so
diagnozed were able to maintain employment (54%), and 57%
had meaningful relationships with non-family members.
Short-term therapy was used, and only 8% of the 103 patients
had to be hospitalized for more than 18 months.

1407.   Valle, J., and Axelberd, M., Police
        intervention into family crisis: A
        training model, Crisis Intervention,
        1977, 8, 117-123.

1408.   Vaughan, W.T., and Downing, J.J.,
        Planning for early treatment
        psychiatric services, Mental Hygiene,
        1962, 46, 486-497.

This paper is based on material presented and discussed at
the Roundtable on Emergency Psychiatric Services, at the
1958 Annual Meeting of the American Psychiatric Association.
The emphasis is placed on early psychiatric treatment with
a strong preventive aim.   Some of the procedures and benefits of the following programs are described: emergency
psychiatric assistance at the scene of a crisis; emergency
psychiatric clinic in a large metropolitan hospital; preadmission home visits by a psychiatric team from a state
hospital; community psychiatric services after a natural
disaster; and psychiatric services in a police department.
Six mental health professionals contribute to the discussion which follows.   (abstract by Deborah Schuller).

1409.   Velhulst, J., Marital change: An
        intensive short-term approach,
        International Mental Health Research
        Newsletter, 1975, 17, 7-10.

1410.   Verinis, J.S., Therapeutic effectiveness
        of untrained volunteers with chronic
        patients, Journal of Consulting and
        Clinical Psychology, 1970, 34, 152-155.

Twenty chronic psychotic patients were divided into a treatment (n=13) and control (n=7) group.   The groups were matched
for age, education, sex, length of hospitalization, and diagnosis.   The treatment group patients had one of 13 non-
professional therapists assigned to them for one session a
week.   Seven of the therapists were given an optimistic
picture of their chance of helping the patient and the
remaining six were given a pessimistic guarded outlook.

The program was continued for five months. Upon termination
it was found that the treatment group showed significantly
more improvement in their interactions with the aides, and
in both the quantity and quality of their social behavior
(less verbal hostility, better sense of humor, and less
withdrawn). There were also five treatment-group patients
discharged from the hospital while none of the control
group left. The initial outlook of the therapists made no
difference. (Journal abstract).

1411.   Viney, L.L., The concept of crisis: A
         tool for clinical psychologists, Bulletin
         of the British Psychological Society,
         1976, 29, 287-295.

1412.   Visher, J.S., Brief psychotherapy in a
         mental hygiene clinic, American Journal
         of Psychotherapy, 1959, 13, 331-342.

The author describes the process of introducing a brief
therapy programe to a mental hygiene clinic. The administrative arrangements, involving elimination of waiting
lists and education of staff toward this treatment modality
are discussed. A specific case history is presented to
highlight the treatment process. The criteria for selecting
patients for brief therapy include: a) readiness for change;
b) definite precipitating factors; c) environmental stability
and evidence of previous adjustment; d) ability to use the
initial interview in a positive way. Not all of these conditions need be met, but if all are the prognosis is good
in short-term treatment. Contraindications are patients
with problems which are part of their character structure
as opposed to being part of a reactive aspect. The need
for the therapist to be focussed on the present, actively-
oriented, placing responsibility on the patient for change,
the belief on the therapist's part that change is possible
within a short span of time, are all stressed. Issues of
termination are also raised. Clinical results reported here
indicate that patients who have had brief therapy apply for
readmission about as frequently as those who have had longer
term approaches.

1413. Volkan, V., A study of a patient's
"re-grief work" through dreams,
psychological tests, and psychoanalysis,
Paychiatric Quarterly, 1971, 45, 255-273.

Over a period of five years, the author has been involved
in treating more than 50 patients in a university setting
who had lost through death a close relative. All patients
exhibited a series of symptoms, and as a result of working
with these patients, an approach labelled re-grief work has
emerged. This approach is described in detail through a
case history, as well as through a theoretical description
of the method. It includes three phases: a) Demarcation:
patient is helped to rationally distinguish between what
belongs to him and what belongs to the deceased (focussing
on the persistent seeking of reunion with the dead); b)
Externalization phase: in which patient is encouraged to
continue detailing aspects of the death and dead person,
and anger usually begins to emerge, first towards others
and then towards the deceased. Disorganization often seen
during this phase; c) Reorganization phase: patient usually
grieves and feels sad, and questions and suggestions about
the future come up. This entire process usually takes about
two months, with four sessions/week. The case history presented includes an analysis of dream material, results of
psychological testing, and the details from a longer analysis
which the patient decided to enter following the re-grief
work.

1414. Volkan, V.D., More on re-grief therapy,
Journal of Thanatology, 1975, 3, 77-91.

The author presents the details of re-grief therapy, a
specifically oriented short-term psychotherapy aimed at
those clients with established pathological grief. Two
case vignettes are presented to highlight the material.

1415.   Volkan, V.D., and Josephthal, D., Brief
        psychotherapy in pathological grief:
        re-grief therapy, in, Karasu, T.B., and
        Bellak, L., (eds.), Special techniques in
        psychotherapy, New York, International
        Universities Press, in press.

This paper concerns adult mourning, its complications, and
therapeutic management. The clinical picture of the person
suffering from established pathological grief is presented.
Such grief is characterized by a chronic hope that the dead
one will return, coupled with equally strong dread of such
an event. Typical behaviours of the pathological mourner
are described. Splitting, internalization, and externalization are identified as the primary intrapsychic mechanisms
underlying established grief. The particular defensive use
of these processes differentiates this clinical entity from
reactive depression, fetishism, and psychosis. Suitability
of patients for re-grief therapy is discussed. Volkan and
Josephthal detail their method of brief but intensive
psychotherapy, which focuses on a circumscribed cluster of
conflicts with respect to content, unconscious processes,
and transference. A case history is reviewed. (abstract
by Deborah Schuller).

1416.   Volkan, V., and Showalter, C.R., Known
        object loss, disturbance in reality
        testing, and "re-grief work" as a method
        of brief psychotherapy, Psychiatric
        Quarterly, 1968, 42, 358-374.

The method described in this paper utilizes as it corner-
stone focalization upon a specific aspect of the patient's
history, namely the lose of an object to which the patient
had developed significant libidinal and aggressive attach-
ments. The paper develops a concept of "re-grief work",
which is a method of short-term psychotherapy in which a
patient suffering from delayed or pathological grief reaction somewhat later in time than would be expected in the
normal course of grief work. (Journal summary).

1417.   Volkan, V.D., et al., "Re-grief" therapy
         and the function of the linking object as
         a key to stimulate emotionality, in, Olsen,
         P., (ed.), Emotional flooding, New York,
         Behavioral Publications, 1975.

This chapter treats in detail theory and method of re-grief
therapy, with particular emphasis to the function of the
"linking object", both within the pathology and the treatment. Established pathological grief is described as a
freezing in the phase of normal adult mourning characterized by the desire to recover the lost person, but pathological grief implies a concomitant dread of that individual's return. The psychodynamics of such grief are
examined in terms of internalization (introjection) and
externalization (via the linking object). Volkan et al.
discuss the selection of patients for re-grief work, and
elaborate on specific goals and steps of the process.
Several case histories illustrate its application. Lastly,
the authors examine why "emotional storms" occur with the
introduction, during the course of treatment, of the
patient's linking object. Dynamic processes underlying the
patient's use of this object are considered in relation to
transitional objects (as per Winnicott), and childhood and
adult fetishes. The authors conclude that the linking
object is a "reactivated variation of the transitional
object", and caution against its injudicious use in treatment as a mere "mechanical aid" or "magical shortcut".
(abstract by Deborah Schuller).

1418.   Voltolina, E.J., et al., Adaptation of
         crisis intervention to navy outpatient
         psychiatric clinic population, Military
         Medicine, 1971, 136, 546-548.

1419.   Wagner, M.K., Parent therapists: An
         operant conditioning method, Mental
         Hygiene, 1968, 52, 452-455.

Through the use of a single case history, the author provides
a detailed description of the use of operant conditioning
procedures in the training of parents to deal with a problem

child. The specific reinforcement procedures are detailed,
including a work-up of what the parents wanted to see happen,
the reinforcement needed, and what behavior they wanted to
see stop and what non-reinforcement or punishment they
needed to use.

1420.   Wagner, M.K., A case of public mastur-
         bation treated by operant conditioning,
         Journal of Child Psychology and Psychiatry,
         1968, 9, 61-65.

This paper describes the treatment of an 11-yr-old girl
reported by her teacher as masturbating publicly in the
classroom as frequently as 7 times per hour. As opposed to
most attempts where the modification of sexual responses has
been with aversive conditioning, this procedure employed the
positive reinforcement of an incompatible response. During
the course of 129 school days, continuous, F.I. and aperiodic
reinforcement schedules were applied to the response of non-
masturbation. After 74 days, the non-masturbatory response
became continuous and persisted until the end of the school
year. This practical demonstration of the effectiveness of
this procedure with a behavior as typically recalcitrant as
'compulsive' masturbation further generalizes the utility
of the operant conditioning model. (Journal summary).

1421.   Wagner,R.F., Short-term counseling in the
         school setting: A diagnostic thera-
         peutic approach, Journal of School
         Psychology, 1963, 1, 42-50.

1422.   Wagner, R.F., Modern child management,
         Johnstown, Pa., Mafex Associates, 1975.

This approach uses a three sessions brief counseling structure, based on Multiple Image Merger Hypothesis (Client,
Parent, School).

1423. Wagner, R.F., Compact counseling,
Valdosta, Ga., Unpublished manuscript,
Valdosta State College Counseling
Center, 1979.

This manuscript presents a structured approach to short-term counseling for student practicum supervision and crisis intervention.

1424. Wahl, C.W., The technique of brief
psychotherapy with hospitalized psychosomatic patients, International Journal
of Psychoanalytic Psychotherapy, 1972, 1,
69-82.

A variety of factors in medically hospitalized patients with psychosomatic disorders particularly lend themselves to an intensification of the doctor-patient relationship and act, therefore, to facilitate short-term insight psychotherapeutic treatment of the prevailing disorder. These include the naive fear of illness and the ego-regression that it produces, the isolating effect of hospitalization, a dimished access to the primary physician, and a corresponding accessibility to the psychiatrist. The taking of the psychiatric history itself, featuring as it does special inquiry into the factors that have molded the patient's character and personality as well as exploration and investigation of the conscious and unconscious stresses that antecede the immediate conflict, also acts as a powerful adjuvant to therapeutic progress.

The particularly intense positive transference that characteristically develops under these circumstances enables a number of modifications to be made in classic psychotherapeutic technique. Resistance, which is greatly reduced, is usually avoided rather than interpreted. Interpretation--educational and genetic--can be accomplished much sooner, and the "working through," necessary in outpatient psychotherapy, seems not to be so necessary.

The implications of these findings in the psychotherapy of psychosomatic disorders is explored and discussed. (Journal abstract).

1425.   Waldfogel, S., et al., School phobia:
         Causes and Management, School Counselor,
         1955, 3, 19-25.

1426.   Waldfogel, S., et al., The development,
         meaning and management of school phobia:
         Workshop, American Journal of Ortho-
         psychiatry, 1957, 27, 754-780.

This article consists of a series of papers resulting from
observations on 53 cases of school phobia. Waldfogel
analyses the particular constellation of family relationships which underlies the development of school phobia.
From a psychoanalytic framework, he discusses basic theoretic issues as specificity of symptom choice, the relation
between personality structure and symptom formation, and the
dynamics of the mother-child-father triad. He reflects
briefly on the dynamics of phobias, noting distinguishing
features of school phobia. Coolidge focusses on typical
reaction patterns manifest during treatment. Although the
child's return to school is regarded as only symptom relief
(the true therapeutic aim being realignment of disturbances
in the family), Coolidge emphasizes the constructive effect
of a first interview; and notes the necessity of viewing
acute symptom formation as a psychiatric emergency--with
minimal delay in initiation of treatment. Phases of treatment and technical problems which may occur are outlined.
Hahn describes the collaborative relation between the clinic
conducting the research and one school system. A program
of school consultation was organized to permit identification
of acute transient cases (for which brief "emergency"
therapy in the school or counseling center was offered) and
chronic, subclinical cases. Data on case-finding and outcome of brief therapy support the value of the program.
Case material is presented by Coolidge and Hahn. A discussion of the three papers is appended. (abstract by
Deborah Schuller).

1427.   Waldfogel, S., et al., A program for
        early intervention in school phobia,
        American Journal of Orthopsychiatry,
        1959, 29, 324-33.

The authors summarize the results of 36 cases seen at the
Judge Baker Guidance Center, a child guidance center. The
aims of the program included identifying as early as possible
school phobia cases, to differentiate the most severe pathological cases from less severe, to refer the very severe
personality disturbances for longer term treatment, and to
develop a crisis intervention model for treating the others.
A program was developed, which involved on-going co-operation
with Newton Public Schools. Criteria for determining method
of treatment are summarized, including degree of emotional
separation and repressed hostility between mother and child,
their initial response to intake, and reactions to various
stresses in the interview. Methods of dealing with school
phobias are presented, along with a case history. Follow-
up evaluation, based on information from teachers, parents,
most children were symptom free. Of those children who did
not receive brief treatment, most continued to report symptoms and a greater number of school problems.

1428.   Wales, E., Crisis intervention in clinical
        training, Professional Psychology, 1972,
        3, 357-361.

The author reviews the changes in role-modelling that have
occurred within clinical psychology training programs, with
an emphasis on the emergence of crisis intervention as an
area which traditional academic training programs have
neglected. Issues of responsibility, self-confidence, and
understanding of the nature of assessments under crisis
conditions are discussed.

1429.   Walfish, S., et al., The development of
        a contract negotiation scale for crisis
        counseling, Crisis Intervention, 1976,
        7, 136-148.

1430.   Walker, R.G., and Kelley, F.E., Short
         term psychotherapy with schizophrenic
         patients evaluated over a three-year
         follow-up period, Journal of Nervous
         and Mental Disease, 1962, 137, 349-352.

The outcome of a group of 44 newly hospitalized schizophrenic patients who had received formal shortterm psychotherapy was compared over a three-year follow-up period
with that of 38 essentially comparable patients who had not
received formal psychotherapy. Similar proportions of
favorable outcome were found for the treated and untreated
groups both with respect to overall length of community
stay and in regard to readmission rates over the three-year
follow-up period. Two-thirds of the patients released
within one year of admission returned to hospital one or
more times over the follow-up period; the median length of
community stay was approximately 30 months. Similarly, with
respect to measures of symptomatic improvement and ratings
of interpersonal relationships in the community, the treated
and control groups were essentially the same. The limitations of the present study and problems associated with
evaluating effectiveness of psychotherapy with schizophrenic
patients were briefly discussed. (Journal summary).

1431.   Wallace, M.A., and Morley, W.E., Teaching
         crisis intervention, American Journal of
         Nursing, 1970, 70, 1484-1487.

Crisis intervention is designed to help a person in trouble
recognize and cope with a specific problem, not to change
his life style. Graduate students in nursing are being
taught the theory and technique in a relatively short time.
Some of the problems encountered by the students, the
patterns into which the problems fall, and the methods of
resolution are discussed in this article. (Journal
abstract).

1432.   Wallace, M.A., and Schreiber, F.B.,
         Crisis intervention training for local
         police officers: A practical program
         for local police departments, Journal
         of Psychiatric Nursing, 1977, 15, 25-29.

The authors report on a training program designed by the
Boulder County Community Mental Health Center in cooperation
with two local police departments focussed on providing
training in crisis intervention principles and techniques
to police. Role playing and the use of videotaping was
incorporated into this program focussed on dealing with the
FDC (family disturbance call). The role playing included
one situation with alcoholism, one with psychotic-like
behavior, and one of a suicide threat. A follow-up
evaluation was conducted, measuring attitudinal and psychological variables related to the crisis calls. Those
officers who had received the training reported a greater
degree of satisfaction in the way they had handled the most
serious FDC's when compared with officers who had not
received such training. Further, the trained group felt
that such emergencies were more predictable than those
officers who did not receive training.

1433.   Walsh, J.A., and Phelan, T.W., People
         in crisis: An experimental group,
         Community Mental Health Journal, 1974,
         10, 3-8.

This paper discusses the efforts of a community mental
health center to respond more swiftly and creatively to
crisis situations. The planning, operation, and termination
of a crisis group are presented. This experiment served 17
people with no one remaining in the group for more than six
sessions. Pre- and post-studies were conducted with group
participants to help evaluate the changes, as the patient
perceived them, that took place as a result of the group.
The experiment covered a six-month period. (Journal
abstract).

1434.   Walsh, J.A., and Wittie, P.G., Police
         training in domestic crisis: A suburban
         approach, Community Mental Health Journal,
         1975, 11, 301-306.

This paper discusses an intervention method that was presented to develop joint police-mental health programs with
seven suburban police departments. A seminar on family
crisis intervention was instituted. The program method and
goals are described and the results of numerous new requests
by police for mental health consultation are discussed.
Results suggest that a training approach different from urban
programs is needed and wanted by suburban police. The initiative for developing such programs falls on the shoulders
of the community mental health practitioners. (Journal
abstract).

1435.   Walter, H., and Gilmore, S.K., Placebo
         versus social learning effects in parent
         training procedures designed to alter
         the behavior of aggressive boys, Behavior
         Therapy, 1973, 4, 367-371.

Using the Patterson parental training behavioral approach
to dealing with behavior problem children, the authors
report a significant difference between two groups, a
control and a treatment, on various change measures, with
the treatment group showing significantly more change in
a positive direction. The control group actually deteriorated during the period of measurement of the study.

1436.   Walton, D., The application of learning
         theory to the treatment of a case of
         somnabulism, Journal of Clinical Psychology,
         1961, 17, 96-99.

A severe and potentially dangerous case of somnabulism is
reported. The attacks had been frequent and covered a
period of six months. A simple method of treatment was
adopted based on learning theory principle of reciprocal
inhibition. The patient made a rapid and positive response
to treatment. A two year follow-up failed to demonstrate a

return of the condition or of any other substitutive symptoms. Only one therapeutic interview was required to effect
such changes. (Journal summary).

   1437.   Walton, D., and Black, D.A., The appli-
            cation of modern learning theory to the
            treatment of chronic hysterical aphonia,
            Journal of Psychosomatic Research, 1959,
            3, 303-311.

A theory is put forward to account for the development of
a chronic hysterical aphonia. This leads to the deduction
of a method of treatment, of which the application in a
specific case is described. The recovery of the patient,
whose condition was of 7 years standing, is tentatively taken
as vindication of the proposed theory. The success of this
method of treatment, based on learning theory, in the face of
the repeated failure of other methods, leads to the discussion of the aetiology of neurotic symptoms. Conclusions
emerge which tend to conflict with much hitherto accepted
psychoanalytic theory, chiefly that of the non-replacement of
the symptom by an alternative, even after 11 months and in
the face of considerable stressful provocation. (Journal
summary).

   1438.   Waltzer, H., Brief crisis-oriented therapy
            in a city hospital setting, American
            Journal of Psychotherapy, 1975, 29, 550-557.

The author defines brief therapy as treatment lasting not
longer than three months,with one or two sessions/week, and
one-half hour/session. The important variables in brief
therapy are: a) the contract: a clear and explicit series
of statements, including time limits, focus of sessions,
responsibility of each participant, etc. b) therapist role:
active, focussed, exploring in initial session extent of
patient's pathology, uncovering and explaining to the patient
the precipitating stress and its effect, etc. c) the precipitating stress: a number of typical events which precipitate
crises are reviewed. d) patient expectations: most patients
are interested in symptom alleviation, and not long term
therapy. e) overall goals of brief treatment: the reestablishment of the previous level of functioning and avoiding
further decompensation. f) supportive techniques: a summary

of some of these is presented, including suggestion, confrontation, environmental manipulation, medication, etc. g)
issues of transference and counter-transference: the importance of transference in determining outcome is reviewed.
h) focus on the here-and-now: delving into patient's past
only when it casts some light on the present difficulty and
behavior. i) the value of a problem-oriented record: in
aiding the therapist clarify the nature of the problem and
treatment directions.

1439.   Waltzer, H., et al., Emergency psychiatric
         treatment in a receiving hospital, Mental
         Hospital, 1963, 4, 595-600.

The authors report on a community service program to reduce
the rate of hospitalization by offering immediate, ambulatory
psychiatric assistance. Treatment procedures and staffing
arrangements are described. Hospitalization is regarded as
a last resort measure, although indicated for certain types
of problems. The emphasis and goals of emergency psychiatric
treatment are delineated. Waltzer, et al. present a summary
of patient-outcome statistics for a six-month period, and
discuss implications of their data. Clinical and technical
difficulties encountered in this program are discussed.
These include lack of follow-up care for patients, questions
concerning duration of treatment, and reluctance of staff to
accept this therapeutic model. (abstract by Deborah Schuller).

1440.   Warkentin, J., and Whitaker, C.A., Time-
         limited therapy for an agency case, in,
         Burton, A., (ed.), Modern psychothera-
         peutic practice: Innovations in technique,
         New, York, Science Behavior Books, 1965.

1441.   Warren, N.C., and Rice, L.N., Structuring
         and stabilizing of psychotherapy for low-
         prognosis clients, Journal of Consulting
         and Clinical Psychology, 1972, 39, 173-181.

Based on the findings of other researchers on the client
variables which predict minimal personality change or early
dropping out of therapy, these researchers attempted to
structure therapy in order to maximize the possibilities

of low-prognosis clients remaining in therapy. The structure involved two approaches, one labelled stabilizing, the
second labelled structuring. The first involved encouraging
clients to talk about any problems he/she may be having
regarding their therapy. The second procedure involved
carefully teaching the client to participate more produc-
tively in the process of therapy. Both operations were
carried out by a non-therapist investigator, prior to the
second, third, fifth, and eighth session. The experimental
group received both procedures, and semi-control received
only stabilizing procedures, and the control received no
extra-therapy help. A total of 55 low prognosis clients
participated. All groups were similar regarding demographic
characteristics. Ten sessions were offered in all, at the
rate of two/week. The results indicated that only those in
the experimental group completed the full block of therapy
session more often than the control group. Further, therapist ratings for the experimental group were significantly
higher than for the other two groups. The authors conclude
that those patients who have an opportunity early in treatment to discuss their therapy relationship will more likely
be able to follow through on the treatment process, and thus
stand a greater chance of gaining from therapy.

1442.   Wattie, B., Evaluating short-term case-
         work in a family agency, Social Casework,
         1973, 54, 609-616.

The author summarizes a study designed, among other things,
to replicate the findings of Reid and Shyne, who compared
the results of continuous service (CS) and planned short-
term service (PSTS). CS had no time limits, while PSTS had
eight sessions/family. Focus in PSTS was on limited aims,
specific focus, and intensive involvement of the therapist
in each interview. A total sample of 84 families was
involved, and samples were matched for the two treatments.
A non-treatment control group was included. Four different
evaluation measures were used, two client-based, two therapist based, Changes occurred in the client group as a
result of treatment, and did not show up in the control
group. There was no greater effectiveness of CS over PSTS
overall. PSTS worked better for those families which were
functioning relatively well at the onset of therapy, while

CS was a more effective therapy approach for those families
who presented a poor level of basic functioning. The
importance of assigning those workers to treatment modalities
which they believe in and are comfortable doing is stressed.

1443.   Watzlawick, P., et al., Pragmatics of
         human communication: A study of inter-
         actional patterns, pathologies, and
         paradoxes, New York, W.W. Norton, 1967.

1444.   Watzlawick, P., et al., Change: Principles
         of problem formation and problem resolution,
         W.W. Norton, N.Y., 1974.

1445.   Watzlawick, P., and Weakland, J.H., (eds.),
         The Interactional View, New York, W.W.
         Norton & Company, Inc., 1977.

This edited text contains a number of articles summarizing
the work of the Mental Research Institute (MRI) in Palo
Alto, California, between 1965 and 1974. The approaches
developed by this group of practitioner/researchers are
presented, with a focus on theory, research, training, and
issues of change.

1446.   Wayne, C.J., How long? An approach to
         reducing the duration of inpatient treat-
         ment, in, Wayne, C.J., and Koegler, R.R.,
         (eds.), Emergency psychiatry in brief
         therapy, Boxton, Little, Brown, 1966.

1447.   Wayne, G.J., Short-term intensive
         psychiatric hospital treatment, Journal
         of the National Association of Private
         Psychiatric Hospitals, 1977, 9, 4-7.

1448.   Wayne, G.J., Clinical aspects of short-
         term hospitalization, Journal of the
         National Association of Private
         Psychiatric Hospitals, 1977, 9, 20-25.

1449.   Wayne, G.J., New hope for old patients
         through brief hospitalization, Journal
         of the National Association of Private
         Psychiatric Hospitals, 1978, 10, 16-21.

1450.   Wayne, G.J., and Koegler, R.R., (eds.)
         Emergency psychiatric and brief therapy,
         Boston, Little, Brown, 1966.

1451.   Waxer, P.H., Short-term psychotherapy:
         some principles and technique, Inter-
         national Journal of Grouo Psychotherapy,
         1977, 27, 33-42.

The author presents a short review of some of the major
contributions in the field of brief treatment, and presents
a discussion and description of brief therapy principles
and techniques. Specifically, the process of explaining
short-term therapy to a prospective client, emphasis on
client responsibility, and the use of a short-term approach
in group therapy are presented. Techniques, such as patient
education, hot seat, role playing, use of video-tape feedback, reality trials, etc. are described. No presentation
is made of research findings.

1452.   Weakland, J.H., "OK - You've been a bad
         mother", in Papp, P., (ed.), Family
         therapy: Full length case studies, New
         York, Gardner Press, 1977.

This chapter presents a case of a 15 year old boy exhibiting
school and behavior problems, of divorced parents, brought
to the Brief Therapy Center in Palo Alto, California, and
seen in therapy by the author. The details of the general
orientation of the Center are presented, along with the
course of brief therapy for this family.

1453.   Weakland, J.H., and Fisch, R., Brief
         therapy, in Ross, D.M., and Ross, S.A.,
         (eds.), Hyperactivity: Theory, research,
         and action, New York, Wiley, 1976.

This chapter contains a short outline of the principles of
brief therapy and a case illustration.

1454.   Weakland, J.H., et al., Brief therapy:
         Focussed problem resolution, Family
         Process, 1974, 13, 141-168.

The authors describe their experiences and approach in
working with 97 cases (a total of 236 individuals) with
widely varying presenting problems in a brief therapy center.
The premises behind their approach are discussed, including
a strong emphasis on interaction as the key to understanding
human behavior and symptomatology, and on everyday difficulties as potentailly leading to such symptomatology.   The
approach is basically pragmatic, symptom-focussed, and
system-oriented.   The operation of the Center is detailed,
along with short case examples.   Such items as introducing
clients to the treatment structure, inquiring into and
defining the nature of the presenting problem, understanding
the behaviors which are maintaining the problem, the setting
of specific goals, the choice of behavioral interventions
and their implementation, and issues of termination are all
reviewed.   Questions of the role of insight and its effect
or lack of effect on change, of the use of idiosyncratic
aspects of an individual client or family, the use of
directed behavioral change and/or paradoxical instructions
(as part of introducing a therapeutic double bind), the use
of interpersonal influence in the form of other team members,
are all discussed.   Based on an average seven sessions/case,
the authors report either success (complete alleviation of
presenting problem) or significant improvement (clear but
not complete improvement) in 72% of the cases treated.

1455.   Weich, M.J., and Robbins, E., Short-term
         group psychotherapy with acutely psychotic
         patients, Psychiatric Quarterly, 1966, 40,
         80-87.

Group psychotherapy was instituted on the acutely psychotic
wards at Bellevue Psychiatric Hospital. Although many
patients attended three to seven sessions, a large number
took part in only one or two. In the first sessions, most
patients spoke as a rule of their protests against hospitalization, directed their hostility toward the therapist, were
very disorganized, denied their illnesses, and were unable
to interact with other patients to any significant degree.
Changes in behavior were often discernible by the second
session, in which the patient demonstrated more composure,
interaction, and organization. Hostility was redirected
from the therapist to other patients and efforts at making
positive contact with the therapist were made by way of
identification and interest in his work. By the third
sessions, there was an autonomous flavor to the group,
discussion of their illnesses was prevalent, more reality
testing could be noted by other members and fewer interventions by the therapist was necessary. The authors'
experience revealed that these stages which usually take
months to unfold in out-patient groups may occur from one
session to another with acuately disturbed patients. Enough
movement in the direction of health warranted a continuation
of this treatment modality. (Journal summary modified).

1456.   Weinberger, G., Brief therapy with
         children and their parents, in, Barten,
         H.H., (ed.), Brief therapies, New York,
         Behavioral Publications, 1971.

This chapter presents an approach with children, adolescents,
and/or their parents. This approach is described as pragmatic, with a focus on current, overt behavior. The therapist seeks actively to modify family relationships by
capitalizing upon the adaptive coping potential of family
members. He does not, within this time-limited frame,
attempt to elucidate traditionally explored intrapsychic
variables. Weinberger first situates brief psychotherapy
with children against the prevailing psychoanalytically-
based model--which he claims is suitable for at best only

5 to 10% of the population. Various steps and theoretic
rationale of brief therapy with children are outlined. The
author presents four case excerpts to illustrate the application of this approach to different ages and different
problems. In a discussion, the author contends that brief
therapy is sufficient for approximately half of all children
seen by a community clinic. (abstract by Deborah Schuller).

    1457.   Weinberger, G., Brief therapy in a child
                guidance setting, in, Parad, Resnick, and
                Parad, (eds.), Emergency and disaster
                management: A mental health source book,
                Maryland, The Charles Press, 1976.

This chapter details the evolution and current operation
within a children's psychiatric center of a brief therapy
delivery system for children, adolescents, and their parents.
The system in operation at this center prior to 1965 had
relied on the traditional, analytic conceptual model and team
delivery system. Restructuring over a two-year period entailed elimination of all formal diagnostic evaluation;
implementation of a six-week (twice weekly) therapy plan;
use of a single therapist rather than a team; and focus on
the family, rather than the child, as the conceptual unit.
Contingencies for treatment beyond the usual six weeks and
emergency treatment were established. On going data
collection for the purpose of evaluating effectiveness was
a final components in the development of this service. The
author reviews four evaluation statistics (drop-out rate,
return rate, satisfaction with treatment, and a problem
checklist) which strongly suggest the value of such a brief
therapy approach. In conclusion, Weinberger examines the
theoretic rationale underlying the delivery system--and
direct implications for the definition of techniques, goals,
and therapist role. (abstract by Deborah Schuller).

    1458.   Weisman, G., et al., Three day hospital-
                ization - a model for intensive inter-
                vention, Archives of General Psychiatry,
                1969, 21, 620-629.

The Emergency Treatment Unit (ETU) was established to
develop a model for brief intensive intervention as an
alternative to longer-term hospitalization. The unit,

located in the Connecticut Mental Health Center, provides
three to five days of hospital care followed by 30 days of
outpatient care. It treated primarily lower socio-economic
patients from emergency room at the Yale-New Haven Hospital.
Specific techniques which promote rapid reintegration include the use of time-limited contracts, intensive daily
involvement with multiple therapists, maximization of
autonomy, and an emphasis on adaptive issues. In addition,
extensive use is made of tranquilizers, individual dyadic
therapy, milieu therapy, and family or marital therapy where
indicated. Of those admitted, 82% are able to return to the
community after a three-day inpatient stay while 18% require
transfer to longer-term treatment settings. A follow-up
study found an additional 19% of admissions were readmitted
for longer-term care within a year of discharge. Thus 63%
of admissions were neither transferred nor rehospitalized.
This compared favourably with other recent follow-up studies.
These data suggest that brief intensive hospital care provides an effective alternative to longer-term hospitalization
for a wide variety of psychiatric disorders. (Journal
summary).

1459.   Weiss, S.D., and Kapp, R.A., An inter-
         disciplinary campus mental health program
         specializing in crisis intervention services,
         Professional Psychology, 1974, 5, 25-31.

The author discusses implication of a campus mental health
program in terms of its impact on other city and campus
agencies, the benefits of an interdisciplinary professional
graduate training division, and the feasibility of the 24-
hour, seven-day-a-week emergency on-call service. (Journal
abstract).

1460.   Weisskopf, S., and Binder, J.L., Grieving
         medical students: Educational and clinical
         considerations, Comprehensive Psychiatry,
         1976, 17, 623-630.

1461.   Weissman, M.M., et al., The efficacy of
         drugs and psychotherapy in the treatment
         of acute depressive episodes, American
         Journal of Psychiatry, 1979, 136, 555-558.

The efficacy of tricyclic antidepressants and various psychotherapies, in comparison with one another or in combination,
has not been fully established in randomized clinical trials.
The authors present a randomized controlled trial comparing
the combination an amitriptyline and short-term interpersonal
psychotherapy, the drug or psychotherapy alone, and nonscheduled supportive psychotherapy in 96, 18-65 yr old
ambulatory patients with acute depression. The Raskin Three
Area Depression Scale was used. It was found that pharmacotherapy and psychotherapy alone were equally efficacious
and better than nonscheduled treatment. The combination
treatment of psychotherapy and pharmacotherapy was more
effective than either treatment alone and delayed the onset
of symptomatic failure. (Journal abstract).

1462.   Weitz, L.J., et al., Number of sessions
         and client-judged outcome: The more the
         better? Psychotherapy, Theory, Research,
         and Practice, 1975, 12, 337-340.

Weitz, et al. present a study to complement and update
information on the relationship between number of sessions
and therapeutic outcome. Subjects were 186 students who
received a minimum of two therapy sessions at a college
counseling center and who responded to a mialed questionnaire
(35% response rate). Client assessed the benefit of treatment on six different variables: specific problem relief,
enhancement of self-respect, improvement in decision-making,
in interpersonal relationships, and grades, and suicide
prevention. Results indicate a significant relation between
duration of therapy and client evaluations of therapeutic
benefit on every criterion except decision-making ability.
Variation in perceived effectiveness as a function of amount
of treatment is most salient on the two measures pertaining
to client self-respect and suicide prevention. The authors
discuss their data, focusing particularly on possible
explanations for the nonlinearity of the self-respect
configuration (which differs strikingly from the basically

linear slopes of the other criteria). Of the subsample who
terminated after six to ten sessions, fewer than 5% report
enhancement of self-respect--in contrast to students receiving more or less therapy (abstract by Deborah Schuller).

1463.   Wellington, Jt, A case for short term
         family therapy, Psychotherapy: Theory,
         Research, and Practice, 1968, 4, 130-132.

The author summarizes a single case study. The identified
patient was a 14 year old female, with a school phobia, and
associated fainting and dizzy spells. She had originally
been seen in treatment when she was seven, and had been in
and out of treatment several times between ages seven and
14. She was seen in short-term family therapy at the
Eastern Middlesex Guidance Center in Massachusetts for a
total of eight interviews. Successful treatment involved
the entire family, with specific focus on instructions to
the parents. A one year follow-up indicated that the gains
had been maintained. The author states that similar short-
term therapy with other families has produced positive
results as well.

1464.   Wellisch, D.K., and Gay, G.R., The
         walking wounded: Emergency psychiatric
         intervention in a heroin addit population,
         Drug Forum, 1972, 1, 137-144.

Significant psychological pathology exists among the members
of the drug using subculture of the Haight-Ashbury district
of San Francisco. Far too often in crisis situations these
"Walking-Wounded" are considered to be "drug users" rather
than as individuals in extreme emotional need and are denied
psychiatric care in conventional public health facilities.
(Journal abstract).

1465.   Wells, R.A., Short-term treatment: An
         annotated bibliography, American Psycho-
         logical Association Catalog of Selected
         Documents, 1976, 6(1), 13 (MS #1189).

This annotated bibliography of short-term treatment
approaches spans 1945-1974, and contains 243 article

abstracts. A short critical review is also included, along
with author and subject indexes.

   1466.   Wells, R.A., et al., Group facilitative
            training with conflicted marital couples,
            in, Gurman, A., and Rice, D., (eds.),
            Couples in Conflict, New York, Aronson,
            1975.

Using the Carkhuff model, couples were given training in
groups. A total of eight, two-hour sessions were held,
with three-four couples in each group. Another three conjoint sessions were permitted for each couple if needed.
Measures of marital adjustment and relationship indices
were taken prior to and following treatment. Outcome
results showed positive outcome across all measures.
Specific techniques used are discussed.

   1467.   Werry, J.S., The conditioning treatment
            of enuresis, American Journal of Psychiatry,
            1966, 123, 226-229.

Werry discusses current attitudes and theories regarding
etiology and treatment methods of enuresis. He notes
specific objections raised by many pediatricians to use of
the conditioning treatment--including the belief that such
a method is psychologically harmful to the child, and may
result in symptom substitution. Learning theorists' explanation of the bed-buzzer treatment is usually placed within
a classical conditioning paradigm, although Werry cites
Lovibond's evidence that therapeutic effects may also be
explained by operant conditioning. The author briefly
summarizes relevant literature and the results of a study
conducted by himself to test the differential effectiveness
of this treatment method. He concludes that the conditioning
treatment is safe and effective; that it should be considered
for any enuretic child, six years of age or above, who is
disturbed by his symptom and who has failed to respond to
less elaborate measures. (abstract by Deborah Schuller).

1468.   Werry, J.S., and Wollersheim, J.P.,
         Behavior therapy with children: A
         broad overview, Journal of the American
         Academy of Child Psychiatry, 1976, 6,
         346-370.

The authors summarize a great deal of literature on behavior
therapy with children. They begin with a review of the
principles of behavior therapy (i.e., problem definition and
analysis, strategy for therapy, motivating patients, shaping
behavior, generalization and stabilization of behavior).
Specific techniques of behavior therapy are discussed
(i.e., manipulation of stimuli through such techniques as
systematic desensitization, attentuation, cue conversion,
modeling, interference with sensory feedback, reciprocal
inhibition, successive approximations, negative and massed
practice, either withholding or providing reward, satiation
and deprivation, and punishment). Research findings in the
use of all of these are summarized. Further, specific types
of conditions (i.e., problems) in which these techniques are
used are discussed, including neurotic symptoms (e.g., fears,
phobias, obsessive-compulsive symptoms), psychophysiological
reactions (e.g., enuresis, vomiting, stuttering, etc.),
psychotic symptoms, conduct disorders (e.g., temper tantrum
and other kinds of oppositional behavior). Indications for
the use of behavior therapy include: a) when there is a
clear and identifiable presenting symptom; b) when client
wishes to focus on symptom removal rather than on insight
into the dynamics of the symptom; c) where insight-oriented
practitioners are in short supply or unavailable.

1469.   Wesselius, L.F., The limitations of crisis
         theory, Journal of the National Association
         of Private Psychiatric Hospitals, 1977, 9,
         17-19.

1470.   Westcott, G.F., Serpasil as an adjunct to
         brief intensive psychotherapy with two
         psychotic patients, Journal of Nervous and
         Mental Disease, 1956, 123, 53-56.

Two cases of schizophrenia have been presented. Treatment
by brief intensive psychotherapy with adjunctive use of

Serpasil has been described. The result in each case is
favourable. Possible factors influencing the remission
have been discussed. (Journal summary).

1471.   Westerman, M., et al., Interpersonal
         style and outcome of brief paradoxical
         versus behavior therapy, Paper presented
         at the American Psychological Association
         Annual Convention, 1979.

1472.   Whitaker, C.A., Communication in brief
         psychotherapy with the non-psychotic
         patient, Diseases of the Nervous System,
         1957, 18, 67-72.

The author provides information about the activities of a
group of therapists at the Psychiatric Institute in Atlanta,
who attempted to vary the signals sent by therapists to
their patients in brief therapy. Specifically, techniques
of free association on the therapists' part (as they relate
to patient material) are presented. Case examples are used
to illustrate this approach, and some of the valuable aspects
are discussed.

1473.   Whitaker, C.A., Psychotherapy of the
         absurd: With special emphasis on the
         psychotherapy of aggression, Family
         Process, 1976, 14, 1-16.

The author summarizes a number of facets of those therapies
which focus on the here and now. Further, he discusses
aggression in interactions in families as the most unacceptable characteristic in interpersonal living. He contends that constructive use of aggression by the therapist
can enhance growth in families in which there is a repetitive pattern of hostility. Specific ways in which the
therapist can positively express this anger are detailed
(e.g., forgiving the patient; counter-attack; one-upping
the situation, not the patient; defusing or redirecting the
aggression, etc.). All of these tactics are aimed at
reducing the guilt and producing a significant decrease in
the level of aggressive affect. The type of approach used

is labelled "therapy of the absurd", in which the patient's
unreasonable behavior is heightened or the situation is
heightened to an absurd level. Caution is stressed concerning the use of this technique - the tactic must be done with
a loving relationship in therapy. The specific steps involved in such a procedure are listed and explained, as
well as possible explanations for the effectiveness of the
approach. In essence the approach is an active, deliberate
attempt by the therapist to break or significantly alter the
old patterns of behavior, thoughts and feelings, through the
use of exaggeration and constructed elaboration. The chaos
and complexity of the situation are increased by this
approach. Specific case examples, some from non-clinical
and some from clinical settings are presented.

   1474.   Whitaker, C.A., et al., A philosophical
            basis for brief psychotherapy, Psychiatric
            Quarterly, 1949, 23, 439-443.

This is a discussion of the use of two therapists in the
treatment of one patient, and the value of such a procedure
in the teaching of the art and science of psychotherapy.
Issues of communication between and the need for continuing
consultation between therapists are highlighted. Three
major principles of brief therapy in relation to the activity
of the therapist are also presented: a) the directive nature
of the therapy; b) the need for the therapist to refuse to
participate in the patient's decisions; and, c) the differences between "healthy counter-transference" and "unhealthy
counter-transference".

   1475.   White, A., et al., An interactive behavior
            index and verbal content analysis, Journal
            of Nervous and Mental Disease, 1968, 146,
            457-464.

The authors report an exploratory study to test the following
hypothesis: neurotic patients classified as changed by
short-term psychodynamic therapy will evidence more interactive behavior (as measured by a three-criterion index) in
the last four hours of treatment than in the first hour;
whereas patients classed as unchanged will not show an
increase in interactive behavior. Criteria for change

were a) significant difference between mean adaptivity
scores in the focus area for the patient, as based on
verbal content analysis; b) nonreqdmission to further
therapy within 10 months of termination; and, c) patient's
report of alleviation of symptoms. Factors comprising the
interactive behavior index are outlined. White, et al.
present and discuss their findings, which support the
initial hypothesis. (abstract by Deborah Schuller).

   1476.   White, A., et al., Measurement of what
            the patient learns from psychotherapy,
            Journal of Nervous and Mental Disease,
            1969, 149, 281-293.

The authors report a study to evaluate the content of psychotherapeutic dialogue as a teaching-learning experience, in
order to provide evidence that verbal learning of specific
insights is related to positive behavioral change. All
therapy sessions and a follow-up interview were taped for
a test sample of 10 neurotic patients who received, on
average, 15 hours of short-term psychodynamically-oriented
therapy in a university mental health clinic. White, et al.
detail the method by which three different instruments
(message learning ratings specific to each patient, a mental
health rating, and an interactive behavior index) were
developed and applied to the analysis of the transcripts.
Data are presented which show the relation of verbal and
behavioral message learning to change in mental health;
the relation of the interactive behavior index to specific
learning and mental health change; and three exploratory
applications of mental health ratings. The findings appear
to support the value of short-term, ego-centered, insight-
oriented therapy. The authors discuss research considerations pertaining to selection of messages for content
analysis, the follow-up interview, and the mental health
rating scale. (abstract by Deborah Schuller).

   1477.   White, K.L., and Sloane, R.B., Drugs in
            brief psychotherapy, Psychiatric Clinics
            of North America, 1979, 2, 171-187.

Treatment combining psychotherapy and pharmacotherapy has
attained widespread use, in spite of the fact that the two

treatments arise from separate theoretical bases. While
clinical experience and observation have convinced many that
their combined use is beneficial, this interaction has not
yet been empirically demonstrated. Some of the controlled
outcome studies of drugs in psychotherapy are re-examined
to see what light they may have cast on such issues. The
focus is on drugs in current use with brief psychotherapy
of the "talking" variety; specialized behavioral techniques
are excluded. (Journal abstract).

1478.   Whitman, R.M., and Young, I.S.,
         Psychiatric social work in a brief
         therapy program in an adult out-
         patient clinic, Journal of Psychiatric
         Social Work, 1955, 24, 210-214.

This paper concerns the contribution of the psychiatric
social worker to both initial formulation of treatment plans,
and the ensuing psychotherapy. The authors present theoretic
and operational background of the approach to brief therapy
taken by one adult outpatient clinic. Goals and specific
procedures are adumbrated. A distinguishing feature is the
collaboration between the psychiatrist and the psychiatric
social worker. Two case summaries illustrate an interactional work-up by the social worker and the psychiatrist,
and the diagnostic value of simultaneous interviewing by the
worker of the relative or friend accompanying the patient to
the clinic. The authors note that, in addition to benefits
in diagnosis and treatment, the program of routinized interviewing of accompanying relatives has been of value in the
areas of teaching and internal consolidation of the psychiatric team. Whitman and Young conclude with a brief
discussion of other advantages of collaborative therapy.
(abstract by Deborah Schuller).

1479.   Whittington, H.G., Transference in
         brief psychotherapy: Experience in a
         college psychiatric clinic, Psychiatric
         Quarterly, 1962, 36, 503-518.

The author examines brief therapy at the Mental Health
Clinic of the Student Health Service of the University of
Kansas. Brief therapy is defined as therapy lasting

between one to 20 hours, usually less than 10 hours. Specifically, the author focusses on the issue of transference
and its role in brief therapy. The therapist in brief
therapy actively participates and responds to the patient's
behavior in the interview, rather than providing an objective analysis of historical aspects and determinants in the
patient's past, as is the case for traditional, long term
psychoanalysis. Thus the patient expresses all of his transference relationships within the emotional relationship
between him and the therapist. The author presents three
case histories, chosen because of the differences among all
of the patients in their use of transference in brief
therapy. In general, the type of brief therapy used here
focusses on present reality, childhood experiences, and the
therapeutic reality in order to produce change. Of interest
in the examples is the author's discussion of the use of non-
verbal behavior through the process of therapist-client
interaction which often produce significant change. The
work of Whitaker and Malone and Alexander is cited in this
regard (e.g., corrective emotional experiences).

1480.   Wiener, D.N., The effect of arbitrary
         termination on returns to psychotherapy,
         Journal of Clinical Psychology, 1959,
         15, 335-338.

The problem of dealing with growing numbers of extremely
long-term or interminable patients in outpatient psychotherapy requires study, particularly since long-term treatment, unspecified as to maximum, is often identified with
successful therapy. A potentially interminable group of
patients was arbitrarily terminated to determine whether
interminability could be controlled in this way, without
dire consequences. A substantial number of these patients
did not return to treatment within six months, and no dire
consequences were observed. The attempt was made to confirm
factors which would predict which of these prospectively
interminable patients would return to treatment, and which
would not. Number of months in treatment did prove significant, with longer treatment indicating greater likelihood of return. (Journal summary).

1481.   Wilder, J.F., and Coleman, D.M., The
         "walk-in" psychiatric clinic: some
         observations and follow-up, International
         Journal of Social Psychiatry, 1963, 9,
         192-199.

One hundred and thirty-eight patients were seen by one
resident in a "Walk-in" Psychiatric Clinic (Albert Einstein
School of Medicine and Bronx Municipal Hospital Center) were
followed during the subsequent year. In race, religion, and
sex ratio this group had a composition similar to the population of our Outpatient Department Medical-Surgical Screening Clinic, although the latter group tended to be older,
contain more foreign-born and have a lower educational background. Social differences seem to become important factors
in referral to long-term psychotherapy. The total group of
patients referred to long-term psychotherapy that year
differed markedly from the Walk-in Clinic population towards
the social characteristics of the referring doctors. Case
histories are discussed by diagnostic category. There is
an overall impression that the Clinic contact was a meaningful event in the lives of many patients. In other cases,
psychotherapy geared to the dynamics of the situation afforded immeasurable relief. This was especially true where
the precipitant was discernible and recent. By using the
most conservative criteria, and if these findings were pro-
jected for the entire Walk-in Clinic, 161 hospitalizations
may have been prevented during the year. (Journal conclusion).

1482.   Williams, C., and Rice, D.G., The
         intensive care unit: Social Work
         intervention with the families of
         critically ill patients, Social Work
         in Health Care, 1977, 2, 391-398.

The value of using a crisis intervention model for social
workers involved with families of intensive care unit
patients is outlined.

1483.   Williams, J., et al., A model for short-
         term group therapy on a children's in-
         patient unit, Clinical Social Work Journal,
         1978, 6, 21-32.

The paper describes the group therapy model which has
evolved over the past two years on the Child Psychiatry
Inpatient Unit of North Carolina Memorial Hospital. It
begins with a brief review of the literature concerning
group therapy with latency-aged children. The setting and
patient population are described. Vignettes from group
sessions are used to illustrate techniques which have
evolved to deal with this particular setting and population.
These include a leadership style characterized by much clarification, modeling, and limit setting; extensive focus on
beginning and terminating; clearly defined behavioral
limits; the use of "time out"; and use of play materials
requiring little skill or attention as anxiety binders as
well as projective media; and observation and supervisory
discussions open to all members of the treatment team. The
paper concludes with a discussion of the potentials and
limitations of group therapy in such a setting. The thesis
is that this model is effective in diagnosing developmental
levels, in developing interpersonal skills, in substituting
verbalization for action, and in mastering separation
anxieties, though the setting limits the extent to which
controlled regression, transference, and group pressures can
develop and be used to produce change. (Journal abstract).

1484.   Williams, S., Short term art therapy,
         American Journal of Art Therapy, 1976,
         15, 35-41.

The author describes the use of art therapy at a short-term
inpatient mental health facility in the San Francisco area.
The average length of stay at the unit was eight days, with
patient participation in facility activities, and involvement in both family and group therapy. Art therapy both in
groups and individually is part of the program. A case is
presented in which a 25 year old male, diagnosed as paranoid
schizophrenic, was seen in individual, short-term art therapy.
The details of the sessions are described, and drawings and
their meaning are also presented. The symptoms of withdrawal, regression, and mutism, were all diminished through

participation in the program, and the staff impressions of
the value of the art therapy in allowing the patient to
open up are detailed.

1485. Williams, W.V., et al., Crisis inter-
       vention on family survivors of sudden
       death situations, Community Mental Health
       Journal, 1976, 12, 128-136.

A controlled study that examined the effect of a short-term
crisis service given to a group of families recently
bereaved through a sudden death within the family is reported. The results reveal that sudden death does have a major
impact on recently bereaved families in terms of increased
risk of ill health, poor coping behavior, and disturbed
social functioning when compared to nonbereaved families.
However, the short-term crisis service appeared to have no
major impact upon post-bereavement adjustment. Discussion
centered around possible reasons for failure of the short-
term crisis service. (Journal abstract).

1486. Willis, R.W., and Edwards, J.A., A study
       of the comparative effectiveness of
       systematic desensitization and implosive
       therapy, Behaviour Research and Therapy,
       1969, 7, 387-395.

Fifty female undergraduate students demonstrating aversive-
ness to mice were assigned to three treatment groups based
on response to two pre-treatment measures. One group
received standard systematic desensitization treatment. A
second group received implosive therapy while a third group
was subjected to control procedures. Six measures were used
to assess the comparative effectiveness of treatment and a
follow-up study was conducted seven to eight weeks following
treatment termination. The results of the present study
indicated that: 1) Systematic desensitization treatment was
significantly more effective than implosive therapy in
reducing avoidant behavior associated with mice; 2) Implosive
therapy treatment was more effective than control procedures
in reducing mouse avoidant behavior; 3) Changes produced by
systematic desensitization were similar for the two thera-

pists employed; 4) Evidence of symptom substitution was absent for a period of seven to eight weeks following treatment. (Journal summary).

1487.   Wilson, C.J., et al., Time-limited
         group counseling for chronic home
         hemodialysis patients, Journal of
         Counseling Psychology, 1974, 21,

This study compared the effects of six sessions of group counseling of nine chronic home hemodialysis patients with a comparable no treatment control group. Comparisons between experimental and control groups on Rotter's locus of control and selected California Personality Inventory scales revealed no significant differences between groups. However, observed changes were noted within the experimental group from pre- to post-testing on two of the measures. Subsequent testing a year later of 11 of the original 18 sample patients suggested that hemodialysis patients use the defensive mechanism of denial in adapting to their condition. (Journal abstract).

1488.   Wilson, R.S., Short term contact in
         social casework, National Travelers
         Aid Association, N.Y., 1937.

1489.   Wiltz, N.A., and Patterson, G.R., An
         evaluation of parent training procedures
         designed to alter inappropriate aggressive
         behavior in boys, Behavior Therapy, 1974,
         5, 215-221.

The authors report on two matched groups of inappropriately aggressive nine year old boys, six in each group. The families used the Patterson and Gullion text on child-management, and were then required to target a single behavior change. The parents collected baseline data, and attended group meetings to discuss problems in gathering information and in managing their children. The researchers report changes in targeted behavior for the experimental group, but no statistically significant generalization to other non-targeted deviant behaviors.

1490. Winkelman, N.W., and Saul, S.D., The
return of suggestion, Psychiatric
Quarterly, 1974, 48, 230-238.

A form of treatment considered outmoded around the turn of
the century, suggestion new plays a considerable role in
general medicine and all contemporary psychotherapies -
including psychoanalysis, behavior therapy, and group encounters. The return of suggestion is dramatically seen in
the community mental health movement, in which centers
dispense brief therapy, help and advice to large portions
of the population previously unreachable. In spite of the
ubiquity of suggestion and the large literature that developed at the end of the 19th and the beginning of the 20th
century, very little is actually known as to how it "works",
and if and when it does. Considerably more research is
needed on the subject, which stands as a basic riddle of
the behavioral sciences. (Journal abstract).

1491. Wiseman, R., Crisis theory and the
process of divorce, Social Casework,
1975, 56, 205-212.

The divorce process is defined as entailing a unique form
of emotional crisis for both spouses. Characteristics of
grieving accompany the process of rejecting a lost object
and constructing new patterns of living. The author conceives the divorce process as a series of five overlapping
stages: denial; loss and depression; anger and ambivalence;
reorientation of life-style and identity; acceptance and a
new level of functioning. She discusses each of these
stages, and includes clinical vignettes to illustrate the
application of brief crisis-oriented interventions. The
therapist's understanding of the client's position relative
to the process described is critical. Other aspects of the
therapist's role which enable the client to maximize the
opportunities implicit within crisis are discussed.
(abstract by Deborah Schuller).

1492. Wolberg, L.R., (ed.), Short-term therapy,
New York, Grune and Stratton, 1965.

1493.   Wolberg, L., Methodology in short-term
         therapy, American Journal of Psychiatry,
         1965, 122, 135-140.

Short-term therapy has more than utilitarian value. Patients
suffering from a wide spectrum of emotional problems, treated
over a short period of time, may obtain not only sustained
relief, but also, in some cases, personality changes of a
reconstructive nature that would have been considered significant had long-term treatment been employed. Four stages
in the course of short-therapy seem apparent: 1) a supportive phase during which homeostasis is brought about through
the healing influences of the relationship with the therapist, the placebo effect of the therapeutic process, and
the decompressive impact of emotional catharsis; 2) an
apperceptive phase, characterized by the ability to understand, even minimally, the meaning of the complaint factor
in terms of the operative conflicts and basic personality
needs and defenses; 3) an action phase distinguished by a
challenging of certain habitual neurotic patterns, facing
them from a somewhat different perspective, and 4) an
integrative relearning and reconditioning phase which continues after termination on the basis of the chain reaction
started during the brief treatment period. The specific
techniques that are outlined in the paper are contingent,
first, on the acceptance of eclecticism, second, on the
existence of flexibility in the therapist; and, third, on
the studied employment of activity in the relationship.
All modalities are employed in those combinations that may
be of value, including psychoanalytic techniques, interviewing procedures, drugs, hypnosis, reconditioning and
group therapy. Among the procedures that might expedite
treatment are the following: 1) establishing a rapid working
relationship (rapport); 2) circumscribing the problem area
as a focus for exploration; 3) evolving with the patient a
working hypothesis of the psychodynamics of his difficulty;
4) employing dream interpretation where the therapist is
analytically trained; 5) altering onself to resistances
and resolving these as rapidly as possible; 6) dealing with
target symptoms like excessive tension, anxiety and depression, through the careful use of drugs; phobic phenomena
by conditioning techniques; obsessive-compulsive manifestations by persuasive tactics, etc.; 7) teaching the patient
how to employ insight as a corrective force; 8) outlining
with the patient a definite plan of action by which he can

use his understanding in the direction of change; 9) searching for transference elements and resolving these quickly
before they build up to destroy the relationship; 10) encouraging the development of a proper life philosophy.
(Journal summary adapted).

1494.   Wolberg, L., Perspectives in short-term
         therapy, Current Psychiatric Therapies,
         1966, 6, 26-34.

The author presents a series of stages which many patients
and therapists go through during short-term therapy. The
initial phase is labelled the supportive phase, followed by
the apperceptive phase, the action phase, and the integrative
phase. Issues of the therapy process and of various therapy
techniques are also discussed.

1495.   Wolberg, L., Psychiatric technics in
         crisis therapy, New York State Journal of
         Medicine, 1972, 72, 1266-1269.

1496.   Wolberg, L.R., Handbook of Short-term
         psychotherapy, New York, Stratton
         Intercontinental Medical Book Corporation,
         1980.

This book reviews the various models of short-term therapy,
and then presents a number of principles which can be used
by therapists of various theoretical persuasions. Such
issues as the criteria for patient selection, methods of
conducting the initial interview, narrowing in on an
immediate focus, as well as choosing a dynamic focus,
specific therapy techniques, the use of hypnosis, use of
self-help materials, and termination questions are all
addressed in this text.

1497.   Wolk, R.L., The kernal interview, Journal
         of the Long Island Consultation Center,
         1967, 5.

A specific therapy technique is presented designed for
socially and/or economically deprived clients. The kernel

interview consists of setting up each therapy session as
if it were an entire treatment, with specific goals, beginnings, endings, etc. Its effect is to leave the client
with a sense of some success based on her/her working and
resolving a specific problem, and an eagerness to return
to work on other difficulties.

1498.   Wolk, R.L., and Reid, R., A study of
         group psychotherapy results with youthful
         offenders in detention, Group Psychotherapy,
         1964, 17, 56-60.

The authors summarize aspects of the method and results of
a study to assess the value of short-term group psychotherapy with delinquent adolescents housed in a correction
facility. Therapy groups met twice-weekly for one and a
half hours, for a total of 16 sessions. Results on several
quantitative measures indicate no significant pre- and post-
testing differences for the experimental group. The authors
affirm, however, that qualitative results did demonstrate
significant and meaningful changes resulting from group
therapy. Wolk and Reid elaborate on some of the changes
with youthful offenders in detention, as well as assist
them in institutional and future community adjustment.
(abstract by Deborah Schuller).

1499.   Wolkon, G.H., Crisis theory, the appli-
         cation for treatment, and dependency,
         Comprehensive Psychiatry, 1972, 13,
         459-464.

The application for treatment was defined as a crisis - a
period of psychological disequilibrium and high anxiety -
in that it is an application for a major role change affecting the core itself. Crisis theory predicts that the
closer the intervention is to the crisis, the greater the
success of the intervention. Specifically, it was predicted that the shorter the delay between the client's
application for treatment and the first scheduled interview,
the more successful the intervention in terms of the interview's actually taking place and the likelihood of the
client's improving at the termination of therapy. Using
the first definition of success, the prediction was confirmed in three different types of treatment agencies.

With the improvement as the definition of success, the
prediction was given encouraging support in two types of
agencies. An argument was made that a necessary but not
sufficient condition for successful crisis intervention is
that a client's dependency and affiliative needs be satisfied . Research directions for understanding dependency
and affiliation in relation to crisis interventions and the
intake process were indicated. (Journal summary).

1500.   Wolkon, G.H., Changing roles: Crises in
        the continuum of care in the community,
        Psychotherapy: Theory, Research, and
        Practice, 1974, 11, 367-370.

Wolkon makes four major points in this paper. He notes that
the current mental health system presents the client with a
confusing array of choice points for entry into treatment;
and that these choices entail not only narrow treatment
considerations, but have broad social psychological meanings
for the individual concerned. Choice points should be considered potential crisis situations, in that they frequently
imply major role change for which the client is unprepared.
Thirdly, Wolkon affirms the usefulness of crisis theory in
providing a rationale for and conceptualization of the
development and restructuring of intake procedures across
the continuum of care. Lastly, Wolkon presents evidence
supporting his contention that successful crisis intervention
implies satisfaction of dependency and/or affiliative needs
for the client. (abstract by Deborah Schuller).

1501.   Wollersheim, J.P., Effectiveness of
        group therapy based upon learning
        principles in the treatment of over-
        weight women, Journal of Abnormal
        Psychology, 1970, 76, 462-474.

Following an 18-wk. base-line period, 79 motivated overweight
female students were randomly assigned from stratified
blocks, on percentage overweight, to one of four experimental
conditions: (a) positive expectation-social pressure; (b)
nonspecific therapy; (c) focal therapy based upon major
learning principles; or (d) no-treatment-wait-control.
Four therapists (two males and two females) each treated

one group of 5 Ss in each of the three treatment conditions
for 10 sessions extending over a 12-wk. period. At both
posttreatment and the 8-wk. follow-up, the focal group was
superior in weight reduction and reduction of reported frequencies of various eating behaviors. Evidence for "symptom
substitution" was lacking. While significant differential
weight reduction occurred for the various treatments, it
did not occur for the different therapists or for the various
therapist-treatment combinations. (Journal abstract).

1502.   Wollersheim, J.P., Follow-up of
         behavioral group therapy for obesity,
         Behavior Therapy, 1977, 8, 996-998.

This study reports the differential weight loss of three
obesity treatment groups at a 16-week follow-up period, a
period of 8 weeks later than the first follow-up reported
in the original study. The differential weight losses from
pretreatment for the three groups at this second follow-up
reached a probability level of between .05 and .10. Specu-
lative hypotheses concerning the differing trends of the
three treatment groups are offered. (Journal abstract).

1503.   Wolpe, J. Reciprocal inhibition as the
         main basis for psychotherapeutic effects,
         Archives of Neurology and Psychiatry,
         1954, 72, 205-225.

The case is presented that conditioned inhibition founded
on reciprocal inhibition is the basis of most fundamental
psychotherapeutic effects. This principle is shown to
explain a large number of widely used therapeutic methods
and has led to some new methods, which are described. Of
122 patients treated by these methods, 110 were apparently
cured or much improved. It is shown that certain other
current theories are unable to account for the same range of
facts as that subsumed by the reciprocal inhibition hypothesis. (Journal summary).

1504.   Wolpe, J. Psychotherapy by reciprocal
        inhibition, Stanford, Stanford University
        Press, 1958.

Wolpe describes the use of the principle of reciprocal
inhibition in psychotherapy. The principle involves the
idea that if a response which is known to counteract or
diminish anxiety can be structured so as to occur in the
presence of anxiety-producing stimulus, such as response
will reduce the strength of the connection between the
stimulus and the anxiety. The author reports on the successful use of this principle in the treatment of a range of
neuroses, especially phobias. The brief amount of time
necessary for the treatment of many patients using this
principle is highlighted.

1505.   Wolpe, J., Psychotherapy based on the
        reciprocal inhibition principle, in,
        Burton, A., (ed.), Case studies in
        counseling and psychotherapy, New York,
        Prentice-Hall, 1959.

1506.   Wolpe, J., The systematic desensitization
        treatment of neuroses, Journal of Nervous
        and Mental Disease, 1961, 132, 189-203.

The desensitization method of therapy is a particular application of the reciprocal inhibition principle to the elimination of neurotic habits. The experimental background and
some theoretical implications of this principle are discussed. A detailed account is given of the technique of
desensitization and an analysis of its effects when applied
to 68 phobias and allied neurotic anxiety response habits
in 39 patients. In a mean of 11.2 sessions, 45 of the
neurotic habits were overcome and 17 more very markedly
improved. Six month to four year follow-up reports from 20
of the 35 successfully treated patients did not reveal an
instance of relapse or the emergence of new symptoms.
(Journal summary).

1507.   Wolpe, J., The prognosis in unpsycho-
         analyzed recovery from neurosis,
         American Journal of Psychiatry, 1961,
         117, 35-39.

A survey of follow-up studies comprising 249 patients whose
neurotic symptoms have either ceased or improved markedly
after psychotherapy of various kinds other than psychoanalysis, shows only 4 relapses (1.6%). This evidence
contradicts the psychoanalytic expectation of inferior durability of recoveries obtained without psychoanalysis and
does away with the chief reason for regarding analysis as
the treatment of choice for neurotic suffering. The facts
presented have gravely damaging implications for the whole
psychoanalytic theory of neurosis, but accord with a theory
based on principles of learning. (Journal summary).

1508.   Wolpe, J., Isolation of a conditioning
         procedure as the crucial psychothera-
         peutic factor, Journal of Nervous and
         Mental Disease, 1962, 134, 316-329.

The treatment by systematic desensitization is described of
a severe case of phobia for laterally approaching auto-
mobiles. The initiation of desensitization required the
introduction of imaginary situations in a fictitious setting
in order to procure anxiety responses weak enough to be
inhibited by the patient's relaxation. Recovery was gradual
and at every stage directly correlated with the specific
content of the desensitization procedures. Certain operations which are usually performed in most systems of
therapy were excluded or modified in order to remove any
basis for arguing that the successful outcome was "really"
due to insight, suggestion, de-repression, or transference.
(Journal summary).

1509.   Wolpe, J., The experimental foundations
         of some new psychotherapeutic methods, in,
         Bachrach, A.J., (ed.), Experimental foun-
         dations of clinical psychology, New York,
         Basic Books, 1962.

1510.   Wolpe, J., The resolution of neurotic
         suffering by behavioristic methods,
         American Journal of Psychotherapy, 1964,
         18, 23-32.

The author begins this article with a short review of
behavior therapy, and specifically delineates the essentials
involved in the principle of reciprocal inhibition. The use
of assertive responses, relaxation responses, and sexual
responses in the treatment of various anxiety-related
conditions is described. The specific value of such
approaches, rooted in learning theory, in the successful
treatment of various neurotic conditions within a short-term
treatment model is summarized. The major features of such
an approach are presented.

1511.   Wolpe, J., New ways to treat sex disorders,
         Sexology, 1964, 31, 16-20.

1512.   Wolpe, J., Direct behavior modification
         therapies, in, Abt, L.E., and Riess, B.F.,
         (eds.), Progress in clinical psychology,
         Vol. 7, New York, Grune and Stratton, 1966.

1513.   Wolpe, J., Behavior therapy, in, Inter-
         national Encyclopedia of Social Sciences,
         New York, MacMillan and The Free Press, 1968.

1514.   Wolpe, J., Psychotherapy by reciprocal
         inhibition, Conditional Reflex, 1968, 3,
         234-240.

Reciprocal inhibition is a process of relearning whereby in
the presence of a stimulus a non-anxiety-producing response
is continually repeated until it extinguishes the old,
undesirable response. A variety of the techniques based on
reciprocal inhibition, such as systematic desensitization,
avoidance conditioning, and the use of assertion, are described in detail. Behavior therapy techniques on the basis
of their clinical efficacy are found to have striking success

over traditional psychoanalytic methods. Currently, more comparative studies are required which will validate the merit of behavior therapy in the psychotherapeutic field while experimental research should continue to refine the techniques. (Journal abstract).

1515.   Wolpe, J., The practice of behavior therapy, New York, Permagon Press, 1969.

1516.   Wolpe, J., Behavior therapy of stuttering: Deconditioning the emotional factor, in, Gray, B., and England, G., (eds.), Stuttering and the conditioning therapies, Monterey, Cal., The Monterey Institute for Speech and Hearing, 1969.

1517.   Wolpe, J., Therapist and technique variables in behavior therapy of neuroses, Comprehensive Psychiatry, 1969, 10, 44-49.

Evidence is presented that specific techniques derived from experimentally established principles of learning are effective in producing lasting diminution in the strength of the habits characteristic of neurosis. There is also evidence that change occurs in the course of psychotherapeutic transactions not involving the deliberate application of these principles. It is suggested that such change is due to the inadvertent operation of the same conditioning principles. (Journal summary).

1518.   Wolpe, J., Basic principles and practices of behavior therapy of neuroses, American Journal of Psychiatry, 1969, 125, 136-141.

The author presents a brief review of the theory and practices of behavior therapy, describing the various methods and their usefulness. He cites several studies which indicate more consistent success for behavior therapy than for analysis, in complex as well as simple neuroses, and also very low rates of relapse or the symptom substitution so often predicted by analysts. (Journal abstract).

1519.   Wolpe, J., Neurotic depression: Experi-
         mental analog, clinical syndromes, and
         treatment, American Journal of Psycho-
         therapy, 1971, 25, 362-368.

Seligman and his colleagues has shown that if an animal is
given a large number of inescapable shocks, he eventually
stops motor responding. If he is subsequently shocked in
a totally different situation where escape is possible, he
does not escape but behaves in a helpless fashion. This
behavior is in many ways similar to that observed in many
human cases of depression. The animal is "cured" only after
being forcibly pulled to safety many times. These experiments provide a basis for understanding human reactive
depressions and for suggesting new methods of treating them.
(Journal summary).

1520.   Wolpe, J., Advances in behavior therapy,
         Current Psychiatric Therapies, 1972, 12,
         27-37.

The author presents a brief overview of the positive results
obtained through the use of behavior therapies. Case
examples are provided to highlight the short-term treatments.
Systematic desensitization and its variants are described,
along with aversive therapy, and operant conditioning
methods. Seventy-five references are included.

1521.   Wolpe, J., et al., The current status of
         systematic desensitization, American
         Journal of Psychiatry, 1973, 130, 961-965.

Systematic desensitization is indicated for phobias, obsessions, compulsions, and anxiety reactions that are maintained by anxiety-reducing defense mechanisms. The technique
involves instruction in deep muscle relaxation, construction
of an anxiety hierarchy, and stepwise pairing of relaxation
with imagined anxiety-provoking scenes. The basic principle
is that relaxation is incompatible with anxiety. Relaxation
can be induced by direct instruction, drugs, carbon dioxide,
hypnosis, positive imagery, and a metronome-conditioned
method. More than 100 outcome studies indicate that systematic desensitization produces significantly better results
than a variety of comparison therapies. ((Journal abstract).

1522.   Wolpe, J., The behavior therapy approach,
         in, Arieti, S., (ed.), American handbook
         of psychiatry, New York, Basic Books, 1974.

1523.   Wolpe, J., Relaxation as an instrument
         for breaking adverse emotional habits, in,
         McGuigan, J., (ed.), Tension control,
         Chicago, University Publications, 1975.
         (American Association for the Advancement
         of Tension Control, First Proceedings,
         Chicago).

Wolpe defines neurosis as a learned, persistent, and unadaptive habit in which anxiety plays a crucial role. Treatment
of neuroses consists of the logical application of learning
principles to facilitate the overcoming (unlearning) of
unadaptive anxiety response habits. The author outlines the
experimental paradigm which led to the development of his
method of treatment--an application of the principle of
reciprocal inhibition. He briefly explains the process of
systematic desensitization and the function of relaxation
in producing autonomic effects counter to anxiety. He notes
that relaxation is not the sole means of counter-conditioning
anxiety; and comments, lastly, on the demonstrated efficacy
of behavior therapy. (abstract by Deborah Schuller).

1524.   Wolpe, J., Laboratory-derived clinical
         methods of deconditioning anxiety, in,
         Thompson, T., and Dockens, W.S., (eds.),
         Applications of behavior modification,
         New York, Academic Press, 1975.

1525.   Wolpe, J., Theme and variations: A
         behavior therapy casebook, New York,
         Permagon Press, 1976.

1526.   Wolpe, J., Desensitization for phobia
         (therapy session), Wandersman, A., et al.,
         (eds.), Humanism and behaviorism: Dialogue
         and growth, New York, Permagon Press, 1976.

1527.   Wolpe, J., How laboratory-derived
        principles have conquered the neuroses,
        in, Serban, G., (ed.), Psychopathology
        of human adaption, New York, Plenum
        Publishing Corporation, 1976.

Maintaining that psychoanalytic theory lacks significantly
acceptable support, and that psychoanalytic practice has an
undistinghished record of results, Wolpe describes "new and
more effective" treatment modes for the neuroses. He defines the nature of neurosis, then reviews his work on
experimental neuroses and their treatment. Similarities
noted between experimental and clinical neuroses led to the
formulation of a therapeutic principle based on reciprocal
inhibition. Wolpe describes various clinical applications
of this principle--i.e., systematic desensitization employing
imagined scenes; the use of assertive training; of sexual
responses; of the patient's emotional responses to the
therapist; flooding; and the use of reciprocal inhibition
in the overcoming of unadaptive habits of thought. Data
from outcome studies of behavior therapy in unselected
neuroses, as well as outcome data of systematic desensitization are presented. (abstract by Deborah Schuller).

1528.   Wolpe, J., Systematic desensitization
        based on relaxation, in, Morse, S.J.,
        and Watson, R.I., (eds.), Psychotherapies:
        A comparative casebook, New York, Holt,
        Rinehart, and Winston, 1977.

1529.   Wolpe, J., Behavior therapy: Learning
        to overcome anxiety in somatic disorders,
        Behavioral Medicine, 1978, 5, 14-18.

This interview with Joseph Wolpe touches briefly on a
number of diverse considerations. He defines behavior
therapy and conditions amenable to it--e.g., anxiety-based
disorders. He discusses "behavior analysis" and the procedure of systematic desensitization, noting the lack of
symptom substitution or relapse. Other issues considered
include median length of treatment; application of behavioral

principles by trained family physicians; psychoses; depression; the use of anti-anxiety drugs; and behavior
therapy as a preventive technique. (abstract by Deborah
Schuller).

1530.   Wolpe, J., Self-efficacy theory and
         psychotherapeutic change: A square
         peg for a round hole, Advances in
         behavior research and therapy, 1978,
         1, 231-236.

Bandura claims that treatments that succeed in eliminating
neurotic fears do so not by directly weakening anxiety
response habits, but through the mediation of expectations
of self-efficacy. Bandura came to this conclusion because
of his success in treating phobic cases by methods involving
modeling and, most particularly, participant modeling.
However, he ignored the fact that emotional reconditioning
processes were also going on during these treatments. It
is argued here that the approach behavior of phobic subjects
to feared objects is inhibited by their anticipation of
aversive consequences in the form of the anxiety that the
approaches entail, and therefore the elimination of anxiety
responses to the primary therapeutic requirement. Bandura's
experiment purporting to show that systematic desensitization
succeeds through raising expectations of self-efficacy is
shown to be unacceptably flawed. In general, the facts dis-
pute the aptness of his theory to the therapeutic context
to which he applies it. (Journal abstract).

1531.   Wolpe, J., and Lazarus, A.A., Behavior
         therapy techniques: A guide to the
         treatment of neuroses, London, Permagon
         Press, 1966.

1532.   Wolpe, J., and Migler, B., Automated
         self-desensitization: A case report,
         Behaviour Research and Therapy, 1967,
         5, 133-135.

1533.   Wolpe, J., and Reyna, L.J., (eds.),
        Behavior therapy in psychiatric practice,
        New York, Permagon Press, 1976.

1534.   Wolpe, J., and Serber, M., Treatment of
        the sexual offender: Behavior therapy
        techniques, International Psychiatry
        Clinics, 1971, 8, 53-68.

1535.   Wolpe, J., and Serber, M., Behavior
        therapy techniques, in, Resnik, H.L.P.,
        and Wolfgang, M.E., (eds.), Sexual
        behaviors: Social, clinical and legal
        aspects, Boston, Little, Brown, and
        Company, 1972.

1536.   Work, H.H., Psychiatric emergencies in
        childhood, International Psychiatry Clinics,
        1966, 3,

1537.   Would, R.L., and Reid, R., A study of group
        psychotherapy results with youthful offenders
        in detention, Group Psychotherapy, 1964, 17,
        56-60.

A total of 40 incarcerated individuals, ranging in age from
17-20 met in therapy groups for 16 sessions, each session
lasting 1 1/2 hours. The results point to some improvement
over the time of the program.

1538.   Wright, K., et al., Time-limited psycho-
        therapy: advantages, problems, outcomes,
        Psychological Reports, 1961, 9, 187-190.

The authors specify criteria for selection of patients for
time-limited psychotherapy--defined as weekly therapy
sessions for not more than one year. Brief psychoanalytically-oriented treatment as practised in the author's clinic
is summarized, and problems and limitations considered. In
conclusion, Wright, et al. outline outcome observations

based on pre- and posttherapeutic Rorschach, TAT, and Draw-
A-Person Test protocols of 10 randomly selected patients.
Interpretation of protocols suggests the following:
strengthening of defences within reduced life space; increased conformity in thinking; reduction in conscious
anxiety; increased conscious hopefulness and unconscious
depression; greater acceptance of dependent feelings in
interaction with others; and in conscious conflict.
(abstract by Deborah Schuller).

  1539.   Wright, M.E., A single-treatment method
          to stop smoking using ancillary self-
          hypnosis: Discussion, International
          Journal of Clinical and Experimental
          Hypnosis, 1970, 18, 261-267.

The remarkable persistence of smoking behavior despite the
generally recognized life-threatening aspects of this
activity is discussed. Certain psychological conditions
must become active for non-smoking status to be achieved.
These include: (a) recognizing the consequences of smoking
to be imminent, (b) identifying oneself as a nonsmoker,
(c) expecting and wanting to participate in a satisfying
future, and (d) adopting a way by which the individual can
gain control over smoking. The technique outlined by Dr.
Spiegel deals with these 4 dynamic aspects and makes a significant contribution to the treatment of the smoker's
problem. (Journal abstract).

  1540.   Wurmser, J.H., The relationships among
          patient variables, therapist variables,
          and outcome in brief psychotherapy with
          children, Dissertation Abstracts Inter-
          national, 1974, 35, 6B, 3045.

  1541.   Yamaguchi, T., A case report of the
          Massachusetts Mental Health Clinic - brief
          psychotherapy dealing with an uncompleted
          termination, Clinical Psychiatry (Tokyo),
          1970, 12, 875-880.

A single case is presented of a 25 year old woman, who had
not completed her long therapy, was accepted in to

brief therapy. A total of eight sessions were held, and
the content of these is presented and discussed. A three
month follow-up was also conducted, and results reported.

1542.   Yamaguchi, T., and Todoroki, S., A
          short-term psychotherapeutic approach
          to cases of school refusal, Japanese
          Journal of Clinical Psychiatry, 1973,
          2, 1293-1301.

The advantages of short term therapy for school phobias are
discussed, along with the short-comings of such an approach.
Previous articles on school phobia are reviewed, and a
classification and the characteristics of school phobia are
presented.

1543.   Yamaguchi, T., and Todoroki, S., Brief
          psychotherapy for maladjusted adolescents,
          Clinical Psychiatry, (Tokyo), 1974, 16,
          491-500.

1544.   Yamamoto, J., and Goin, M.K., On the
          treatment of the poor, American Journal
          of Psychiatry, 1965, 122, 267-271.

The poor patient with his special needs requires special
psychiatric treatment. In the past, clinics have not considered this fact and have rejected them too often as
unsuitable or unmotivated. We have developed techniques
for a flexible, active, brief, supportive and reality-
oriented treatment approach. These techniques include
changes in administrative procedures such as appointment
scheduling and in efforts to create a warm, friendly social
context in which to offer help. We have modified group
therapy and have focussed on not only insight but education,
social interaction, and group support. Minimal supportive
therapy with drugs as indicated serves a portion of our
patient population. With all these changes, the responses
of our patients have been much more often enthusiastic than
those of our professional colleagues. (Journal summary
adapted).

1545.   Yates, A.J., The application of learning
         theory to the treatment of tics, Journal
         of Abnormal and Social Psychology, 1958,
         56, 175-182.

A theoretical model was proposed to show that some tics may
be conceptualized as drive-reducing conditioned avoidance
responses, originally evoked in a traumatic situation. From
this model, a method of treatment was derived. It was predicted that if the tics were evoked voluntarily under condition of massed practice a negative habit of "not doing the
tick" should be built up, resulting ultimately in the extin-
tion of the tics and that this extinction should generalize
beyond the test situation. The results of a number of
experiments support the validity of the theory. There was
a significant decline in the ability to respond voluntarily
under various conditions of massed practice and rest. The
optimum condition for the growth of the negative habit
appeared to be the combination of very prolonged massed
practice followed by prolonged rest. Subjective reports of
the patient indicated considerable clinical improvement
outside the immediate test situation. (Journal summary).

1546.   Yung, C., Research strategies in short-
         term dynamic psychotherapy, in, Davanloo,
         H., (ed.), Basic principles and techniques
         in short-term dynamic psychotherapy, New
         York, Spectrum Publications, 1978.

This chapter deals in great detail with two major issues:
a) the selection of appropriate patients for short-term
dynamic psychotherapy, and, b) issues related to the classification of therapy outcome measures.

1547.   Zadik, A., The approach of brief conjoint
         psychotherapy - a case of separation
         anxiety, Journal of Child Psychotherapy,
         1973, 3, 71-82.

Zadik describes the treatment of a mother and her four-year
old daughter, together. Background and history of the
family are carefully outlined. The author then relates
the first seven sessions of conjoint therapy, conducted by

the author and a social worker with the two patients both
present. After three months of conjoint weekly therapy,
the social worker continued with the mother; and the author
was able to work alone with the child. Although therapy
with the child continues, Zadik notes a great deal of
improvement in the girl's developing object relations, both
internal and external. Borrowing from Esther Bick's conceptualization of psychic "skins", Zadik discusses her
theoretic understanding of this case. (abstract by
Deborah Schuller).

   1548.   Zeiss, A.M., et al., Nonspecific
            improvement effects in depression
            using interpersonal skills training,
            pleasant activity schedules, or cog-
            nitive training, Journal of Consulting
            and Clinical Psychology, 1979, 47,
            427-439.

Depressed outpatients received treatment focusing on either
interpersonal skills, cognitions, or pleasant events. In
each treatment modality, approximately half of the patients
received immediate treatment and half received delayed
treatment. Patients were assessed at four intervals to
determine response to treatment and follow-up status.
Results indicated that all treatment modalities significantly
alleviated depression. However, no treatment modality had
specific impact on the variables most relevant to its treatment format. Instead, all patients improved on most dependent variables, regardless of whether the variables were
directly addressed in treatment. Results are discussed in
terms of Bandura's self-efficacy model. (Journal abstract).

   1549.   Zitrin, C.M., et al., Comparison of short-
            term treatment regimens in phobic patients,
            A preliminary report, in, Spitzer, R.L.,
            and Klein, D.F., (eds.), Evaluation of
            psychological therapies, Baltimore, John
            Hopkins University Press, 1976.

The authors report, in preliminary form, on a double-blind
study comparing three different combinations of treatment:
behavior therapy paired with administration of imipramine,

paired with a placebo, and a supportive therapy intervention
paired with imipramine. The subject total was 57, which the
authors described differentially in terms of presenting
symptomatology; agoraphobics, phobic neurotics, and mixed
phobics. The different reactions of each of these groups
are reported. The positive effect of imipramine is hypothesized to relate to its ability to eliminate the spontaneous panic attacks experienced by many phobics, which
when used enables psychotherapeutic intervention to be more
effective.

1550.   Zonano, H., et al., Psychiatric emergency
         services a decade later, Psychiatry in
         Medicine, 1973, 4, 273-290.

The changes in the functioning of the psychiatric component
of a general hospital emergency room were assessed over the
past decade. The effect of its incorporation into a community mental health center as its emergency service was
seen to exert a significant increase in its utilization.
Admissions increased threefold over the ten year period and
the 15-21 age group increased by twice that amount. Analysis
of census and social class data showed a significant effect
of distance on only the lower socioeconomic groups. Diagnostic and dispositional shifts were seen as showing an
increase in utilization by less disturbed patients who use
the emergency room as their primary treatment resource.
The rise in the drug addictions is striking and may mask
other diagnoses. (Journal abstract).

1551.   Zusman, J., Emergency room psychiatry,
         Current Psychiatric Therapies, 1965,
         9, 182-185.

Zusman describes the approach to providing emergency psychiatric care devised by one general hospital in a large
urban setting. The hospital's psychiatry department provided a variety of services during daytime hours. At all
times when these units were closed, a psychiatrist was
available in the emergency room. His responsibilities
included seeing all patients arriving in emergency who requested psychiatric help, answering consultation requests

from the emergency room and the wards, and providing a
maximum of five therapy sessions or referring a patient to
another facility. More general goals consisted of reducing
the gap between the emergency room service and the department
of psychiatry, and improving the psychiatric skills of emergency room staff. The author discusses various stages in
the implementation of this service, specifically the evolution of a working relationship between emergency staff and
the psychiatrist. He concludes with a comparison of the
advantages of emergency room psychiatry over a walk-in
clinic. (abstract by Deborah Schuller).

1552.   Zusman, J., The psychiatrist as a member
         of the emergency room, American Journal
         of Psychiatry, 1967, 123, 1394-1401.

A psychiatrist was made a part-time member of the emergency
room staff in a 600-bed general hospital. He was available
for consultations and referrals and to do brief psychotherapy. He also attempted to influence the attitudes of
physicians and others on the emergency room staff toward
psychiatry and psychiatric patients. The findings and
impressions from the first year of this program are presented
and discussed. The value of this approach compared to a
walk-in clinic is discussed. (Journal summary).

Late Additions

Bernard, H.S., and Klein, R.H., Some perspectives on time-limited group psychotherapy, Comprehensive Psychiatry, 1977, 10, 71-88.

Bernard, H.S., et al., Relationship between patients' in-process evaluations of therapy and psychotherapy outcome, Journal of Clinical Psychology, 1980, 36, 259-264.

Dube, S., and Mohan, D., Towards a distinction between psychopathology and sociopathology in short term conjoint marital therapy, Indian Journal of Behaviour, 1977, 1, 30-34.

Fogelman, E., and Savran, B., Brief group therapy with off-spring of Holocaust survivors: Leader's reactions, American Journal of Orthopsychiatry, 1980, 50, 96-108.

Hasenbush, L., Successful brief therapy of a retired elderly man with intractable pain, depression, and drug and alcoholic dependence, Journal of Geriatric Psychiatry, 1977, 10, 71-88.

Padfield, M., Depression: Not getting what turns you on, Personnel and Guidance Journal, 1976, 55, 20-23.

Saposnek, D.T., Aikido: A model for brief strategic therapy, Family Process, 1980, 19, 227-237.

Strupp, H.H., Success and failure in time-limited psychotherapy: A systematic comparison of two cases, Archives of General Psychiatry, 1980, 37, 947-954.

Author Index

Abend, S. - 1
Abrahams, E. - 388
Abramovitz, A. - 800
Abramson, H.A. - 2
Ackerman, M. - 3
Ackerman, S. - 3
Adams, H.B. - 4
Adams, N.M. - 1075
Adelman, C.S. - 5
Adler, K.A. - 6
Adsett, C.A. - 7
Affleck, D.C. - 8, 475
Aguilera, D.C. - 9-13
Ahumada, J.L. - 14-15
Aja, J.H. - 16
Albers, D.A. - 1052
Albronda, H.F. - 17
Aldrich, C.F. - 18-20
Alexander, F. - 21-24
Alexander, J.F. - 25, 885, 1051
Allgeyer, J.M. - 26, 666, 1343
Alpern, E. - 27
Alpert, J.J. - 28
Alvord, J.R. - 29, 910
Amada, G. - 30-31
Amster, F. - 32-33
Anchor, K.N. - 34-35
Anderson, L. - 142
Andolfi, M. - 36-37
Andre, J.M. - 895
Andrews, D.A. - 38
Annon, J. - 39-42, 1082
Ansbacher, H.L. - 43
Applebaum, S.A. - 44
Argles, P. - 45
Argyle, M. - 46
Argyris, C. - 47
Arthur, G.L. - 48
Atkins, M. - 49
Atkins, R.W. - 50

Auerbach, R. - 52
Auerbach, S. - 51, 727
Augenbraun, B. - 53
Auld, F. - 996
Avnet, H.H. - 54
Axelbred, M. - 1407
Axelrod, B.H. - 55
Ayer, W.H. - 56
Ayllon, T. - 57-64
Azrin, N.H. - 65-75
Azrin, N.H. - 58-59, 440, 655

Babad, E.Y. - 76
Bach, G.R. - 77
Bach, T.R. - 989
Bailey, M.A. - 78
Baird, S.H. - 170
Baker, E. - 79
Baldwin, B.A. - 80-84, 622
Baldwin, K.A. - 85
Balint, K. - 86
Ball, J.D. - 87
Balson, P.M. - 88
Balter, L. - 104
Baker, B. - 695
Bambrick, A.F. - 491
Bandler, B. - 89-90
Bandura, A. - 91
Barcai, A. - 1206
Bard, M. - 92
Barrera, M. - 93
Barrett, C.L. - 94
Barten, H.H. - 95-100
Barten, H.H. - 123
Barten, S.S. - 100
Bartoletti, M.D. - 101-102
Bartolucci, G. - 103
Bassuk, E. - 503
Bauer, F. - 104
Baum, C. - 105
Baum, M. - 106
Baum, O.E. - 107-108

Subject Index

All numbers in the Subject Index refer to abstract numbers, and not to page numbers.

Abortion
140, 210, 308, 540, 541, 1283,

Accelerated interaction
1328,

Addiction (see also Alcoholism; Drug abuse)

Adlerian therapy
6, 43, 99, 100, 489, 984, 1221, 1222, 1223, 1227,

Adolescence
1, 38, 98, 109, 134, 166, 198, 204, 263, 317, 338, 350, 374, 375, 376, 393, 412, 424, 462, 463, 490, 539, 545, 576, 583, 617, 654, 721, 733, 757, 774, 864, 865, 944, 945, 953, 968, 1033, 1039, 1049, 1053, 1129, 1156, 1157, 1172, 1206, 1212, 1263, 1267, 1307, 1383, 1452, 1498, 1537, 1543, 1550,

Adoption
268, 286, 1039,

Affective disorders (see Psychosis)

Aftercare
1175, 1178,

Aging (see Geriatrics)

Alcoholics/Alcoholism
65, 89, 168, 249, 339, 436, 494, 655, 749, 852, 1011, 1198, 1322,

Anger
191, 199, 306,

Anorexia
156, 383, 583, 1036, 1037, 1117,

Anxiety (as symptom)
88, 155, 176, 197, 250, 270, 281, 290, 324, 342, 357, 438, 466, 467, 522, 536, 610, 719, 727, 952, 1065, 1093, 1101, 1136, 1137, 1170, 1332, 1351, 1360-1366, 1547,

Anxiety arousing therapy (see also Short-term anxiety
275, 609, 937,   provoking psychotherapy)

Woman/Women
341, 346, 548, 726, 915, 931, 932, 939, 1004, 1016, 1212,
1283, 1299, 1347, 1501, 1502,